Entrepreneurship, Innovation, and Sustainable Growth

T0300562

Entrepreneurship and innovation play a vital role in fostering sustainable development. Advances in technology and communications have both transformed the process of business and strengthened the role of entrepreneurship in developed and developing countries. This new edition of *Entrepreneurship, Innovation, and Sustainable Growth* provides the fundamental concepts and applications for faculty and students in this field, and also serves as a professional reference for practicing entrepreneurs and policymakers.

Each chapter provides a clear guide to the conceptual and practical elements that characterize entrepreneurship and the process of new venture formation, including functional strategies in key areas such as marketing, information technology, human resources management, and accounting and finance. Updated throughout to take account of recent developments in topics such as environmental impacts, diversity and inclusion, and COVID-19, the book is a comprehensive and holistic approach to the theory, policy, and practice of entrepreneurship and innovation. Keeping practicality as the book's core aim, all chapters include a long case study to set the scene and then draw upon shorter cases from both developing and developed countries to reinforce key learning objectives and the real-world application of the book's core concepts.

With new questions and exercises presented throughout in order to encourage discussion and problem-solving, quick summaries of the important concepts and definitions, and extensive support for lecturers and students, *Entrepreneurship, Innovation, and Sustainable Growth*, Second Edition, is ideal for students at undergraduate and postgraduate level.

Nader H. Asgary is Professor of Management and Economics at Bentley University, USA, and founder and President of the CYRUS Institute of Knowledge.

Emerson A. Maccari is Professor and the former dean of the Graduate School of Management at UNINOVE University, São Paulo, Brazil.

Heloisa C. Hollnagel is Professor at the Federal University of São Paulo, Brazil.

Ricardo L.P. Bueno is Associate Professor at the Federal University of São Paulo, Brazil.

Entrepreneurship, Innovation, and Sustainable Growth

Theory, Policy, and Practice

Second Edition

Nader H. Asgary, Emerson A. Maccari, Heloisa C. Hollnagel, and Ricardo L.P. Bueno

Routledge
Taylor & Francis Group

LONDON AND NEW YORK

Designed cover image: © Getty Images

Second edition published 2024
by Routledge
4 Park Square, Milton Park, Abingdon, Oxon, OX14 4RN

and by Routledge
605 Third Avenue, New York, NY 10158

Routledge is an imprint of the Taylor & Francis Group, an informa business

© 2024 Nader H. Asgary, Emerson A. Maccari, Heloisa C. Hollnagel,
and Ricardo L.P. Bueno

First edition published by Routledge 2019

British Library Cataloguing-in-Publication Data
A catalogue record for this book is available from the British Library

Library of Congress Cataloging-in-Publication Data
Names: Asgary, Nader H., author. | Maccari, Emerson A., author. | Hollnagel,
    Heloisa C., author.
Title: Entrepreneurship, innovation and sustainable growth : theory, policy and practice /
    Nader H. Asgary, Emerson A. Maccari, Heloisa C. Hollnagel and Ricardo L.P. Bueno.
Description: Second Edition. | New York, NY : Routledge, 2024. | Revised edition of
    Entrepreneurship, innovation and sustainable growth, 2020. | Includes bibliographical
    references and index.
Subjects: LCSH: Entrepreneurship. | Sustainable development. | Technological
    innovations—Economic aspects.
Classification: LCC HB615 .A84 2024 (print) | LCC HB615 (ebook) |
    DDC 658.4/08—dc23/eng/20230731
LC record available at https://lccn.loc.gov/2023035347
LC ebook record available at https://lccn.loc.gov/2023035348

ISBN: 978-1-032-52247-0 (hbk)
ISBN: 978-1-032-52243-2 (pbk)
ISBN: 978-1-003-40574-0 (ebk)

DOI: 10.4324/9781003405740

Typeset in Times New Roman
by Apex CoVantage, LLC

Dedicated to our family members!

Contents

SECTION IV
Process 259

About the authors

Nader H. Asgary is Professor of Management and Economics at Bentley University.

Dr. Asgary specializes in economic development and international business. He serves as an associate provost for international relations at Bentley, where he developed a unique understanding of the needs for a book that would enrich economic development through entrepreneurship. He has led several successful entrepreneurship and leadership-based development projects in El Sauce, Nicaragua; Rio de Janeiro, Brazil; Iran; the Netherlands; and the United States. His extensive publication record coupled with his teaching and practical experiences in both public and private sectors enrich this textbook.

Dr. Asgary is also the founder and President of the CYRUS Institute of Knowledge (CIK; http://cyrusik.org/), a think tank that focuses on research in business development, sustainability, and economic development. Some of CIK's activities include annual international conferences, executive training, and research/consulting services. This role continues to provide Dr. Asgary with insights and experiences that impart a rapt purview and timely focus upon his writing that would otherwise be impossible.

Emerson A. Maccari is Professor and the former Dean of Graduate School of Management at UNINOVE University, São Paulo, Brazil.

Dr. Maccari has led proposals in preparation for the development of new master's and doctorate programs in the fields of administration, accounting, economics, tourism, education, engineering, law, and healthcare. Since 1999, he has led and advanced graduate programmes, master's, and doctorate programs at UNINOVE University and the University of São Paulo.

In 2013 Dr. Maccari helped to create the first master's in entrepreneurship program in Brazil at the University of São Paulo. Additionally, he has assisted in the creation and development of scientific journals in the platform Open Journal System (OJS). He is a consultant to the CAPES, a Brazilian agency that is in charge of developing and evaluating graduate programs. Dr. Maccari has organized and led several international conferences, in particular the International Symposium on Project Management, Innovation and Sustainability (SINGEP). He has developed international courses for graduate students in the United States, Germany, France, Portugal, and China in the areas of entrepreneurship, innovation, project management, strategy, sustainability, smart cities, sport management, and healthcare management.

Heloisa C. Hollnagel graduated in biological sciences from the Federal University of Rio Grande do Sul and in mathematics with an emphasis in informatics from Universidade Paulista, and attained master's and PhD (2000) in sciences from the University of São Paulo. Since 2001, she has been a professor and coordinator of traditional and technological undergraduate, and graduate courses in several institutions, participating in several university extension projects and sustainability research. Has more than two decades of experience in third sector organizations' fundraising to carry out socio-environmental projects, some of them with grants of national and international development agencies.

She is a tenured professor at the Federal University of São Paulo (UNIFESP) Campus Osasco in the Accounting Department, lecturing courses like "Entrepreneurial Experience," "Social and Environmental Accounting," and "Elaboration and Viability of Socio-environmental Project for SMEs." She is also a member of the professional master's program in civil engineering at Universidade São Judas Tadeu.

Ricardo L.P. Bueno is Associate Professor at the Federal University of São Paulo (UNIFESP) and holds bachelor's, master's, and PhD in business management from Universidade Federal of Rio Grande do Sul (2010). He has experience lecturing in MBA, undergraduate, and graduate courses focusing on business creation and entrepreneurial decision-making. He has 20 years of executive business experience supporting relevant spin-offs from established corporations.

Preface

This book amalgamated with the revolution in information technology and communications are transforming the way businesses innovate and initiate processes around the world. This new approach, which is both creative and pioneering, is leading to significant economic efficiencies and improvements in the quality of life for billions of people globally. Many policymakers are initiating policies supporting entrepreneurial startups that result in job creation and economic development. The aim of this book is to contribute to the advancement of knowledge in the aforementioned areas and share experience with stakeholders, thus helping the advancement of economic development.

The first edition of this book, titled *Entrepreneurship, Innovation, and Sustainable Growth: Opportunities and Challenges*, evolved from 2012, during which the authors were involved in a few international entrepreneurial studies and projects. The content of the book has grown and been enriched through comments and suggestions from faculty, graduate, and PhD students from institutions of higher education such as Bentley University, UNINOVE University, and MIT. Dr. Marcos Mazieri, who contributed in the early stage of the book, is acknowledged and appreciated. We acknowledge and greatly appreciate contributions of Rajat Sharma Subedi, Diana Kontsevaia, Zlatina Aleksandrova, Ashley Acosta, Jairo Oliveira, Luis Zanin, Evelyn Bernardo, Tatiana Manolova, Poorya Hosseini, Jonathan Sales, Tarek Hatem, Eugenio Briales, and Alf Walle, who have assisted in the review of the content and deserve special thanks. Additionally, the enormous contributions from Bhaskar Nandina, Pang Hsu, Neeka Asgary, and Mazdak Asgary in content creation, editing, organization, formatting, and design are acknowledged and appreciated. It would not be possible to have such a book which has a global depth and breadth without their efforts. Their support, dedication, and talent in this process are greatly appreciated. The support from the CYRUS Institute of Knowledge is acknowledged.

In this second edition, Drs. Asgary and Maccari invited Drs. Ricardo L.P. Bueno and Heloisa C. Hollnagel as coauthors to enrich the content of the book. The second edition contains significant modifications to the first edition in terms of literature survey, case studies, and examples for every chapter. We also added a new chapter about sustainability as a strategy for business operation to the first edition of the book. Additionally, we added a chapter at the end of the book comprising three unique cases: a company, a higher education institution, and a nonprofit organization.

A team of scholars and specialists in the field who reviewed our proposed revision for this edition supported our modifications. We incorporated valuable suggestions and comments by students into this edition. We also acknowledge the contributions of Patricia Cardoso Da Silva from the UNIFESP. The second edition proposed revisions were developed after the first edition was utilized by authors in their classrooms. We concluded that appropriate title for this edition would be *Entrepreneurship, Innovation, and Sustainable Growth: Theory, Practice, and Policy.* The book provides valuable content in every chapter that is named in the title.

This book is organized into four main sections: environment, individual characteristics, organizational setup, and processes. Each section contains from two to four chapters, totaling 12 chapters, which includes a case chapter. In a nutshell, this book provides a systematic, logical, and practical approach to scholars, students, policymakers, and entrepreneurs who seek to enhance their knowledge and support entrepreneurial instigation. Each chapter provides basic definitions, theoretical background, real-world examples, applications, and implications of the concepts discussed. Each chapter begins with the chapter's learning objectives and ends with questions for discussion. Quick reviews summarizing the main topics are present within many of the chapters. Also, all chapters have an opening case that highlights the key concepts and a few questions for class discussion. Furthermore, the book displays more than 50 real-world examples from both the developing and the developed countries in the form of short case studies, containing elegant images about individuals, organizations, companies, and more.

Introduction

Overview

Entrepreneurship and innovation play a vital role in fostering sustainable growth and development. Advances in technology and communications have transformed the process of business initiations and accelerated entrepreneurial operations in developed and developing countries. In this book, we examine the link between entrepreneurship and innovation from both a practitioner's and a scholar's perspective. We discuss entrepreneurship and innovation by placing entrepreneurial practice within broader contexts such as the economical, institutional, and technological circumstances.

In the second edition, we made significant modifications to the first edition in terms of literature survey, case studies, and examples for every chapter. We also added a new chapter about sustainability as a strategy for business operation to the first edition of the book. This new chapter will enhance the book by highlighting the important role entrepreneurs can play to advance sustainability. A team of scholars and specialists in the field who reviewed our proposed revision for the second edition supported our modifications. The second edition's proposed revisions were developed after the first edition was utilized by authors in their classrooms. We incorporated valuable suggestions and comments by students into the second edition. We realized the appropriate title for this edition would be *Entrepreneurship, Innovation, and Sustainable Growth: Theory, Practice, and Policy*. The book provides valuable content in every chapter that is named in the title.

In the introductory chapter we briefly describe thoughts, ideas, and process that most entrepreneurs perform prior to moving forward to start a new venture. Topics of discussion in the later chapters include the characteristics of entrepreneurs, economic and technological environments, institutional and cultural infrastructure, and the process of new venture formation, which includes functional strategies in key areas such as marketing, information technology, human resources management, and accounting and finance. There are also broader strategic issues discussed, such as ethics, corporate social responsibility (CSR), strategy, institutions, and governance. We have provided questions that would encourage discussions and quick reviews that summarize topics within each chapter. Long and short case studies and videos of entrepreneurs, organizations, companies, etc. are incorporated within each chapter from both developing and developed countries. They help to reinforce key learning objectives and provide real-world examples.

Overall, we present a comprehensive perspective of the entrepreneurial ecosystem that is composed of interdependent players and factors that are coordinated and enable productive entrepreneurship. The six players in this ecosystem are government, corporations, non-governmental organizations (NGOs), foundations, academia, and investors. Their roles are essential and complementary in the creation of an ecosystem in which entrepreneurship can flourish. In future chapters, we will discuss these issues in detail. These players can both complement and advance entrepreneurship by enabling, celebrating, training, and funding existing and upcoming entrepreneurs, and in this process – in the words of Adam Smith – serving their self-interests and society at large.[1]

This book is unique for its presentation of entrepreneurship and development within the institutional and technological context of developing regions. The role of entrepreneurship and innovation in the context of ongoing economic growth and development is discussed, taking into consideration the expanding globalization. Constraints and opportunities are discussed in a proactive manner. Each chapter contains lessons to be learned from successful entrepreneurs and firms. In addition, the book provides conceptual and practical guidance to entrepreneurs who seek greater knowledge and control over their careers and organizations, thus advancing sustainable development. The book provides an exceptional and lucrative contribution to economic growth and development literature.

Aims and contributions

In addition to the introductory chapter, the book consists of four parts: environment, individual characteristics, organizational setup, and processes. The introductory chapter provides an overview of the book and links the entrepreneurs' objectives and challenges to a road map that ultimately leads to the creation of a new venture. Chapter 3, titled "Technology, Communications, and Entrepreneurship," has an overarching impact on all parts of the textbook. The summary of all chapters and parts are briefly described in the following. In a nutshell, the book provides a systematical, logical, and practical approach for scholars, students, and entrepreneurs who seek to enhance their knowledge and support entrepreneurial initiation.

Who should read this book?

This book is a vital resource for those concerned with the relations between entrepreneurship, innovation, and sustainable development. Its aim is to be a primary text that provides fundamental concepts and applications for faculty and students, and also serves as a professional reference for practicing entrepreneurs and policymakers. Professional jargon is kept to a minimum for the benefit of aspiring entrepreneurs and is suitable for both undergraduate and MBA courses geared towards topics such as entrepreneurship, business development, small and medium enterprises (SMEs), and economic development and growth.

Introductory chapter

The introductory chapter defines and describes the steps involved in the development of a business model. We will describe in brief the influence of an individual's personal and professional characteristics, and public circumstances on opportunity recognition. We will discuss frameworks about the processes of idea discovery to the development of a business model. Future chapters in the book will provide details of theoretical and empirical evidence on each section of the business model.

Section I: The environment and entrepreneurship

In this part, we discuss the entrepreneurial ecosystem in the context of developing economies. Chapter 1 provides an explanation of the association between entrepreneurship, innovation, and development in an era of globalization with reference to both micro and macro variables. Chapter 2 focuses on both formal and informal institutional environments, with information on the government policies that support entrepreneurship and other related institutions. Chapter 3 focuses on the role of technology and communication and its overarching impact on all elements in the ecosystem.

Section II: Individual characteristics and training

In this part, we examine an individual's intent on pursuing entrepreneurial initiatives in developing economies. Chapter 4 discusses topics such as competencies, spirit, training, personality, and professional experience of entrepreneurs. Chapter 5 focuses on the entrepreneur's creativity and the ability to innovate. The ability to innovate and be creative is strongly associated with entrepreneurial opportunities. Creative ideas serve as the link between observing problems or needs and creating solutions to these needs. Entrepreneurs are the opportunists who search for answers and in this process, advance themselves and society.

Section III: The organization

This part comprises Chapters 6, 7 and 8, which present important information on building organization with good principles. In Chapter 6 we will discuss how to build institutions and governance, and to develop a viable road map to grow and be successful. Chapter 7 provides best practices, including social entrepreneurship, competitive advantage, and the triple bottom line. In Chapter 8, we describe how businesses can thrive and grow through sustainability as a strategy for business operation. We examined different business models and gained an understanding of the broader landscape, including the role of government, investors, and customers in advancing the Sustainable Development Goals of the United Nations (UN).

Section IV: Process

In the final part, comprising Chapters 9, 10, and 11, we present the process for venture creation. To create a sustainable enterprise, the entrepreneur needs to educate themselves on aspects of business such as marketing, finance, and accounting. Understanding concepts in these chapters are vital for creating a functioning business.

Note

1 Smith, A. (1776). *An Inquiry into the Nature and Causes of the Wealth of Nations.*

A brief overview of each chapter

Introduction: entrepreneurial discovery, creationary, and business model development

The introductory chapter provides concepts and techniques that entrepreneurs perform prior to the start of a new venture. The steps involved result in the development of a model that encompasses all concepts of the new business. Many factors influence the start of a venture; some of them are individuals' characteristics, personal and public circumstances, and market research, all of which influence the process of opportunity discovery and creation and development of the model. We will set the stage for an in-depth presentation of theoretical and empirical corroborations in the areas of entrepreneurial environment, personal characteristics, organization structure, and process that is involved to succeed.

Section I: The environment and entrepreneurship

Chapter 1: Entrepreneurship and development in the era of globalization

In this chapter, the role that entrepreneurship plays in advancing sustainable development is analyzed, setting the stage to discuss distinctive skills, perceptions, orientations, and environmental challenges that impact entrepreneurship. Relevant theoretical principles are illustrated, using examples from both developing and developed economies. Fundamental economic theories of development are also presented while the positive and negative impacts of globalization on entrepreneurship are examined.

There are fundamental questions that scholars, policymakers, NGOs, and citizens ask about the impact of growing globalization on development and especially about entrepreneurship. Some questions include: Does globalization accelerate development by advancing entrepreneurship in developing countries? What is the impact of entrepreneurship on innovation in developing countries? What are the effects of entrepreneurship on employment and income? How has entrepreneurship in developing countries been impacted by the revolution of technology? In this chapter, we will provide an overview of these topics, which we will discuss in more detail over subsequent chapters.

Chapter 2: Culture, entrepreneurship, and development

This chapter introduces the concept of the entrepreneurial ecosystem and focuses on critical components of this ecosystem. Critical components include the national culture of entrepreneurship, formal and informal institutional framework, and government policies in support of entrepreneurship. The cultural context of entrepreneurial activities and traditions harmonize with innovation, motivations, and entrepreneurial endeavors. The concept of cultural convergence and its relation to both entrepreneurship and development is presented. With the help of models by Hofstede and other scholars, we examine the link between entrepreneurship and development. Numerous examples in the chapter identify ways policymakers in developing countries can enhance cultural traits to encourage and support entrepreneurial efforts. We consider it vital for growth-oriented entrepreneurship, as it is an important vessel for innovation and job creation. Therefore, governments should encourage entrepreneurship and help it grow and contribute to the country's economy.

Chapter 3: Technology, communications, and entrepreneurship

This chapter presents the roles of technology and communications in an entrepreneurial ecosystem by analyzing their efficiency to create links for entrepreneurial activities. Technological advances and their applications are pervasive in world economics and are constantly changing. Technology has nurtured and advanced entrepreneurship since the dawn of the industrial revolution. The current digital revolution has exponentially expanded the impact of technology. Technological innovations have led to increased production and communication efficiency, allowing for better quality goods and services to be produced and delivered at lower costs. The production of new goods and services has become easier and more innovative, making it a catalyst for entrepreneurship in both developed and developing countries.

Technology is an overarching and constantly evolving phenomenon that changes the economic realm by transforming business and consumer demands. Technology, in this context, refers to making, modifying, and using knowledge, tools, and operational systems in order to solve problems. This chapter focuses on the influence that technology and communications have had and continue to have on creating value and new opportunities.

Section II: Individual characteristics and training

Chapter 4: Personality, experience, and training

In this chapter, the nature of entrepreneurs and entrepreneurship, also called the entrepreneurial spirit, is discussed. We focus on personal characteristics, educational backgrounds, and prior experiences of entrepreneurs, while also dealing with ecological and social factors that influence entrepreneurial activities. The different perspectives surrounding entrepreneurs and entrepreneurship are discussed, from basic definitions to factors such as the education and experience that influence them. The chapter explores the importance of entrepreneurship and the role that experience, training, social and cultural connections, and networking play in shaping an entrepreneur's life. Most definitions of entrepreneurship agree on individuals' behaviors, such as taking initiative, continuous organization of social and economic mechanisms, turning resources and situations into something practical, and the acceptance of risk or failure.

Chapter 5: Creativity, innovation, and development

Creativity and the ability to innovate are strongly linked to entrepreneurship and economic development. Creativity and innovation are key factors that contribute to an enterprise's ability to thrive in an increasingly global marketplace. Creative ideas are connections between problems and solutions. A vital role of entrepreneurs is to find creative solutions to these problems. Innovation is not just about solving a problem, but the solution must also fit the customers' specific needs and desires. In this chapter, a deeper understanding of links between creativity, innovation, economic development, and entrepreneurship are discussed. The impacts of culture on creativity and innovation are examined and cultural influences on public policy are analyzed. The attitudes towards creativity and innovation vary widely from culture to culture, as does the access to and adoption of modern information and communication technology. Cultural attitudes towards creativity can facilitate or impede an enterprise's ability to bring an innovative product to market, thus affecting their economic success. The role of governments and public policy in offering incentives and creating rules, regulations, and rights are critical in this process.

Section III: The organization

Chapter 6: Institutions, governance, and strategy

In this chapter, we will present definitions of institutions, governance, and strategy, as well as their relationship to entrepreneurial activities and sustainable development. A strategic guide for the formation of a sustainable enterprise is presented. Understanding the role that institutions and governance play in articulating and implementing successful strategies is discussed in this chapter. Knowledge of these key concepts is necessary on both the micro and macro levels for building a sustainable and transparent organization with a credible system of governance. Good governance and relevant supporting institutions advance entrepreneurial activities in a society. When rules, regulations, and a clear and transparent road map for operations are designed and implemented, they will lead to a flourishing economy.

Chapter 7: Ethics and corporate social responsibility

Definitions are provided for the concepts of ethics and corporate social responsibility (CSR). The implications in the era of globalization on businesses and entrepreneurial activities are discussed. The chapter describes the stakeholders' theory with distinct emphasis on human resources management. It also addresses how ethical solutions to issues and adhering to CSR in developing countries create conditions for fairness and shared values, which will help the development of enterprises to create fair market conditions.

Section IV: Process

Chapter 8: Sustainability as a strategy for business operation

Social injustice, income inequality, ecological footprint, and climate change are some of the major problems of the 21st century. In this chapter, we will examine how businesses can thrive and grow while playing a significant role in solving named challenges. Entrepreneurs can be at the forefront of these activities. Addressing these challenges is the concerns of the majority of citizens, thus policymakers are responding to it through public policies. Therefore, there are some financial incentives for entrepreneurs to focus their innovation in these domains. Additionally, we will examine different business models that examine the role of government, investors, and customers in aiding the UN's Sustainable Development Goals (SDGs).

Chapter 9: Marketing, technology, and entrepreneurship

In the era of globalization and fierce competition, marketing is essential to the survival and success of an organization. Increase in the means for marketing in this era seems to have created "a flat world" in which to advertise products, services, and ideas. The focus of this chapter is on the know-how and tools necessary for entrepreneurs, particularly those in developing countries, to market their products or services. Both marketing concepts and their application help an entrepreneur advance their objectives. The role of marketing in the success of the business, the characteristics of marketing, and the essential application of technology in developing countries are described. Concepts such as the marketing mix (price, place, product, and promotion) and customer loyalty programs are explored. New means of communication provide a degree of competitive advantages for entrepreneurs and SMEs over large corporations.

Chapter 10: Financing opportunities and challenges

In this chapter, we take a detailed look at the opportunities and constraints facing entrepreneurs in their pursuit of financial resources. Emphasis is placed on the importance of obtaining appropriate and affordable streams of funding. Both direct and indirect constraints are discussed, from a global perspective, on both the micro and macro levels. The micro opportunities and constraints are the acquisition of funding opportunities in support of startups, while the macro opportunities and constraints concern generally with government policies. Comparing them in scale differentiation is made between startup entrepreneurs and large enterprises in their quest to secure financing.

Chapter 11: Essentials of bookkeeping

This chapter addresses two important questions related to bookkeeping for an entrepreneur: first, why must an entrepreneur keep financial records; and second, what are its important components? It is hard to acquire the necessary assistance for growth without knowledge of financial feasibility of the enterprise. The importance of both financial and managerial accounting from the entrepreneurial perspective are discussed. Precise record keeping is essential for tax purposes and for acquiring additional funding. The benefits of thorough accounting as well as the problems that arise from it are underlined in the chapter. It is very difficult to evaluate an idea or a business without being able to quantify its value in the marketplace. Therefore, a budget is one of the most important documents an entrepreneur must create, which depends upon the detailed records of expenditures and revenues. In developing economies, entrepreneurs often operate in the informal sector, reducing the need to keep financial records for tax purposes.

Chapter 12: Cases

This chapter comprises three interesting and diverse cases. The cases are about the Philips Company in the Netherlands; ESCA Ecole de Management in Casablanca, Morocco; and CYRUS Institute of Knowledge, a nonprofit organization, in Cambridge, Massachusetts. The aim of these unique cases is to provide examples and applications of organizations for some chapters of the book as a complement. For example, the Philips Company case reviews the progress and strategy of the company to operate and grow for more than 100 years.

Introduction

Entrepreneurial discovery, creationary, and business model development

The introductory chapter provides an overview of concepts and process that most entrepreneurs perform prior to the formation of a new venture. This chapter discusses all of the incremental stages, starting from ideation to business model, involved in venture creation. The final stage which is recognized as a functioning "business model" encompasses all essentials of a new business, especially financial viability. Factors that influence the start of a venture such as ideation, individuals' characteristics, personal and public circumstances, evaluation, and financing are discussed. This chapter sets the stage for a more in-depth presentation of a theoretical and empirical study that has been conducted in the future chapters. The chapter will end with a brief description of each section of the book.

Learning objectives

1 Define a business opportunity
2 Discuss the indicator of the ease of doing business index
3 Differentiate internal and external stimulated opportunities
4 Analyze evaluation of the viability of an idea
5 Describe the business model and its essential role in building a viable business.

Introduction

The opening chapter will present an overview of the concepts and practices that entrepreneurs perform prior to the start of a business venture. It defines and describes all the steps involved from the formation of a business idea to the development of a business model. At each stage in the developmental journey, the entrepreneur discovers vital business concepts that govern the creation and substance of the new business venture. A brief discussion of the methods in starting entrepreneurial activities, discovery, and creation are highlighted. The chapter also discusses how an entrepreneur's individual characteristics, personal and public circumstances influence decisions that lead towards a successful opportunity recognition.

Each step of the creation process is an attempt by the entrepreneur to reach the goal of "enterprise formation." Each step is vital to the realization of a successful business model that has considered most aspects in business formation. Also, this chapter will provide a business model that combines the theoretical and applied knowledge discussed in the following sections. This chapter will end with a brief description of each section of the book. Future chapters will provide details on theoretical and empirical evidence in the areas of entrepreneurial environment, personal characteristics, organization, and process.

DOI: 10.4324/9781003405740-1

Seetharaman (2020) discusses the impact of the unprecedent and unexpected shock of COVID-19 on their business models. The author examines a multi-dimensional assessment of the impact of COVID-19 on businesses and states that "I also present some anecdotal evidence of attempts to alter business models in these circumstances in order to address the challenges that certain product characteristics impose but at the same capitalize on the business opportunities presented by the essentiality of the products."[1] COVID-19 caused individuals, organizations, and governments to reevaluate and modify their self-interests, operational model, and approach to public policies, respectively.

The role and applications of communications tools, including the evolving artificial intelligence (AI), has become significantly important. The recent evolution and competition (i.e., Google and Microsoft) in the AI domain seems to represent a new era of innovation that shall impact many aspects of our lives.[2] Of course, concerns about AI powers and applications need to be carefully evaluated.

Defining a business opportunity

Scholars have used different terminologies such as recognition,[3] identification,[4] discovery,[5] and finding[6] to explain an opportunity. The business opportunity is defined as the process that leads to an end goal. The end goal depends on what each entrepreneur considers as a worthy achievement. According to De Bono,[7] a business opportunity is a "course of action" worth pursuing using non-linear creative thinking. De Bono's non-linear thinking characterizes a business opportunity as an effort to reach a solution(s) by expanding thinking in multiple directions, rather than in one direction. Based on the concept that there are multiple starting points from where one can apply logic to a business problem, you can ultimately end at multiple valid solutions. Kirzner[8] described a business opportunity as an entrepreneur's ability to recognize commercial value of products or services to be sold in new markets at a profit. Others scholars[9] see business opportunity as a detail plan to translate the "business concept into reality." In their search to understand an opportunity, Hulbert, Brown, and Adams[10] define it as the goal to "meet an unsatisfied need in a profitable manner." Ardichvili, Cardozo, and Ray[11] emphasized that the end goal is to deliver superior value to the end-user. While we observe that scholars have some degree of differences in their definition of the business opportunity, perhaps business discovery can be summarized as a process to achieve an expected positive outcome and gain.

Furthermore, the definition of business opportunity can be described as an end goal where a new functioning "business model" has been created. We achieve the end goal by following three consecutive processes, namely discovery, development, and model-creation. In realizing the process we take into consideration the role of the entrepreneur both as a creative thinker and an acute businessman. Further, we also examine entrepreneurs' strategies in conjunction with their surrounding environment.[12] A functioning business concept can be developed to the following five outcomes:[13]

1   An invention looking to become a commercialized product
2   Expanding products or services to new markets
3   Commercializing an unmet market need
4   Businesses trying to create differentiated products or services for an existing market
5   Testing a novice business approach in the matured industry.

The process of opportunity recognition is considered an iterative process where each of the steps (discovery, development, and business model) is repeatedly tested as time progresses.[14] Iteration gives a greater advantage for fine tuning and staying relevant to the potentially

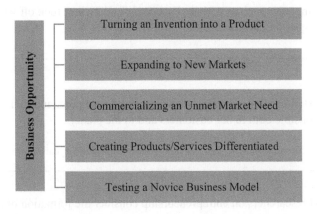

Figure 0.1 Defining opportunity

changing market environment. While the model in this chapter is specified for the creation of new ventures, many aspects of the model apply to existing business strategies. As the recurring process of idea discovery and its development, the business model is further strengthened with newer concepts and approaches that become relevant to changing market dynamics (see Figure 0.1). Finally, the process of opportunity recognition favors improvement of business processes, the discovery of products, and recognition of trends and acknowledgment of changing market situations.

Environmental condition and entrepreneurship

The environment condition plays a significant role in the creation and the rate of success of entrepreneurial activities. Conditions that best suit venture creation are analyzed and presented using "the ease of doing business index." It is an index created by Simeon Djankov at the World Bank Group[15] and is widely regarded as an indicator that suggests entrepreneurial environment across countries around the world. Each country tries to improve its index rankings to portray itself as having business-friendly regulations. The index's comprehensive use of 11 indicator sets measure aspects of business regulation that matter for entrepreneurship. An important finding is that better performance in doing business is associated with lower levels of unemployment and poverty.

Opportunity formation: discovery versus creation

Opportunities come in various forms. From a customer's point of view, it might mean unmet needs or changes in spending habits and preferences. From a market's perspective, they include the discovery of a new resource or scarcity of the existing resource, opening of new local/international markets, or expansion of market size. Opportunities in the macroeconomic perspective include a change in government policies such as regulation, privatization, employment objectives, etc. Therefore, public policy revisions, social and demographic changes, and technological evolution are events that can disrupt the existing competitive equilibrium in a marketplace. These revisions, changes, and evolution will provide opportunities for entrepreneurial acceleration. Some of the most recent inventions such as the iPhone/iPad have evolved from entrepreneurs who exploited technological advances to meet future customer needs. Thomas Friedman, in his book titled *Thank You for Being Late*,[16] states that in 2007 several new and innovative businesses and companies such as Airbnb, Facebook, and Twitter took off when their founders understood business opportunities created.[17]

TED Talk

Maya Penn started her first company when she was 8 years old, and thinks deeply about how to be responsible both to her customers and to the planet.

Source: www.ted.com/talks/maya_penn_meet_a_young_entrepreneur_cartoonist_designer_activist

---

Academics and researchers on entrepreneurship consider the formation of an opportunity as a function of two separate theories. It is widely accepted that entrepreneurial opportunities are formed by the application of either the discovery theory[18] or the creation theory.[19] However, both discovery and creation theories[20] assume that the goal of entrepreneurs is to form an enterprise and exploit opportunities.[21] Some scholars have provided a historical perspective of entrepreneurship, growth, and development.[22]

The discovery theory interprets all opportunities as objective phenomena. The theory considers "change" as a constant in the market, therefore opportunities to be ever-present. Opportunity discovery theorists argue that opportunities are independent of entrepreneurs in the marketplace and are waiting to be discovered.[23] It is the task of ambitious entrepreneurs to discover these opportunities by using different sources of information. Entrepreneurs use data collection techniques to identify any/all changes that are currently happening in the market and develop strategies to then exploit them. By considering opportunities to be objective the entrepreneur can use a variety of techniques to understand the expected potential outcomes associated with an opportunity. Other conditions inherent in discovery theory include decision-making to be dependent on the credibility of the knowledge source, the importance of opportunity cost, and an exploitation strategy which is relatively complete and unchanging.

The discovery approach sometimes occurs when entrepreneurs stumble across existing problems which they attempt to find a solution to. They could be existing unmet customers' needs that require fulfilling or access to new resources that can build into a business or an efficient method to conduct business. These opportunities may be in the domain that the entrepreneur has prior experience in. With years of knowledge and understanding of an industry, the entrepreneur develops skills to recognize either growth in the customer segment, advancement of technology in the industry, gaps between cost and selling price, or gaps in the supply chain, which can lead to an efficient business model. Companies such as Airbnb and Uber are business opportunities where the founders identified an opportunity to create an entirely new and efficient business model around existing products/markets.

Most established businesses go through an external opportunity recognition process, being alert to changes in the market and actively analyzing opportunities to upsell or cross-sell to their customers. They gather information of markets and conduct tests by either creating new products or new subsidiaries around newer opportunities.[24] Companies also keep track of their own procedures by performing detailed observation and evaluation of their supply chain system, technology, government regulation, and their competition.

Creationists are those who believe that opportunities are endogenous and, therefore, are created by the actions, reactions, and enactment of entrepreneurs discovering ways to produce new products or services.[25] An entrepreneur's actions are the competitive imperfections in markets that generate opportunities. The theory applies the Schumpeterian perspective of opportunities as thoughtful efforts by an entrepreneur to create new combinations of ideas, knowledge, and resources.[26] Entrepreneurs act on exogenous shocks that create opportunities and form organizations to exploit it.[27]

Chetty et al. (2018) argue that there is not enough study which examines the impact of the internationalization process on advancing discovery and creation of opportunities especially for small firms. Also, they investigated the internalization opportunities and identified and constructed it in the process of foreign market entry (FME). Authors stated that "therefore studies how opportunities become connected during small firms' FME. By incorporating the concept of duality, this article conceives of the discovery and creation of opportunity as mutually enabling rather than opposed. From this duality perspective, opportunity discovery and creation facilitate each other during internationalization processes." In their case study they used data from five high-tech Australian firms and 30 FMEs. Their findings "show that knowledge, networks, and capabilities enable opportunities in the FME context."[28] Jones and Barnir (2019) argue that nature and new ventures that entrepreneurs operate have an important influence on their outcome in the context of discovery and creationist. In their empirical study they "capture the relevance of these two perspectives ad hoc by linking the assumptions of the formation process to specific properties of entrepreneurial actions under different environmental contexts of innovativeness. "Their results show that the environmental context that entrepreneurs operate in is important. They state that "we find that search activities and formal funding are utilized more in a discovery context whereas entrepreneurial experience is more relevant in a creation context."[29] Dencker et al. (2021) apply motivational theory to examine the entrepreneur as the founders' basic needs, endowments of human capital, and the supporting instructional levers. The authors stated that "we seek to reconceptualize the necessity entrepreneurship construct by drawing on a motivational theory of necessity to predict how variation in founders' basic needs influences the entrepreneurial process, conditional on the level of their human capital endowments, the environmental context in which they are embedded, and the presence of supportive institutional levers." They conclude that there are some potential approaches that their theory "can be tested and extended."[30]

Opportunities where entrepreneurs deliberately create ideas happen when they are engaged in creative thinking.[31] The techniques of creative thinking are a way of generating solutions to current and future foreseen problems through the use of unconventional creative thinking. Decision-making in creationist theory is an iterative, inductive, incremental method that uses the rule of thumb, educated guess, and common sense to find diverse solutions. The creative process of new business ideas formation follow four stages[32] of maturity (see Figure 0.2):

1 *Preparation*: The first stage involves gathering information. An entrepreneur tries to learn things using attention, reasoning, and planning to gather information.
2 *Incubation*: It is the unconscious recombination of information that results in novel ideas in the future. It is the unconscious part of a process whereby an intuition may become validated as an insight.
3 *Illumination*: As ideas begin to mature, entrepreneurs have an epiphany regarding how to piece their thoughts together in a manner that makes sense. The moment of illumination can happen unexpectedly.
4 *Verification*: Creative ideas are subjected to critical thinking in order to become polished and persuasive. This stage involves actively creating and testing diverse business ideas.

The fundamental differences in process of opportunity formation between discovery and creation theory are the actions taken by the entrepreneurs from the two groups of scholars who

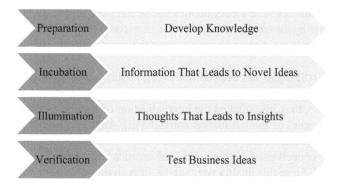

Figure 0.2 Creative approach

Table 0.1 Discovery and creation approach

	Discovery	*Creation*
Leadership	Based on expertise and experience	Based on charisma
Decision-making	Dependent on data; scientific Values opportunity cost	Iterative, inductive, incremental decision-making
Human resource practices	Recruitment of specialized human capital	General and flexible human capital recruited from networking
Strategy	Relatively complete and set to move on	Emergent and changing
Finance	External capital sources such as banks and venture capital	"Bootstrapping," "friends, family"
Marketing	Changes in marketing mix as new information gets accumulated	Marketing mix fundamentally differs from existing channels
Sustaining competitive advantage	Speed, secrecy, and erecting barriers to entry may sustain advantages	Tacit learning is a path-dependent process which may sustain advantages

have articulated the theories. Management and construction of the business model have different contexts when considering both the approaches. Table 0.1 shows the different approaches that an entrepreneur might take depending on which approach the opportunity is generated in.[33]

Role of information

While all entrepreneurs actively keep track of opportunities, experienced entrepreneurs develop greater pattern recognition skills of noticing connections between trends, changes, and events.[34] It is widely regarded by researchers[35] that entrepreneurs' superior intellectual skills and alertness are what makes them sensitive towards exploring new opportunities. Experienced entrepreneurs also quickly recognize the value in opportunities based on gut feeling rather than formal evaluation framework. This acquired skill set is the interaction of factors that combine individual characteristics, societal, cultural and institutional stimulation, which will be discussed in detail in future chapters. The aim of this book is to provide entrepreneurs with principles and frameworks for flourishing in the formation of the business.

Business ideas generated either through discovery or by creation are only as good as the information they are based on. Successful entrepreneurs have superior access to information that includes quality sources of search behavior, market gaps[36] which come from industry insiders,

Table 0.2 Generating ideas

	Themes	Illustrative key findings
Internal stimulation	Personal desire and interest	Interest in the certain business sector and business idea from the beginning
	Family members	Encouragement and advice by parents and relatives
	A deliberate search of ideas	Series of activities to explore new business ideas and testing them
	New inventions/discovery	Series of trial and error to find a market for a novice idea
External stimulation	Personal work experiences	Ideas generated observing current/past markets
	Personal experiences as customers	The desire to correct problems of products or services which were experienced as a consumer
	Evaluation	Growth in the product line, availability of new resources, new technology, or gaps in the supply chain
	Market evaluations	New markets, government regulation, and challenging competition

government connections, and financial institutions. Access to quality information depends on various factors, but the most important factor in emerging economies is an entrepreneur's status in the social ladder. Superior social ties and high-income groups have enhanced access to high-quality information about entrepreneurial opportunities.[37] However, entrepreneurs are alert to recognize the possibility of making money out of their existing business or new ventures by evolving their strategies through guesswork, analysis, and actions that test their initial findings. Entrepreneurs invest in building diverse social networks to improve the quantity and quality of information and to increase the speed of acquiring additional information.[38] Following either a deliberate search for a business idea or stumbling across an opportunity requires having credible knowledge, vigilance, and risk-taking.

Table 0.2 summarizes where ideas come from. Ideas can be broadly categorized into internally or externally stimulated by separating them on how deliberate the entrepreneur was in discovering the opportunity. Each of the two categories is divided into themes or techniques that contain recognized methods of idea generation. These techniques are highly influenced by the culture in which the individual lives or works. An individual's desire to create a venture can be influenced by both family members and their company's culture of innovation. Other techniques look at how a functioning venture creates ideas for new products and services by analyzing their market/customer needs. Each technique contains a series of activities that result in idea generation and have multiple factors (family, experience, reports) influencing the process.

Opportunity development and evaluation

Business opportunity can be realized by executing distinct processes of discovery, development, and creation (business model). Discovery is the process of creating or perceiving current and/or future market needs and/or underemployed resources. The customers' needs previously discussed, the presence of resources, and new venture ideas arise from various channels ranging from personal expertise to deliberate research process. Opportunity development is the process where entrepreneurs perform "due diligence" by committing resources and investment for further development of an idea.[39] In this stage, entrepreneurs attempt to craft, shape, mold, and reconstruct the discovered opportunities by carrying out different fit and balance between resources and teams (human capital) to get the odds in their favor.[40] The important criteria are to consider the opportunity as moving targets where business strategies evolve through guesswork, analysis, and actions that the entrepreneur takes in an attempt to find a "fit."[41] Lichtenthaler (2021) examines crisis management that companies went through during COVID-19 and evolved with new businesses. Author states that "contributes to research into innovation, strategic planning, managing AI, and entrepreneurial marketing."[42] Clausen (2020) developed a conceptual model process about how founders advance their ideas into opportunities. For the study, the author utilizes translation theory in which the three are interlinked. The model presents "a triple-looped process driven by distinct types of translation, lateral, vertical and empirical." The author stated that "a process of translation between three interlinked but distinct entities over time: ostensive ideas (abstract entrepreneurial ideas), performative ideas (context-specific entrepreneurial ideas) and venture offerings."[43]

Development is the iterative process of "discovering fit" between particular market needs and specified resources, and in the process, the opportunity grows into a business model. The created business model compares market needs and resources until they match the entrepreneur's ambitions or objectives. The following are evaluation methods that can be applied to an idea to discover its business value.

An evaluation procedure known as feasibility analysis examines opportunities by stating the uniqueness/value of the discovery for prospective stakeholders. The method implies the existence of a business model, even one that might be basic in form. This basic business model contains the perceived market needs or resources that were discovered and conceptually creates a business model that is feasible[44] in its abstract form. Feasibility analysis works in situations where business needs or underutilized resources are well defined, easy to comprehend, and the knowledge of the market need is universally acknowledged.

However, for many opportunities, an entrepreneur discovers there is a need to define many of the aspects of a business model. Opportunities do not come with a defined market need, a fully functional product/service, or any prior evidence of its value to the stakeholders. Because the idea of the product/service is nascent, entrepreneurs face circumstances where the evaluation procedure has to define business concepts that make the business model. A popular procedure that may be adapted to a wide range of circumstances is the "stage-gate" procedure.[45] The procedure explicitly calls for evaluation of an opportunity at each level of its discovery, where at each level the entrepreneur answers an integral business question. An opportunity to pass through each of the "gates" goes through a number of tests that aim to answer questions of its objective, problems it aims to solve, risks, technology/resource requirements, financials, the entrepreneur's responsibilities, and their personal objectives.

The entrepreneur is likely to conduct evaluations several times, and at every stage a piece of the business venture is realized. Evaluation of resources to market needs happens even after the creation of a business venture and can often lead to useful revisions of business concepts or rethinking of business objectives for the venture to sustain. Additionally, the process also could lead to recognition of additional opportunities or adjustments to the initial vision of the business ideas. At the same time, it can result in the aborting of opportunities at any level of development. It is natural that the number of market needs and underemployed resources perceived greatly exceeds the number of successful businesses formed. Evolution of a business opportunity is summarized in Figure 0.3.

Business model

The business model is defined as "the architecture of a venture – soup to nuts – that lead to a financial outcome."[46,47] A business model contains viable and relatively reasonable financial details of the business opportunity. Formal cash flows, schedules of activities, and resource

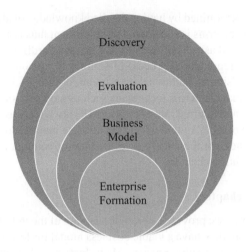

Figure 0.3 Evolution of opportunity

Figure 0.4 Business model

requirements are added to the continuously evolving venture creation process. Precision lays the foundation for cash flow statements and for identifying the major risk factors that could affect cash flow; all of these additions enable the business concept to transform into a full business plan. Figure 0.4 summarizes a business model.

Definitions[48]

Business concept: An idea for a business that includes basic information about the service or product, the target demographic, and a unique selling proposition that gives a company an advantage over competitors. A business concept may involve a new product or simply a novel approach to marketing or delivering an existing product.

Business model: A business model is a company's plan on how it will generate revenues and make a profit. It explains what products or services the business plans to manufacture and market, and how it plans to do so, including what expenses it will incur.

Financial plan: A financial plan is a comprehensive evaluation of an investor's current and future financial state by using currently known variables to predict future cash flows, asset values, and withdrawal plans. These metrics are used along with estimates of venture growth to determine if the entrepreneur's financial goals can be met in the future.

A comprehensive business model includes not only a detailed report of the need, the resources, and the market size, but also a financial model estimates the value of the product or service that is being created and how that value might be distributed among stakeholders.[49] Financial reports can be considered as final steps of the development process as they require forecasting of cash flows which can be only determined by having detailed knowledge of all aspects of the business. The opportunity in financial terms is considered as investment thus is given a numerical value in currency denomination as all aspects of the business are standardized to financial terms.

Beyond the typical entrepreneurial process of venture formation, some new businesses are also formed through acquisitions, additional investment, or through loans. Methods of evaluating opportunities using financial terms/techniques such as payback, simple interest, discount or net present value (NPV), and internal rate of return (IRR) are widely used by venture capitalists, bankers, and financial experts.[50] An understanding of these methods of evaluation is important for the entrepreneur as they are the widely used medium of communication. Financial dimensions are covered in the future chapters.

Conclusion and future chapters

In this introductory chapter, we provided a brief description of the initial stages that an entrepreneur will go through before they have a viable business model for forming a new venture. These stages shall take place for most entrepreneurs. Many factors such as an individual's character, personal knowledge, and public circumstances will have a significant impact on how an entrepreneur proceeds in these stages. The next ten chapters will provide theoretical and empirical presentations in the areas of entrepreneurial environment, personal characteristics, organization structure, and process that will enlighten these important subjects.

We have developed questions that would motivate discussions and quick reviews that summarize key subjects for each chapter. Long and short case studies, videos of entrepreneurs, organizations, companies, etc. are incorporated within each chapter to share experiences and advance discussions. Additionally, they will reinforce the key learning objectives of each chapter.

The remainder of the book is summarized according to the Figure 0.5, showing an overarching impact on all sections of the textbook. The following shows each of the four parts of the book and the chapter titles. In summary, the book provides a systematic, logical, and practical

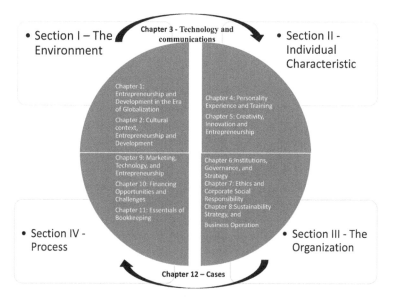

Figure 0.5 Textbook framework

Source: Adapted from Gartner, W.B. (1985). A conceptual framework for describing the phenomenon of new venture creation. *Academy of Management Review*, 10(4), 696–706.

approach for scholars, students, and entrepreneurs who seek to enhance their knowledge in the field and support entrepreneurial initiation.

Supporting materials

This book offers an entrepreneurial approach for faculty and students in terms of teaching and learning. In the second edition, we have tested the book in classrooms and therefore, we have enhanced and improved its content, approach, examples, and readability. We provide essential content and supporting materials for presentation and discussion while leaving a significant degree of creativity and innovation for faculty and students to incorporate cases and content that in their view best fits for their approach. The following is a summary of supporting materials.

1 *Case studies*: Each chapter has an opening case study that summarizes the essence of the chapter and follows with a few questions for discussion. Also, three longitudinal cases that provide examinations of the life cycle of two companies and a higher education institution are added as the last chapter of the book. These cases will provide a holistic perspective of entrepreneurship through time and domain. We have included more than 50 international short case studies that display a real-life perspective of important topics that are covered. Additionally, we have a good number of TED Talks in the book. The aim for including these cases and TED Talks is to stimulate discussion and debates in class.
2 *Video clips*: We have included seven interesting TED Talks about important subjects of the book that will highlight fascinating perspectives for class discussion.
3 *Quick reviews*: We have developed quick reviews at the end of some chapters.
4 *PowerPoint slides*: We have developed a comprehensive set of interesting and interactive PowerPoint slides for each chapter. Each chapter has about 30 slides. The slides intend to assist instructors in their presentation of the materials and enable students to comprehend the concepts and their applications.
5 *Exam questions*: About 15 thoughtful essay questions are developed for each chapter to facilitate class discussion and usage by the instructor for quizzes and exams. Faculty will have access to multiple choice and true/false questions for each chapter.

Notes

1 Seetharaman, P. (2020). Business models shifts: Impact of Covid-19. *International Journal of Information Management*, 54, 102173.
2 www.wsj.com/articles/google-ai-chatbot-bard-chatgpt-rival-bing-a4c2d2ad
3 Tang, J., Kacmar, K.M., & Busenitz, L. (2012). Entrepreneurial alertness in the pursuit of new opportunities. *Journal of Business Venturing*, 27(1), 77–94. https://doi.org/10.1016/j.jbusvent.2010.07.001
4 Ardichvili, A.A., Cardozo, R., & Ray, S. (2003). A theory of entrepreneurial opportunity identification and development. *Journal of Business Venturing*, 18(1), 105–123. https://doi.org/10.1016/S0883-9026(01)00068-4
5 Alvarez, S.A., & Barney, J.B. (2010). Entrepreneurship and epistemology: The philosophical underpinnings of the study of entrepreneurial opportunities. *The Academy of Management Annals*, 4(1), 557–583. https://doi.org/10.1080/19416520.2010.495521
6 Venkataraman, S., Sarasvathy, S.D., Dew, N., & Forster, W.R. (2012). Reflections on the 2010 AMR decade award: Whither the promise? Moving forward with entrepreneurship as a science of the artificial. *Academy of Management Review*, 37(1), 21–33. https://doi.org/10.5465/amr.2011.0079
7 De Bono, E. (1978, September). When opportunity knocks. *Management Today*, 102–105.
8 Kirzner, I. (1979). *Perception, Opportunity and Profit*. Chicago, IL: University of Chicago Press.
9 Long, W., & McMullean, W. (1984). Mapping the new venture opportunity identification process. In *Frontiers of Entrepreneurship Research* (pp. 567–590). Wellesley, MA: Babson College.
10 Hulbert, B., Brown, R.B., & Adams, S. (1997). Towards an understanding of opportunity. *Marketing Education Review*, 7(3), 67.

11 Ardichvili, A., Cardozo, R., & Ray, S. (2003). A theory of entrepreneurial opportunity identification and development. *Journal of Business Venturing*, 18(1), 105–123.

12 Shane, S., & Venkataraman, S. (2000). The promise of entrepreneurship as a field of research. *Academy of Management Review*, 25, 217–226.

13 Kirchhoff, B.A. (1994). *Entrepreneurship and Dynamic Capitalism: The Economics of Business Firm Formation and Growth*. Westport, CT: Praeger.

14 Alvarez, S.A., & Barney, J.B. (2007). Discovery and creation: Alternative theories of entrepreneurial action. *Organizational Context*, 3(6), 123–152.

15 Doing Business. (2011). Retrieved May 20, 2013, from www.doingbusiness.org/

16 Friedman, T. (2007). *Thank You for Being Late: An Optimist's Guide to Thriving in the Age of Accelerations*. New York: Farrar, Straus and Giroux.

17 Friedman, T. (2007). *Thank You for Being Late: An Optimist's Guide to Thriving in the Age of Accelerations*. New York: Farrar, Straus and Giroux.

18 Chandra, Y., Styles, C., & Wilkinson, I.F. (2009). The recognition of first time international entrepreneurial opportunities: Evidence from firms in knowledge-based industries. *International Marketing Review*, 26(1), 30–61.

19 Alvarez, S.A., & Barney, J.B. (2007). Discovery and creation: Alternative theories of entrepreneurial action. *Organizational Context*, 3(6), 123–152.

20 Kirzner, I. (1973). *Competition and Entrepreneurship*. Chicago, IL: University of Chicago Press.

21 Shane, S. (2000). Prior knowledge and the discovery of entrepreneurial opportunities. *Organization Science*, 11(4), 448–470.

22 Walle, A. (2018). *Beyond Heroic Paradigms: Expanded Models of Entrepreneurship*. Cambridge, MA: CYRUS Institute of Knowledge.

23 McMullen, J., Plummer, L., & Acs, Z. (2007). What is an entrepreneurial opportunity? *Small Business Economics*, 28(4), 273–283. Retrieved from www.jstor.org/stable/40229532

24 Louth, J.D. (1966). The changing face of marketing. *McKinsey Quarterly*.

25 Baker, T., & Nelson, R.E. (2005). Creating something from nothing: Resource construction through entrepreneurial bricolage. *Administrative Science Quarterly*, 50(3), 329–366.

26 Dodgson, M. (2011). Exploring new combinations in innovation and entrepreneurship: Social networks, Schumpeter, and the case of Josiah Wedgwood (1730–1795). *Industrial and Corporate Change*, 20(4), 1119–1151.

27 Sarasvathy, S.D. (2001). Causation and effectuation: Toward a theoretical shift from economic inevitability to entrepreneurial contingency. *Academy of Management Review*, 26(2), 242–263.

28 Chetty, S., Karami, M., & Martín, O.M. (2018). Opportunity discovery and creation as a duality: Evidence from small firms' foreign market entries. *Journal of International Marketing*, 26(3), 70–93.

29 Jones, R.J., & Barnir, A. (2019). Properties of opportunity creation and discovery: Comparing variation in contexts of innovativeness. *Technovation*, 79, 1–10.

30 Dencker, J.C., Bacq, S., Gruber, M., & Haas, M. (2021). Reconceptualizing necessity entrepreneurship: A contextualized framework of entrepreneurial processes under the condition of basic needs. *Academy of Management Review*, 46(1), 60–79.

31 THINKING Methods. (2018). Retrieved from www.ideaconnection.com/thinking-methods/

32 Stillman, J. (2014, October 1). *The 4 Stages of Creativity*. Retrieved from www.inc.com/jessica-stillman/the-4-stages-of-creativity.html

33 www.google.com/search?rlz=1C1GCEB_enUS815US815&q=discovery+and+creation+approaches+comparison&tbm=isch&source=univ&sa=X&ved=2ahUKEwjb7Lzm78HkAhVDu1kKHXMwDPUQsAR6BAgAEAE&biw=853&bih=406#

34 Baron, R.A. (2007). Behavioral and cognitive factors in entrepreneurship: Entrepreneurs as the active element in new venture creation. *Strategic Entrepreneurship Journal*, 1(1–2), 167–182.

35 Gaglio, C.M. (1997). Opportunity identification: Review, critique and suggested research directions. In J.A. Katz, & R.H. Brockhaus (Eds.), *Advances in Entrepreneurship, Firm Emergence and Growth* (Vol. 3). Greenwich, CT: JAI Press.

36 Kaish, S., & Gilad, B. (1991). Characteristics of opportunity search of entrepreneurs vs. executives: Sources, interest and general alertness. *Journal of Business Venturing*, 6, 45–61.

37 Arenius, P., & De Clercq, D. (2005). A network-based approach on opportunity recognition. *Small Business Economics*, 24(3), 249–265.

38 Aldrich, H.E., & Zimmer, C. (1986). Entrepreneurship through social networks. In D.L. Sexton, & R.W. Smilor (Eds.), *The Art and Science of Entrepreneurship* (pp. 3–23). Cambridge, MA: Ballinger.

39 Venkataraman, S. (1997). The distinctive domain of entrepreneurship research: An editor's perspective. In J. Katz, & R. Brockhaus (Eds.), *Advances in Entrepreneurship, Firm Emergence, and Growth* (Vol. 3, pp. 119–138). Greenwich, CT: JAI Press.

40 Timmon, J.A., & Spinelli, S. (2009). *New Venture Creation: Entrepreneurship for the 21st Century* (7th ed.). New Delhi, India: Tata McGraw-Hill Education Pvt. Ltd.

41 Bhide, A. (1994, March–April). How entrepreneurs craft strategies that work. *Harvard Business Review*, 72(2), 150–161.

42 Lichtenthaler, U. (2021). A conceptual framework for innovation and new business opportunities in the post-pandemic period. *Innovation*, 7, 74–89.

43 Clausen, T.H. (2020). Entrepreneurial thinking and action in opportunity development: A conceptual process model. *International Small Business Journal*, 38(1), 21–40.

44 Ardichvili, A., Cardozo, R., & Ray, S. (2003). A theory of entrepreneurial opportunity identification and development. *Journal of Business Venturing*, 18(1), 105–123. https://doi.org/10.1016/S0883-9026(01)00068-4

45 Ardichvili, A., Cardozo, R., & Ray, S. (2003). A theory of entrepreneurial opportunity identification and development. *Journal of Business Venturing*, 18(1), 105–123. https://doi.org/10.1016/S0883-9026(01)00068-4

46 FourWeekMBA. (n.d.). *What is a Business Model? 30 Successful Types of Business Models You Need to Know*. Retrieved from https://fourweekmba.com/what-is-a-business-model/

47 Mayer, M., & Crane, F. (2011). *Entrepreneurship: An Innovator's Guide to Startups and Corporate Venture*. Thousand Oaks, CA: SAGE.

48 What is Business Concept? Definition and Meaning. (n.d.). Retrieved November 3, 2018, from www.businessdictionary.com/definition/business-concept.html

49 Ardichvili, A., Cardozo, R., & Ray, S. (2003). A theory of entrepreneurial opportunity identification and development. *Journal of Business Venturing*, 18(1), 105–123. https://doi.org/10.1016/S0883-9026(01)00068-4

50 Forrest, C. (n.d.). *Glossary: Startup and Venture Capital Terms You Should Know*. Retrieved from www.techrepublic.com/article/glossary-startup-and-venture-capital-terms-you-should-know/

Section I

The environment and entrepreneurship

1 Entrepreneurship and development in the era of globalization

There are essential questions about the impact of globalization on entrepreneurship and economic growth and development, such as: Does globalization accelerate growth and development by advancing entrepreneurship? What is the impact of entrepreneurship on innovation in developing countries? How can evolution of technology in the developed nations influence entrepreneurship in the developing countries? The devastating effects of COVID-19 on humanity seem to have revised the perspectives of citizens, companies, and policymakers regarding globalization, as we knew it. This chapter will discuss these questions by defining entrepreneurship, growth, and development in the era of globalization. We will employ relevant theories to understand incentives that drive growth and development at both micro and macro levels. The chapter takes into consideration the influences of key factors such as culture, public policies, innovation, and competition on entrepreneurial activities. Also, we will discuss the impact of COVID-19 on the aspects of these relevant issues. With the use of case studies, examples, and illustrations readers will gain a deeper understanding of importance of influences of globalization on entrepreneurship.

Learning objectives

1 Understand definitions of entrepreneurship, development, and globalization
2 Comprehend the relationships between entrepreneurship, development, and globalization
3 Discuss the major theories of economic development
4 Evaluate entrepreneurship operations in developing countries
5 Examine the influences of globalization on entrepreneurship
6 Discuss the impact of COVID-19 on globalization and entrepreneurship.

Box 1.1   Special economic zones and their impact on local economy

Special economic zones (SEZs) have been growing in the global economic landscape. Special industrial privileges have been granted since centuries ago and helped guarantee free exchange along trade routes. The first "modern" SEZ is considered to be in Shannon Airport in Clare, Ireland.[1] From about the 1970s, many SEZs were established for labor-intensive manufacturing, mostly in Latin America and East Asia.[2] Indeed, we find that the building of SEZs in modern times has exploded since about 2005.

DOI: 10.4324/9781003405740-3

Why are SEZs attractive?

The phrase "special economic zone" encompasses a broad range of special zones such as tax-exempt zones, free trade zones, export-processing zones, free ports, industrial parks, high-tech zones, economic and technology development zones, science and innovation parks, enterprise zones, and others. Special regions within a country are designated as SEZs, where business and trade laws are different from the rest of the country with the purpose of attracting foreign investment and developing infrastructure and technology.

If implemented properly, SEZs can be an effective instrument to promote industrialization and development. In many developing countries, this strategy has paid off, particularly for countries in East Asia. Seeing results from this strategy, more countries implemented this tool as part of their development plans.

What is it about SEZs that enables countries to increase the pace of economic development of the country as a whole? SEZs generally include the following characteristics:

- It is a specifically separated area which is also mostly physically secured.
- It has its own separate management or administration from the rest of the country.
- It provides benefits for investors physically within the zone.
- It has its own customs area (duty-free benefits) and own special procedures.[3]

Generally, SEZs are established to achieve one or more of the following policy objectives: (a) attract foreign direct investment (FDI); (b) help alleviate large-scale unemployment; (c) support economic reform strategies; and (d) serve as an experiment for new policies. In this summary, we focus on the first objective, attraction of FDI, and use it as part of our basic definition for a "successful" SEZ.

Despite initial investment and development, most SEZs take 5–10 years to become effective. While some countries have exhibited rapid growth, many SEZs, especially in Africa, failed to develop local economies, even after 10 years of operation (although it is still too early to tell for some).

Duranton and Venables (2018) set to analyse the effects of place-based policies that intend to stimulate private sector investment and economic growth. They examine it in the contexts of transport improvements, economic corridors, special economic zones, lagging regions, and urban policies. However, they state that it is hard to assess the social values of these policies.[4]

Questions for discussion

1 Analyze the role of SEZs on the development of communities and countries.
2 Are there any drawbacks for having SEZs in the long run?
3 Why do SEZs have different outcomes in different regions of the world?
4 Examine the claim of Duranton and Venables (2018) for one SEZ of your choosing.

Introduction

In this chapter we will describe the relationship between entrepreneurship, growth, and development, as well as how globalization has influenced this relationship.

Figure 1.1 SEZ worldwide

There are many fundamental questions scholars, policymakers, NGO activists, and others are asking about the impact of globalization on the relationship between entrepreneurship and economic growth and development. Some examples include: Does globalization accelerate development by advancing entrepreneurship in developing countries? What is the impact of entrepreneurship on innovation in developing countries? What is creativity and how does it relate to innovation and development? What are the effects of entrepreneurship on employment and income in the era of globalization? How has entrepreneurship in developing countries been influenced by the revolution in technology? How has COVID-19 impacted the evolution of globalization and development? We will attempt to provide answers to these questions by applying relevant theories and discussing their practical entrepreneurial implications.

By the end of this chapter, you will be able to understand the profound link between entrepreneurship, globalization, and sustainable growth and development. Case studies, examples, and illustrations will help guide readers towards a deeper understanding of the role of entrepreneurial business formation on growth and development.

Box 1.2   Major themes of research on entrepreneurship, innovation, and sustainable growth

Scholars, policymakers, and NGOs are examining the relationship between globalization, geopolitical tensions, entrepreneurship, and sustainable development goals. These are new frontiers to be explored.

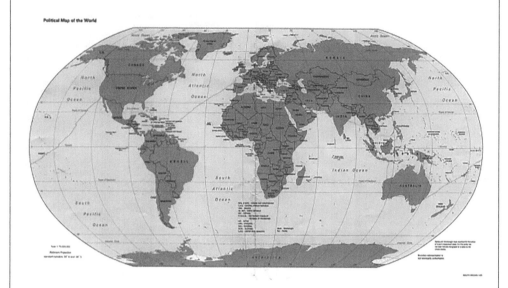

Figure 1.2 Research without borders

Defining entrepreneurship

There is a lack of agreement among stakeholders on what constitutes entrepreneurship. Some scholars view entrepreneurship as a process of new venture creation.[5] Others conceptualize it as the process of opportunity recognition, opportunity creation, and opportunity exploitation[6] or, more broadly, as "a dynamic interaction between entrepreneurial attitudes, entrepreneurial activity, and entrepreneurial aspiration that varies across stages of economic development."[7]

Still others define entrepreneurship, specifically strategic entrepreneurship, as a social process of mobilizing and orchestrating resources, creating value and generating wealth, etc. For the purposes of this textbook, we will follow a mid-range theoretical lens, and conceptualize entrepreneurship as a socially embedded and context-specific process of resource mobilization and opportunity exploitation, culminating in the creation of a new venture, whose purpose is to create value and generate wealth and other social enhancement benefits.[8] This approach provides a broad and theoretically robust framework with which we can critically review and integrate conceptual developments and empirical evidence that may highlight the unique characteristics of new venture creation when aligned with developing countries.

Box 1.3   Contextual of entrepreneurial activities

Social and contextual aspects influence the fundamental way that entrepreneurship functions. For example, what works in India may not work in other countries.

The term "entrepreneur" was coined by French economist Jean-Baptist Say and was originally translated as "adventurer." In 1821 in his book, *A Treatise on Political Economy, or the Production, Distribution, and Consumption of Wealth*, Say described entrepreneurs as agents of change who seek opportunities for profit and, by doing so, create both new markets and fresh opportunities.[9]

Joseph A. Schumpeter, an Austrian-born American economist and political scientist, was perhaps the first scholar to theorize about entrepreneurship. In his 1911 book, *The Theory of Economic Development*, Schumpeter described entrepreneurs as being at the heart of a dynamic system of creative destruction, by which the economy as a whole is continuously reinvented. Another influential scholar in the study of entrepreneurship was Frank H. Knight. In his 1921 book, *Uncertainty and Profit*, Knight used the concepts of risk and uncertainty to explain the process by which entrepreneurs acquire resources.

Friedrich Hayek, in his 1945 book, *The Use of Knowledge in Society*, focused on the limited information available to individuals as the source of differential realization for entrepreneurial opportunities. Israel Kirzner, in his 1973 book, *Competition and Entrepreneurship*, posited that entrepreneurs are alert to profit opportunities and thus strive to help restore economic equilibrium rather than disturb it. The influential management and strategy scholar Peter F. Drucker also theorized on the importance of entrepreneurship. In his 1985 book, *Innovation and Entrepreneurship*, Drucker delved into classifications of entrepreneurial opportunities and provided practical advice to entrepreneurs, institutions, and the emerging entrepreneurial economy. William Baumol, in his 2002 book, *The Free-Market Innovation Machine*, described the key features of the free-market system that allowed for such incredible economic growth, including the important role played by independent entrepreneurs and the routinization of innovative activities by large corporations.

Fairlie and Fossen (2020) provide an explanation that business creation will increase during recession and two components are the driving factors, the opportunity and necessity. They state that there is some agreement on the conceptual definition of entrepreneurship. However, there is little agreement in the literature on empirical definitions. Applying their proposed definition of the opportunity entrepreneurship is generally procyclical while the necessity is mostly counter-cyclical.

Defining economic development

The World Bank defines economic development as the "qualitative change and restructuring in a country's economy in connection with technological and social progress."[10] The main indicator of economic development is increasing gross national product (GNP) per capita or gross domestic product (GDP) per capita, reflecting an increase in the economic productivity as well as average material well-being of a country's population. In the report, *Our Common Future*, written by the Brundtland Commission on Environment and Development, it was defined as "development that meets the needs of the present without compromising the ability of future generations to meet their own needs."[11]

Economic development is closely linked with economic growth. Economic growth is conventionally measured as the percentage increase in GNP or GDP for one year. Economic growth comes in two forms: an economy can either grow "extensively" by using more resources (e.g., physical, human, or natural capital) or "intensively" by using the same amount of resources more efficiently (productively). When economic growth is achieved through the use of greater labor, it does not result in the growth of per capita income.

But, when economic growth is achieved by more productive use of all resources, labor included, it results in higher per capita income and improvement in individuals' standard of living.[12] On the other hand, the 1998 Nobel Prize winner Professor Amartya Sen abandons the idea of measuring development through economic growth. Instead, he views "development as freedom."[13] His approach is mainly focused on "human flourishing," which he defines as the cornerstone of solving the problems of poverty and global inequality.[14]

He challenges the conventional understanding of development by changing the viewpoint of its meaning: "Development consists of the removal of various types of unfreedoms that leave people with little choice and little opportunity of exercising their reasoned agency."[15]

He further identifies the factors causing the "un-freedoms" as "poverty, tyranny, poor economic opportunities, systematic social deprivation, and neglect of public facilities and intolerance or overactivity of repressive states."[16] Some of the essential freedoms that he defines include "economic opportunities, political freedoms, social facilities, transparency guarantees and protective security," which he argues need to be interconnected in order to function efficiently and effectively.

Sen's view of development was crucial for the 20th century and played a significant role in redefining the concept of development to include human rights as a constitutive part.[17]

In the context of international organizations aiming to end extreme poverty and promote shared prosperity in a sustainable way, the World Bank Group[19] is a major player, with their 189 member countries, staff from more than 170 countries, and offices in over 130 locations being a unique global partnership consisting of five institutions working for sustainable solutions in developing countries.

Van Dam and Frenken (2020) propose a combinatorial model of economic development by acquiring new capabilities that allows production of a greater variety of products, given the increasing complexity of the era. In their study they show that "variety first increases and then decreases in the course of economic development" which is consistent with the empirical pattern.[20] Kostetska et al. (2020) examined the international trends and directions of inclusive growth which is composed of an index of the environmental, economic, social, and technological components. These are considered to be the prerequisites for inclusive environmental factors for management. The main objective of this study was the formation of prerequisites for inclusive growth and their follow-up methodological support.[21]

Major theories of economic development

Over the past century, several economists have articulated theories and relevant policies and practices to accelerate development. Understanding these theories and their applications will help recognize incentives that drive development at both micro and macro levels. Additionally, they will provide an understanding of the societal change that will emerge in developing countries.

Box 1.4   Development as a freedom

Amartya Sen is an Indian economist and philosopher currently working at Harvard University. He has made vast contributions to the studies of welfare economics, social choice theory, economic and social justice, economic theories of famines, and indexes of the measure of well-being of citizens in developing countries. These contributions awarded him a Nobel Memorial Prize in Economic Sciences in 1998.[18]

Figure 1.3 Social choice, welfare distributions, and poverty

Box 1.5   Major theories of economic development

1   Rostow's theory
2   The Harrod-Domar model
3   Lewis structural change
4   Chenery's patterns of development approach
5   Dependency theory
6   Neoclassical theory.

Rostow's theory[22]

Rostow's theory is one of the major historical models of economic growth, which was developed by W.W. Rostow in 1960. The model proposes that economic growth occurs in five basic stages of varying lengths:

1   Traditional society
2   Preconditions for take-off
3   Take-off
4   Drive to maturity
5   Age of high mass consumption.

Each stage can only be reached through the completion of the previous stage. Rostow asserts that all developed countries have gone through these stages. These stages are as follows:

The traditional society: This is typically a society with no access to science and technology where most of its resources are dedicated to agricultural use. Agricultural productivity is mostly at the subsistence level and there is limited market interaction.

Preparatory stage: There is an expansion in output which extends beyond agricultural produce to manufactured goods. This is the result of higher savings levels and investments in education. In this stage, there are lower levels of market specialization.

Take-off stage: At this stage, revolutionary changes occur in both agriculture and industry to attain self-sustaining economic growth. There is greater urbanization and increased human capital accumulation.

Drive to maturity: This stage takes place after a long period of time. The population involved in agriculture declines while industry becomes more diverse. Overall income per capita

Figure 1.4 Rostow's theory

increases. The rate of savings and investments is such that it can automatically sustain economic growth.

Stage of mass consumption: At this stage, a country's demand shifts from food, clothing, and other basic necessities to demand luxuries. To satisfy these needs, new industries involve themselves in mass production to match consumption.

Rostow's theory became one of the important concepts in the theory of modernization of America during John F. Kennedy's presidency, but his thesis was criticized because it could not be replicated in places like Latin America or sub-Saharan Africa.

The Harrod-Domar model

The Harrod-Domar model is an early post-Keynesian model of economic growth that explains its growth rate in terms of the level of saving and productivity of capital. The implications are that growth depends on the quantity of labor and capital. More investment leads to higher capital accumulation which generates economic growth. The Harrod-Domar model was developed independently by Sir Roy Harrod in 1939 and Evsey Domar in 1946.

Box 1.6   The future of mobility

Innovation of Uber, Lyft, and many other similar car sharing models in developing countries will have a significant impact on employment and the environment, which requires public policies in development and developing countries. Incoming autonomous driving will have an enormous impact on several industries in developed countries and in the future of developing countries. These innovations, which are the practical application of innovation and technologies, will take societies to uncharted territory. Get ready and prepare yourself!

Box 1.7   Quick review on entrepreneurship and economic development

- There is a lack of agreement on what constitutes entrepreneurship among stakeholders.
- This book conceptualizes entrepreneurship as a socially embedded and context-specific process of resource mobilization and opportunity exploitation, culminating in the creation of a new venture, whose purpose is to create value and generate wealth and other social enhancement benefits.
- Economic growth comes in two forms: an economy can either grow "extensively" by using more resources (i.e., physical, human, or natural capital) or "intensively" by using the same amount of resources more efficiently (i.e., productively).
- "Development consists of the removal of various types of unfreedoms that leave people with little choice and little opportunity of exercising their reasoned agency."[23]

Lewis structural change

This model stresses the transformation from a traditional, agricultural economy to a modern, industrial economy. The Lewis model is attracting attention due to its linkages between traditional agriculture and modern industry through migration of workers from rural to urban areas. However, it is criticized for incorrectly assuming that real urban wages will not rise. Arthur Lewis believed that since the industrialized economy is run by capitalists, wages paid for labor are fixed instead of being paid according to the value imparted on the goods during production. He also believed that migration and modern sector employment grows proportionately to urban full employment.[24] Van Neuss (2019) provided a comprehensive literature survey aiming to identify the key drivers of structural changes. The author generally defined the process of "reallocation of economic activity across the three broad sectors agriculture, manufacturing and services." Van Neuss used the GGDC 10-Sector Database to present the empirical facts associated with structural change in different regions of the world: Europe, the United States, Asia, Latin America, and Africa.[25]

Chenery's patterns of development approach

Hollis Burnley Chenery's findings of the patterns of development are presented in an empirically styled visual and include the shift in production from agriculture to industry and services. It also shows the accumulation of physical and human capital, as well as the shift to material consumption, investment, and the growth of trade, which are presented as a share of GNP. See Figure 1.5.

Dependency theory

This theory stipulates that resources flow from poor (periphery), underdeveloped states to wealthy (core) states and therefore enrich the latter at the expense of the former. The central argument of this theory is that poor states are impoverished and rich ones enriched (see Figure 1.7).[26]

Neoclassical theory

The neoclassical-dependent school emphasizes unequal power relationships between the developed and less developed countries. It blames the reason for underdevelopment in a few countries (conscious or unconscious) on exploitation by the developed country. This is preserved by a small

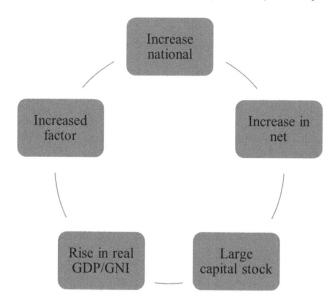

Figure 1.5 Chenery's patterns of development approach

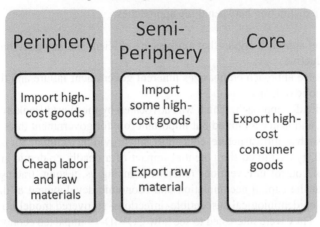

Figure 1.6 Andre Gunder Frank dependency theory

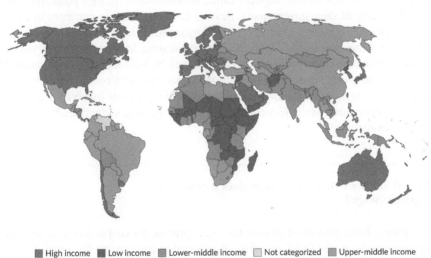

Figure 1.7 World Bank income classification

elite ruling class within such developing countries. Andre Gunder Frank, the leading dependency theorist, "suggests that lack of development is because western nations have deliberately under-developed them." The international trading system and multinational companies practice is creating conditions that means less developed countries are dependent on western aids and markets.[27]

This theory of the 1980s is termed *neoclassical counterrevolution*, and it emphasizes corruption, inefficiency, and a lack of economic incentives within developing countries as being responsible for the lack of development.

We can make a distinction between three approaches:

1 The free market approach argues that markets are efficient and any government intervention is counterproductive.
2 The public choice approach emphasizes inherent government failure and the self-interested behavior of public officials.
3 The market-friendly approach, which was advocated by the World Bank, recognizes market imperfections, and hence a limited but important role for government through non-selective interventions such as infrastructure, education, and providing a climate for private enterprise. Gori et al. (2021) examined the potential impact of a deadly epidemic and its main non-pharmaceutical control interventions (social distancing vs. testing, tracing, and isolation). They looked at the capital accumulation and economic development at different times by integrating an epidemiological susceptible–infectious–recovered model utilizing the Solow growth model. They were interested to see how COVID-19 impacted economic performance and the application of different approaches.[28]

Definition and classification of countries

According to the World Bank, developing economies are countries with low to mid-levels of GNP per capita; five high-income developing economies – Hong Kong (China), Israel, Kuwait, Singapore, and the United Arab Emirates – also fall into this category. These five economies are classified as developing, despite their high per capita income because of their economic structure or the official opinion of their governments. Several countries that are currently in transition from a centrally planned economy to a market economy are sometimes grouped with developing countries because of their low to mid-levels of per capita income. In a few cases, they sometimes are grouped among the developed countries because of their high level of industrialization. More than 80 percent of the world's population lives in more than 100 developing countries.[29]

The World Bank classifies all the developing countries into heavily indebted poor countries (HIPCs), low-income, lower-middle-income, and middle-income economies.[30,31] Figure 1.7 shows the classifications.[32]

Box 1.8   What is a living wage? How does it compare to the minimum wage?

The living wage is the amount of income needed to provide the cost of living in any location for anyone who works full-time, which is adjusted to compensate for inflation.

The purpose of a living wage is to make sure that anyone who works full-time should have enough money to live above the federal poverty level and avoid homelessness.

Source: Definition from www.thebalance.com.

The World Economic Forum, which is recognized by the Swiss authorities as an international body, provides a similar classification of countries at different levels of economic development. This classification places a country at three major stages of economic development: factor-driven economies, efficiency-driven economies, and innovation-driven economies. There also exist two transition stages: the transition from factor driven to efficiency driven, and the transition from efficiency driven to innovation driven. See Figure 1.8.

Table 1.1 presents the countries/economies at each stage of development, based on the World Economic Forum's 2015–2016 Global Competitiveness Index.[33]

Figure 1.8 Development classification factors

Table 1.1 Countries/economies at each stage of economic development

Stage 1: *Factor driven (35* *economies)*	*Transition from* *stage 1 to stage 2* *(16 economies)*	*Stage 2:* *Efficiency driven* *(31 economies)*	*Transition from* *stage 2 to stage 3* *(20 economies)*	*Stage 3:* *Innovation driven (38* *economies)*
Bangladesh	Algeria	Albania	Argentina	Australia
Benin	Azerbaijan	Armenia	Brazil	Austria
Burundi	Bhutan	Bolivia	Chile	Bahrain
Cambodia	Botswana	Bosnia and Herzegovina	Costa Rica	Belgium
Cameroon	Gabon	Bulgaria	Croatia	Canada
Chad	Honduras	Cape Verde	Hungary	Cyprus
Cote d'Ivoire	Iran	China	Latvia	Czech Republic
Ethiopia	Kazakhstan	Colombia	Lebanon	Denmark
Gambia, The	Kuwait	Dominican Republic	Lithuania	Estonia
Ghana	Moldova	Ecuador	Malaysia	Finland
Guinea	Mongolia	Egypt	Mauritius	France
Haiti	Nigeria	El Salvador	Mexico	Germany
India	Philippines	Georgia	Oman	Greece
Kenya	Saudi Arabia	Guatemala	Panama	Hong Kong SAR
Kyrgyz Republic	Venezuela	Guyana	Poland	Iceland
Lao PDR	Vietnam	Indonesia	Romania	Israel
Lesotho		Jamaica	Russian Federation	Italy
Liberia		Jordan	Seychelles	Japan
Madagascar		Macedonia, FYR	Turkey	Korea Republic
Malawi		Montenegro	Uruguay	Luxembourg
Mauritania		Morocco		Malta
Mozambique		Namibia		Netherlands
Myanmar		Paraguay		New Zealand
Nepal		Peru		Norway
Nicaragua		Serbia		Portugal
Pakistan		South Africa		Qatar
Rwanda		Sri Lanka		Singapore
Senegal		Swaziland		Slovak Republic
Sierra Leone		Thailand		Slovenia
Tajikistan		Tunisia		Spain
Tanzania		Ukraine		Sweden
Uganda				Switzerland
Zambia				Taiwan, China
Zimbabwe				Trinidad and Tobago
				United Arab Emirates
				United Kingdom
				United States

Entrepreneurship in the developing countries

The link between entrepreneurship and economic development is complex. On one hand, the level of a country's economic development determines the nature of entrepreneurial initiatives available to its aspiring entrepreneurs. On the other hand, the entrepreneurial activity itself is seen by many as a major vessel for self-employment, empowerment, poverty alleviation, economic growth, and social progress. In the following, we discuss both aspects of the relationship.

Stage of economic development and entrepreneurial activity

The stage of a country's economic development determines, to a large extent, the scope of its entrepreneurial activity, as well as the nature of feasible entrepreneurial initiatives. As mentioned earlier, countries can be classified into five stages of economic development: factor driven; in the transition from factor driven to efficiency driven; efficiency driven; in the transition from efficiency driven to innovation driven; and innovation driven. Companies present in countries that are in the first stage of economic development compete on the basis of price. They sell basic products or commodities with low productivity, which reflects their lower prices. As business becomes more competitive, the countries move into the efficiency-driven stage of development. Companies begin to develop more efficient production processes and also improve their product quality. The wages rise due to the requirement of a skilled workforce, but yet they do not see any increase in prices. Finally, as countries move into the innovation-driven stage, wages will have risen so much that they reach an equilibrium, thus improving the standard of living. Businesses that are able to produce new and unique products survive. At this stage, companies have to compete by producing new and different goods and services using the most sophisticated production processes and invention methods.

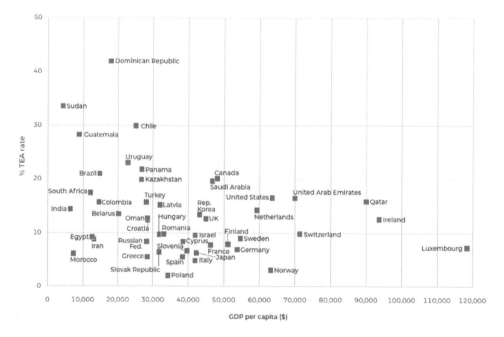

Figure 1.9 GDP per capita and Total Entrepreneurial Activity (TEA) rate, 2022

Source: Global Entrepreneurship Monitor (2023).[37]

In terms of scope, the entrepreneurial activity in an economy follows a curvilinear, U-shaped relationship with GDP, as shown in Figure 1.9. At low levels of per capita GDP, the entrepreneurial sector provides job opportunities and potential for the creation of new markets. The per capita income increases and the emergence of new technologies and economies of scale allow larger and more established firms to satisfy the increasing demand for growing markets. Therefore, increase in their relative role in the economy and the role of smaller and newer firms may decline.

Finally, in the third stage, the role played by the entrepreneurial sector in countries with higher GDP increases again, as more individuals have the resources to go into business in an economic environment that may present high-potential opportunities.[34]

Box 1.9   Uber operation in developing countries

Catherine Cheney wrote a piece for www.devex.com titled "What Is Driving Uber's Global Impact?," in which she discusses the evolution of Uber, shared cars, accelerating expansion and employment, etc. She states that "Uber Nigeria is a locally incorporated company that hires employees, runs support services, and adapts the platform to meet the demands of local consumers." While Uber riders in most markets pay via credit card through the app, riders in Nigeria and across sub-Saharan Africa have the option to pay in cash, which means adjusting to local market conditions. The most populous cities in the world cannot afford a future in which ridesharing and carpooling are not available.

Source: Cheney (2016).[35]

Thus, in terms of the nature of entrepreneurial initiatives, at lower levels of economic development, entrepreneurship is predominantly necessity driven.

Necessity-based entrepreneurship occurs when individuals participate in entrepreneurial activities because all other employment options are either absent or unsatisfactory.[36]

The relationship between the level of economic development and level of entrepreneurial activity is presented in Figure 1.9.

At higher levels of economic development, technological and institutional sophistication (e.g., the United States) gives rise to opportunity entrepreneurs, those who are driven by the achievement of success through exploiting an opportunity for some form of gain often believed to be economic.[38]

Opportunity-driven entrepreneurship is more desirable because it is more likely to be both technology and innovation based with high growth orientation, thus contributing to economic growth and development. As the level of economic development of the country increases, the ratio of necessity-to-opportunity entrepreneurship goes down.

Entrepreneurial activity and economic development

Entrepreneurship in emerging markets is much different than its presence in developed countries. Of particular interest is the growth-oriented entrepreneurship, which has a greater capacity to create sustainable economic growth than microenterprises.[39] Entrepreneurship has played an important role in economic growth and innovation, while increased competitiveness has also played a key role in poverty alleviation over time.

Opportunities for entrepreneurs in developing countries are broader in scope than in developed countries because entrepreneurs in developing markets face different sets of environmental restrictions than those in developed economies. These differences are rooted in the underlying fundamental economic differences, cultural characteristics, and the role of governments. Most developing countries lack stable and clearly defined market mechanism rules, regulations, ownership rights, and enforcement instruments. Thus, the opportunity for entrepreneurship is not only broader, but also more challenging in the building of successful and sustainable organizations. It is broader due to higher demand for better quality of goods and services and the availability of certain factors of input. It is challenging due to the scarcity of resources, regulations, and enforcement capabilities. Of course, the level of educational completion of the population also plays a critical role in the extent of challenges.

From an economic development point of view, entrepreneurship raises two major issues: (1) economic development and growth and (2) the progress of nations. The mechanism of development has been the subject of a continuing lively debate among scholars.[40] The validity of any economic policy is measured by its impact on economic development and growth. The progress of a nation is taking place when there is a need for improvement in social conditions, citizenship rights, and political transparency. Many developing countries are trying to implement prescriptions of development theories or replicate the process that most developed economies pursued. Of course, most developing countries are trying to find ways to expedite the process by applying new tools such as technology and educational advancement in order to accelerate economic development.

Figure 1.10 Educational advancement to accelerate economic development

---

Box 1.10 When globalization meets entrepreneurship, it can be a force for good

Entrepreneurship is described as the pursuit of opportunities and is often seen as a hero of the global economy. On the other hand, globalization is criticized. Entrepreneurship and globalization go hand in hand in three ways. First, globalization facilitates technology because it fosters the innovation of ecosystems. Second, it facilitates transnational entrepreneurship when corporations use what they know to create new businesses. Third, it facilitates social entrepreneurship by addressing societal problems. Many multinationals have concluded globalization is a powerful tool to gain new ventures.

Source: Prashantham (2018).[41]

Sustainable economic development leads to diminishing illiteracy, reduction of unemployment, a higher standard of living, and overall better quality of life for current and future generations. An important factor that can lead to sustainable economic development is the degree of entrepreneurial activity. Most developing countries aspire to boost the enriching environment for entrepreneurship by enacting entrepreneur-friendly policies.

In turn, entrepreneurs spur economic development through a constant process of economic experimentation and efficiency. Startup companies can engage in economic experimentation because they are not constrained by the limits of old technologies, the traditional ways of organizing production, or the need to serve established markets. Instead, entrepreneurs can be more aggressive than established organizations in pursuing radical approaches to the creation of economic value.

Globalization provides opportunities for such economic experimentation. Digital startups, for example, require far less capital than, say, building a factory, and a brilliant piece of software can be distributed to millions at a minimal cost. Digital technologies have allowed young Russian entrepreneurs to set up a virtual talent agency for models (www.castweek.ru); Asian-American electric cellists to teach people how to make new sounds using a laptop (www.danaleong.com); and young Nigerians to start a new publishing house for African romantic novelists (www.ankarapress.com).[42] The value of startup activity is not limited to the substantial value created by new businesses, but also includes the benefits from increased competitive pressure on established firms.

Box 1.11 Quick review on country classification

- The World Bank classifies the developing countries into countries with low or mid-levels of GNP per capita.
- The World Bank further classifies developing countries into heavily indebted poor countries (HIPC), low-income, lower-middle-income, and middle-income economies.
- The World Economic Forum provides a similar classification of countries at two transition stages: transition from factor driven to efficiency driven, and transition from efficiency driven to innovation driven.
- The stage of a country's economic development determines, to a large extent, the scope of entrepreneurial activity in an economy, as well as the nature of feasible entrepreneurial initiatives.

Table 1.2 Major types of economic experiments

Technological experiments	Market experiments	Organizational experiments
Attempts to exploit a scientific discovery of engineering opportunity for economic gain.	Attempts to identify and exploit the market applications where the technology may be most valuable.	Attempts to link together individuals and organizations in the pursuit of exploiting the interaction between market and technical opportunities.

We can differentiate between three major types of economic experiments in Table 1.2.

To sum up, by playing a fundamental role in the process of economic experimentation, entrepreneurship contributes decisively to the range and diversity of economically useful knowledge, which is at the base of economic prosperity. Some scholars have suggested that it does not change among existing businesses and entities that generate the greatest transformations, but rather the creation of new firms and competition that does.[43]

Entrepreneurial activity contributes to a country's economic development through innovative products, services, and ideas, increased competition leading to productivity gains, consumer benefits, and increased learning capacity.[44] Entrepreneurship is credited for being the "engines of growth" and for "providing catalyst" for economic development in both developed and developing countries.[45] In fact, according to Ernst & Young CEO Jim Turley, some statisticians show that "100% of the net job growth over many years came from entrepreneurs."[46]

Key factors of entrepreneurship and development

The value of entrepreneurship to the contributions of a nation's wealth is becoming increasingly significant. In an era of globalization, countries are leaning on entrepreneurship as a sustainable way to improve their economy. Culture affects how individuals in a society view entrepreneurship, which is a key influencer of the likelihood of a person becoming an entrepreneur. The culture of a country also helps to explain why certain countries have an environment that fosters entrepreneurship, while others rely on partnerships, corporations, or state-run institutions.

The role of government is significant when shaping the future of entrepreneurship in a country. Leaders must examine the type of culture that exists before making regulatory changes that will impact entrepreneurs. For example, in an individualistic culture, governments attempt to reform by strengthening institutions, engaging with private sector, and legitimizing small informal businesses. This is typically well-received and can result in new ventures and economic development. Encouraging innovation through competition and monetary incentives have proven successful as well.

Box 1.12   Uganda entrepreneurship power

Entrepreneurship has different definitions depending on which part of the world you are in. For the western countries, it might mean a lavish lifestyle and money, while for other countries it is a tool for survival. Starting a business involves taking financial risk, which most countries cannot afford. Even though people believe that the United States leads in entrepreneurship, it's actually Uganda that is the most entrepreneurial. Uganda has a 28 percent growth in entrepreneurial startups each year; coming second is Thailand with 16 percent. Even though a large percent of young adults are unemployed, Uganda still manages to have great entrepreneurial success, largely due to training and support from the government and other non-government organizations.

For most people in the west, starting a new business is based upon an existing job or good finances. But for developing countries it means earning the essential income for family needs and also challenges of poor economic conditions.

Source: Rajna (2015).[47]

However, a more incremental approach may be necessary for collectivist cultures – particularly in areas where society is apprehensive towards government regulation. Encouraging new ventures to be created as formal businesses, for example, is a more indirect, hands-off approach that will likely have more success. By identifying a society's cultural values, the government can provide monetary and non-monetary motivators that enable entrepreneurship and innovation. Entrepreneurship has become one of the primary mechanisms in the transformation of many economies. Developing countries have begun to examine the role of entrepreneurship in their potential development.

With this shift in developmental policy, a greater focus on the role of the private sector as a vital engine for economic growth in emerging economies and a de-emphasis on the role of government is becoming evident. Entrepreneurship in emerging markets is much different from that in developed nations. Of particular interest are new and growth-oriented entrepreneurship, which has a greater capacity to create sustainable economic growth.

Entrepreneurship has played an important role in economic growth, innovation, and competitiveness and it will also play a role over time in poverty alleviation. The focus has been on describing the attributes of entrepreneurship in developing countries, but it has to be on providing a framework in which entrepreneurs and policymakers can plan and execute innovative business models. Existing models of entrepreneurship are based largely on research conducted in the United States and other developed countries and do not adequately describe how entrepreneurship is carried out in developing countries. Opportunities for entrepreneurs in developing countries are broader in scope than in developed markets because entrepreneurs in developing countries face a different set of circumstances than their counterparts in developed economies. These differences are rooted in the underlying political, economic, cultural, and social environments that they operate.

For example, Mexico has made a commitment to transform itself into a competitive nation by privatizing state-owned industries, reducing tariffs, making it easier for foreign investment, and setting up free-trade agreements (NAFTA) with neighbors such as the United States and Canada.

Box 1.13   How women in rural India turned courage into capital: Chetna Gala Sinha

When bankers refused to serve her neighbors in rural India, Chetna Gala Sinha did the next best thing: she opened a bank of her own, the first ever for and by women in the country.

In this inspiring talk, she shares stories of the women who encouraged her and continue to push her to come up with solutions for those denied traditional financial backing.

You can check out more details in the full TED Talk at www.ted.com/talks/chetna_gala_sinha_how_women_in_rural_india_turned_courage_into_capital/details

However, to sustain the changes and expand them, there needs to be a thriving private sector, where new entrepreneurs are needed. The informal sector in some developing countries is an important source of entrepreneurial and economic activity. Brazil, for example, has a substantial share – about 60 percent by some measures – of its employees working without a labor registry. In addition, 58 percent of the country's population below the poverty line live in families headed by informal workers. In Brazil, formal employment usually implies that the worker is an employee with a signed employment booklet (card). Informal employment in Brazil is understood to imply that the worker is an employee without a signed employment booklet (no card), which means that these employees are not registered with the ministry of labor and therefore not legally covered by labor codes (meaning that the worker probably does not receive certain benefits and protections). These are mostly mom-and-pop enterprises, which is generally more common in most developing countries. Most developing countries have certain provisions to provide free primary school education to children. Training students through an initiative-driven learning and teaching environment inspires the discovery of new ideas, problem-solving, creative thinking, experimentation, and collaborative student projects, which will prepare students to think in entrepreneurial manners in their daily learning processes.

The two dimensions of developing entrepreneurs are through the educational system and through the creation of incentives and reduction of costs in starting the business.

There are entrepreneurs who have not been to school or college yet are extremely successful in their endeavors, such as setting up a small roadside business, working with street vendors, and many other forms of enterprise. This is the most prevalent mode of entrepreneurship in India and many other developing countries. The scope of such a business in terms of revenues is limited but is sufficient to support or contribute to the livelihood of such entrepreneurs and their families on a day-to-day basis. These entrepreneurs operate in rural as well as urban areas. Entrepreneurship is required in all facets of society and economy such as education, research, agriculture, and business.

Box 1.14   Cambridge incubator

Cambridge Innovation Center (CIC)'s flagship location was founded in Cambridge, Massachusetts, in 1999 in Kendall Square, and has since become an established critical mass of thriving innovative companies. More than 800 startups are housed in the CIC. Dozens of successful companies have grown to prominence while housed at CIC, including Hubspot, MassChallenge, GreatPoint Energy, and Android. CIC Cambridge's One Broadway location is home to more than $7 billion of venture capital, putting this single CIC location ahead of many nations in terms of total venture capital.

Defining globalization

The Merriam-Webster dictionary defines globalization as "the development of an increasingly integrated global economy marked especially by free trade, free flow of capital, and the tapping of cheaper foreign labor markets."

Box 1.15   Globalization

Stiglitz (2007) defines globalization as "the expanding scale, growing magnitude, speeding up and deepening impact of transcontinental flows and patterns of social interaction."[48]

In other words, globalization can be observed as the increased freedom for movement of goods (or the visible trade), services (or the invisible trade), capital (investment flows), and people (migration). Globalization has been spurred by developments in the worldwide political situation, reduction in the barriers to trade, advancement in communication and transportation, the establishment of global institutions such as the World Bank, the International Monetary Fund, World Trade Organization, etc.

Box 1.16   Informal marketplace

Entrepreneurship without a formal education is common, especially in developing countries, such as the roadside business shown here.

Box 1.17   Quick review on entrepreneurship and economic growth

- Most developing countries aspire to boost the environment for entrepreneurship by enacting entrepreneur-friendly policies.
- Entrepreneurs can be more aggressive than established organizations in pursuing radical approaches to the creation of economic value.
- According to Ernst & Young, some statisticians show that "100% of the net job growth over many years came from entrepreneurs."
- Information technology enhancements affect customer relationships.
- Cloud computing and globalization have created virtual teams that must focus on continuous innovation.

These organizations and their relevant domestic and international institutions facilitate globalization. Reduction in trade barriers has led to an improvement in the overall standards of living. A major boost to globalization is provided by the improved communications and transportation technology. In the following, we provide two examples of the rapid pace of globalization.

Figure 1.11 Informal marketplace

Figure 1.12 illustrates the accelerated growth of world trade as a percentage of GDP between 1960 and 2015. Figure 1.12 reports the percentage of people in different areas of the world who would consider emigrating from their home country in search of better opportunities.

Globalization and entrepreneurship

The rapid transformation of the economic landscape across the globe has had a significant impact on economic, political, cultural, and social issues both within and among countries. Globalization, which started with the economic theories of efficient allocation of resources by reducing and eliminating barriers to trade, has led to various economic opportunities and created challenges for citizens and their governments (see Table 1.3).

The reduction and elimination of barriers of movement of capital, goods, and services, and in some instances (e.g., European Union) labor, provided opportunities for businesses to establish themselves throughout the world. Some scholars introduce new indexes to investigate the attitude and the capacity of communities. These indexes were entrepreneurial attitude and

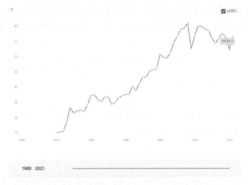

Figure 1.12 World trade as a percentage of world GDP: 1960–2021

Source: World Bank Group. Trade (% of GDP). (2023). Retrieved from https://data.worldbank.org/indicator/NE.TRD.GNFS.ZS

Table 1.3 Global desire to migrate rebounds in some areas

	Desire to migrate, 2010–2012, in %	*Desire to migrate, 2013–2016, in %*	*Change, in pct. pts.*
Sub-Saharan Africa	30	31	+1
Europe (outside European Union)	21	27	+6*
Latin America and Caribbean	18	23	+5*
Middle East and North Africa	19	22	+3*
European Union	20	21	+1*
Commonwealth of Independent States	15	14	−1
Australia/New Zealand/Oceania	9	10	+1
Northern America	10	10	0
South Asia	8	8	0
East Asia	8	7	−1
Southeast Asia	7	7	0
Global	13	14	+1*

Source: Esipova et al. (2017).[49]

Note: * = *Significant change*

entrepreneurship capacity, and they proposed a non-linear regression approach to examine the relationship between these indexes. These indexes will be able to improve the economic categorization of countries.[50]

Innovations in communications, transportation, and technology have brought millions of citizens of the world closer to one another. Multinational enterprises (MNEs) are tapping into workforces and consumers around the globe. This rapid movement has brought its own economic, cultural, and social challenges that require careful attention. Throughout this process, the role of national governments and international organizations are being redefined.

Across the globe, entrepreneurs exchange ideas, collaborate, and compete. Entrepreneurs and entrepreneurship are getting prizes from policymakers and are rewarded by both the public and private sectors. Rising pressure and the desire of citizens in developing countries to attain the quality and living standards of developed nations have forced a major transformation in most developing governments. As a result, institutions and other non-state actors have come to fill the governance void. In developed countries, institutions and private organizations are generally powerful and integrated into society, while in developing countries they are slowly evolving.

Box 1.18   Globalization promises

Globalization makes our world seem smaller, increasing the pace that ideas, goods, services, and people move around the globe.

Globalization and entrepreneurship interact in multifaceted ways. In Table 1.4, we present both the positive and the negative effects of globalization on entrepreneurship.[51]

COVID-19 and globalization

Globalization has significantly changed the way we live and manage our lives. Trade and travel have led to a higher degree of connectivity, which has led to many economic and social benefits; however, these high degrees of connectivity caused the spread of diseases such as COVID-19.

Table 1.4 Positive and negative effect of globalization on entrepreneurship

Positive impacts of globalization on entrepreneurship	*Negative impacts of globalization on entrepreneurship*
Reduction of trade barriers acts as strong incentive for innovation to flourish in attempts to meet demand.	Competition from cheaper imported products and against companies that have access to lower cost infrastructures and resources makes it more challenging for entrepreneurs in developing countries.
Continuous innovation to meet demand and quality of the global markets.	Late globalization might lead to insufficient time for innovate domestically, thus losing to competitors from the developed countries.
In terms of large-scale production, jobs are created domestically.	Technical and managerial difficulties of producing standardized goods by entrepreneurs for markets and being differentiated to meet the needs of any specific costumer simultaneously.
Globalization facilitates the flow of technology between nations by increasing the mobility of production factors. Consequently, the borrowing process of ideas and methods for entrepreneurs gets easier.	It prepares an opportunity for developed countries to dump goods that are substandard to developing countries. It makes the competition hard for entrepreneurs.
The mobility of most of the production factors as well as reduction of trade boundaries would provide incentives for entrepreneurs to operate globally.	Globalization depletes the production resources (e.g., brain drain, raw material) of developing countries by providing them with a way out from their home country.
The window of communication opened by globalization led to the collaboration of entrepreneurs with foreign investors or other entrepreneurs by joint venture contracts. Getting managerial and technical consultations got easier.	

Source: Akpor-Robaro (2012).[52]

Of course, urbanization and closer integration are other important factors that increased the spread of the disease. The COVID-19 pandemic caused an unprecedented burden on the world economy and impacted globalization.

The COVID-19 pandemic at the end of 2019 significantly altered human lives, creating drastic changes which rippled into economic and organizational structure remodeling that the world has not confronted since 1918. People were facing an unknown way of life, while companies and policymakers faced many uncertain challenges of how to function and address this pandemic. Pharmaceutical companies began to develop vaccinations. The enormous and rapid scientific advances in different parts of the world led to new vaccines which began to minimize the number of people who were killed and became ill. By October 2022 in many parts of the developed world, life began to become partially normal. However, in many areas of the world COVID-19 still is causing death and disruptions. As of October 10, 2022, Johns Hopkins University reported that total cases numbered 621,571,762, total related deaths numbered 6,557,896, and 9,063,634,485 vaccine doses have been administered. As of the time of writing, this is the highest number of deaths due to a pandemic since 1918.

When the effects of globalization are operationalized in terms of mobility, economy, and healthcare systems, some parts of the world were more impacted than others. The economic impact was dependent on the levels of development and public policies of the governments in power and their health quality system. Authors have examined the data on international travel restrictions of 185 countries from January to October 2020 due to COVID-19.[53] They evaluated the relationship between globalization and the timing of travel restriction implementation.

Overall, COVID-19 has impacted significantly both developed and developing countries. The supply chain disruption for many products froze many economies for a few years. Country-specific studies are required to identify the quality of healthcare systems and prepare for better future responses. The impact of COVID-19 on the expansion of globalization remains to be seen. It seems some countries are focusing on regionalization and production of essential healthcare, industrial and national securities products that are considered necessities to be produced in the home countries. For example, the United States is subsidizing production of high-end chips.

Concluding remarks

The definitions, theories, and concepts of economic development, entrepreneurship, and globalization were described and the relationship between entrepreneurship and development was analyzed. Additionally, the role of globalization in this process was discussed.

In the opening case of the chapter, SEZ, we provided an overview of entrepreneurial policies with objectives of creating jobs and development. Additionally, several short cases about different countries and issues are presented to enhance our understanding of the concepts and their applications. In the history of humanity, every generation has been unique in its own ways, learning, achieving, and experiencing life shaped by global occurrences and trends. Each generation has had a storehouse of "human experiences," values, attitudes, skills, and practical knowledge passed on to them through seasoned intellectual minds such as their parents, grandparents, teachers, mentors, coaches, etc.

From a microscopic view, each youth's "human experiences" become learned aspects of their personality. The youth today, primarily the millennial generation, have grown up in a globalized and dynamically interconnected world, where it is, for example, possible for a student at a university in India to virtually connect with peers, professors, and experts at a university in the United States without very little cost.[54] The significant negative impact of COVID-19 on the world's health, economic, and public policies led to a more careful evaluation of globalization as we knew it which was mainly focused on economic efficiency. It seems some countries are focusing on more regionalization and production of essential healthcare, industrial, and national securities products to be produced in the home countries. The impact of COVID-19 on entrepreneurship seems to be positive because of the advancement of new technology and communications and its applications.

Box 1.19   Quick review on entrepreneurship and globalization

- What constitutes entrepreneurship among stakeholders?
- Entrepreneurship is a socially embedded and context-specific process of resource mobilization and opportunity exploitation, culminating in the creation of a new venture, whose purpose is to create value and generate wealth and other social enhancement benefits.
- Economic growth comes in two forms: an economy can either grow "extensively" by using more resources (e.g., physical, human, or natural capital) or "intensively" by using the same amount of resources more efficiently (productively).
- What does development consists of?
- What is a living wage? How does it compare to the minimum wage?
- What categories does the World Bank classify developing countries into?
- What does the World Economic Forum provide?
- What determines the stage of a country's economic development?
- How do most developing countries aspire to boost the environment for entrepreneurship?
- How do information technology enhancements affect customer relationships?
- How can cloud computing and globalization lead continuous innovation?
- How has COVID-19 impacted the evolution of globalization?
- How has COVID-19 impacted the public policies in some of the developed countries?

Discussion questions

1   What were the main points of this chapter?
2   What has been the influence of globalization on entrepreneurship in developing countries?
3   Are there differences in entrepreneurial initiation in developed versus developing countries?
4   Analyze the impact of entrepreneurial activity on sustainable development.
5   Discuss positive and negative impacts of globalization on entrepreneurship.
6   Examine the impact of COVID-19 on globalization.

Table 1.5 Key terms

Entrepreneurship	Chenery's patterns of development approach
Economic development	Dependency and neoclassical theory
Gross national product (GNP)	Heavily indebted poor countries (HIPCs)
Rostow's theory	Factor-driven economies and efficiency-driven economies
The Harrod-Domar model	Sustainable economic growth
Lewis structural change	Globalization

Table 1.6 Glossary

Entrepreneurship	Entrepreneurship is the process of starting and running a business, typically with a focus on innovation and growth.
Economic development	Economic development refers to the process by which a country's economy improves over time, typically characterized by increased productivity, higher living standards, and a growing economy.
Gross national product (GNP)	GNP is a measure of a country's total economic output that takes into account the total value of all goods and services produced by a country's residents, including those working abroad.
Rostow's theory	Rostow's theory of economic development, also known as the "stages of growth" model, is a linear-staged model that outlines the stages a country must go through to become a developed economy.
The Harrod-Domar model	The Harrod-Domar model is a theory of economic growth that explains the relationship between savings, investment, and economic growth.
Lewis structural change	The Lewis structural change theory, developed by economist W. Arthur Lewis, is a theory that explains the transformation of an economy from a subsistence agricultural economy to an industrialized one.
Chenery's patterns of development approach	The Chenery pattern of development approach is a framework for understanding the process of economic development, developed by economist Hollis Chenery.
Dependency and neoclassical theory	Dependency theory and neoclassical theory are two competing approaches to understanding the process of economic development and the relationship between rich and poor countries.
Heavily indebted poor countries (HIPCs)	The HIPC initiative was a program launched by the International Monetary Fund and the World Bank in 1996 to provide debt relief to the poorest, most heavily indebted countries in the world.
Factor-driven economies and efficiency-driven economies	Factor-driven economies and efficiency-driven economies are two concepts used to describe different stages of economic development and the factors driving economic growth in a particular country.
Sustainable economic growth	Sustainable economic growth refers to a type of economic growth that meets the needs of the present without compromising the ability of future generations to meet their own needs.
Globalization	Globalization refers to the increasing interconnectedness and interdependence of the world's economies, societies, and cultures, driven by advancements in transportation, communication, and technology.

Notes

1 Zeng, D.Z. (2015). *Global Experiences with Special Economic Zones: Focus on China and Africa.* World Bank. Retrieved from http://documents.worldbank.org/curated/en/810281468186872492/pdf/WPS7240.pdf

2 Boyenge, J. (2007). ILO database on export processing zones. *International Labour Office.*

3 FIAS. (2008). *Special Economic Zones: Performance, Lessons Learned, and Implications for Zone Development.* Washington, DC: World Bank.

4 Duranton, G., & Venables, A.J. (2018). Place-based policies for development (No. w24562). *National Bureau of Economic Research.* Retrieved from www.nber.org/system/files/working_papers/w24562/w24562.pdf

5 Gartner, W.B. (1985). A conceptual framework for describing the phenomenon of new venture creation. *Academy of Management Review,* 10(4), 696–706.

6 Alvarez, S.A., & Barney, J.B. (2010). Entrepreneurship and epistemology: The philosophical underpinnings of the study of entrepreneurial opportunities. *The Academy of Management Annals,* 4, 557–577; Shane, S., & Venkataraman, S. (2000). The promise of entrepreneurship as a field of research. *Academy of Management Review,* 25(1), 217–226.

7 Acs, Z.J., & Szerb, L. (2009). The global entrepreneurship index (GEINDEX). *Jena Economic Research Papers No. 2009-028.* Retrieved from https://ideas.repec.org/p/jrp/jrpwrp/2009-028.html

8 Hitt, M.A., Ireland, R.D., Sirmon, D.G., & Trahms, C.A. (2011). Strategic entrepreneurship: Creating value for individuals, organizations and society. *Academy of Management Perspectives*, 25(2), 57–75.

9 Beattie, A. (2018, May 17). *Who Coined the Term "Entrepreneur"?* Retrieved December 14, 2018, from www.investopedia.com/ask/answers/08/origin-of-entrepreneur.asp

10 Retrieved from www.worldbank.org/

11 Sustainable Development. (2018, November 29). Retrieved December 14, 2018, from www.iisd.org/topic/sustainable-development

12 www.worldbank.org/

13 Sen, A.K. (1999). *Development as Freedom*. Oxford: Oxford University Press.

14 Clifton, H. (2013). *Amartya Sen on Development*. Retrieved from WordPress.com.

15 Sen, A.K. (1999). *Development as Freedom*. Oxford: Oxford University Press.

16 Sen, A.K. (1999). *Development as Freedom*. Oxford: Oxford University Press.

17 Uvin, P. (2010). From the right to development to the rights-based approach: How human rights entered development. In A. Cornwall, & D. Eade (Eds.), *Deconstructing Development Discourse. Buzzwords and Fuzzwords* (pp. 163–174). Oxford: Practical Action Publishing Ltd.

18 www.nobelprize.org/prizes/economic-sciences/1998/press-release/

19 www.worldbank.org/

20 Van Dam, A., & Frenken, K. (2020). Variety, complexity and economic development. *Research Policy*, 103949. Retrieved from www.sciencedirect.com/science/article/pii/S0048733320300299

21 Kostetska, K., Khumarova, N., Umanska, Y., Shmygol, N., & Koval, V. (2020). Institutional qualities of inclusive environmental management in sustainable economic development. *Management Systems in Production Engineering*, 28(1), 15–22. Retrieved from https://sciendo.com/pdf/10.2478/mspe-2020-0003

22 Rostow's Model. (2015, April 30). Retrieved from www.emaze.com/@ALRQOZWQ/Rostow's-Model. Economic Development Models. Dorfman, R. (1991). *Economic Development from the Beginning to Rostow*. Retrieved from www.jstor.org/stable/pdf/2727524.pdf

23 Sen, A.K. (1999). *Development as Freedom* (p. xii). Oxford: Oxford University Press.

24 Structural Changes Models. (2011, January 12). Retrieved December 14, 2018, from https://erik-krantz.wordpress.com/2011/01/12/structural-changes-models/

25 Van Neuss, L. (2019). The drivers of structural change. *Journal of Economic Surveys*, 33(1), 309–349. Retrieved from https://web.s.ebscohost.com/ehost/pdfviewer/pdfviewer?vid=0&sid=cb974e58-178e-40cd-93c0-8bfa5169a6ad%40redis. GGDC stands for the Groningen Growth and Development Centre (GGDC).

26 Unit 2 People and the Planet – Linear. (2013, December 12). Retrieved December 14, 2018, from https://geogyourmemory.wordpress.com/unit-2/

27 Kiely, R. (2010, March). Dependency and world-systems perspectives on development. *International Studies* (online November 2017). https://doi.org/10.1093/acrefore/9780190846626.013.142

28 Gori, L., Manfredi, P., Marsiglio, S., & Sodini, M. (2021). COVID-19 epidemic and mitigation policies: Positive and normative analyses in a neoclassical growth model. *Journal of Public Economic Theory*. Retrieved from https://onlinelibrary.wiley.com/doi/pdf/10.1111/jpet.12549

29 www.worldbank.org/

30 Retrieved February 20, 2016, from www.worldbank.org/depweb/english/beyond/global/glossary.html

31 Countries and Economies. (n.d.). Retrieved from https://data.worldbank.org/country

32 World Economic Forum. (2016). *Global Competitiveness Index 2015–2016*. Retrieved February 20, 2016, from https://reports.weforum.org/global-competitiveness-report-2015-2016/appendix-methodology-and-computation-of-the-global-competitiveness-index-2015–2016/; https://devex.com/news/what-is-driving-uber-s-global-impact-88419

33 The Global Competitiveness Report 2015–2016. (n.d.). Retrieved February 20, 2016, from http://reports.weforum.org/global-competitiveness-report-2015-2016

34 Audretsch, D. (2007). Entrepreneurship capital and economic growth. *Oxford Review of Economic Policy*, 23(1), 63–78; Acs, Z.J., & Szerb, L. (2009). The Global Entrepreneurship Index (GEINDEX). *Jena Economic Research Papers No. 2009-028*. Retrieved from www.jenecon.de; Wennekers, S., Van Stel, A., Thurik, A.R., & Reynolds, P. (2005). Nascent entrepreneurship and the level of economic development. *Small Business Economics*, 24(3), 293–309.

35 Cheney, C. (2016, August 5). *What is Driving Uber's Global Impact?* Retrieved December 14, 2018, from www.devex.com/news/what-is-driving-uber-s-global-impact-88419

36 Acs, Z.J. (2006). How is entrepreneurship good for economic growth? *Innovations*, 1(1), 97–107.

37 GEM (Global Entrepreneurship Monitor). (2023). *Global Entrepreneurship Monitor 2022/2023 Global Report: Adapting to a "New Normal."* London: GEM.

38 Kelley, D.J., Bosma, N., & Amorós, J.E. (2011). *Global Entrepreneurship Monitor: 2010 Global Report*. Wellesley, MA: Babson College and Santiago Chile, Universidad Del Desarrollo. Retrieved from www.av-asesores.com/upload/479.PDF

39 Acs, Z.J., Desai, S., & Hessels, J. (2008). Entrepreneurship, economic development and institutions. *Small Business Economics*, 31(3), 219–234.

40 Todaro, M.P., & Smith, S. (2011). *Economic Development* (11th ed.). New Jersey: Prentice Hall.

41 Prashantham, S. (2018, September 19). *When Globalisation Meets Entrepreneurship, It Can Be a Force for Good.* Retrieved December 14, 2018, from http://theconversation.com/when-globalisation-meets-entrepreneurship-it-can-be-a-force-for-good-64415

42 The Economist. (2016). *The Walled World of Work.* https://www.economist.com/special-report/2016/01/21/the-walled-world-of-work

43 Jackson, J., & Rodkey, G. (1994). The attitudinal climate for entrepreneurial activity. *The Public Opinion Quarterly*, 58(3), 358–380.

44 Eunni, R.V., & Manolova, T.S. (2012). Are the BRIC economies entrepreneur-friendly? An institutional perspective. *Journal of Enterprising Culture*, 20(2), 171–202. https://doi.org/10.1142/S0218495812500082

45 Steenhuis, H.-J., & Gray, D.O. (2006). The university as the engine of growth: An analysis of how universities can contribute to the economy. *International Journal of Technology Transfer and Commercialization*, 5(4), 421–432.

46 http://business.slu.edu/news-and-events/events/event/2016/04/21/vasquez-wuller-accounting-lecture-presents-james-turley-former-chairman-and-ceo-of-ernst-young/

47 Rajna, T. (2015, August 6). *Uganda Named the World's Most Entrepreneurial Country.* Retrieved December 14, 2018, from www.virgin.com/entrepreneur/uganda-named-worlds-most-entrepreneurial-country

48 Stiglitz, J.E. (2007). *Making Globalization Work*. New York: W.W. Norton & Company.

49 Esipova, N., Ray, J., & Pugliese, A. (2017, June 8). Number of potential migrants worldwide tops 700 million. *Gallup*. Retrieved from https://news.gallup.com/poll/211883/number-potential-migrants-worldwide-tops-700-million.aspx

50 Faghih, N., Bonyadi, E., & Sarreshtehdari, L. (2019). Global entrepreneurship capacity and entrepreneurial attitude indexing based on the Global Entrepreneurship Monitor (GEM) dataset. In *Globalization and Development* (pp. 13–55). Cham: Springer.

51 Asgary, N., Frutos, D., & Samii, M. (2015). *Introduction to Foundations of Global Business*. Charlotte: Information Age Publishing Inc.; Asgary, N., Frutos, D., Samii, M., & Varamini, H. (2019). *Global Business: Economic, Social and Environmental Approach* (2nd ed.). Charlotte: Information Age Publishing Inc.

52 Akpor-Robaro, M.O.M. (2012). The impact of globalization on entrepreneurship development in developing economies: A theoretical analysis of the Nigerian experience in the manufacturing industry. *Journal of Management Science and Engineering*, 6(2), 1–10.

53 Bickley, S.J. et al. (2021). How does globalization affect COVID-19 responses? *Global Health*, 17, 57. https://doi.org/10.1186/s12992-021-00677-5

54 In the knowledge economy that we are currently moving towards, it is critical to develop entrepreneurial characteristics at all levels of educational process. Entrepreneurship education in most countries is limited to university level education. In the United States, according to a survey conducted by the Gallup organization, it was discovered that 70 percent of the high school students in the sample wanted to start their own business, and yet only 44 percent had basic knowledge about entrepreneurship.

2 Culture, entrepreneurship, and development

In this chapter we define culture and analyze its essential and complex role in entrepreneurial activities. The complexity and distinctness of cultures can shape entrepreneurship and development significantly. Hofstede's model of cultural variation plays a significant role in understanding the various aspects of culture that can affect and be affected by entrepreneurship, innovation, and technology, such as power distance, individualism/collectivism, masculinity level, and uncertainty avoidance.

Policies enacted by policymakers can help shape attitudes towards entrepreneurial activities. Drawing on the conclusion that some cultures are less entrepreneurial than others, the authors have examined the underlying cultural traits. Since government policies play a large role in shaping attitudes towards entrepreneurship, the chapter examines countries such as Spain, the Philippines, and Vietnam as examples of a cultural move towards stronger entrepreneurship. By offering several cases from various countries, we illustrate a few examples of these relationships to help in clarifying the effects and interactions that government, entrepreneurial activities, culture, and technology have on each other.

Learning objectives

1 Learn the definition of culture
2 Understand the relationship between culture and entrepreneurship
3 Examine the relationship between innovation, motivations, and culture in relation to entrepreneurial activities
4 Examine the influence of technology on culture
5 Comprehend the role of government in shaping entrepreneurial culture
6 Study the role of culture on development.

Box 2.1   We believe that we can

MehrGiti is an NGO and philanthropic (assistantship) institution consisting of various units with the basic objective of trying to build an Iran free of discrimination and cultural poverty.

Everything began from a visit to deprived areas of Sistan and Baluchistan province in Iran. In 2005, Ms. Zahra Giti Nezhad visited a few rural schools during her visit to the schools in Mirjaveh Town.

DOI: 10.4324/9781003405740-4

Figure 2.1 Fostering Education, Culture and Development

Our mission is to help the establishment of educational and cultural spaces, in particular schools, in deprived needy areas, as well as financial, spiritual and cultural support for talented and deprived students in different parts of the country.

The fundamental topic of good affairs in Mehre Giti [*sic*] is the cultural and educational affairs, which are presently carried out in the form of the following plans:

The construction of schools, dormitories, multi-purpose salons, libraries, etc. in all the country's less-favored areas:

- Educational support for less-favored students and college students
- Donation of books to schools in less-favored areas of the country

- Donation of computers to schools in less-favored areas of the country
- Equipping schools in less-favored areas of the country
- Educational and cultural activities.

Mehrgiti Charity Foundation is a nonprofit, non-governmental and non-political NGO, and this has been and will be an integral part of the policy of Mehre Giti [*sic*] Charity Foundation. . . .

Transparency, accountability, respect, and expansion of hope in society are the main values of the Mehre Giti [*sic*], and all our activities are formed and performed in accordance with these principles.

https://mehrgiti.com/en/about-us/

Questions:

1 Analyze this case in terms of its mission, ethics, and policies.
2 Examine its successes and challenges.
3 What do you find unique about this nonprofit organization?

Introduction

This chapter explores how diverse cultures influence the outcome of a country's/region's entrepreneurship, and economic development. The means and policies will be discussed that culture can be influenced (e.g., government policies and interventions) in ways that cannot only encourage and reduce entrepreneurial barriers, thus contributing to the growth of a country. Overcoming and encouraging entrepreneurial and risking taking down cultural barriers is a serious question to be answered.

The chapter discusses traits and traditions that complement innovation, motivation, and entrepreneurial endeavors. The concept of cultural convergence and its relationship to entrepreneurship are presented. The application of Geert Hofstede's model of cultural variation largely connects the chapter's concepts and conclusions.

Culture definition

National culture can be separated into three levels (see Figure 2.3).

The cultural attitude varies to a great extent among various countries and societies. Geert Hofstede developed a model for cultural analysis intended for business purposes. Hofstede's model is discussed in the next section.

Business or organizational culture is the set of values and beliefs that exist within an organization. These include, among others, the relationship between managers and workers, the degree of formality of an organization, the degree of risk-taking, and the attitude towards social responsibility. Organizations with a strong social culture have an alignment between the value system and the belief of the employees, while organizations with a weak social culture have little alignment between the two.

Both the culture of the organization and the overall culture of a country influence and affect each other. The organization's culture initially takes to a great extent the form of the home country value system. The degree of this influence obviously varies from organization to

Box 2.2   MIT's center for entrepreneurship

The Martin Trust Center for MIT Entrepreneurship is one of the largest research and teaching centers at the MIT Sloan School of Management. It nurtures many student-run startups inside the campus. Most MIT ventures get initial funding and mentoring services. California, with its experienced IT and technology environment, is another favorite destination. Both Boston and California locations contain a skilled workforce with intelligent minds.

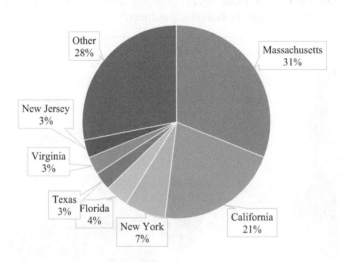

Percentage of total ventures

Figure 2.2 Percentage of total ventures – MIT

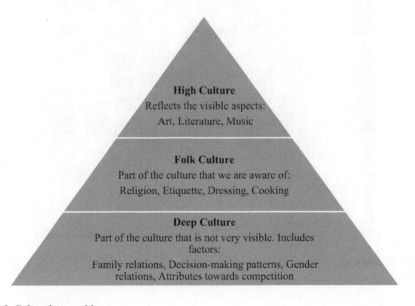

Figure 2.3 Cultural pyramid

organization. For example, if a society is characterized by entrepreneurship and risk-taking, it is inevitable that such an attitude would not be reflected in the enterprises operating in that country. Obviously, the degree of entrepreneurial tendency varies and depends on a number of factors that are firm specific.

Box 2.3   The role of culture

Aristotle said, "We are what we repeatedly do." This view elevates repeated behavior or habits as the core of culture and deemphasizes what people feel, think, or believe. It also focuses our attention on the forces that shape behavior in organizations, and so highlights an important question: are all those forces (including structure, processes, and incentives) "culture," or is culture simply the behavioral outputs?[1]

Figure 2.4 Aristotle

Source: "Aristotle" by maha-online is licensed under CC BY-SA 2.0.

Anthropologist Edward Hall, in his 1976 book *Beyond Culture*, defines culture as "the way of life of a people, the sum of their learned behavior patterns, attitudes and material things" and articulates the following "ideas and metaphors":[2]

1 Culture = models, templates.
2 Culture is the medium we live in; like the air, we breathe.
3 Culture is innate but learned (i.e., we are born with the physical necessity and capacity to specialize our bodies, brains, and hearts in line with cultural patterns).
4 Culture is living, the interlocking system(s) – touch one part and the rest moves.
5 Culture is shared; it is created and maintained through relationships.
6 Culture is used to differentiate one group from another. (In other words, division into groups comes first; deliberate differentiation via cultural symbols comes second.)

Therefore, Hall's ideas of cultures are systems that "extend" the abilities of the human being.

Kluckhohn and Strodtbeck (1961) define culture as "a shared, commonly held body of beliefs and values that define the 'should' and 'ought' of life."[3] Spradley et al. (2015) defined culture as "the acquired knowledge people use to interpret experience and generate behavior."[4] Hofstede et al. (2010) defines culture as "the collective programming of the mind distinguishing the members of one group or category of people from others."[5] Culture is seen in groups and can be defined as a pattern of basic assumptions shared and learned by the group that works well enough to be considered valid and therefore taught to new members.[6]

We can draw the conclusion that culture is the accepted values and norms that influence the way in which people think, feel, and behave in their everyday life. Every society has its own culture that affects the spirit of its people. It is transferred from one generation to another, thus it can be difficult to change or influence. However, evaluation of globalization and, therefore, a higher level of cultural interactions among different cultures will lead to cultural conversion.

Table 2.1 is a cultural map from the perspectives of four teams of scholars in four related areas: cultural elements (Hall), value patterns (Hofstede),[7] sociological and anthropological framework (Trompenaars), and variations in value orientations (Kluckhohn & Strodtbeck).[8]

Culture, entrepreneurship, and development

Culture has a critical impact on entrepreneurial activities. Therefore, cultural characteristics of a developing country or community will be carefully studied in order to identify its degree of openness to entrepreneurship. Table 2.2 shows Hofstede's six cultural differences that influence

Table 2.1 Cultural maps

Cultural elements (Hall)	Value patterns (Hofstede)	Sociological and anthropological framework (Trompenaars)	Variations in value orientations (Kluckhohn & Strodtbeck)
• Time • Space • Things • Friendships • Agreement • Interpersonal behavior	• Power • Risk • Individualism • Masculinity • Time • Management theories – practice	• Universalism vs. particularism • Collectivism vs. individualism • Affective vs. neutral relationships • Achievement vs. ascription • Orientation towards time • Internal vs. external control	• Relation to nature • Orientation to time • Belief about human nature • Mode of human activity • Relationships • Space • International business practice

Table 2.2 The Hofstede model

Trait	Description
Power distance	Refers to the distance between social classes and groups in the society
Individualism/collective	Level of interdependence among members of society
Masculine/feminine	Masculinity vs. femininity: Motivation by competition vs. motivation by interest
Uncertainty avoidance	Extent to which society is tolerant of unknown situations and attempts to avoid them
Long-term orientation	Societal long-term, future-oriented perspective rather than a short-term outlook
Indulgence/restraint	How freely one can fulfill their needs and desires

Source: Hofstede (1991, cited in Marcus, A., & Gould, E.W. [2000]). Crosscurrents: Cultural dimensions and global web user-interface design. *Interactions ACM*, 7(4), 32–46. https://doi.org/10.1145/345190.345238

entrepreneurial activities. Holding everything else constant, we can draw the conclusion that some cultures are less open and familiar to entrepreneurial activities than others. Therefore, public policies can begin to influence entrepreneurial activities in a developing country that has interest.

Box 2.4   "No culture can live if it attempts to be exclusive" (Mahatma Gandhi)

We need:

- Partnership between people of north and south (of India)
- Ownership by marginalized people at the grassroots level
- Participation of people with disabilities so that no groups are at risk of being left behind.

Does Gandhi's ideology apply to organizations as well?

The effects that culture has upon entrepreneurship can be highlighted using various examples that often refer back Hofstede's attributes (see Table 2.2). A useful general theory advanced by Nguyen et al. (2009) provides comparative analyzes which enable entrepreneurship activities.[9]

The logic for such a theory embraces the following chain of thought: (1) countries such as the United States that show high levels of individualism are motivated by competition and personal achievement; (2) these traits tend to support higher individual contributions, innovation, and new ideas; (3) this, and the other traits listed earlier, tend to both support and create a fertile environment for entrepreneurship.

Cultures that have low uncertainty avoidance, furthermore, are more comfortable with ambiguous situations such as those that involve risk-taking. Thus, some cultures encourage risk-taking while others do not. As a result, cultures in which risk avoidance is the norm may have difficulty developing a tradition of strong and vital entrepreneurship because people hesitate to take the risks that fuel entrepreneurial efforts. Thus, those who choose to reduce risk taking (by, for example, choosing job security) cease to be candidates for entrepreneurial enterprises.[10]

Figure 2.5 Gandhi

Source: "Mahatma Gandhi" by dbking is licensed under CC BY 2.0.

This type of response can dampen the economic development and growth that entrepreneurial activity could trigger. Ernst & Young CEO Jim Turley, for example, suggests that South Korea's "fear of failure" is the first thing that must change if the country is to maintain its economic momentum and attract entrepreneurs and innovators.[11,12]

Low power distance

Cultures that have a low power distance have lesser distinctive social classes and partake in more intimate social interactions. This environment may provide a greater degree of freedom for people throughout society, and therefore will foster more entrepreneurial activities. Many developed western countries are characterized by a low power distance. Established democracies in which officials are elected rather than appointed tend to have cultural, social, and legal environments that nurture a relatively low power distance.

High masculinity

Cultures that are defined as high in masculinity promote competition and recognition. These cultures place a higher value on success and innovation than cultures that tend to be more feminine and value their personal interests and rank quality of life higher than individual "success" or "achievement." The more masculine, developed countries in Western Europe and North America, for example, tend to be more motivated by monetary incentives and competition than most developing countries. A country high in masculinity not only promotes an environment of competition but also can foster a culture of selfishness. Of course, this could be for selfish reasons as well. Countries where feminine cultural values are dominant should have more partnerships and alliances. A country's culture is often intimately linked to its heritage, traditions, and historical foundation. Table 2.3 summarizes organizational cultural traits.

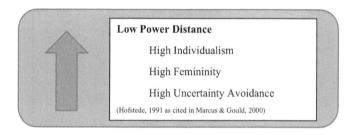

Figure 2.6 Low power distance

Table 2.3 Organizational cultural traits

Masculine	Feminine
Connect compensation with power	Encourage equity with parity
Maintain rigid control of staffing	Provide equal opportunity for all
Focus on material rewards	Focus on relationships

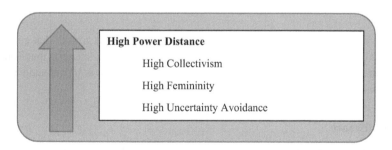

Figure 2.7 High power distance

Source: Veltri, N.F., & Elgarah, W. (2009). The role of national cultural differences in user adoption of social networking. In *Southern Association for Information Systems Conference*. Charleston, SC.

History and culture is more important than profits

Marta is a small business artist in Rio de Janeiro, Brazil. Her values, for example, are symbolic of her country's deep-rooted passion for displaying and maintaining one's history and culture, and putting this before profits. As a Brazilian, Marta is proud of her heritage and is willing to make business decisions to preserve this heritage at the risk of failure. This is an example of having low masculinity – following passion and interests rather than money or competition. This helps to explain why Brazil tends to lean towards the feminine end of Hofstede's masculinity index (Hofstede et al., 2010).[13] Marta receives a lot of respect in Rio de Janeiro for not only being a successful entrepreneur, but for being a successful Afro-Brazilian female entrepreneur. While many countries would also praise this, there are developing countries that would not give Marta the respect she finds in Brazil. It seems there is significantly less praise for entrepreneurs in Russia than in Brazil. The contrast between Russia and Brazil illustrates how culture and government can breed an environment that favors or hinders entrepreneurship. Compounding the lack of respect for entrepreneurs in Russia, the uncertainty index is also very high, resulting in a strong fear of failure. Russia's entrepreneurial activity is thus less favorable than a society that praises successful ventures.[14]

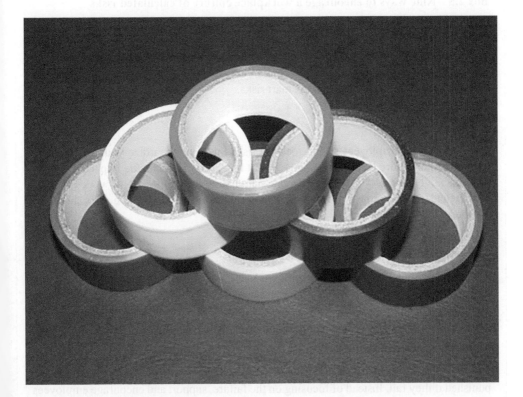

Figure 2.8 Value of thinking differently

Source: Image by laverrue on flickr.

Sweden, as an example, is a developed country with a history of cooperation and strong interpersonal skills among its traders and seafarers.[15] This history has shaped its culture, as it is considered one of the most feminine cultures in the world, according to Hofstede's country analysis.[16] This tradition helps to explain why intrapreneurship – behaving like an entrepreneur within a large company – drives innovation in Sweden rather than entrepreneurship, which presupposes a greater degree of independence.[17] Braunerhjelm (2012) defines intrapreneurship as the act of "behaving like an entrepreneur while working within a large organization."

In 1998, Professor Amartya Sen, the recipient of the Nobel Memorial Prize in Economic Sciences, observed that culture has wrongfully been understated for its role in economic development. Instead, the dominant paradigm of neoclassical economists has focused on rational thought and the maximization of self-interest.

Sen reminds us that culture exerts a strong influence because it reflects and guides the way people live their lives. As a result, it can exert a significant influence on economic development. Policymakers of any country that would like to boost its entrepreneurial activities will identify its cultural characteristics and articulate relevant policies. There is no question that policymakers will highlight the positive impact of entrepreneurship for the well-being of society and create a relevant atmosphere. They can have an influence on educational institutions, from elementary to college, and support the creation of other institutions that support entrepreneurship. For example, in the United States there are small business development offices in towns and cities whose roles are to provide professional, and in some cases financial, support to entrepreneurs.

Box 2.5   Nine ways to encourage a workplace culture of calculated risks

1. Lead by example

To create a culture of measured risk-taking, senior leadership teams must give their full buy-in. You also need to set a good example by challenging the status quo and showing that you're willing to take measured, smart risks.

2. Define a smart risk

You do not want employees taking reckless risks that can jeopardize your business. To avoid this, make sure you define what a "smart risk" is and explain the impacts risks can have on the business. This helps to create parameters for employees to work between, so they understand the procedures, where they can take risks, and where risks should be avoided.

3. Spread the message

A workplace culture isn't changed overnight. Make sure you regularly encourage employees to take risks and experiment. You could hold weekly meetings, for example, where you encourage employees throughout the organization to put forward new ideas.

4. Create a safe environment for risk-taking

Create an environment where employees feel trusted and know they won't be judged or punished if they fail. Instead of focusing on the failure, support and encourage employees to learn from their experiences. This not only encourages risk-taking to continue, but their learnings can help ensure risks are more successful in the future. This can also help to develop their career prospects.

5. Reward risk-takers

Offer praise and promotions to those employees who have been brave enough to take calculated risks, even if those risks didn't pay off. Other employees will see this and are more likely to take risks themselves in the future.

6. Identify risk-takers in your business

Some people may be more comfortable taking risks than others. Focus on encouraging these employees to take risks. They will act as mentors, encouraging others to take smart risks too.

7. Recruit born-to-be risk-takers

Risk-taking behavior can be learned, but it's not something that everyone will feel comfortable doing. It's therefore important to keep this in mind during your recruitment process so you hire people who are willing and able to take smart risks for your business going forward.

8. Start small and build up

Rather than instantly expecting employees to take big risks, start small. Once employees feel trusted and able to handle these smaller risks, they will feel more comfortable handling much larger risks.

9. Set "creative time"

Encourage employees to take time from their standard workday where they come up with new ideas, or brainstorm ideas with others. Fostering a workplace culture that supports calculated risks not only provides business benefits, but can help support the individual career growth of your staff, and eventually your ability to retain top talent.

Source: Robert Half (August 29, 2022).[18]

Jackson and Rodkey state that besides parents, educators and institutions are most influential in forming children's attitudes and culture.[19] Between parents, school, society, and the government, it is a very difficult and arduous process to change the culture of a region. An alternative vision also exists: a United Nations "systems task team" agrees that "culture can be a powerful driver for development, with community-wide social, economic and environmental impacts."[20]

In congruence with the UN Millennium Development Goals, this team at the UN is focused on the social and economic development of weak, developing countries. Instead of identifying ways to change the culture of society like prior researchers, this team is identifying ways that countries can harvest their own cultural background into a plan for further development. Developing countries often have both a large labor force and a culture-rich heritage. Using their unique culture and labor force to promote tourism, cultural infrastructure, or promoting their cultural heritage, countries can create sustainable revenue growth. Cultural tourism will revive cultural heritage and generate employment in the segment of the economy. Of course, it will revive entrepreneurial initiation in this domain. There are many success stories in countries such as Brazil, China, Iran, and Turkey. The following is an example of how culture and development are linked. More effective development policy interventions that lead to an increase in entrepreneurship development could have economic benefits in terms of employment and wealth creation for entrepreneurs who are engaged. However, problems could also arise, such as inclusiveness, equity, and diversity. Therefore, policymakers should address these issues over time through appropriate policies to maximize the benefits for larger segments of the society and to minimize its negative impacts.[21]

In the past, governments have often tried to influence entrepreneurial attitudes (even if only indirectly) through cultural intervention. Various examples of this sort are discussed in order to identify ways in which the leaders of developing countries can use and enhance cultural traits in ways that encourage and support entrepreneurial efforts (see Table 2.3). Doing so can be vital because entrepreneurship is an important economic engine in many contemporary societies. Although many experts believe that globalization is leading to greater cultural homogeneity, some nations and cultures appear to have cultures and traditions that embrace innovation and entrepreneurship. Tian et al. have conducted a systematic literature survey and analyzed the impact of culture on innovation. They used 37 years (1980– 2017) of peer-reviewed articles for this study. They stated that their "findings highlight the complex and idiosyncratic relationship between culture and innovation."[22] Yun et al. have studied the role of culture as a critical driver of innovation. Their focus is to provide some perspective into the role of "culture for open innovation dynamics." They state that this study "helps organizations and entrepreneurs to better understand the role that culture plays in boosting open innovation dynamics."[23]

The evolution of globalization has reduced barriers to cross-cultural interactions and understanding and therefore the advancement of entrepreneurship. The role that culture plays in the advancement or discouragement of entrepreneurship and economic development can have serious social and economic ramifications on a developing country or region. This results because the heritage and traditions of a people can influence innovation, motivations, and incentives for entrepreneurs.[24] The continuous growth of entrepreneurship can culminate in a material impact on the economic development of a country. There are various measurements of culture and evidence suggests that certain cultural tendencies affect the entrepreneurial potential for a culture, region, and/or country. It is therefore important to study which cultural behaviors, tendencies, and traits influence entrepreneurial potentials. Building this understanding can help societies to leverage their cultural traits in ways that encourage entrepreneurship. Birukou et al. attempt to provide a new formal definition of culture. They argue that "globalization makes culture no more bound to a geographical area, race or religion. Multi-national companies, software developers, scientists need to take into account cultural differences when delivering products to people." Furthermore, they state that AI plays a significant role in this process.[25] Ergashev and Farxodjonova analyze the process of integration of national culture and evaluate the positive and negative impact of it on the development of the culture. They state that "the general rule of law is that a nation that expresses its own national culture should not lose its identity in the reflection of the characteristics of the spiritual heritage of these peoples in the national traditions inherent and corresponding to that or that of that nation." Also, they state that it is important to develop and become rich and modern, which will serve both national and universal development. Furthermore, they argue that culture needs to be open to changes caused by globalization.[26]

Believing in entrepreneurship can encourage economic growth; public policies often strive to encourage entrepreneurial behavior. Worries about social engineering aside, governments often play an important role in affecting cultural and social change. How intervention of this type can both foster and deter entrepreneurial activities requires study. The analysis of culture is not only used to examine the entrepreneurial potential of a country, but entrepreneurial behavior can be viewed as an artifact or expression of it.

Drawing upon an individual's or a region's cultural heritage can provide a sustainable means by which an entrepreneur in a developing country can contribute to economic development.

Scholars have shown that the prevalence of entrepreneurial activity is closely related to cultural and social considerations.[27] The United States, often seen as a classic example of an entrepreneurial culture, exhibits a long tradition of valuing hard work and individual achievement, which is the most important precondition for entrepreneurial cultures.[28] They state that two basic positions exist regarding the relationship between culture and entrepreneurship:

1 Culture as a precursor to entrepreneurship
2 The other discounted culture's affect altogether.

Figure 2.9 Diversity and female entrepreneurs
Source: CYRUS Institute of Knowledge.

Box 2.6   Female entrepreneurs

The role of females in entrepreneurship is varied among cultures and religions. Debate how your community and the government have encouraged female entrepreneurs.

The lack of adequate and appropriate entrepreneurial activities is one of the most important obstacles for sustainable development and growth in most developing countries. It appears that the relatively small entrepreneurial group in developing countries is engaged. Focus and sustainable public policies that provide financial and educational incentives for entrepreneurial activities and influence cultural perceptions can impact positively on startups growth.

It is important to notice that, before the industrial revolution, economic development and growth was slow and basically non-existent. Robert Lucas (2004) reported that annual growth rates "of 1 percent for the entire 19th century, of one-third of 1 percent for the 18th century."[29] In some cultures, hard work and workers themselves were looked down upon by the elite. However, with the advancement of capitalism and globalization, this view has been changing. Due to the revolution in technology and communication, societies are becoming more interconnected. Additionally, countries that have been more entrepreneurial have had a higher rate of growth and standard of living. In this process, the perspectives of elites are changing. The Global Entrepreneurship Monitor (GEM) survey shows these advances in recent years.[30]

A respect for the value of work, however, is not enough to fuel a robust embrace of entrepreneurship. Other aspects that are at least partially related to culture exert impacts, including the society's view on individual achievement and the ability for commercial activities to have sufficient freedom in which to operate. Such cultural aspects are often reflected in the legal and regulatory environment of a country.

The conclusion that follows from these observations is that, from a cultural perspective, the preconditions for entrepreneurial activity include placing a high value on hard work, a generally positive attitude towards those who function as an entrepreneur, and the freedom to experiment and innovate.

Figure 2.10 History of opportunity

Source: One Way Stock, licensed under CC BY-SA 2.0.

Box 2.7   Innovative entrepreneurship trait

Since the beginning of time, entrepreneurs have always found ways to innovate. Debate what is the most important trait of an entrepreneur from your perspective.

Culture and innovation

Country culture

Country culture is like our immune system: it is woven into all aspects of life. Country culture, in its broadest sense, is cultivated behavior, or the totality of what a person has accumulated in experience through social learning. Thus, different cultural groups may think, feel, and act differently towards topical issues such as innovation.

Hofstede (1991, cited in Marcus & Gould, 2000)[31] defined a schema for describing a culture using four key dimensions: power distance, individualism/collectivism, masculinity, and uncertainty avoidance.

Power distance: The degree to which less empowered members accept the power distribution within a culture.

Individualism/collectivism: The degree to which a member of a culture is oriented towards the needs of the individual versus the needs of the group.

Masculinity: The degree to which the culture places value on masculine (assertiveness, competition) versus feminine (home, people) concerns.

Uncertainty avoidance: The degree to which a culture tolerates ambiguity and creates strategies to manage it.

Each of these dimensions has possible ramifications towards innovation. Power distance, for instance, can affect how comfortable employees feel communicating new ideas with their employers. Collectivism over individualism would indicate a culture in which design is done by committee and therefore possibly does not generate as many unique ideas as a culture that supports individualism. A masculine culture would be more competitive than a feminine culture and would thereby foster creativity and innovation through such competition. A risk-averse culture would avoid making creative, but risky, decisions that would foster innovation.

Thirty-eight countries were surveyed and ranked against each other along these dimensions (Hofstede, 1991, cited in Marcus & Gould, 2000).[32] By analyzing the scores for each country, we can predict the impact of cultural attitudes on innovation through each element's effect on creativity.

For example, Spain can be characterized as having a culture with dimensions of low power distance. The factors that work well for Spanish innovation are low power distance and high individualism. Low power distance indicates that subordinates and supervisors work closely together as equals, and organizational structures may be flatter hierarchies. This has a positive impact on the innovation in an organization, as employees may feel comfortable to share ideas freely with their supervisors and work together on implementation (see Figure 2.6 and Table 2.2).

High individualism also predicts positively towards innovation, indicating that the society places higher relative value on freedom of personal self-expression, which is crucial for the generation of ideas.

Box 2.8   The 2017 Nobel Prize in Economic Science for human behavior

Figure 2.11 Richard H. Thaler, from the Booth School of Business at the University of Chicago, was awarded the Nobel Memorial Prize in Economic Science for his contributions to behavioral economics. He concluded that it is important for policymakers to consider human behavior as an important factor, and that humans may act irrationally. Professor Thaler stated that the basic premise of his theories was that "in order to do good economics you have to keep in mind that people are human." He named this phenomenon an "endowment effect." You can read more at www.nytimes.com/2017/10/09/business/nobel-economics-richard-thaler.html

---

The cultural factor that could negatively affect innovation is high uncertainty avoidance. In this type of culture, formal structure is preferred to ambiguity, and familiarity is preferred to what is different. This is problematic towards the development of a culture of innovation, where failure and experimentation are encouraged, and innovators should take risks.

According to a recent study of creativity and design in European countries, Spain is ranked 13 of 27 countries overall and is consistently ranked slightly higher than the median in each dimension taken into account for the scoring.[33] Self-expression is one of the lower-ranked areas, ranked at 17, suggesting that cultural factors could be obstructing the generation of ideas.

Morocco, as a developing country, can be characterized as a culture with high power distance (see Figure 2.7). These characteristics predict that Morocco may have cultural barriers conducive of a less innovative environment in comparison to Spain. High power distance suggests a high inequality of power between employees and employers. The primary attitude is that knowledge resides in the hands of those who are empowered or esteemed, such as teachers or supervisors, and obedience is expected from employees (Hofstede, 1991, cited in Marcus & Gould, 2000).[34]

A culture holding collectivism highly values the needs of the group over the individual and places low emphasis on personal autonomy or challenges. Individuals raised within these cultural settings tend to be less assertive and competitive in a business setting, as compared to other societies (Hofstede, 1991, cited in Marcus & Gould, 2000).[35] Generally speaking, highly collectivist societies are less likely to be innovative.[36]

As a country with relatively high uncertainty avoidance, Morocco would tend to prefer the "tried and true path" versus taking risks.

Similar to Spain, experimentation would be discouraged, and rules and policies are geared towards managing uncertainty rather than encouraging creativity.[37] Innovation and permissiveness to experiment could even be viewed as an attack on the culture's traditions, morals, and values. Therefore, culture, especially national culture, is a crucial factor in the process of innovating.

Box 2.9   Working together

Figure 2.12 Flat organizations
Source: Wonderlane, marked with CC0 1.0.

Valve is a gaming company responsible for classics such as Half-Life, Counter-Strike, Portal, and many others. At Valve there are no job titles, and nobody tells you what to work on. Instead, all the employees at Valve can see what projects are being worked on and can join whichever project they want. If an employee wants to start their own project, then they are responsible for securing funding and building their team. For some, this sounds like a dream; for others, their worst nightmare.

Country culture is like our immune system; its job is to kill intruders before they can harm the body. Unless the country culturally honors ideas and supports risk-taking, innovation will be suppressed before it even has a chance to commence. Therefore, the knowledge of cultural factors that promote or constrain innovation will have an important impact on the development of a country.

Culture demission and innovation

The relationships between cultural dimension and innovation have been discussed previously.[38,39] There is a negative relationship between power distance and innovation. Holding everything else constant, it seems that higher levels of innovation are positively correlated with higher levels of the spread of information.

This social culture is also accepted by companies. There is a process of validation of the culture that individuals acquire in the external environment. The leadership of an organization and the culture that is built can transmit its culture, such as a culture of innovation.[40]

In low power distance societies, communication across functional or hierarchical boundaries is easier and more common, which makes it possible to connect different thoughts and creative ideas which lead to breakthroughs.[41] However, given a large power distance, the sharing of information can be constrained by the hierarchy.[42]

There is a positive relationship between individualism and innovation. The process of initiating innovation is often regarded as the act of an individual. The initial ideas emerge in the head of an individual, while the group can only be supportive or not. Since individualistic cultures value freedom more than collectivistic cultures, people in individualistic societies have more opportunities to try something new.[43] There is a negative relationship between masculinity and innovation. In feminine societies, people focus on humanity and relationships that can lead to a more supportive climate. A warm and kind environment, with mutual trust, low conflict, and socio-emotional support helps employees cope with uncertainty in relation to new ideas.[44]

Box 2.10   Impact of culture in entrepreneurial attitude

- Holding everything else constant, we can draw the conclusion that some cultures are less entrepreneurial than others.
- Cultures that have a low power distance are in more intimate contact in social encounters, government interactions, and business.
- A country high in masculinity not only promotes an environment of competition, but also can foster a culture of selfishness.
- More feminine countries will tend to have partnerships and alliances.
- Jackson and Rodkey state that besides parents, educators and institutions are the most influential in forming children's attitudes and culture.
- Governments have often tried to influence entrepreneurial attitudes.

There is a negative relationship between uncertainty avoidance and innovation. Innovations are always associated with some risk and uncertainty. As a result, cultures with strong uncertainty avoidance are more resistant to innovations.[45] To avoid changes, these cultures adopt rules to minimize ambiguity, and rules in return constrain the opportunities to develop new solutions. There is a strong correlation between innovation and entrepreneurial activities and creativity. Therefore, we can conclude that the previous arguments are also applicable to cultural characteristics, and entrepreneurial behavior and will influence development.

Based on the relationship between cultural dimension and innovation mentioned earlier, we can conclude that innovation will flourish in a creative environment. It seems horizontal organizations are more conducive to innovation. Low power distance index and high individualism are positive in the way of treating others in the first stages of innovation. Creative people should be comfortable volunteering their opinions and motivated to exploring new ideas. Some examples show China and Morocco to have high power distance and low individualism. This means that people in China and Morocco do not feel comfortable speaking up when it comes to idea creation relative to people in the United States, which has a low power distance.

Although generally having a low power distance and high individualism are better for innovation, it does not mean each country does not innovate only in accordance with these gauges. Low uncertainty avoidance is also an important factor that affects innovation. It indicates that, for example, in China, employees prefer to search for solutions for unstructured situations. Unstructured situations are unknown, surprising, and different from the "norm" situations. In Spain, employees, on average, have a high uncertainty avoidance compared to China and Morocco. Spanish citizens seem to prefer to plan everything carefully to avoid uncertainty.

Innovation faces cultural constraints for various reasons, such as shaping the mentality and patterns people deal with, as well as human behaviors concerning risks and opportunities.

Box 2.11   "In Afghanistan, an entrepreneur thrives"

Figure 2.13 Hassina Syed

Edward Girardet (2009) highlights micro, macro, and cultural challenges that exist in Afghanistan, especially for women.[46] One of these brave entrepreneur's stories is that of Ms. Hassina Syed, who is an outspoken 42-year-old former refugee and mother of two. Giradet states that "despite numerous obstacles, including threats by warlords, government officials and rival male interests who deeply resent a female in their presence, Hassina now ranks as one of the most successful entrepreneurs in Afghanistan."

Girardet reports that Hassina Syed has created several companies and is the founder of the nonprofit Afghan National Women's Organization (NOW). NOW's aim is to help women develop their own livelihoods. Significantly, she is the only female member of the powerful Afghan Chamber of Commerce and Industry (ACCI), which has taken official trade delegations overseas with President Hamid Karzai.

The key issue is to what extent and in what ways culture influences individual and group phenomena in organizations.[47] Figure 2.14 demonstrates the importance of corporate frameworks in building an innovational culture.[48]

Figure 2.14 shows the link between creativity, design, and innovation, and its influence on culture. Creativity and design are important strategic resources for an enterprise and a key differentiator for a business. A creative climate in a country or a business organization leads to

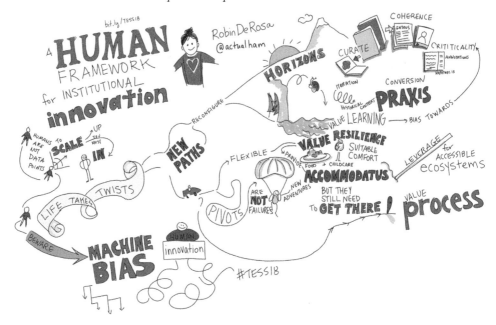

Figure 2.14 Corporate innovation framework
Source: giulia.forsythe, licensed under CC BY 2.0.

the generation of ideas, which can be turned into innovative products or services. Swann and Birke argued that a creative climate in an organization is an important selling point for the organization.[49] The application of creativity and design to innovation is well-defined and should be well-managed. Organizations that have a clear road map for this process will have a competitive advantage over their competitors. In the global economy, creativity and design as drivers of innovation are important for handling economic uncertainty and can help ensure global acceptance of a product.[50] Creativity and design are not only important enablers of innovation in the context of an organization, but are also important features of a knowledge economy, and necessary for a society to be economically competitive.[51] Creativity, design, innovation, and entrepreneurial activities are positively linked and can play a critical role in the development of an economy.

Entrepreneurship, culture, and government

The government can play a large role in shaping the attitudes in an entrepreneurial environment. The regulatory framework and establishment of policies and institutions can encourage the process of creating new businesses as well as helping to ensure property rights, intellectual property, and so forth are protected.[52] Governments at all levels can create incentives for entrepreneurship, doing so in ways that are designed to reflect the culture and its society.

Vietnam provides a good example of this possibility. Vietnam's culture, as a whole, is similar to African, Latin American, and Middle Eastern cultures in the sense that it possesses collectivist tendencies. A strong individual approach is atypical and the country tends to be quite low on the masculinity index.[53]

These characteristics seemingly indicate that Vietnamese culture would not produce many entrepreneurs. However, there are two reasons why the Vietnamese culture has become a stronghold for entrepreneurship. Based on Hofstede's assessment, the country scores very low for "uncertainty avoidance" or fear of failure. The culture views uncertainty as an opportunity, whereas Latin American culture tends to view it as a risk. The government's current "socialist-oriented market economy," furthermore, has created institutions, regulations, and infrastructure to support the private sector and entrepreneurial activity.[54] Although the government once discouraged private enterprises, strategic changes in governmental policies have created a vibrant entrepreneurial spirit. During the French colonial period from the 18th century until 1954, many aspects of capitalism and entrepreneurial culture were introduced there and influenced the culture characteristics of Vietnam.

Box 2.12   Egypt's first university-based incubator

AUC Venture Lab is Egypt's long-standing university-based incubator and accelerator at the American University in Cairo (AUC). The lab enables startups to capitalize on AUC's intellectual capital, world-class facilities, and research capacities. It connects innovative startups with AUC's network that includes alumni, faculty, mentors, and investors. Through this, it fosters a thriving ecosystem of innovation, education, and responsible business.

The mission of the AUC Venture Lab is twofold: to help Egyptian startups commercialize their innovative technologies and business models into viable ventures that contribute to economic growth, competitiveness, and job creation; and to provide a learning and research platform for the AUC community to connect with entrepreneurs.

As the government of Vietnam once did, nations can develop laws and regulations that act as a deterrent to entrepreneurship. The long-standing socialistic culture of the former Eastern bloc, for example, tends not to nurture entrepreneurial activity. In some regions of the world, profiting from private enterprises is considered unfavorable and is viewed as being selfish.[55] This notion can inhibit private innovation and entrepreneurship.

Russia, for example, has a strong developing economy, supported by substantial energy resources, but relatively few have significantly benefited. The high power distance, going all the way back to czarist times and continued through the socialist era, resulted in a society generally not prone to taking risks. This helps to explain why uncertainty avoidance is very high in Russia and, as a result, why as a society they do not encourage entrepreneurship and bottom-up development.[56]

In the case of Brazil, the government has fostered an unfavorable business market through its regulatory system, or lack thereof. Many entrepreneurs and small businesses are considered "informal" and do not report themselves in any way to the government. This results in less tax revenue for the government and creates an environment where formal tax abiding businesses must compete with smaller, informal businesses on an uneven playing field. Currently, a reported 50 percent of the Brazilian economy is operating informally so as to avoid the high tax rates of formal businesses.[57]

This may be an additional reason why a small business leader does not want their business to grow. When we asked a few informal entrepreneurs in Brazil about their organizational and operational strategies, they did not feel as though they were doing anything wrong, observing "it's simply the way it is." Brazil has created an environment where being an informal entrepreneur or small business is the norm rather than the exception.

All of these informal entrepreneurial activities create jobs and generate income that is good for a developing economy. Because self-interest and needs are combined to improve the quality of life, governments should support this outcome. If governments have the ability to clamp down on the informal sector to collect taxes, then the unemployment rate may increase, which could be a bigger challenge for the government.

Box 2.13   Impact of culture in entrepreneurial innovation

- From a cultural perspective, the preconditions for entrepreneurial activity include placing a high value on hard work, a generally positive attitude towards entrepreneurship, and the freedom to experiment and innovate.
- Hofstede (1991, cited in Marcus & Gould, 2000)[58] defined a schema for describing a culture using four key dimensions: power distance, individualism/collectivism, masculinity, and uncertainty avoidance.
- High individualism also predicts positively towards innovation.
- High uncertainty avoidance could impact innovation negatively.
- Generally speaking, high collectivist societies are less likely to be innovative.
- Unless the country culture honors ideas and supports risk-taking, innovation will be stifled before it begins.
- There is a negative relationship between masculinity and innovation.
- There is a strong correlation between innovation and entrepreneurial activities and creativity.
- Culture affects innovation because it shapes the mentality and patterns people deal with novelty, as well as human behaviors in regards to risks and opportunities.
- Creativity and design are important strategic resources for an enterprise and a key differentiator for a business.

This is a period of development in some developing countries. The institutions of government are not developed adequately and are not able to collect taxes to build infrastructure and provide basic services. Therefore, the informal economy and government may coexist in the short run for the purpose of growth and employment.

However, by transcending an informal status, entrepreneurs and small businesses should theoretically benefit. Evidence from countries such as Uruguay and Argentina furthermore legitimizes the claim that informal micro-enterprises and entrepreneurs can jump-start an economy. In 1989, Uruguay and Argentina were two economically and culturally similar countries. Argentina reformed its policies to legitimize its informal entrepreneurs and small businesses, while Uruguay did not.[59] As a result, Uruguay's economy fell behind while Argentina's flourished.[60] The growth proved that legitimization of micro-enterprises could have a much more significant effect on the large Brazilian economy today. In addition to regulatory action, governments of developing countries can also benefit from the experiences of developed countries when seeking to provide relevant incentives for entrepreneurship.[61]

Box 2.14   Cultural tourism and entrepreneurship

Figure 2.15 Brazilian burial ground of African slaves

The owner of the Instituto de Pesquisa e Memória Pretos Novos in Rio de Janeiro is just one example of an entrepreneur capitalizing on Brazil's rich culture. After identifying the site as a burial ground of African slaves, the owner uncovered buried artifacts and turned the house into a museum to display the rich history of the region. Many of Brazil's entrepreneurs exhibit their history and traditions in the products they make or services they render. One woman sells her acarajé, a traditional snack with black-eyed peas and shrimp, in Rio de Janeiro as a tribute to her cultural traditions in northern Brazil. Not only is it something she knows very well, but it allows her to make money while expressing her culture. These "cultural and creative industries" are generating strong growth in most developing regions. By incorporating culture into a national development plan can work towards economic and human rights purposes while making the plan more relevant to the needs of the people and linking to their heritage and self-interest.

Case study

Box 2.15   Women and entrepreneurship case

According to a survey conducted by IIT-Delhi, in recent years in developed countries like the United States and Canada, one-third of women owned small businesses. Women in

Figure 2.16 Women in business

Asian countries led 40 percentage of the total workforce. In Britain and China the women workforce preceded dramatically from men. In a 15-year period, 1980–1995, Japanese women entrepreneurs increased 2.4 percentage points. Women entrepreneurship has a significant role in developing countries. However, in the same developing countries, women encounter many obstacles at the initial stages of commencement of their own business. The majority of top management positions are held by men, and even the most professional women entrepreneurs have the least chance to make it through the commercial market. Traditionally, it is believed that only men could have an entrepreneurship role in society, while women's part is limited to paid employees. Presuming that a woman deviates from the norm of society and initiates their own business, in the running process of her business she would be suppressed by other male competitors or if not, society would do it. Lack of experiments in entrepreneurship for women would be another hassle. Some women involve themselves in training programs without having sufficient entrepreneurial aptitude. Predominance in financial markets, gaining financial resources, complicated loan procedures, and managing working capital in business are financial issues that, to some extent, perhaps men would be structured to perform better than women. Severe competition in the marketplace would be a repellent for vulnerable genders. The main hindrance is the double role of women: first motherhood in family then business women in society. Balancing between these roles is too demanding. Sometimes women spend too much time on their motherhood role that their inability to attend the workplace would add conflicts. It seems women are take risks less often than men, therefore the capital structure they are making would involve less risky capital. They rarely accept credit from bankers for the simple reason of a lack of collateral security.

Questions for discussion

1 Take multiple examples of major companies across industries and evaluate the role/ number of women in top management.
2 Explain why these numbers differ across cultures, countries, and industries.

Conclusions

The influence of culture on entrepreneurship and development was discussed in this chapter. We presented perspectives of scholars and practitioners regarding the relationship between culture, entrepreneurship, and development. We can draw conclusions that government policies can impact behavior by enacting policies which will provide incentives to accept and accelerate entrepreneurial activities.

We examined cultural traditions that are more or less complementary entrepreneurship activities. Additionally, the concept of cultural convergence and its relationship to entrepreneurship and development were discussed.

We provided several cases from different countries to showcase these relationships, including the case about MIT – a higher education institution with a strong entrepreneurial culture.

Discussion questions

1 What is the definition of a culture?
2 What is the relationship between culture and entrepreneurship, and is it relevant?
3 Provide examples of cultures that are open to innovation, motivational techniques, and entrepreneurial happenings.
4 Conduct a case study of two different cultures whose response to entrepreneurship is different. Provide public policies that may alter their entrepreneurial behavior.
5 What is cultural convergence? Is it good or bad? Make your arguments.
6 Is technology altering cultural behavior? How has it influenced you?
7 Does the government have a role in shaping entrepreneurial cultures?

Table 2.4 Key terms

Culture	Uncertainty avoidance
Cultural map	Long-term orientation
Power distance	Indulgence/restraint
Individualism/collectivism	UN Millennium Development Goals
Masculine/feminine	

Table 2.5 Glossary

Culture	Culture as the way of life of a people is composed of learned behavior, attitudes, and material things; thus articulates the following ideas and metaphors.
Cultural map	A visual representation of the different cultural practices, beliefs, and values that exist within a particular society or region.
Power distance	The distance between social classes and groups in a society.
Individualism/ collectivism	The level of interdependence among members of a society.
Masculine/feminine	Motivation by competition versus motivation by interest.
Uncertainty avoidance	The extent to which society is tolerant of unknown situations and attempts to avoid them.
Long-term orientation	Societal long-term, future-oriented perspective rather than a short-term outlook.
Indulgence/restraint	How freely one can fulfill their needs and desires.
UN Millennium Development Goals	Goals created by the UN that are focused on the social and economic development of weak, developing countries.

Notes

1 Watkins, M. (2013). *The First 90 Days*. Boston, MA: Harvard Business Review Press.
2 Hall, E.T. (1976). *Beyond Culture*. Garden City, NY: Anchor Press.
3 Kluckhohn, F.R., & Strodtbeck, F.L. (1961). *Variations in Value Orientations*. Evanston, IL: Row, Peterson.
4 Spradley, J.W., McCurdy, D.W., & Shandy, D. (2015). *Conformity and Conflict: Readings in Cultural Anthropology* (15th ed.). London: Pearson.
5 Hofstede, G., Hofstede, G.J., & Minkov, M. (2010). *Cultures and Organizations: Software of the Mind* (3rd ed.). New York: McGraw-Hill Education.
6 Schein, E.H. (2010). *Organizational Culture and Leadership* (Vol. 2). New Jersey: John Wiley & Sons.
7 Hofstede, G., Hofstede, G.J., & Minkov, M. (2010). *Cultures and Organizations: Software of the Mind* (3rd ed.). New York: McGraw-Hill Education.
8 Lane, H.W., Maznevski, M., DiStefano, J., & Deetz, J. (2009). *International Management Behavior: Leading with a Global Mindset*. New Jersey: Wiley Publishing.
9 Nguyen, T.V., Bryant, S.E., Rose, J., Tseng, C.-H., & Kapasuwan, S. (2009). Cultural values, market institutions, and entrepreneurship potential: A comparative study of the United States, Taiwan, and Vietnam. *Journal of Developmental Entrepreneurship*, 14(1), 21–37. https://doi.org/10.1142/S1084946709001120
10 Jackson, J., & Rodkey, G. (1994). The attitudinal climate for entrepreneurial activity. *The Public Opinion Quarterly*, 58(3), 358–380.
11 Da-ye, K. (2012). Entrepreneurial culture begins with a tolerance for failure. *Korea Times*.
12 Smit, C. (2016, October 21). *What is Uncertainty Avoidance?* Retrieved December 14, 2018, from https://culturematters.com/what-is-uncertainty-avoidance/; Noort, M.C., Reader, T.W., Shorrock, S., & Kirwan, B. (2015). The relationship between national culture and safety culture: Implications for international safety culture assessments. *Journal of Occupational and Organizational Psychology*, 89(3), Version of Record online: December 12, 2015.
13 Hofstede, G., Hofstede, G.J., & Minkov, M. (2010). *Cultures and Organizations: Software of the Mind* (3rd ed.). New York: McGraw-Hill Education.
14 Eunni, R.V., & Manolova, T.S. (2012). Are the BRIC economies entrepreneur-friendly? An institutional perspective. *Journal of Enterprising Culture*, 20(2), 171–202. https://doi.org/10.1142/S0218495812500082
15 Steensma, H.K., Marino, L., & Weaver, K.M. (2000). The influence of national culture on the formation of technology alliances by entrepreneurial firms. *The Academy of Management Journal*, 43(5), 951–973.

16 Hofstede, G., Hofstede, G.J., & Minkov, M. (2010). *Cultures and Organizations: Software of the Mind* (3rd ed.). New York: McGraw-Hill Education.

17 Braunerhjelm, P. (2012). *Swedish Entrepreneurs Prefer to be Employed.* Global Entrepreneurship Monitor. https://www.gemconsortium.org/file/open?fileId=48326

18 www.roberthalf.com.au/blog/employers/9-ways-encourage-workplace-culture-calculated-risks

19 Jackson, J., & Rodkey, G. (1994). The attitudinal climate for entrepreneurial activity. *The Public Opinion Quarterly*, 58(3), 358–380.

20 UN System Task Team. (2012). *Culture: A Driver and an Enabler of Sustainable Development.* Paris: UNESCO. https://www.un.org/millenniumgoals/pdf/Think%20Pieces/2_culture.pdf

21 UN System Task Team. (2012). *Culture: A Driver and an Enabler of Sustainable Development.* Paris: UNESCO. https://www.un.org/millenniumgoals/pdf/Think%20Pieces/2_culture.pdf

22 Tian, M., Deng, P., Zhang, Y., & Salmador, M.P. (2018). How does culture influence innovation? A systematic literature review. *Management Decision*, 56(5), 1088–1107. https://doi.org/10.1108/MD-05-2017-0462

23 Yun, J.J., Zhao, X., Jung, K., & Yigitcanlar, T. (2020). The culture for open innovation dynamics. *Sustainability*, 12(12), 5076.

24 La Porta, R., Lopez-de-Silanes, F., & Shleifer, A. (2008). The economic consequences of legal origins. *Journal of Economic Literature*, 46(2), 285–332.

25 Birukou, A., Blanzieri, E., Giorgini, P., & Giunchiglia, F. (2013). A formal definition of culture. In *Models for Intercultural Collaboration and Negotiation* (pp. 1–26). Dordrecht: Springer.

26 Ergashev, I., & Farxodjonova, N. (2020). Integration of national culture in the process of globalization. *Journal of Critical Reviews*, 7(2), 477.

27 Ondracek, J., Bertsch, A., & Saeed, M. (2011). Entrepreneurship education: Culture's rise, fall, and unresolved role. *Interdisciplinary Journal of Contemporary Research in Business*, 3(5), 15–28.

28 Ondracek, J., Bertsch, A., & Saeed, M. (2011). Entrepreneurship education: Culture's rise, fall, and unresolved role. *Interdisciplinary Journal of Contemporary Research in Business*, 3(5), 15–28.

29 Robert Lucas (2004) reported: "The striking thing about postwar economic growth is how recent such growth is. I have said that total world production has been growing at over 4 percent since 1960. Compare this to annual growth rates of 2.4 percent for the first 60 years of the 20th century, of 1 percent for the entire 19th century, of one-third of 1 percent for the 18th century. For these years, the growth in both population and production was far lower than in modern times. Moreover, it is clear that up to 1800 or maybe 1750, no society had experienced sustained growth in per capita income. (Eighteenth century population growth also averaged one-third of 1 percent, the same as production growth.) That is, up to about two centuries ago, per capita incomes in all societies were stagnated at around $400 to $800 per year. But how do we know this? After all, the Penn World Tables do not cover the Roman Empire or the Han Dynasty. But there are many other sources of information" (Lucas, R.E. (2004, May 1). *The Industrial Revolution: Past and Future, 2003 Annual Report Essay (Chapter 5 of His Lectures on Economic Growth).* Cambridge: Harvard University Press, 2002).

30 "GEM is a trusted resource on entrepreneurship for key international organisations like the United Nations, World Economic Forum, World Bank, and the Organisation for Economic Co-operation and Development (OECD), providing custom datasets, special reports and expert opinion" (Global Entrepreneurship Monitor. (n.d.). Retrieved from www.gemconsortium.org/).

31 Marcus, A., & Gould, E.W. (2000). Crosscurrents: Cultural dimensions and global web user-interface design. *Interactions ACM*, 7(4), 32–46. https://doi.org/10.1145/345190.345238

32 Marcus, A., & Gould, E.W. (2000). Crosscurrents: Cultural dimensions and global web user-interface design. *Interactions ACM*, 7(4), 32–46. https://doi.org/10.1145/345190.345238

33 Hollanders, H., & Van Cruysen, A. (2009). Design, creativity and innovation: A scoreboard approach. *Pro Inno Europe, Inno Metrics: Holanda*, 26, 1–36.

34 Marcus, A., & Gould, E.W. (2000). Crosscurrents: Cultural dimensions and global web user-interface design. *Interactions ACM*, 7(4), 32–46. https://doi.org/10.1145/345190.345238

35 Marcus, A., & Gould, E.W. (2000). Crosscurrents: Cultural dimensions and global web user-interface design. *Interactions ACM*, 7(4), 32–46. https://doi.org/10.1145/345190.345238

36 Veltri, N.F., & Elgarah, W. (2009). The role of national cultural differences in user adoption of social networking. In *Southern Association for Information Systems Conference*. Charleston, SC, USA.

37 Veltri, N.F., & Elgarah, W. (2009). The role of national cultural differences in user adoption of social networking. In *Southern Association for Information Systems Conference*. Charleston, SC, USA.

38 Shane, S. (1993). Cultural influences on national rates of innovation. *Journal of Business Venturing*, 8, 59–73.

39 van Everdingen, Y.M., & Waarts, E. (2003). The effect of national culture on the adoption of innovations. *Marketing Letters*, 14(3), 217–232. https://doi.org/10.1023/A:1027452919403

40 Schein, E.H. (2010). *Organizational Culture and Leadership* (Vol. 2). New Jersey: John Wiley & Sons.

41 Shane, S. (1993). Cultural influences on national rates of innovation. *Journal of Business Venturing*, 8, 59–73.

42 van Everdingen, Y.M., & Waarts, E. (2003). The effect of national culture on the adoption of innovations. *Marketing Letters*, 14(3), 217–232. https://doi.org/10.1023/A:1027452919403

43 Waarts, E., & van Everdingen, Y. (2005). The influence of national culture on the adoption status of innovations: An empirical study of firms across Europe. *European Management Journal*, 23(6), 601–610.

44 Nakata, C., & Sivakumar, K. (1996). National culture and new product development: An integrative review. *Journal of Marketing*, 60(1), 61–72.

45 Waarts, E., & van Everdingen, Y. (2005). The influence of national culture on the adoption status of innovations: An empirical study of firms across Europe. *European Management Journal*, 23(6), 601–610.

46 Girardet, E. (2009). In Afghanistan, an entrepreneur thrives. *Forbes*, October 12. Retrieved from www.forbes.com/2009/10/12/afghanistan-women-hassina-syed-forbes-woman-entrepreneurs-mega-finance.html#6ee83b1824a7

47 Aycan, Z. (2000). Cross-cultural industrial and organizational psychology. Contributions, past developments, and future directions. *Journal of Cross-Cultural Psychology*, 31, 116–128.

48 Swann, P., & Birke, D. (2005). *How do Creativity and Design Enhance Business Performance? A Framework for Interpreting the Evidence* (pp. 1–45). London: UK Department of Trade and Industry.

49 Swann, P., & Birke, D. (2005). *How Do Creativity Enhance Business Performance? A Framework for Interpreting the Evidence* (pp. 1–45). London: Think Piece for DTI Strategy Unit.

50 Swan, K.S., Kotabe, M., & Allred, B.B. (2005). Exploring robust design capabilities, their role in creating global products, and their relationship to firm performance. *Journal of Product Innovation Management*, 22(2), 144–164.

51 Djeflat, A. (January 2011). Innovation systems and knowledge economy in North Africa: New opportunity for innovation take off? In *Maghtech Network, Lab. CLERSE/CNRS* (pp. 16–44). London: University of Lille 1-France.

52 Nguyen, T.V., Bryant, S.E., Rose, J., Tseng, C.-H., & Kapasuwan, S. (2009). Cultural values, market institutions, and entrepreneurship potential: A comparative study of the United States, Taiwan, and Vietnam. *Journal of Developmental Entrepreneurship*, 14(1), 21–37. https://doi.org/10.1142/S1084946709001120

53 Hofstede, G., Hofstede, G.J., & Minkov, M. (2010). *Cultures and Organizations: Software of the Mind* (3rd ed.). New York: McGraw-Hill Education.

54 Nguyen, T.V., Bryant, S.E., Rose, J., Tseng, C.-H., & Kapasuwan, S. (2009). Cultural values, market institutions, and entrepreneurship potential: A comparative study of the United States, Taiwan, and Vietnam. *Journal of Developmental Entrepreneurship*, 14(1), 21–37. https://doi.org/10.1142/S1084946709001120

55 Eunni, R., & Manolova, T. (2012). Are the BRIC economies entrepreneur-friendly? An institutional perspective. *Journal of Enterprising Culture*, 20(2), 171–202.

56 Nguyen, T.V., Bryant, S.E., Rose, J., Tseng, C.-H., & Kapasuwan, S. (2009). Cultural values, market institutions, and entrepreneurship potential: A comparative study of the United States, Taiwan, and Vietnam. *Journal of Developmental Entrepreneurship*, 14(1), 21–37. https://doi.org/10.1142/S1084946709001120

57 Eunni, R., & Manolova, T. (2012). Are the BRIC economies entrepreneur-friendly? An institutional perspective. *Journal of Enterprising Culture*, 20(2), 171–202.

58 Marcus, A., & Gould, E.W. (2000). Crosscurrents: Cultural dimensions and global web user-interface design. *Interactions ACM*, 7(4), 32–46. https://doi.org/10.1145/345190.345238

59 "Although Uruguay has natural resources similar to those of Argentina, innovative entrepreneurs and economic development have been seriously stunted by excessive government intervention as well as

by high inflation" (University of Canterbury. (n.d.). Retrieved December 14, 2018, from www.canterbury.ac.nz/).

60 Nguyen, T.V., Bryant, S.E., Rose, J., Tseng, C.-H., & Kapasuwan, S. (2009). Cultural values, market institutions, and entrepreneurship potential: A comparative study of the United States, Taiwan, and Vietnam. *Journal of Developmental Entrepreneurship*, 14(1), 21–37. https://doi.org/10.1142/S1084946709001120

61 Instituto de Pesquisa Econômica Aplicada. (2010). *Brasil em Desenvolvimento: Estado, planejamento e políticas pública. 00 p. 3 v.: gráfs., mapas, tabs. (Brasil: o Estado de uma Nação)*. Retrieved from www.ipea.gov.br/bd/pdf/Livro_BD_vol2.pdf

3 Technology, communications, and entrepreneurship

This chapter examines the impact of technology on entrepreneurship and its relationship with globalization. We provide a brief background on the evolution of technology and share different platforms of IT that entrepreneurs can take advantage of. We describe how technology is shaping and transforming all aspects of today's life, along with its use to overcome challenges for humanity. The chapter outlines the knowledge and information that are essential factors of production. By the use of technology, the chapter provides a framework of novice practices and tools that can solve contemporary problems. We discuss resources (IT, internet, e-commerce, and mobile technology) that entrepreneurs can take advantage of to achieve their objectives. With the idea that technology provides incremental improvements and transformation of business processes, short case studies on successful entrepreneurs who have achieved greater efficiencies are provided.

Learning objectives

1 Understand the relationship between entrepreneurship, technology, and communications
2 Comprehend the role of technology on entrepreneurship in developed and developing countries
3 Understand the different platforms of IT
4 Examine the relationship between technology and the knowledge economy
5 Study the valuation of IT in a business
6 Explain the role of technology for startups.

Creativity, innovation, and development

Ryan the social robot: technological innovation and barriers to adoption

Case study: DreamFace Technologies and Ryan

DreamFace Technologies, LLC (DFT), founded by Dr. Mohammad Mahoor of the University of Denver, specializes in robotics and advanced technologies development in artificial intelligence and computer vision. Their flagship product, the social robot named Ryan, was created to meet the developmental needs of aging older adults and their caregivers. Ryan has been successfully piloted with over 50 older adults with mild cognitive impairment or early-stage Alzheimer's disease (AD) since 2017.

 Research demonstrates that Ryan is an effective companion for older adults who may otherwise spend a significant time alone as a result of understaffed senior living facilities

---

DOI: 10.4324/9781003405740-5

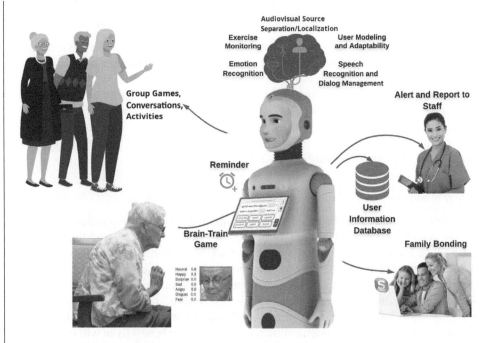

Figure 3.1 General overview of Ryan's functionalities and features

or overworked family members. Ryan forges a bond with users through developmentally appropriate conversation, physical activity (e.g., chair yoga), serious brain games, and a litany of other features (see Figure 3.1). Human-robot interaction is made possible by leveraging state-of-the-art facial expression recognition and synthesis, advanced conversational technologies and natural language processing, and human body tracking.

DFT is launching Ryan in the second quarter of 2023, making available this novel technology to the public at large. Their target customers are senior care facilities exploring their options for staffing, resident caregiving, and market differentiation.

The opportunity: The world population is aging at an unprecedented rate, shifting the landscape of the healthcare industry and the demand for caregiving services.

The number of individuals worldwide over the age of 60 is expected to reach more than 1.4 billion by 2030. Because of an unprecedented increase in life expectancy, healthcare industries in myriad countries are facing significant challenges to care for older adults, particularly those diagnosed with mental illnesses like AD, dementia, depression, or anxiety. In the United States, projections show that as many as 8.2 million staffing jobs in long-term care will need to be filled by 2028. With an unemployment rate below 4 percent at the time of publication (2023), the healthcare industry is facing a historic employment constraint. In fact, industry surveys suggest that 3 in 5 assisted living facilities are concerned that they may have to close due to staffing shortages. Plunkett Research notes:

Healthcare is one of the world's largest and fastest-growing industries, and virtually all of the government and private health initiatives that pay for health care are desperately seeking ways to improve patient care outcomes, cut billing fraud, create operating efficiencies and generally slow the growth of costs overall.

Addressing the gap in care: socially assistive robots and other innovative technologies

Innovative technologies such as artificial intelligence, robotics, wearable devices, and internet of things devices have emerged to satisfy the employment gap affecting the healthcare industry. Socially assistive robotics (SAR) is a field within robotics that aims to use social robots to engage older adults with social interactions, cognitive games, exercise, and companionship. Research has demonstrated that social robots can impact older adult cognition, mood, sociality, and quality of life. Nonetheless, like most emerging technologies, social robots must overcome significant consumer and institutional barriers before their adoption by the public.

Barrier to adoption

Foremost, robot-based technologies have a perception problem: there is a chasm separating the actual present-day functionality of social robots and the perceived functionality generally presented in Hollywood movies and science fiction writing. This separation distorts reality and creates barriers to technology adoption for even the most advanced robots like Ryan who cannot match the imagination of potential consumers. For example, Ryan's response to common commands is limited to those commands that have been programmed by its developers. If you say "stop" to Ryan, it will stop speaking. However, if you say an unrecognized command such as "scratch your head," Ryan will ignore that command and simply switch topics. While seemingly innocuous, such limitations can be a letdown to potential customers who perceive robots to be more adaptable or advanced than modern technology and funding constraints allow for. Other barriers to adoption include high research and development costs, expensive maintenance of hardware and software components, and the advent of competing non-robot technologies such as Chat-GPT, a new artificial intelligence chatbot developed by OpenAI.

Questions for discussion

1   What is the market opportunity for social robots in the senior care industry?
2   What are the barriers in American society to using a social robot as a caregiver?
3   Are there drawbacks to utilizing social robots in the senior care industry?
4   Identify and analyze potential international markets for Ryan.
5   Who do you conceptualize creating a bond with a non-human entity?
6   What differentiates novel technologies that are adopted or discarded?

Introduction

In this chapter, we will examine the impact of technology on entrepreneurship and development and its relationship with globalization. A brief background on the evolution of technology is provided. We will present different platforms of IT that entrepreneurs can take advantage of to advance their objectives.

Globalization was largely made possible by a radical innovation that occurred about 300,000 years ago which was by the daily use of fire. In the book *Sapiens: A Brief History of Humankind*, by Yuval Noah Harari, the main events that may explain about how the domestication of fire led *Homo sapiens* to the top of the food chain is discussed.[1] For us, the fire can be thought of as one of the first radical innovations that is known that made it possible to cook. Cooking was the technology developed from the radical innovation "domain of fire" that allowed us to introduce non-digestible foods through the intestine of the human organism. For humans, two capacities were developed: we spend less time per day preparing food to feed ourselves and increase the chances of survival by ingesting food. While a chimpanzee took 5 hours to eat raw food, a *Homo sapiens* took a single hour to eat cooked food. The energy involved in the digestion of food eaten by chimpanzees, obviously, was far greater than the energy involved in the digestion of food eaten by a human. When cooking food, many other ingredients were introduced into the diet of humans, which would not be if they had not achieved this technology (cooking). As we know chimpanzees did not achieve cooking.

Approximately 230,000 years after the start of the daily use of fire, humans began to migrate to Europe and Australia from Africa; perhaps a kind of entrepreneurship that led to a first globalization, keeping the specificities of the time. Entrepreneurship can be seen as a multidimensional phenomenon involving economic, technological, political, and cultural aspects, among others. Thus, the world is configured by regions according to their level of economic development: developing, emerging, and developed. There is certainly much discussion around the criteria for levels of development. However, there is some consensus that these three blocs make some sense to understand the world from an economic point of view. What we can understand is that the footprint of entrepreneurship intrinsically presents economic development as part of the characteristics of its trajectory. We can also infer that when developing solutions for needs or desires, technologies are designed (high, intermediate, or low technology) and these technologies are elements to support entrepreneurial activities. By technologies, we understand here that they are the practices and the tools that solve or facilitate addressing many problems; just as 300,000 years ago, a radical innovation (fire domain) may have made possible the rise of *Homo sapiens* to the top of the food chain and its prominence as a dominant species (expansion of *Homo sapiens* from Africa to Europe and Australia). Throughout history, humans have made many significant innovations that have drastically changed the way we live. Some of the main human innovations include stone tools, agriculture, writing, wheel, printing press, electricity, and aviation. In 1947, another radical innovation developed that defined the contours of technology and entrepreneurship of the 21st century: the invention of the transistor that allowed the emergence of the internet that has played a central role in the disruption of business today, which we will examine next.

Transistor: the father of the digital age

Before the transistor, the processing and communication equipment operated by means of valves. The problems were mainly the cost of each valve, the heating, the consequent consumption of energy, and the space that the equipment occupied. We can imagine without much exaggeration that for a single smartphone in 1940, it would require a building of some floors to process all the data and the communication. In other words, without transistors, without microchips, without computers, without mobile phones, and without the internet, it would not be easy to operate.

The fact is that the transistor is a radical innovation. Professor Fitzgerald et al. (2011) from MIT published a book titled *Inside Real Innovation*.[2] He describes the invention of the X-ray and the transistor as the two fundamental innovations (radicals) in the strictest sense. From this point of view, all these applications you use on your smartphone, or perhaps the e-reader you're using to read this book, were only possible after we invented the transistor, in particular.

To invent the transistor, it was necessary to learn to master the transmission of electric current through a material different from the conductors; of the semiconductor type (germanium and silicon). In 1947, scientists Bardeen, Brattain, and Shockley invented the transistor while working for Bell Telephone Laboratories.

Figure 3.2 Paper, scissors, stone

Source: rockindave1, licensed under CC BY 2.0.

Making paper from stone – innovation and caring for environment

"Stonepaper" (also known as rock paper, lime paper, or mineral paper) is a new generation of paper that was first developed by Taiwan Lung Meng Tech Co. in Taiwan during
the late 1990s. The primary material of this paper is calcium carbonate powder, which
replaces the use of wood for the production of paper. Its properties are waterproof, tear
resistance, its magic effect of colors on it, and finally its reversibility to the soil. BS Group
in Iran is the fourth company in the world which is making papers from stone (Figure 3.2).

The relationship between entrepreneurship and technology is complementary, one supporting the other and vice versa. Still, in analyzing technologies that originate from a radical innovation such as the domestication of fire 300,000 years ago or the invention of the transistor
70 years ago, we can infer that these technologies begin to delineate the contours of both entrepreneurship and economic development. By inventing the transistor to advance to data-pro-
cessing devices (integrated circuit and then microprocessors), we came to transistor-powered
computers in 1950. Soon after, in 1960, developments began in the United States, the United
Kingdom, and France of the communication protocols called the Advanced Research Projects
Agency Network (ARPANET). This system used packet switching to allow multiple computers
to communicate on a single network. The way we are doing this chronological description is to
explain from another perspective of entrepreneurship, innovation, and development.

In just 20 years, starting with the invention of the transistor, it was possible to get to computers in 1950 (hardware), to begin to processing data (software), and to make feasible the principles of data transmission in 1960 (telecommunications). The internet protocol suite (TCP/IP) was introduced (1982) as ARPANET's standard communication protocol, almost at the same time as the Swiss Tim Berners-Lee developed the concept of the World Wide Web (WWW) that consisted of the inclusion of documents based on hypertext within an information system that was accessible to any node of this network. In the late 1980s and early 1990s, the internet became available to society and not only to universities and research centers. This mass diffusion of a low-cost communication technology (internet) can be considered as one of the essential benefits for entrepreneurship. Society responds when more information is at its disposal. The phenomenon of dissemination of information, initiated with the availability of a network (internet), drastically reduces information asymmetry, provoking impacts on society, on companies, on governments, and consequently influencing the way in which economic development has taken place.

- Entrepreneurship, technology, and globalization are directly and intimately related, beginning with the use of fire and leading to the first case of entrepreneurship and globalization – the migration to Europe and Australia from Africa.
- Entrepreneurship can be seen as a multidimensional phenomenon involving economic, technological, political, and cultural aspects, among other phenomenon.
- The world is configured by regions according to their level of economic development: developing, emerging, and developed.
- The relationship between entrepreneurship and technology is complementary, one supporting the other and vice versa.
- The culmination and mass diffusion of a low-cost communication technology (internet) can be considered as one of the most essential benefits for entrepreneurship.

This explains why technology nurtures entrepreneurship after the industrial revolution. The main aspects that demonstrate the "replacement" of the industrial revolution by the technological revolution has been an inducer of entrepreneurship. By understanding the relationship between information, communication technology, and entrepreneurship, we can explain the ramifications of entrepreneurship in the context of developed and developing countries, which seem to have different nuances.

Thomas Friedman, *New York Times* columnist and the author of several bestselling books including *Thank You for Being Late*, presented data that in 2007, many new innovations evolved. However, due to the 2008 financial crises this did not get the attention it deserved. During 2007, 15 revolutionary inventions such as the iPhone and the Kindle were unveiled. Most of these innovations have revolutionized our means of communications (e.g., iPhone) and ways of our lives.[3]

Social and contextual aspects influence the fundamental way that entrepreneurship functions. For example, what works in India may not work in other countries.

Figure 3.3 Yahoo offices in Bangalore
Source: eirikref, licensed under CC BY 2.0.

Entrepreneurship in developed and developing countries

Since the dawn of the industrial revolution, technology has nurtured entrepreneurship. The current digital revolution seems to expand it exponentially. Through technological innovations, the efficiency of communication has increased. The production of goods and services is now cheaper and broader as compared to the previous decades. The production of new products and services has become easier and more innovative. No wonder it is a catalyst for entrepreneurship in the developed as well as in the developing countries.

Technological advances and applications are becoming ubiquitous because they are constantly evolving at an increased speed. Even the definition of technology is being modified in the process. This chapter focuses on traditional views such as production, modification, usage, and knowledge of tools and systems that solve problems in a systematic manner. Technology is shaping and transforming all aspects of life. It is creating newer dimensions for expansion of entrepreneurship as an actor and also as a class of leaders and innovators.

BusinessDictionary.com describes that technology can be divided into five categories as demonstrated in Table 3.1.

This table highlights the different aspects of technology valuation and usages. Different segments of society use technology to serve their basic needs for communication to advance projects. What is clear is that more and more of the world citizens are finding that it is an amazing tool to use and gain knowledge.

Table 3.1 The range of technology

Aspect	Discussion
Tangible	Blueprints, models, operating manuals, and prototypes
Intangible	Consultancy, problem-solving, and training methods
High	Fully or semi-automated and intelligent technology that manipulates ever finer matter and ever powerful forces
Intermediate	Semi-automated, partially intelligent technology that manipulates refined matter and medium-level forces
Low	Labor-intensive technology that manipulates only coarse or gross matter and weaker forces

Information technology

The contemporary digital age is changing the way business is being conducted. It is universally understood that all types of information and transactions pass through the internet at great speeds. In addition, IT plays various roles in business and entrepreneurship. For example, computers, equipment, software, and other technologies have found their way into all areas of business including finance, marketing, sales, distribution, and others. IT plays an indispensable role in making a company successful during uncertain and turbulent economic conditions.[4] IT is used to encompass a range of new technologies and their applications including in all aspects of the use of computers, microelectronic devices, satellites, and communication technology. IT can affect a firm's products, services, markets, producing costs, and product differentiation. Hence, the success of innovative firms critically depends on the implementation and creative use of IT. The rapid evolution of artificial intelligence and its application to all aspects of human life will be drastic. A good example of the use of artificial intelligence is the ChatGPT application reached about 100 million active monthly users in January 2023, just 2 months after launch, earning the rank of fastest growing consumer application in history. For comparison, it took Tik-Tok about 9 months after its global launch to reach 100 million users and Instagram 2½ years.[5]

As it was discussed in previous chapters, entrepreneurs are risk-takers who develop new ideas, organizations, products, and services. Novelty and innovativeness are the outcome of entrepreneurship while uncertainty is always present during the process of achieving such milestones. Success requires opportunity, timing, hard work, and perhaps some luck. Entrepreneurs tend to embody several traits such as being proactive innovators and risk-takers, who are willing to do what is necessary in order to bring their ideas to fruition.[6] In the contemporary world as in the past, technology provides the emerging tools that allow entrepreneurs to achieve their goals by gaining a competitive edge at a reduced cost. It is widely recognized that any new business venture creates jobs in the economy and improves the general economic conditions in both developing and developed countries. Moreover, these organizations generate new ideas, new business models, and new ways of selling goods and services, and technology has been the essential factor in all of them.

Although many obstacles pose as challenges for entrepreneurs, most of them can be mitigated through the effective use of IT. IT plays a significant positive role in firms' performance.[7] They highlight that through dynamic capabilities of the organization (i.e., agility, digital options, and entrepreneurship), alertness and strategic processes are derived from IT. Enterprises will improve their course of strategic actions, which in turn impact the firms' performance.

Modern-day IT offers a wealth of tools, which entrepreneurs can use to lower the risks, reduce costs, and serve their customers and clients better. Information technologies are significantly changing the global economy and conventional businesses are becoming more and more dependent on technology for their continued success.

IT, particularly the internet, is having a significant impact on the operations of all organizations, especially for entrepreneurs and SMEs.

Careers of the future

In the article "Career in Information Technology: Future Prospects," Jason Wong wrote that we humans have included the use of operating systems from mobile phones to automated company tasks.[8] He expected a growth of 32 percent by 2018 for jobs in computer software engineering, according to the Bureau of Labor Statistics (Figure 3.4). And with change in the US economy, a greater number of opportunities and wealth are available for experts in computer science and technology. Currently, more students are interested in an IT or computer science degree, but still the industry grows at a faster pace. He explains that in the field of IT and CS, you do not have to be a tech person to get involved in the industry. Like many other skills, technology skills can be learned on the job.

He lists five of the most trending jobs in IT: consultant, mobile/web application developer, system administrator, network architect, and data/business analyst.

Figure 3.4 Action adult augmented reality

Source: "756439" by toptenalternatives is licensed under CC BY 2.0.

IT has become essential for economic growth in general and for the success of enterprises because they provide the tools for communication. Compared to the conventional way of doing business, new technologies facilitate and increase interactivity, flexibility, lowers cost, and also improves the linkage between customers/clients and suppliers.[9] IT is having a significant positive impact on entrepreneurial activities by improving linkages between stakeholders in both business-to-business (BTB) and business-to-consumer (BTC) companies.

Knowledge economy

The digital age has had a great impact on the global society/economy by changing the process and the speed of communication, and also on how organizations conduct business. In the last two decades of the 20th century, globalization of the world economy, as well as technological developments, transformed the majority of the wealth-creating methods from physically based to knowledge based.[10] These days, the economic environment is increasingly dependent on new technologies and, therefore, making knowledge and information essential is the key factor of production.[11] In this knowledge-based economy, ideas, processes, and information are the foundation of trade and the catalyst triggering improvements in the quality of life experienced by the people. This transformation (that continues to broaden and deepen) has greatly enhanced the value of information to business organizations by offering new opportunities and solutions to problems. Business organizations, of course, revolve around two factors of production: labor and capital. Although this may still be true, however, an evolution is occurring where information and knowledge have altered the labor market significantly. Especially in developed countries, technology is replacing many "low skilled" jobs with positions requiring specialization and skill.

A basic principle for entrepreneurs is the ability to effectively use knowledge and information to advance their power. An entrepreneur who can attain rapid and relevant information will have a great competitive advantage over those who cannot. IT plays a critical role in delivering this information. Entrepreneurs should be able to tap into this information and create a competitive advantage. Therefore, technologies that support decision-making, which provides an effective interface between users and computer technology and other advantages to entrepreneurs, will be better off. The new technologies, especially the internet, are changing the business environment in trade, investment, and the competitive advantage of industries.[12] These changes, combined with the need for information, are requiring all enterprises, no matter their size, to invest in new technology. Not only are entrepreneurs to adopt these technologies, but also their business sustainability and survival depends on it. With the successful integration of IT, enterprises enhance the availability of information in ways that improve the quality, effectiveness, and efficiency of their operations.

Therefore, many entrepreneurs in the age of IT work to produce high-quality goods and services by using communication and technology tools. These entrepreneurs use the fruit of IT to transform knowledge and their assets into products and services that meet customer/client needs. In this knowledge society, businesses require high-quality information so that they can gain a competitive edge in quality, price, and service.[13]

IT as resources

There are various resources such as the internet, e-commerce, wireless/mobile technology, and social media that can facilitate the advancement of a firm.[14] They state what drives a firm's performance is their processes, which in turn influence their earnings. Linna and Richter (2011) examined the use of technology as a potential engine for economic and social transformation in Kenya.[15] They concluded that young Kenyan tech entrepreneurs are using mobile technologies to overcome challenges at the bottom of the pyramid. While most of the studies have focused on mobile service, the business models are from the developed economy.[16,17] There are few studies that have examined the opportunities and challenges in emerging markets.[18,19]

The conclusion is that the approach and applications tend to be different between the developed and the developing countries because each faces a different set of opportunities and constraints. In a developing country's setting, "benefits of mobile services may not only include profits but also less tangible societal benefits such as the empowerment of users, improving access to the use of information, improving coordination among agents and increasing market efficiency."[20,21]

Strategizing IT expenditure

Schilke (2015) discusses key components to answer before investing the budget on information technology in one's business (Figure 3.5).[22] Most people see expenditure on technology taking higher importance than other factors, but fall behind and look at the big picture outcome.

Most businesses spend between 0.5 percent and 10 percent of their revenue on technology. If the company is not spending enough on technology, it probably means they are not taking advantage of all the benefits available. On the other hand, businesses may be spending more than they need to on proprietary solutions. Thus the author is using her experience with various businesses to come up with questions every business should ask before budgeting money or time on technology, questions such as "Is there a core business benefit to be gained?," "Why do it in the first place?," and others.

Figure 3.5 Budget

Source: "Budget on Keyboard" by SurveyHacks is licensed under CC BY 2.0.

Deciding on which area to spend resources is also an important question. Infrastructure is one of the main areas where businesses spend their budgets, from computers, to networking equipment, to internet service providers. It is important to know when a business should make the changes because it will affect employees and customers. Finally, she advises on adapting to small things little by little over changing everything at once. Read the full article to learn more: http://teamstrength.com/information-technology-in-business-the-big-picture/

By providing the tools and information for innovation in a distributed and accessible way, there has been a great revolution in the models of innovation in terms of cost and format. One of the responses to an observable restrictive context (ORC) is the frugal innovation. Frugal innovation is the response to an observable restrictive context, with drastic resource savings that focus on the inclusion of the unattended demographic masses.[23]

Some regions have attracted special interest in frugal innovation since these countries (regions) still have the presence of significant restrictions on both financial and human resources. It seemed, in fact, that in this new scenario, these countries would have access to other ways to innovate.[24, 25] These regions or countries are the so-called emerging countries, those that have severe restrictions to access innovation or to produce innovation in a structured innovation model. The structured innovation model requires consistent financial investments, offering resources on a long-term basis, but in these regions, financial resources are not available.

Changes in the flow of capital between regions of the world have reordered economies by raising the block of emerging markets, those with a strong GDP growth and market economy orientation.[26]

Mobile technology is a way to reduce the effects of some constraints. On one hand, mobile technologies are enablers of information for people. On the other hand, mobile technology represents a relevant platform for entrepreneurs developing a new business model, for instance.

The world is demanding many applications that run on a mobile platform to solve quotidian problems of society. Some entrepreneurs could observe problems locally and create a new big software solution on a mobile platform. The dissemination of a mobile application is fast and unlimited because they use the internet structure to do so.

Finally, it is important to verify that mobile technology is different when we compare it in developed countries and developing countries. In developed countries, mobile technology is not only a platform for entrepreneurial activities but also a way to address lifestyle and attend to the desires of the people. In developing countries, normally, the mobile platform is used as a platform for entrepreneurial activities by focusing on problem-solving. Despite the different visions, the catalytic effect on entrepreneurial activities is relevant for both countries, developed and developing, and it plays an important role in entrepreneurial behavior and in entrepreneurship.

- Technology is a catalyst for entrepreneurship in the developed, as well as in the developing, countries.
- Technology can be categorized into five types based on their aspects: tangible, intangible, high, intermediate, and low.
- Information technology (IT) plays various roles in business and entrepreneurship.

- IT encompasses a range of new technologies and their applications. IT affects a firm's products, services, markets, producing costs, and product differentiation.
- IT is having a significant positive impact on entrepreneurial activities and has improved the linkages between stakeholders in both business-to-business (BTB) and business-to-consumer (BTC) companies.
- The majority of wealth-creating methods shifted from physically based to knowledge based.
- Entrepreneurs use IT to transform knowledge and their assets into products and services that meet customer/client needs.

Internet

Most of us know what the internet is and what it does. Perhaps we may find it very hard to operate without it. The internet is a global system that connects computer networks together through wireless and electronic means. The internet serves as a key component and point of access for a wealth of IT resources and applications. It has grown from being a tool for military communication into a digital web, serving over 5.3 billion users: a number that continues to grow.[27] A tool of this magnitude is obviously of vital importance and its power continues to grow. Table 3.2 provides estimate internet usage of different regions of the world in December 2023. The usage in all regions from 2000 to 2023 has increased by 1392 percent, which is a significant increase. For all developing countries, the growth has been very high and still is increasing. The increase in internet usages from 2000 to 2023 for regions of Africa, the Middle East, and Asia has been 13,233 percent, 6194 percent, and 2452 percent, respectively, which is the highest increase. The same regions have the highest potential for growth.

This kind of increase in internet usage has great economic, political, and social impacts.

The reach of the internet coupled with its low cost allows smaller firms to reduce their transactional costs and levels the playing field against larger organizations. Common benefits of the internet include expanding the scope of marketing, wider and richer communication, reaching new markets, and partnering with suppliers and collaborators. It is evident that the adoption of the internet can help entrepreneurs tremendously by giving them resources that in the past only the larger business organizations could attain. Yet, many SMEs and entrepreneurs, especially in

Table 3.2 World internet usage and population statistics (2023 estimate)

World regions	Population (2022 est.)	Population% of world	Internet users (31 Dec 2021)	Penetration rate (% pop.)	Growth 2000–2023	Internet users %
Africa	1,394,588,547	17.6%	601,940,784	43.2%	13,233%	11.2%
Asia	4,352,169,960	54.9%	2,916,890,209	67.0%	2452%	54.2%
Europe	837,472,045	10.6%	747,214,734	89.2%	611%	13.9%
Latin America/ Caribbean	664,099,841	8.4%	534,526,057	80.5%	2858%	9.9%
Middle East	372,555,585	4.7%	347,916,694	93.4%	222%	6.5%
North America	268,302,801	3.4%	206,760,743	77.1%	6194%	3.8%
Oceania/Australia	43,602,955	0.5%	30,549,185	70.1%	301%	0.6%
WORLD TOTAL	7,932,791,734	100.0%	5,385,798,406	67.9%	1392%	100.0 %

Source: Internet World Statistics (n.d.).[28]

Table 3.3 Levels of internet penetration

Level	Definition	Descriptions
Level 0	The firm only has an email account but no website	The firms have an email account that they use to establish connectivity with customers and business partners.
Level 1	The firm has a web presence	Though web presence exists, it remains underutilized. Websites at this stage only have the capacity to provide information and brochures and normally tend to be non-strategic in nature.
Level 2	Prospecting websites exist within the firm's structure at this level	At this stage, firms use websites to provide information regarding product specifications, news, and interactive content to customers. The firms using a website at this stage do not relate it in business strategy.
Level 3	Firms at this level incorporate web applications in business strategies	The firm uses website and internet to establish a cross-functional link with its customers and suppliers. The firm also integrates web strategy in their business plan.
Level 4	The level represents the application of web adoption in business transformation	This level represents the highest level of web adoption with the ability to transform business model throughout the organization. The focus is on building relationships and seeking new business opportunities.

Source: The authors

developing countries, fail to realize the benefits of adopting the internet. The degree of usage of the internet can be organized as per Table 3.3.

E-commerce

Electronic commerce (e-commerce) facilitates the buying and selling of products and services over the internet. Doing so can provide substantial benefits to entrepreneurs and SMEs largely by improving efficiencies and raising revenue.[29] It can also create new business opportunities and serve as a vital tool for new businesses. E-commerce enables electronic transactions to occur, and can also help to transform internal systems management, control, data mining, and research in ways that can help build relationships with customers and other stakeholders. E-commerce can cheaply facilitate buying and selling by reducing barriers such as time and place. Despite these benefits, many entrepreneurs have not been able to take full advantage. It is quite important for entrepreneurs to realize the importance of e-commerce for their growth and success. E-commerce allows entrepreneurs to sell their products and services from their home, decreasing infrastructure and other costs. Through its low-cost, low-risk features, e-commerce creates tremendous opportunities for entrepreneurs to start up, expand, and sustain the growth of their businesses.

Wireless/mobile technology

Mobile communication devices offer entrepreneurs a way to overcome the challenges of doing business because it will create linkages.[30] The mobile phone offers more flexibility and efficiency but has its own constraints compared to other means of communication. It will also improve access to capital and market information, facilitate mobile payments, and help to reach new customers. Mobile phones can help entrepreneurs communicate with one another, access market information, sell products across geographic areas, reach new consumers, and enter mobile payment systems. Furthermore, researchers have found that each "one percent increase in mobile penetration is associated with 0.5–0.6 rate of FDI/GDP growth."[31] Mobile technology is a key part of IT and is playing a critical role in improving opportunities for entrepreneurs throughout the world.[32]

Technological inertia

The company Sepahan, which produces disposable plastic containers in Iran, is facing multiple challenges to grow (Figure 3.6). While the imposition of sanctions on the country has negatively impacted the price of raw materials, there also exists the difficulty in incorporating technology in the company's sales and distribution activities. The focus in this short case is to analyze benefits and challenges in opening a direct online channel of sales to the final users.

Sepahan is a small partnership company which has been in operation for about 15 years. It currently (2015) has 30 employees who work three shifts 7 days a week. The management constitutes three key personal, the director of marketing, the director of operations, and the director of human resources. The hardware consists of three imported machines

Figure 3.6 Silicon form for muffins

from China, which in a relatively short process turns the powder of raw materials to usable containers.

Since inception, the output has been sold to middlemen, who in turn sell them to final users who are mostly yogurt producers. The company in this process makes about 20 percent of profit. Their marketing and sales processes remain old fashioned, having no real contact with end-users. Therefore, the company is considering a strategic shift that aims at eliminating its dependence on middlemen. By setting up their website and sales teams, the company aims to reach the final user(s) via the promise of lower prices and better services. Evaluate the company's case by considering opportunity and challenges that it might face during this process.

Figure 3.7 shows the role of wireless technology (WT) in advancing entrepreneurial activities in certain countries. It indicates that WT plays a bigger role in entrepreneurship in the developing countries (e.g., Indonesia, India, China) rather than the developed countries.

It appears that WT is the primary means for conducting most aspects of a business (e.g., communication, marketing) in developing countries. There are more choices for communication in developed countries and it does require more professional networking, fundraising, marketing, and communications.

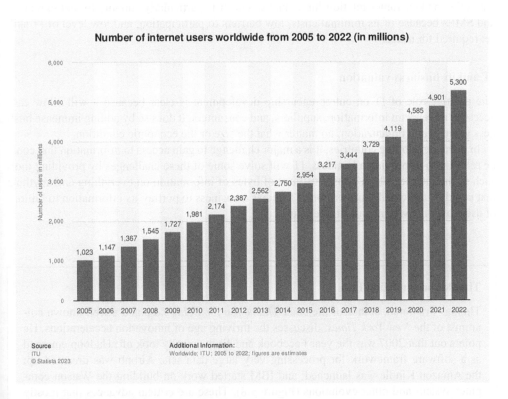

Figure 3.7 Number of internet users worldwide 2022

Source: www.statista.com/statistics/273018/number-of-internet-users-worldwide/

A Time Mobility Poll, which surveyed 4250 entrepreneurs in eight countries, shows the following results: 93 percent believe that wireless/mobile technology is very or somewhat important for entrepreneurship. The survey revealed that 81 percent of those interviewed reported that mobile technology helped them search for the lowest available price for something they wanted to buy; 78 percent felt it gave them access to a larger group of potential customers; 78 percent believed it helped them follow up with their customers; 77 percent thought it granted access to financial service information; 74 percent believed it allowed them to find where they could sell goods for the best price; and 63 percent believed it strengthened the economy in their home country.[33]

Social media

For many entrepreneurs across the globe, one of the biggest challenges is mass marketing. Large corporations have immense marketing budgets and the manpower to conduct marketing campaigns. So how can a small enterprise start and compete?

The answer lies in social media. Social media technology, which is a platform based on the internet, allows people to create, share, and exchange information with other people. Social media facilitates the exchange of information as well as more effective interaction between businesses and their customers. Examples of social media include Facebook, Twitter, and weblogs. Social media has billions of users worldwide and these users are highly interactive.

Social media can be used by businesses for a range of functions, including but not limited to marketing and customer relationship management. It is particularly suitable for entrepreneurs and SMEs because of its minimal costs, low barriers to participation, and low level of IT skill set required for usage.

IT and its business valuation

The positive role of IT on entrepreneurship development is clear because it will allow easy access to all relevant information, suppliers, and consumers. It does so by adding immense business value to any organization, no matter what the size or the economic condition.

In many developing countries, it is a major challenge to gain access to information that could be relevant to improving a business. IT will solve some of these challenges by providing tools such as the internet which houses trillions of bytes of information on everything and anything that could be fathomed. Furthermore, IT allows a business to portray its information to billions of users over the web at an extremely low cost.

Thank You for Being Late

Thomas Friedman, author of the book *Thank You for Being Late* and a well-known columnist of the *New York Times*, discusses the thriving age of innovation accelerations. He points out that 2007 was the year Facebook and Twitter really took off; Hadoop emerged as a software framework for processing very large data sets; Airbnb was dreamed up; the Amazon Kindle was launched; and IBM started work on building the Watson computer system and other evolutions (Figure 3.8). These are critical advances that mostly

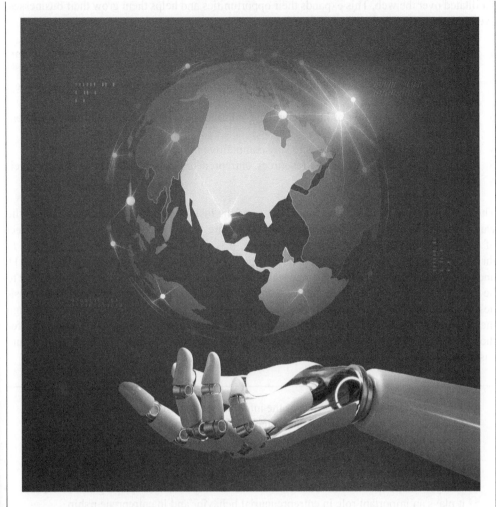

Figure 3.8 Era of revolution in knowledge

Source: www.freepik.com/free-vector/technology-global-ai-race-information-networkconnection_17850519.htm

happened in one year and have led to accelerations of more innovations which are drastically impacting our way of living. Friedman highlights that these technological innovations are moving in such a rapid speed that they are outrunning society's ability to adapt. Combining globalization and climate change has led to an uncharted domain that people find threatening and sometimes frightening.

IT helps entrepreneurs serve broader geographic areas and reach new consumers. It does so by reducing the barriers of physical boundaries. Because of the nature of IT, one does not need to be physically present to share information and conduct transactions, as all of this is now facilitated over the web. This expands their opportunities and helps them grow their businesses. We can summarize the value of IT as follows:

1   Access to IT is essential for entrepreneurship, which will have a positive impact on economic development.
2   Some of the resources IT provides are the internet, e-commerce, wireless/mobile technology, and social media.
3   IT is facilitating the flow of knowledge and information which is replacing many conventional jobs.
4   Entrepreneurs utilize IT resources to stay competitive in their industry at a very low cost.
5   With the correct usage of these IT resources, entrepreneurs can add tremendous value to their business.

The rapid growth of technological innovations and the fusion of IT have drastically changed the way companies compete. Entrepreneurs and SMEs are widely recognized as a critical aspect of developed and developing economies. Hence, it is vital that entrepreneurship continues to thrive. One way to gain a competitive advantage is by utilizing (efficiently and effectively) IT and all the resources it provides. As new technologies are introduced in businesses, they have to be mutually adaptive for them to generate profitability and survivability, otherwise these businesses could face collapse brought by changes of the newly introduced technologies.[34] Through the appropriate usage and combination of these resources, entrepreneurs can create value for their customers and prosper as a result. Doing so can help pave the way for future growth and sustainability.

- There are various resources such as the internet, e-commerce, wireless/mobile technology, and social media that can facilitate the advancement of a firm.[35]
- Frugal innovation is the response to an observable restrictive context, with drastic resource savings and focuses on the inclusion of the unattended demographic masses.
- Mobile technology is the way to reduce the effects of some constraints and serves as a catalyst on entrepreneurial activities for both developed and developing countries, and it plays an important role in entrepreneurial behavior and in entrepreneurship.
- The usage of the internet in all regions from December of 2000 to March 2017 has increased by 924 percent.

Technology and culture

As internet penetration rates in the developing economies increase, so does the ability to be linked with the developed countries. Through this process, exposure to foster innovation is enhanced in developing countries. In 2006, just 18 percent of the world's population was online. according to the UN Millennium Development Goals Report of 2014.

By the end of 2014, penetration rates of mobile cellular subscriptions in developing countries will reach 90 percent, compared with 121 percent in developed countries. Similarly, growth in internet usage in developing countries continues to outpace that in developed countries. Further, by the end of 2014, 711 million people in the world are expected to have fixed-broadband subscriptions – twice as many as in 2009.[36] The internet can foster innovation by connecting merchants, educating entrepreneurs, and establishing a global marketplace. The growing success of eBay and Amazon globally is an indication of the role of technology. As the world becomes a global marketplace, citizens of developed and individualistic countries overlook the entrepreneurs in the developing and collectivist countries that value their lifestyle and relationships.

Holding everything else constant, actually, there are higher desires for entrepreneurial activities in developing countries for the purpose of improving the quality of life. And as they migrate to developed countries, they are determined to make it. Many Laos Hmong war refugees resettled in the United States following the communist takeover of Laos in 1975. When they were relocated, the government spread them throughout the country to avoid concentrations of this group in one place. The Hmong, however, used the internet to get in touch and moved to where other Hmong lived. There are now large Hmong communities in cities such as East Lansing, Michigan.

The role of technology for startups

Startups are initiatives of certain groups of people aiming at building untested business models (new business models). Such a definition helps us to achieve some of the key features of a startup, such as high risk, high potential for return on investment, and often in contexts of great uncertainty. Since the 2000s the term *startup* has ceased to be just one of the initial phases of a business or enterprise and has become a term that self-describes as being a company that uses technology intensely. Each startup is unique, as well as in a company with a traditional business model, which denotes the complexity derived from this idiosyncrasy.

What is common among startups is the strong propensity to use technology. In a startup company, technology provides support for both the middle activities and the final activities. These are therefore technology intensive initiatives, whether for the design of the business or for the operation and management process itself, as well as for the design of the product or service that the startups intend to deliver to the market. Perhaps there are still arguments that a company that exploits a more traditional sector can use some innovations and therefore claim for themselves the title of startups.

As time passes (and goes by fast) we can see that the definition of startups is those involved with technology in their final product, being nanotechnology, biotechnology or information, and communication technology most often found in incubators and accelerators. Thus, we have observed the tendency for the definition of startup to evolve more and more to describe business initiatives intensely related to technology.[38]

Of course, the movement that made mass accessible hardware, software, and communication (internet) outlined many of the opportunities sought by startups. These opportunities are enabled on the one hand by the use of IT and communication to work in the startup itself (processing of office tasks, such as email, electronic workflow, low-cost websites, and smartphones), and, on the other hand, the massive democratization of access to information. Another aspect related to the role of technology in startups is the software market, whether in the client-server, web, or app architecture. Virtually anyone with internet access, anywhere in the world, can learn some programming language and develop the next big billion-dollar application. Initial investments to develop web or app software have become almost zero, reducing the entry barrier, producing real armies of young and not-so-young entrepreneurs in the field of information and communication technology.

The mobility of information access, favored by the cheap access to the mobile internet and smartphones, not only enabled the emergence of startups that offer their new products and services to the market: they also outlined new markets. Mobile internet access has placed at least one-third of the world on a single network, with potentially accessible consumers instantly generating and consuming products, services, and content using digital channels. Yes, today we are generating information 24 hours a day, 7 days a week.

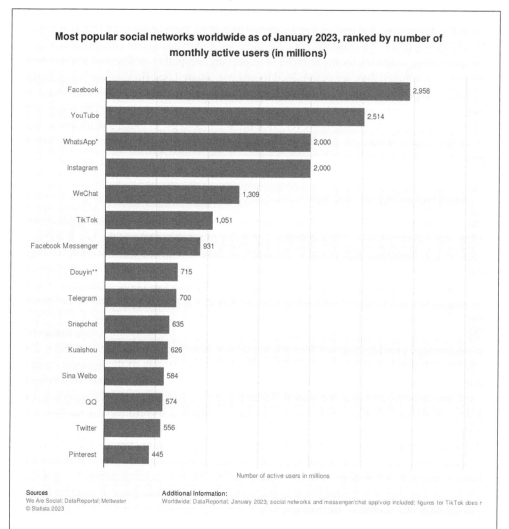

Figure 3.9 Most popular social networks worldwide as of January 2023, ranked by number of monthly active users

Source: www.statista.com/statistics/272014/global-social-networks-ranked-by-number-of-users/ Worldwide; DataReportal; January 2023; social networks and messenger/chat app/voip included; figure for TikTok does not include Douyin.[37]

"How China is changing the future of shopping"

China is a huge laboratory of innovation, says retail expert Angela Wang, and in this lab, everything takes place on people's phones. Five hundred million Chinese consumers – the equivalent of the combined populations of the United States, the United Kingdom, and Germany – regularly make purchases via mobile platforms, even in brick-and-mortar stores. What will this transformation mean for the future of shopping? Learn more about the new business-as-usual, where everything is ultra-convenient, ultra-flexible, and ultra-social in the full TED Talk at

  www.ted.com/talks/angela_wang_how_china_is_changing_the_future_of_ shopping#t-806182

Everywhere we go, every restaurant in which we have lunch or dinner, or every time we go to university, we provide our position, time of arrival, etc. By carrying a smartphone connected to the internet, we form a network of 3 billion people who generate and consume information.

Startups have been working hard to fill this network with service offerings that solve the problems of people connected with entertainment and lifestyle proposals. Social networks for all interests are available, but also applications that can be installed according to the interest of each user. Smartphone applications can be especially understood as a disruption in distribution channels. By developing "virtual" products like apps and making them available in an app store, billions of people will be able to "consume" it right away. Of course, this possibility changes the entire cost structure related to the distribution of a new product.

The startups, therefore, have the information and communication technology and the elementary parts (information, market access, and automation of office routines and communication) to start a potential company. The platform to develop the business model, generate the product (which is also technological), and distribute the channel itself is available to new entrepreneurs, with virtually no entry barriers related to cost. From this point of view, technology plays a central role in startups. Let us take a moment to look at the technological aspects of one of the most valuable companies in the world: Google. It is very difficult to discuss entrepreneurship and technology without involving any case related to Google. This is due to two main factors. First, most of us use almost any product from Google, especially its search engine. Second, because of the company's example of economic success, challenging companies from both the media and other powerful industries. What we are saying is that Google has more market value than oil companies. Google was worth $558 billion in 2017. Apple, Amazon, Facebook, Alibaba, eBay, Microsoft, etc., in terms of users reach, services, and capitalization, show the revolution in technology and its influence in the economic, political, and social issues.

Failure is the foundation of successful innovation

Success is not final, failure is not fatal.

Winston Churchill

In 2012, a group of friends in Mexico City got together to talk about why their business ventures had gone awry. It was a strange thing to do, as entrepreneurs were usually asked to share how they succeeded, not how they failed. Each speaker shared their major business failure – or fuckup as they called it – and the lessons learned. And so Fuckup Nights was born.

Since 2012, Fuckup Nights has turned into a worldwide phenomenon, where entrepreneurs of all walks of life share how they failed. There are monthly events in cities all over the world that invite startup founders to share their failures – and their eventual way to success. The event was deemed as a way to "reveal the honest side of entrepreneurship."[39] Indeed, the curious thing is, no one had to explain why it was important to talk about failure. In fact, most speakers and attendees wondered why this hasn't started sooner, especially given the fact that 50 percent of startups fail in their first 5 years, and 70 percent fail in the first 10 years.[40]

This case study is continued later in this chapter.

Furthermore, there are about 220 startups called "unicorns." Unicorns are the startups with the market value from $1 billion.[41] In Table 3.4, we can observe that of the eleven listed unicorn startups, five (4, 6, 8, 9, and 10) provide services with IT and communication in the final product, four (1, 2, 5, and 7) provide services on-demand, using information and communication technology as a means to transact its services and one (3) manufactures smartphones, therefore, offers mobile internet access infrastructure. We also noticed that both the United States (six startups) and China (four startups) dominate the list, in these top 11 positions.

Figure 3.10 Startup fails

Source: "Mistakes are proof you're trying" by Dasapta Erwin Irawan under CC BY 2.0.

Table 3.4 Startup valuations

No.	Startup	Valuation (billions)	Date joined	Country	Industry	Select investments
1	Uber	$68	8/23/2013	United States	On-demand	Lowercase Capital, Benchmark Capital, Google Ventures
2	Didi Chuxing	$50	12/31/2014	China	On-demand	Matrix Partners, Tiger Global Management, Softbank Corp.
3	Xiaomi	$46	12/21/2011	China	Hardware	Digital Sky Technologies, QiMing Venture Partners, Qualcomm Ventures
4	Airbnb	$29.3	7/26/2011	United States	Commerce/ marketplace	General Catalyst Partners, Andreessen Horowitz, ENIAC Ventures
5	SpaceX	$21.2	12/1/2012	United States	Other transportation	Founders Fund, Draper Fisher Jurvetson, Rothenberg Ventures
6	Palantir Technologies	$20	5/5/2011	United States	Big data	RRE Ventures, Founders Fund, In-Q-Tel
7	WeWork	$20	2/3/2014	United States	Facilities	T. Rowe Price, Benchmark Capital, SoftBank Group
8	Lu.com	$18.5	12/26/2014	China	Fintech	Ping An Insurance CDH Investments, Bank of China
9	China Internet Plus Holding	$18	12/22/2015	China	e-Commerce/ marketplace	DST Global, Trustbridge Partners, Capital Today
10	Pinterest	$12.3	5/19/2012	United States	Social	Andreessen Horowitz, Bessemer Venture Partners, Firstmark Capital
11	Flipkart	$11.6	8/6/2012	India	e-Commerce/ marketplace	Accel Partners, SoftBank Group, Iconiq Capital

Source: The Global Unicorn Club. (n.d.). Retrieved March 23, 2023, from www.cbinsights.com/research-unicorn-companies

Technology and economic growth

Technology is defined by the Merriam-Webster dictionary as "the practical application of knowledge in a particular area." The modern era, named the "information age," is marked by technological advancements. Therefore, success is based on knowledge, which in turn leads to efficient production methodologies. To compete in this framework and the new era marketplace, businesses need communicative networks, an educated workforce, and management support of technology.

Technology is an important component of economic growth. Labor, capital, and technology combine to form the production function. Robert Solow, the Economic Sciences Nobel Prize winner, theorizes that:

$$Q = A(t) f(K/L)$$

where Q is the output, $A(t)$ is an index of technology, K is capital, f states for a function, and L is labor in total hours worked. Thus, the index of technology combines with the ratio of capital and labor to account for a significant percentage of the production output.[42] In addition to increasing productivity, technology improves the quality of products and operational efficiency. Financially, IT systems help companies produce goods at a lower cost, through efficiency and the incorporation of robotic systems in production. Operational improvements, such as identifying new organizational structures or processes that decrease costs and provide efficiencies, lead to competitive advantages through low costs and improved quality. IT enhancements affect customer relationships when they identify new segments for direct marketers or provide cutting-edge experiences to purchasers. Moreover, IT is a gateway to new markets. New value propositions and newly created products for information innovation can be very profitable. If competitors also have access to information, it leads to an information-driven culture that results in the fight to obtain first-mover advantage and patents.

Technology can provide incremental improvements or transformational innovation, thus making international expansion easier to access and more reliable, increasing real-time data communications. Technology has become increasingly portable. Mobile phones and remote desktop setups have provided flexible work options for most stakeholders. Moreover, cloud computing and a globalized workforce have created virtual teams that focus on continuous innovation. Technology also opened up constant feedback funnels, connecting consumers to the company through social media channels. Employees are now asked to solve trans-discipline problems using vast amounts of information. It is evident that good quality education is needed to manage this kind of large cognitive load. This connectivity also allows companies to gather the opinions of multiple stakeholders before making decisions and create clear expectations for consumers. Customers have become continuously informed about how companies operate and expect ethical conduct from them.

This creates a need for companies to manage their brand reputation worldwide.[43]

Technologies are helping to reshape our economies by bringing significant improvements in communication and efficiencies.

- Entrepreneurs and SMEs are widely recognized as a critical aspect of developed/developing economies.
- There are about 220 startups called "unicorns." Unicorns are the startups with market value above $1 billion.
- Technology is an important component of economic growth. Labor, capital, and technology combine to form the production function.
- Technology improves the quality of products and operational efficiency. It helps companies to produce goods at a lower cost, through efficiency and the incorporation of robotic systems in production.
- Growth will continue in the areas of information and communication technology, development of e-businesses, manufacturing, and technological design. These will help businesses to compete effectively in the global market.

Future IT developments will be measured by their quality, usability, ergonomics, and ultimately, user satisfaction. Processes are becoming increasingly automated, yet also are successful in providing a personalized service to their customers. Value is being placed on the human experience.

Growth will continue in the areas of information and communication technology, development of e-businesses, manufacturing, and technological design. These improvements will help businesses compete effectively in the global market, which will directly influence economic growth. Technology mediates productivity, but it takes technology and innovation to raise the economy to its desired level.

Concluding remarks

In the recent past, technology has nurtured and advanced entrepreneurship through a significant evolution in technology. It has been the most important tool in building bridges, repairing them, and perhaps questioning their values. The digital revolution is expanding exponentially and leading to new innovations and higher efficiencies. The production of new products and services has become easier and more innovative, thus expediting entrepreneurship in developed as well as developing countries.

Failure is the foundation of successful innovation

These founders realized that failure is much more instructive than success. In fact, success and failure can be much more similar, and greatly depends on how each is being measured and defined to truly distinguish between the two.[44] Yet, how do you recognize or define which one is which? And how do you change people's mindset: that failure can also be success?

Entrepreneurs start their businesses because of their desire for change and innovation. On their journey, they frequently hear from the people who were successful, and then they learn about all the reasons why a startup may fail. A good number of studies have analyzed the reasons behind startup failure. For example, top reasons according to *Statistic Brain* are things such as lack of focus, lack of motivation, too much pride, and taking the wrong advice.[45] In another study, *CB Insights* mentions the more economic reasons behind failure, such as no market need, running out of cash, and not having the right team.[46] These are all aggregated reasons that a founder might take to heart – but ultimately, they are vague, hard to relate to, and even harder to apply to avoid the problems in the entrepreneurs' own unique situations. What has thus far been missing is how everyday people dealt with the challenges. And most importantly, how they have redefined failure in order to move on.

While acceptance of failure has grown in recent years, there is still much work to do to make it an acceptable, educational part of entrepreneurship. It's not that entrepreneurs should be encouraged to fail, rather they should be encouraged to create in the best way possible without being ashamed or scared of failure.[47] Popular business outlets have started to suggest that failure is a vital component of innovation, but none has gone deep enough to study the positive effects of failure.

Following the success of Fuckup Nights, the team behind the worldwide phenomenon founded the Failure Institute in recognition of the educational value of failure. The institute is dedicated to studying why and how failure affects businesses. In 2017, they launched the "Global Failure Index," which will help gather more ground level information about why businesses fail, what ideas work and which ones do not, and what do to about it. Most importantly, they're on a mission to redefine what it means to be successful – by ensuring failure is seen as the foundation and the best teacher of success.

During the COVID-19 pandemic, the business world had to face a very harsh reality, with many companies having to move from the analog model to the digital model practically overnight. This reality was felt in practically all sectors, from universities that needed to remodel their entire curricular matrix, with the drastic expansion of the offer of online courses, to the food and beverage sector, in which delivery became the only possibility of survival. In this sense, the following case illustrates the change in the model of a Brazilian company that operates in the supermarket sector, which used technology to face the COVID-19 pandemic crisis.

Impact of COVID-19 on the business model – use of e-commerce as a competitive strategy

The ALPHA group comprises six physical stores and has an economic activity established in the retail trade (supermarket) with annual revenues of R$50 million and has more than 200 employees.

The company began its activities in 1963, as a result of the entrepreneurial attitude of its founder. Currently, the ALPHA group has a modern structure, with a strategic location, as the stores are located on high-traffic roads and in densely populated areas in two cities belonging to Greater São Paulo. One of its differentials is the pioneering performance in the region in the supermarket sector, through the sale of products with a wide variety and high quality. In 2020, with the advent of the COVID-19 and the necessity for social

Figure 3.11 Physical store

distancing imposed by the authorities, the company was forced to look for an alternative to stay alive in the business during health crisis. In this sense, it chose to implement the e-commerce strategy for online sales, through a multiplatform application for the delivery of its products. Additionally, a personalized loyalty club was implemented, offering promotions, advantages and benefits, whose customer registration is integrated with its e-commerce operation system.

Caieiras/SP
Franco da Rocha/SP

Characteristics of the system implemented in the company

The system implemented was a white-label type, a standard system that can be customized to meet the specific needs of the acquirer. It is noteworthy that white-label technology is usually adopted when a company wants to expand its operations but does not have the expertise to do so. Therefore, this type of platform allows the company to buy a ready-made, tested, and approved technological solution, without the necessity to invest effort and money in the integral development of the system.

The white-label platform adopted by the company ALFHA was a logistical model created exclusively for the food retail sector, available on multiple platforms: desktop, tablet, and smartphone. This system was customized to reflect the company's identity to offer a customized experience to customers. As for the characteristics of the system, it involves an intuitive navigation structure, with the purpose of leading customers to the content quickly in order to promote sales and make it possible to store information about the consumption habits of these customers. The white-label platform involves advantages and limitations as discussed in the mind map presented in Figure 3.12.

There is a perception in the market that the company that has experience in the commercial area will be able to carry out its sales easily through the internet. However, this is not what happens in the real world. In the view of the owner of ALPHA, especially in the period of resumption of economic activities, after the COVID-19, the support of the company supplying the system (the app) would be essential for the success of its implementation. This commitment by the supplier company had to be contained in a detailed contract, with all implementation phases well described, with a high number of hours dedicated to training the internal team. This was necessary for the system to be fully implemented and for it to reach its full potential.

Results of deploying the application for e-commerce

The operation of an e-commerce requires its own infrastructure, differentiated logistics designed for the business in the new format. In a food trade, some precautions are even more specific. Because ALPHA was already operating in the retail trade through the physical channel, there was no need for the validation process of the business model. System deployment also involved the prototyping and testing phase, which played a vital role in determining the quality and performance of the application. With the release in version beta, the customer became a participant in the process of identifying failures and points of

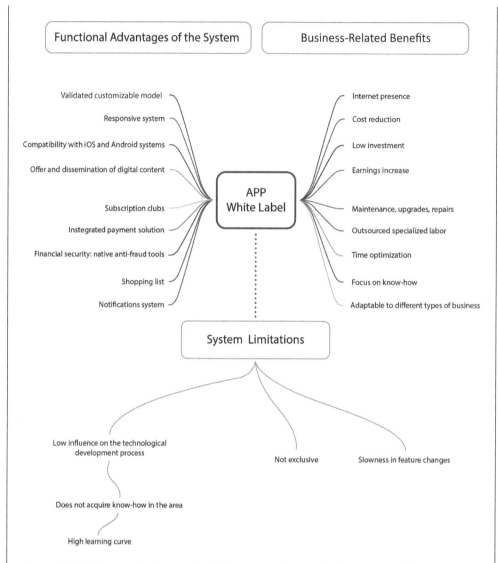

Figure 3.12 Mind map of business-related advantages, functional advantages, and limitations

improvement, both in the app settings (its functionalities) and in the service offered. It was at this stage that the company identified the possibility for customers to buy through the app and pick up at the store, or even if the customer was in the store, they could activate special discounts using the app – for customers belonging to the "loyalty club," paying with these discounts directly at the cashier in the physical store.

After the adoption of the multiplatform system (website and app), ALPHA identified an increase of 17 percent in revenue and 9.4 percent in the number of customers who started making purchases through digital means. In 2022, the company found that interactions and adherence to online purchases continued to grow. These results also involved an increase in the average ticket for purchases made through the app. Therefore, ALPHA began to serve a new customer profile, with greater purchasing power and demand for imported products. These customers – who made their purchases online during the COVID-19 pandemic – became regular customer, which enabled ALPHA to continue investing in new technologies, making it more prepared to face the demands of new times and the advances provided by technology.

Questions for discussion

1   What are the challenges for small and medium-sized companies in the adaptation and innovation process, in crisis scenarios?
2   How can new technologies help small and medium-sized companies to develop in an increasingly competitive market?

Discussion questions

1   How has technology impacted entrepreneurship and development?
2   What is the relationship between IT and globalization?
3   What are the different platforms of IT? What do you think would be the future platforms?
4   How would you do a valuation of IT in a business?
5   Are you planning to start a business that applies technology?

Table 3.5 Key terms

Transistor	Internet
Advanced Research Projects Agency Network (ARPANET)	Levels of internet penetration
Internet Protocol Suite (TCP/IP)	E-commerce
The range of technology	Wireless technology
Frugal innovation	Technology

Table 3.6 Glossary

Transistor	A transistor is a key semiconductor device in modern electronics, crucial for amplifying, controlling, and generating electrical signals. Integral to integrated circuits, transistors are ubiquitous in electronic devices, including computers and telecommunications systems, due to their dual function as switches and amplifiers. Their commercial application began in the 1950s, initially in hearing aids and pocket radios. This marked the beginning of their widespread use in various electronic applications.
Advanced Research Projects Agency Network (ARPANET)	The Advanced Research Projects Agency Network (ARPANET), funded by the U.S. Defense Department's Advanced Research Projects Agency (ARPA) in the late 1960s, was an experimental computer network and the precursor to the Internet. Its initial goal was to connect computers at Pentagon-funded research institutions via telephone lines. ARPANET's development signified the beginning of the concept of a globally interconnected network of computers, laying the groundwork for the modern Internet.

Internet Protocol Suite (TCP/IP)	Developed by the United States Department of Defense through research at DARPA (Defense Advanced Research Projects Agency), TCP/IP has become the global standard for computer-to-computer communication. Despite its widespread use and scalability, it can be complex to set up and manage. TCP/IP ensures that data is delivered effectively, controlling the size and flow rate of data to prevent network congestion.
Frugal innovation	Frugal innovation refers to the process of reducing the complexity and cost of a good and its production, typically to make products more accessible in developing countries. It emphasizes resourcefulness, affordability, and sustainability, often leading to innovative solutions that address basic needs in constrained environments.
Internet	Internet is a transformative system architecture enabling global interconnectivity of computer networks. It revolutionizes communication and commerce, underpinning services like the World Wide Web, email, and e-commerce. This network transcends geographical boundaries, democratizing information access and fostering a globally interconnected society. It's integral to modern digital communication, media, and business operations.
Levels of internet penetration	The "Levels of Internet Penetration" or "Internet Penetration Rate" is the percentage of a country or region's population using the Internet. This includes those with Internet access and basic web technology knowledge. This metric is vital for assessing Internet spread and access across different areas, offering a quantitative view of societal Internet use and accessibility.
E-commerce	E-commerce, or electronic commerce, is the practice of conducting business activities like selling goods and services through computer networks, especially over the internet. It encompasses a wide range of commercial activities, including both business-to-consumer and business-to-business transactions, as well as the internal processes that support these exchanges.
Wi-Fi - Wireless technology	Wi-Fi, a type of wireless technology, facilitates high-speed data transmission over short distances using radio waves. Wi-Fi is crucial for creating cable-free local area networks and providing internet access in "hotspots." Its widespread use spans from home and business networks to public spaces, allowing various devices like smartphones and laptops to connect to the internet wirelessly.
Technology	Technology encompasses the application of scientific knowledge for practical purposes, especially in industry. It involves the use of techniques, skills, methods, and processes to create tools, systems, or devices that solve problems or achieve specific objectives.

Notes

1 Harari, Y.N., & Perkins, D. (2014). *Sapiens: A Brief History of Humankind*. London: Harvill Secker.
2 Fitzgerald, E., Wankerl, A., & Schramm, C.J. (2011). *Inside Real Innovation: How the Right Approach Can Move Ideas from R&D to Market – and Get the Economy Moving*. Hackensack, NJ: World Scientific. ISBN 978-9814327985.
3 15 Revolutionary Inventions of 2007. (2008, August 19). Retrieved December 14, 2018, from www.entrepreneur.com/slideshow/188038
4 Deans, P.C., & Kane, M.J. (1992). *Information Systems and Technology*. Boston, MA: PWS-Kent Publishing.
5 www.reuters.com/technology/chatgpt-sets-record-fastest-growing-user-base-analyst-note-2023-02–01/

6 Morris, M.H., & Sexton, D. (1996). The concept of entrepreneurial intensity: Implications for company performance. *Journal of Business Research*, 36(1), 5–13.
7 Sambamurthy, V., Bharadwaj, A., & Grover, V. (2003). Shaping agility through digital options: Reconceptualizing the role of information technology in contemporary firms. *MIS Quarterly*, 27(2), 237–263.
8 Wong, J. (2015, April 2). *Career in Information Technology: Future Prospects*. Retrieved December 14, 2018, from https://info.focustsi.com/it-services-boston/topic/managed-services/career-in-information-technology-future-prospects
9 Beley, S.D., & Bhatarkar, P.S. (2013). The role of information technology in small and medium sized business. *International Journal of Scientific and Research*, 3(2).
10 Berisha-Namani, D.M. (2009). The role of information technology in small and medium sized enterprises in Kosova. *Small Places Can Change the World*, 1–8.
11 Berisha-Namani, D.M. (2009). The role of information technology in small and medium sized enterprises in Kosova. *Small Places Can Change the World*, 1–8.
12 Lucey, T. (2005). *Management Information Systems* (9th ed.). London: Thomson Learning; Miles, R.E., & Snow, C.C. (1978). *Organizational Strategy, Structure, and Process*. New York: McGraw-Hill.
13 Pollard, D. (2006). *Promoting learning transfer, developing SME marketing knowledge in the Dnipropetrovsk Oblast, Ukraine. South East European Journal of Economics & Business* (1840118X), (1).
14 Teece, D.J., Pisano, G., & Shuen, A. (1997, March). Dynamic capabilities and strategic management. *Strategic Management Journal*, 18, 509–533.
15 Linna, P., & Richter, U. (2011). Technology entrepreneurship-potential for social innovation? The case of Kenyan mobile industry companies. *International Journal of Business and Public Management*, 1(1), 42–50.
16 Hedman, J., & Kalling, T. (2003). The business model concept: Theoretical underpinnings and empirical illustrations. *European Journal of Information Systems*, 12(1), 49–59.
17 Pateli, A., & Giaglis, G. (2004). A research framework for analysing business models. *European Journal of Information Systems*, 13, 302–314.
18 Anderson, J. (2006). A structured approach for bringing mobile telecommunications to the world's poor. *The Journal of Information Systems in Developing Markets*, 27, 1–9.
19 Ivatury, G., & Pickens, M. (2006). *Mobile Phone Banking and Low Income Consumers: Evidence from South Africa, CGAP, UN Foundation, Vodafone Group Foundation*. Retrieved from www.cgap.org/publications/mobilephonebanking.pdf
20 Aker, J.C., & Mbiti, I.M. (2010). Mobile phones and economic development in Africa. *Journal of Economic Perspectives*, 24(3), 207–232.
21 Howard, P.N., & Mazaheri, N. (2009). Telecommunications reform, internet use and mobile phone adoption in the developing world. *World Development*, 37(7), 1159–1169.
22 Schilke, S. (2015, July 24). *Information Technology in Business: The Big Picture, Website*. Retrieved from https://teamstrength.com/information-technology-in-business-the-big-picture/
23 Mashelkar, R.A., & Prahalad, C.K. (2010). Innovation's Holy Grail. *Harvard Business Review*, 116–126.
24 Tiwari, R., & Herstatt, C. (2012). Assessing India's lead market potential for cost-effective innovations. *Journal of Indian Business Research*, 4(2), 97–115.
25 Tiwari, R., & Herstatt, C. (2014). *Emergence of India as a Lead Market for Frugal Innovation*. Hamburg: Consulate General of India.
26 UNCTAD. (n.d.). Retrieved December 14, 2018, from https://unctad.org/en/pages/home.aspx
27 Internet World Statistics. (n.d.). Retrieved March 23, 2023, from www.internetworldstats.com/stats.htm
28 Internet World Statistics. (n.d.). Retrieved March 23, 2023, from www.internetworldstats.com/stats.htm
29 Pease, W., & Rowe, M. (2003). E-commerce and small and medium enterprises (SMEs) in regional communities. The Future of Marketing with Particular Reference to Asia and the Antipodes. https://research.usq.edu.au/item/9xx52/e-commerce-and-small-and-medium-eenterprises-smes-in-regional-communities
30 Andjelkovic, M. (2010, Summer–Fall). The future is mobile: Why developing country entrepreneurs can drive internet innovation. *SAIS Review*, 30(2).
31 Daine Coyle. (2004). *Moving the debate forward*. The Vodafone Policy Paper Series: Number 2, March 2005 Africa: The Impact of Mobile Economist (1999), Survey: Telecommunications, October 9th.

32 West, D.M. (2014). *Going Mobile: How Wireless Technology is Reshaping Our Lives*. Retrieved from https://books.google.com/books?isbn=0815726260

33 Time. (2012, August 27). *How Has Wireless Technology Changed How You Live Your Life?* (pp. 1–26). The Time Mobility Poll was undertaken in cooperation with Qualcomm. August. https://www.qualcomm.com/content/dam/qcomm-martech/dm-assets/documents/TimeMobilityPollResults.pdf

34 Linton, J.D., & Solomon, G.T. (2017). Technology, innovation, entrepreneurship and the small business – technology and innovation in small business. *Journal of Small Business Management*, 55(2).

35 Teece, D.J., Pisano, G., & Shuen, A. (1997, March). Dynamic capabilities and strategic management. *Strategic Management Journal*, 18, 509–533.

36 www.un.org/millenniumgoals/reports.shtml

37 Retrieved March 23, 2023, from www.statista.com/statistics/272014/global-social-networks-ranked-by-number-of-users/

38 Blank, S. (2012). *The Startup Owner's Manual: The Step-by-Step Guide for Building a Great Company*. Pescadero:, K&S Ranch Press, ISBN: 978-0-9849993-7-8

39 Narvey, J. (2016, October 7). Fuckup Nights reveal the honest side of entrepreneurship. *Betakit*. Retrieved from betakit.com/fuckup-nights-reveal-the-honest-side-of-entrepreneurship/

40 Henry, P. (2017, February 18). Why some startups succeed (and why most fail). *Entrepreneur*. Retrieved from www.entrepreneur.com/article/288769

41 Rungi, M., Saks, E., & Tuisk, K. (2016). Financial and strategic impact of VCs on start-up development: Silicon Valley decacorns vs. Northern-European experience. In *Industrial Engineering and Engineering Management (IEEM), 2016 IEEE International Conference*. Bali, Indonesia, (pp. 452–456). IEEE. doi: 10.1109/IEEM.2016.7797916

42 McCombie, J.S.L. (2001). What does the aggregate production function show? Further thoughts on Solow's "second thoughts on growth theory." *Journal of Post Keynesian Economics*, 23(4), 589–615.

43 Asgary, N., & Li, G. (2015). Corporate social responsibility: Its economic impact and link to the bull-whip effect. *Journal of Business Ethics*, 81(1), 223–234.

44 Farson, R., & Keyes, R. (2003, July). *The Innovation Paradox: The Success of Failure, the Failure of Success*. New York: Simon and Schuster.

45 Statistic Brain. (2017, May 5). *Startup Business Failure Rate by Industry*. Retrieved from www.statisticbrain.com/startup-failure-by-industry

46 CB Insights. (2017, September 27). *The 20 Reasons Startups Fail*. Retrieved from www.cbinsights.com/research/startup-failure-reasons-top/

47 Harvard Business Review. (2015, October 19). *To Encourage Innovation, Stop Punishing Failure*. Retrieved from hbr.org/tip/2015/10/to-encourage-innovation-stop-punishing-failure

Section II

Individual characteristics and training

4 Personality, experience, and training

Learning objectives

1 Understand the definition of entrepreneurship and personal characteristics impact
2 Study the classification of entrepreneurs
3 Examine the role of the big five personal characteristics of an entrepreneur
4 Analyze the role of academic education and job experience on entrepreneurship
5 Comprehend the role of financial, environmental, and cultural infrastructure on entrepreneurship.

Box 4.1   Story of a young, dedicated entrepreneur

Entrepreneurship does not necessarily involve building a brand or a firm from scratch. For example, the franchise business model essentially constitutes an entrepreneur purchasing a branch of a preexisting, successful brand. This is the story of the Quality Group of brands in India. Tharun Rao, the founder and managing director of the Quality Group, has proudly assembled an eclectic portfolio of franchises composed of different brands competing in diverse industries.

Tharun describes his style of entrepreneur who considers association with brands as essential. It is based upon acquiring franchises with the plan of introducing these preexisting brands into new markets. His understanding of entrepreneurship is derived from his graduate education in business at the Royal Holloway University. During his time in England, Tharun studied foundational business disciplines such as marketing and financing, branding, accounting, networking, management, and situational analysis. However, he also learned skills essential to entrepreneurship, including how to identify business opportunities, ideas, and planning; strategic and organizational models behind new venture innovation and strategic renewal; and finance and marketing of both small and large organizations. These studies taught Tharun the dispositive influence that a firm's culture can have on a firm, and how to adapt an international franchise's culture when introducing the concept in India.

Tharun graduated in 2014 with a degree in entrepreneurship. Since that time, he has successfully grown the Quality Group into six diverse brands, including clothing, automobiles, and agricultural products. Together, the Quality Group franchises gross more than $9 million annually.

DOI: 10.4324/9781003405740-7

Figure 4.1 Story of an Indian entrepreneur

Despite the Quality Group's early success, startup funding was not easy. Tharun was unable to secure funding for his early ventures from conventional financial institutions. This was based on his lack of an established track record as an entrepreneur. Accordingly, the Quality Group was forced to derive its early capital from Tharun's family and friends. Today, these circumstances have changed. The Quality Group's planed growth is supported by banks.

There is no scarcity of people aspiring to become an entrepreneur by applying the franchise business model. However, Tharun successfully differentiates himself by learning everything about the franchisor's brand, including the customer value proposition (CVP) of the brand (i.e., the problem it solves for the consumer) and how consumers perceive the brand. This comprehensive understanding of the brand and the franchise forms a strong foundation for Tharun's business proposals. His approach towards entrepreneurship is influenced by his education, which distinguishes him from virtually all competitors.

Questions for discussion

1 What were the unique challenges Tharun Rao faced during the initial stages of establishing the Quality Group?
2 How would skills acquired by an entrepreneur differentiate them from the competition?
3 Discuss all the advantages and disadvantages of starting a venture without prior experience.
4 Construct a set of prerequisites that each entrepreneur should possess and discuss each skill's influence in advancing their cause.

Introduction

In this chapter, we will consider the nature of entrepreneurship with a focus on personal characteristics, educational backgrounds, and prior experiences of entrepreneurs. We will also consider the ecological and social factors that impact entrepreneurial activities. It is essential to understand evolving definitions of entrepreneurship and the impact of experience and training in shaping an entrepreneur.

Definitions of entrepreneurship

The definition of entrepreneurship has been debated for centuries. At the beginning of the 18th century, the definitions presented entrepreneurship as an economic concept that describes process of taking the risk of buying at certain prices and selling at uncertain prices.

At the beginning of the 19th century, French economist J.B. Say provided that entrepreneurship "shifts economic resources out of an area of lower into an area of higher productivity and greater yield."[1] Others broadened the definition to include the concept of bringing together the factors of production.[2]

These definitions led others to question whether entrepreneurship was a unique organizational form of business, or whether it was simply a management philosophy.

Discussion about the nature of entrepreneurship activity found an ambiguous relationship between economic conditions and entrepreneurship. The operational distinction between opportunity entrepreneurship and necessity entrepreneurship is based on the prior job situation of the entrepreneur (e.g., prior unemployment), with opportunity entrepreneurship being linked to the development of growth-oriented enterprises.[3]

Over the past few decades, the innovation has become a prominent component of the definition of entrepreneurship. Conceptually, process innovation, market innovation, product innovation, factor innovation, and organizational innovation are all included in the spectrum of the innovation concept. As we will consider later in this book, even the business model itself may represent significant innovation and constitute the source of sustainable competitive advantage.

Box 4.2   Iranian proverb

A father, Ramezon, told his sons to go out daily and try to generate some value and bring it back home; if you could not make it, bring in a small piece of rock so you feel you have achievement. A mother, Khadija, told her kids to be optimistic and persistence; don't give up.

The symbiosis of innovation and entrepreneurship are a central characteristic of most contemporary definitions of entrepreneurship. These definitions emphasize the founding of new businesses in this sense and refer to the founders as entrepreneurs. Virtually all of the definitions share common ideas: initiative taking, risk-taking or the possibility of failure, and the process of value creation (which is derived from organizing and reorganizing of social and economic mechanisms, resources, and situations).[4] Entrepreneurs are viewed from slightly different perspectives in each of the previous descriptions. Each of the foregoing definitions views entrepreneurs from a slightly different perspective. However, they all contain similar notions, such as newness, organizing, creation, wealth, and risk-taking.

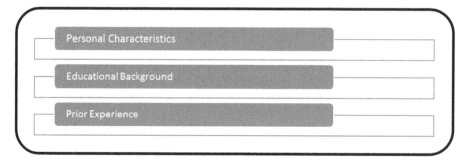

Figure 4.2 Entrepreneur qualities

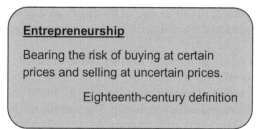

Figure 4.3 Endeavor

Entrepreneurs do not come from the same social groups. Rather, they are a diverse group from all walks of life which are prone to calculated risk-taking. Additionally, their entrepreneurial endeavors are not confined to conventional for-profit firms. Instead, they are found in all professions, including medicine, research, law, architecture, engineering, social work, distribution, and government – and even in nonprofit or hybrid organizations.

In sum, a contemporary definition should capture the view that entrepreneurship is the process of creating new or different value by devoting the necessary time and effort; assuming the associated financial, intellectual, and social risks; and obtaining net benefits, whether monetary, in-kind, tangible, or intangible rewards (including personal satisfaction and independence).[5] Figures 4.2 and 4.3 show qualities that make a successful entrepreneur.

Schumpeter distinguishes between inventor and innovator. An inventor envisages new products and services. In contrast, an innovator exploits invention in distinctive combinations that provide and create new value. Additionally a person functions as an entrepreneur only when they actually carry out new combinations and lose that as soon as they have built up their business and later settles down to running it as other people run their business.

The risk-taking appetite and dealing with uncertainty are key components of entrepreneurship. Richard Cantillon, a 17th-century economist, provided that an "entrepreneur is an agent who buys means of production at certain prices and sells them at uncertain prices."[6] Entrepreneurs must balance potential losses against potential gains under uncertainty.

Contemporary authors also see that in a context of continuous change the traditional rational logics of decision-making may adequately represents the entrepreneur mindset at later stages. The traditional paradigm on entrepreneurship called causation derives from the idea that decision-making process flows from defining, diagnosing, designing, and then finally choosing an alternative. But in the initial stages of ventures an entrepreneur uses the resources they have at

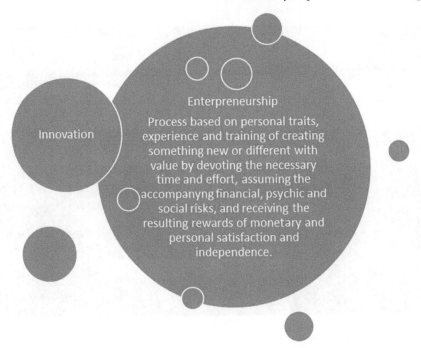

Enterpreneurship
Process based on personal traits,
experience and training of creating
something new or different with
value by devoting the necessary
time and effort, assuming the
accompanyng financial, psychic and
social risks, and receiving the
resulting rewards of monetary and
personal satisfaction and
independence.

Innovation

Figure 4.4 Definition

their disposal and embraces uncertainty to control an unpredictable future rather than predicting an uncertain one. This logic of strategic decision-making is called effectuation.[7]

Peter Drucker stated that "maximization of opportunities" is a meaningful, indeed a precise, definition of the entrepreneurial job.[8] It implies that efficacy and effectiveness rather than efficiency is essential in business. The pertinent question is not how to do things right, but how to find the right things to do and to concentrate resources and allocate attention to them.

An entrepreneur should be a person who are problem-solving oriented and who is expected to make smart decisions about the solution offered by business design that fulfill customer needs. They must perceive upcoming opportunities and chose the correct move in given situations. The previous sections of the book describe the historical evolution of the definition of entrepreneurship, which is clearer and is becoming more concise.

Box 4.3   Outstanding entrepreneur

Steve Jobs is known for creating a company under the assumption that his Apple products and services would revolutionize the world. Since the beginning, he had an unbelievable imagination; he always envisioned that his company would change how people communicated, worked, and lived.

The ability that Steve Jobs had to develop and design products was incredible, unlike anyone else. He is recognized as a legend in innovation and interactive design. The certainty that he had of believing that having the perfect design was the most important factor in the evolution of a new generation of products such as the iPhone.

Figure 4.5 Apple headquarters

He was known for being passionate and fearless in regard to developing what is known today as Apple. The decisions and actions that he took and made could have been risky in the development of the company, but that did not stop him. Every employer must find a way to push their company and employees without crossing any unnecessary boundaries.

The dedication for perfection that Steve Jobs had regarding his company and design shows you that each individual has some traits that if used in the right direction can lead to success. To complete our goals it is important to believe and trust ourselves in the same way that Steve Jobs believed in perfection.[9]

Classifications of entrepreneurs

The following is Galindo and Ribeiro's (2012) entrepreneur classification summary, which highlights who is and who is not considered to be an entrepreneur:[10]

1 An entrepreneur innovates on a regular basis and consistently introduces new products, organizations, or processes. In this class, entrepreneurship is seen as a characteristic which could appear or disappear in any individual. The key point is understanding the difference between an inventor and an entrepreneur; that's the structure destroying and creating simultaneously by the entrepreneur on the organizational (firm) level.
2 An entrepreneur is a speculator or an opportunist. Their role is to keep the economic system in equilibrium. Institutions facilitate the competitiveness and incentives that entrepreneurs need.
3 An entrepreneur is not a risk manager, instead, they manage uncertainty; this differs from risk by being insurable or not. While there is no frequency related to recent events, the entrepreneur (uncertainty manager) tries to ensure the success of their subjects. Profit is a reward for managing uncertainty.

4 Entrepreneurs are environmentally oriented and have to be productive or nonproductive depending on the environmental opportunities that are available to them. This point of view could be applicable to developing countries because there are fewer entrepreneurs per capita than in developed countries. Overall, in developing countries, there are more environmental challenges compared with most developed countries. However, developing countries need more economic and social entrepreneurs to develop.

5 An entrepreneur possesses charismatic, Protestant, and bureaucratic or non-bureaucratic characteristics. This point of view combines interpersonal skills, religious, and knowledge aspects of the personality of an entrepreneur.

Therefore, entrepreneurship could be seen from an individual or organizational perspective. At the individual level, entrepreneurs have the unusual ability and belief to articulate resource in an innovative approach. At the organizational level, decision-making and strategy execution lead to an original way to production, marketing, etc. It should be feasible to expand further classifications of entrepreneurs.

Balachandran and Sakthivelan define *netpreneurship* as a person who runs their business on the internet.[11] The primary requirements for this kind of entrepreneur are "connectivity" and "intellectual capital" as the main variable factors of input and "connectivity infrastructure" as the only physical input. It is clear that the internet has created the greatest revolution in science and technology with so many benefits. The netpreneur provides service to the community in all aspects of life and employment. In fact, the most used portals or search engines like Yahoo, eBay, and Amazon are examples of netventures.

Adopting an evolutionary perspective today, *digital entrepreneurship* is defined as the third wave on ventures related with digital technologies as stated by Zaheer, Breyer, and Dumay[12] the second wave essence, which is called e-entrepreneurship, is exemplified by the digitization of traditional organizations' physical transactions, whether some or all, and exploring new ways of relationships with Facebook and other social media sites.

Amazing changes are happening with the advent of today's digital entrepreneurship. This wave includes transforming business models in ubiquitous connectivity and saturated usage environments. We use tablets and smartphones to create entrepreneurial ecosystems that foster shared and decentralized entrepreneurial agencies, processes, and outcomes, as in the example of Uber and Airbnb. Figure 4.6 presents a graphical presentation of this discussion.

A social entrepreneur is driven to improve and transform economic, social, environmental, and educational conditions to improve social value. Their main traits and characteristics are the ambition to change for the better and rejection of accepting the world as it is. For example, issues such as reduction and elimination of poverty are one of their objectives. They seek to develop innovative solutions to global problems that can be replicated.

Box 4.4   Social entrepreneurship and enterprise

Academia has struggled to reach a consensus on some definitions of social entrepreneurship, social entrepreneurship, and social business. A recent definition follows:

1 Social entrepreneurs are people who use innovative, risky, and efficient behaviors to identify opportunities, launch new businesses, adopt business procedures, and make the most of limited resources in order to become and stay sustainable in their attempts to deliver social value.

2 Social enterprises identify opportunities, stimulate innovation, exploit, and allocate resources that individuals and organizations adopt through social enterprises to meet social needs, create social value, and achieve sustainable social benefits in communities and regions.

3 A social enterprise is a for-profit, nonprofit, or hybrid organization that serves as a vehicle for social participation to create and maintain social value by leveraging resources within the business in innovative ways.

Wu, Y.J., Wu, T., & Sharpe, J. (2020). Consensus on the definition of social entrepreneurship: a content analysis approach. *Management Decision*.

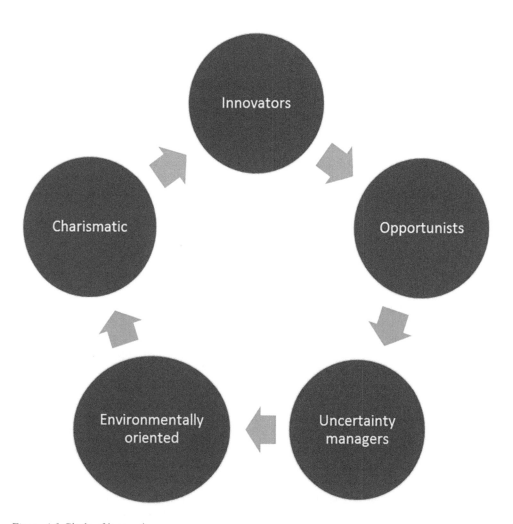

Figure 4.6 Circle of innovation

They are also driven to create social and caring values for the community. Zahra et al. said that "social entrepreneurs make significant and diverse contributions to their communities and societies, adopting business models to offer creative solutions to complex and persistent social problems."[13] They offer a typology of entrepreneurs' search processes that lead to creating opportunities for social ventures and highlight ethical concerns in the societies. Table 4.1 shows some statistics regarding social entrepreneurship from around the world.

A serial entrepreneur is a person who continuously generates new ideas and starts a new business. These individuals have a high propensity for risk-taking and are innovative and drivers for achievement and change. A typical entrepreneur will often come up with an idea and build on it to make it successful and functional as a new company. Most of these typical entrepreneurs hold leadership positions in the organization and some of them may see entrepreneurship as a transaction stage of their careers at corporations, which in turn is more likely when the labor market is less inflexible for non-habitual entrepreneurs. On the other hand, a serial entrepreneur will often articulate an idea and get things started; thereafter, they will give responsibility to others to move it forward. A person who places passion ahead of other factors and combines personal interests and talent to earn a living is defined as "lifestyle entrepreneur."

Table 4.1 Country statistics[14]

Country	Statistics
Australia	• 20,000 social enterprises • 37% growth over the past 5 years • 2%–3% of GDP[15]
Belgium	• 63% self-generated • Over 50% of their revenues through fees or sales (2014)[16]
Canada	• 57% are less than 3 years old (2015) • 45% operate to achieve a cultural purpose • 26% work towards employment development • 27% focus on the environment (2016)
European Union	• 1 out of 4 new enterprises set up every year are social enterprises
India	• More than 89% are less than 10 years old • 88% in the pilot, startup, or growth stage (2012)
Indonesia	• 80% are small-scale enterprises (2012)
Malaysia	• 21% lack adequate funding (2015)
Middle East	• 75% of universities teaching social entrepreneurship (2009) • Estimated 78 globally recognized social entrepreneurs operating in the region (2010) • 20%–30% of business plan competition submissions are social enterprises (2013)
Philippines	• 25% are "multi-organizational systems": amalgamations of for-profit and nonprofit organizations (2015)
Scotland	• 42% formed in the last 10 years • 54% generate half or more of their income from trading • 60% are led by a woman (2015)
Senegal	• 18.1% of the population are pursuing social entrepreneurial activity (2015)
Vietnam	• 68% are working towards poverty reduction and 48% have environmental objectives (2012)
United Kingdom	• 73% earn more than 75% of their income from trade • 27% have the public sector as their main source of income (2015)
United States	• 22% have over $2 million in revenue • 89% have been created since 2006 • 90% focus on solving problems at home (2012)

They may become self-employed because they can have higher personal freedom and work on projects that inspire them. It can be a combination of hobby and profession that will bring satisfaction and financial means. They also may like a good work/life balance and owning a business without shareholders.

Personal characteristics

From humanistic perspective entrepreneurship is based on a set of behavior including exploration of opportunities, innovation and value creation, this desire to start a business is referred in literature as entrepreneurial intention (EI) which is determined by a set of specific psychological traits such as need for achievement, tolerance for ambiguity, risk-taking, and beliefs.[17]

Another common debate in literature is whether the entrepreneurial personality is something a human is inherently born with or something that can be learned. Fisher and Koch (2008) have studied both genetic evidence and survey data and concluded that a considerable share of entrepreneurial behavior is genetically inherited.[18] They cite the characteristics of risk-taking, innovation, optimism, extraversion, high energy levels, self-confidence, competitiveness, and a motivating vision of an entrepreneur.

The authors also explained that certain entrepreneurship characteristics will enhance the probability of entrepreneurial success but are not the sole determinants of success. Research also has shown the entrepreneurship personality. Most characteristics have centered around three of the "big five" personality traits.

Box 4.5   Comparing entrepreneurship in Europe and in the United States

Writer and entrepreneur Babs Carryer claims that Europe is falling behind in entrepreneurship. She writes that after the 1950s, only seven new big companies have been founded compared to 52 in the United States. She gives five main reasons for this phenomenon:

1 Strong European labor and union laws
2 Bankruptcy being harshly punished in Europe
3 Europe's fragmented markets making it difficult to reach a substantial number of customers
4 Absence of startup hubs around the European Union compared to the United States
5 Lower venture capital investment due to the bubble burst in year of 2000.

The article concludes with an opinion that Europe has to think hard about this problem and try to fix it now; otherwise there will be serious consequences for the economy in the future.

Source: Carryer (2014).[19]

The big five[20] are the five broad factors (dimensions) of personality that are based on empirical research (see Figure 4.8).

Recent research has found that there are similarities in the profiles of college students and true entrepreneurs when it comes to traits that are strongly associated with entrepreneurial behavior; those possessing traits of extraversion, conscientiousness, openness, emotional intelligence,

Figure 4.7 Comparing entrepreneurship in the European Union and the United States

and ambiguity tolerance are more likely to engage in entrepreneurial activities. In contrast, low scores on agreeableness and neuroticism have been linked to entrepreneurial behaviors as well. These findings imply that certain individuals may be more predisposed to entrepreneurship, but the negative consequences of entrepreneurship, known as entrepreneurship dark side, should not be overlooked.

Entrepreneurship dark side encompasses a range of negative outcomes that can result from entrepreneurial activities, including fraud, exploitation, abuse of power, and illegal or unethical practices. Personality traits, such as narcissism, psychopathy and Machiavellianism,[21] as well as organizational culture, social norms, and weak institutions, have been identified as factors that contribute to the emergence of entrepreneurship dark side.[22] Addressing these factors is essential for promoting sustainable and ethical entrepreneurship and mitigating its negative impacts.

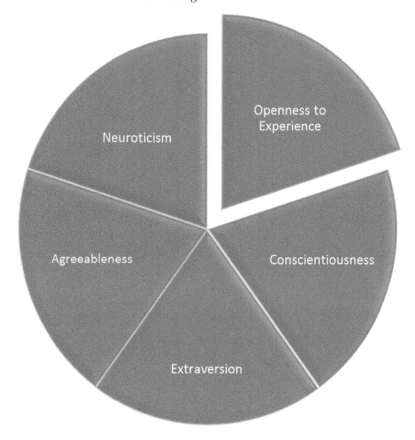

Figure 4.8 Big five

By nurturing positive traits associated with entrepreneurial behavior while acknowledging the potential risks and implementing measures to promote ethical and sustainable entrepreneurship, we can contribute to a more positive and socially responsible business landscape. In this regard, understanding the factors that give rise to entrepreneurship dark side is a crucial step towards designing interventions. Additionally, individuals with a strong internal locus of control believe they are in control of their destiny (see Figure 4.9). By contrast, individuals with a weak external locus of control believe that fate is the form of chance that events outside their control have a dominating influence on their lives.

While it is wise for an entrepreneur to be aware of how other forces may affect their business, it seems entrepreneurs encompass more of an internal locus of control, which would work in cooperation with their need for achievement and desire to be independent.

In Table 4.2, common characteristics of entrepreneurs, their definition, and a brief analysis are provided.

More recently, Hmieleski and Sheppard examined gender effects on entrepreneurship and identified that some personal traits are important for well-being and venture performance which differs from one to another. Creativity is especially important for women, and teamwork is important for men. It is possible that other factors and shared personality traits also differ in the

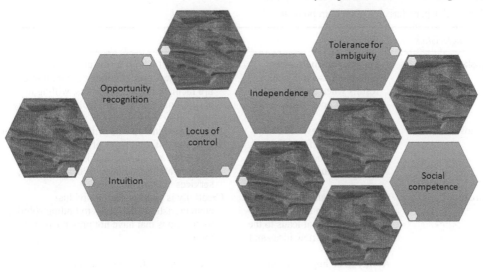

Figure 4.9 Locus of control

extent to which they promote the ability of female and male entrepreneurs to thrive, achieving high levels of both subjective well-being and new entrepreneurial achievements.[23]

Training for entrepreneurship

This section provides descriptions and examples for training and learning how to become an entrepreneur. Many will identify their passion and belief to succeed in entrepreneurial activities while they may have had very little education or training on starting an enterprise. There has been increasing skepticism in the United States about whether or not college is necessary to succeed in the entrepreneurial world. Granted, some of the greatest US entrepreneurs (e.g., Steve Jobs, Mark Zuckerberg, and Bill Gates) are not college graduates but are embedded in an entrepreneurial culture of the United States. The examples of these college dropouts have good economic reasons for their decisions. It is the concept of economic opportunity cost and choices that individual is making at the given time. Either one of the previously mentioned entrepreneur's gained knowledge from continued education would be significantly lower compared to them dropping out and implementing their ideas.[24]

The teaching of entrepreneurship has become widespread throughout universities and has even been integrated into other subjects such as engineering and the arts. It has expanded throughout the educational system and can now be found in elementary and high schools in various countries. The study of entrepreneurship, which was once mainly focused in North America, has now gained significant attention in European and Asian countries and has become a significant part of many educational policies.[25]

Modern entrepreneurship education is an evolving paradigm in the last three decades from instructor-oriented classes based on theoretical approach to a self-directed approach allowing students to get the wheel of their own development by offering authentic learning by doing opportunities whereby students are stimulated to mimic the work of professionals, train in the decision-making process, and be empowered through choosing relevant projects.[26]

Table 4.2 Characteristics of an entrepreneur

Characteristics	Definition	Analysis
Risk-taking	A personal attribute where individuals seek to achieve results when there is a high degree of uncertainty in the outcome.	An individual who is a risk-taker is willing to explore new opportunities even though they are facing many uncertainties; willing to accept financial risk and look for efficiency.
Innovative	Generation of new ideas leading to the formation of new products, services, organizations, etc.	Innovators think outside of the box and look for new and different ways of solving problems. The innovative individual is vital for the creation and formulation of new products, services, and organizations.
Creative	Creativity means thinking outside of the box and the imagination that leads to the generation of new ideas and solutions.	Creativity is an important individual characteristic which leads to finding solutions to questions that have not previously been thought of.
Optimistic	Ability to be hopeful even without a clear path to success.	The expectation for a positive outcome; cheerfulness. An indication of being hopeful amidst uncertainties.
Extraverted	Friendliness, the sense of being preoccupied with an external locus.	It enables growth based on changing market dynamics.
Self-confident	Being confident in one's thoughts and actions.	It is a feature to possess because it creates a sense of assurance in the completion of tasks.
Competitive	The ability to perform competitively in a large setting.	Being competitive gives an individual or organization the impetus to perform better.
Persistent problem-solver	Being resilient in seeking ways to achieve the outcome.	The need for persistent problem-solving is an important component for entrepreneurs seeking to define their standing in a new endeavor within the market.
Goal-directed	It is a characteristic of focusing on achieving goals.	Portray certain behavioral properties that mark the consistency of processes to achieve a particular goal.
Emotionally stable	The ability to make logical decisions without emotional influence.	A moderation buffer where the individual or organization is capable to manage smoothly during critical times.
Passionate	A serious commitment to a particular idea, event, or entity.	A serious commitment to an idea or belief. Love and have an inherent zeal to achieve.
Visionary	Formation of a clear agenda aimed at a goal.	A visionary entrepreneur can clearly articulate the current status of an idea or organization to point to the direction where it wishes to be.
Able to communicate well	Ability to convey information in a clear and convincing manner.	Ability to communicate well and clearly the goal and/or the objective is critical to success.

Lesonsky discusses the non-academic skills learned in school and emphasizes that the social and networking skills that are gained in college are more important nowadays than the academic lessons that may be learned.[27] Considering the current development of the artificial intelligence (AI) revolution could act as an enabler of a fresh entrepreneurial training. They could take advantage by using AI to improve opportunity recognition and exploitation, the decision-making process, and business performance.[28]

In addition, we must also realize that in order to start a business you should have some skills sets, especially business functioning. For example, if Steve Jobs knew nothing about computers, it would have been rather difficult for him to develop a computer business. So, while going to school to earn a degree in entrepreneurship may not be the most accepted path to running your own business, learning skills at college are vitally important to the running of a new business. That is not to say that people without a college degree cannot succeed in the business; it is evident that they can. In fact:

the entrepreneurship activity rate among the least-educated group (high school dropouts) decreased from 0.59 percent in 2010 to 0.57 percent in 2011 but remains significantly higher than for groups with other educational levels. The largest decrease in entrepreneurial activity occurred for college graduates.[29]

The COVID-19 pandemic and the shift to digital have brought some positive changes to entrepreneurial education. First, the rise of remote work and virtual communication has made it more convenient and accessible for students to attend entrepreneurship classes and communicate with teachers. Second, the pandemic has highlighted the importance of entrepreneurial skills, increasing the demand for such training. This has led to the creation of new entrepreneurship courses and programs at the university. Third, increased use of technology has made it easier for students to access a wide range of resources such as online courses, webinars, and virtual instructional programs. Additionally, it has provided students with valuable insight into real-world business practices through the opportunity to interact with successful entrepreneurs from around the world. The pandemic and the rise of digitization have had a profound impact on entrepreneurial education, and these changes are likely to continue to shape the field.

Unfortunately, the COVID-19 pandemic also has brought about numerous negative impacts on education and human interaction. In-person classes have been disrupted, leading to a shift towards virtual learning, which can be challenging for some students and lacks the social interaction and hands-on experience of in-person classes. Furthermore, the pandemic has caused economic hardship for many families, making it difficult for them to afford education. The restrictions on travel and gatherings have also limited the opportunities for students to connect with each other and build relationships, leading to feelings of isolation and loneliness. The pandemic has also caused strain on the mental health of students, teachers, and families, which can further hinder the education process. Overall, the COVID-19 pandemic has had a profound impact on education and human interaction, with many negative consequences.

> **Box 4.6   COVID-19's impact on a Brazilian major research funding agency**
>
> When the pandemic was declared, the Coordination for the Improvement of Higher Education Personnel (CAPES) consulted its scholarship holders about their desire to stay abroad. As soon as the first requests to return to Brazil were submitted, the International Relations Office (DRI) created a task force and a crisis room to provide support and special attention to affected scholarship holders and their families.
>
> The constantly changing scenario led the DRI to seek legal support for various situations. The federal prosecutor's office at CAPES provided legal security for the support

and accommodation of DRI scholarship holders abroad. The DRI also renegotiated agreements and calls for scholarships to adapt to the pandemic.

Out of the 3332 CAPES scholarship holders abroad at the beginning of the pandemic, 612 expressed their desire to return to Brazil, but 24 were unable to do so due to border closures or flight cancellations. The remaining 2395 scholarship holders were monitored and supported, including 141 who received a monthly allowance called "Covid Aid" due to their inability to return to Brazil.

This support included the purchase of airplane tickets and the provision of information through various channels, such as a hotline and FAQs. The DRI also provided training for its technicians to ensure the quality of the support and repatriation of scholarship holders, even during the pandemic.

Source: Coordination for the Improvement of Higher Education Personnel (CAPES) international case. https://www.ncbi.nlm.nih.gov/pmc/articles/PMC9168409/

We can see that high school dropouts are still more likely to begin an entrepreneurial venture as opposed to college graduates. This may be due to the knowledge gained in college and the risk of uncertainty. Students who have completed college are most likely going to have a better view of startups and the risks associated with starting a new business. Additionally, high school dropouts have less choice to be employed because of lower skill sets and therefore have lower risk premium.

There are numerous people that have started businesses who do not hold a degree in entrepreneurship (they may or may not hold a degree in another field), and scholars are split on whether or not a business education can actually help entrepreneurs. At the Tuck Business School at Dartmouth College, only a small percentage of recent graduates start their own businesses, but about half of the school's alumni are entrepreneurs two decades after graduation. "We have entrepreneurship, but it comes a little later in life when they have more experience, more money, and more networks."[30] So, while a business degree may not inspire someone to start their own business right after graduation, it does give them the skills to get the experience, money, and networks that they need in order to build a business later on in life.

Box 4.7   Choosing a different path

Patrice Motsepe learned at a young age that he must choose a career that would keep him away from his family business of selling liquor. He went on to earn a BA from Swaziland University and an LLB from Wits University, and in 1994 he became the first black lawyer to be made a partner at the law firm Bowman Gilfillan. At Wits he specialized in mining and business law, which led him to shift into the mining industry where he started his own business. Today, Patrice Motsepe is executive chairman of African Rainbow Minerals Limited (ARM), a leading niche-diversified mining and minerals company based in Johannesburg, South Africa.

Forbes magazine ranked him as the 642nd richest man and the first African-American billionaire. Patrice is an example of how even at a young age we can set our goals and work hard to achieve them. He also shows us that sometimes we must make our own paths and not follow what our family wants for us, but instead do what makes you happy.

Figure 4.10 Choosing a different path (HalfTone)

There are strong indications that an entrepreneurial education will produce more and better entrepreneurs than were produced in the past. Tomorrow's educated entrepreneurs will know better when, how, and where to start their new ventures. They will know how to better pursue their careers as entrepreneurs, and how to maximize their goals as entrepreneurs, not just for themselves, but also for the betterment of society.[31]

While a business education does not automatically translate into entrepreneurial success, it does give graduates the necessary skills to better improve their chances of starting their own successful business.

Box 4.8   Quick review on entrepreneurial traits and behavior

- Entrepreneurial mindset changes over time.
- An entrepreneur sees profitable opportunities and exploits them.
- An innovator uses creativity to make a new combination, which gives them more profit.
- An entrepreneur innovates on a regular basis and consistently introduces new products, organizations, or processes.
- An entrepreneur is a speculator or an opportunist.

- An entrepreneur deals with uncertainty.
- Entrepreneurs are environmentally oriented and have to be productive or non-productive depending on the environmental opportunities that are available to them.
- Entrepreneurs possess charismatic, Protestant, and bureaucratic or non-bureaucratic characteristics.
- Digital entrepreneur is a person who runs their business in a digital ecosystem.
- Social entrepreneurs adopt business models to creatively solve complex and persistent social problems, aiming to increase social value.

Colleges and universities also have the advantage of having the resources to promote entrepreneurship to their own staff as well. Academics have the advantages of experience and strong networks which can help them build their own businesses with the skills and capital gained from a university. Colleges have a large stake in the success of many entrepreneurial ventures as well. In 2009, The Economist reported that:

> America's universities are economic engines rather than ivory towers, with proliferating science parks, technology offices, business incubators, and venture funds. Stanford University gained around $200m in stock when Google went public. It is so keen on promoting entrepreneurship that it has created a monopoly-like game to teach its professors how to become entrepreneurs. About half of the startups in Silicon Valley have their roots in the university.[32]

Higher education institutions like colleges and universities have a lot to gain from educating the next group of entrepreneurs. Not only do well-known alumni provide schools with credit and higher prestige, but they also give the colleges opportunities to invest and benefit from alumni success through investments and donations. College and university are not the only organizations jumping on the entrepreneurship bandwagon; many other organizations are promoting entrepreneurship and education as well.

This shows that while a college education is the most traditional way to gain knowledge about entrepreneurship and other fields, there are other options for people who are interested in starting their own businesses. In addition to private organizations encouraging entrepreneurship through their own form of education, public organizations are now becoming involved as well.

The Federal Deposit Insurance Corporation (FDIC) and Small Business Administration (SBA) have developed a program called "Money Smart for Small Businesses," which is "10-step instructional guide for financial institutions and other stakeholders to teach budding entrepreneurs the basics of running a business." This instructor-led program is designed to be taught to financial institutions and small business development centers which in turn give the training to entrepreneurs.[33]

While there are different opinions on the best ways to entrepreneur development, they share some aspects that there are skills that can be gained from receiving an education, whether it is in entrepreneurship or another field. This education can be learned at a formal institution, in a community program, or even through life experience, but an education of some sort is necessary to succeed. The resource-based view (RBV) in strategic management complements this approach, with the formal learning providing the practical skills and knowledge to develop resources and capabilities, and life experience providing the theoretical framework for understanding how a

Figure 4.11 Entrepreneur connections

company's resources and capabilities contribute to its success. By combining both concepts, individuals are equipped with a comprehensive understanding of what it takes to build a successful business.[34]

Education, innovation, and creativity

Education influences innovation from early ages throughout college and within organizations. Education that employees receive prior to employment and how the company continues to educate employees after hire play a big role in creating and continuing innovative culture. Many from developing countries come to the United States to acquire education and exposure to innovation. For example, the founder of Hmizate, an e-commerce business, was educated in the United States and was exposed to innovative culture. He returned to Morocco, where he applied the concepts and behaviors that he learned from experience abroad.

Moreover, executing an educational training program at the organization level has shown positive effects on entrepreneurial orientation, risk-taking, proactiveness, and more relevance in innovativeness which leads to increased performance. There is stronger evidence of positive impact of entrepreneurship training on intention/creation, emotional attitudes, self-efficacy, and self-reliance.[35]

The way in which companies educate their employees after hire also influences the innovation abilities of the companies. For example, Intel provides workshops and classes for its employees in order to keep them fresh and current. In an industry such as marketing, companies, brands, and trends change on a daily basis; keeping employees educated on a constant basis is the only way to maintain their knowledge base and inspire innovation.

Figure 4.12 Company success

Experience and repertoire

The experience of an individual is seen to have an important influence on that person's performance in new endeavors. Normally educational and job experience are common requirements for finding a job in general as they are designed to standardize the performance of individuals. However, the backgrounds of business owners are heterogeneous, which has led to the suggestion that differences in the experiences of owners might explain variance in the performance of their enterprises. Entrepreneurs could use their experience to identify possible innovations and how to capitalize on the experience they have, such as entering certain industries. In addition, previous industry experience will help entrepreneurs build relationships, network, identify new products and markets, and acquire funding (see Figure 4.12).

Box 4.9   Training of entrepreneurs' competencies in higher education – Brazil

A teaching project in entrepreneurship was created in 2013 for undergraduate students of pharmacy from the State University of the West of Paraná–UNIOESTE, located in the city of Cascavel, Brazil. The objective of this entrepreneurship consisted of teaching, extension, and research activities, which were (1) creation of the discipline "Entrepreneurship in Pharmaceutical Sciences"; (2) implementation of the teaching project "Entrepreneurial Experiences in Pharmaceutical Sciences"; and (3) conducting surveys to evaluate the profile of students and undergraduate alumni of the pharmacy course. The purpose of this project is to contribute to the higher education courses for the training of entrepreneurial skills of its academics, and to the formation of an entrepreneurial culture that has reflexes in the external environments to the institutions promoting the regional development.

Surveys and research of investors in the developed countries who invest in new companies consistently reveal that industry experience for startup companies are among the most important determinants of new company success.

This suggests that experience enhances the performance and sustainability of new ventures. Therefore, we can draw conclusions that experience is a good education for entrepreneurs.

However, industry experience remains a controversial topic in aiding entrepreneurial success. One can argue that industry experience can lead entrepreneurs to run their firms better, as suggested earlier, but it is also possible that industry experience has no impact at all. If entrepreneurial performance is driven by the value of available opportunities and not by an entrepreneur's abilities, then industry experience can be seen in a different view. By taking this view, people with industry experience may have a greater ability to identify opportunities which will help them to succeed, but they may not perform better than other entrepreneurs with less experience; they are just making better-informed risks. This reasoning would also help break down the myth that experience is key to performing better for entrepreneurs.

Environmental infrastructure

The entrepreneurial environment is characterized by rapidly changing and uncertain markets, making the application of contingency theory particularly important. In this context, entrepreneurs must be able to quickly adapt to new situations, identify and respond to new opportunities, and make decisions that align with the specific contingencies of their environment. Contingency theory suggests that there is no one-size-fits-all approach to organizational design and management, but rather the appropriate approach depends on the unique combination of factors present in a given situation, including the organizational context and the environment in which it operates. By recognizing the need for flexibility and adaptability, entrepreneurs in the entrepreneurial environment can better position themselves for success in an ever-changing business landscape.[36]

Environmental infrastructure comprehends economic factors, finance, and social and cultural aspects inside that entrepreneurship flourish or perish. The business environment as a role could be seen as a multifaceted factor that influences economic growth and wealth; to a higher extent they include the macroeconomics settings, regulations, capital availability, and social and cultural expectations.

Economic factors

Market dynamics and the strength of competition are central to the entrepreneurial spirit and the driving force of economies. The importance of entrepreneurship in economic success has been acknowledged since the early days of economics. In a thriving market economy, the entrepreneurial mindset is widely embraced and passed down as a part of the open-minded culture. Media often celebrates successful entrepreneurs, and there are numerous individuals who serve as inspirational figures in this regard. Under capitalism (the basis of many developed nations' economies), innovative activity becomes somewhat of a given.

For no other reason, that market economy has been recommended for developing nations. For example, one of the issues that Central and Eastern European countries faced in the transformation from centrally planned into market economies was the need to develop a private business sector which allows entrepreneurs to create their own businesses. The transformation occurred in three ways. First, on the firm level, there needs to be a change from government ownership to private ownership, which can be achieved through the direct transfer of formerly state-run businesses to private ownership or by starting a new business from scratch, reducing the obstacles for entrepreneurship. The second is the liberalization of markets, which increases market opportunities as well as in the level of competition. The third involves the creation of market institutions, such as banks, other financial intermediaries, and business and training support services, which are an integral part of the external environment for business development in mature market economies.[37]

Undoubtedly, the experience of privatizing industries in the former Soviet Union and Eastern Europe holds valuable lessons that should not be overlooked. While the transfer of public ownership to the private sector was aimed at fostering a market economy, it was not necessarily done in a manner that promoted a fair and equitable market system. The proliferation of oligarchs in Russia is a testament to the shortcomings of this privatization process.

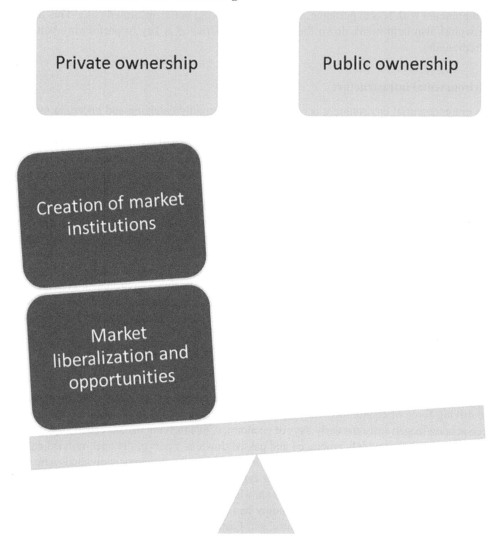

Figure 4.13 Environmental infrastructure

While innovation and entrepreneurship are the drivers for economic growth, in developing countries, there are also ways where entrepreneurship can actually hinder economic development due to the misallocation of entrepreneurial talent. This misallocation arises from the absence of good institutions (see Figure 4.13).

Financial structure

Access to capital is one of the biggest hurdles to start and grow a new business. Entrepreneurs may not be aware of the financial loan products available to them. If they are aware of financial institutions, entrepreneurs also need to provide valuable collateral and meet interest obligations which might be difficult. In addition, financial institutions may be reluctant to lend to entrepreneurs or SMEs due to a lack of reliable credit information and limited capacity to appropriately assess credit risks. In the future chapters, we will discuss this subject in detail.

Box 4.10   Quick review on training and experience

- Entrepreneurial education prior to employment and during employment in the company plays a big role in venture performance.
- Previous industry experience will help entrepreneurs build relationships, network, identify new products and markets, and acquire funding.
- In a developed market economy, entrepreneurial knowledge is transmitted as a part of the open culture.
- Misallocation of entrepreneurial talent arises from the absence of good institutions.
- Financial institutions may be reluctant to lend to entrepreneurs or SMEs due to a lack of reliable credit information and limited capacity to appropriately assess credit risks.

The advent of market economies has fostered greater competition among banks, enabling a freer flow of capital towards the most promising ventures. In the absence of traditional banking options, entrepreneurs in developed countries can explore alternative financing methods such as small business associations, crowdfunding, venture capital, angel investors, bond markets, and others. Additionally, many entrepreneurs rely on their personal wealth and income to fund their business initiatives. It is this plentiful access to financial capital that has fueled developed nations to promote entrepreneurship. In Chapters 9 and 10, we will discuss funding sources and challenges that entrepreneurs are facing in developing countries. While there are different sources of funds available for entrepreneurs in developed countries, this is not the case in most developing countries.

Social structure

The relationship between institutions, entrepreneurship, and economic growth has been studied extensively over the past 25 years.[38] The findings indicate that there is a strong connection between them, with institutions playing a crucial role in fostering entrepreneurship and driving economic growth.

For public policies to be effective in promoting economic growth, it's important to understand the specific institutional factors that support entrepreneurship. This may involve exploring the effects of regulations, access to financing, cultural attitudes towards risk-taking and innovation, and the provision of human capital and infrastructure.

To support entrepreneurship and drive economic growth, policymakers must develop targeted strategies that consider the intricate relationship between institutions, entrepreneurship, and economic growth. This requires a comprehensive and interdisciplinary approach, as these relationships are complex and may involve multiple interconnected mechanisms.

Culture

Although some countries have made great strides in economic development, many still struggle to foster an entrepreneurial culture. A prime example is Russia, where despite the implementation of a new economic system, the country has yet to see significant entrepreneurial success. The root cause of this lies in the lack of a cultural shift that supports and encourages entrepreneurial behavior. To truly cultivate a thriving entrepreneurial community, a shift in cultural attitudes is crucial.

As such, a national culture that supports and encourages entrepreneurial activity is needed. Borozan and Barkovic described the rules of the games that developed nations have established as important for creating an entrepreneurial environment. They include adequate knowledge, adequate human resources, appropriate institutional organization, appropriate entrepreneurial infrastructure, and a value system and social norms suitable to entrepreneurship (see Figure 1.3). Adequate knowledge refers to the training and education that is offered in a country that would aid in competitiveness.[39] Education needs to be flexible to the demands of the current business environment in order to continue to provide development and sustainability of competitive advantage. A lack of education will lead to a lack of prepared human resources. Having satisfactory human resources is vital in entrepreneurship. An entrepreneurship culture also needs to have the appropriate institutional infrastructure, such as legal and government institutions, in order to prevent corruption and create competition.

Box 4.11   Why Germany is so much better at training its workers

Apprenticeship is different in the United States than in Europe. Today in the United States, only 5 percent train as an apprentices, while in Germany it is closer to 60 percent. Many companies in Europe use dual training to ensure that students learn the work habits and responsibilities necessary to succeed in the workplace. Germans see this training as useful for everyone, not only for struggling students. You can also see that both employers and employees benefit more by an apprenticeship than a short-term training.

One of the reasons that it might be hard for the United States to transition is the cost. In Germany the range of cost per apprentice is between $25,000 and $80,000. Other reasons are the differences in centralization in both countries. It's hard to imagine the level of state control that Germany has compared to the United States. The last difference is also how Americans see education and training in comparison to how Germans do.

Source: Jacoby (2014).[40]

Entrepreneurs require assurance that laws and regulations will be upheld, especially with respect to contractual agreements and protection of intellectual property. A lack of faith in these intuitions creates business uncertainty, which undermines entrepreneurship. An appropriate entrepreneurial infrastructure also includes a support system for entrepreneurs such as business incubators, technological parks, and development centers. These elements need to work together to provide services that support entrepreneurship development in each context.

In Table 4.3, Heinonen and Poikkijoki summarize the relationship between individual characteristics, process, and behavior for entrepreneurial activities. There is the consensus that a framework for creating an entrepreneurship culture should include the variables described in the table.

Table 4.3 Framework for culture

Characteristic	Definition	Analysis
Education	Acquiring know-how and processes with new ideas.	Investment in education is critical because it encourages critical thinking and helps address the challenges faced in the process.
Entrepreneurial knowledge	The possession of relevant information related to entrepreneurship.	Entrepreneurial knowledge is critical because it fosters experience and good practices. Building networking among entrepreneurs, institutions, organizations, and universities.
Self-achievement	Ability to realize personal goals.	Being independent; confident in solving problems.
Entrepreneurial climate	A nurturing and rewarding atmosphere.	Needs to cater to which self-achievement and social responsibility will be nurtured, rewarded, and promoted; government policies and regulations and culture play a significant role.
Legal ramifications	Consequences faced when guilty of business irregularities.	This helps monitor activity in the business environment including corrupt activities, entry regulations, and obstacles faced when seeking finances.

Source: Heinonen, J., & Poikkijoki, S.-A. (2006). An entrepreneurial-directed approach to entrepreneurship education: mission impossible? *Journal of Management Development*, 25(1), 80–94.

Box 4.12   Creative problem-solving in the face of extreme limits

Navi Radjou has spent years studying "jugaad," also known as frugal innovation. Pioneered by entrepreneurs in emerging markets who figured out how to get spectacular value from limited resources, the practice has now caught on globally. You can learn more in the full TED Talk at www.ted.com/talks/navi_radjou_creative_problem_solving_in_the_face_of_extreme_limits

---

Social connections

Networks are often defined as relationships between individuals, groups, or organizations. Networks may take many forms including strategic alliances, joint ventures, licensing arrangements, subcontracting, etc.

An organizational network is a voluntary arrangement between two or more firms that involves an exchange, sharing, or co-development of new products and technologies.[41]

An example of a network for entrepreneurs is a trade organization (see Figure 4.14) in which many entrepreneurs are members. To meet challenges, an entrepreneur must develop a network, which results in connections to resource providers (e.g., clients, partners, consultants, governments). Entrepreneurs require information, capital, skills, and labor in order to start their new business. While they hold some of these resources themselves, they often complement their resources by accessing their contacts. These contacts are often informal work and non-work connections. These relations may extend across professional networks, reaching friends and colleagues from earlier collaborations. Research has shown that networks are very useful for entrepreneurs. The first is size. Entrepreneurs can enlarge their networks to get crucial information and other resources from knowledgeable others. The next is positioning. Entrepreneurs

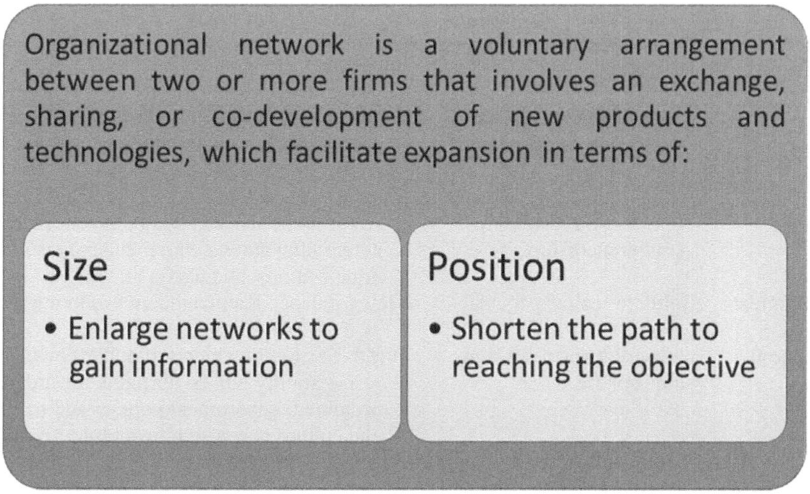

Organizational network is a voluntary arrangement between two or more firms that involves an exchange, sharing, or co-development of new products and technologies, which facilitate expansion in terms of:

Size

- Enlarge networks to gain information

Position

- Shorten the path to reaching the objective

Figure 4.14 Organizational networks: considering joining a trade organization

position themselves within a social network to shorten the path to get what they need. Over time, entrepreneurs accumulate social capital, which is crucial for starting a new business.

The phenomenon of firms clustering in certain locations, referred to as industrial concentration, is prevalent in entrepreneurship. While some see clustering as having benefits such as increased knowledge spillovers and access to specialized resources, it may not always be a result of firms' intentional behavior. Advances in communication technology and increased interconnectedness through social networks have enabled entrepreneurs to access information and resources from remote locations. Despite this, industries tend to concentrate in a few places. This can be attributed to various factors like historical precedent, presence of specialized resources, and supportive social networks. Although clustering may not necessarily benefit individual firms, it remains a distinctive characteristic of the geography of entrepreneurship.[42]

The role of the family in networking and entrepreneurship is to acquire resources and/or information. But the role of the family in aiding entrepreneurs has a long history and it seems to have a mixed outcome. Generally, entrepreneurs draw on their family and friends for input and in many cases as a role model (e.g., SMEs) or to acquire financial support. Entrepreneurial parents provide emotional encouragements and unique skills to their children's initiations and are an easily accessible resource.[43, 44] Some scholars have explored the factors associated with the scope of startup activities among young emerging entrepreneurs. They have found that the effects of family support on "young nascent entrepreneurs' start-up activity are complex and multi-faceted."[45]

Type of business most common to entrepreneurship

The global economy is witnessing significant growth in several high-potential industries that are expected to generate substantial revenue in the near future. With the current technology boom, it would be thought that the most common entrepreneurial ventures would take place in technological fields which include, but are not limited to, technology and software development, e-commerce, healthcare and biotechnology, and renewable energy.

A recent report about the United States stated that:

By industry, construction had the highest entrepreneurial activity rate at 1.68 percent, continuing an upward trend over the past several years, followed by the services industry at

Table 4.4 High growth industries in the near future

Internet services (data processing)	Science
Computer systems	Technical consulting
AI software	Home healthcare
Employment services	Personal financial advisory
Management	Childcare services, arts and entertainment

0.42 percent. The manufacturing startup rate was the lowest among all industries, with only 0.11 percent of non-business owners starting businesses per month during 2011.[46]

Therefore, in the recent past construction businesses are the most prominent businesses for entrepreneurs in the United States. However, it would not be unlikely for this to change in the coming years.

Using the Bureau of Labor Statistics'[47] job-growth projections for 2002 to 2012, Inc.com came up with a list of the ten industries (see Table 4.4) "that are projected to have enormous growth-and opportunities."[48]

From this list, we can see that technology companies are going to be more prominent in the coming years, although we cannot say for sure that they will be the most lucrative entrepreneurial business. However, we can see from the success of Silicon Valley that technology is likely to be the field with the most growth in the coming years, and therefore the best industry in which to start a new company. We can see already the success that technology-driven entrepreneurs have had with companies such as Apple, Google, and Facebook. One interesting factor to consider when determining the growth of an industry is to look more closely at who these entrepreneurs are and where they have received their training. More recently the AI global market is expected to grow at a rate of 35 percent in 2022, reaching $190 billion in revenue.[49]

There is no question that technology and communications are influencing most, if not all, businesses in developed and developing countries. Technology as a tool is continually reinventing itself through entrepreneurial work. This is influencing developing countries in many ways. In Appendix 4A, we have provided the top ten high-growth industries for a few countries and regions.

Industries experience growth differently across regions due to various factors such as economic conditions, infrastructure, government policies, and resources. In Asia, the technology industry has grown significantly, with countries like China, Japan, and South Korea leading the way in areas such as e-commerce, fintech, and artificial intelligence. The expansion of the middle class and consumer demand has also boosted industries like automotive and retail. Meanwhile, in Europe, the services sector dominates, particularly in the information and communication technology industry, as countries like Ireland, Denmark, and the UK invest in research and development. The renewable energy sector has also experienced significant growth in countries like Germany and Denmark.

Africa's fastest-growing industries are driven by natural resources such as oil and mining, with countries like Nigeria, Angola, and South Africa leading the way. The construction and engineering sectors are also seeing significant growth due to infrastructure development, with Ethiopia becoming a hub for road, railway, and airport construction. In Latin America, the agriculture and food industry, the automotive industry, and fintech are the fastest-growing sectors, with countries like Brazil, Mexico, and Argentina exporting large quantities of soybeans, corn, and beef, and global car manufacturers establishing production facilities in the region.

In summary, the fastest-growing industries vary by region, reflecting the unique economic conditions, resources, and policies in each region. The sectors driving growth include natural resources, infrastructure, technology, and services, providing opportunities for businesses and entrepreneurs to innovate, expand, and create jobs. Despite challenges such as access to finance and skills shortages, the potential for growth and development across different regions of the world remains significant.

Concluding remarks

In this chapter, discussed entrepreneurs' midset approach, traits and characteristics. Many traits and characteristics are common globally. Factors such as education, government regulations and policies, and cultural characteristics have significant influences on entrepreneurial initiation. The need for experience is also important because it emerges after acquiring certain levels of knowledge and training has occurred. Characteristics such as openness of mind are important because they influence an entrepreneurial agenda. A perception of self-achievement and a curious mindset that delves into various aspects of organizational development, including production processes, marketing, and product design, form the foundation of this profile. Other features related to entrepreneurial attributes are acting as market speculators and exhibiting abilities to manage risks. For entrepreneurs, the need to understand the basic is important because it reinforces the need for consistency once certain characteristics are integrated. The importance of formal education is emphasized for the development of critical thinking and specialization. Various support avenues should be sought with particular emphasis on capital acquirement.

Discussion questions

1 Define entrepreneur and entrepreneurship.
2 What are the different classifications of entrepreneurship? Do they make sense to you? Which classifications might you be in?
3 What are your thoughts in terms of the role of education and experience in relation to entrepreneurship?
4 Which one of the personal characteristics do you think you have?
5 Write a short case about an entrepreneur that you admire.

Table 4.5 Key terms

Entrepreneurship	Lifestyle entrepreneur
Classifications of entrepreneurs	Characteristics of an entrepreneur
Serial entrepreneur	Money Smart for Small Businesses

Table 4.6 Glossary

Entrepreneurship	Entrepreneurship is the process of starting and running a business, typically with a focus on innovation and growth.
Classifications of entrepreneurs	Entrepreneurs can be classified based on various factors such as their motivations, goals, and the types of businesses they start.
Serial entrepreneur	A person who continuously generates new ideas and starts a new business.
Lifestyle entrepreneur	A person who places passion ahead of other factors and combines personal interests and talent to earn a living.
Characteristics of an entrepreneur	Entrepreneurs are individuals who start and run their own businesses, often taking calculated risks to pursue opportunities and create value.
Money Smart for Small Businesses	A program developed by the Federal Deposit Insurance Corporation (FDIC) and Small Business Administration (SBA) which is ten-step instructional guide for financial institutions and other stakeholders to teach budding entrepreneurs the basics of running a business.

Appendix 4A – top 10 high-growth industries in different regions of the world

Top 10 high-growth industries in the Middle East

1. Construction and infrastructure	6. Consultancy services
2. E-commerce solutions	7. Hotel chains and restaurants
3. Tourism and travel	8. Fashion products and jewelry
4. Real estate	9. Marketing and advertising
5. Health and hospitality	10. Security services

Notes:
• Free trade zones make business easier in UAE.
• UAE ranked #27 on list of countries likely to attract foreign direct investment in 2018.
• UAE authorities allow registration of offshore companies.

Source: www.danburitecorp.com/top-10-fastest-growing-business-sectors-and-leading-industries-in-the-uae-2022/nw-159

Top 10 high-growth industries in India

1. Advanced engineering and manufacturing	6. Construction
2. Pharmaceutical industry	7. Telecom
3. Digital marketing and social media	8. Retail
4. Artificial intelligence and automation	9. Media and entertainment
5. Energy sector	10. Tourism industry

Notes:
• India's GDP growth is the one of highest in the world in the past decade, an average of 5.5 percent.
• India's economy is expected to be among the top 3 world economy by 2027.

Source: https://businesstalkmagazine.com/blog/fastest-growing-industries-in-india/; www.morganstanley.com/ideas/investment-opportunities-in-india

Top 10 high-growth industries in Africa

1. Fishing	6. Oil
2. Textiles	7. Finance
3. Mining	8. Transport
4. Infrastructure	9. Healthcare
5. Agriculture	10. Space

Notes:
• There has been an expansion of exclusive economic zones (EEZs).
• More than 250 startups have already started working towards the democratization of space activities.

Source: www.ariseiip.com/top-10-fastest-growing-industries-in-africa/

Top 10 high-growth industries in Europe

1. Technology services/development	6. Retail services
2. Tourism	7. Automotive industry
3. Financial services/technology	8. Manufacturing industries
4. Food services/industry	9. Aerospace and space technology
5. Energy services/electric power	10. Digital health

Notes:
• The European Union (EU) has created a single market across its member states, which allows for the free movement of goods, services, capital, and people. Companies can easily access a market of over 500 million people without facing barriers such as tariffs or different regulatory requirements.

Source: Globalization Partners. (2021). *The European Tech Sector: Trends and Opportunities*. Retrieved from www.globalization-partners.com/blog/europe-tech-sector/#gref; Statista. (2021). *Travel and Tourism in Europe – Statistics & Facts*. Retrieved from www.statista.com/topics/3848/travel-and-tourism-in-europe/#topicOverview

Top 10 high-growth industries in China

1. Manufacturing industry	6. Construction/development industry
2. Mining industry	7. E-commerce
3. Energy industry	8. Healthcare
4. Agriculture industry	9. Transportation and logistics
5. Real estate	10. Entertainment

Notes:
• Large domestic market provides many opportunities for businesses to grow and expand, with a growing middle class creating a large and increasingly affluent consumer base.
• Manufacturing hub: major manufacturing hub for the world, with low labor costs and a large pool of skilled workers, leading to significant economic growth and job creation.

Source: www.worldatlas.com/articles/which-are-the-biggest-industries-in-china.html

Notes

1   Say, J.B. (1997). *An Economist in Troubled Times*, selected and translated by R. Palmer. New Jersey: Princeton University Press.
2   Hisrich, R.D., Peters, M.P., & Shepherd, D.A. (2005). *Entrepreneurship* (6th ed., paperback). McGraw-Hill.
3   Fairlie, R.W., & Fossen, F.M. (2020). *Defining Opportunity Versus Necessity, Entrepreneurship: Two Components of Business Creation*. Bingley: Emerald Publishing Limited.
4   Hisrich, R.D., Peters, M.P., & Shepherd, D.A. (2005). *Entrepreneurship* (6th ed., paperback). McGraw-Hill.
5   Hisrich, R.D., Peters, M.P., & Shepherd, D.A. (2005). *Entrepreneurship* (6th ed., paperback). McGraw-Hill.
6   Mises Institute. (2010). Richard Cantillon: Founder of political economy. *Mises Institute*. Retrieved from https://mises.org/library/richard-cantillon-founder-political-economy.
7   Sarasvathy, S.D. (2001). Causation and effectuation: Toward a theoretical shift from economic inevitability to entrepreneurial contingency. *The Academy of Management Review*, 26(2), 243–263.
8   Himmel, R. (2013). What personality traits made Steve Jobs successful? *Entrepreneur.com*. Retrieved from www.entrepreneur.com/answer/226410
9   Himmel, R. (2013). What personality traits made Steve Jobs successful? *Entrepreneur.com*. Retrieved from www.entrepreneur.com/answer/226410
10 Galindo, M.-Á., & Ribeiro, D. (2012). *Women's Entrepreneurship and Economics: New Perspectives, Practices, and Policies*. New York: Springer, Edited book.
11 Balachandran, V., & Sakthivelan, M.S. (2013). Impact of information technology on entrepreneurship. *Journal of Business Management & Social Sciences Research*, 2(2), 50–56.
12 Zaheer, H., Breyer, Y., & Dumay, J. (2019). Digital entrepreneurship: An interdisciplinary structured literature review and research agenda. *Technological Forecasting and Social Change*, 148, 119735.

13 Zahra, S.A., Gedajlovic, E., Neubaum, D.O., & Shulman, J.M. (2009). A typology of social entrepreneurs: Motives, search processes and ethical challenges. *Journal of Business Venturing*, 24(5), 519–532. https://doi.org/10.1016/J.JBUSVENT.2008.04.007

14 Boolkin, J. (2016). *Social Enterprise: Statistics from around the World – Social Good Stuff*. Retrieved from http://socialgoodstuff.com/2016/08/statistics-from-around-the-world/

15 Social Enterprise in Australia. (2016). Retrieved from www.socialtraders.com.au/about-social-enterprise/ fases-and-other-research/social-enterprise-in-australia/

16 Ip, M. (2014). *5 Facts about Social Enterprise in Belgium*. Retrieved from www.socialenterprisebuzz. com/2014/05/06/5-facts-about-social-enterprise-in-belgium/

17 López-Núñez, M.I., Rubio-Valdehita, S., Aparicio-García, M.E., & Díaz-Ramiro, E.M. (2020). Are entrepreneurs born or made? The influence of personality. *Personality and Individual Differences*, 154, 109699.

18 Fisher, J.L., & Koch, J.V. (2008). *Born, Not Made: The Entrepreneurial Personality*. Greenwood Publishing Group.

19 Carryer, B. (2014, November 14). *Comparing Entrepreneurship in Europe and in the US*. Retrieved December 15, 2018, from http://newventurist.com/2012/11/comparing-entrepreneurship-in-europe-and-in-the-us/

20 Oliver, A., Schneider, B.H., Galiana, L., Puricelli, D.A., Schwendemann, M., & Tomás, J.M. (2022). Entrepreneurship attitudes and the Big Five: A cross-cultural comparison between Spain and the United States. *International Journal of Psychology*, 50(6), 449–455. https://scielo.isciii.es/pdf/ap/ v38n1/1695-2294-ap-38-01-119.pdf

21 Jonason, P.K., & Webster, G.D. (2010). The dirty dozen: A concise measure of the dark triad. *Psychological Assessment*, 22(2), 420–432. https://doi.org/10.1037/a0019265

22 Peixoto, Â., Gouveia, T., Sousa, P., Faria, R., & Almeida, P.R. (2023). Dark personality traits and tolerance towards unethical behaviors on entrepreneurship: A comparison between entrepreneurs and non-entrepreneurs. *Journal of White Collar and Corporate Crime*, 4(1), 5–13. https://doi.org/10.1177 /2631309X211029877

23 Hmieleski, K.M., & Sheppard, L.D. (2019). The yin and yang of entrepreneurship: Gender differences in the importance of communal and agentic characteristics for entrepreneurs' subjective well-being and performance. *Journal of Business Venturing*, 34(4), 709–730.

24 Krugman, P., & Wells, R. (2013). *Microeconomics* (3rd ed.). London: Worth Publishers.

25 Morselli, D. (2019). *The Change Laboratory for Teacher Training in Entrepreneurship Education: A New Skills Agenda for Europe* (p. 143). Springer Nature.

26 Aadland, T., & Aaboen, L. (2020). An entrepreneurship education taxonomy based on authenticity. *European Journal of Engineering Education*, 45(5), 711–728.

27 Lesonsky, R. (n.d.). Is college necessary for young entrepreneurs? *MSN: Business on Main*. Retrieved June 23, 2012, from http://businessonmain.msn.com/browseresources/articles/smallbusinesstrends. aspx?cp-documentid=29202016#fbid=ZXwbJs0Clh8

28 Giuggioli, G., & Pellegrini, M.M. (2022). Artificial intelligence as an enabler for entrepreneurs: A systematic literature review and an agenda for future research. *International Journal of Entrepreneurial Behavior & Research* (ahead of print). https://doi.org/10.1108/IJEBR-05-2021-0426

29 Pruitt, B. (2012, March 19). New business startups declined in 2011, Annual Kauffman study shows. *Ewing Marion Kauffman Foundation*. Retrieved June 16, 2012, from www.kauffman.org/newsroom/ new-business-startups-declined-in-2011-annual-kauffman-study-shows.aspx

30 Wecker, M. (2012, June 12). Skip business school, MBA entrepreneurs say. *US News-Education*. Retrieved June 16, 2012, from www.usnews.com/education/best-graduate-schools/top-business-schools/ articles/2012/06/12/skip-business-school-mba-entrepreneurs-say

31 Kent, C.A. (1990). *Entrepreneurship Education*. Westport, CT: Quorum Books.

32 *The Economist*. (2009, March 12). The United States of entrepreneurs. Retrieved June 16, 2012, from www.economist.com/node/13216037

33 Adler, J. (2012). FDIC, SBA take on small-business training. *American Banker*, 177(64).

34 Kellermanns, F., Walter, J., Crook, T.R., Kemmerer, B., & Narayanan, V. (2016). The resource-based view in entrepreneurship: A content-analytical comparison of researchers' and entrepreneurs' views. *Journal of Small Business Management*, 54, 26–48. https://doi.org/10.1111/jsbm.12126

35 Al-Awlaqi, M. (2021). The effect of entrepreneurship training on entrepreneurial orientation. *The International Journal of Management Education*, 19(1), 100267. Retrieved from www.sciencedirect.com/ science/article/pii/S1472811718302234

36 Harmeling, S.S., & Sarasvathy, S.D. (2013). When contingency is a resource: Educating entrepreneurs in the Balkans, the Bronx, and beyond. *Entrepreneurship Theory and Practice*, 37(4), 713–744. https://doi.org/10.1111/j.1540-6520.2011.00489.x

37 Smallbone, D., & Welter, F. (2001). The distinctiveness of entrepreneurship in transition economies. *Small Business Economics*, 16(4), 249–262. https://doi.org/10.1023/A:1011159216578

38 Urbano, D., Aparicio, S., & Audretsch, D. (2019). Twenty-five years of research on institutions, entrepreneurship, and economic growth: What has been learned? *Small Business Economics*, 53, 21–49.

39 Borozan, D., & Barkovic, I. (2005). Creating entrepreneurial environment for SME's development: The case of Croatia. *Silicon Valley Review of Global Entrepreneurship Research*, 1, 44–55.

40 Jacoby, T. (2014, October 20). *Why Germany Is So Much Better at Training Its Workers*. Retrieved December 16, 2018, from www.theatlantic.com/business/archive/2014/10/why-germany-is-so-much-better-at-training-its-workers/381550/

41 Groen, A.J. (2005). Knowledge intensive entrepreneurship in networks: Towards a multi-level/ multi dimensional approach. *Journal of Enterprising Culture*, 13(1), 69–88. https://doi.org/10.1142/S0218495805000069

42 Sorenson, O. (2018). Social networks and the geography of entrepreneurship. *Small Business Economics*, 51(3), 527–537.

43 Greve, A., & Salaff, J.W. (2003). Social networks and entrepreneurship. *Entrepreneurship Theory and Practice*, 28(1), 1–22. https://doi.org/10.1111/1540–8520.00029

44 El Jadidi, J., Asgary, N., & Weiss, J. (2017). Cultural and institutional barriers for western educated entrepreneurs in Morocco. *CYRUS Chronicle Journal: Contemporary Economic and Management Studies in Asia and Africa*, 2, 61–75.

45 Edelman, L.F., Manolova, T.S., Shirokova, G., & Tsukanova, T. (2016). The impact of family support on young nascent entrepreneurs' start-up activities. *Journal of Business Venturing*, 31(4), 365–484.

46 Pruitt, B. (2012, March 19). New business startups declined in 2011, Annual Kauffman study shows. *Ewing Marion Kauffman Foundation*. Retrieved June 16, 2012, from www.kauffman.org/newsroom/new-business-startups-declined-in-2011-annual-kauffman-study-shows.aspx

47 United States Department of Labor. (n.d.). Business employment dynamics: Entrepreneurship and the U.S. economy. *Bureau of Labor Statistics*. Retrieved June 10, 2012, from www.bls.gov/bdm/entrepreneurship/entrepreneurship.htm

48 Steiman, J. (2005, April 6). *Top 10 Industries to Start and Grow a Business*. Retrieved June 23, 2012, from Inc.com; www.inc.com/articles/2005/04/top10.html

49 Statista Research Department. (n.d.). Artificial intelligence – world market revenue. *Statista*. Retrieved February 10, 2023, from www.statista.com/outlook/373/129/artificial-intelligence/worldwide#market-revenue

5 Creativity, innovation, and development

Creativity and innovation are essential components of an organization's and a country's culture for sustainable development. Creativity and innovation are a tangled web; neither one works well without the other. This chapter attempts to examine the web in detail. Creative design contributes to the expansion of available ideas and to the increased chances of successfully commercializing these ideas. By defining creativity and innovation, the chapter answers how organizations can have an integrative view of these two essential thoughts. The chapter also examines cultural and environmental constraints that hinder their progress. A few discussed constraints include lack of qualified human capital, inadequate financial capital, weak legal systems, infrastructure, and other resources.

Learning objectives

1 Define and analyze creativity and innovation
2 Examine the role of culture on creativity and innovation
3 Describe the predominant types of innovation
4 Discuss the 4Ps of innovation
5 Understand the role of human resources on creativity
6 Examine the five factors of stagnation.

Al Capizza: a creative and unique pizza restaurant, São Paulo, Brazil

Everybody likes a hot fresh pizza, but nobody wants an order; not as before!

Background

It was the year 2000 when Mr. Corleone decided to open a pizzeria in Blumenau, a southern city of Brazil. Having paternal roots from Italy and a childhood love for Italian food inspired him to find recipes for the first pizzas. Mr. Corleone took great care of every detail, starting from the purchase of the ingredients to the preparation of pizzas. His customers soon arrived, and thus began the Don Corleone pizzeria. The pizzeria started to serve its Blumenau customers, through services like home delivery and customer pick up. Though Don Corleone had a few tables where customers could eat the pizza on the spot, it was not the focus of the business. His two children Sonny and Michael soon acquired their father's love for pizza and promptly joined the family pizza business. A few years later,

---

DOI: 10.4324/9781003405740-8

Figure 5.1 Al Capizza road map

Source: Authors.

the two brothers saved enough money from their work at Don Corleone and with $3000 in initial funds opened a second Don Corleone pizzeria, also in Blumenau. While Michael runs the business, Sonny went to study abroad in the United States.

Growth and current challenges

Building on the initial success, by 2016 the family owned five Don Corleone pizzerias in Blumenau. One is run by Mr. Corleone and the other four by his son Michael. As of 2016, the sales from all five pizzerias amounted to ten million pizzas. Their delivery process starts with the customer making the call to choose the flavor and the crust. The pizzeria always prepares the pizza with fresh ingredients and delivers on time to the customer's address. This model has been successfully implemented for more than 20 years. However, the Corleone family have identified customer preference changes, especially from the new generations who ask for much better use of information and communication technologies (e.g., mobiles, apps, tracking). Also, the arrival of brands of multinational pizzerias in Brazil are new challenges and concerns for the Corleone family.

This case study is continued later in this chapter.

Introduction

Creativity and innovation are essential components of an organization and a culture for economic development. However, both creativity and innovation can be constrained by cultural factors, in turn inhibiting a country's ability to live up to its potential. These cultural factors run deep, and they are expressed in the inner workings of an office, in the innovation processes

Figure 5.2 Creativity definition
Source: www.freepik.com/free-vector/illustration-light-bulb-ideas_2605671.htm

that a company has chosen to foster, and even in the development of a business model itself, as discussed in earlier chapters. There are many questions regarding the relationship and impact of creativity and innovation on economic development which will be addressed in this chapter.

Economic development is dependent upon many factors, which include creativity and innovation. These are the focus of this chapter. As we discussed in the earlier chapters, the most significant determinants of economic development are human capital, capital stock, and technology. To ensure economic development, countries should nurture creativity and innovation. We examine the role of creativity and its relationship with innovation and culture. We examine its impact on entrepreneurial activities and economic development. Creativity and the ability to innovate are closely linked to entrepreneurial activities and therefore to economic development.

Creativity design and innovative technology are important factors that contribute to an enterprise's ability to succeed in an increasingly global marketplace. However, attitudes towards creativity and innovation are culturally constructed and vary widely from country to country, as is the access to and adoption of modern information and communication technology. Cultural attitudes towards creativity can facilitate or impede an enterprise's ability to bring an innovative product to market, thus directly impacting their economic success, as discussed in Chapter 2.

Creativity is often described as technological, economic, and artistic innovation, but fundamentally it is the desire to express oneself, which can only take place in an open environment that is oriented towards the exchange of ideas.

The degree of creativity in a culture is difficult to measure for lack of quantifiable evidence, but attempts have been made to assess cultural attitudes towards creativity and to infer a composite creativity score based on other measurable and related markers.[1,2]

Hollanders and Van Cruysen's study shows that creative education is linked most closely to a country's ability to innovate. This being the case, it's important to understand further how culture impacts innovation. Creative ideas are connections between problems and solutions for the

Figure 5.3 Creativity

Source: www.freepik.com/free-photo/top-view-idea-written-black-notepad-keyboard-lupa-binder-clip-light-bulb-cal-culator-dark_17235217.htm#query=Idea%20concept%20with%20light%20bulb&position=46&from_view=search&track=ais

first time. When working on understanding the voice of the customer, producers have to identify customers' needs. People typically ask for an idea or solution to problems. However, it is the role of entrepreneurs to be creative and find the solution. Innovation aims to answer a question or solve a problem; it is best if it fits customers' needs.

Creativity can be defined as the inherent ability of all human individuals to generate novel ideas. Creativity could be defined as the human mind conceiving new ideas and bringing them into being. The new Oxford Dictionary of English defines innovation as "making changes to something established by introducing something new." This definition does not suggest that innovation is only related to a "thing." It has a broader definition and implications.

When Alexander the Great visited Diogenes and asked whether he could do anything for the famed teacher, Diogenes replied: "Only stand out of my light." Perhaps some day we shall know how to heighten creativity. Until then, one of the best things we can do for creative men and women is to stand out of their light.

What did Diogenes mean by "Only stand out of their light"?

John W. Gardner

Definition of creativity

To explain the concept of creativity, it is important to consider the most common objects of analysis in the literature of creativity.[3] Usually creativity as an object of analysis can be associated with an individual, a group, and an organization.[4] This scope of study has been designed especially because the individual, the group of individuals, and the organization are interdependent constituent parts, when creativity is thought of as a system.[5] Acar et al. (2019) discussed generating creative ideas and turning them into innovations is key for competitive advantage. However, advancement towards creativity and innovation are bounded by many constraints; among them are rules and regulations, deadlines, and scarce resources. The authors state that "we develop a taxonomy of constraints and mediating mechanisms and provide an integrative synthesis that explains how constraints affect creativity and innovation."[6]

The focus at this stage will be on organizational creativity and its proximity to the concept of economic development, which is the focus of this textbook. However, the presence of an individual's or a group's creativity is found for better understanding of the overall creativity of the organization. Organizational creativity can be understood as the creation of a new product, service, idea, procedure, or process that is valuable and useful, and is developed by individuals working together in a complex social system.[7] The article by Puccio and Cabra has the general objective that contributes to understanding the formation of the individual components of creativity through a systemic approach, basing itself from the works of other authors such as Woodman and his colleagues.[8] The definition of creativity has strong proximity to the concepts of innovation. Innovation is what was done previously on various issues such as product, process, marketing, or organizational arrangement and it generates an economic value.[9] Creativity and innovation can be understood as integrated skills which apparently have different cut-off points, as argued by Anderson et al. (2014).[10] Creativity does not have to generate economic value necessarily, but should be considered useful.[11] They claim innovation necessarily has to generate economic value to be considered as such. Puccio et al. (2010) discuss fostering creativity and creating demand and economic value.[12] In fact, it seems that generating economic value is not a condition for the existence of creativity, but rather the generation of a useful idea. The distance of a more objective definition of the term "useful idea" seems to highlight the challenge or the distance between the two concepts, useful and idea in practice. A useful idea can be understood as the idea that generates economic value, concluding that creativity is in fact innovation.

This conclusion was obviously incorrect, since these are concepts of a different nature and essence and this could be the dominant opinion. On the other hand, considering that innovation creates economic value in the form of interest income (income) while creativity does not generate any economic value will result in creativity to be viewed as a spillover effect. Therefore, we can distinguish them in terms of their ultimate goal, which is not discussed permanently in any of the cited articles, although the three articles have workings of the two concepts in the same context of discussion. The arguments in this textbook consider that innovation has its aim of income (i.e., financial income), while creativity has its ultimate goal as the outcome, or as they say in economics, the spillover effects.

The spillover can occur in the form of social impact, the environment, improving the organizational climate, or other outcomes that may not be financial.

Promoting organizational creativity

Organizational behavior specialists have deemed that creativity, lateral thinking, and communication are the key skills to innovation and success in the business world. Thus various companies conduct creative building events throughout the year: Manchester Metropolitan University has an annual "Engage Week," Cognizant Business Consulting hosts "Insight Days," and every year Virgin Management asks their employees for suggestions on how to improve the workplace, of which one to three suggestions are implemented. Companies believe the best way to earn employee loyalty and engagement is to give them a voice and show them that their ideas matter.

For more information, see Manchester Metropolitan University (2017).[13]

In this line of reasoning, one can seek to evaluate the organizational creativity from the results obtained and these will be analyzed from the recognition and measurement of generated spillovers. In this context, ambidexterity is the ability to adapt, bring together, and manage complex and conflicting demands, in order to promote engagement between fundamentally different activities. Despite many approaches and visions of creativity, we can show in Figure 5.4 Amabile's approach, defining the components of individual creativity or for small groups.

Definition of innovation

It is clear that innovation plays an important role around the globe, but it looks very different when it occurs in developing countries compared to advanced economies such as the United

Figure 5.4 Manchester Metropolitan University

Source: https://openverse.org/image/920e4ce0-bf86-427b-b693-1840d2bfcf9e?q=manchester%20metropolitan%20university

States. The realities of developing countries can render innovation much less likely to occur, more difficult to bring to market, and limited to only modest success. We will explore these specific factors later in this chapter. Despite these challenges, innovation is essential to the advancement of our world. Not only can it cure diseases and save lives, it can combat climate change and has an undeniable impact on economic growth. Even with limited resources, technological advancements have the ability to improve efficiency.

Technological innovations (e.g., low-cost tablet computers) can lead to increased access to education, greater employment rates, and solutions to everyday problems. Most importantly through the economic perspective, innovation is a creator of wealth and of jobs, with the potential to escalate national economies to higher levels of growth. "Thus, it has been claimed that entrepreneurship is the main vehicle of economic development."[14] The more entrepreneurs there are in an economy, the faster it will grow; the engine of this economic growth is the entrepreneur.[15,16,17] Innovation is defined as "the act of inventing new processes, products, services, or solutions that can be brought to market, implemented within an existing organization, or used to contribute value to society."[18] In this chapter we argue that innovation should be promoted in all countries, especially in the developing countries who are desperately in need of advancement, as it is our most powerful tool for achieving a higher global standard of living.

Narvekar (2023) focuses on artificial intelligence (AI) in the sphere of entrepreneurship. It takes us back to the 1990s during the dot-com bubble. Entrepreneurs, seeing this as an opportunity for lots of money to be made, created countless dot-com firms. This eventually culminated in a crash bursting the dot-com bubble. At the time people understood that the new version of the internet would change their lives as they knew it, and people today are saying the same about AI.[19] The author predicts and hopes for an AI bubble. He anticipates another bubble, this time for AI, will bring about unimagined technology and advancements. While the author notes that some investors will lose money, they predict that overall, more people will benefit.

Entrepreneurship and innovation have not been addressed in an integrated way, however, since 1911 and, especially from the perspective of Schumpeter, it can be seen that they are related to large overlapping themes.

In this section, we intend to address more aspects related predominantly to innovation, and in the final section of this chapter to perform the integrated approach to innovation and entrepreneurship.

Schumpeter identified the value of the migration phenomenon between the traditional factors of production to a new emerging production factor called "knowledge." The new logic showed that land or capital – financial resources – would not be enough to sustain the growth of the economic world in the future. The economy, however, is the result of social changes carried out at different times in the past.[20] When we look at rates or economic factors, we are checking what has already happened (past). The logic proposed by Schumpeter, which is based on economic concepts, demonstrated the need to consider "knowledge," and classified it as a new form of power and as an input for economic development.

Therefore, Schumpeter epitomized that "new things" or "differentiation" would result from recombination of skills and competencies of the companies. These recombination would be a history of a kind of creative destruction.[21] The definition of innovation has evolved over time. Innovation is a modification of any previous inventions and methods, whether it be product, marketing, organization, or arrangement process. An invention becomes an innovation through diffusion processes – ways in which innovation spreads and becomes available for usage (see Figure 5.5). The adoption and valuation of the invention by users who are willing to pay for it are the determinants of success.[22] When the value of innovation is recognized, people decide to pay for it, and they make up the market. The market in this particular case is the set of people

Figure 5.5 Innovation definition
Source: www.flickr.com/photos/67526850@N00/418049088

who have their problems solved by this innovation. By this definition, considering the principles set out in the Oslo manual, to be called innovation, the goal is to generate economic value. Some classifications of innovation have been developed in a very useful way to help your understanding. The Oslo Manual, issued in 1992, is the global innovation data collection and use guide. The next versions of the manual incorporates a wider range of innovation phenomena and recent innovation surveys in OECD nations and partner economies and organizations.

Scholars have discussed about a recent innovation in the realm of AI which called DALL-E that reveals about human creativity. The program is able to create images based off some present text, as well as its scanning of images across the internet.[23] Apple Newsroom (2023) report that creativity and innovation as crucial elements to Apple's success. Apple was originally told that creating a phone without a physical keyboard would not work since cell phones always had a physical keyboard and that was what consumers liked. Thankfully Apple decided to ignore this advice and disrupt the market and turn into the powerhouse that it is today. Apple is the role model for entrepreneurs hoping to establish and create an innovative culture at their company. This article shows that funding innovation is crucial for the success of a company and for the overall success of an economy.[24] The importance of innovation in a world that is constantly changing due to technological, economic, and political transitions has also been discussed. The consultant Peter Drucker exclaimed, "Innovate or die." In fact, to remain competitive in the age of digital technology, companies must innovate frequently to add value to their product or service and to avoid being outdone by their competitors. However, how can a company stay innovative? This process is mainly developed through an innovative corporate culture. Companies should integrate it into their values and way of operating in each employee to be innovative.[25] Scholars investigate disruptive innovation through the underexplored relationship between two ecological concepts, exaptation and ecosystems. Exaptation-driven innovation involves exploiting unintended latent functions of pre-existing technologies. Digital innovation ecosystems account for industry-spanning co-operative and competitive dynamics among firms related to innovations that combine physical and digital elements, such as 3D printing.[26]

Identified in the literature are four predominant types of innovation described as incremental innovation, radical innovation, modular innovation, and architectural innovation, whose differences lie in the combination of knowledge and skills of the innovator – current or future knowledge – and the locus of change – if the central or peripheral concept.[27] Widely studied by Christensen, disruptive innovation is the innovation that comes from unmet needs in already established markets that are not addressed by large corporations and therefore exposes them to risks when they are overcome by smaller companies which take advantage of the identified opportunity.[28,29,30,31,32] Through the models of Henderson, his colleagues and Christensen have not been compared by the authors at the time; other later studies of the authors have identified some complementarities between them, or both appear to argue that their theories are

Figure 5.6 Hydroponics

Source: https://openverse.org/image/4a8babf3-8a08-4b35-a273-1b0240d7fc9e?q=hydroponics

complementary and in a convergent way. It can be seen in the case of disruptive innovation that the emergence of opportunities related to market shares are not satisfied.

Such dissatisfaction, according to Christensen, is related to the logic of the development of products and services in the enterprise. This logic is to constantly increase the amount of features of products and services to add value and raise the price the market will pay for them, thus increasing profit margins by increasing the surplus (surplus is the term for perception of consumer value and is the reason why the consumer pays the price charged by the manufacturer or supplier of a product or service).

Developing a countrywide solution

Droughts and floods are widely known to completely destroy farms in Kenya, leaving the country unsure how to repair the land. Peter Chege, a Kenyan man, wanted to design a solution that could lead to more productive, resilient farming and potentially boost the entire economy.

Hydroponics Kenya (2011) developed a method of hydroponic farming, which uses water containing mineral solutions to grow crops. This method uses ten times less water than traditional farming, leaving more water for other needs such as drinking and bathing.[33] It also gives the farmer much more control over their crops, since they grow in trays inside sheds or greenhouses. The crops also grow significantly faster and are higher quality. Chege used his findings to develop entire systems he could sell to farmers, including humidity-controlled greenhouses, hydroponic sheds, trays, mineral solutions, seeds, and the associated training.

Chege caught the attention of the Kenyan CIC (Climate Innovation Center), an aid program funded by the World Bank that gave $10 million per year in the form of private donations. The CIC provided Chege with the funding he needed in addition to office space, business guidance, assistance with tax registration, legal support to protect his intellectual property, and a computer to do research, budget, and create a website.

Source: Company website.[34]

Disruptive innovation and ambidextrous organization

As the value of innovation continues to grow and organizations begin to invest in more initiatives to attain a competitive advantage over their competitors, leaders must be wary of disruptive innovations. Disruptive innovation is a development that helps to form a new market and value network. These advancements eventually begin to disrupt the existing markets and displace older technologies, rendering them obsolete.

Clayton Christensen, who coined the term *disruptive innovation*, explains that today, many organizations are innovating "faster than their customers' needs evolve."[35] This causes them to produce products that can be considered too sophisticated, too expensive, or even too complicated for the customers in their market. Christensen continues to explain that companies who try to monetize these innovations by selling them to the higher tiers in their markets can leave them susceptible to "disruptive innovations." As corporations begin to focus their innovation efforts on market segments where they can maximize profitability, leaders often lose sight of the developments in the external environment. It is important for future leaders in innovative firms to understand how to balance the challenges of "dualism."[36]

Dualism is the ability to function efficiently in the present to sustain the success and bottom line of their organizations while preparing for the long term by investing in innovation and, at the same time, developing their own forms of disruptive innovation. "Not only must business organizations be concerned with the financial success and market penetration of their current mix of products and services, but they must also focus on their long-term capabilities to develop or commercialize."[37]

- Creativity and innovation can be constrained by cultural factors, in turn inhibiting a country's ability to live up to its potential.
- To ensure economic development, countries should nurture creativity and innovation.
- Creativity is often described as technological, economic, and artistic innovation, but fundamentally it is the desire to express oneself.
- Creativity could be defined as the human mind conceiving new ideas and bringing them into being; there are six most prominent theories (see Table 5.1) that define creativity.
- Innovation is defined as "the act of inventing new processes, products, services, or solutions that can be brought to market, implemented within an existing organization, or used to contribute value to society."[38]

Regardless of how an organization is structured, leadership with the help of human resources must find ways to manage both operations at the same time. Still on dualism, O'Reilly and Tushman presented the concept of ambidextrous organization.[39] The vision of ambidextrous organization discusses the managerial challenge of looking at almost the same time to the past, depleting products, processes, organizational arrangements, and developed marketing (exploitation) and for the future, exploring market opportunities and demands of consumers that are not yet met by the organization. On the one hand, it is needed to pay diligent attention to issues related to efficiency, such as reducing costs and incremental improvement of the quality of the mix of current products and services; on the other hand, managers need to identify threats to the business considered by O'Reilly as "emerging business." Looking at the bias of strategic

Table 5.1 Prominent theories of creativity

Amabile's theory	Highlights the influence of working environment on creativity. The elements of working environment include knowledge, creative thinking skills, and intrinsic motivation.
Interactionist perspective	Proposes that creativity is a complex relationship between the individual and their work situation at different levels: individual, team, and organizational configurations.
Individual's model of creative action	Explained with the individual as the starting point of creativity, influenced by processes that make sense, motivation, knowledge, and skill.
Fourth prominent theory	Describes creativity with a construct explained by cultural differences, including listing the differences between the East and the West.
Fifth prominent theory	Describes four factors (vision, participative safety, guidance, and support innovation task) related to the climate for the innovation team. The most relevant issue of this theoretical perspective is in the care of the process of criticism and judgment among the team members.
Sixth theory	Deals with the ambidextrous related mediation and conflict management at multiple organizational levels and as a factor that explains the innovative success.

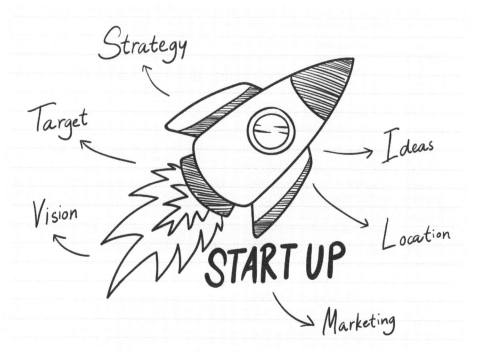

Figure 5.7 Disruptive innovation

Source: www.freepik.com/free-vector/start-up-scribbled-notepad_3109353.htm

planning in a more superficial way, one might think that this is macro-environment mapping, considering the matrix SWOT (strengths, weaknesses, opportunities, and threats) a possible threat. The point is that the SWOT matrix mapping could identify possible threats that were not detailed.

The vision of ambidextrous organization brings the understanding of the need to develop integrated management structures in exploitation (past) and exploration (future). It is considered, therefore, that ambidextrous organizations are those with organizational structures that address in an integrated way these two views that can be antagonistic. The ambidextrous organization was defined as one that has organizational structure with culture and resources with the focus on exploitation and exploration whose integration is the management.

It can be noticed that there is no sharing between structures, manufacturing, sales, and R&D, as shown in Figure 5.8.

Creativity and innovation

The personal characteristics and ability of exploring and identifying ideas is defined as *creativity*.[40] Design can be described as the application of creativity in the relevant context of an issue. Knight defines innovation as "the adoption of a change, which is new to an organization and to the relevant environment."[41]

All innovations aren't necessarily positive, however. We will focus on innovation as defined by Whyte et al.: "the successful application of new ideas."[42] Design leads to innovation by

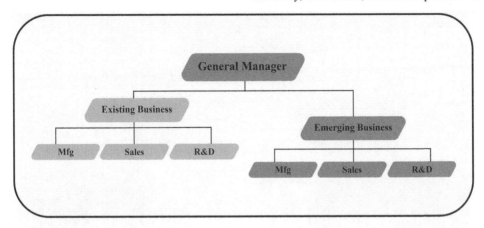

Figure 5.8 Ambidextrous organization

Source: Authors; O'Reilly, C.A., & Tushman, M.L. (2004). The ambidextrous organization. *Harvard Business Review*, 82(4), 74–81, 140. Retrieved from www.ncbi.nlm.nih.gov/pubmed/15077368

bringing together user needs, form, and function in a new way. Innovation does not necessarily have to be technological; it can be in the realm of aesthetics, function, sustainability, reliability, or manufacturability. However, technology plays a key role in the modern design process. The computer and other tools are not only the medium in which many design activities are carried out, but also enable simulation and testing of concepts prior to production, thus speeding up the time to market for a product.

"Creativity and design can thus be linked to innovation as the first contributes to the expansion of available ideas and the second to increased chances of successfully commercializing these ideas."[43] The main difference between creativity and innovation is the outcome. Creativity is about the human mind conceiving new ideas. These ideas could show themselves in the form of something we can imagine, observe, hear, smell, touch, taste, and feel. It is not easy to measure creativity because it is a subjective matter; however, innovation is measurable and output oriented. Innovation is about making changes that lead to revised and different outcomes. It also deals with the work required to make an idea into a viable outcome. By identifying either an unrecognized, unmet, or prospective need, an individual or organization can innovate and use resources to design an appropriate practical solution and gain from its investment. Innovation is the applied knowledge that is preceded by invention and creation of a new product or approach of delivery. Innovation is required to keep the discovery relevant in light of changing times. However, not all inventive progress referred to as innovations end up succeeding.[44] Innovations do not happen in isolation.

Dubina et al. (2012) state that mediums or intermediaries need to account for associated risks and offer distribution platforms to ensure that these novelties get the exposure in the marketplace, thereby influencing changes and making their contributions towards economic growth.[45] Innovations require market exposure to public and private institutions and their agents to become relevant and therefore influence economic development. These institutions serve to distribute risks associated with innovation and provide the necessary financial support in a manner that makes sustainable innovation possible.[46] They are the intermediaries in facilitating active participation of innovations, an outcome that spurs economic growth.[47] Governance has a direct effect on the level of risks that a particular innovation encounters in its formation and

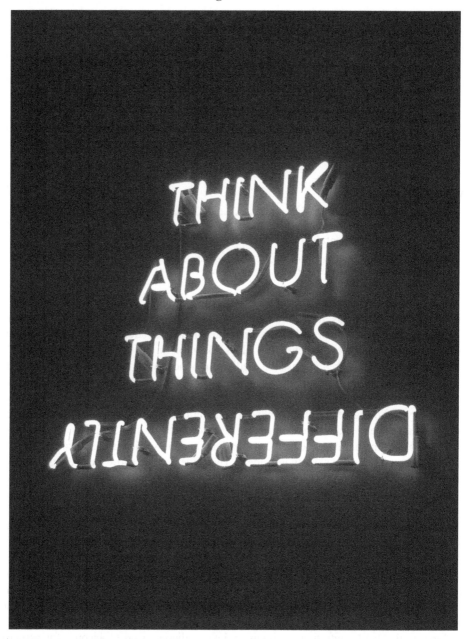

Figure 5.9 Design thinking

Source: www.pexels.com/pt-br/foto/sinalizacao-de-neon-2681319/

implementation. Economic and environmental factors are associated with launching innovations and will impact its outcome.[48] Risk mitigation measures are characterized by economic policies and government protection measures that ensure the launching of innovations is met with minimal resistance in the marketplace.

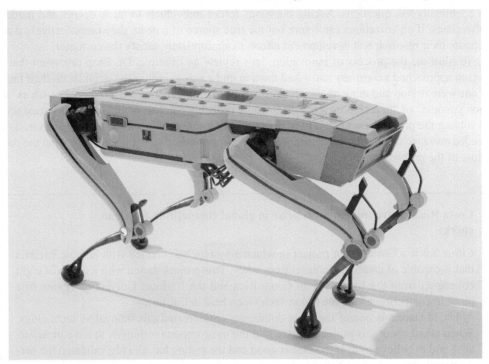

Figure 5.10 Innovation
Source: www.freepik.com/free-photo/3d-rendering-biorobots-concept_29317104.htm

For decades, innovation has been a key driver of competitiveness between the major cities in the United States. It is considered one of the most important factors underlying economic growth in today's global economy and is an important source of new technologies, products and services, industries, jobs, and income. Often people consider that innovation begins with a creative idea or the introduction of new technologies or methodologies, for example, the internet or Apple's iPhone and iPad. However, this is a common misconception as innovation does not actually begin with an idea of creating something new. A simple idea is nothing more than connecting two pieces of already known information together. A creative idea, however, is slightly different as it takes these existing elements and combines them in a new way. This may seem like the construction of a solution to a current need, but it cannot be considered innovation. One relevant vision of Amabile is the integrative vision between organizational innovation and individual creativity, shown in Figure 5.10.

It is important that a leader who is looking to promote improvement in an organization understands that innovation does not come from creative ideas, but rather proper information. In an organization, when a customer is faced with a specific need, the company will match that need to a technology that adequately addresses the problem. However, if that technology does not exist, then innovation is required.

A leader who asks their team to brainstorm and come up with innovative ideas to satisfy the customer's need is operating inefficiently and does not understand the true concept of innovation. This is a common problem for many organizations. To be an innovative leader, they must stress to their employees to learn as much information about the problem as possible and to continually ask questions. Asking questions forces individuals to think deeper and harder. Oftentimes, if organizations can figure out the true source of a need, they can effectively concentrate their research and development efforts to appropriately satisfy the customer.

To illustrate the process of innovation, let's review an example. Dr. Paap discussed that a person approached a company and asked them to find a way to reduce the wrinkles on their face. If one were to stop and think about what the true need of this request was, responses such as "to look younger" or "to feel more attractive" would probably come to mind. This was a great start to solving the problem because it gave the company information to work with. However, they needed more, so the employees began to ask more questions, digging deeper into what the root cause of the problem might be.

Costa Rican entrepreneur wins prize in global competition for clean energy

Citrus 3.0 is a Costa Rican project in which a system was created with aerobic bacteria that is capable of creating biodiesel from whey. This project started with a group of eight colleagues from the University of Costa Rica and the National University. It won first place in competitions like the Clean Tech Open held in California.

David Garcia is one of the eight colleagues who created this innovative technology. When asked about this project, Garcia said the most important thing is to have perseverance and to believe in it. If the idea is good and the testing has already validated the performance, then you must believe so other people will believe in you and your idea.

This project and hard work of the group of individuals promotes and encourages us to never stop believing in ourselves. No matter what others say, if you believe in what you can do, others will support you and help you achieve your goals.

Source: *Costa Rica News* (2013).[49]

Ultimately, the company found that the true problem was not actually to reduce the size of their wrinkles, but simply the appearance of them. Wrinkles are visible because of shadows caused by direct light on a particular area on the body. After the company gathered this information, they were able to come together as a team and brainstorm ideas for a new technology that reduced the appearance of wrinkles rather than the physical size. They ultimately created a form of makeup with microscopic mirrors imbedded within it to reflect the pathways of light, reducing the presence of shadows. This is true innovation. The solution came from a team who gathered as much information about the problem as possible and came together focusing their efforts on the defined need. This method is significantly more efficient than investing time and money into multiple ideas hoping somebody comes up with a creative idea.

Innovation has become a global idea and many people, companies, and governments are exploring it. Innovation is present in most, if not all, industries. Most people around the world are beginning to understand the effects of innovation on their daily life. The true meaning of international innovation is shown when governments display how their innovation made the lives of people better. Strong and effective risk management policies serve to promote the implementation of innovation considering intellectual property rights. Competition is a key factor for successful innovations because it will ensure that the best ideas are given the chance to succeed.

Open trade and investment for business and/or financial environments ensures that innovations get the necessary support and guarantee of success. Research and development infrastructure and resources will advance innovation and therefore will have a positive influence on economic growth. Of course, government and institutional commitment through funding and policy formulation is necessary.

Education is the cornerstone of creativity and innovation, and its role in sustainable economic growth has been documented. Advancements in science and innovation will create and nurture constant flow of ideas and technological knowledge to promote sustainable growth.[50] Transparent and efficient regulatory systems are needed to ensure the implementation of innovations that adhere to the rule of law and are ethical.

Innovation has become the primary source of competitive advantage for companies in all industries, driving efficiency and productivity. Recent history shows innovative entrepreneurs who have created new products and services and therefore have changed the economic, political, and social landscapes.

With the exponential growth of technology, its role in innovation has become increasingly important as a powerful driving force in innovative capacity. This is true in both the evolution of innovation and in the way these innovations proliferate. Economic theory revealed that labor, capital, and technology are the main drivers of production process.[51] Assessing and understanding how to foster innovation are essential in defining the trajectory of a country's economic development (see Figure 5.11).

Innovation is the development of values through developing solutions that meet new requirements or needs. This is accomplished through the construction of better products, services,

Figure 5.11 Invention versus innovation
Source: Authors.

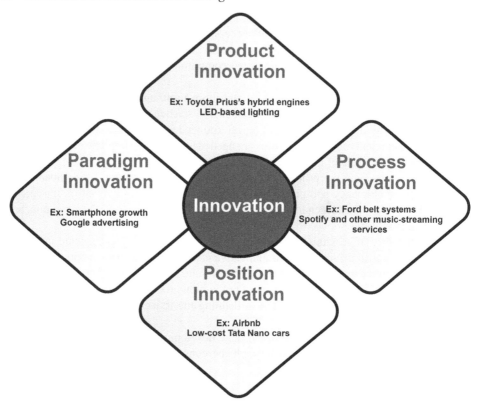

Figure 5.12 The four Ps of innovation

Source: Authors.

processes, technologies, or ideas. As discussed earlier, innovation differs from invention in that innovation refers to the use of a better, novel idea or method, whereas invention refers more directly to the creation of the idea or method itself (see Figure 5.12).

Innovation also differs from improvement in that innovation refers to the notion of doing something different rather than doing the same thing better. Tidd and Bessant discuss the 4Ps of innovation, which are paradigm, process, products, and position.[52] Figure 5.12 describes the relationship between the 4Ps.

The importance of the human side is clear in both definitions of creativity and the different dimensions observed in innovation. It was decided to summarize the role of human resources in this next section, understanding that it is one of the connection points between creativity innovation and entrepreneurship.

Creative use of the "Prime" model by Amazon

Despite Amazon's tough Six Sigma workplace reputation, the company is a pioneer when it comes to creativity and innovation. The open secret to Amazon's success is the expansion of their Prime model. CEO Jeff Bezos believes that the only way Amazon builds customer loyalty is by always offering the best deal, which the company made possible through Amazon Prime. Amazon's creativity in expansion of Amazon Prime and brand innovation in new industries has earned the company $100 billion in annual sales and stock that has skyrocketed over 300 percent over the past 5 years. There are 40–50 million Prime members in the United States alone. Although Amazon has a strict corporate work environment, there is no lack of creativity that has led to superior innovation within the company.

Source: Robischon (2017).[53]

Human resources and innovation

The human resources departments within organizations play a significant role in fostering innovation. Over the last decade in business, the value of a well-functioning human resources department has significantly increased.

Along with organizing initiatives, recruiting high caliber talent, and structuring employee compensation, to list a few, the department has become responsible for aligning organizations appropriately to ensure long-term success. Promoting innovation has been a proven methodology to gain a competitive advantage. This process has since become a responsibility of human resources. "HR leaders should strive to build and strengthen the unique set of organizational capabilities that give an organization its competitive advantage."[54]

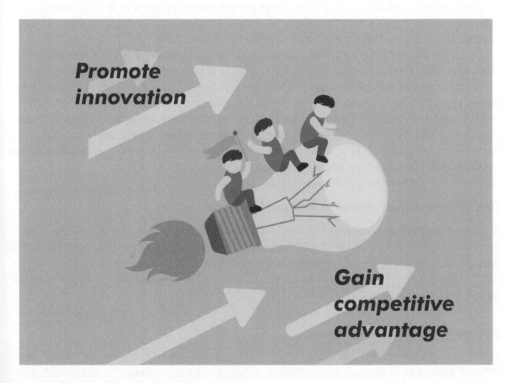

Figure 5.13 Innovation and competitive advantage

Source: Authors.

As Hughes et al. (2018) state, "Leadership is a key predictor of employee, team, and organizational creativity and innovation." They report the review of a large number of empirical studies (N = 195) that explore the role of leadership and workplace for creativity and innovation.[55] Peter Drucker highlights that to remain competitive in the age of digital technology, companies must innovate frequently and add value to their product or services continuously. However, the challenge is how can a company stay innovative? This process is mainly developed through an innovative corporate culture. Each employee must develop this idea of inventing new products, services, or solutions that can be brought to market, used to add value, and can fix an unmet need of the customer. Thus, human resources departments are now the key to developing this culture by recruiting employees who fit this mindset. Originally, every company needed to innovate to remain competitive and viable in the long term. However, in a world in transition and constant improvement, innovation seems a necessity, especially in the digital and the technology sector with for example the importance of the cloud, machine learning, and artificial intelligence.

A survey conducted by IBM for global human resource leaders indicates that driving creativity and innovation is one of the greatest challenges for businesses. The survey also pointed out that of a majority of the people surveyed, close to 70 percent felt that human resources play a significant role in fostering innovation.

However, "71 percent said they don't use any screening tools designed to bring in creative and innovative candidates."[56] Additionally, it was shown that nearly 53 percent do not tie performance management systems to even help promote or drive innovation. What this information is doing is showing leaders in human resources that the topic of innovation is an issue that truly matters to many people, but initiatives are not taking place to do anything about it. Promoting innovation is much easier said than done.

There are three initiatives human resources professionals can adopt to help encourage continuous innovation within their organizations: hiring for innovation, creating a culture of innovation and training, and rewarding for innovation (see Figure 5.14).

One of the most crucial operations that human resources is responsible for is the recruitment and acquisition of talent for their firms. Innovation is created by people who have the ability to look at problems differently than others. If an organization has aspirations to become more pioneering, then efforts on recruiting individuals who carry the capabilities of innovation must be a top priority. They should recruit employees who ask questions, welcome co-workers' points of view, and are open-minded about new ideas. If human resources departments focus efforts on recruiting individuals who have these capabilities, then they will have built a solid foundation on which their companies can foster innovation.

Developing countries: structured for stagnation

In contrast to developed countries, the rest of the world must overcome both the inherent risk of innovation as well as significant obstacles posed by the local environment. Not considering the issues of international trade, we have identified five factors of stagnation which create these barriers (Figure 5.15): (1) deficiency of resources, (2) absence of demand, (3) inadequate financial capital, (4) lack of human capital, and (5) weak legal systems.

Deficiency of resources and infrastructure

Developing countries are often unable to innovate due to a lack of resources or infrastructure to bring their ideas to fruition. As mentioned earlier, developing countries typically lack modern technology or access to the internet. High-tech manufacturing centers, climate-controlled

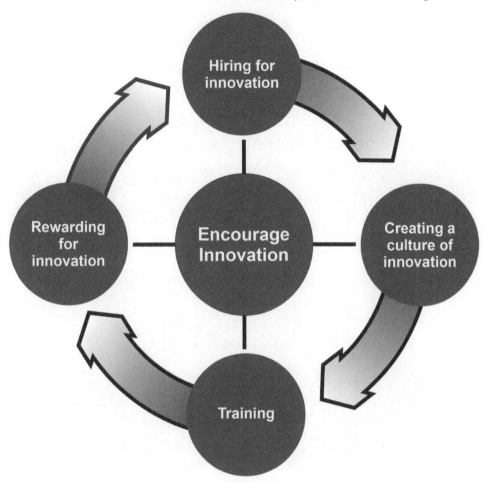

Figure 5.14 Cultural for innovation
Source: Authors.

warehouses, and even modern office spaces can be entirely inaccessible. Many times, raw mate-rials cannot be sourced locally and innovators do not have the network to overcome these obstacles. Due to natural disasters and extreme poverty, even finding clean drinking water can be a challenge. According to the UN News Centre, "Some 70 to 83 percentage of countries are reportedly falling significantly behind the trends required to meet their national targets for access to sanitation and drinking water, respectively."[57] Further, certain innovations can never be effectively brought to market because there is an absence of complementary indus-tries. For example, the country of Chad has one of the worst shortages of healthcare workers in the world, with only one doctor for every 20,000 people and four hospital beds for every 10,000 people. Because the healthcare industry is so underdeveloped, certain types of innova-tion which thrive in developed countries are unthinkable. There is no value in innovating new batteries for medical devices, because medical devices are so rarely purchased by hospitals. It's not feasible to create a software to manage medical records, because most doctor's offices

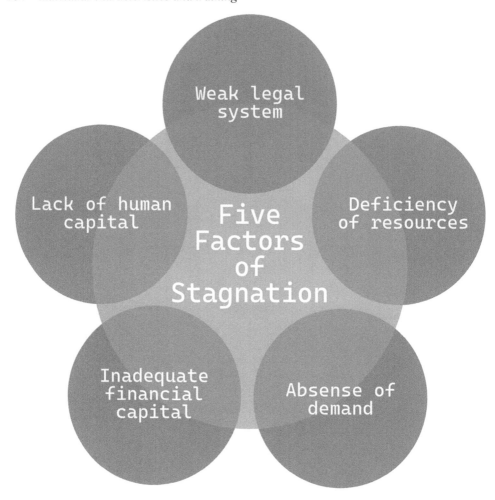

Figure 5.15 Factors of stagnation
Source: Authors.

don't have computers. Even inventing a new vaccine could be futile given a weak supply of syringes. Without complementary industries and resources, many types of innovation become nearly impossible to successfully create. Lema et al. (2018) investigates how combining global value chain and innovation system approaches may lead to the possible change the trajectories of performance in developing countries. Utilizing empirical evidence, they "find that, in some cases, there is an improvement in local innovation capabilities with potentially positive effects on overall competitiveness, while in others there is little progress or even a loss of previous innovation capacity."[58]

In addition, there is often a lack of infrastructure to support transportation. This can affect consumers' ability to travel to buy a product, an innovator's ability to coordinate an efficient supply chain, and the possibility of trading internationally. Latin America has struggled with this issue for decades.

Until recently, investment in infrastructure actually had been declining as a percentage of GDP, from 4 percent of South America's GDP in 1980–85 to 2.3 percent of its GDP in 2007–08. The region's weak infrastructure has hurt its competitiveness in various respects, including productivity, international trade volume and foreign direct investment.[59]

- An invention becomes an innovation through diffusion processes and adoption so that when the value of innovation is recognized, people decide to pay for it; thus they make up the market.
- Disruptive innovation is a development that helps to form a new market and value network.
- The vision of ambidextrous organization brings the understanding of the need to develop integrated management structures, in exploitation (past) and exploration (future).
- "Creativity and design can thus be linked to innovation as the first contributes to the expansion of available ideas and the second to increased chances of successfully commercializing these ideas."[60]
- Innovation is the applied knowledge that is preceded by invention and creation of a new product or approach of delivery.
- Amabile model shows the organizational innovation model and individual creativity.

As a result, South America has the lowest proportion of paved roads out of any region in the world.

Kotschwar writes, "Latin America's greatest disadvantage, by far, is in railroads, an area in which the region has invested very little."[61] Brazil, Colombia, and Peru have specifically suffered due to a lack of ports and roads, making manufacturers reluctant to set up shop in non-urban areas of these countries. Innovation suffers when regional transportation costs are unreasonably high and there is no affordable way to bring your innovation to a large geographic market.

An absence of demand

As discussed earlier, innovation is primarily incentivized by the promise of future success and consumption. Without the presence of local demand, there is very little motivation to innovate. To illustrate, Karnani writes,

Half of the world's population on average needs to wear spectacles. But in India the penetration of eyeglasses is dramatically lower at only 7% because the poor do not have access to eyeglasses and/or cannot afford them. It is often concluded from this that there must be a huge business opportunity for a firm to market eyeglasses to the needy. The major flaw in this logic is that an unmet need does not constitute a market. A market exists only to the extent that there are buyers willing and able to pay a price higher than the total costs, including the opportunity cost of capital, of the sellers.[62]

In addition to being unable to pay for products, people in developing countries are often uneducated and unable to perceive value in new innovations. For example, if a scientist were to design a new type of eyeglass lens that could be customized to different types of astigmatism, most impoverished individuals in India do not have the medical literacy to understand the value of the new innovation. The innovator would need to take on a significant marketing effort to educate the public on ophthalmology, which could quickly become expensive and eliminate any hope of a profit margin. Without an educated public capable of paying a fair price for products, there is little incentive for innovative ventures.

Inadequate financial capital

In most poor developing countries, finding wealthy investors to fund innovation is nearly impossible and because the governments are already strained under limited tax revenue, it's difficult for them to provide incentive programs. The UN reports that expenditures on innovation in most developing countries are at a much lower scale than in developed countries. Of course there are a few exceptions such as China, the Republic of Korea, and Singapore. In these Asian countries, innovation is aggressively funded by the government. However, for the rest of the developing countries, it's extremely difficult for aspiring entrepreneurs to find the funding to innovate.

Lack of human capital

Access to quality education is also sparse in developing countries. Tertiary or college-level education is very rare in developing countries, which face a lack of funding, transportation, educational materials, building infrastructure, technological tools, and qualified professors.[63] In addition, local customs and traditions, particularly in the Middle East, prohibit female enrollment. This further limits the educational potential for a large segment of the population. Teaching methods are also often outmoded or the focus is more on theoretical ideas. The students, who are frequently unable to afford a textbook, must then transcribe the notes into a notebook, and those students who regurgitate a credible portion of their notes from memory achieve exam success. These passive approaches to teaching have little value in a world where creativity and flexibility are at a premium. Creativity, critical thinking, and mental agility are at the heart of all innovation.

Without companies like Uber or Netflix to employ and excite those in developing countries who beat all odds to become skilled and well-educated, "brain drain" tends to occur.

Joseph Stiglitz defines this concept by saying, "Without appropriate jobs, developing countries will lose this much-needed intellectual capital, their brightest children, in whom they have invested enormously through elementary and secondary education and sometimes even through college, to developed countries."[64]

- Promoting innovation has been a proven methodology to gain a competitive advantage, the process of which is a responsibility of human resources.
- There are three initiatives human resource professionals can adopt to help encourage continuous innovation within their organizations: hiring for innovation, creating a culture of innovation and training, and rewarding for innovation.
- In developing countries, five factors of stagnation create barriers posed by the local environment: (1) deficiency of resources, (2) absence of demand, (3) inadequate financial capital, (4) lack of human capital, and (5) weak legal systems.

At an alarming rate, developing countries are losing their skilled labor to developed countries like the United States and Canada, who accept them under skilled worker visas. However, in many cases it's hard to blame the migrants. They have a much larger chance at success in their destination countries and are more likely to find other bright thinkers with whom to collaborate and hire as employees. Brain drain benefits developed countries even further.

Ngoma and Ismail write,

> it was established that brain drain raised the education and income levels of the destination countries at the expense of the source countries. . . . In addition, when labor productivity and wages depends on the average level of human capital, voluntary skilled migration lowers the average level of human capital and productivity performance in the source countries.[65]

It's clear that brain drain negatively affects the innovators in developing countries, along with their potential employees (or employees of their supply chain).

Weak legal systems

In developing countries, legal systems that protect innovators often do not exist, are poorly formed, or are not properly enforced. Among others, these systems include property law, contract law, and intellectual property law. It's nearly impossible to incentivize innovation or entrepreneurship when an aspiring individual is rightfully worried about a neighbor stealing their inventory or a debtor has no legal obligation to repay them. Cooter writes,

> Written contract law in poor countries mostly resembles written contract law in rich countries. . . . The writing is similar, but its application is dissimilar.
>
> Applied law is weakened by high court fees that discourage meritorious suits, low court fees that encourage meritless suits, long delays in trials, formalistic proceedings, the absence of streamlined courts for small claims, judges who are corrupt or politicized, and clumsy procedures to execute court judgments by corrupt officials.[66]

The judges in developing countries are frequently appointed arbitrarily or based on social status and have no real training of the law. As a result, legal statutes are upheld in an inconsistent, inefficient manner with much bias. High-income countries tend to have shorter legal delays and quicker judgments compared to low-income countries.

Creative work space

Google is the frontrunner in building whacky workplaces that promote creativity within the company. Stories of Google's pool tables, bowling alleys, free food, gym memberships, and colorful decor are well-known, which means every year, Google gets thousands of applicants for openings in their offices. Google's "chief happiness officer" boasts that these creative workplaces keep employees happy, productive, loyal, and motivated, which drives innovation for the company. More and more companies are following Google's lead by engaging employees in creative activities through fun and social breakrooms and through excursions or classes that teach their employees new creative skills (see Figure 5.16).

Source: Coleman (2016).[67]

Figure 5.16 Google campus
Source: www.flickr.com/photos/92082510@N04/9565917396

It's often impossible for impoverished individuals to afford legal counsel or court fees in the first place.[68] Even if an entrepreneur is able to sue a business partner for breach of contract, the chances of them being made whole are slight. Cooter continues,

> Collecting damages from poor people is impractical. People in poverty do not have the money to pay damages, or the little money that they have is easily hidden, or they work informally without any records of their earnings, or they have no bank accounts where wages can be garnished, or their property cannot be separated from the property of their relatives.[69]

The legal systems in developing countries are inefficient and impractical when compared to rich countries like the United States where the threat of being sued or prosecuted typically keeps businesses and individuals playing by the rules.

This issue is especially pertinent in the former Soviet nations of Eastern Europe. Transitioning from communist control, these countries had a somewhat developed judicial system with courts and judges, but it had only ever operated in the interest of the state. In other words, there was no precedent of a legal system truly intended to protect individuals or private enterprises.

Development and innovation

Innovation is traditionally considered to be a function of creativity and curiosity to find new or different solutions. Organizations and companies tend to conceive of innovation as a function of their research and development (R&D) departments and allocate funding for it. In 2011 the European Commission allocated 3 percent of its total budget to R&D to kick-start innovation in the framework for research and innovation called "Horizon 2020."

Innovation results from organizational learning as much as from R&D. It also always involves investment in developing skills and knowledge. Therefore, analyzing a country's total expenditure on R&D as a percentage of its total GDP (R&D intensity) can be a good indicator of its innovation level. Increased investment in R&D may originate from a variety of reasons, such as an increasing number of skilled workforces and the opening up of new technology enterprises.

Scientists must be free to learn, to speak, and to challenge

"You do not mess with something so fundamental, so precious, as science," says Kirsty Duncan, Canada's first minister of science. In a heartfelt, inspiring talk about pushing boundaries, she makes the case that researchers must be free to present uncomfortable truths and challenge the thinking of the day – and that we all have a duty to speak up when we see science being stifled or suppressed. Learn more in the full TED Talk at www.ted.com/talks/kirsty_duncan_scientists_must_be_free_to_learn_to_speak_and_to_challenge

---

Innovation undeniably plays a key role as one of the critical roots that determines the willingness of organizations to spend on R&D. For example, Morocco, Spain, and China had higher total expenditure on R&D as a percentage of its total GDP in 2011, in the range of 1.0–1.9 percent. This indicates that Spain and China have a higher innovation level than Morocco.

Innovation has been a strong indicator for long-term economic growth as it creates opportunities for tomorrow's jobs. Fundamentally speaking, there are two ways to increase output in an economy (see Figure 5.17).

The second point is where innovation can play a role in the growth of an economy. In this capacity, technology is one factor of innovation aiding the development of economies.

In order to invest in technology, a culture of innovation is a necessity. Data lies at the heart of appropriate decision-making. The ability to make decisions faster based on relevant information as well as the ability to provide the right messages to the right customers would lead to competitive advantage for the firm. Business processes will evolve by using sensors, and computational power will expand to gather information at every step of the supply chain and evolution and application of artificial intelligence.[70] These technological innovations thus pave the way for development. However, so far, most of the benefits have been gained by educated workforces in developed countries.

In addition to cultural factors, there is also organizational structure that impacts innovation. The first challenge is to reduce economic hardship. With the great need to improve welfare and living conditions of their population, a country needs to balance the allocation of resources aimed at the basic necessities of its citizens against the needs of the newly emerging knowledge workers. Improving the standing of impoverished citizens in developing countries should rightfully take priority. However, lack of opportunity and poor policy choices for those who do have access to higher education have a causal effect on the emigration of the very resources that are able to innovate and effect change.[71]

For a country to be viewed as a competitor in the global economy, innovation should be seen relative to the local context and capitalize on the unique cultural advantages that the country offers. By identifying strengths and turning them into economic advantages, a country can

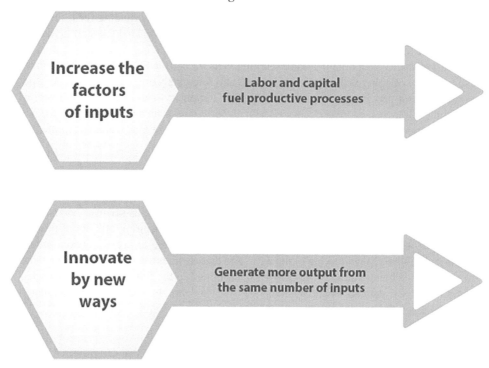

Figure 5.17 Factors of input

Source: Authors.

position itself for success.[72] Each country needs to identify strengths and develop an innovation strategy.

A culture that has some barriers to innovation can be influenced by public policy. Innovation policies have to blend new and old cultural paradigms while still respecting traditional values and ways of doing business. These new cultural patterns should correct some of the more problematic areas while preserving cultural strengths. For example, Morocco does not have formal education or innovation systems in place and faces significant challenges to innovate.

Conclusion

We have presented factors that influence creativity and innovations. The examples of cultural factors in China, Spain, and Morocco that played an important role in the ability to innovate were analyzed. As a developed nation, Spain's focus is on fostering the development and exchange of ideas as a function of corporate process.

As developing nations, China and Morocco are not as far down the path and emphasize creative problem-solving and market development rather than the creation of radically new ideas. There is a clear positive relationship between innovation and economic standing and innovation and culture. Culture comes from its history and form of government. Some culture promotes innovation while others do not. However, economic growth requires innovations of some sort to stay competitive. As discussed earlier, there is an undeniable relationship between the study of Hofstede's dimensions and innovations; the four dimensions provide an approximate measurement of innovative level. Nevertheless, this does not conclude that a country or a company has to model its culture differently to promote economic growth. Different companies in the same industry and country may have different cultures and thrive equally.

The definition of innovation is covering a wide range, which includes both improvements in technology and better methods of doing things. It can also manifest in product changes, process changes, new approaches to do business, new forms of distribution, and new conceptions of scope.

However, we know that one size does not fit all. Business innovation is becoming a central research topic in management. Based on the relationship between Hofstede's cultural dimensions and innovation, it will help the company to provide an environment for continuous, collaborative "what if" modeling. It will also help the company to increase the ability of adapting to change. To add value in today's rapidly changing, increasingly complex, and global business environment, the management system must be able to quickly adapt to all kinds of change. Such changes include organizational, market, competitive, and regulatory change.

Discussion questions

1 Do culture characteristics impact creativity and innovation in a society?
2 Define creativity and innovation.
3 What are the predominant types of innovation?
4 What are the 4Ps of innovation?
5 Could micro or macro factors impact creativity and innovation?

Al Capizza: a creative and unique pizza restaurant, São Paulo, Brazil

World pizza market

The world market for pizza is valued at $141.4 billion as of 2020. Market growth rates for the 2017–2025 period are projected to exceed the GDP rate in all of the regions that can be verified, whether they be developed markets (United States, European Union) or emerging markets (Latin America, Africa, Russia, China).[73]

In the emerging and developing markets, especially, growth is forecast to be in the double digits. The biggest explosion will happen in Eastern Europe (12.7 percent growth) and Latin America (12.2 percent). There is a good potential for increasing revenues, but it is a very competitive market.

According to Aaron Allen,[74] the main players in terms of market share, as of 2020 were:

1 Domino's Pizza: $16.1 billion in global sales, with 52 percent in the United States and 48 percent internationally. More than 70 percent of US sales were achieved via digital channel.
2 Pizza Hut: $12.0 billion in global sales; 45 percent of sales take place in the United States and more than 30 percent in Asia (including China and India).
3 Little Caesars Pizza: $4.8 billion in sales.
4 Papa John's International: $3.5 billion in sales, with 60 percent in the United States.
5 Papa Murphy's International: more than $800 million in sales.

Figure 5.18 Forecast 2022 world pizza market

Source: Euromonitor for pmq.com. www.pmq.com/pizza-power-report-2022/

Together, these companies represent over 25 percent of market share.

Brazil world market share

The Brazilian pizza market is one of the largest in the world in terms of revenue. With a turnover of more than $5 billion a year, the market remains highly fragmented. The city of São Paulo by itself has over 6000 pizzerias that together sell 1 million pizzas a day. In 2017, Sonny and Michael, realizing the potential of the Brazilian pizzas market, installed the first Al Capizza in São Paulo, with the aim of generating a model of franchise.

The business model should consider the profile of new customer (millennials) that was changing the way that they use to buy pizzas, from the analogue way (telephone) to the digital one (website): alcapizza.com.br, app: Alcapizza Oficial, whatsapp, and Marketplace (order aggregators) like: (Ifood, Uber Eats, Rappi).

Customer behavior research

Both Sonny and Michael understand the millennials' "technological" demands, and their love for pizza. Having researched in-depth the trends of consumption, they found that nearly 41 percent of millennials now eat pizza once a week, a big jump from 26 percent in 2017. The following are key findings of the Technomic's 2016 Pizza Consumer Trend Report:

- Pizza is the number one favorite comfort food, earning twice as many votes as any other dish. (Take that, chocolate!)

- The pizza industry, in fact, forged ahead in the past year, even with the presence of independents who are bound to decades of proud tradition. Pizza makers are slow to adopt newer technologies and continued to lag behind other chains in the food industry.
- The signs point to modest growth in this segment, with fast-casual chains leading the charge with the availability of online ordering technology and third-party delivery.
- According to research done by PMQ Pizza Magazine, 63 percent of self-identified "pizza lovers" are women. The average consumer is now health conscious and works out twice a week. This change reflects the broader movement among the population to live a healthier, more balanced lifestyle.
- The 80 million millennials buying pizza are expected to outspend baby boomers by 2017. Not only do they look for the healthier options, but they also consider themselves as "foodies" – interested in the experience of eating more than the sustenance. They love custom, build-your-own pizzas with interesting and unique tastes, textures, and ingredients. And they like to talk about their food online.
- Today's consumers have developed a social consciousness towards the brands they connect with. They feel good about supporting establishments that focus on sustainability and natural ingredients. Companies like Pizza Hut have announced a commitment to reduce their energy and water consumption and have begun using more environmentally friendly packaging.

Trends forecasts for 2023, according to Pizza Today,[75] reveal that a key insight for the pizza market is the increasing use of technology in the pizzeria industry. Technology plays an important role in how pizzerias do business, from online ordering and delivery systems to kitchen automation and point-of-sale systems. This trend is expected to accelerate in the coming years, as more and more pizzeria owners look to technology to streamline their operations and improve their bottom line.

Pizza Today also incorporated consumer insights and outlooks on the pizza industry with data sourced from the 2022 Technomic Pizza Consumer Trend Report by Technomic Inc. As consumers become more adventurous in their food choices, pizzeria owners are responding by offering a wider range of toppings and flavor combinations. Thirty-one percent of consumers want organic ingredients, while 22 percent want restaurants to offer plant-based items. Consumers are also looking for more accessibility and convenience. Forty-two percent find an online ordering system where they can track their pizza order to be appealing, and 38 percent want curbside pickup availability. And 23 percent of American consumers would like to order pizza from their smart TVs, which is a 20 percent increase from 2020.

Considering trends for the next years, the brothers Sonny and Michael invested $1 million to create the concept of Al Capizza: pizza to be more convenient, healthier, and fairly priced, and aligned to the trends of the world markets. Competition has ceased to be local and has become global. The use of manufacturing and transportation techniques combined with information technologies, especially social networks and mobile ordering software (mobile commerce), became the basis of Al Capizza's business model.

The new concept developed by the brothers does not give up on the quality and freshness of the ingredients and innovates deeply with ordering procedures (90 percent online) and in the process of assembling the pizza.

The business model

"If the pizza is for delivery, you cannot get to the customer's house dismantled because the cheese went all to one side, leaving the rest of the pizza uncovered," Sonny points out.

The family has always insisted on quality as being a differentiating factor of all their pizzerias. And to prove this point, the new unit improvised on the traditional L-shaped restaurant to be assembled with clear glass. Now, all customers who pass by on the street can see the workings of the pizzeria kitchen. This concept called "Pizza Aquarium" or fish bowl. Therefore, consumers are able to see everything that is happening inside. The model store opened in February 2017. Around 90 percent of orders are generated through digital channels such as website, app and WhatsApp, social networks, and third-party marketplaces (order aggregators). Total cumulative revenue is $1.2 million with a monthly net profit margin of 7.5 percent on average. Revenue ramp up more than twice the projection set in the business plan. In 2023 customer satisfaction is measured by the digital ordering channel ranging from 1 to 5. Customers evaluate on four dimensions: delivery time, packaging, food, and price/benefit. There have been more than 10, 000 evaluations so far and the average score for each item is 4.7 on the digital ordering channel. All complaints and suggestions are answered by Sonny; this enables him to understand common problems and can address solutions quickly.

Plans for the new challenges

Sonny and Michael want more. They intend to open franchising of their business model throughout Brazil in the next years. Domino's announced that it intends to open 500 new units in Brazil in the near future. When interviewed, the brothers said that the more Domino's expands, the better it will be for the pizza market. They feel that "the pizza market has invested little in technology." In general, only the large chains of pizzerias have observed the need to innovate both in relation to the customer and in relation to the gastronomy involved. Sonny and Michael intend to invest in R&D, about 5 percent of their financial revenue to strengthen their digital presence and food technology. It is expected that in 10 years they will have the same reach as some big four chains, which took 50 years to achieve.

Impact of COVID-19 in Al Capizza's business model

The situation caused by the COVID-19 pandemic resulted in a crisis in the labor market in several countries around the world. In the United States as for the labor crisis, in 2022 some pizzeria operators were considering an option to minimize the human touch in the pizza making process through automation. Several robotics companies and several pizza chains from around the world are counting on tech to change the industry in dramatic fashion. Will robots soon begin taking over the jobs that people don't want?[76]

In Brazil, the sanitary crisis brought an increase of competition, because every pizzeria had to adapt their business model to also support delivery. For Al Capizza, which has been digitally oriented since the beginning, it has been using technology to capture order and manage efficiently pizza delivery, and the pandemic situation brought new opportunities. The increase in pizza orders was supported by multiple digital channels such as marketplaces, Al Capizza's app, website, and WhatsApp. Just to get an idea, the order numbers had more than doubled in a short period of time (first quarter of 2020), so more stores had to be opened to cope with customer demand. By the beginning of 2020, Al Capizza was available in five locations; by the end of the year, additional five stores had opened.

The next year two more stores came to operation. As the business had 12 stores, the brothers decided to split the group in two business. After this separate, one group was under the Al Capizza brand and the other under the Corleone brand. In the division process, geographical position among stores (to improve logistics), revenue, and the number of stores were taken in account.

In the owners' point of view, this new design allows efficacy of management, because there was an existing record of consumer behavior in each territory, and each of the brands could address these challenges differently, keeping the business growing.

As a lesson from pandemic situation, it was natural to improve the business model with restaurant and delivery store (eat on spot) to delivery only (pick up and take away), turning the organization structure to a more flexible. To support this model, the following strategic decisions were made. (1) Increased investment in marketing for online sales in the Al Capizza's app. This strategy made it possible to reduce the number of people needed to take order and allowed Al Capizza to sell pizza anywhere, without the necessity be present at addresses listed on highly busy avenues where rents are more expensive. (2) Automation/mechanization of the pizza production process. The usage of automatic oven door opener reduced 50 percent in the need for labor, which resulted in lowering the cost of the entire operation.

This redesign adjusted the business to a higher profit level, without disappointing the regular customers. It is important to highlight that the flagship restaurant remained in the same geographical location, highlighting the brand, values and mission, even in this new configuration of the business model.

Finally, the investment in the business model with a digital footprint enabled Al Capizza to grow, even during the pandemic, because the company already knew the customer profile (more digital) and took advantage of the situation to expand business and consolidate the brand as a modern company aligned with the new reality of the pizza industry.

Questions for discussion

1 What are the creativity and the innovation of Al Capizza? Do these differentiations provide competitive advantages for them?
2 What is the role of the "pizza aquarium" concept in Al Capizza's business model? In your opinion, how will millennials perceive this?
3 What are the roles of information and communication technologies in the success of Al Capizza as a startup?
4 Analyze the impact of the arguments about millennials' demand for different services.
5 Analyze the impact of COVID-19 on Al Capizza's business model.
6 In your opinion, how is the future of the pizza industry in terms of order, production, and delivery?
7 Provide a road map of how Al Capizza could compete globally.

Summary of main ideas

Creativity and innovation can be constrained by cultural factors and educational systems which may not enable people to live to their potentials.

- To ensure economic development, countries should nurture creativity and innovation through educational system and public policies.
- Creativity is often described the desire to express oneself.
- Creativity could be defined as the human mind conceiving new ideas and bringing them into being.
- Innovation is defined as "the act of inventing new processes, products, services, or solutions that can be brought to market."
- Disruptive innovation is a development that helps to form a new market and value network.
- The vision of ambidextrous organization brings the understanding of the need to develop integrated management structures, in exploitation (past) and exploration (future).
- Creativity and design can be linked to innovation which is an outcome.
- Innovation is the applied knowledge that is preceded by invention and creation of a new product, service, or approach.
- Combining global value chain and innovation system approaches may lead to the possible change in the trajectories of performance in developing countries.

Table 5.2 Key terms

Creativity	Radical, modular, and architectural innovation
Prominent theories on creativity	Disruptive innovation
Innovation	Dualism
Knowledge	Intellectual property (IP)
	Artificial intelligence (AI)

Table 5.3 Glossary

Creativity	Creativity is a complex and multifaceted concept that encompasses the ability to generate, develop, and express ideas that are novel, original, and valuable. It's considered a crucial skill in numerous fields, from the arts to science, business, and education
Prominent theories on creativity	The Investment Theory posits that creative individuals behave like good investors, making novel ideas popular and vice versa. Amabile's Componential Theory emphasizes the role of expertise, creative thinking skills, and intrinsic task motivation.
Innovation	Innovation involves the creation, development, and implementation of new ideas, processes, products, or services, often leading to significant improvements or the creation of something entirely new. It is a critical component in various fields, driving growth, efficiency, and competitive advantage.
Knowledge	Knowledge refers to the collection of information, skills, and understanding that individuals accumulate through experiences, education, and perception. It encompasses facts, truths, and principles acquired and retained by the human mind.
Radical, modular, and architectural innovation	Radical innovation introduces breakthrough changes, creating new industries or revolutionizing existing ones. Modular innovation involves significant changes to one component of a product or system, while the overall design remains unchanged. Architectural innovation reconfigures the way components interact, altering the overall system architecture without changing the individual components.

Disruptive innovation	Disruptive innovation refers to a process where a smaller company, typically with fewer resources, successfully challenges established incumbent businesses by creating a new market and value network. This innovation often starts by targeting overlooked segments, eventually displacing established market-leading firms, products, or alliances.
Dualism	Dualism is a philosophical concept asserting the existence of two distinct, often contrasting, principles or realms, such as mind and body or good and evil. It suggests a binary nature to certain aspects of existence or reality, where two fundamentally different categories coexist.
Intellectual property (IP)	Intellectual property refers to creations of the mind, such as inventions; literary and artistic works; designs; and symbols, names, and images used in commerce. It is legally protected by intellectual property laws, enabling individuals or businesses to earn recognition or financial benefit from their inventions or creations.
Artificial intelligence (AI)	Artificial Intelligence (AI) refers to the simulation of human intelligence in machines that are programmed to think and learn like humans. This field encompasses the development of algorithms and technologies that enable machines to perform tasks requiring cognitive functions typically associated with human minds, such as learning, problem-solving, and decision-making.
Radical, modular, and architectural innovation	Radical innovation introduces breakthrough changes, creating new industries or revolutionizing existing ones. Modular innovation involves significant changes to one component of a product or system, while the overall design remains unchanged. Architectural innovation reconfigures the way components interact, altering the overall system architecture without changing the individual components.

Notes

1 Marcus, A., & Gould, E.W. (2000). Crosscurrents: Cultural dimensions and global web user-interface design. *Interactions ACM*, 7(4), 32–46. https://doi.org/10.1145/345190.345238.
2 Hollanders, H., & Van Cruysen, A. (2009). Design, creativity and innovation: A scoreboard approach. *Pro Inno Europe, Inno Metrics*: Holanda, 26, 1–36.
3 Lee, S.K. (2008, June 7). *Optimum Performance Technologies*. Retrieved December 16, 2018, from http://optimumperformancetechnologies.blogspot.com/2008/06/organisational-creativity-top-10.html
4 Amabile, T.M. (1988). A model of creativity and innovation in organizations. *Research in Organizational Behavior*, 10, 123. Retrieved from http://web.mit.edu/curhan/www/docs/Articles/15341_Readings/Group_Performance/Amabile_A_Model_of_CreativityOrg.Beh_v10_pp123-167.pdf
5 Puccio, G.J., & Cabra, J.F. (2010). Organizational creativity: A systems approach. In *The Cambridge Handbook of Creativity* (p. 508). Cambridge University Press. https://doi.org/10.1017/CBO9780511763205
6 Acar, O.A., Tarakci, M., & Van Knippenberg, D. (2019). Creativity and innovation under constraints: A cross-disciplinary integrative review. *Journal of Management*, 45(1), 96–121.
7 Kaufman, J.C., & Sternberg, R.J. (2010). *The Cambridge Handbook of Creativity. International Journal* (p. 508). Cambridge University Press. https://doi.org/10.1017/CBO9780511763205
8 Woodman, R.W., Sawyer, J.E., & Griffin, R.W. (1993). Toward a theory of organizational creativity. *The Academy of Management Review*, 18(2), 293. https://doi.org/10.2307/258761
9 Willis, R. (2014, December 17). *Creativity vs Innovation!* Retrieved December 16, 2018, from www.linkedin.com/pulse/creativity-innovation-robert-willis
10 Anderson, N., Potočnik, K., & Zhou, J. (2014). Innovation and creativity in organizations. *Journal of Management*, 40(5), 1297–1333. https://doi.org/10.1177/0149206314527128
11 Amabile, T.M. (1997). Motivating creativity in organizations: On doing what you love and loving what you do. *California Management Review*, 40(1), 39–58.
12 Puccio, G.J., Cabra, J.F., Fox, J.M., & Cahen, H. (2010, May 1). Creativity on demand: Historical approaches and future trends. *Artificial Intelligence for Engineering Design Analysis and Manufacturing*, 24(2), 153–159
13 Manchester Metropolitan University. (2017). *Engage Week Timetable of Events 3rd–7th July*. Retrieved December 16, 2018, from www.mmu.ac.uk/staff/docs/MMU2286_Engage-week-2017-V7.pdf

14 Anokhin, S., Grichnik, D., & Hisrich, R.D. (2008). The journey from novice to serial entrepreneurship in China and Germany: Are the drivers the same? *Managing Global Transitions*, 6, 117–142.

15 Dejardin, M. (2000, November). Entrepreneurship and economic growth: An obvious conjunction? *The Institute for Development Strategies*, 1–14. Retrieved from http://econwpa.repec.org/eps/dev/papers/0110/0110010.pdf

16 Holcombe, R.G. (1998). Entrepreneurship and economic growth. *The Quarterly Journal of Austrian Economics*, 1(2), 45–62. https://doi.org/10.1177/097135570801700202

17 Gries, T., & Naudé, W. (2009). Entrepreneurship and regional economic growth: Towards a general theory of start-ups. *Innovation: The European Journal of Social Science Research*, 22(3), 309–328. https://doi.org/10.1080/13511610903354877

18 Gries, T., & Naude, W. (2008). Entrepreneurship and regional economic growth: Towards a general theory of start-ups. *Innovation: The European Journal of Social Science Research*, 22. https://doi.org/10.1080/13511610903354877

19 Narvekar, A. (2023, February 2).Why entrepreneurs need to become early birds of AI revolution. *Forbes India*. Retrieved from www.forbesindia.com/article/sp-jain-school-of-global-management/why-entrepreneurs-need-to-become-early-birds-of-ai-revolution/82931/1

20 Fitzgerald, E., Wankerl, A., & Schramm, C. (2011). Inside real innovation: How the right approach can move ideas from R&D to market – and get the economy moving. *World Scientific*. https://doi.org/10.1142/7985

21 Schumpeter, J.A. (1911). *The Theory of Economic Development*. New Jersey: Routledge. https://doi.org/10.4324/9781315135564

22 Rogers, E.M. (2010). Diffusion of innovations. *Recorded Books, Inc*. Retrieved from www.simonandschuster.com/books/Diffusion-of-Innovations-4th-Edition/Everett-M-Rogers/9781451602470

23 Slack, G. (2023, January 17). *What DALL-E Reveals about Human Creativity*. Stanford HAI. Oxfordshire: Routledge. Retrieved February 25, 2023, from https://hai.stanford.edu/news/what-dall-e-reveals-about-human-creativity

24 Apple Newsroom. (2023, February 9). Apple commits $430 billion in US investments over five years. *Apple Newsroom*. Retrieved from www.apple.com/newsroom/2021/04/apple-commits-430-billion-in-us-investments-over-five-years/

25 Goel, A. (2022, December 6). Innovation in a world in transition. *Forbes*. Retrieved from www.forbes.com/sites/forbesbusinessdevelopmentcouncil/2022/12/06/innovation-in-a-world-in-transition/?sh=2bf9a20c3487

26 Beltagui, A., Rosli, A., & Candi, M. (2020). Exaptation in a digital innovation ecosystem: The disruptive impacts of 3D printing. *Research Policy*, 49(1), 103833.

27 Henderson, R.M., & Clark, K.B. (1990). Architectural innovation: The reconfiguration of existing product technologies and the failure of established firms. *Administrative Science Quarterly*, 35(1), 9. https://doi.org/10.2307/2393549

28 Bower, J.L., & Christensen, C. (1995). Disruptive technologies: Catching the wave. *Harvard Business Review*, 73(1), 43–53.

29 Christensen, C. (2013). *The Innovator's Dilemma: When New Technologies Cause Great Firms to Fail (Management of Innovation and Change) eBook*. Harvard Business Review Press.

30 Christensen, C.M. (2006). The ongoing process of building a theory of disruption. *Journal of Product Innovation Management*, 23(1), 39–55. https://doi.org/10.1111/j.1540-5885.2005.00180.x

31 Christensen, C.M., Bohmer, R., & Kenagy, J. (2000, October). Will disruptive innovation cure health care? *Harvard Business Review*, 78(5), 102–112. https://doi.org/10.1016/0002-9610(92)90118-B

32 Christensen, C.M., & Overdorf, M. (2000, March–April). Meeting the challenge of disruptive change. *Harvard Business Review*, 1–10. https://doi.org/10.1002/rwm3.20019

33 infoDev. (2014). *infoDev Annual Report 2012–2013*. Retrieved from www.infodev.org/annual-report

34 Hydroponics Kenya. (n.d.). *About Us*. Retrieved December 16, 2018, from http://hydroponicskenya.com/about-us/

35 Christensen, C. (2012, October 23). *Disruptive Innovation*. Retrieved December 16, 2018, from www.claytonchristensen.com/key-concepts/

36 Paap, J., & Katz, R. (2004). Anticipating disruptive innovation. *Research-Technology Management*, 47(5), 13–22. https://doi.org/10.1080/08956308.2004.11671647

37 Paap, J., & Katz, R. (2004). Anticipating disruptive innovation. *Research-Technology Management*, 47(5), 13–22. https://doi.org/10.1080/08956308.2004.11671647

38 Shaver, E. (2014). *The Many Definitions of Innovation*. Retrieved from www.ericshaver.com/the-many-definitions-of-innovation/
39 O'Reilly, C.A., & Tushman, M.L. (2004). The ambidextrous organization. *Harvard Business Review*, 82(4), 74–81, 140. Retrieved from www.ncbi.nlm.nih.gov/pubmed/15077368
40 Whyte, J., Bessant, J.R., & Neely, A.D. (2005). *Management of Creativity and Design within the Firm*. UK Department of Trade and Industry. Retrieved from www.ericshaver.com/the-many-definitions-of-innovation/
41 Knight, K.E. (1967). A descriptive model of the intra-firm innovation process. *The Journal of Business*, 40(4), 478–496. https://doi.org/10.1086/295013
42 Whyte, J., Bessant, J.R., & Neely, A.D. (2005). *Management of Creativity and Design Within the Firm* (pp. 31–73). London: DTI - Department of Trade and Industry.
43 Hollanders, H., & Van Cruysen, A. (2009). Design, creativity and innovation: A scoreboard approach. *Pro Inno Europe, Inno Metrics: Holanda*, 26, 1–36
44 Lazzeretti, L. (2012). *Creative Industries and Innovation in Europe: Concepts, Measures and Comparative Case Studies*. Routledge. Retrieved from www.routledge.com/Creative-Industries-and-Innovation-in-Europe-Concepts-Measures-and-Comparative/Lazzeretti/p/book/9780203112571
45 Dubina, I.N., Carayannis, E.G., & Campbell, D.F.J. (2012). Creativity economy and a crisis of the economy? Coevolution of knowledge, innovation, and creativity, and of the knowledge economy and knowledge society. *Journal of the Knowledge Economy*, 3(1), 1–24. https://doi.org/10.1007/s13132-011-0042-y
46 Howells, J., & Bessant, J. (2012). Introduction: Innovation and economic geography: A review and analysis. *Journal of Economic Geography*, 12(5), 929–942. https://doi.org/10.1093/jeg/lbs029
47 Batten, D.F. (1995). Network cities: Creative urban agglomerations for the 21st century. *Urban Studies*, 32(2), 313–327. https://doi.org/10.1080/00420989550013103
48 Krätke, S. (2012). *The Creative Capital of Cities: Interactive Knowledge Creation and the Urbanization Economies of Innovation*. Wiley. https://doi.org/10.1002/9781444342277
49 Costa Rica News. (2013, November 27). *Costa Rican Entrepreneur Wins Prize Global Competition Clean Energy*. Retrieved December 16, 2018, from www.mycostaricanews.com/costa-rican-entrepreneur-wins-prize-global-competition-clean-energy/
50 Lebel, C., Walker, L., Leemans, A., Phillips, L., & Beaulieu, C. (2008). Microstructural maturation of the human brain from childhood to adulthood. *Neuroimage*, 1044–1055. Retrieved from www.ncbi.nlm.nih.gov/pubmed/18295509
51 Krugman, P.R., Wells, R., & Graddy, K.J. (2013). *Essentials of Economics* (3rd ed.). Worth Publishers. Retrieved December 16, 2018, from www.mycostaricanews.com/costa-rican-entrepreneur-wins-prize-global-competition-clean-energy/
52 Tidd, J., & Bessant, J.R. (2009). *Managing Innovation: Integrating Technological, Market and Organizational Change*. Wiley.
53 Robischon, N. (2017, October 11). *Why Amazon is the World's Most Innovative Company of 2017*. Retrieved December 16, 2018, from www.fastcompany.com/3067455/why-amazon-is-the-worlds-most-innovative-company-of-2017
54 Stanleigh, M. (n.d.). *Innovation: A Strategic HR Imperative*. Retrieved July 13, 2015, from https://bia.ca/innovation-a-strategic-hr-imperative/
55 Hughes, D.J., Lee, A., Tian, A.W., Newman, A., & Legood, A. (2018). Leadership, creativity, and innovation: A critical review and practical recommendations. *The Leadership Quarterly*, 29(5), 549–569.
56 Stanleigh, M. (n.d.). *Innovation: A Strategic HR Imperative*. Retrieved July 13, 2015, from https://bia.ca/innovation-a-strategic-hr-imperative/
57 UN News. (2012). *Lack of Resources Threatens Water and Sanitation Supplies in Developing Countries – UN*. Retrieved from https://news.un.org/en/story/2012/04/408532-lack-resources-threatens-water-and-sanitation-supplies-developing-countries-un
58 Lema, R., Rabellotti, R., & Gehl Sampath, P. (2018). Innovation trajectories in developing countries: Co-evolution of global value chains and innovation systems. *The European Journal of Development Research*, 30(3), 345–363.
59 Field, A.M. (2013). *Infrastructure in South America: Fits and Starts*. Retrieved from www.joc.com/international-trade-news/infrastructure-news/south-america/infrastructure-south-america-fits-and-starts_20130319.html

60 UN News. (2012). *Lack of Resources Threatens Water and Sanitation Supplies in Developing Countries – UN*. Retrieved from https://news.un.org/en/story/2012/04/408532-lack-resources-threatens-water-and-sanitation-supplies-developing-countries-un

61 Kotschwar, B.R. (2012). Transportation and communication infrastructure in Latin America: Lessons from Asia. *Peterson Institute for International Economics Working Paper*, 12–16.

62 Karnani, A. (2010). Selling to the poor. *World Financial Review*, 30–37.

63 World Bank Group. (2017). *Education Public Expenditure Review Guidelines*. Retrieved from http://documents.worldbank.org/curated/en/155861497609568842/pdf/116334-REVISED-Education-PER-Guidelines.pdf

64 Stiglitz, J.E. (2006). *Stability with Growth: Macroeconomics, Liberalization and Development*. Oxford University Press. https://doi.org/10.1093/0199288143.001.0001

65 Ngoma, A.L., & Ismail, N.W. (2013). The impact of brain drain on human capital in developing countries. *South African Journal of Economics*, 81(2), 211–224. https://doi.org/10.1111/saje.12014

66 Cooter, R. (2008). Doing what you say: Contracts and economic development. *Alabama Law Review*, 59(4), 1107–1133.

67 Coleman, A. (2016, February 11). Is Google's model of the creative workplace the future of the office? *The Guardian*. Retrieved from www.theguardian.com/careers/2016/feb/11/is-googles-model-of-the-creative-workplace-the-future-of-the-office

68 Cooter, R. (2008). Doing what you say: Contracts and economic development. *Alabama Law Review*, 59(4), 1107–1133.

69 Cooter, R. (2008). Doing what you say: Contracts and economic development. *Alabama Law Review*, 59(4), 1107–1133.

70 Future Work Skills. (2020). Retrieved from www.iftf.org/futureworkskills/

71 Djeflat, A. (2005, October–November). *Innovation Systems and Knowledge Economy in North Africa: New Opportunity for Innovation Take Off? Third GLOBELICS Conference* (pp. 285–303). Pretoria, South Africa.

72 Aubert, J.E. (2005). *Promoting Innovation in Developing Countries: A Conceptual Framework. World Bank Policy Research Working Paper* (Vol. 3554).

73 www.pmq.com/pizza-power-report-2022

74 https://aaronallen.com/blog/pizza-industry

75 https://pizzaexpo.pizzatoday.com/show_news/new-study-reveals-key-insights-trends-forecasts-for-the-2023-pizza-industry/

76 www.pmq.com/pizza-power-report-2022

Section III

The organization

6 Institutions, governance, and strategy

Learning objectives

1 Learn the definitions of institutions, governance, and strategy
2 Understand why appropriate institutions are necessary for nurturing an entrepreneurial ecosystem
3 Examine the role of governance for a well-functioning business environment
4 Discuss the relationship between corporate governance and institutions
5 Analyze why business strategy is necessary for sustainable growth.

Micro and macro startup challenges facing Iran

In this case, many aspects of institutions, governance, and strategy have been highlighted for the country of Iran. In an article by Alireza Jozi, the entrepreneurial and startup ecosystem challenges of Iran are analyzed.[1] In this study of Iran's startup ecosystem, he has divided the challenges into six different categories: market challenges, capital challenges, human resource challenges, knowledge resource challenges, governance challenges, and infrastructure challenges. These sets of micro, macro, and cultural challenges also exist for most developing countries.

Market challenges

1 Startups don't have ambitions to target the international market (though Iran's market is already large)
2 Sanctions! There is no easy and direct way to access the international market
3 Political instability and uncertainty.

Capital challenges

1 Not enough funding in seed-stage startups.

Human Resource challenges

1 Talent exists, but not the type startups are looking for
2 Not enough lawyers experienced in startup legal structures
3 Huge rate of brain drain (talent leaving the country); human capital is the most important factor of production and job creation.

DOI: 10.4324/9781003405740-10

Knowledge resource challenges

1 Not enough opportunities for private sector involvement in academia
2 Limited university curriculum in startups and tech entrepreneurship
3 Not enough investment in R&D.

Infrastructure challenges

1 Slow internet speed
2 Lack of proper legal framework for startup registrations and investments
3 Long and lengthy process of company registration
4 Limited payment options.

Governance challenges

1 No proper policy and regulation structure to ease the way of entrepreneurs and encourage them
2 Twenty-four months of mandatory military service for men – and yes, that includes entrepreneurs!

Questions

1 Analyze this case study main points.
2 Evaluate similar challenges for a set of low- and medium-income countries.
3 Compare and contrast between developed and developing countries for the previously stated challenges.
4 Examine the role of institutions for a set of developed and developing countries.
5 If you are a policymaker, how would you overcome these challenges? What kind of strategy would you propose? What kind of institutional and governance changes need to be implemented, especially in the case of Iran?
6 In what ways was the Iranian uprising of 2022–2023, led by women, a reflection of the challenges highlighted in this case?

Introduction

It is important to understand the essential role that institutions and governance play on the development of sustainable growth. Also, it is essential to develop strategies at the micro and macro levels. These are key elements for creating transparent and sustainable organizations which are indispensable for entrepreneurial activities that drive the country's development. The entrepreneurial activities in society will flourish under good governance and with relevant supporting institutions that make the rules and regulations. Regardless of past and current scenarios, having a futuristic strategy is necessary for any country. These strategies are a road map for reaching a certain outcome. In this chapter, we will present definitions and applications of institutions, governance, and strategy, and their relationship with entrepreneurial activities.

Institution definition

The institution is defined as the rules of the game that shape human interaction. However, institutions are not external to human action; they have a reflexive relationship with human interaction.[2] Clear and transparent rules that are applied equally to all lead to institutions of better quality, and institutional quality holds the key to prevailing patterns of prosperity around the world.[3]

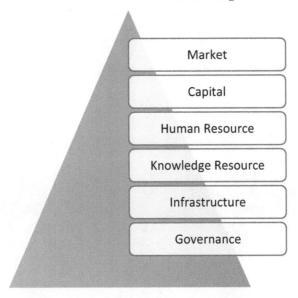

Figure 6.1 Challenges

Developed nations are those where institutions allow investors to feel secure about their property rights, have prevailing laws, and have monetary and fiscal policies that are grounded in solid macroeconomic institutions. They also contain risk-mediating policies and the country's citizens have civil liberties and participate in government.[4]

Formal institutions (e.g., regulations, policies, and sanctions), as well as informal institutions (e.g., norms and values), need to be considered in development. For example, research in the sociology of culture has documented that communism has left a heavy print on the informal institutions in the transition countries which are not quite conducive to entrepreneurial activity.[5] Baumol was among the first ones to pay due diligence to the idea that institutions could represent an obstacle to entrepreneurial activity. He further emphasized the importance of the institutional environment on the attitudes and propensities for new business endeavors.[6]

Recently the concept has been examined by a number of economists including McMillan and Woodruff, who found that if an entrepreneur does not have the needed trust in the court's rulings and inability to enforce contracts efficiently, their entrepreneurial spirit deteriorates leading to a negative effect on employment growth. Nevertheless, distrust in the judicial institutions of a country could have a degrading effect not only on entrepreneurial activity but also on the business environment overall, leading to a decrease in new investment levels and entrepreneurial confidence.[7,8] He and Tian (2020) review the recent literature that links institutions and innovation and the role of culture, demographic characteristics, and other social issues to development.[9] Bosma et al. (2018) study the relationship between the institutions, entrepreneurship, and economic growth empirically. They conclude that productive entrepreneurship enhances economic growth.[10]

In 2002, the Pakistani government implemented a judicial reform that cost $350 million, or 0.1 percent of Pakistan's 2002 GDP. This reform did not involve increased incentives for judges to improve efficiency but merely provided them with more training. Nonetheless, the reform had dramatic effects on judicial efficiency and consequently on entrepreneurship: judges disposed of a quarter more cases and entry rate of

Figure 6.2 Judicial reform and GDP effects case of Pakistan

Source: Sheba. "Scales of Justice Courts-1+" by Sheba Also 18 Million Views is licensed under CC BY-SA 2.0.

new firms increased by half due to the reform. Using data from the World Bank Group Entrepreneurship Database, estimates suggest that this translates into an increase of Pakistan's GDP by 0.5 percent.

Source: Chemin (2009).[11]

Many authors indicated that institutional characteristics that are most prescribed to affect the entrepreneurial environment in a country are as follows.[12,13,14] Property rights, as an institutional indicator for entrepreneurial ventures, are essential to the business environment not only because they encompass a certain social security of the status quo, but also because they make up the "find and keep" component, which is vital for the entrepreneurship aspects associated to discovery, innovation, and creation of new resources, all of which also impact the entrepreneurial activity in low- and middle-income economies.[15,16] Acemoglu and Johnson (2005), for example, illustrate the direct impact of property rights institutions on investment, financial development, and long-term economic growth, all of which have a considerable impact on the business environment and entrepreneurship.[17]

Political systems and class struggles influence the process of law formulation and, thus, shape institutional order which later on forms the framework for economic activity and entrepreneurship.[18,19] The informal institutions (e.g., social norms and culture) also influence the business environment in a given country to a high extent by shaping the structure of corporate governance on the micro level.[20] Therefore, the interdependency between the micro and macro levels is well established as they are interconnected and influence each other to a high extent. This is why governmental efficiency and institutions' effectiveness lay the foundations for successful entrepreneurial strategy.

Conditions for entrepreneurial success

Estrin and Mickiewicz (2011) argue that transitional economies, such as the former Soviet Union and Central and Eastern Europe, have lower rates of entrepreneurial activity and business development due to the legacy of communist planning, which, according to them, needs to be substituted with formal market-supporting institutions.

Figure 6.3 Conditions for success

The communist heritage left a particular legacy of serious institutional weakness, especially with respect to entrepreneurial activity, and that could be due to a centrally planned economy controlled by government through production and policies, and incentives and rewards. However, it seems it has been real improvements to entrepreneurial activity, especially in the European Union accession economies such as Poland in recent years.

Source: Adekoya (2014).[21]

Figure 6.4 Communism and it legacy of weak institution
Source: iStock: btgbtg.

Furthermore, they claim that even though most of this transition has already occurred, entre-preneurship levels have not increased in some of these countries. According to the authors, the main culprit for this is the so-called lack of institutional memory due to the prolonged Soviet rule. They argue that the lack of generalized trust in these transition economies also contributes to the low levels of entrepreneurial entry. The phenomenon of "insider entrepreneurship" is observed in transition economies as well.

"Insider entrepreneurship" refers to the idea that new enterprise undertakings are more likely to be started by the ones who have already established themselves in the business world.[22] The generational effect – "the bridge between the influences of the past and the future" – is also worth mentioning as it entails a prolonged period of transition as changes in the norms and culture of the people could be slow-paced. Therefore, it is one of the characteristics of informal institutions.[23]

Meanwhile, an institution can be broadly defined as "a set of humanly devised behavioral rules that govern and shape the interaction of human beings, in part by helping them to form expectations of what other people will do,"[24] or as "systems of established and prevalent social rules that structure social interactions."[25] This will lead to a higher degree of certainty and expectations of human nature which promote entrepreneurial activities.[26]

As explained earlier, both country governance and institutions are essential sets of cultural and organizational regulations that play an important role in the development, growth, and suc-cess of entrepreneurial initiatives. More than that, both institutions and governance, respec-tively, provide meaning and the rules of social interaction. Therefore, the meaning and way of the entrepreneurial activity itself is a result of institutions and governance structures. For instance, in countries where entrepreneurial activity has more legitimacy, the governance struc-ture itself creates higher entrepreneurial activities.[27]

Figure 6.5 Morocco port
Source: Farid Mernissi.

Macro governance efforts

The Tanger-Med is a brand-new major cargo port located in Tangier, Morocco. The $10 billion project was started by the Moroccan government with the intent of creating jobs and improving the Moroccan economy. About 4000–5000 employees work there. The port provides storage and shipping capabilities for Morocco's major export products: phosphates, agricultural items, and fish/sardines. It also includes 29 storage containers for oil, natural gas, and a passenger area. The second phase of the port will take several years to complete, and it is estimated that it will take 9–10 years before the port will become profitable. The port is connected with the newly constructed transportation infrastructure (railway and highway), providing easy access to key distribution channels within the country.

The concept of the port is not inherently innovative, but the business has demonstrated some innovative thinking in its approach to managing government controls and regulation. In order to maximize the speed and efficiency of the building process, the Moroccan government created a dedicated ministry to handle the affairs of the port. This allowed matters, including budgets, permits, and regulations, to be handled within a single organization, avoiding excessively bureaucratic restrictions.

This case will continue at the end of the chapter.

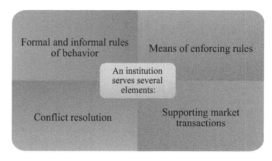

Figure 6.6 Institution elements

Source: https://techcrunch.com/2014/08/02/political-yield/ featured by Bryce Durbin.

Having a clear and developed governance structure and strong institutions will positively impact entrepreneurial initiatives. Unfortunately, many developing countries lack viable institutions and governance.

World Trade Report (2009) highlights that "institutions can create or destroy incentives for individuals to engage in trade and invest in human and physical capital, and engage innovation."[28] Thus, institutions have always played an essential role in governmental regulation, but their role has grown considerably since the fall of the former Soviet Union and the advent of globalization. In democratic societies, institutions are better developed and are mostly anchored towards good governance. However, in non-democratic societies, institutions are rigid, and the process of incentives for entrepreneurial actions is more selective and more dependent on an alignment with the dominant logic.

Governance definition

Governance is defined as the "processes of interaction and decision-making among the actors in an enterprise."[29] Denis and McConnell define corporate governance as a "set of mechanisms – both institutional and market-based – that induce the self-interested controllers of a company to make decisions that maximize the value of the company to its owners (the suppliers of capital)."[30]

Country governance, on the other hand, also plays an essential role in the development of an entrepreneurial ecosystem in any given country. Governance refers to all processes of governing that describe rules, laws, norms, and power that is applied by a government, market, family, tribe, or formal or informal organization.[32] A study by Omri (2020) advances the literature on how formal and informal entrepreneurship in emerging economies is linked to financial conditions and governance.[33] International organizations such as the International Monetary Fund (IMF) have become key watchdog organizations for the fight against corruption in different forms.[34] The IMF, through its powerful positions and policies, pressures countries to enact anticorruption policies and reduce corruption in areas such as the privatization of state-owned enterprises, etc.[35]

In the recent past, most governments encourage programs and policies which support the entrepreneurial spirit in the country. This trend is not new; it owes its origins to a report from 1979 by David Birch of MIT called "The Job Generation Process."[36] Most essential was the fact that job creation was coming more from small businesses than from large ones. Thus, entrepreneurship was claimed to be a trigger for economic growth and most of the governments worldwide started encouraging it, some sooner and others later.

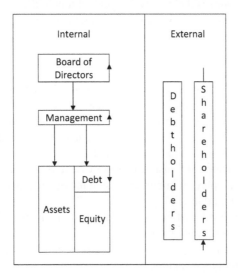

Figure 6.7 Corporate governance and the balance sheet model of the firm

Source: Adapted from PowerPoint slides accompanying Ross, S.A., Westerfield, R.W., & Jaffe, J. (2005). *Corporate Finance* (7th ed.). New York: McGraw-Hill Irwin; Jensen, M.C. (1993). The modern industrial revolution, exit, and the failure of internal control systems. *Journal of Finance*, 48, 831–880.

The board of directors, at the apex of internal control systems, is charged with advising and monitoring management and has the responsibility to hire, fire, and compensate the senior management team.[31] External governance arises from a firm's need to raise capital. Further, it highlights that in the publicly traded firm, a separation exists between capital providers and those who manage the capital. This separation creates the demand for corporate governance structures.

Nevertheless, creating a sustainable entrepreneurial ecosystem is more complex than it sounds. It demands close attention to a number of factors including the reform of the legal, bureaucratic, and regulatory frameworks. Such reforms require leadership by government institutions such as ministers who can support small businesses through their public policies. A bottom-up or top-down approach should be undertaken from already existing industries in the different countries. A single model of building a strong and sustainable entrepreneurial system could hardly be applied to a lot of countries, mainly due to their significant differences in culture, governance, and business trends. Therefore, a country's government overall plays an essential role in the growth and stability of a sustainable entrepreneurial ecosystem.

For instance, some of the means for the effective encouragement of entrepreneurship in a country by a government could be helping to sustain small firms, motivating a competitive culture, and alleviating unfair taxation on small firms.[37]

Democracies are traditionally seen as having the best level of governance for promoting development.[38] In the UN System Task Team on the Post-2015 UN Development Agenda, reference is made to democratic governance as "a process of creating and sustaining an environment for inclusive and responsive political processes and settlements."

The success of governance is defined by the goal, although there isn't a standard or point at which we can say that a country's governance is good; the success of governance is defined by whether the country reaches its desired outcomes.

- The entrepreneurial activities in a society will flourish under good governance and having relevant supporting institutions that make the rules and regulations.
- An institution is defined as the rules of the game that shape human interaction.
- Formal institutions (e.g., regulations, policies, and sanctions) and informal institutions (e.g., norms and values) need to be considered in development.
- Both country governance and institutions are essential sets of cultural and organizational regulations that play an important role in the development, growth, and success of entrepreneurial initiatives.
- Having a clear and developed governance structure and strong institutions will positively impact entrepreneurial initiatives.
- Governance within an enterprise can be described as the process of interaction and decision-making among key actors.

Governance: a micro perspective

Hufty (2011) describes governance as "the processes of interaction and decision-making among the actors involved in a collective problem solving that lead to the creation, reinforcement, or reproduction of social norms and institutions."[39] Denis and McConnell define corporate governance as a "set of mechanisms – both institutional and market-based – that induce the self-interested controllers of a company to make decisions that maximize the value of the company to its owners (the suppliers of capital)."[40] This definition differentiates between internal and external mechanisms of corporate governance by integrating the economy with the organization to guide the empirical investigation.[41] La Porta et al. (1997) have shown that the legal tradition (home country conditions and concentration of ownership) of a country impacts corporate governance.[42,43,44] Mallin et al. state that from a global perspective, corporate governance seems to be a 21st-century phenomenon which is supported by Stiglitz's view that "economic liberalization has outpaced political globalization and the globalization of our mindsets."[45]

Governance refers to the process of decision-making and implementation (and sometimes rejection). Analysis of governance focuses on understanding the formal and informal actors involved in decision-making and implementation of decisions. Governments are just one of the actors in governance; other actors include influential landlords, associations of peasant farmers, cooperatives, NGOs, research institutes, religious leaders, finance institutions, political parties, the military, etc., depending on the circumstances.

Nature and role of economic institutions

Institutions should:

Provide the "rules of the game" in economic life
Provide the underpinnings of a market economy

Include property rights and supervise contract enforcement
Work for the improvement of coordination among players
Restrict coercive, fraudulent, and anti-competitive behavior
Provide access to opportunities for the broad population
Constrain the power of elites and manage conflicts
Be providers of social insurance
Work towards a predictable macroeconomic stability.

Source: Rodrik (2008).[46]

Governance and entrepreneurship: a macro perspective

Governance refers to all processes of governing that are based on rules, laws, norms, and power applied by a government, market, family, tribe, and formal or informal organizations.[47] The impact country governance has on entrepreneurship in the current era of globalization has been explored and discussed in recent years. Nevertheless, some of the research results have shown a negative relationship between a country's level of governance and entrepreneurship, and some have found a positive one. The discrepancy in results between negative and positive studies is explained by Thai and Turkina.[48,49,50,51] The argument is that on one hand, studies proving negative relationships have used a general level of entrepreneurship data provided by the Global Entrepreneurship Monitor (GEM), which includes both formal and informal entrepreneurship. On the other hand, studies which show the positive relationship between the quality of governance and entrepreneurship are mostly based on variables using the number of registered businesses in a given country. In both cases, however, it could be established that the government plays an essential role in the creation of sustainable entrepreneurship. Therefore, the question becomes what could the government do in practice to encourage the entrepreneurial spirit? For example, Isenberg (2010) insists that governments should emphasize a few key points (illustrated in Table 6.1) in order to successfully encourage sustainable entrepreneurial ecosystems.[52]

Table 6.1 Government recommendations

Do	Do not
Use existing industries and build on their foundations, skills, and capabilities.	Assume one model applies to all strategies.
Encourage self-sustainable firms with strong root systems.	Flood the system with "easy money" (e.g., government grants, venture capital).
Encourage institutional entrepreneurs to act as managers for programs and policies regarding entrepreneurship.	Direct them towards only one specific industry (e.g., high-tech sector).
Ensure all industry sectors are influenced by the programs.	Treat entrepreneurship the same as small businesses. The policy for the first is "relational" and for the latter "transactional."

Figure 6.8 Economic institutions
Source: Brunosan.

Economic institution

Furthermore, Isenberg also puts forward recommendations for governments in encouraging the sustainable entrepreneurial ecosystem, which is in Table 6.1.

The main challenge for governments, in this case, would be to support the growing entrepreneurs without intervening too much in the business culture of the country. Contrary to Isenberg (2010),[53] who supports the claim that government efficiency cultivates entrepreneurship, Friedman (2011)[54] denies it. According to Friedman (2011), there is a negative relationship between the perception of government effectiveness and entrepreneurship on a country level. He reaches this conclusion after scrutinizing the six Worldwide Governance Indicators, developed by the World Bank Project, the GEM. Using descriptive statistics and Pearson correlations, he analyzes the results of 36 countries across the world and concludes that most of the entrepreneurs in these countries started their businesses not due to higher perceptions of opportunities offered by the external macro environment, but out of necessity.

Therefore, the macro environment (e.g., government efficiency) did not allure young entrepreneurs through being benevolent, but the nascent entrepreneurship was born as a result of the individual need for economic prosperity. In other words, most of the nascent entrepreneurs were motivated by the necessity created by the government or market failure to employ them properly. Friedman (2011) uses data from the Worldwide Governance Indicators to analyze the impact of the following variables:

• Voice and accountability
• Political stability and absence of violence
• Government effectiveness

- Regulatory quality
- Rule of law.

He concludes that countries with high governance effectiveness have less favorable attitudes towards entrepreneurship when compared to countries with less effective governance.[55] The finding might be due to the fact that countries with a higher GDP per capita had fewer entrepreneurial opportunities. High employment levels and individual job satisfaction could keep people distant from the idea of creating a new business. Also, the market in developed countries is well saturated in comparison to developing countries.

As a result, the motivation for starting a business in the developed countries would be decreased by the variety of businesses that already exist. Another explanation could be that well-developed countries have higher barriers for entry due to higher regulations and taxes. For instance, Denmark and Finland, which are among the developed countries with high WGI scores and heavy taxation, have lower levels of entrepreneurship when compared to countries such as Thailand or China, which have the lowest WGI scores in the study but reported higher levels of entrepreneurship due to their decreased level of taxation.

Groşanu et al. (2015) explored which characteristics of country-level governance most strongly influence the business environment and the entrepreneurship levels from a sample of 132 countries from around the world, using 792 observations in a 6-year period from 2007 to 2012. They have found that the government impacts the ease of doing business. As displayed in Table 6.2 the main premise here is that good quality governance in the country stimulates a well-developed and high ranked business environment with more entrepreneurial opportunities.[56]

Essentially, the macro factors most influencing the entrepreneurial framework are as follows:

- A 1-point increase in political stability would bring, on average, a 21.3 percent increase in Entrepreneurship (Density).
- A 1-point increase in regulatory quality would bring a 34.4 percent increase in Entrepreneurship (Density).
- A 1 percent increase in income (GNI) per capita would bring about a 0.5 percent increase in Entrepreneurship (Density).

From the earlier study, we can conclude that well-established property rights institutions and market-friendly government policies are an essential framework for the sustainable development of entrepreneurship. A 1-point increase in political stability would bring, on average, a

Table 6.2 Macro factors that impact entrepreneurial activities

Factors	Coefficient	p-value	95% confidence interval	
			Lower limit	Upper limit
Constant	−4.492	<0.001	−6.073	−2.912
Political stability	0.213	0.001	0.088	0.337
Regulatory quality	0.344	0.001	0.142	0.546
Income (log of GNI)	0.518	<0.001	−6.073	−2.912
$R^2=0.51$				

Note: Dependent variable: Entrepreneurship (Density).
Panel data: 95 countries and 6 years 2007–2012 (GLS estimates).

Source: Groşanu, A., Boţa-Avram, C., Răchişan, P.R., Vesselinov, R., & Tiron-Tudor, A. (2015). The influence of country-level governance on business environment and entrepreneurship: a global perspective. *Amfiteatrur Economic*, 17(38), 60–75.

21.3 percent increase in entrepreneurship, and a 1-point increase in regulatory quality would bring a 34.4 percent increase. A 1-point increase in income (GNI) per capita would result in about a 0.5 percent increase. Other characteristics that good country governance should have in order to attract new businesses include accountability, transparency, and the rule of law. These are the foundations of good governance and thus, economic growth and entrepreneurial development.[57,58]

In either case, it is clear that the government's role is essential. In one case, if it is efficient enough it will encourage the sustainable development of entrepreneurship, and in the other case, it will spark it through its own failure. Developing countries would experience more difficulties

Figure 6.9 Iraqi center

Source: Richie Diesterheft.

in sustaining good levels of entrepreneurship if the government is not transparent and fair as investors would be discouraged.

Moreover, entrepreneurs are even more afflicted by high levels of corruption and ineffective regulatory frameworks, as compared to multinational corporations, because of their lack of bargaining power vis-à-vis the bureaucracy. This could explain the reasons for low levels of entrepreneurship in transitioning and developing countries.

Therefore economic development, a stable political environment, and the capacity of governments to promote and implement business-friendly regulations are all macro factors which are greatly related to a higher level of entrepreneurship and the stimulation and encouragement of the private sector. Therefore entrepreneurship, when measured in terms of new registrations and entry rates, is highly affected and positively correlated with the quality of government and economic growth.[59,60] Scholars Rodrik and Melo stated that numerous links and interdependencies between politics, institutions, and a country's history are highly important to the business environment and entrepreneurial activity.[61,62]

3D printed hand at RiTS

Aim of the Iraqi Entrepreneurship Center

At the website "Bite.tech," the CEO of RiTS, Aziz Alnassiri, talks about reasons for the current economic stagnation in Iraq. Given the lack of funds available, he believes that entrepreneurship is the only means of increasing economic activities. He suggests that a massive number of entrepreneurial projects be initiated, incubated, and supported through a network of organizations dedicated to the cause of successful startups.

He writes about how RiTS, an Iraqi entrepreneurial company, has spent most of 2016 establishing Iraq's first incubator dedicated to the graduates of Al Mansour University College. It has also established Iraq's first crowdsourcing gathering, which is currently hosted on LinkedIn. It plans shortly to go on the air as an independent self-contained resource that brings together Iraqi entrepreneurs and experienced professionals from around the world to combine their efforts, knowledge, and money to support new start-ups in Iraq. This initiative has already led to two new ventures being established. A new division within RiTS produces 3D printed mechanical prosthetic hands for Iraqi disabled children. Further, RiTS proposes to take the Iraqi entrepreneurship to the next level by expanding to other areas of technology and also establishing an international presence.

Source: Alnassiri (2017).[63]

Furthermore, the macro perspective of corporate governance has a historical connotation as it originates not from the rational choices and reforms, but is rather a product of historical processes that have occurred in the past in relation to politics, society, law, and economics.[64]

Governance: good and bad

Let's examine what constitutes good and bad governance in order to better understand the operational framework entrepreneurship that could exist in transitioning, developing, and developed countries. Every country has to have a set of good governance to operate regardless of its degree

Figure 6.10 Gears

of efficiency and responsiveness. Good governance promotes community, gives confidence to elected members, leads to better decisions, and supports ethical decision-making. But what happens when lax and ineffective governance leads to corruption, cash transfers, and abused power?

This is the case of most of the economically "transitioning" Eastern European countries. They usually have a lower level of entrepreneurship activities than in most developed and developing countries due to government incompetence and many other issues including corruption.

Even if countries performing well on the entrepreneurial level, a change in the corruption level could influence them positively or negatively.[65]

Good governance comes with addressing many issues at both macro and micro levels and is concerned with the transparency and long-term well-being of its citizens. Good governance should also be efficient. If it takes too much time and/or funding, the public sector and the citizens may lose interest and sight of the direction the intervention is supposed to be taking the country in. For these reasons, it is crucial that governance finds the crucial balance between good, efficient, and fair.

However, much like ethics, there are some basic principles that successful governance must have. First, it is fundamental to have transparent linkages between the public and private sectors, delivery and ease of access to public services, and the implementation of citizens' views when making critical decisions. In addition to this linkage, goals have to be developed in line with the key factors of a developing country, which include education, finance, and health. The second basic principle of good, successful governance is its judicial efforts, everything from implementing the law, implementing equality before the law, electoral integrity, and freedom of expression both for the media and citizens, among many other democratic concepts. Although democratic governance has some soft and doubtful spots, and despite being seen as the universally superior form of governance, a developing country should strive for a democratic government. This will allow for freedom of expression and decisions and a connection with transparent accountable institutions which support each other and help promote development.

This kind of governance brings success to those in power and politics since resources are priced and allocated to those in politics, and the leader always has to have eyes and ears everywhere due to the probable rise of patrons looking to either revolt or slowly take the leader out of power. Although the allocation of resources for the government is good politics, it is disastrous for the people and the economy of the country since it leaves patrons resourceless, usually in poverty, and basically without the right to anything.

The private sector will mostly be used for services, instead of the public sector, which means the country will not have money to get out of the hole they have been dug into.

The IMF classifies 51 countries as "resource-rich." These are countries which derive at least 20 percent of exports or 20 percent of fiscal revenue from nonrenewable natural resources. Common characteristics of 29 of these countries include (1) extreme dependence on resource wealth for fiscal revenues, export sales, or both; (2) low savings rates; (3) poor growth performance; and (4) highly volatile resource revenues.

Source: Venables (2016).[66]

Bad governance is created when resources, income, and political power have no correlation and are distributed unfairly. To improve governance, we first must identify the main issue that is the basis of the problem and why these problems slow down development, especially in poor, resource-rich countries, often also called "resource-cursed" countries.[67,68] These are countries that are rich in terms of natural resources but fall short when it comes to standard of living and overall economic level. Thus, bad governance, in this case, leads to poverty, inequality, and deprivation. There are more than 20 countries, especially in the Middle East, that derive a significant amount of their exports from oil and gas but are not real democracies.

Hence, the accountability of the government to its citizens is diminished, leading to increased levels of corruption and an enormous economic discrepancy between the social clusters of society. Instead of taxes and social benefits, the governments of such countries usually tend to facilitate corruption and "patronage networks."

Another factor contributing to the "curse" of rich natural resources is the proclivity to social violence it brings with itself. In combination with bad governance, the consequences and results are highly visible in oil-rich countries.[69] What can be done? Recently, a number of organizations and institutions worldwide started trying to combat the so-called curse.

For instance, the Extractive Industries Transparency Initiative is trying to improve revenue management in about 30 resource-rich countries. The Open Government Partnership objectives are to fight corruption by securing tangible national plans against it.[70] Nevertheless, due to the fact that most of them are voluntarily based, no accountability or enforceability is incorporated. On a global level, members of organizations such as the Group of Eight (G8) and the Group of Twenty (G20) meet annually to discuss further remedies for the minimization of corruption and the support of democratic transparency which will contribute to the accountability in business and governance, thus attempting to transform the "curse" to a "blessing."[71,72] It is not surprising that non-governmental actors are the ones taking over the role of good governance to help these countries.

Nevertheless, instead of completely reforming governance we should focus on the exact problem governance has so it is more effective, and the change can occur quicker; for example, if the problem is corruption, an anti-corruption agency might help. Directly and gradually reforming some aspects of governance such as formal institutions – private or public – or property rights could result in dysfunctional, ineffective, and perhaps even counterproductive measures to some countries.

The reforms should be undertaken incrementally and over the long run in order to be effective. Overall, for a reform change to be effective, changes in institutions need to be complemented by changes in de facto political power. Improved governance occurs when the costs and benefits of different stakeholders and the relevant institutions are changed and, therefore, will impact their action. For example, the World Bank intervened in policies and policymaking.[73]

Although democracies are seen as the basis of good governance, Scandinavian countries such as Norway and Sweden strive to achieve good governance with a socialist government style, which proves the point that any government style can be effective; all that is necessary is the backing of citizens and the appropriate allocation of resources. The Nordic model of governance has proved to be effective and efficient for all stakeholders.

On the other hand, dictatorships in South Korea and Taiwan evolved through good governance and democracy. Socialism in Scandinavian countries is also seen as good governance, as it promotes equality for its citizens. Most systems of government can evolve with good governance, if rule of laws is dominating and there is a representative government.

Globalization and governance

Globalization has caused national governments to think and act globally, and it is making it hard for some governments to operate under secrecy.[74] Governments need to adjust to a new normal which is a more transparent system of governance. International pressure and the desire of citizens of developing countries to reach the quality and living standards of developed nations are forcing many governments to go through a major transformation.

The national governments are losing their influence and power in decision-making to non-state actors due to innovation in technology and communication. The role of national governments is crucial for development because of their macro position. Some countries in Asia (e.g., Singapore and South Korea) play an active role in advancing the education and evaluation of relevant institutions and governance, including the creation of opportunities for entrepreneurial activities. Supporting good governance, rule of law, and transparency is a necessary condition for sustainable development. Hassan et al. used panel data to "analyze the effect of competitiveness, governance and globalization on poverty in case of 73 developing countries from 2005 to 2016." The estimated results "confirmed that all governance indicators have a negative impact on poverty. Similarly, globalization, competitiveness and development expenditures also assist in poverty alleviation."[75]

Large-scale and accelerated growth has rendered the statist model of governance unviable and encouraged the emergence of polycentric regulations, however the state remains crucial in this new polycentric regulation because although globalization has led to the empowerment of non-state actors such as multinational corporations, non-governmental organizations, and transnational activist network states remain the primary actors for handling social and political externalities created by globalization. Powerful states will use a range of foreign policy substitutes to advance their desired preferences into their desired outcomes. Globalization undercuts state sovereignty and weakens governments' ability to effectively regulate their domestic affairs.

- Governments are just one of the actors in governance; other actors include influential landlords, associations of peasant farmers, cooperatives, NGOs, research institutes, religious leaders, finance institutions, political parties, the military, and so on.
- Well-established property rights institutions and market-friendly government policies form an essential framework for sustainable development of entrepreneurship.
- Entrepreneurs are even more afflicted by high levels of corruption and ineffective regulatory frameworks compared to multinational corporations.
- When performing well on the entrepreneurial level, a change in corruption level could influence entrepreneurs positively or negatively.
- Good governance comes with addressing many issues at both macro and micro levels and is concerned with the transparency and long-term well-being of its citizens.

As state power has waned, globalization has simultaneously enhanced the power of non-state actors (i.e., multinational corporations, or MNCs). [76] The impact of globalization on national and local governments is clear, and the issue of decentralization and evolving institutions has become significantly important. There are different degrees of citizen participation in the political process in most developed and developing countries. It appears that the globalization impact on undemocratic systems of government has been significant; it is questioning the existence of their system of government.

However, in countries with a democratic system of government, the question concerns the degree of government participation in economic and social issues, which essentially deals with reallocation of resources. Finally, given the shifts in the power of national governments, the question is how these decentralized institutions will evolve and are able to operate and serve the interest of citizens.

Globalization has significantly impacted the way that nations are managed. It is becoming harder for countries to set policies without consulting with other nations and being considerate of the impact of its policies. Therefore, some governments have lost their influence in providing a "conventional" model of governance. This is changing the traditional structure of governance and is being distributed in new and different manners. Some scholars argue that in order for us to become more globalized, voters and citizens need to start thinking globally rather than locally.[77] In this process, governance and institutions should converge to some form of similarity. Nevertheless, when local services are not being provided, it may cause citizens to start rejecting the idea of globalization and may resist the move towards globalization. The example of Greece is a unique and obvious one.

The most recent example is the national referendum in the United Kingdom (Brexit, 2016), in which 51.9 percent of the British people have decided that they prefer not to be part of the European Union, the economic and social union of Europe, thus making the UK the first to leave the EU in 2019. By breaking its formal relationship with the union, the UK will replace the existing EU laws with UK domestic laws. This is one of the first bold steps against globalization.

There are three main themes that need to be highlighted regarding the transformation of governance and the role of government in the globalization era: globalization, devolution, and the role of government. These three themes have transformed the role of government in two ways: (1) they have strained the traditional role of all players and (2) a new era has challenged the capacity of governments and their non-governmental partners to deliver high-quality public services. Globalization has decreased the effectiveness of individual governments' policies and procedures as governments see themselves responsible for their citizens and are considerate of them on an international level. In addition, the creation of international organizations and institutions such as the World Trade Organization (WTO), the UN, and NGOs have also risen to power and have been offering some services better than some local governments. As a result, governments are losing their ability to act alone and have less control in their decision-making.[78]

UK NGOs could miss out on €140 million ($150 million) of funding a year from the European Union as a result of Brexit, according to new research by Bond, the UK NGO network.

Source: Edwards (2017).[79]

Figure 6.11 Brexit
Source: muffinn.

When the leaders of a nation, developed or underdeveloped, recognize governance as a possible aid to the struggling economy, it becomes necessary to determine how much is the right amount. With a high level of intervention, there will be ample controls to keep growth on track and remove the threat of corruption in profitable industries. Good governance can protect those who are less privileged while keeping the playing field level and preventing the wealthiest from suppressing the growth of those beneath them. Nonetheless, it is apparent from the arguments made earlier in this chapter that a given level of governance is not only necessary but beneficial for the country as a whole.

Determining what the proper level is comes down to balance, changing traditional approaches, and receiving buy-in. There is a balance that needs to occur when determining the level of governance for each nation, developed or not, in order to ensure that the internal interests of the nation are preserved. When the nation is attempting to achieve an effective level of governance, it is not uncommon for them to focus only on the economic and political plights and opportunities within the nation itself. While focusing solely on the needs of one's own nation could yield the quickest results when the level of governance is heightened, it can be extremely difficult to implement that kind of change based solely on the struggles of the developing nation. Simply put, the nation has been struggling for some time economically or politically, so it would be difficult to use solely internal resources to implement a change in governance. For the advancement of globalization, emerging or emerged economies should assist developing countries in this process. This resistance to external help from successful nations, while it will preserve the goals and resources of the nation itself, will make it extremely difficult to foster relationships with foreign institutions that can not only help the developing country but could be allies when it comes time to trade or expand economically. It is for that reason that some help can go a long way when trying to improve the economic status of an entire nation.

Oftentimes, when a developing nation is looking to make significant changes, they turn to a developed nation for assistance. This assistance most often comes from foreign institutions that are designed to help developing nations with this sort of improvement (i.e., WTO, World Bank) or from successful foreign entities.[80] With several benefits to this strategy, including heightened resources, expertise, and information, reaching to developed institutions for help may yield positive outcomes.

The investment logic for sustainability

Sustainability is pretty clearly one of the world's most important goals, but what groups can really make environmental progress in leaps and bounds? Chris McKnett makes the case that it is large institutional investors. He shows how strong financial data isn't enough, and reveals why investors need to look at a company's environmental, social, and governance structures, too. Learn more in the full TED Talk at www.ted.com/talks/kirsty_duncan_scientists_must_be_free_to_learn_to_speak_and_to_challenge

---

Krasner (2015) recognizes the shortcomings of high levels of governance by noting that leaders seeking rapid economic growth or drastic political intervention often "have no interest in sustaining accountable governance."[81] The quick fix for governance could yield great payoffs at the onset, but in the long run it is not invested in sustainable growth of the nation. Respecting the way in which the country operated traditionally and utilizing governance to improve those traditional methods will create the greatest chance for successful change. Additionally, those leaders seeking a quick fix that will exploit the resources of a developing nation are poised to corrupt the political system in the process of growing the economic one. Traditionally, countries that focus solely on one system but neglect the other are subject not only to corruption but also to an economy that becomes cutthroat and relies on the greediness of the haves and the complacency of the have-nots. The economic agenda of a country must align with the political ideals in order for long-term success to be possible, and it is the role of governance to bring that alignment into perspective.[82]

Transparency International (TI) has published the Corruption Perceptions Index (CPI) since 1996, annually ranking countries on perceived levels of corruption. The CPI currently ranks 176 countries "on a scale from 100 (very clean) to 0 (highly corrupt)."

Source: Transparency International (2016).[83]

Figure 6.12 Corruption
Source: https://ccPixs.com.

Newig et al. (2016) describe governance as learning to update beliefs based on evidence, experience, and additional information. They note that participation in the planning for intervention helps to shape the design and eventual effectiveness of the intervention plan. It should be noted that the aforementioned authors specifically discussed the installation of flood risk planning, but the principles and ideology hold true for a larger-scale situation.[84]

Borrowing from the authors' analysis, buy-in is easiest to achieve when those in power are transparent. Transparency around the need for governance within a nation and transparency around the desired results of that governance are what the different groups requiring buy-in will need to be equipped with in order to get on board for the change. Achieving nationwide buy-in includes having targeted objectives. And with knowledge comes the ability to discuss what will be needed and what can wait for later.

Economic development and entrepreneurship

The economic development of a country is in relation to well-developed institutions that contribute to increased levels of entrepreneurial activity.[85] Porter and his colleagues illustrate competitiveness in accordance with a given country's economic development by differentiating between three specific stages: the factor-driven stage, the efficiency-driven stage, and the innovation-driven stage.[86,87]

Factor-driven stage

Countries in this stage of economic activity have based their competitive advantage on low-cost efficiencies in the production of commodities or low value–added products. Almost all economies go through this phase where neither innovation knowledge nor use knowledge is exploited.[88]

Efficiency-driven stage

Countries in this stage usually increase their production efficiency and, furthermore, educate their workforce labor to be accustomed to applying new technologies and adapting to the globalized environment. In order for competition to exist on this stage, countries must have efficient production and manufacturing practices on large markets, thus allowing companies to exploit economies of scale. This economic stage is typically marked by low levels of entrepreneurial activity due to the increasing returns to wage work. Therefore, people are more willing to move from self-employment to wage employment. As when an economy becomes richer, the average firm size usually increases as well, leaving enough room for labor expansion and diminished levels of nascent entrepreneurship. In other words, this stage of the economy encourages individuals to join an already existing profitable business than to create their own. Thus, contrary to conventional wisdom, the more developed an economy becomes, fewer individuals are pursuing self-employment opportunities.

Innovation-driven stage

This stage of economic development encompasses an increase in entrepreneurial activity. It is characterized by a decrease in the share of manufacturing in the economy and an increase in technological development and globalization. Technological advancements have directly affected the entrepreneurial environment throughout the world, making it both less expensive and less time-consuming for geographically and physically separate individuals to exchange information and work together.

Although most developed countries are in the innovation-driven stage, most developing economies (e.g., Brazil, Russia, India, China) are still in the efficiency-driven stage where manufacturing and exporting is what drives the economy.

Figure 6.13 Asunción

Source: Image by Tetsumo on flickr.

Moreover, as innovation is important for competition in foreign markets, developed countries usually are better integrated globally than developing countries. Thus, it is essential for economies to move into the innovation-driven stage in order to develop the necessary environmental conditions conducive to entrepreneurship. Some of the countries that have already achieved this transition include Korea, Ireland, Israel, and Taiwan.[89]

Incubator of companies in the National University of Asunción: INCUNA

In 2009, the companies' incubator called INCUNA was created and managed by the National University of Asunción–UNA, in the Paraguayan capital. The incubator emerged with the need to support university entrepreneurs and undergraduates with the interest to undertake entrepreneurships. Its mission is focused on technology-based ventures in an attempt to minimize their errors and failures. The INCUNA has captured business ideas among university students and supported the formation of innovative technology-based companies, applying management tools to ensure the sustainability of projects. Its main objectives are to create an entrepreneurial culture within the academic environment, promote development throughout the country, and form groups and productive chains to improve the regional economy. With the target audience within the university itself, it opens up opportunities for academic jobs if they become successful companies.

A business and entrepreneurial environment is highly determined by the interdependencies between economic development and institutions which could impact other country governmental characteristics such as:

- Quality of governance
- Access to capital and other resources
- Perceptions of entrepreneurs.

Thus, institutions could be accepted as critical to the overall setting of economic behavior and transactions as they can impose both direct and indirect effects on the supply as well as the demand of entrepreneurs in a given country. Figure 6.14 illustrates the Nascent Entrepreneurship Rate for 2015, according to the Global Entrepreneurship Monitor.[90]

- Transparent linkages between the public and private sectors, delivery and ease of access to public services, and the implementation of citizens' views when making critical decisions, as well as a principle of good, successful governance in its judicial efforts, are some of the basic principles to achieve successful governance.
- Governments need to adjust to a new normal that is a more transparent system of governance.
- The impact of globalization on national and local governments is clear, and the issue of decentralization and evolving institutions has become significantly important.
- Globalization has significantly impacted the way that nations are managed.
- There are three main themes that need to be highlighted regarding the transformation of governance and the role of government in the globalization era: globalization, devolution, and the role of government.

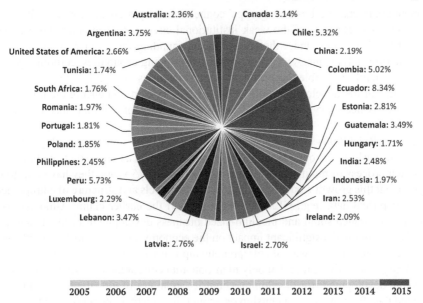

Australia: 2.36%
Canada: 3.14%
Argentina: 3.75%
Chile: 5.32%
United States of America: 2.66%
China: 2.19%
Tunisia: 1.74%
Colombia: 5.02%
South Africa: 1.76%
Ecuador: 8.34%
Romania: 1.97%
Estonia: 2.81%
Portugal: 1.81%
Guatemala: 3.49%
Poland: 1.85%
Hungary: 1.71%
Philippines: 2.45%
India: 2.48%
Peru: 5.73%
Indonesia: 1.97%
Luxembourg: 2.29%
Iran: 2.53%
Lebanon: 3.47%
Ireland: 2.09%
Latvia: 2.76%
Israel: 2.70%

2005 2006 2007 2008 2009 2010 2011 2012 2013 2014 2015

Figure 6.14 Countries percentages

Corporate governance and institutions in developing economies

Development and advancement of governance are necessary conditions for a flourishing entrepreneurial atmosphere. Some scholars have argued that developing economies are using economic liberalization as their primary engine for economic growth and that institutional theory has become the predominant theory for examining management.[91,92] Others have argued that institutions affect organizational routines and help frame the strategic choices facing organizations.[93,94,95,96,97]

In other words, institutions help determine the firm's course of actions and, therefore, determine the outcomes and effectiveness of the organization. The institutions that influence organizational actions in developing economies are not stable and developed, so that will impact the actions of firms.

Additionally, the existing formal institutions often do not promote mutually beneficial impersonal exchanges between economic actors.[98] Therefore, organizations in developing economies are to a greater extent guided by informal institutions.[99] For example, in the case of corporate governance, most developing economies do not have a clear and effective rule of law which, in turn, creates a "weak governance" condition.[100,101]

Most developing economies have laws dealing with corporate governance, but those laws are not as clear and enforced as in developed economies. Some developing economies have tried to adopt legal frameworks of developed economies, in particular, those of the Anglo-American system, either as a result of internally driven reforms or as a response to international market demands. In the existing formal institutions, enforcement is either absent, inefficient, or does not operate as intended with laws and regulations regarding accounting requirements, information disclosure, and securities trading.

Therefore, standard corporate governance mechanisms have relatively little institutional support in most developing economies.[102,103] Thus, informal institutions such as family connections, government contracts, and business groups' connections play a greater role in influencing corporate governance. Because of the weak institutional environment in emerging economies, it is common for firms to be under the control of the founding family or retain control through other (often informal) means. As a result, in most developing economies, corporate governance structures frequently resemble those of developed economies in form but not in substance. We can conclude that the development of institutions that support and ensure the implementation of governance is necessary, especially if the aim is to advocate and advance entrepreneurial activities.

Koster and Rai (2008) created a model that predicts that entrepreneurship levels would decrease in the early stages of economic development based on a case study from India. As India has been in a process of rapid economic growth for the last 15 years, they have questioned the assumption that this growth would have an effect on the levels and structure of entrepreneurship. However, empirical data (e.g., GEM) does not support the earlier claim. Although economic growth has encouraged small and medium-sized business development in India, entrepreneurship levels have not had a significant impact on the economy of the country. Nevertheless, they also note that a more formal way of entrepreneurship is not (yet) noticeable in India.[104]

Thus it might actually be true that only high-potential entrepreneurship has a positive impact on economic development for developing countries in an era of globalization.[105] Prieger et al. investigated the effect of entrepreneurship on economic growth, concluding that less developed countries have more small businesses than wealthier countries. This idea is somehow confusing, as their empirical evidence also shows that low- and middle-income countries do not have increased levels of entrepreneurship; there are three possible reasons for this controversy:[106]

- Economic growth in less developed countries might require even more entrepreneurship.
- Other factors might be influencing the impact of entrepreneurship on growth.
- Less developed countries might be encouraging entrepreneurship of a negative kind.

Furthermore, Prieger et al. (2016) advise policymakers in less developed countries to be more responsive to the changing roles of entrepreneurs and overall environment; for instance, through the encouragement of a new formation of businesses with high potential and growth.[107]

Strategy

A strategy can be defined as "the creation of a unique and valuable position, involving a different set of activities." A strategic position arises from "three distinct sources: the work of deciding which target group of customers and needs to serve requires discipline, the ability to set limits, and forthright communication." Of course, strategy and leadership are strongly linked and require making competing choices of what to do and what not to do to have a competitive advantage. Leadership and strategy play an even more important role for an entrepreneur than for a large company. These issues even become more critical in developing countries than in developed countries.[108]

To be able to develop and implement successful strategy it does require viable institutions and good governance. These concepts are established and advanced in most developed countries, thus leading to a higher level of prosperity and transparency in these societies. These sets of micro and macro factors re-enforce each other in creating a well-functioning and transparent advanced society.

Some developing nations are able to revise the rules of the game in the direction of strengthening its governance and institutions, which would lead to an increase in its productive capacity.[109] Unfortunately, many developing countries are ending up being led by a strongman, a dynasty, a family, or other non-democratic forms where democratic institutions and values are undermined. The self-interest of the leadership of these countries does not permit the development of quality institutions, transparent governance, and the rule of law.

These issues are essential for the development of entrepreneurial activities that require clear and transparent rules of law – that define rewards and penalties – and their enforcement. The success rates among startups in developing countries are much lower than in developed countries due to the absence of good governance and appropriate institutions. Holding everything constant, there is a continual entrepreneurial brain drain from developing countries (e.g., India, China, Iran) to developed countries for some of the same reasons. In most developing countries, there are very few successful examples of private companies that have grown to become mature, multinational, and multigenerational. Most large multinational companies from developing countries tend to be supported by their government (e.g., Petrobras, Brazil; Aramco, Saudi Arabia).

- Innovation is important for competition in foreign markets, with developed countries usually better integrated globally than developing countries.
- There are three distinct stages to a given country's economic development: the factor-driven stage, the efficiency-driven stage, and the innovation-driven stage.
- Institutions help determine firm courses of action and therefore determine the outcomes and effectiveness of organizations.
- Development of institutions that support and ensure implementation of governance is necessary, especially if the aim is to advocate and advance entrepreneurial activities.
- In most developing countries, there are very few successful examples of private companies that have grown to become mature, multinational, and multigenerational.

Covi (2016) explores strategies for coping with globalization through an analysis of the "new competitive framework" small and medium-sized enterprises are operating in. He further introduces the concept of "complete productive process" to describe the environmental factors influencing innovation and entrepreneurship in the era of globalization. Moreover, Covi recognizes "local systems" as "cognitive systems" which need to embrace globalization not individually but rather as one comprehensive system. The main prerequisite is "collective and cooperative behavior" which is embodied by the concept of "collective local entrepreneurship."[110]

A recent report by the Organisation for Economic Co-operation and Development (OECD) concludes that some of the most important factors influencing the creation and sustainability of competitive advantage are as follows:

Knowledge networks and innovation are essential features in modern competitive regional economies. This has been recognized over the years and more formal approaches have been developed to encourage the networking and the spread of innovation.[111]

Just as Porter has established, competitive advantage development is highly dependent on the specific details, the "know-how," and the feeling of belonging to a particular space. As the business environment is affected differently in every country by politics, culture, and legal systems, it is not surprising that different countries would need different strategies for the encouragement of nascent entrepreneurship and small and medium-sized businesses.[112]

Covi further emphasizes the benefit of incremental innovation in comparison to radical innovation, which encompasses the fact that small and medium-sized firms do not have the needed resources to perform a radical innovation. The opposite process has been labeled as "creative destruction" by Schumpeter. Thus, Covi proposes the idea of "local collective entrepreneurship," which would allow for small firms and entrepreneurs to compete in the framework of globalization. Globalization has created an entrepreneurial strategy which is based on the possession of technical and organizational knowledge, well-developed learning ability, and human capital.

Nonaka and Takeuchi (1995) have long concluded that "knowledge is the most important strategic factor of production"; thus, managers should aim at its production, acquisition, movement, retention, and most of all, application.[113] Arrow (1994) has argued that in the current globalized world, it is more important to possess technical knowledge than to own goods.[114] Covi (2016) has furthermore discussed the sources of competitive advantage through the perspective of different schools of thought (see Figure 6.15).

Covi (2016) claims that the global economy of the world nowadays is mainly based on different competitive systems and competitive advantages, meaning that there is no one "best way" or strategy to organize the industrial operations in the different countries and economies as their competitive advantages are intangible and significantly marked by their past.

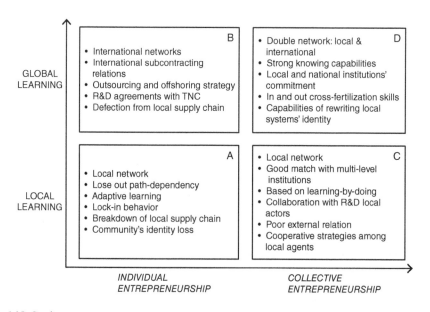

Figure 6.15 Covi strategy

Source: Covi, G. (2016). Local systems' strategies copying with globalization: Collective local entrepreneurship. *Journal of the Knowledge Economy*, 7(2), 513–525. https://doi.org/10.1007/s13132-014-0225-4

For instance, the rapid technological development of the century has allowed for globalization to offer easier access to new production at the transnational level. However, this is not a strategy for success as it does not contribute towards the decrease of the growth rates among the countries and regional economies. In other words, it does not provide for an equal or same model apply-to-all strategy. Knowledge and skill sets are in the foundation of entrepreneurship; the different levels of local government directly impact entrepreneurial levels in the country. For instance, local, national, regional, and municipal governments impact the learning skills of people on a local level, thus directly contributing or harming the country on a macro level.

Covi (2016) proposes the strategy as shown in Figure 6.15.

In Figure 6.15, Case A depicts a situation in which a local system, under the influence of the competitive forces of globalization, has broken its connections to the local supply chain in order to go global. Unless applied to avoid a lock-in situation, this kind of a business action could be regarded as harmful to the sense of identity of the community.

Case B illustrates a situation in which the entrepreneurs had a breakthrough, which has helped them escape Case A. They have gained access to an international subcontracting chain and international network.

Case C shows the struggles endured by mature and well-structured local clusters when competing with global markets.

Case D represents "a short list of ingredients for success," as Covi (2016) calls it (see Figure 6.15). Moreover, he argues that the main purpose here would be to possess the capabilities and the resources to "rewrite the identity" of their territory. Thus, he claims that it is essential for the cluster to provide a double network on a local and international level.

Conclusion

In sum, globalization has had positive effects on the governance and institutions of some developing countries. Traditional forms of governments are no longer effective in light of globalization, where there is the higher focus in governance and institutions in theory and practice.[115] Globalization has caused national governments to think and act globally; however, it also causes these governments to become less effective in providing governance. As a result, institutions and other non-state actors have come to fill in this gap.

The result of this can either help countries to develop further, like some Asian countries, or to fall behind, like most Middle Eastern and Latin American countries. What has been effective thus far is a balance between representative governments and the relevant institutions to help deliver good governance. It seems that globalization has had more influences on governance at the micro level, such as corporate governance. In some developing economies, corporate governance is evolving more towards the Anglo-American model which is more transparent and generally has good governance.

An important component of rule of law and by-products of good governance has a positive impact on entrepreneurial activities. A combination of good governance and institutions with thoughtful strategies will lead to sustainable development. A democratic system empowers its citizens to engage in building institutions, which enhances development. This allows for the voices of many to be incorporated into the government and governance and thus incorporate stakeholders' interest. Many developing countries' governments need to support and create space so institutions and good governance are developed. Of course, without the active participation of citizens, this will not be achieved.

Discussion questions

1 Why is understanding the definitions of institutions, governance, and strategy important?
2 Why is having appropriate institutions and governance essential for advancing entrepreneur-ial activities?
3 Is a well-functioning business environment an indication for good institutions?
4 Compare and contrast a few developed and developing countries from the perspective of institutions, governance, and entrepreneurial activities.
5 Compare and contrast the strategies of a few enterprises from developed and developing countries.
6 Write a short case that applies at least two important topics in this chapter.

Macro governance efforts

Within the confines of the port area, port-based businesses are given a grace period during which they are exempt from import tariffs, making importation of goods more affordable and enabling businesses to take advantage of the port's services.

Unlike most Moroccan business, which is conducted in French, the maritime business is in English. This is an important consideration as the port's strategic geographical loca-tion positions it to do business with companies around the world.

In conclusion, and based on the earlier case studies, there are several identifiable trends related to innovation. The culture of the countries in which the company resides, the way that employees at the companies are educated, and the innovative processes of the company all greatly influence the way that innovation is realized with the evaluated companies.

Questions

1 What is the degree of public versus private management and ownership of ports and its affected organization in developed and developing countries?
2 Does this kind of public ownership lead to sustainable and multilayered employment?
3 What type of employment is this, skilled or unskilled?

Table 6.3 Key terms

Institution	Factor-driven stage
Governance	Efficiency-driven stage
Global Entrepreneurship Monitor (GEM)	Innovation-driven stage
Resource-cursed countries	

Table 6.4 Glossary

Institution	Is defined as the rules of the game that shape human interaction.
Governance	The processes of interaction and decision-making among the actors in an enterprise.
Global Entrepreneurship Monitor (GEM)	Is a research program that aims to provide insights into the state of entrepreneurship and entrepreneurial activity worldwide.

Resource-cursed countries	Is a term used to describe countries that are rich in natural resources, such as oil, gas, minerals, and timber, but are plagued by economic underdevelopment, political instability, and social unrest.
Factor-driven stage	The first stage of economic development in a country when factors drive development.
Efficiency-driven stage	In the second stage of economic development, economic efficiency is the driver.
Innovation-driven stage	In the final stage of economic development, innovation is the driver.

Notes

1 Jozi, A. (2015). 15 challenges of Iran's startup ecosystem. *Techrasa*. Retrieved from https://techrasa.com/2015/12/25/15-challenges-of-irans-startup-ecosystem/
2 North, D.C. (1990). *Institutions, Institutional Change, and Economic Performance*. New York: Cambridge University Press. https://doi.org/10.1017/CBO9780511808678
3 World Trade Organization. (2009). *World Trade Report 2004: Governance and Institutions*.
4 Rodrik, D. (2007). *One Economics, Many Recipes: Globalization, Institutions, and Economic Growth*. Princeton University Press. Retrieved from https://press.princeton.edu/titles/8494.html
5 Estrin, S., & Mickiewicz, T. (2011). Entrepreneurship in transition economies: The role of institutions and generational change. *The Dynamics of Entrepreneurship*, 181–208. https://doi.org/10.1093/acprof:oso/9780199580866.003.0009
6 Baumol, W.J. (1990). Entrepreneurship: Productive, unproductive, and destructive. *Journal of Political Economy*, 98(1), 893–921. https://doi.org/10.2307/2937617
7 McMillan, J. (1999). Dispute prevention without courts in Vietnam. *Journal of Law, Economics, and Organization*, 15(3), 637–658. https://doi.org/10.1093/jleo/15.3.637
8 McMillan, J., & Woodruff, C. (2002). The central role of entrepreneurs in transition economies. *Journal of Economic Perspectives*, 16(3), 153–170. https://doi.org/10.1257/089533002760278767
9 He, J., & Tian, X. (2020). Institutions and innovation. *Annual Review of Financial Economics*, 12, 377–398.
10 Bosma, N., Sanders, M., & Stam, E. (2018). Institutions, entrepreneurship, and economic growth in Europe. *Small Business Economics*, 51(2), 483–499.
11 Chemin, M. (2009). The impact of the judiciary on entrepreneurship: Evaluation of Pakistan's "Access to Justice Programme." *Journal of Public Economics*, 93(1–2), 114–125. https://doi.org/10.1016/j.jpubeco.2008.05.005
12 De Soto, H. (2000). *The Mystery of Capital*. New York: Basic Books.
13 Djankov, S., LaPorta, R., Lopez-de-Silanes, F., & Shleifer, A. (2002). The regulation of entry. *Quarterly Journal of Economics*, 117(1), 1–37.
14 Sobel, R.S. (2008). Entrepreneurship. In D.R. Henderson (Ed.), *The Concise Encyclopedia of Economics*. Indianapolis: Liberty Fund.
15 Estrin, S., & Mickiewicz, T. (2011). Entrepreneurship in transition economies: The role of institutions and generational change. *The Dynamics of Entrepreneurship*, 181–208. https://doi.org/10.1093/acprof:oso/9780199580866.003.0009
16 Aidis, R., Estrin, S., & Mickiewicz, T. (2009). Entrepreneurial entry: Which institutions matter? *CEPR Discussion Paper No. DP7278*. Retrieved from https://papers.ssrn.com/sol3/papers.cfm?abstract_id=1405075
17 Acemoglu, D., & Johnson, S. (2005). Unbundling institutions. *Journal of Political Economy*, 113(5), 949–995. https://doi.org/10.1086/432166
18 Botero, J., Djankov, S., LaPorta, R., López-de-Silanes, F., & Shleifer, A. (2004). The regulation of labor. *Quarterly Journal of Economics*, 119(4), 1339–1382.
19 Deeg, R., & Jackson, G. (2007). Towards a more dynamic theory of capitalist variety. *Socio-Economic Review*, 5(1), 149–180.
20 Melo, L. (2015). *Firm-Level Corporate Governance in the Context of Emerging Market Firm Internationalization*, Bentley University, PhD Dissertation.
21 Adekoya, R. (2014). How the EU transformed Poland. *The Guardian*. Retrieved from www.theguardian.com/commentisfree/2014/may/01/eu-poland-10-years-economic

22 Estrin, S., & Mickiewicz, T. (2011). Entrepreneurship in transition economies: The role of institutions and generational change. *The Dynamics of Entrepreneurship*, 181–208. https://doi.org/10.1093/acprof:oso/9780199580866.003.0009

23 Sztompka, P. (1996). Looking back: The year 1989 as a cultural and civilizational break. *Communist and Post-Communist Studies*, 29(2), 115–129. https://doi.org/10.1016/S0967-067X(96)80001-8

24 Lin, J.Y., & Nugent, J.B. (1995). Institutions and economic development. In J. Behrman, & T.N. Srinivasan (Eds.), *Handbook of Development Economics* (Vol. 3A, pp. 2301–2370). New York, North Holland: Elsevier Science.

25 Hodgson, G.M. (2006). What are institutions? *Journal of Economic Issues*, 40(1), 1–25.

26 North, D.C. (1995). The new institutional economics and third world development. In J. Haapiseva-Hunter, C.M. Lewis, & J. Harriss (Eds.), *The New Institutional Economics and Third World Development* (p. 360). Oxfordshire: Routledge.

27 Díez-Martín, F., Blanco-González, A., & Prado-Román, C. (2016). Explaining nation-wide differences in entrepreneurial activity: A legitimacy perspective. *International Entrepreneurship and Management Journal*, 12(4), 1079–1102. https://doi.org/10.1007/s11365-015-0381-4

28 World Trade Organization. (2009). *World Trade Report 2004: Governance and Institutions*. Geneva.

29 www.igi-global.com/dictionary/governance/12372

30 Denis, D.K., & McConnell, J.J. (2003). International corporate governance. *The Journal of Financial and Quantitative Analysis*, 38(1), 1. https://doi.org/10.2307/4126762

31 Jensen, M.C. (1993, January 5–7). The modern industrial revolution, exit, and the failure of internal control systems. *The Journal of Finance*, 48(3), Papers and Proceedings of the Fifty-Third Annual Meeting of the American Finance Association: Anaheim, California.

32 Melo, L. (2015). *Firm-Level Corporate Governance in the Context of Emerging Market Firm Internationalization*, Bentley University, PhD Dissertation.

33 Omri, A. (2020). Formal versus informal entrepreneurship in emerging economies: The roles of governance and the financial sector. *Journal of Business Research*, 108, 277–290.

34 Addink, H. (2019). *Good Governance: Concept and Context*. Oxford University Press.

35 Reinsberg, B., Stubbs, T., Kentikelenis, A., & King, L. (2020). Bad governance: How privatization increases corruption in the developing world. *Regulation & Governance*, 14(4), 698–717.

36 Mazzarol, T. (2014, April 11). Does it matter if Australia no longer manufactures things? *Enterprise Society: The Conversation*.

37 Mazzarol, T. (2014). How do Australia's universities engage with entrepreneurship and small business? *CEMI Discussion Paper No. DP1401*. Centre for Entrepreneurial Management and Innovation.

38 Sen, A. (1999). *Development as Freedom*. Oxford: Oxford University Press.

39 Hufty, M. (2011). Investigating policy processes: The governance analytical framework (GAF). In U. Wiesmann, H. Hurni et al. (Eds.), *Research for Sustainable Development: Foundations, Experiences, and Perspectives* (pp. 403–424). Bern: Geographica Bernensia.

40 Denis, D., & McConnell, J. (2003, March). International corporate governance. *Journal of Financial and Quantitative Analysis*, 38(1), 1–36, 5.

41 Melo, L. (2015). *Firm-Level Corporate Governance in the Context of Emerging Market Firm Internationalization*, Bentley University, PhD Dissertation.

42 La Porta, R., Lopez-de-Silanes, F., Shleifer, A., & Vishny, R.W. (1997). Legal determinants of external finance. *The Journal of Finance*, 52(3), 1131–1150. https://doi.org/10.1111/j.1540-6261.1997.tb02727.x

43 La Porta, R., Lopez-de-Silanes, F., Shleifer, A., & Vishny, R.W. (1998). Law and finance. *Journal of Political Economy*, 106(6), 1113–1155. https://doi.org/10.1086/250042

44 La Porta, R., Lopez-De-Silanes, F., & Shleifer, A. (1999). Corporate ownership around the world. *The Journal of Finance*, 54(2), 471–517. https://doi.org/10.1111/0022-1082.00115

45 Mallin, C., Michelon, G., & Raggi, D. (2013). Monitoring intensity and stakeholders' orientation: How does governance affect social and environmental disclosure? *Journal of Business Ethics*, 114(1), 29–43. https://doi.org/10.1007/s10551-012-1324-4

46 Rodrik, D. (2008). *One Economics Many Recipes: Globalization, Institutions, and Economic Growth*. New Jersey: Princeton University Press.

47 Melo, L. (2015). *Firm-Level Corporate Governance in the Context of Emerging Market Firm Internationalization*, Bentley University, PhD Dissertation.

48 Thai, M.T.T., & Turkina, E. (2014). Macro-level determinants of formal entrepreneurship versus informal entrepreneurship. *Journal of Business Venturing*, 29(4), 490–510. https://doi.org/10.1016/j.jbusvent.2013.07.005

49 Friedman, B.A. (2011). The relationship between governance effectiveness and entrepreneurship. *International Journal of Humanities and Social Science*, 1(17), 221–225.

50 Isenberg, D. (2016). The big idea: How to start an entrepreneurial revolution. *Harvard Business Review*. Harvard Business School Publishing, June 2010. Retrieved from https://hbr.org/2010/06/the-big-idea-how-to-start-an-entrepreneurial-revolution

51 Groşanu, A., Boţa-Avram, C., Răchişan, P.R., Vesselinov, R., & Tiron-Tudor, A. (2015). The influence of country-level governance on business environment and entrepreneurship: A global perspective. *Amfiteatrur Economic*, 17(38), 60–75.

52 Isenberg, D. (2010). The big idea: How to start an entrepreneurial revolution. *Harvard Business Review*. Harvard Business School Publishing, June 2010. Retrieved from https://hbr.org/2010/06/the-big-idea-how-to-start-an-entrepreneurial-revolution

53 Isenberg, D. (2010). The big idea: How to start an entrepreneurial revolution. *Harvard Business Review*. Harvard Business School Publishing, June 2010. Retrieved from https://hbr.org/2010/06/the-big-idea-how-to-start-an-entrepreneurial-revolution

54 Friedman, B.A. (2011). The relationship between governance effectiveness and entrepreneurship. *International Journal of Humanities and Social Science*, 1(17), 221–225.

55 Friedman, B.A. (2011). The relationship between governance effectiveness and entrepreneurship. *International Journal of Humanities and Social Science*, 1(17), 221–225.

56 Groşanu, A., Boţa-Avram, C., Răchişan, P.R., Vesselinov, R., & Tiron-Tudor, A. (2015). The influence of country-level governance on business environment and entrepreneurship: A global perspective. *Amfiteatrur Economic*, 17(38), 60–75.

57 Rodrik, D. (2008). *One Economics Many Recipes: Globalization, Institutions, and Economic Growth*. New Jersey: Princeton University Press.

58 Groşanu, A., Boţa-Avram, C., Răchişan, P.R., Vesselinov, R., & Tiron-Tudor, A. (2015). The influence of country-level governance on business environment and entrepreneurship: A global perspective. *Amfiteatrur Economic*, 17(38), 60–75.

59 Brander, J., Hendricks, K., Amit, R., & Whistler, D. (1998, July). *The Engine of Growth Hypothesis: On the Relationship between Firm Size and Employment Growth Work*. Washington: University of British Columbia, Department of Economics. Manuscript.

60 Klapper, L., & Quesada Delgado, J.M. (2007). *Understanding Entrepreneurship: Influences and Consequences of Business Creation*. New Jersey: World Bank Viewpoint.

61 Rodrik, D. (2008). *One Economics Many Recipes: Globalization, Institutions, and Economic Growth*. Waltham: Princeton University Press.

62 Melo, L. (2015). *Firm-Level Corporate Governance in the Context of Emerging Market Firm Internationalization*, Bentley University, PhD Dissertation.

63 Alnassiri, A. (2017). *Iraqi Entrepreneurship Center*. Retrieved from www.bite.tech/news/iraqi-entrepreneurship-center

64 Morck, R., Shleifer, A., & Vishny, R.W. (1988). Management ownership and market valuation: An empirical analysis. *Journal of Financial Economics*, 20, 293–315.

65 Avnimelech, G., & Zelekha, Y. (2011). The impact of corruption on entrepreneurship. international business ethics and growth opportunities. *IGI Global*, 282–294. October 2008. Web. October 3, 2016. http://link.springer.com/article/10.1007%2Fs11187-008-9135-9

66 Venables, A.J. (2016, February). Using natural resources for development: Why has it proven so difficult? *Journal of Economic Perspectives*, 30(1), 161–184. https://doi.org/10.1257/jep.30.1.161

67 Stiglitz, J. (2008). The $3 trillion war. *New Perspectives Quarterly*, 25(2), 61–64. https://doi.org/10.1111/j.1540-5842.2008.00980.x

68 Farooqi, H., & Asgary, N.H. (2016). Natural resources and economic development: The case of Afghanistan. *CYRUS Chronicle Journal*, 1(1), 38–48. https://doi.org/10.21902/2573-5691/2016.v1i1.5

69 Asgary, N. (2016). Role of institutions in sustainable and socially equitable development. *CYRUS Chronicle Journal: Contemporary Economic and Management Studies in Asia and Africa*, 1(1).

70 Other such institutions include "Publish What You Pay" and the World Bank–sponsored Stolen Asset Recovery (StAR) Initiative.

71 Lawson-Remer, T. (2012). *Beating the Resource Curse: Global Governance Strategies for Democracy and Economic Development*. New York: Council on Foreign Relations.

72 Lechner, R. (2009, March 10). The seven pillars of a "green" corporate strategy. *Environmental Leader*. Retrieved November 15, 2014, from www.environmentalleader.com/2009/03/10/the-seven-pillars-of-a-greencorporate-strategy.

73 Baland, J.-M., Moene, K.O., & Robinson, J.A. (2009). Governance and development. In *Handbook of Development Economics* (Vol. 5, pp. 4597–4656). Waltham. https://doi.org/10.1016/B978-0-444-52944-2.00007-0

74 Asgary, N. (2016). Role of institutions in sustainable and socially equitable development. *CYRUS Chronicle Journal: Contemporary Economic and Management Studies in Asia and Africa, MA*, 1(1).

75 Hassan, M.S., Bukhari, S., & Arshed, N. (2020). Competitiveness, governance and globalization: What matters for poverty alleviation? *Environment, Development and Sustainability*, 22(4), 3491–3518.

76 Drezner, D.W. (2001). Globalization and policy convergence. *International Studies Review*, 3(1), 53–78.

77 Stiglitz, J.E. (2006). *Stability With Growth: Macroeconomics, Liberalization and Development*. Oxford: Oxford University Press.

78 Kettl, D.F. (2000). The transformation of governance: Globalization, devolution, and the role of government. *Public Administration Review*.

79 Edwards, S. (2017, April 4). *140 Million Euros of EU Funding a Year at Risk for UK NGOs after Brexit*. Retrieved December 16, 2018, from www.devex.com/news/140-million-euros-of-eu-funding-a-year-at-risk-for-uk-ngos-after-brexit-89932

80 The Nation. (2013, February 22). The World's Political and Economic Landscape is Undergoing Major Adjustments and Changes. Although Some Progress Has Been Made in the Reform of Global Economic Governance, the Financial Crisis is Not Yet Behind Us and the Structural Problems Exposed by Th. Thailand Edition ed. China Daily, Asia News Network. Web. December 10, 2015.

81 Krasner, D. (2015). *Why We Aren't Winning Wars*. Retrieved from www.ohio.com/akron/editorial/stephen-d-krasner-why-we-aren-t-winning-wars

82 Ragab, A. (2016, September 15). *Why Does Corruption Exist?* Retrieved December 16, 2018, from www.linkedin.com/pulse/why-does-corruption-exist-alaa-ragab?articleId=6182106880798662656

83 Transparency International. (2016). Retrieved August 14, 2017, from https://en.wikipedia.org/wiki/Transparency_International

84 Newig, J., Kochskämper, E., Challies, E., & Jager, N.W. (2016). Exploring governance learning: How policymakers draw on evidence, experience and intuition in designing participatory flood risk planning. *Environmental Science & Policy*, 55, 353–360. https://doi.org/10.1016/j.envsci.2015.07.020

85 Acs, Z.J., Desai, S., & Hessels, J. (2008). Entrepreneurship, economic development and institutions. *Small Business Economics*, 31(3), 219–234. https://doi.org/10.1007/s11187-008-9135-9

86 Porter, M.E. (1990). *The Competitive Advantage of Nations*. London: Macmillan.

87 Porter, M., Sachs, J., & McArthur, J. (2002). Executive summary: Competitiveness and stages of economic development. In M. Porter, J. Sachs, P.K. Cornelius, J.W. McArthur, & K. Schwab (Eds.), *The Global Competitiveness Report 2001*.

88 Acs, Z.J., Desai, S., & Hessels, J. (2008). Entrepreneurship, economic development, and institutions. *Small Business Economics*, 31(3), 219–234.

89 Acs, Z.J., & Szerb, L. (2006). Entrepreneurship, economic growth and public policy. *Small Business Economics*, 28(2–3), 109–122. https://doi.org/10.1007/s11187-006-9012-3

90 Nascent phase entrepreneurship levels: Source: Global Entrepreneurship Monitor – Adult Population Survey Measures (2015).

91 Hoskisson, R.E., Eden, L., Lau, C.M., & Wright, M. (2000). Strategy in emerging economies. *Academy of Management Journal*, 43(3), 249–267. https://doi.org/10.2307/1556394

92 Wright, M., Filatotchev, I., Hoskisson, R.E., & Peng, M.W. (2005). Strategy research in emerging economies: Challenging the conventional wisdom – introduction. *Journal of Management Studies*, 42(1), 1–33. https://doi.org/10.1111/j.1467-6486.2005.00487.x

93 Carruthers, B.G., Hollingsworth, J.R., & Boyer, R. (1998). Contemporary capitalism: The embeddedness of institutions. *Contemporary Sociology*. New York: Cambridge University Press. https://doi.org/10.2307/2655178

94 Feldman, M.S., & Rafaeli, A. (2002). Organizational routines as sources of connections and understandings. *Journal of Management Studies*, 39(3), 309–331. https://doi.org/10.1111/1467-6486.00294

95 Peng, M.W. (2003). Institutional transitions and strategic choices. *Academy of Management Review*, 28(2), 275–296. https://doi.org/10.5465/AMR.2003.9416341

96 Peng, M.W., Lee, S.H., & Wang, D.Y.L. (2005, July 1). What determines the scope of the firm over time? A focus on institutional relatedness. *Academy of Management Review*. Academy of Management. https://doi.org/10.5465/AMR.2005.17293731

97 Powell, W.W. (1991). Expanding the scope of institutional analysis. In *The New Institutionalism in Organizational Analysis* (pp. 183–203). Chicago: The University of Chicago Press. Retrieved from http://ci.nii.ac.jp/naid/10030010601/

98 North, D.C. (1994). Economic performance through time. *The American Economic Review*, 84(3), 359–368. https://doi.org/10.2307/2118057

99 Peng, M.W., & Heath, P.S. (1996). The growth of the firm in planned economies in transition: Institutions, organizations, and strategic choice. *Academy of Management Review*, 21(2), 492–528. https://doi.org/10.5465/AMR.1996.9605060220

100 Zahra, S.A., Dharwadkar, R., & George, G. (2000, May, August). Entrepreneurship in multinational subsidiaries: The effects of corporate and local environmental contexts. In *Published in Conference Proceedings, Entrepreneurship* (Vol. 2130, pp. 4–9). Toronto, Canada: Academy of Management.

101 Mitton, T. (2002). A cross-firm analysis of the impact of corporate governance on the East Asian financial crisis. *Journal of Financial Economics*, 64(2), 215–241. https://doi.org/10.1016/S0304-405X(02)00076-4

102 Peng, M.W. (2004). Institutional transitions and strategic choice (Vol. 28, p. 278, 2003). *Academy of Management Review*, 29(3), 278.

103 Peng, M.W., Buck, T., & Filatotchev, I. (2003). Do outside directors and new managers help improve firm performance? An exploratory study in Russian privatization. *Journal of World Business*, 38(4), 348–360. https://doi.org/10.1016/j.jwb.2003.08.020

104 Koster, S., & Rai, S.K. (2008). Entrepreneurship and economic development in a developing country: A case study of India. *Journal of Entrepreneurship*, 17(2), 117–137.

105 Wong, T.A. et al. (2005). Membrane metabolism mediated by Sec14 family members' influences Arf GTPase activating protein activity for transport from the trans-Golgi. *Proceedings of the National Academy of Sciences, USA*, 102(36), 12777–12782.

106 Prieger, J.E., Bampoky, C., Blanco, L.R., & Liu, A. (2016). Economic growth and the optimal level of entrepreneurship. *World Development*, 82, 95–109. https://doi.org/10.1016/j.worlddev.2016.01.013

107 Prieger, J.E., Bampoky, C., Blanco, L.R., & Liu, A. (2016). Economic growth and the optimal level of entrepreneurship. *World Development*, 82, 95–109. https://doi.org/10.1016/j.worlddev.2016.01.013

108 Porter, M. (1996). What is strategy? *Harvard Business Review*, 74(6), 61–78.

109 Rodrik, D. (2007). *One Economics, Many Recipes: Globalization, Institutions, and Economic Growth*. Princeton University Press. Retrieved from https://press.princeton.edu/titles/8494.html

110 Covi, G. (2016). Local systems' strategies copying with globalization: Collective local entrepreneurship. *Journal of the Knowledge Economy*, 7(2), 513–525. https://doi.org/10.1007/s13132-014-0225-4

111 Innovation, Higher Education and Research for Development. (2012). *Research Universities: Networking the Knowledge Economy*. Retrieved from www.oecd.org/sti/Session%205_Networking%20the%20Knowledge%20Economy.pdf

112 Covi, G. (2016). Local systems' strategies copying with globalization: Collective local entrepreneurship. *Journal of the Knowledge Economy*, 7(2), 513–525. https://doi.org/10.1007/s13132-014-0225-4

113 Nonaka, I., & Takeuchi, H. (1995). *The Knowledge-Creating Company: How Japanese Companies Create the Dynamics of Innovation*. New York: Oxford University Press.

114 Arrow, K. (1994). Methodological individualism and social knowledge. *The American Economic Review*, 84(2), 1–9. Retrieved from www.jstor.org/stable/2117792

115 Melo, L. (2015). *Firm-Level Corporate Governance in the Context of Emerging Market Firm Internationalization*, Bentley University, PhD Dissertation.

7 Ethics and corporate social responsibility

Learning objectives

1 Understand the definition of ethics in business and some of the relevant theories
2 Comprehend some of the theories related to corporate social responsibility (CSR)
3 Realize the difference between CSR and environmental, social, and governance practices of enterprises
4 Evaluate the impact of CSR on entrepreneurship and competitiveness
5 Discuss the relationship between CSR, human resource management, and strategy.

Introduction

In this chapter, basic definitions like ethics, corporate social responsibility (CSR), environmental, social, and governance (ESG) practices, and human resource management (HRM) and their implications for businesses and entrepreneurial activities in the era of globalization will be presented. The ethical conceptions of virtue, caring, and justice are crucial for enterprises operating in a global environment, which could be evidenced by the practices in organizations. This issue is a societal demand reinforced by government acts and social control mechanisms. Discussions on globalization are oftentimes shaped by nationalized interests which also includes ethical decision-making processes. Organizations can, therefore, succeed in any environment providing that decision makers make an effort to adhere to standards that are moral, fair, caring, and just. Every unethical behavior should be condemned. There will also be a discussion of the role of communications and technology in providing the instruments that improve transparency and good governance. We will discuss how CSR and CSE (corporate social entrepreneurship) are related and examine how they work together, such as in hybrid organizations. We will also look at the fundamental connection between CSR and HRM. Finally, we will cover various topics, such as social entrepreneurship, competitive advantage, and the triple bottom line, related to the effective managerial application of CSR/ESG practices. Some considerations about ethics and HRM/business adaptation due to the COVID-19 pandemic will close this chapter.

Cryptocurrencies, like Bitcoin, are trending. They are spread in the financial market and on the internet, and those who invested in or mined Bitcoin early are sitting on small fortunes. The concept of easy money is always tempting.

As in every entrepreneurial project, one of the primary requisites is to have a legal team on staff to ensure continuous compliance. The second is venture capital; startups sometimes fail to prepare for the future, resulting in modest first raises that may cover development costs but deprive the business of the vital operating capital required until they achieve profitability. Besides, in the case of cryptocurrency, optimum security practices are mandatory, such as offline

DOI: 10.4324/9781003405740-11

Figure 7.1 Bitcoin – BTC
Source: www.flickr.com/photos/105644709@N08/10307527573

cold storage wallets, two-factor authentication, and encrypted databases, since cryptocurrencies are now a prime target for hacking and fraud. However, business ethics is the most crucial feature of successful and long-time entrepreneurship.

Box 7.1   Brazil's "Bitcoin King" arrested over 7000 missing BTC: who was the thief?

In Brazil, a startup cryptocurrency entrepreneur deceived justice and clients in a billionaire fraud scheme. Cláudio José de Oliveira, known as the "Brazilian King of Bitcoin," was convicted in 2022 by the federal court for embezzlement and crimes against the national financial system. The judge determined a sentence of 8 years and 6 months in prison in a closed regime, in addition to paying a fine.

Oliveira described himself as a successful businessman with European relatives and heir to fortunes, a description still used today. When he opened Bitcoin Banco, he even claimed that he obtained a PhD in financial engineering in Switzerland. Everywhere he went, Oliveira, with "advanced deceit techniques," sought to relate to wealthy people (or influencers) and convince them to hand over money.

Bitcoin Banco Group (BBG) reportedly lured investors with promises of exorbitant daily returns. But, according to police, alarm bells began ringing early in 2019 when the platform started blocking withdrawal requests. After this, the alleged fraudster's crypto brokerage filed for bankruptcy, claiming to have been the victim of a hack. At the time, the values of all creditors were blocked by the company.

As the investigations progressed and with the lack of cooperation from the company owner, the civil police, and the public ministry suspected that the cyber-attack was fake and that the group had committed crimes, such as embezzlement.

After denouncing the alleged cyber-attack, the suspected group promised creditors that it would return the blocked amounts in installments. Despite this, according to the PF (Federal Bureau of Investigation), the amounts were never settled.

The 1st Court of Bankruptcy and Judicial Recovery of Curitiba (capital of the Brazilian state Paraná) decreed the bankruptcy of the companies that make up the Bitcoin Banco Group in 2021. In the same week, the group's owner, Oliveira, was arrested for fraud in negotiations that simulated the buying and selling of cryptocurrencies.

Later, investigations showed that the group used this court order to stop the civil cases the company was responding to. During the process, according to the federal police agents consulted, the group provided false information and deceived the judiciary. While applying for judicial recovery, Bitcoin Banco Group allegedly continued to conduct business as usual, and it failed to comply with its responsibilities to the bankruptcy court, including neglecting to pay creditors. Even after not being registered with the Brazilian Securities Commission, the platform launched "public collective investment contracts" to attract new users.

The investigation into Bitcoin Banco Group, dubbed "Operation Daemon," found that investors' funds had been "diverted according to the interests of the criminal organization leader."

A leaked tax return from 2018 showed that Oliveira had then claimed 25,000 BTC, a Lamborghini, and 14 Brazilian properties among his assets.

The "Bitcoin King" is accused of committing billionaire fraud of R$1.5 billion (roughly $300 million) in cryptocurrency trading simulations. According to investigations, around 7000 people were victims of a scam carried out by brokerages controlled by him (one of them declared a loss of almost R$1 million in 4 months of investment), and the "Bitcoin King" has already claimed victims in Switzerland, Portugal, and the United States: Oliveira is being investigated for crimes such as embezzlement, crime against the popular economy and money laundering.

The alleged fraudster's crypto brokerage filed for bankruptcy in 2019 after claiming to have been the victim of a hack.

Questions for discussion: BBG's case

1 It is well known that Mr. Oliveira had previous convictions in other countries (Switzerland and United States). So what do you expect to learn about a startup or an entrepreneur's past before lending them money?
2 Imagine yourself as a social media influencer engaged in a startup promotion in which unethical behavior is suddenly discovered. What will be your public version of the facts?
3 Financial pyramids are operations that depend on new people joining in sustaining the earnings of the first ones. But at some point, the cycle will break as it becomes unsustainable. What is the lesson learned with cryptocurrencies?

4 In Brazil, there is a regulation agency for cryptocurrencies – the Associação Brasileira de Cryptoeconomia (ABCripto) – which is responsible for the market's self-regulation in the country. There are rules that must be followed by member companies, such as preventing money laundering and reporting suspicious activities to Coaf. Before investing in cryptos, it is worth checking if the company you are looking for is associated with ABCripto. But, if your country does not have an organization with a database, what do you suggest for an investor to increase confidence in the operator?

It is common sense that in entrepreneurial activity, money is always necessary, but be wary of excessive profits offered in the financial market

If the promise of profit is unreliable, exorbitant gains should also be viewed with reservations. When you find an operator that sells cryptocurrencies with ads like "Up to 1000% return in X time," it is prudent to turn on the warning signal. It is even possible to get rich with cryptocurrencies, but caution is fundamental.

Theories of ethics and management implications

Ethics is a widely used term and is synonymous to a moral code, morals, morality, values, rights and wrongs, principles, ideals, standards (of behavior), value systems, virtues, and dictates of conscience. Therefore, it is not easy to define ethics clearly and concisely because they may have different meaning and understanding by different stakeholders, locally and globally. Simply put, ethics is the behavior that is concerned with "ought" and "ought not." It extends above and beyond the standards set forth by the law or those which are commercially profitable.

Integrating theoretical ethics with practical decision-making is a major challenge for academics and practitioners of organization and management. The complexity of business environments urges responsible and conscientious decision-making processes in organizational management domestically and globally. In this sense, ethical decision-making in an organization is derived from applying ethical theories to practical dilemmas from the top down and that predominant decision-making paradigms require more than a single ethical theory.[1,2]

In literature, the theories on ethics and management have evolved into two parallel streams. Theories of management have been discussed mainly by management scientists, practitioners, economists, and business administrators whose primary concerns remain economic efficiency, organizational effectiveness, and product or service innovation. Some scholars have discussed it in virtual isolation from the ethical implications of management decisions.[3,4] This mechanistic approach expects managers and employees to follow ethics policies and procedures without having a logical justification for why ethical behavior is essential, beneficial, or desirable.

On the other hand, theories of ethics have been studied by social scientists and philosophers who explain ethics in abstract terms such as "axios," "deontos," or "teleos," with little attention to the practical implications for organizations.[5,6] In other studies, models of ethics have been proposed and key components of ethical behavior were identified for MNCs in isolation from the conceptual foundations of ethics or management.[7] Cultural relativism indicates how morals and ethics changed over time and among different cultures, but some believe that what makes the difference is how each society practices those values.[8]

Theories of ethics such as deontology and utilitarianism have been utilized for performing ethical behavior in organizations.[9,10,11,12] However, these efforts are scattered and have a glaring gap in business ethics literature when considering the relationship between the acclaimed frame-works of ethics and dominant theories of management.

Table 7.1 summarizes the main theories of ethics and their implications for business management.[13]

Table 7.1 Main theories of ethics and their implications for business management

Theory	Definition/characteristics	Implications for businesses
Axiological ethics "Axiä" (Greek) – *"Value"/"Worth"*	The science of determining the value of an idea or object for an individual or organization. It differentiates between "instrumental" values or what is good as a means, and "intrinsic" value" which is what is good as an end.	Actions are right or wrong based on their intrinsic goodness regardless of their economic consequences. It emphasizes the inherent happiness of the stakeholders generated from the decisions made by employees or managers.
Teleological ethics **"Virtue ethics"** "Teleos" (Greek) – *"brought to its end or purpose"*	Considers an action proper or improper according to the desirability of its outcome. Actions are right and justified if the consequences are good regardless of the intentions and means of achieving the action. Served as basis for the "utilitarianism" of the 19th century.	Main objective of ethical action is to achieve an appropriate and advantageous end or goal. Considers an action good if it promotes the greatest happiness possible in economic terms and treats human beings as economic creatures (homoeconomics).
Deontological ethics "Deontos" (Greek) – *"that which is obligatory"*	Focuses on the obligations and duties that various members of society have towards one another. The Kantian version of deontological ethics dictates that these duties could be determined by a rational process called the "categorical imperative" – a universal principle of ethics regardless of individual interests, organizational objectives, or economic consequences.	According to Kantian deontology which subordinates individual interest to higher principles, the ultimate purpose of being for business organizations becomes the development of rational and moral capabilities of the organization's stakeholders, not the maximization of profits or stockholder's equity.[14]
Perfectionist ethics	Concerned with the application of principles of moral perfectionism to ethical conduct of individuals and organizations. Expects individuals to live and promote lives that are objectively good.	Dimensions of perfections have been defined, and rationality in decision-making has been identified as one of them.[15]
Utilitarian ethics *"The greatest happiness principle"*	Based on the premise that moral worth of an action depends entirely on its contribution to overall perceivable utility for society. Thus, the highest objective of ethical conduct is to maximize the utility of the outcome of an action in terms of happiness, pleasure, or some other satisfaction of desired objectives.	"The greatest good for the greatest number of people." Suitable for business decision-making in that it provides a sound economic basis for testing the efficacy of ethical decisions, clearly identifies the stakeholders, and provides an objective approach to conflict resolution in decision-making.[16]

Theory	Definition/characteristics	Implications for businesses
Existentialist ethics	Human freedom is the foundation of the understanding of all motives, reason, morals, and values.[17] Key features include freedom of choice, subjectivity of human experience, and values, which are seen as consequences and not determinants of human moral decisions and choice.[18]	The requirement of individuals' awareness of freedom and responsibility to distinguish between choices makes existentialism a highly individualistic ethical doctrine.
Naturalistic ethics	Based on British empiricism, which implies that all knowledge is derived from experience and sensory perception.	Suggests that true propositions of ethics are derived from objective features of nature independent of any moral judgement, opinions, or subjective values. Highly applicable in tourism and hospitality industries.[19]
Relativistic ethics	Ethical behavior cannot be defined or prescribed in universally applicable absolute terms. An action can be considered "ethical" in one set of social, cultural, and individual circumstances and "unethical" in a different set of circumstances.	The requirement of giving fair wages while employing fewer workers can be justified on ethical grounds in an economy where there is a better balance between the demand and availability of workers. On the other hand, in countries such as India, where the oversupply of labor is chronic, this choice may not be very ethical.

Source: Authors.

The classic approach of ethical decision-making in business advises applying an initial set of principles to a particular problem and attempting to instinctively balance them if they collide. Nevertheless, in the lack of law enforcement, behaving ethically could be challenging when unexpected outcomes with substantial financial damage occur.

Box 7.2   Africrypt and South Africa's most significant financial robbery

As cryptocurrency startups are being created worldwide, some similar outcomes for Brazilian BBG investors are happening in other countries. For example, in South Africa it was discovered in 2021 that $3.6 billion in Bitcoin and the founders of a South African cryptocurrency investment firm were missing. Africrypt's loss would rank among the biggest-ever crypto heists.[20]

An essential issue in this context is the lack of a regulatory framework for digital assets in South Africa, which does not view cryptocurrencies as a financial instrument, limiting the government's ability to supervise (and investigate) the matter and the user to check the investment's safety (although it is always relative). Digital currencies are assets that vary freely based on supply and demand. No central bank, ministry of finance, exchange rate policy, or other mechanisms provide predictability.

Africrypt vanished along with 69,000 bitcoins, estimated to be worth $3.6 billion, and its creators, the brothers Ameer (age 20) and Raees Cajee (age 17) in 2021.

Investors in Africrypt received an email in April of that year informing them that the platform was freezing all accounts and closing down due to a hack that had exposed their wallets and personal data. Also, investors were encouraged to refrain from informing law enforcement about the hack because the founders believed this would impede the restoration process (i.e., reporting the alleged hack to the police might delay getting their money back).

The founders allegedly transferred the pooled investor cash from Johannesburg's First National Bank (FNB) account, but they headed to the United Kingdom shortly after the claimed hack. Moreover, the Cajee brothers reportedly shut down Africrypt's website after the accounts were frozen and did not return investors' calls.

The alleged crime has been reported to the Hawks, a specialty division of the South African police force that deals with organized and economic crime. It is not a surprise that in 2022 the country's financial regulator was planning to unveil a framework covering cryptocurrencies to help protect vulnerable members of society.

According to Chainalysis's "2021 Crypto Crime Report,"[21] the incident occurred shortly after the South African Mirror Trading International (MTI) cryptocurrency scam robbed investors of approximately $589 million. Of course, cryptocurrency scams are nothing new, but Africrypt might be the biggest in recent memory.

In 2022, a mystery benefactor emerged to repay some of the lost cash, even though a group of investors started the process of liquidating Africrypt and are pushing for the brothers to be charged with fraud, theft, and possibly money laundering. Furthermore, they can get 10–15 years for a first-time offense.

The Africrypt fallout has highlighted the lack of scrutiny over the country's burgeoning crypto industry, so the South African financial watchdog intends to put cryptocurrency exchanges under regulatory control. Remember, a watchdog can be an individual or group that monitors the activities of another entity (e.g., an individual, corporation, nonprofit group, or governmental organization) on behalf of the public to ensure that entity does not behave illegally or unethically.

Nevertheless, their sentencing could lead founders to be more careful about what they do or advertise to investors in the future because ethics and business should walk together.

Questions for discussion: ethics in business

1 In your opinion, what were the positive aspects of this startup considering the South African entrepreneurial environment?
2 If everyone gets their money back (other help from the anonymous benefactor), do you think the case against Africrypt could be closed?
3 What are the limitations in South Africa to investigate the Cajee brothers that could happen in your country?
4 Identify some similarities and differences between Brazilian and South African BTC cases.

Ethics and business discipline

The social responsibility movement of the 1960s gave rise to what is now known as the management discipline of business ethics. The concept of business ethics emerged from this movement as doing what is suitable for the company's stakeholders. This phrase, frequently used to define ethics, is known as corporate social responsibility (CSR).[22, 23] Although it deals with different categories or levels of economic, legal, and discretionary activity, CSR also relates to the moral standards that society expects from businesses.[24, 25]

Furthermore, the perception of ethical issues has changed thoroughly in business despite the evident importance of financial aspects. Nowadays, a company should also be perceived as a reliable business partner and presenting a high level of institutionalization of business ethics principles and practices, even more in the industry at controversial sectors of the economy (e.g., pharmaceutical, tobacco, alcohol).

For many reasons, there is now much more pressure on firms to act ethically and with social responsibility. Stakeholders' importance has increased, and they demand more from companies than they did in the past due to the expansion of American corporations. The emergence of a new nobility that expects morality and generosity from influential people and corporations like Gates, Clinton, Omidyar, and Soros is another development (e.g., Microsoft, Facebook). The final reason that the demands have increased is that business institutions have become so powerful that their domain has expanded to include some of the areas that were once covered by government agencies.

Companies must make moral decisions that consider the numerous social problems included in the role of corporations in light of the changes in business and American society. While profitability by itself frequently does not indicate overall effectiveness, solid ethics undoubtedly will over time. Businesses will engage in ethical behavior either out of a desire to be moral, out of concern for stakeholder interests, or occasionally because of regulations.[26]

Box 7.3   A global network for a more peaceful world

Applied Ethics, Inc. is a US-based nonprofit organization established in 2007 with the mission to seek ethical solutions to significant social issues through projects, education, counseling, and advocacy. The principal project of Applied Ethics has been Pax Populi, its people-to-people peacebuilding program. The mission of Pax Populi (which is Latin, for "the people's peace") is to put the tools of peacebuilding into the hands of ordinary people through education and economic development within a framework of human rights and moved by a spirit of love and respect for all people and the world in which we live. Since 2010, Pax Populi has delivered on its mission by creating an online school, Pax Populi Academy, through which teachers and tutors have provided free educational services to students in Afghanistan and Afghan refugees who fled the country after the Taliban takeover in August 2021.

Source: Pax Populi – People-to-People Peacebuilding.[27]

A just and decent society should result from the significance of having individuals uphold and enhance their ethical values in combination with recent movement of business ethics and corporate social responsibility. Ethical values became the topic of discussion at human-resource meetings, and the outcomes of these discussions affect the surrounding community, thus coming to play a role in company decisions.[28]

When companies use their ethical behavior as a leading indicator of profitability, they gauge profit according to their integrity, morality, justice, and social contribution.[29, 30, 31] Van der Merwe et al. (2003) examined what ethics is and how they apply to the business world. They also discussed if it is important to consider the question of why a company should practice ethical behavior.[32]

Peters and Waterman's study explored the relationship between corporate ethics and the concept of excellence as defined under the definition of excellence. According to their study, excellence in a company was dependent on eight characteristics.[33] These qualities were then evaluated by self-administered, anonymous questionnaires that were generated from a large commercial database and then sent to a sample of companies operating in industrial markets in the UK. The second component of these self-administered surveys referenced the ethical qualities possessed by the companies. This survey defined ethics as "a set of moral principles or values." The questionnaires were used to assess managerial perceptions of excellence and the perception these chosen managers had regarding the attitudes that their company held to business ethics. The results of this study showed that there was a highly significant correlation between ethics and excellence. It was identified that many of the components of excellence are associated with an ethical culture. It also revealed that many of the excellent companies were also ethical companies.[34]

Ahmed et al. (2003) examined ethical beliefs on a global level in an effort to contend that people in different environments shared differed expectations as to what was ethical and acceptable. They used scenarios and surveyed students in business courses in China, Egypt, Finland, Korea, Russia, and the United States. Though all respondents viewed the ethical problems in a similar manner (the basic concepts of right vs. wrong and good vs. bad), they found that the potential harms resulting from the practices were viewed differently. For instance, when asked whether participating in the unethical behavior would have a negative effect, it was viewed differently across cultures.[35, 36]

Globalization of the business environment, accompanied by rapid technological changes, has given rise to a new paradigm where company accomplishment is determined by the effective use of resources and applying appropriate strategies while adopting the concept of CSR and business ethics in management processes. Although the degree of institutionalization of business ethics (e.g., the presence of a code of conduct, an employee appointed to deal with ethical issues, ethical training, and so on), the perceived ethical behavior of the firms (e.g., preventing and handling corruption cases), and their relationship with their key stakeholders may have relativity in their importance in different countries,[37] business ethics is regarded as a determining factor influencing business success and the corporate image of companies from the sectors in question in Central European countries like Poland and Hungary.

Box 7.4   Advantages of ethical behavior for business

Ethical behavior and CSR can bring significant benefits to a business. For example, they may

- Attract customers to the company's products, thereby boosting sales and profits;
- Ensure that employees want to stay with the business, reducing labor turnover and therefore increasing productivity;
- Attract more employees wanting to work for the business, thus enabling the company to hire the most talented employees;
- Attract investors and keep the company's share price high, thereby protecting the business from takeover.

Source: Włodzimierz Sroka, M.L. (2015). The perception of ethics in business: Analysis of research results. *Procedia Economics and Finance*, 34, 156–163. https://doi.org/10.1016/S2212-5671(15)01614-7

In this section, it was demonstrated that intangibles like reputation and brand has become important to the local and global market; nevertheless, academic research is still struggling to differentiate business ethics and CSR through the lens of customer behavior in this issue. An interesting finding was that for adults living in the United States, 74.9 percent of 351 respondents of an exploratory study[38] suggested that both ethics and social responsibility are equally important. In this sense, it seems that customers value both of these behaviors but, when descriptive constructs were developed from organizational practice, ethics had more impact on brand attitudes than CSR.

Corporate social responsibility definition and implications

Although the definition of CSR is intuitive, the online business dictionary defines CSR as "a company's sense of responsibility towards the community and environment (both ecological and social) in which it operates."[39] Freeman (1984) defined stakeholders as "any group or individual who can affect or is affected by the achievement of the firm's objectives."[40] Other academics proposed the disclosure of relevant information for all company stakeholders and suggested some voluntary standards, establishing codes of ethics for global corporations. According to the stakeholder theory, businesses should take into account the interests of both internal and external actors when making decisions about their operations. Internal stakeholders include owners, customers, employees, and suppliers, while external stakeholders include governmental bodies, environmentalists, special interest groups, and local community organizations. The main idea of this theory is that the success of an organization depends upon the degree of satisfaction of all stakeholders under consideration.[41, 42, 43]

The stakeholder theory is defended by Donaldson and Preston (1995) using three arguments, which are descriptive, instrumental, and normative. The descriptive defense provides evidence of what businesses are actually doing. The instrumental argument is that the theory is vital for their business strategy. And it is normative because it is the "right" thing to do – considering everybody that is impacted by it. Therefore, businesses that consider stakeholders' interests will be more successful in creating a long-term, more sustainable, and lucrative organization.[44]

In the past, businesses, organizations, and entrepreneurs were taught that their primary goal should be to turn a profit; however, CSR contends that companies should also consider their total influence on their stakeholders. In other words, businesses must realize that every action they take affects the public at large, including customers, investors, the environment, workers, and communities. It does not, however, imply that businesses cannot turn a profit while implementing CSR measures. The three most common justifications for using CSR are boosting earnings, helping the environment, and enhancing brand perception. In addition, revenue-driven CSR participants can combine their commercial operations with philanthropic endeavors by implementing CSR techniques like the "seven strategies for delivering profits with ethics."[45]

Besides stakeholders' theory, some others sustain the importance of CSR for organizations. Theoretical debate points out that CSR activities could result in an agency problem having a negative effect on corporate financial performance, where managers may benefit themselves using firm resources through corporate philanthropy while shareholders incur a loss by spending on charity. Agency theory focuses upon relationships between parties where one delegates some decision-making authority to the other. The agency theory of corporate governance was put forward by Alchian and Demsetz (1972)[46] and Jensen and Meckling (1976).[47] They argued that firms can be regarded as a nexus for a set of contracting relationships among individuals, whereas classical economics regards firms as single-product entities with the purpose of maximizing profit. So, it is another academic point of view related to Freeman (1994) stakeholders' perspective. Agency theory addresses disputes that arise primarily in two key areas – a difference in risk aversion or a difference in goals (where the shareholders may play a role) – but it has been discussed that CSR has a positive effect on corporate financial performance due to firms' social cost reduction by improving stakeholder relationships and increasing market opportunities after an increase in social spending.

Another theory related to CSR activities and its disclosure benefits is the natural resource–based view of the firm (RBV), which suggests that if this is voluntarily adopted, it signalizes the virtue of management, as well as the quality of the firm's financial strategy, to its investors. In a context of increased demand for transparency of firm activities, governance, environmental and social responsibility performance may influence a firm's value.[48]

One should remember that at the beginning of the 21st century, there was a surge in social, environmental, and governance-related scandals, ranging from accounting malpractice (e.g., Enron in 2001 and WorldCom in 2002); to environmental violations (e.g., the Volkswagen emissions case of 2015, the Duke Energy oil spill of 2017, the Apple product obsolescence case of 2019); and data breaches (Uber in 2018 and British Airways in 2019) (https://doi.org/10.1016/j.jcorpfin.2021.102066). A connecting element across these incidents was the lack of CSR and corporate governance (CG).[49]

The former definition of CG included regulations that gave boards of directors, shareholders, and managers a legal structure to settle alleged agency conflicts between principals and agents as proposed by Berle and Means (1932).[50] The rights and obligations of the parties with an interest in the company as well as the organizational process configurations that affect both financial and non-financial firm-level results must also be included in a larger perspective on CG. Despite the abundance of studies on CG and CSR, there has yet to be a consensus on the relationship between these or how they presents themselves in different institutional contexts. A study based on the national business systems examined the literature about the nature of the CG-CSR relationship, with (1) CSR as a function of CG and (b) CG as a function of CSR, in order to shed light on the full range of this relationship. Interesting findings are that in advanced emerging economies, the majority of studies have investigated CSR as a function of CG (91 percent) and find support for stakeholder and agency theory arguments, and predominantly focus on the effects of board structures on CSR. On the other hand, a paper published in 2022 by Zaman et al.[51] in the context of LME (liberal market economies), the authors found that, broadly speaking, board networking capacity, board diversity on age and race parameters, and multiple directorships positively affect CSR showing support for resource dependence theory (RDT) and that firms with an audit committee that exhibits higher expertise positively influences CSR.

In the Arab oil economies, Habbash (2016)[52] finds that whereas family and government ownerships are positively related to CSR, institutional ownership has no significant effect. Furthermore, it is also suggested that western mechanisms of sound governance practices, such as the existence of an audit committee and independent directors on boards, do not impact CSR in this context as expected.

Box 7.5   Quick review on ethics, business, and CSR implications

- Ethics is the behavior that is concerned with "ought" and "ought not."
- If good business ethics can lift the revenue, unethical behavior can bring it down.
- There are eight main theories of ethics that implicate business management.

- Corporate social responsibility (CSR) is often utilized in defining ethics and is basically doing what is right for the company's stakeholders, but there is no agreement in the literature over which theory explains it.
- Preserved and enhanced individual ethical values combined with the recent movement of business ethics and CSR should lead to a fair and decent society.
- When companies apply ethical conduct as a seal of their profitability, they measure profit on the scale of ethical integrity, morality, and social contribution.
- Corporate governance (CG) positively influences CSR practices.

It is important to highlight the role of the public sector and the future direction of sustainable development by integrating CSR in its principles and practices. Moreover, the public sector plays a critical role in creating an enabling environment for responsible business to thrive. For example, public policy in a wide range of areas impacts on CSR and businesses management (e.g., the environment, labor markets, community development, human rights, anti-corruption, and governance reporting). The Irish government recognizes its role in 2017 launching the second National Action Plan on CSR, *Towards Responsible Business*,[53] with a propose agenda that includes (1) endorsing and supporting the concept of CSR in enterprises; (2) adhering to good CSR practice in its own operations; and (3) having relevant regulatory roles.

This concern is observed in Asian countries as well. China has experienced remarkable economic growth since the 1980s, but this growth was obtained with high social and environmental costs. To overcome this challenge, the government has been playing an important role in incorporating CSR into company laws to help them develop faster a socially responsible business approach. Despite this, a recent study displays a remarkable situation: the market responds neutrally to state-owned enterprises (SOEs) but favorably to CSR by market-oriented non-SOEs, demonstrating the important role of ownership in the dynamic CSR-performance relationship.[54]

Governments are genuinely interested in fostering CSR, and some policy instruments can be used (legal, economic, informational, partnering, and hybrid) and four thematic domains of action are possible (raise awareness, improve transparency, foster socially responsible investment, and lead by example).[55]

In addition, governments seek to play a more active role in defining the concept and promoting the respective practices positively with softer, non-binding initiatives. As a result, the number of corporations adjusting financial performance while looking out for a broader community is increasing. Microsoft (Figure 7.2) is one example of a corporation that demonstrates that businesses with outstanding CSR will have high efficiency and happy employees, their main stakeholders.

Examples of companies that focus on the environmental effect as their CSR and also make a profit are plentiful in the market. By using a "green" strategy, the companies can reduce their financial burdens/risks due to environmental blunders and improve their brand image, as done by Starbucks and Costco. Additionally, since more and more customers base their purchase decisions on a company's CSR track record, businesses benefit from enhancing their brand image. Therefore, companies must have a suitable CSR strategy to maximize their beneficial effects while limiting adverse consequences on their stakeholders.[56]

Figure 7.2 Microsoft Office

Source: https://openverse.org/image/1524167e-54ef-4a3f-a7f3-00814510c175

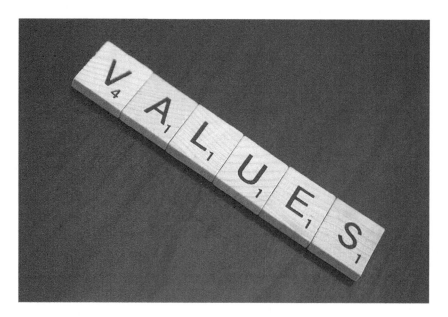

Figure 7.3 Values

Source: https://openverse.org/image/5dde58ef-0bf4-48e2-a0fa-0d3edcbc9038

Box 7.6   CSR disclosure

These days most company websites have a "corporate responsibility" page which communicates the company's social efforts. It also contains information to educate its customers on the company's ethical policies and standards.

Chevron's CSR web page[57]

As an example of commitment, the organization policies to engage CSR should be public. The following text was obtained at one of most traditional corporations in the United States (which traces its history back to the 1870s). Chevron is an American multinational energy corporation active predominantly in oil and gas. Its actual slogan is "the human energy company" and considers its compromise with the triple bottom line: people, profit, and planet. Remembering that was not always the case, Chevron's most widely known scandal involves Texaco's activities in the Lago Agrio oil field, for which Chevron is deemed responsible for due to its acquisition of Texaco in 2001.

The description of one of the corporate governance mechanisms is the existence of the Public Policy and Sustainability Committee (the "Committee") of the board of directors of Chevron Corporation (the "Corporation") that has the following purposes:

- To assist the board of directors in overseeing environmental, social, human rights, political, and public policy matters, including those related to sustainability and climate change, that are relevant to the corporation's activities and performance;
- To assist the board of directors in devoting appropriate attention and effective response to stockholder concerns regarding environmental, social, human rights, political, and public policy matters that are relevant to the corporation's activities and performance;
- To perform such other duties and responsibilities enumerated in and consistent with this charter.

In addition, the website has comprehensive information for different stakeholders' needs. The sustainability annual report of Chevron is of public domain in the website.[58] Considering the disclosure of CSR, companies, organizations, and entrepreneurs individually should consider the following three things: make a frank assessment of their ethos, determine the strategic value that social responsibility activities provides for their firm, and understand the company's industry and competitive CSR landscape. By making an honest assessment of the firm's ethos, the company can ensure that its actions will not contradict its CSR brand identity. Along with these three considerations, CSR ranking, geography, and the industry type should also be considered. "Corporates' communication of their social initiatives could assist a corporation in developing a reputation that might safeguard or help restore its image against damaging publicity."[59] All of these fundamentals are applicable to both entrepreneurs and SMEs as well.

Entrepreneurs will therefore have a greater chance of success if they base the core of their business on ethics and CSR.

Companies known for a strong CSR brand identity will bring positive media attention for themselves (e.g., Starbucks, Costco).

Figure 7.4 Costco and CSR
Source: www.flickr.com/photos/39160147@N03/15430692891

Negative media coverage can have a material impact on a firm's business bottom line. Due to varying levels of authenticity, the company must also consider if and how its CSR-related efforts would affect the target audience and to what degree. Besides raising profit, benefiting the environment, and bettering the company brand image, CSR can aid in attracting workers, keeping consumers, lowering manufacturing costs, and enhancing reputation in addition.

By implementing a CSR-oriented strategy, a company may maximize its stakeholders' benefits while minimizing drawbacks in the marketplace. For instance, Facebook co-founder and CEO Mark Zuckerberg donated $25 million to the fight against the Ebola virus.[60] This is a perfect example of why the concept of CSR is so crucial in the modern world. Zuckerberg can use his firm to change the world, and he decided to do so. Additionally, this donation (leadership behavior) is the best example of why organizations must embrace CSR to emulate Zuckerberg in a win-win game.

Revenue drove CSR companies to focus on performance that allows for "the better good." According to Jackson and Nelson, a business must adhere to seven strategies to grow its profits while upholding its principles: harness innovation for the public good, put people at the center, spread economic opportunity, engage in new alliances, be performance driven in all aspects, practice superior governance, and pursue purpose beyond profit.[61]

The pursuit of these seven strategies promotes profitable and competitive activities while focusing on making the world a better place. In order to maximize its profit, a company should measure the success of its processes for these seven strategies through financial and social outcome metrics. A company that is focused on profit should integrate its business activities with charitable activities so that its participation in CSR produces a profit.

Figure 7.5 Strategies for profit linked to CSR

Source: http://pixr8.com/wp-content/uploads/2015/10/Rohit-Bansal-2-e1446023817609-1170x480.png

Business and charitable activities must be one and the same for participation in socially responsible activities to increase company profit. Another important consideration is profit with no environmental damage. Companies that are environmentally conscious in their processes and participate in activities which benefit the environment make themselves more competitive, successful, and socially responsible.[62]

Additionally, a "green" corporate strategy bolsters success as it allows for fewer financial burdens due to environmental blunders (e.g., litigation, cleanup costs) and therefore can be more profitable over the long run. By adopting a corporate environmental strategy, most firms will advance their company performance.[63] A "green" strategy may make a company more competitive as it can lead to an "improved brand image" in the eye of the company's stockholders.

Companies can use marketing to establish an association between philanthropic efforts and a brand or product. More consumers look for philanthropic or CSR elements when choosing a product or service. However, it is important for these efforts to be sincere, as social media allows consumers to see through artificial philanthropic activities that are only used for selfish gains of the enterprise.[64] Companies who choose to generate brand loyalty through sincere philanthropic activities hope to see increases in profit due to this connection between the consumer and their CSR strategy.

A business accomplishes this through marketing campaigns where it associates itself and its product with a particular cause. Dove's "Real Beauty" campaign, developed to establish a new beauty standard, one that does not conform to social standards of beauty, illustrates this kind of marketing strategy. To improve its brand's reputation and a cause (enhancing self-esteem through a contemporary sense of beauty), Dove's approach (in particular its 2006 Super Bowl commercial) in linking its brand and a sensitive cause (improved self-esteem through a modern sense of beauty) had an end goal of strengthening its relationship with its consumers and, therefore, increasing profits, besides the relevant emotional aspect.

CSR and entrepreneurship

Due to their connections and effects on the corporate environment, entrepreneurship and CSR have recently been the focus of many researchers. The century's technological advancements have increased the market's exposure to the effects of globalization, which have had a significant impact on both entrepreneurship and CSR. This has contributed to the recognition of the notion of corporate social entrepreneurship (CSE), which incorporates within itself entrepreneurship, corporate entrepreneurship, and social entrepreneurship.[65,66] CSE could be regarded as a facilitator of a significant transformation in how the company is operated, where entrepreneurship is considered from the perspectives of an individual founder and a well-established organization.

Corporate social entrepreneurship has been defined by Austin and colleagues (2006) as "the process of extending the firm's domain of competence and corresponding opportunity set

---

Box 7.7   What really motivates people to be honest in business?

Each year, 1 in 7 large corporations commits fraud. Why? To find out, Alexander Wagner takes us inside the economics, ethics, and psychology of doing the right thing. Join him for an introspective journey down the slippery slopes of deception as he helps us understand why people behave the way they do: www.ted.com/talks/alexander_wagner_what_really_motivates_people_to_be_honest_in_business

---

through innovative leveraging of resources, both within and outside its direct control, aimed at the simultaneous creation of economic and social value."[67] According to the authors, an effectively implemented CSE consists of three key elements:

- *An enabling environment*: Top management should adopt an entrepreneurial mindset and a shared sense of purpose throughout the organization.
- *Corporate social entrepreneurs (mainly change agents)*: They are distinct from other management roles as they will be the main facilitators of the internal organizational transformation.
- *Corporate purpose of a value-based organization*: A consistency between words and actions should be prominent in order for the firm to create more value.

However, how startups inform their (quasi)shareholders of their responsible behavior remains varied. For instance, Achleitner et al. (2013)[68] developed some empirical research with social venture capitalists to investigate this question. According to the existing CSR literature, future research should examine the responsible entrepreneurs' websites, press releases, and op-eds and the materiality of their disclosure and suggest that sustainability reports may become mandatory for all organizations, which depend on external funding.[69]

Moreover, new businesses have historically been found to harm the environment and break the law more frequently than their more seasoned corporate counterparts.[70] Startups like the renowned Uber and Airbnb are receiving public rebukes for their reckless behavior and running into opposition from both authorities and customers. The literature show that investors, who place greater importance on corporate responsibility, follow this societal trend.[71] Responsibility made its way into the world of for-profit commercial startups, which were once the exclusive domain of the mission-driven social entrepreneur. Beyond the obvious social and environmental benefits this change will have today, it has the potential to change how the corporate world looks in the future as startups turn into well-established businesses.

Box 7.8   Leadership and CSR

Starbucks commitment to uplift humanity through connection and compassion has long distinguished the company, building an unrivaled, globally admired brand that has transformed the way we connect over coffee. I am humbled to be joining this iconic company at such a pivotal time, as the Reinvention and investments in the partner and customer experiences position us to meet the changing demands we face today and set us up for an even stronger future.

Source: Laxman Narasimhan, CEO of Starbucks Coffee (September, 2022).[72]

Figure 7.6 Starbucks

Source: https://openverse.org/image/c670b4ae-85d2-4800-bf46-68b00f3ed42d

A company must lay the foundations from the highest position of power in any given company to develop a sustainable CSE. The main focus or goal of CSE is to serve as the basis for a sustainable and robust organizational transformation into a dynamic generator of societal improvement. In other words, an increasing number of businesses today might profit from establishing and maintaining a balance between accumulating "economic wealth" and improving the standard of living for society. Consistent CSR initiatives could contribute a broader non-financial value because an organization's vision and values significantly impact how a corporation behaves in the marketplace. Consequently, it is encouraged to engage in strategic and entrepreneurial initiatives. Successfully integrating social issues into a company's agenda requires top-level strategic management. Other preconditions for the encouragement of entrepreneurial activities across an industry include a conducive regulatory climate and political stability.

Building a company's reputation, which eventually transforms into a direct non-financial added value, depends heavily on the external and internal quality of an organization's relationship. As a result, a company must be "responsible while successful," or, to put it another way, to attempt and address particular societal needs while making a profit. Such organizations are often referred to as "hybrid" organizations. These groups often combine several types of organizational structures in an effort to build and preserve both social benefits and financial wealth. Organizations which aim to create social value independent of financial wealth are typically nonprofit and non-governmental organizations. For-profit organizations are on the other side and the hybrid ones are in the middle, combining both sets of values.

Figure 7.7 Venture capital

Source: https://openverse.org/image/7f7c2766-184b-4638-8306-d7882f88106e

---

Box 7.9   Investing in social causes: venture capital group

Omidyar Network is an early seed-funding venture capital group. The company primarily invests in entrepreneurs who share their commitment to advancing social good at the pace and scale the world needs today. The company claims to be focused on five key areas they believe are building blocks for prosperous, stable, and open societies: education, emerging tech, financial inclusion, governance and citizen engagement, and property rights.

Pierre Omidyar experienced this firsthand as the founder of eBay. Just as eBay created the opportunity for millions of people to start their own businesses, the company believes market forces can be a potent driver for positive social change. That's why Omidyar Network invests in both for-profit businesses and nonprofit organizations, whose complementary roles can advance entire sectors.

Socially responsible investment (SRI) includes both ethical and financial concepts. Environmental, social, and governance (ESG) measurements are one of the pillars of SRI. Some researchers reaffirm the significance of ESG indicators in the field of SRI, where they serve as both a market enabler and a proxy for sustainability performance. But there are two fundamental problems with ESG metrics that make them less reliable: a lack of transparency and a lack of convergence.[73]

CSR and competitiveness

A company must be socially responsible if it wants to maintain its competitiveness both locally and globally, and its financial capacity provides an opportunity for a company to be independent from creditors, enhancing technological capability, introducing innovations, strengthening brand, and simultaneously holding a dominant position in a competitive market. Aspects as better reputation: strengthening of the brand, consumer loyalty, highly competent workers, increase market share (penetrate in new markets), work efficiency, consumer satisfaction, cost reduction and risk reduction had been related to CSR and its materialization in ESG achievements, which are described in the sustainability reports or correlated documents.

A study conducted in Lithuania[74] with Global Compact network members investigated the influence of different social responsibility dimensions on separate elements of competitiveness, confirming that environmental, social, economic, shareholder, voluntariness differently affects the elements of competitiveness (e.g., financial capacity, quality of production, satisfied needs of consumers, efficiency, introduction of innovations, and company's image). In this research, the environmental aspect of CSR and related areas are relevant to a company's financial capacity, image, and reputation, providing a competitive advantage. Despite of this, neither the quality of production nor the possibilities for introduction of innovations in a company are affected by the dimensions of social responsibility.

The three aspects, CSR, competitiveness, and firm value, seem to be entangled in the business strategy of the 21st century. Yoon et al. (2018)[75] analyzed whether a firm's CSR plays a significant role in Korea, a developing market, and presented a scenario where CSR performances evidenced by environmental, social, and corporate governance (ESG) scores have a favorable and considerable impact on a firm's market, consistent with earlier research on developed nations. Nevertheless, the value-creating impact of CSR is less pronounced for environmentally sensitive businesses than for businesses in unaffected industries. Corporate governance practices, in particular, have a detrimental impact on the firm value of environmentally conscious businesses. Additionally, only *chaebols*' (conglomerates) governance practices significantly increase market value, whereas investors place little importance on the governance practices of other enterprises. Therefore, the Korean government's engagement in the reformation of conglomerates may have an economic justification if CSR has a more substantial valuation effect in chaebols.

Scholars have also shown that companies such as Costco, Whole Foods, Nestlé, and Starbucks, who were able to clearly identify their companies' shared values with their stakeholders and incorporate CSR within their strategic business decisions, have gained competitive advantages over their competitors.[76,77] According to Porter and Kramer, combining business and CSR necessitates alterations to organizational structure, reporting connections, and incentive structures. Performance metrics must also be changed from short-term income generation to long-term revenue generation.[78] They indicated that "the more closely tied a social issue is to a company's business, the greater the opportunity to leverage the firm's resources – and benefit society."[79] Therefore, to achieve a sustainable CSR impact, a company needs to be hands-on and tailor (customize) its operational process. A list of suggestions based on the finest CSR practices in various industries has been provided by several academics.[80,81,82]

One major motivation for businesses to create a CSR strategy that could aid in reputation building and brand protection is developing a favorable brand image. However, evidence also suggests that maintaining a company's image is more complicated than creating a CSR brand identity. For example, when British Petroleum (BP) was promoting CSR programs, such as its "Beyond Petroleum" program, they were more commonly picked up for negative media exposure because of big oil spills in the Gulf of Mexico. When choosing stories to publish, editors consider both the novelty of an event and whether it conforms to widely held beliefs.[83]

Companies known for a strong CSR identity that commit an act detrimental to their brand identity will bring media attention to their issue due to the novelty of the event's occurrence. While a firm cannot afford to behave unethically or ignore CSR altogether, there is a risk that accompanies being a CSR leader as the firm takes on a heightened sense of scrutiny from the media.

A wealthy individual can also make a difference when it comes to social responsibility. Mark Zuckerberg declared that he would donate 99 percent of Facebook shares, which might be worth up to $45 billion, for the "advancement of human potential" and the "promotion of equality." In addition, he gave the Newark Public School District $100 million in 2010. Even though it was a generous and benevolent act intended to serve good, Mark was highly criticized by public officials for it, as such an action was viewed to be inconsistent with his devotion to the "promotion of equality." To address this, he founded the Chan Zuckerberg Initiative, which is distinct from conventional foundations because it allows funding to nonprofit organizations, makes private investments, and participates in political debates. Thus, Mr. Zuckerberg connected his beliefs to his deeds and increased his popularity as a CSR activist.[84]

Social media can help ethical behavior (by making everything public) and benefit society as a social control mechanism. It can help individuals connect and deepen their relationships, exchange impressions, and share opinions. Social media also encourages us to identify role models and to understand different cultures and their communication signs. And it can empower businesses to build their audiences, boost their bottom line, and also bring them down.

Box 7.10   The power of the commons: social media

According to a report by Freshfields Bruckhaus Deringer, more than one-quarter of crises spread to international media within an hour and over two-thirds within 24 hours. Despite 6 out of 10 cases providing days if not months of notice, it still takes an average of 21 hours for companies to respond, leaving them open to "trial by Twitter."[85]

Source: www.freshfields.com/49fabb/globalassets/campaign-landing/cyber-security/containing-a-crisis.pdf

Figure 7.8 Social media: spreading news

Source: "Social media icons on an iPhone 7 screen" by stacey.cavanagh is licensed under CC BY 2.0. https://openverse.org/image/69fb3fe6-4c6a-42f1-af1e-6ea721cc15a4

Geography and industry type should also be considered when developing a CSR strategy. Cohn and Wolfe (2014) show that "authenticity" has different meanings for consumers, contingent upon their geographic location and industry sector type.[86] Authenticity here is defined by the individual taking the poll but was loosely defined as a "company with values and morals and stands by them no matter what challenges are encountered." The study shows industries that have high degrees of authenticity are supermarkets, electric companies, retailers, and coffee shops. See the full report by Freshfields Bruckhaus Deringer (n.d.).[87]

Authentic companies are companies that the consumer sees and experiences on a regular basis with repeated satisfaction. Companies on the bottom end of the authenticity scale are alcohol companies, fast-food chains, and social media providers. These authenticity rankings also vary by geographic location. A firm must consider whether its CSR-related efforts will impact its target audience and to what degree. In some cases, the firm may be in a sector where CSR strategies may directly support creating a positive, authentic brand identity, generating loyal consumers; or on the other hand, the firm may be in a market where CSR efforts will go relatively unnoticed but morally it has done well.

Most of the discussion about the CSR and competitive advantages are applicable for all organizations and entrepreneurial activities. Because of the sheer size of the MNCs' market share and competitors, they will get more widespread attention about CSR than smaller companies and entrepreneurs. Applying CSR is more critical for survivability for SMEs and entrepreneurs due to resource constraints and limitations. For example, a developing country offering quality products at a reasonable price will bring positive attention to the community. Actually, entrepreneurs who are authentic in applying CSR will get more attention whether they are in the developed or developing country.

Perhaps being ethical and authentic stands out more in developed countries than developing because of the advancement in information exchanges.

Human resources management and entrepreneurship

In general, an entrepreneur who intends to establish an organization has to manage two important sets of challenges: internal and external. Some of the internal factors could be the gathering of creative, innovative, and cooperative staff, a well-developed rewards system, and employee assessment, all of which could contribute to a well-functioning organization. Schneider et al. (2013) examined the interrelationships between HRM, organizational climate, and culture factors that impact them.[88, 89] They investigated empirical data from a cross-sectional dataset of 214 knowledge-intensive German SMEs[90] and concluded that "the strong impact of staff selection, staff development, and training as well as staff rewards on Corporate Governance." This means having a successful team is essential for running the shop.

Overcoming internal challenges of organizational structures and processes leads to appropriate and timely decision-making, which is essential for entrepreneurs.[91] Therefore, entrepreneurs will be able to respond effectively to the external challenges of continuous change on issues such as developing markets, technological evolution, and sophisticated competitors.[92, 93] Additionally, entrepreneurs need to evaluate economic, political, and social changes that impact its core business. Nurturing and training entrepreneurs to prepare and recognize these challenges will increase their success rate.

For the better comprehension of the next topic, check again Box 7.4, as human resource management deals with the affirmative moral obligations of the employer towards employees to maintain equality and equity justice.

CSR and HRM

The importance of ethics in human resources management is also relevant because of the globalization of the companies, which has affected the organizational policies to work in the world economy; the growing competition which forces the company to find a competitive advantage and increase profitability in different markets. Incorporating ethical practices in human resource management and ethical values in individuals empowers an organization to maintain and increasing trust. Also, HRM has a significant role in defining ethical standards, policies, and procedures and implementing ethics-related activities in the workplace. In this way, HR experts must improve organization efficiency and employee performance and address ethical infractions. There is a need for building a corporate behavior code to which all officials, employees, contract workers, and agents must adhere. Ethics at both personal and professional levels are related to CSR, but on the professional level, it is heavily influenced by HRM. Ethical violations can occur in any department, but when they appear in the human resource department, they can immediately impact the entire organization. The upper echelon must recognize the importance of ethics in human resource management and support it.

As highlighted previously, one aspect related to CG is the diversity of the board and the social aspect of ESG, the workforce composition. Organizations have evolved into multicultural communities in the modern economic environment and, companies with CSR commitment are including DEI (diversity, equity, and inclusion) in their HRM goals on daily bases, like recruitment, remuneration, and promotion policies. Through the years, regardless of its terminology, D&I, I&D, EDI, JEDI (justice, equity, diversity, and inclusion), and DEIB (diversity, equity, inclusion, and belonging). DEI refers to policies and programs that promote the inclusion and involvement of people of all ages, races, ethnicities, abilities and disabilities, genders, faiths, cultures, and sexual orientations, to create a better working environment for everyone,[94] regardless of their different identities and experiences.

Related to this, companies with CSR commitment are including increasing policies of DEI in their HRM goals because, highly qualified job candidates, employees, clients, and communities place a high value on businesses that have incorporated diversity into their organizational cultures.[95] Norman and Johnson (2022)[96] propose practical steps for HR professionals to help improve cultural inclusiveness in their workplaces. To implement DEI, HRM should consider (re)evaluating the workplace culture, establishing KPIs (key performance indicators: quantifiable measures used to evaluate the success of an organization in meeting objectives for performance), considering employee incentives, engaging the entire team, pay attention to pay equity, develop a fair hiring process, sponsor employee resource groups, and respond to team member input.

A recent study at an UK division of a multinational professional services organization examines the efforts made by executives in an organization with a strategic business case for diversity and inclusion to close the implementation gap for equity improvement.[97] The authors identify difference between what is declared and what is actually done considering gender and ethnicity in internal human resource development processes in the perspective of agency theory. The study demonstrates how increased control through required diversity training, diversity targets, and diversity monitoring can push managers towards taking progressive steps but is ultimately constrained by the need for management discretion. These contradictions reflected the need for attitudinal development with behavioral control as well as the boundaries of control (CG, for example). Because of managers' agency conflict, the implementation gap for equity can be reduced but never eliminated.

Diagnosis and assessment over the time, like Global Report Initiative[98] (a framework to elaborate CSR reports) proposes can help HRM to evaluate its policies. It is worth to mention that GRI Sustainability Reporting Standards (GRI Standards) are designed to be used by organizations to report about their impacts on the economy, the environment, and society.

According to the Women in the Workplace study,[99] at the start of 2021 women of color represented 17 percent of entry-level positions versus 30 percent represented by white women. At the

VP level, women of color held 7 percent of representation, and white women held 25 percent, while white men held 56 percent of VP level positions, in a study conducted by LeanIn and McKinsey which collected information from 333 participating organizations employing more than 12 million people, surveyed more than 40,000 employees published in 2022. Another highlight of this report[100] is that it is increasingly important to women leaders that they work for companies that prioritize flexibility, employee well-being, and DEI.

As stated before, the company must choose its goals considering CSR and HRM and keep tracking them constantly. WPP began life as a maker of wire shopping baskets, as in 1985 Sir Martin Sorrell took a controlling stake in a small UK manufacturer of wire baskets and teapots called Wire and Plastic Products, the company was renamed simply WPP. Today it is a world leader in communications, experience, commerce and technology. The WPP group declare in its website[101] that they have made "significant progress in driving gender equality, with women now representing 51% of our senior managers. We are working hard to improve in all aspects of diversity, equity and inclusion (DE&I) at WPP. Success relies on accountability so, for the first time, we have included DE&I goals in the remuneration plans."

Consequently, it is not surprising that we see a significant increase in the interest of researchers on the topic of CSR and HRM.[102] The globalizing business environment has contributed to the rapid change in institutional conditions, organizational forms, and power relations, which have called for a deeper understanding of the implementation of a sustainable long-term CSR program.[103, 104]

Nevertheless, applying efficient CSR strategies in managerial practices is considered a challenge.[105, 106] A variety of organizations are struggling with the implementation of a viable CSR

Figure 7.9 Diversity in workplace

Source: "Diverse Workplace" by Direct Media is marked with CC0 1.0. https://stocksnap.io/photo/diverse-workplace-2UIILTYHZX

strategy in managerial practices. This is where effective HRM practices could prove helpful.[107] A recent study into the field of HRM and CSR has offered different frameworks and theoretical perspectives for the conceptualization of the underlying connection between CSR and HRM.[108,109,110] Both CSR and HRM are highly relevant in the formation of the company's brand image, comprehending the role of the organization, and the sensitive employer-employee relationship. This is why understanding the underlying connection is essential for the success of the company. Moreover, HRM deals with the internal microenvironment of the organization, while CSR is more externally oriented with a focus on the macro environment. Efficient HRM practices could contribute to the understanding, development, and enactment of sustainable and effective CSR application.

HRM, ethics, and COVID-19

The COVID-19 pandemic brought unprecedented challenges for HRM across many areas of their operations, like shifting to remote work environments or implementing new workplace policies and procedures to limit human contact while monitoring well-being and performance measures. In addition to making it harder to keep work and personal life separate, the closing of childcare facilities and schools has increased parental expectations for workers, further distorting the distinction between work and family life. While single and childless workers may not be immune to the adverse effects of such altered working conditions, as they may be most at risk of loneliness, a sense of purposelessness, and associated negative effects on well-being, these work-family interconnections seem particularly demanding for employees with children.

One other aspect of HRM was to experience a transition from presence to virtual forms of recruitment, selection, and training.[111] This adaptation to the information and communication technologies (ICT) environment, on the other hand, was not automatic, so HR experts had to evaluate the outcomes of these activities being conscious and fair considering the limitations of the actors and technologies involved.

Additionally, from the perspective of the expanding trends of virtual work brought on by the COVID-19 pandemic, home tasks, and domestic responsibilities still appear to fall disproportionately on women due to long-held gender preconceptions. Literature (Ganeshan & Vethirajan, 2022) mentioned this happens even in two-parent heteronormative households. Therefore, HRM and equity policies will become more and more important as the requirements of the changing workforce and its environment. Regarding working from home, there are different infrastructure conditions and scenarios to be into consideration. Because of this, it's crucial to remember that employees will need different kinds of support based on their specific circumstances.

As presented below, HR policies were different depending on the economic activity. One of the most impacted in 2020–2021 (and sometimes 2022) due to the problems that arose, and the following policies implemented was the hospitality sector and tourism industry. However, there was a global advancement in many other industries (e.g., food, sport, and agriculture) during that period.

When a pandemic occurs hospitality employees are exposed to health/safety risks while, simultaneously, sharing the responsibility for carrying out crisis response tasks[112] but, as the authors reinforce it could be "deep" (mindful awareness and careful application of safety procedures) or "surface" compliance (demonstrating compliance with minimal effort). Regardless, it was essential for businesses to keep a careful eye on employee safety since doing so shows the organization's commitment to preventing the virus's spread and determines its ability to survive the current crisis. Having as a case study object our a small-medium sized private restaurant group in northern China in 2020–2021 which managed to survive COVID-19 without massive layoffs or restructuring and was operating at full capacity at the time of the study. In response to COVID-19, ABC management implemented a number of new health and safety procedures and practices. The main findings are individuals' engagement in deep compliance started with heightened risk and health awareness and a combination of management demonstrates to the team a genuine commitment to workplace health and their safety. Another important conclusion was that in response to the economic threat, the organization pivoted its core mission, emphasizing the business's survival from the perspective of social responsibility, building stronger relationships with the workforce's effective safety responses during a difficult period. Table 7.2 summarize some strategies employed in a restaurant in China.

Table 7.2 Strategies employed in a restaurant in China during the COVID-19 pandemic

Specific group of individuals	Moment	Measures
Employees	Before work	Fill out travel history form Compulsory temperature check 7-step handwashing
	During work	All staff must wear face masks and food-handling gloves during work. Practice social distancing during the lunch break, meetings, and trainings.
	Off work	During the lockdown period, set up a WeChat group for daily check of travel history, temperature, and symptoms. Managers send daily COVID-19 safety reminders to employees who take public transportation.
Customers	At the entrance	Require customers to read COVID-19 prevention notice and dine-in notice. Scan health QR code or fill out register form, including name, contact number, address, and travel history in past 2 weeks. Take temperature check. Apply disinfectant spray. Encourage customers to take away instead of dine in other business of the group (take away/ stand tables). Require customers to wear face masks when they enter the restaurant.
	During dining	Provide a "public" pair of chopsticks to transfer food to customers' own bowl instead of using own chopsticks to share the food. Cancel reservations for the private dining room.
Other measures for customers (take away/stand units)		Put marks on the floor to remind of social distancing. Keep 1.5–2 m distance between tables.
	After dining (restaurant and take away units)	Encourage WeChat pay or Alipay, not cash.

Sanitization of the working places: disinfect the entire premises at least two times a day; disinfect all eating utensils and the dining table/chairs after each meal; disinfect toilet every 30 minutes; update disinfection notice and present it at the front door.

Source: Adaptation from Hu, X., Yan, H., Casey, T., & Wu, C.-H. (2021). Creating a safe haven during the crisis: How organizations can achieve deep compliance with COVID-19 safety measures in the hospitality industry. *International Journal of Hospitality Management*, 92, 102662. https://doi.org/10.1016/j.ijhm.2020.102662

It can be observed in the descriptions in Table 7.2 that some of these measures occurred in several countries, but in normal situations, they would be considered unethical, like temperature checking and knowing the whereabouts of employees and temperature measurements and QR code solicitation of customers for example.

Government guidance on personal protective equipment (PPE) and immunity testing for the safe delivery of aesthetic services is one strategy, but among healthcare staff and the public regarding the risk of transmission of COVID-19 in healthcare settings this was not enough as had been discussed in a paper in UK.[113] The use of lateral flow serology provides a clinically convenient approach for the assessment of prior infection with COVID-19. However, its widespread adoption in organizations seeking to use it is both controversial based on uncertainty of what the test result means a creates for management and staff the need to respond and deal with the information it generates. One ethical aspect was the legitimacy of sharing the results to the group. Not only to plan the schedules and tasks but the psychological impact of this in their work and personal lives. The authors pointed out that once the tests results are made available to employees, the potential conflict should be managed carefully to avoid a dysfunctional outcome that can leave behind negative effects on trust and group cohesiveness.

One study presented perceptions of front-line hotel staff regarding their ability and willingness to report to work during the COVID-19 epidemic.[114] This qualitative research concluded that front-line hotel employees generally felt a sense of duty to work during the pandemic. Most barriers to willingness (transport to work, family obligations, risk to self/family, lack of pandemic planning, erosion of goodwill) seem to form a continuum ranging from negotiable to insuperable barriers. From the authors point of view, the key to reducing absenteeism during the pandemic is take preventive action so that barriers to willingness do not become perceived as barriers to ability to work. Additionally, childcare is perceived as a barrier to ability to report to work and should be considered too.

The lesson obtained from this experience is to make the employees part of the decisions and transparency in the orientations, supported by HRM. Each individual has its own circumstance resulting from a combination of personal beliefs/circumstances and external constraints and should be respected considering the principles of CSR. Efforts should also be made to develop a communication policy, encouraging the feeling that the needs of employees are acknowledged. Guidance from the employer is also mandatory in a pandemic planning development, like training about the correct use of the equipment and other precautions or being made aware of what would be expected from them if the crisis escalates.

CSR and strategy

Despite CSR's rise to seemingly ubiquitous application across many companies due to increased profit, environmental benefit, and improved brand image, developing a CSR program or strategy should not be taken lightly. Poorly executed CSR programs may not only waste valuable resources that could be deployed elsewhere in the firm, but a poorly managed CSR presence can be detrimental to the firm.

In terms of stakeholders, most companies have educated and trained their executives on the importance of CSR and entrepreneurs should make it an important aspect of their vision and mission. For example, organizations need to extend CSR training and education to their suppliers and employees.

Box 7.11   Quick review on HRM, business, and CSR implications

- The three most popular reasons for applying CSR are raising profits, benefiting the environment, and bettering the company brand image.
- Having a successful team is essential for organizations.
- Nurturing and training entrepreneurs to prepare and recognize these challenges will increase their success rate.
- HRM deals with the internal microenvironment of the organization, while CSR is more externally oriented with a focus on the macro environment.
- Corporate social entrepreneurship (CSE) is a facilitator of a significant transformation in how the company is operated, where entrepreneurship is considered from the perspectives of an individual founder and a well-established organization.
- Austin et al. (2006) state that a successfully implemented CSE consists of three key elements: creating an enabling environment, fostering the corporate social entrepreneur, and corporate purpose of a value-based organization.[115]
- Most of the discussion about the CSR and competitive advantages is applicable for all organizations and entrepreneurial activities. Applying CSR is more critical for survivability for SMEs and entrepreneurs due to resource constraints and limitations.
- Organizations are facing an increasingly dynamic environment in which they must interact, and HRM should rapidly respond to changes.

In terms of decision levels, most companies conclude the importance of CSR on the relationship with the public, but few seem to have found a proper balance between their objectives in CSR and their performance in global supply chains. This has shown that their economic losses can become significant if they are not transparent.[116] A few key elements to consider when developing an appropriate CSR strategy for the firm to attempt to align CSR efforts with company profits include:

- An honest assessment of the firm's philosophy
- Determining strategic value CSR adds to firm profitability
- Understanding the company's industry and competitive CSR landscape.

Developing a CSR strategy is very important and has more elements than the previous list. However, these are key areas to consider to maximize the potential benefits in developing a CSR strategy while also minimizing negative impacts from implementing an ill-planned CSR strategy.

Applications of CSR: a few examples

Consumers in most countries live in a globalized world with access to information at will, and actions by companies in this environment speak louder than words. Media outlets exist in more forms than ever with an ever-increasing amount of information available for the end-user. In

Figure 7.10 Woman farmer

Source: www.flickr.com/photos/44760652@N05/42757540094

addition to regular media reporting, there are multiple independent CSR rating agencies and self-published CSR reporting by firms (e.g., Transparency International).

In this easily accessible and rich information environment, firms need to be more careful than ever to align their company ethos with a brand identity and actions that firms take. If not, consumers can easily discover the marketing guise of the CSR branding strategy from the company and see that its actions are not concurring with the claims of CSR principles from the company. Furthermore, consumers will become skeptical of the true intentions of the firm despite its CSR brand identity.

Box 7.12   Agriculture entrepreneurship in Mali by Niang brothers

Brothers Salif Romano Niang and Mohamed Ali Niang have created a social enterprise known as Malô which aims to revolutionize the processing and distribution of rice in Mali. Malô is based on creating a partnership model where rice is purchased from farming cooperatives instead of individual rice farmers to assure that people get a fair price.

When asked about how they believe that their company could advance the agricultural sector in Mali, Salif said:

It is funny, because our relatives in Mali told us we were crazy when we left the United States to start Malô, and work with rural rice. But Mohamed and I saw a real opportunity in our home country, and it was clear that momentum was being built in the African countries agricultural sector.

These brothers have created a business in which their philosophy was to create a partnership with communities and work to achieve their goals while maintaining the vision of sustainable agricultural growth and food security. The hard work that these young entrepreneurs are doing to establish a business was profitable, but more importantly had a main focus to help the community. This shows that dreams and goals can always be achieved.

Consider examples of social entrepreneurship in your area/state/city. Explain how they have improved the existing strategy/culture to bring in safer/efficient products or services.

Companies need to take a careful assessment of their core corporate values to ensure that their actions will not contradict their CSR brand identity. There are examples of companies that have recognized this and changed their behavior. For example, BMW, which promotes sustainability as a core part of its brand identity, stopped racing Formula 1 because it felt this was not aligned with sustainability. This change in behavior was an attempt to align its brand identity with its actions despite the potential loss of branding opportunities through Formula 1 racing.[117] On the other hand, Bank of America is a noted example of a company that has let business

Figure 7.11 New business paradigm

Source: https://openverse.org/image/28aed9aa-deca-4766-8c9f-cbe5f6d7fa58

strategy conflict with their CSR strategy, thus opening the door to public criticism and negative publicity. According to the Bank of America website (2013), two of their primary CSR missions are "responsible business practices" and creating "strong economies through lending, investing, and giving."[118]

Despite Bank of America stating that their fundamental beliefs revolve around creating a strong economy through lending and investing, Bank of America was a central player in the 2008 financial crisis when they sold financial products backed by risky subprime mortgages. Arguably, Bank of America created a profit for the firm at the expense of the US economy, which is in direct contradiction with Bank of America's stated CSR beliefs. This inconsistency between actions and stated beliefs discounts any believability for their CSR identity by the consumer public.

The conflict between their actions and beliefs is tangibly demonstrated by a Harris Poll where the US consumer listed Bank of America as the number one "worst reputation" firm.[119] This example underscores the need for a company to align corporate actions with the firm's CSR identity to ensure they are not wasting valuable resources on a fruitless endeavor.

A well-defined and developed CSR could, on the other hand, highly benefit any institution. By consistently and genuinely following their CSR mission statements, any organization could reach the top of their abilities. This is why it is important that educational institutions provide the necessary tools for the proper preparation of leaders who will be devoted and will contribute to the successful implementation of the company's CSR activities.[120]

Box 7.13   Entrepreneurship and collaboration in Nicaragua: Enlace

Strategic partnerships could transform a region and improve welfare in emergent economies. The Enlace entrepreneurial and development project in Nicaragua has been a successful collaboration between faculty, students, an institution of higher education (State University of New York–Geneseo), and private contributors. This project started in 2005 from a few team research projects in an economics course and then was supported by the institution and a couple of dedicated entrepreneurial and caring students who built on the initial initiation and accelerated its growth. Examining the impact of this collaborative effort shows the role of some key stakeholders in truly making a big impact in a small town after 10 years by advancing education.

CSR and the bottom line

Is a well-developed CSR strategy the same as a business plan to maximize profits? Karnani (2011) discusses the critical views of Milton Friedman's perspective on CSR.[121] Milton Friedman indicates that:

> there is one and only one social responsibility of business – to use its resources and engage in activities designed to increase its profits so long as it stays within the rules of the game, which is to say engages in open and free competition without deception or fraud.[122]

Friedman argues that firms should be focused on activities that drive profitability and would likely view many CSR related activities as ancillary business activities that are not central to the business objective of the firm. This is further supported by Friedman's argument that a business's socially responsible activities are notable for their "analytical looseness and lack of rigor."[123] The lack of a clear correlation between a firm's CSR efforts and profitability is supported by some scholars, which further proves Friedman's point of focusing on profit generation.[124] The argument is that it is difficult to quantify CSR efforts and a firm's financial performance. Therefore, it is important to develop a CSR strategy that displays potential profit opportunity for a company rather than deploying firm resources to assist activities without clear lines of strategic firm opportunity.

Some companies choose not to focus on CSR as a core practice due to the lack of alignment of their business strategy and are doing well! Apple is one example as it experienced some of its most lucrative earnings while managing manufacturing plants like Foxconn in immoral labor conditions, which included explosions leading to death, underage employment, and suicides.[125]

CSR strategy continues to grow with increasing importance in today's media-rich environment, but it may be a strategy at the margin. That is to say that all companies should concern themselves with developing a social strategy but careful consideration should be given to how and to what degree. The firm needs to commit to resources dedicated to supporting CSR activities while also supporting the core business objectives of the firm. In some instances, a company's core business objective simultaneously supports both the social welfare and the economic benefit of the firm. In this case, there is a positive relationship between CSR investment and the profitability of the firm.[126]

Box 7.14   Quick review on HRM, strategy, and CSR implications

- Companies are losing out on significant opportunities if they don't foster a diverse and inclusive culture, so HRM should comply with this societal demand.
- Entrepreneurs who build the foundation of their organization on ethics and CSR will have higher potential success.
- Developing a CSR program or strategy shouldn't be taken lightly, as poorly executed CSR programs can be detrimental to the firm.
- The firm needs to dedicate resources to supporting CSR activities while also supporting the core business objectives of the firm.
- Research has proven that diversity drives innovation and employee engagement, and that companies with greater gender and racial diversity financially outperform their peers.

This is referred to as the "zone of opportunity" by Karnani (2011), who contends that investing in this area is just wise business practice because it enables the firm to capitalize on all market opportunities. Businesses should carefully consider integrating their CSR strategy into their business strategy to maximize revenues, concentrating on synergistic alignments between profit growth and social responsibility.

A Brazilian door-to-door sale business based on sustainable growth values has expanded its strategy to flagship stores and global brands, believing that a beauty brand can do everything to make the world more beautiful and contribute to keeping the forest standing. Natura is a benchmark for CSR as a strategy leading to outstanding financial performance.

Figure 7.12 Natura plant – Cajamar-SP/Brazil
Source: www.flickr.com/photos/82289802@N00/3908986015

Box 7.15   Entrepreneurship and Amazonian rainforest protection: Natura

Brazilian cosmetics company Natura, founded in 1969, has grown from a small regional player operating mainly through door-to-door to a global powerhouse and the fourth-largest consumer segment in the cosmetics market (present in 100 countries in all continents with a network of over 6.3 million independent consultants and representatives, 35,000 employees and associates, and 200 million consumers around the world). The company is known for its innovative business model, which includes a direct-to-consumer sales network and a multi-brand portfolio of cosmetics, personal care, and fragrance brands.

In 2013, Natura acquired 65 percent capital of Emeis Holdings, owner of Aesop, an Australian organic luxury cosmetics brand, for the sum of €54.7 million (A$68.25). Aesop revenue was estimated at €51 million. In the meantime, the two companies will continue to function independently, keeping their respective teams. Later, Natura paid in 2017 an estimated value of €1 billion ($1.1 billion) to the French group L'Oreal, which has owned The Body Shop for the past 11 years. The Body Shop was established in the UK in 1976 by the late Dame Anita Roddick and pioneered manufacturing and selling cosmetics that have not been tested on animals and use natural ingredients. In 2020, Natura & Co closed the acquisition of Avon (its main rival), creating the world's fourth-largest pure-play beauty group. The negotiation involved approximately $3.7 billion, which led to creating of a group of $11 billion in annual revenues.

Today, Natura & Co is a publicly traded company with a market capitalization of over $20 billion and is widely recognized as one of the leading cosmetics companies in the world. The company remains committed to sustainability and continues to use natural ingredients in its products, making it a popular choice among consumers who value environmentally friendly products.

Regarding such trends and the right acquisitions, Natura & Co was founded on the idea of employing natural resources as essential components in its products and has long been recognized for its commitment to ethical, socially conscious business practices. Natura was the first Brazilian publicly traded company to obtain the B Corp seal (www.bcorporation.net/en-us/certification), recognizing companies committed to integrating financial results with the generation of socio-environmental results.

In addition, since 2000, it has been committed to developing sustainable and inclusive alternatives in the Amazon. In 2011, all initiatives to transform socio-environmental challenges into business opportunities were brought together in the "Amazônia Program." As a result, between 2012 and 2020, R$1.5 billion in new business was generated in the region, strengthening partnerships for conserving the environment and biodiversity chains.

By 2030, as part of the Natura & Co group – formed by Avon, Natura, The Body Shop, and Aesop – its goals aimed at a positive impact on the Amazon region, including expanding the area conserved with partnerships to 3 million hectares and mobilizing collective efforts for zero deforestation by 2025 too.

Today, they contribute to the conservation of 2 million hectares of standing forest and, in the last 10 years, have increased by seven times the use of Amazonian bio-ingredients extracted in partnership with agro-extractivist communities in their product portfolio.

Questions for discussion: Natura's case

1 Branding, multiplatform approach and environment, and social purpose: Natura's strategy inspires and serves as a reference for companies that want to stand out in the market. Considering ethics and business, what can Natura's strategy teach?

2 Change of sales strategy: after beginning with consultant support and magazine sales, it was understood that it was necessary to put sensory experiences on paper and get even closer to his audience! In this way, it opened physical stores across the country and the transformation of the company into a multichannel. The phase followed a market trend, with the aim of:

   a Enabling experimentation and immersion in Natura's ambiance
   b Allowing direct contact between customers and products
   c Creating a physical product display/showcase
   d Keeping the company's established model with catalog sales.

3 Considering the analysis of ten trends for 2023, explain the alignment of these strategies of Natura to them.

Concluding remarks

This chapter discussed three important topics – ethics, CSR, and HRM – which are deeply linked concepts with clear implications. Their influences on entrepreneurial and business reputations and outcomes were highlighted. The definition and theories of ethics, CSR, HRM, and their implication for entrepreneurial activities and development have been examined. CSR is more than a combination of activities; it should be the compass to build an organization's strategy. ESG and metrics are the mirrors of a CSR well conducted. The role of communications and technology as tools for transparency and good governance are analyzed. And social media helps to separate the wheat from the chaff. DEI is growing in importance in high-performance companies. Finally, we have provided some real-world examples related to the subjects. While all three main topics that were discussed in this chapter are essential, unfortunately, due to the limitation of space, we had to combine them into one chapter with a summary of each.

Discussion questions

1 What is the relationship between ethics and the longevity of a business? Give some examples.
2 Which ethical theories are more relevant to the discussion of this chapter? Defend your argument with examples.
3 What is the relationship between different theories which frame CSR and entrepreneurship?
4 How are CSR and human resource management issues applicable to entrepreneurial activity?
5 Provide a few examples of entrepreneurial activities that have applied CSR as a strategy.
6 Write a short case that applies at least two important topics in this chapter.

Table 7.3 Key terms

Axiological ethics	Utilitarian ethics	Corporate social responsibility (CSR)
Teleological ethics	Existentialist ethics	Corporate social entrepreneurship (CSE)
Deontological ethics	Naturalistic ethics	Environmental, social, and governance (ESG)
Perfectionist ethics	Relativistic ethics	Zone of opportunity

Table 7.4 Glossary

Axiological ethics	The science of determining the value of an idea or object for an individual or organization.
Teleological ethics	Considers an action proper or improper according to the desirability of its outcome.
Deontological ethics	Focuses on the obligations and duties that various members of society have towards one another.
Perfectionist ethics	Concerns the application of principles of moral perfectionism to ethical conduct of individuals and organizations.
Utilitarian ethics	Based on the premise that moral worth of an action depends entirely on its contribution to overall perceivable utility for society.
Existentialist ethics	Human freedom is the foundation of the understanding of all motives, reason, morals, and values.
Naturalistic ethics	Based on British empiricism, which implies that all knowledge is derived from experience and sensory perception.
Relativistic ethics	Ethical behavior cannot be defined or prescribed in universally applicable absolute terms.
Corporate social responsibility (CSR)	A company's sense of responsibility towards the community and environment (both ecological and social) in which it operates.
Corporate social entrepreneurship (CSE)	The process of extending the firm's domain of competence and corresponding opportunity set through innovative leveraging of resources, both within and outside its direct control, aimed at the simultaneous creation of economic and social value.
Environmental, social, and governance (ESG)	Refers to a set of three criteria used to evaluate the sustainability and societal impact of companies, organizations, and investments, measurements are one of the pillars of socially responsible investment (SRI).
Zone of opportunity	A term used in business and entrepreneurship to refer to the space or area in which a company can create value by identifying and pursuing opportunities that align with its strengths, values, and purpose. In this case, there is a positive relationship between CSR investment and the profitability of the firm.

Notes

1 Geva, A. (2000). Moral decision making in business: A phase-model. *Business Ethics Quarterly*, 10(4), 773–803. https://doi.org/10.2307/3857833
2 Thomas, J. (2020). Ethics in organization and management: The application of contemporary theories of ethical decision-making in global conditions. *International Journal of Business Strategy and Automation (IJBSA)*, 1(3), 67–74. https://doi.org/10.4018/IJBSA.20200701.oa1
3 Taylor, F.W. (1911). *The Principles of Scientific Management*. New York: Harper & Brothers. Print.
4 Van Buren, H.J. (2008). Fairness and the main management theories of the twentieth century: A historical review, 1900–1965. *Journal of Business Ethics*, 82(3), 633–644.
5 Foot, P. (2003). *Natural Goodness*. Oxford: Oxford University Press; Guyer, P. (2002). Ends of reason and ends of nature: The place of teleology in Kant's ethics. *Journal of Value Inquiry*, 36, 161.
6 Jackson, K. (2005). Towards authenticity: A Sartrean perspective on business ethics. *Journal of Business Ethics*, 58, 307–325.
7 Asgary, N., & Mitschow, M. (2002). Towards a model for international business ethics. *Journal of Business Ethics*, 36(3), 239–247.
8 Rachels, J. (2003). *The Elements of Moral Philosophy* (4th ed.). New York: McGraw-Hill Company Inc.
9 Garofalo, C. (2003). Toward a global ethic. *International Journal of Public Sector Management*, 16(7), 490–501. https://doi.org/10.1108/09513550310500373
10 Yaman, H.R. (2003). Skinner's naturalism as a paradigm for teaching business ethics: A discussion from tourism. *Teaching Business Ethics*, 7(2), 107–122. https://doi.org/10.1023/A:1022636929914
11 Tännsjö, T. (2007). Against sexual discrimination in sports. *Ethics in Sport*, (Ed. 2), 347–358. Retrieved from www.cabdirect.org/cabdirect/abstract/20073163457
12 Van Buren, H.J. (2008). Fairness and the main management theories of the twentieth century: A historical review, 1900–1965. *Journal of Business Ethics*, 82(3), 633–644.
13 Asgary, N., Walle, A., & Saraswat, S.P. (2014). Ethical foundations and managerial challenges: The strategic implications of moral standards. *Journal of Leadership, Accountability and Ethics*, 11(2).
14 Gotsis, G., & Kortezi, Z. (2008). Philosophical foundations of workplace spirituality: A critical approach. *Journal of Business Ethics*, 78(4), 575–600. https://doi.org/10.1007/s10551-007-9369-5
15 Foot, P. (2003). *Natural Goodness* (p. 136). Oxford: Clarendon Press. ISBN 019926547X.
16 Barry, N.P. (1979). *Hayek's Social and Economic Philosophy*. London: Palgrave Macmillan UK. https://doi.org/10.1007/978-1-349-04268-5
17 Sartre, J.-P. (1956). *Being and Nothingness: An Essay on Phenomenological Ontology*, translated by H.E. Barnes. New York: Philosophical Library Inc.
18 West, A. (2008). Sartrean existentialism and ethical decision-making in business. *Journal of Business Ethics*, 81(1), 15–25. https://doi.org/10.1007/s10551-007-9477-2
19 Yaman, H.R. (2003). Skinner's naturalism as a paradigm for teaching business ethics: A discussion from tourism. *Teaching Business Ethics*, 7(2), 107–122.
20 Henderson, R., & Prinsloo, L. (2021, June 23). South African brothers vanish, and so does $3.6 billion in Bitcoin. *Bloomberg (online)*. Retrieved from www.bloomberg.com/news/articles/2021-06-23/s-african-brothers-vanish-and-so-does-3-6-billion-in-bitcoin?leadSource=uverify%20wall
21 Retrieved February 2, 2023, from https://go.chainalysis.com/2021-Crypto-Crime-Report.html
22 Joyner, B., & Payne, D. (2002). Evolution and implementation: A study of values, business ethics and corporate responsibility. *Journal of Business Ethics*, 41(3), 297–311.
23 Lawrence, A., & Weber, J. (2011). *Business and Society: Stakeholders, Ethics, Public Policy* (13th ed.). New York: McGraw-Hill Irwin.
24 Joyner, B., & Payne, D. (2002). Evolution and implementation: A study of values, business ethics and corporate responsibility. *Journal of Business Ethics*, 41(3), 297–311.
25 Lawrence, A., & Weber, J. (2011). *Business and Society: Stakeholders, Ethics, Public Policy* (13th ed.). New York: McGraw-Hill Irwin.
26 Joyner, B., & Payne, D. (2002). Evolution and implementation: A study of values, business ethics and corporate responsibility. *Journal of Business Ethics*, 41(3), 297–311.
27 www.paxpopuli.org/
28 Badaracco, Jr. J.L. (1995). *Business Ethics Roles and Responsibilities*. Chicago: Irwin.
29 Joyner, B., & Payne, D. (2002). Evolution and implementation: A study of values, business ethics and corporate responsibility. *Journal of Business Ethics*, 41(3), 297–311.
30 Asgary, N., & Walle, A.H. (2002). The cultural impact of globalisation: Economic activity and social change. *Cross Cultural Management: An International Journal*, 9(3), 58–75. https://doi.org/10.1108/13527600210797433

31 Asgary, N., & Li, G. (2016). Corporate social responsibility: Its economic impact and link to the bull-whip effect. *Journal of Business Ethics*, 135(4), 665–681. https://doi.org/10.1007/s10551-014-2492-1

32 van der Merwe, R., Pitt, L., & Berthon, P. (2003). Are excellent companies ethical? Evidence from an industrial setting. *Corporate Reputation Review*, 5(4), 343–355. https://doi.org/10.1057/palgrave.crr.1540183

33 Peters, T., & Waterman, R. (1988). *In Search of Excellence: Lessons from America's Best-Run Companies*. New York: HarperCollins Publishers.

34 van der Merwe, R., Pitt, L., & Berthon, P. (2003). Are excellent companies ethical? Evidence from an industrial setting. *Corporate Reputation Review*, 5(4), 343–355. https://doi.org/10.1057/palgrave.crr.1540183

35 Ahmed, M.M., Chung, K.Y., & Eichenseher, J.W. (2003). Business students' perception of ethics and moral judgment: A cross-cultural study. *Journal of Business Ethics*, 43(1/2), 89.

36 Gowing, M., & Islam, M. (2003). Some empirical evidence of Chinese accounting system and business management practices from an ethical perspective. *Journal of Business Ethics*, 42(4), 353–378.

37 Sroka, W., & Szántó, R. (2018). Corporate social responsibility and business ethics in controversial sectors: Analysis of research results. *Journal of Entrepreneurship, Management and Innovation*, 14(3), 111–126. https://doi.org/10.7341/20181435

38 Ferrell, O.C., Harrison, D.E., Ferrell, L., & Hair, J.F. (2019). Business ethics, corporate social responsibility, and brand attitudes: An exploratory study. *Journal of Business Research*, 95, 491–501. https://doi.org/10.1016/j.jbusres.2018.07.039

39 www.businessdictionary.com/definition/social-responsibility.html

40 Freeman, R.E. (1984). *Strategic Management: A Stakeholder Approach*. Boston: Pitman.

41 Adam, M. et al. (2001). H2A.Z is required for global chromatin integrity and for recruitment of RNA polymerase II under specific conditions. *Molecular and Cellular Biology*, 21(18), 6270–6279.

42 Asgary, N., & Mitschow, M. (2002). Towards a model for international business ethics. *Journal of Business Ethics*, 36(3), 239–247.

43 Sethi, S.P. (2003). Globalization and the good corporation: A need for proactive coexistence. *Journal of Business Ethics*, 43(2), 21–31.

44 Donaldson, T., & Preston, L.E. (1995). The stakeholder theory of the corporation: Concepts, evidence, and implications. *Academy of Management Review*, 20(1), 65–91.

45 Jackson, I., & Nelson, J. (2004). *Values-Based Performance: Seven Strategies for Delivering Profits with Principles. Corporate Social Responsibility Initiative Working Paper No.7*. Cambridge, MA: John F. Kennedy School of Government, Harvard University.

46 Alchian, A., & Demsetz, H. (1972). Production, information costs, and economic organization. *American Economic Review*, 62, 777–795.

47 Jensen, M.C., & Meckling, W.H. (1976). Theory of firm: Managerial behavior, agency costs and ownership structure. *Journal of Financial Economics*, 3, 305–360.

48 Widyawati, L. (2019). A systematic literature review of socially responsible investment and environmental social governance metrics. *Business Strategy and the Environment*, 29(2), 619–637. https://doi.org/10.1002/bse.2393

49 Zaman, R., Atawnah, N., Baghdadi, G.A., & Liu, J. (2021). Fiduciary duty or loyalty? Evidence from co-opted boards and corporate misconduct. *Journal of Corporate Finance*, 70, 102066. https://doi.org/10.1016/j.jcorpfin.2021.102066

50 Berle, A., & Means, G. (1932). *The Modern Corporation and Private Property*. New York: Commerce Clearing House.

51 Zaman, R., Jain, T., Samara, G., & Jamali, D. (2022). Corporate governance meets corporate social responsibility: Mapping the interface. *Business & Society*, 61(3), 690–752. https://doi.org/10.1177/0007650320973415

52 Habbash, M. (2016). Corporate governance and corporate social responsibility disclosure: Evidence from Saudi Arabia. *Social Responsibility Journal*, 12(4), 740–754. https://doi.org/10.1108/SRJ-07-2015-0088

53 Ireland, Ministry for Enterprise and Innovation. (2017). *Ireland's National Plan on Corporate Social Responsibility 2017–2020. Towards Responsible Business*. Dublin. Retrieved from https://enterprise.gov.ie/en/publications/publication-files/towards-responsible-business-ireland%E2%80%99s-national-plan-csr-2017-2020.pdf

54 Kao, E.H., Yeh, C., Wang, L., & Fung, H. (2018). The relationship between CSR and performance: Evidence in China. *Pacific-Basin Finance Journal*, 51, 155–170. https://doi.org/10.1016/j.pacfin.2018.04.006

55 Steurer, R. (2010). The role of governments in corporate social responsibility: Characterising public policies on CSR in Europe. *Policy Sciences*, 43, 49–72. https://doi.org/10.1007/s11077-009-9084-4

56 Taylor, J., Vithayathil, J., & Yim, D. (2018). Are corporate social responsibility (CSR) initiatives such as sustainable development and environmental policies value enhancing or window dressing? *Corporate Social Responsibility and Environmental Management*, 25(5), 971–980. https://doi.org/10.1002/csr.1513

57 Chevron Charter of *Public Policy and Sustainability Committee*. Retrieved October 2, 2023, from www.chevron.com/investors/corporate-governance/public-policy

58 www.chevron.com/-/media/shared-media/documents/chevron-sustainability-report-2021.pdf

59 Vanhamme, J., & Grobben, B. (2008). "Too good to be true!": The effectiveness of CSR history in countering negative publicity. *Journal of Business Ethics*, 85(S2), 273–283, 276. https://doi.org/10.1007/s10551-008-9731-2

60 Phillip, A. (2014). Facebook's Mark Zuckerberg and wife Priscilla Chan donate $25 million to Ebola fight. *The Washington Post*. Retrieved from www.washingtonpost.com/news/to-your-health/wp/2014/10/14/facebooks-mark-zuckerberg-and-priscilla-chan-donate-25-million-to-ebola-fight/?utm_term=.1a85e74b14bc

61 Jackson, I., & Nelson, J. (2004). *Values-Based Performance: Seven Strategies for Delivering Profits with Principles. Corporate Social Responsibility Initiative Working Paper No.7*. Cambridge, MA; John F. Kennedy School of Government, Harvard University.

62 Wunsch, C., & Lechner, M. (2008). What did all the money do? On the general ineffectiveness of recent West German labour market programmes. *Kyklos*, 61(1), 134–174.

63 Curcio, R.J., & Wolf, F.M. (1996). Corporate environmental strategy: Impact upon firm value. *Journal of Financial and Strategic Decisions*, 9(2), 21–31.

64 Vallaster, C., Lindgreen, A., & Maon, F. (2012). Strategically leveraging corporate social responsibility to the benefit of company and society: A corporate branding perspective. *California Management Review*, 54(3), 34–60. ISSN 0008-1256

65 Zahra, S.A. (2015). Corporate entrepreneurship as knowledge creation and conversion: The role of entrepreneurial hubs. *Small Business Economics*, 44(4), 727–735. https://doi.org/10.1007/s11187-015-9650-4

66 Austin, J., & Reficco, E. (2008). Corporate social entrepreneurship. *International Journal of Not-for-Profit Law*, 11, 86.

67 Austin, J.E., Leonard, H., Reficco, E., & Wei-Skillern, J. (2006). Social entrepreneurship: It's for corporations too. *Social Entrepreneurship New Models of Sustainable Social Change*, 169–180, 175.

68 Achleitner, A.-K., Lutz, E., Mayer, J., & Spiess-Knafl, W. (2013). Disentangling gut feeling: Assessing the integrity of social entrepreneurs. *Voluntas: International Journal of Voluntary and Nonprofit Organizations*, 24(1), 93–124. https://doi.org/10.1007/s11266-012-9264-2

69 Tiba, S., van Rijnsoever, F.J., & Hekkert, M.P. (2019). Firms with benefits: A systematic review of responsible entrepreneurship and corporate social responsibility literature. *Corporate Social Responsibility and Environmental Management*, 26(2), 265–284. https://doi.org/10.1002/csr.1682

70 Fuller, T., & Tian, Y. (2006). Social and symbolic capital and responsible entrepreneurship: An empirical investigation of SME narratives. *Journal of Business Ethics*, 67, 287–304. http://link.springer.com/article/10.1007/s10551-006-9185-3

71 Bocken, N. (2015). Sustainable venture capital – catalyst for sustainable start-up success? *Journal of Cleaner Production*, 108, 647–658. https://doi.org/10.1016/j.jclepro.2015.05.079

72 https://stories.starbucks.com/press/2022/starbucks-names-laxman-narasimhan-as-next-chief-executive-officer/

73 Widyawati, L. (2019). A systematic literature review of socially responsible investment and environmental social governance metrics. *Business Strategy and the Environment*, 29(2), 619–637. https://doi.org/10.1002/bse.2393

74 Li, J., Ren, L., Yao, S., Qiao, J., Mikalauskiene, A., & Streimikis, J. (2020). Exploring the relationship between corporate social responsibility and firm competitiveness. *Economic Research-Ekonomska istraživanja*, 33(1), 1621–1646. https://doi.org/10.1080/1331677x.2020.1761419

75 Yoon, B., Lee, J.H., & Byun, R. (2018). Does ESG performance enhance firm value? Evidence from Korea. *Sustainability*, 10, 3635. https://doi.org/10.3390/su10103635

76 Porter, E., & Kramer, M.R. (2006, December). Estrategia y sociedad. *Harvard Business Review-America Latina*, 3–15.

77 Kiran, R., & Sharma, A. (2011). Corporate social responsibility and management education: Changing perception and perspectives. *Global Journal of Management and Business Research*, 11(6). https://journalofbusiness.org/index.php/GJMBR/article/view/517

78 Harris, P. (2012). Apple hit by boycott call over worker abuses in China. *The Guardian*. Retrieved from www.guardian.co.uk/technology/2012/jan/29/apple-faces-boycott-worker-abuses

79 Porter, M.E., & Kramer, M.R. (2006). Strategy and society. *Harvard Business Review*, 84(12), 78–92.
80 Gonzalez, M.C., & Martinez, C.V. (2004). Fostering corporate social responsibility through public initiative: From the EU to the Spanish case. *Journal of Business Ethics*, 55(3), 275–293.
81 Perez-Aleman, P., & Sandilands, M. (2008). Building value at the top and the bottom of the global supply chain: MNC-NGO partnerships. *California Management Review*, 51(1), 24–49.
82 Asgary, N., & Li, G. (2016). Corporate social responsibility: Its economic impact and link to the bullwhip effect. *Journal of Business Ethics*, 135(4), 665–681.
83 Luo, W., Li, Y., Tang, C.H., Abruzzi, K.C., Rodriguez, J., Pescatore, S., & Rosbash, M. (2012). CLOCK deubiquitylation by USP8 inhibits CLK/CYC transcription in Drosophila. *Genes & Development*, 26(22), 2536–2549.
84 Byruch, G. (2016). *Corporate Social Responsibility: Mark Zuckerberg Makes a Statement.* Medium, December 7, 2015. Web. November 8. https://medium.com/@geoffreybyruch/corporate-social-responsibility-mark-zuckerberg-makes-a-statement-138bf3f42c6e
85 www.freshfields.com/49fabb/globalassets/campaign-landing/cyber-security/containing-a-crisis.pdf
86 BCW. (n.d.). *BCW*. Retrieved from https://bcw-global.com/
87 Freshfields Bruckhaus Deringer. (n.d.). *Containing a Crisis: Dealing with Corporate Disasters in the Digital Age.* www.freshfields.com/49fabb/globalassets/campaign-landing/cyber-security/containing-a-crisis.pdf
88 Schneider, B., Ehrhart, M.G., & Macey, W.H. (2013). Organizational climate and culture. *Annual Review of Psychology*, 64, 361–388.
89 Nguyen, H. (2016, October 17). *CSR and When to Come to Marketing Strategy.* Retrieved from www.linkedin.com/pulse/csr-when-come-marketing-strategy-lee-nguyen
90 Schneider, B., Hanges, P.J., Smith, D.B., & Salvaggio, A.N. (2003). Which comes first: Employee attitudes or organizational financial and market performance? *Journal of Applied Psychology*, 88(5), 836.
91 Hammer, M., Champy, J., & Künzel, P. (1994). *Business Reengineering: Die Radikalkur für Das Unternehmen* (p. 120). Frankfurt: Campus.
92 Kemelgor, B.H. (2002). *A Comparative Analysis of Corporate Entrepreneurial Orientation between Selected Firms in the Netherlands and the U.S.A.* (pp. 67–86). London: Taylor & Francis.
93 Kuratko, D.F., Hornsby, J.S., & Goldsby, M.G. (2004). Sustaining corporate entrepreneurship. *International Journal of Entrepreneurship and Innovation*, 5(2), 77–89.
94 Itam, U., & Bagali, M.M. (2018). Diversity and inclusion management: A focus on employee engagement. In *Management Techniques for a Diverse and Cross-Cultural Workforce* (pp. 149–171). https://doi.org/10.4018/978-1-5225-4933-8.ch009
95 Ganeshan, M.K., & Vethirajan, C. (2022, June 10–12). Diversity, equity, and inclusion in the workplace in human resource management. In M. Günes Açikgöz, & Z. Alimgerey (Eds.), *International Congress on Social Sciences, China to Adriatic-XIV, Proceedings Book.* Kayseri, Turkey: IKSAD Global. ISBN 978-625-8323-42-9. Retrieved from https://iksadyayinevi.com/
96 Norman, M.V., & Johnson, K.M. (2022). The importance of employee inclusion: Lessons for HR managers. *Strategic HR Review*, 21(1), 20–24. https://doi.org/10.1108/SHR-11-2021-0052
97 Noon, M., & Ogbonna, E. (2020). Controlling management to deliver diversity and inclusion: Prospects and limits. *Human Resource Management Journal*, 31(3), 619–638. https://doi.org/10.1111/1748-8583.12332
98 www.globalreporting.org/
99 www.mckinsey.com/featured-insights/diversity-and-inclusion/women-in-the-workplace
100 LeanIn.Org and McKinsey & Company. (2022, October). *Women in the Workplace 2022.* Retrieved from https://womenintheworkplace.com/
101 www.wpp.com/
102 DeNisi, A.S., Wilson, M.S., & Biteman, J. (2014). Research and practice in HRM: A historical perspective. *Human Resource Management Review*, 24, 219–231.
103 Hagiwara, N., Wessel, J.L., & Ryan, A.M. (2012). Race and gender acknowledgment in the presidential election 2008: When did stigma acknowledgment hurt or benefit the candidates? *Journal of Applied Social Psychology*, 42, 2191–2212.
104 Stone, D.L., & Deadrick, D.L. (2015). Challenges and opportunities affecting the future of human resource management. *Human Resource Management Review*, 25(2), 139–145.

105 Matten, D., & Moon, J. (2008). "Implicit" and "explicit" CSR: A conceptual framework for a comparative understanding of corporate social responsibility. *Academy of Management Review*, 33, 404–424.

106 Jamali, D., & El Dirani, A. (2013). CSR and HRM for workplace integrity: Advancing the business ethics agenda. In W. Amann, & A. Stachowicz-Stanusch (Eds.), *Integrity in Organizations: Building the Foundations for Humanistic Management* (pp. 439–456). London: Palgrave Macmillan.

107 Jamali, D.R., Dirani, A.M., & Harwood, I.A. (2014). Exploring human resource management roles in corporate social responsibility: The CSR-HRM co-creation model. *Business Ethics: A European Review*, 24(2), 125–143. https://doi.org/10.1111/beer.12085

108 Voegtlin, C., & Greenwood, M. (2016). Corporate social responsibility and human resource management: A systematic review and conceptual analysis. *Human Resource Management Review*, 26(3), 181–197. https://doi.org/10.1016/j.hrmr.2015.12.003

109 Jamali, D.R., Dirani, A.M., & Harwood, I.A. (2014). Exploring human resource management roles in corporate social responsibility: The CSR-HRM co-creation model. *Business Ethics: A European Review*, 24(2), 125–143. https://doi.org/10.1111/beer.12085

110 Gond, J.-P., Igalens, J., Swaen, V., & El Akremi, A. (2011). The human resources contribution to responsible leadership: An exploration of the CSR – HR interface. *Journal of Business Ethics*, 98(S1), 115–132. https://doi.org/10.1007/s10551-011-1028-1

111 Carnevale, J.B., & Hatak, I. (2020). Employee adjustment and well-being in the era of COVID-19: Implications for human resource management. *Journal of Business Research*, 116, 183–187. https://doi.org/10.1016/j.jbusres.2020.05.037

112 Hu, X., Yan, H., Casey, T., & Wu, C.H. (2021). Creating a safe haven during the crisis: How organizations can achieve deep compliance with COVID-19 safety measures in the hospitality industry. *International Journal of Hospitality Management*, 92, 102662. https://doi.org/10.1016/j.ijhm.2020.102662

113 Davies, S., White, G.R.T., Samuel, A., & Martin, H. (2021). Dialectics and dilemmas arising from Covid-19 immunity testing: Presenting a workforce management paradox. *JWAM*, 13, 227–240. https://doi.org/10.1108/JWAM-11-2020-0052

114 Stergiou, D.P., & Farmaki, A. (2020). Ability and willingness to work during COVID-19 pandemic: Perspectives of front-line hotel employees. *International Journal of Hospitality Management*, 93, 102770. https://doi.org/10.1016/j.ijhm.2020.102770

115 Austin, J.E., Leonard, H., Reficco, E., & Wei-Skillern, J. (2006). Social entrepreneurship: It's for corporations too. *Social Entrepreneurship: New Models of Sustainable Social Change*, 169–180.

116 Asgary, N., & Li, G. (2016). Corporate social responsibility: Its economic impact and link to the bullwhip effect. *Journal of Business Ethics*, 135(4), 665–681.

117 Vallaster, C., Lindgreen, A., & Maon, F. (2012). Strategically leveraging corporate social responsibility: A corporate branding perspective. *California Management Review*, 54(3), 34–60. https://doi.org/10.1525/cmr.2012.54.3.34

118 Bank of America. (2013). *Corporate Social Responsibility 2013 Report*. Retrieved from https://about.bankofamerica.com/assets/pdf/Bank-of-America-2013-Corporate-Social-Responsibility-Report.pdf

119 Reputation Quotient. (n.d.). Retrieved from https://theharrispoll.com/reputation-quotient/

120 Enlace Project. (n.d.). Retrieved from www.enlaceproject.org/; and SUNY Geneseo. (n.d.). Retrieved from www.geneseo.edu/

121 Karnani, A. (2011). "Doing well by doing good": The grand illusion. *California Management Review*, 53(2), 69–86.

122 Friedman, M. (1970, September 13). The social responsibility of business is to increase its profits. *New York Times Magazine*, 32–33, 122–124.

123 Karnani, A. (2011). "Doing well by doing good": The grand illusion. *California Management Review*, 53(2), 69–86.

124 Aupperle, K.E., Carroll, A.B., & Hatfield, J.D. (1985). An empirical examination of the relationship between corporate social responsibility and profitability. *Academy of Management Journal*, 28(2), 446–463.

125 Duhigg, C., & Barboza, D. (2012, January 26). In China, the human costs that are built into an iPad. *The New York Times*, A1.

126 Karnani, A. (2011). "Doing well by doing good": The grand illusion. *California Management Review*, 53(2), 69–86.

Section IV

Process

8 Sustainability as a strategy for business operation

Learning objectives

1 Understand what is an entrepreneur as a social change agent
2 Critically examine how different models of entrepreneurship aligned with the UN Sustainable Development Goals could be applied to low-income country contexts and poverty reduction
3 Recognize the importance of a planned transition to a low-carbon economy for business
4 Evaluate the value creation of a business from an ethical and sustainability perspective
5 Analyze social and ecological problems as entrepreneurial opportunities.

Box 8.1 Agricultural innovation in South America: propelling Peru's sustainable growth

Figure 8.1 Cusco-Puno Raqchi woman

Source: "Cusco-Puno Raqchi woman on Inca Trail" by Yandi is licensed under CC BY 2.0. www.flickr.com/photos/87337695@N00/364125769

DOI: 10.4324/9781003405740-13

World Bank Group (WBG) is a global partnership with 189 member countries working for sustainable solutions that reduce poverty in developing countries. Using global experience and in collaboration with the Inter-American Development Bank, WBG replaced in Peru the traditional linear model (dominated by public agencies, where research institutes eventually transfer improved technologies to public extension agencies for distribution to end-users) with a multi-actor innovation network in which public agencies, private firms, civil society organizations, and end-users could interact through iterative feedback loops, allowing innovations originating in different locations to flow throughout the system in response to supply and demand forces.

The National Agricultural Innovation Project (known as PNIA from its Spanish acronym) funded efforts on multiple fronts to foster the creation of a new multimodal innovation network. One set of initiatives centered on bolstering National Institute of Agricultural Innovation position as the national agricultural innovation system leader by rehabilitating aged infrastructure, updating equipment, training personnel, and revising institutional policies and processes. A second set of initiatives centered on constructing the national agricultural innovation system by establishing regional bodies and facilitating the development of locally tailored innovation agendas. A third set of operations focused on supporting innovation on the ground, most notably through a demand-driven competitive grants program that directed financing to innovative activities via 541 subprojects carried out around the nation.

The generated innovations were adopted by approximately 32,000 farmers, resulting in an average 34 percent increase in their revenues. In addition, researchers and extension personnel received more than 75,000 training days, and 57 agriculture-related master's degrees, including 25 for women, were awarded.

The World Bank, through the International Bank for Reconstruction and Development (IBRD), approved a loan in the amount of $40 million to finance this project. Project preparation activities came through a grant in the amount of $350,000 financed by the Spanish Fund for Latin America (SFLAC), a region-specific trust fund program and a critical instrument of the Bank's work in the Latin America and Caribbean region. Besides, an additional $40 million (parallel funding) was offered from the Inter-American Development Bank. So, teams from the two banks coordinated their efforts to pursue a common development goal.

Counterpart funding by the government of Peru provided approximately $37.4 million to finance project costs. Project beneficiaries (individual farmers, producer organizations, and agribusiness enterprises) also actively participated in the design and implementation of subprojects, giving about $24.1 million in cash or in kind to access subproject finance through the competitive grant windows.

PNIA, implemented between 2015 and 2021, achieved the following key results in Peru:

- Strengthened INIA's capacity
- Raised awareness of the innovation agenda
- Consolidated the national agriculture innovation system
- Financed demand-driven innovation
- Trained the next generation of innovators.

As an example, Carmen Chavez, a veterinary student from Peru's Amazonas Region, is one of the 189 students who participated in PNIA's worldwide internship program. She spent 6 months at Sassari University in Sardinia, Italy, studying enhanced management strategies for sheep milk production as part of the curriculum. She selected this project because she is interested in discovering solutions for intensive livestock production that could help prevent deforestation in the Peruvian Amazon. Carmen performed fieldwork at Caseificio Deidda for the first 3 months, where she learned how to produce dairy products. Then, she worked on the Cuscusa farm for the final 6 months of the internship, handling, feeding, and caring for goats and sheep. Carmen adds, "Thanks to this internship, I have realized my responsibility as a professional to contribute to the development of our country and particularly my region: Amazonas."

The outstanding results produced by PNIA demonstrate conclusively that sector-level innovation support may be highly effective. Maintaining the results of PNIA and building upon its established foundation would require strong ownership of the project by the Peruvian government and continuous political and financial support. The relative advantages and disadvantages of promoting innovation at the sectoral level versus concentrating efforts within a single, more centralized agency or program are currently the subject of heated discussion in Peru. The outcome of this debate will likely determine whether or not the PNIA's results can be sustained in the future.

Source: www.worldbank.org/en/results/2021/11/04/fueling-an-engine-of-sustainable-growth-agricultural-innovation-in-peru

---

This project's outcomes reinforce the idea of Sustainable Development Goals – the implementation of SDGs requires great support from policymakers (government) especially by introducing new policies and measures, as well as the private sector (business) and civil society participation. SDG 17: Strengthen the means of implementation and revitalize the Global Partnership for Sustainable Development is exemplified by PNIA.

A Partnership Accelerator Guidebook was recently launched by the UN (2020)[1] which aims to convey how multi-stakeholder at the country level can deliver extraordinary results towards the Sustainable Development Goals and provide clear guidance on building the most robust, effective collaborations.

This Guidebook presents the key building blocks of successful partnerships and the underlying processes – from initial stakeholder engagement to partnership review – necessary to develop and keep them in place and to maximize partnership impact.

Partnership and SDG-related subjects will be more profoundly discussed in the following items of this chapter.

Box 8.2 Questions for discussion: PNIA's case

1 Cite two advantages and two disadvantages of the Peruvian traditional public agency model.
2 Due to climate change it is necessary to improve research skills and firm-level innovation in the agriculture sector. Discuss the experience that occurred in Carmen's internship.

3 Rank the results obtained in PNIA's considering the goal of strengthening the science, technology, and innovation system in Peru. Justify your answer.
4 How can multilateral funds improve the support of a green and resilient development policy in emerging economies?

Learn more

Peru National Agricultural Innovation Project (World Bank's Project Page)

Multimedia

Video: ¿Qué son los fondos concursables del PNIA? (in Spanish)
Video: Proyecto introducción de razas de cuyes para mejorar el mercado (in Spanish)

Introduction

Our Common Future, often known as the Brundtland Report, was released by the UN and Oxford University Press in October 1987. This book was published in recognition of former Norwegian Prime Minister Gro Harlem Brundtland's role as chair of the World Commission on Environment and Development. (WCED).

Its ambition was to promote multilateralism and interdependence among nations in pursuing a path to sustainable development. The study intended to revive the spirit of the Stockholm Conference (1972), which pushed environmental concerns into the realm of formal political growth. Finally, this book proposes to analyze the environment and development as a single issue for better results.

In 1992, the UN Conference on Environment and Development (UNCED), popularly known as the Rio Conference or the Earth Summit (Portuguese: ECO92), was held in Rio de Janeiro, Brazil. It was conducted as a venue for member nations to collaborate on sustainability concerns, as individual member states could not address them independently. Since its inception, many others in the field of sustainability, including non-governmental organizations (NGOs), have developed similarly to the topics presented at these conferences. An agreement on the Climate Change Convention, which led to the Kyoto Protocol and the Paris Agreement, was a major outcome of the meeting. Another commitment was to "not conduct any activities on indigenous peoples' lands that would degrade the environment or be culturally inappropriate." Also, at the Earth Summit, the Convention on Biological Diversity was opened for signatures, marking the beginning of a reinterpretation of measures that do not intrinsically support the destruction of natural ecoregions and so-called uneconomic growth.

The UN Conference on Sustainable Development – or Rio+20 – took place in Rio de Janeiro, Brazil on June 2012. It resulted in a focused political outcome document which contains clear and practical measures for implementing sustainable development. Different from the previous one (1992), its practical results were less than expected.[2] This negative evaluation is the consequence of failed expectations for a bold, ambitious collective global vision or treaty to address the increasing urgency of modern environmental issues.

At the beginning of the 21st century, half of the world's population lived on less than $2 a day, and nearly a billion people lacked access to adequate water sources (i.e., safe drinking water and basic sanitation). Over 30,000 people die daily from avoidable illnesses.[3] After more

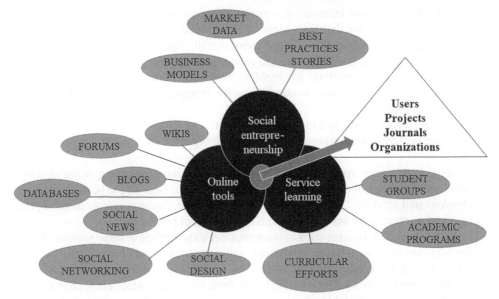

Figure 8.2 Information Technology and Open Sustainability Network (OSN)

Source: Pearce et al. (2019, p. 202).

than two decades, there has been some improvement due to individuals, nonprofit organizations, community groups, schools, corporations, governments, and other organizations which have been advocating for equitable, sustainable development. These factions developing relevant technologies, small enterprises, and goods contribute to constructing a sustainable and just world.

Pearce and colleagues (2019)[4] presented a strategy to improve the results towards the sustainable development achievements: the Open Sustainability Network (OSN). OSN could links relevant individuals, programs, courses, projects, and organizations aimed at just sustainable development (Figure 8.2). The proposed OSN could help to (1) develop partnerships with sites with online tools to alleviate some of the technological overhead; (2) help inform entrepreneurs and expanding businesses about the challenges and opportunities presented in social entrepreneurship; and (3) benefit service learning implementation by acting as a repository for appropriate technologies, systems, and policies, while also acting as a clearinghouse for international and local collaborations.

Nowadays, millions of online tools exist, many of which could be employed to addressing sustainable development issues. The primary categories of online tool types are described here as examples of each type in the arena of sustainability as mentioned by Pearce et al. (2019, p. 203).

- *Blog*: An often updated online diary or journal, sometimes with multiple editors.
- *Wiki*: A site that allows users to collectively edit pages.
- *Forum*: An online community of users posting questions, answers, and rants on topics of common interest.
- *Journal*: A periodical publication, dedicated to a specific topic, which contains scholarly manuscripts usually written by students, professors, or experts and reviewed by peers.

- *Database*: A collection of information organized in a particular, often searchable, manner.
- *Social networking*: A site that links users together based on similar interests by providing social tools, such as profiles, chats, and network visualizations.
- *Social news*: A website that allows users to submit, vote on, and filter relevant news.
- *Social design*: A online platform for enabling individuals, teams, and communities to co-design by providing tools such as community file storage, online whiteboards, and some social networking.
- *Project*: Any website dedicated to a specific project.
- *Organization*: Any website representing a particular organization.

Additionally, building on appropriate technology creation and prototyping being developed online via collaborative technology, entrepreneurship offers a unique way to scale up the impact of technology and services. Consequently, social entrepreneurship uses entrepreneurial principles to organize, create, and manage a venture to solve social problems.

The term *sustainable* is being used in numerous contexts, including sustainable living, sustainable transportation, sustainable agriculture, and sustainable economic growth. Therefore, students should ideally comprehend the philosophy of sustainable development and be able to see how the notion may be used on multiple levels, from the micro (a sustainable chair or pair of shoes) to the macro (a sustainable city or economic system).[5] (Development Education Project, 2007). *Service learning* can be defined as a teaching method that combines community service with academic instruction as it focuses on critical, reflective thinking and civic responsibility. In this sense, service-learning programs address local needs while developing students' "academic skills, sense of civic responsibility, and commitment to the community" (Pearce et al., 2019, p. 207).

Sustainable Development Goals and entrepreneurial activity

Entrepreneurs can be the change agents of sustainable development, aligned with the UN Millennium Development Goals, (MDGs); Sustainable Development Goals (SDGs) and Agenda 2030, and this will be presented in the following sections of the present chapter.

In the literature and among experts and governmental agencies, entrepreneurship has emerged as a vital factor for generating economic value and having a beneficial social and environmental impact in many countries. Sustainability-oriented entrepreneurship is primarily driven by entrepreneurial expertise, understanding of the natural and communal surroundings, and motivation. In addition, new business paradigms and innovation can motivate entrepreneurs to develop answers to long-standing problems and significantly impact their community and society as a whole. Nonetheless, social and environmental effects goals are highly different and dependent on each country's socioeconomic and political conditions for fostering entrepreneurship.

Entrepreneurship has become recognized as a means of transforming economic sectors towards sustainable development.[6,7,8] Sustainable businesses that simultaneously pursue environmental preservation, social welfare, and economic viability are considered increasingly influential change agents.[9,10] However, due to the multitude of aims inherent to sustainable entrepreneurship, the effective exploitation of sustainable business prospects can be viewed as more complex than the successful exploitation of opportunities driven only by economic factors achieving concurrent economic, social, and environmental objectives (Hall et al., 2010;[11] Sarango-Lalangui et al., 2018[12]).

The goal of sustainable development is economic efficiency (economic growth), social responsibility (social progress), and environmental protection, integrated, being the pillars of a so-called triple-bottom-line (Elkington, 1998[13]). A plan for achieving a better future for human-kind was created in September 2015 by all 193 Member States of the UN, outlining a path to end extreme poverty, combat inequality and injustice, and safeguard our planet over the next 15 years. At the core of Agenda 2030 are the 17 SDGs that define the desirable world – encompassing all nations and leaving no one behind (see Table 8.1 for a description).

The new Global Goals, which substitute the Millennium Development Goals, are the outcome of a process that has been more inclusive than ever before, with businesses, civil society, and individuals participating from the beginning. As a result, there is a consensus on the direction the world must take. However, realizing these goals would require extraordinary effort from all sectors of society, with business playing a crucial role in the process.

Table 8.1 The 17 UN Sustainable Development Goals

Goal	Description
1. No poverty	Economic growth must be inclusive to provide sustainable jobs and promote equality.
2. Zero hunger	The food and agriculture sector offers key solutions for development, and is central to hunger and poverty eradication.
3. Good health and well-being	Ensuring healthy lives and promoting the well-being for all at all ages is essential to sustainable development.
4. Quality education	Obtaining a quality education is the foundation for improving people's lives and sustainable development.
5. Gender equality	Gender equality is not only a fundamental human right, but a necessary foundation for a peaceful, prosperous and sustainable world.
6. Clean water and sanitation	Clean, accessible water for all is an essential part of the world we want to live in.
7. Affordable and clean energy	Energy is central to nearly every major challenge and opportunity.
8. Decent work and economic growth	Sustainable economic growth will require societies to create the conditions that allow people to have quality jobs.
9. Industry, innovation and infrastructure	Investments in infrastructure are crucial to achieving sustainable development.
10. Reduced inequalities	To reduce inequalities, policies should be universal in principle, paying attention to the needs of disadvantaged and marginalized populations.
11. Sustainable cities and communities	There needs to be a future in which cities provide opportunities for all, with access to basic services, energy, housing, transportation and more.
12. Responsible consumption and production	It is about promoting energy efficiency and providing access to basic goods and services. It means accelerating green jobs and therefore, better quality of life.
13. Climate action	Climate change is a global challenge that affects everyone, everywhere.
14. Life below water	Careful management of this essential global resource is a key feature of a sustainable future.
15. Life on land	Sustainably manage forests, combat desertification, halt and reverse land degradation, and halt biodiversity loss.
16. Peace, justice and strong institutions	Access to justice for all, and building effective, accountable institutions at all levels.
17. Partnerships for the goals	Revitalize the global partnership for sustainable development.

Source: Sachs et al. (2018).[14]

Environmentally relevant market failures (e.g., public goods, externalities, monopoly power, inappropriate government intervention, and imperfect information) may present opportunities for entrepreneurs to simultaneously achieve profitability and reduce the environmental degradation of economic behavior.[15]

In some countries, opportunity entrepreneurs are subject to stringent regulation that compels them to use more sustainable production methods; consequently, their businesses will be designed to take advantage of this opportunity to increase their market share or enter new markets, which was not possible before the change in regulation, and to contribute to sustainable development at the same time they profit.

However, researchers point out that stronger regulations may be so onerous for many entrepreneurs to adapt their businesses that they abandon their entrepreneurial endeavors.[16]

To support them to overcome this challenges, initiatives like the UN Global Compact,[17] can help them to:

- Conduct business responsibly by aligning their strategies and operations with ten principles on human rights, labor, environment, and anti-corruption;
- Take strategic actions to advance broader societal goals, such as the UN Sustainable Development Goals, with an emphasis on collaboration and innovation.

There are two important tools to evaluate entrepreneurship and the achievement of SDGs of a country: the Global Entrepreneurship Monitor (GEM; www.gemconsortium.org/) database and the SDGs (www.sdgindex.org/) Index.

The GEM database is the most comprehensive study of entrepreneurship globally. Data is collected annually by the Adult Population Survey (APS), resulting from a questionnaire given to at least 2000 adults in each GEM country. The SDG Index constitutes a yearly summary of the country's performance on the 17 Sustainable Development Goals compiled by the Bertelsmann Stiftung and Sustainable Development Solutions Network; the ranking of 2022 is displayed in Table 8.2. It is interesting that the leading positions belong to Scandinavian countries. Missing countries on this list are due to their lack of SDG Index calculation in the website.

With some exceptions, the leading places are occupied by European Community countries or developed nations with relatively strong economic growth and stability. Their high income per capita or GDP, the level of industrialization, the general standard of living, and the amount of technological infrastructure along with noneconomic indicators, such as the Human Development Index (HDI), which quantifies a country's levels of education, literacy, and health benefits.

As mentioned earlier in this chapter, one of the biggest challenges of the 21st century is to reconcile economic growth with social progress and environmental sustainability. Climate change is already exerting pressure on shared natural resources and triggering devastating weather events. And in some countries, conflicts and governance issues persist, exacerbated by weak social cohesion, ethnic tensions, and violent extremism. To address some of these problems, entrepreneurship has been generally acknowledged as a crucial road to sustainable development, positively contributing to the growth of a nation's economy.

For example, the data from the GEM indicate that entrepreneurship is a significant component in promoting sustainability, particularly for opportunity-driven and innovative entrepreneurial activities. In this sense, entrepreneurship should become a national priority by introducing new laws and initiatives, that is, by creating the conditions for entrepreneurship to contribute significantly, leading to sustainable development goals consecution. On the organizational level, there are some examples showing that it is feasible to build an organization that generates financial

Table 8.2 Sustainable Development Index by country: ranking in 2022

Rank	Country	Score	Rank	Country	Score	Rank	Country	Score
1	Finland	86.51	56	China	72.38	111	Lao PDR	63.39
2	Denmark	85.63	57	North Macedonia	72.31	112	Honduras	63.07
3	Sweden	85.19	58	Peru	71.93	113	Gabon	62.83
4	Norway	82.35	59	Bosnia and Herzegovina	71.73	114	Namibia	62.72
5	Austria	82.32	60	Singapore	71.72	115	Iraq	62.25
6	Germany	82.18	61	Albania	71.63	116	Botswana	61.43
7	France	81.24	62	Suriname	71.59	117	Guatemala	61.00
8	Switzerland	80.79	63	Ecuador	71.55	118	Kenya	60.96
9	Ireland	80.66	64	Algeria	71.54	119	Trinidad and Tobago	60.41
10	Estonia	80.62	65	Kazakhstan	71.14	120	Venezuela, RB	60.34
11	United Kingdom	80.55	66	Armenia	71.05	121	India	60.32
12	Poland	80.54	67	Maldives	71.03	122	Gambia, The	60.17
13	Czech Republic	80.47	68	Dominican Republic	70.76	123	Sao Tome and Principe	59.42
14	Latvia	80.28	69	Tunisia	70.69	124	Rwanda	59.42
15	Slovenia	79.95	70	Bhutan	70.49	125	Pakistan	59.34
16	Spain	79.90	71	Turkey	70.41	126	Senegal	58.70
17	Netherlands	79.85	72	Malaysia	70.38	127	Cote d'Ivoire	58.42
18	Belgium	79.69	73	Barbados	70.34	128	Ethiopia	58.01
19	Japan	79.58	74	Mexico	70.20	129	Syrian Arab Republic	57.37
20	Portugal	79.23	75	Colombia	70.13	130	Tanzania	57.37
21	Hungary	79.01	76	Sri Lanka	70.03	131	Zimbabwe	56.77
22	Iceland	78.87	77	Uzbekistan	69.93	132	Mauritania	55.83
23	Croatia	78.79	78	Tajikistan	69.68	133	Togo	55.57
24	Slovak Republic	78.66	79	El Salvador	69.60	134	Cameroon	55.55
25	Italy	78.34	80	Jordan	69.41	135	Lesotho	55.06
26	New Zealand	78.30	81	Oman	69.19	136	Uganda	54.86
27	Korea, Rep.	77.90	82	Indonesia	69.16	137	Eswatini	54.63
28	Chile	77.81	83	Jamaica	69.02	138	Burkina Faso	54.47
29	Canada	77.73	84	Morocco	68.98	139	Nigeria	54.23
30	Romania	77.72	85	United Arab Emirates	68.84	140	Zambia	54.16
31	Uruguay	77.00	86	Montenegro	68.81	141	Burundi	54.05
32	Greece	76.81	87	Egypt, Arab Rep.	68.66	142	Mali	54.05
33	Malta	76.77	88	Iran, Islamic Rep.	68.59	143	Mozambique	53.57
34	Belarus	75.99	89	Mauritius	68.40	144	Papua New Guinea	53.56
35	Serbia	75.89	90	Bolivia	67.99	145	Malawi	53.25
36	Luxembourg	75.74	91	Paraguay	67.43	146	Sierra Leone	52.98
37	Ukraine	75.69	92	Nicaragua	67.14	147	Afghanistan	52.49
38	Australia	75.58	93	Brunei Darussalam	67.10	148	Congo, Rep.	52.33
39	Lithuania	75.42	94	Qatar	66.78	149	Niger	52.20
40	Cuba	74.66	95	Philippines	66.64	150	Yemen, Rep.	52.08
41	United States	74.55	96	Saudi Arabia	66.56	151	Haiti	51.91
42	Bulgaria	74.29	97	Lebanon	66.30	152	Guinea	51.27
43	Cyprus	74.23	98	Nepal	66.18	153	Benin	51.24
44	Thailand	74.13	99	Turkmenistan	66.05	154	Angola	50.94
45	Russian Federation	74.07	100	Belize	65.73	155	Djibouti	50.31
46	Moldova	73.93	101	Kuwait	64.53	156	Madagascar	50.12
47	Costa Rica	73.76	102	Bahrain	64.27	157	Congo, Dem. Rep.	50.00
48	Kyrgyz Republic	73.72	103	Myanmar	64.27	158	Liberia	49.89
49	Israel	73.51	104	Bangladesh	64.22	159	Sudan	49.63
50	Azerbaijan	73.45	105	Panama	64.00	160	Somalia	45.57
51	Georgia	73.35	106	Guyana	63.89	161	Chad	41.29
52	Fiji	72.93	107	Cambodia	63.75	162	Central African Rep.	39.28
53	Brazil	72.80	108	South Africa	63.72	163	South Sudan	39.05
54	Argentina	72.78	109	Mongolia	63.51			
55	Vietnam	72.76	110	Ghana	63.44			

Source: https://dashboards.sdgindex.org/rankings

benefits, improves people's lives, and protects the environment. At the national level, a combination of institutional reforms, activities designed to improve capability, and supporting investments is needed.

Huđek and Bradac Hojnik (2020)[18] found that opportunity-driven entrepreneurial activity and innovative entrepreneurial activity show positive relations to the SDG Index, so having a positive impact on sustainable development, while the necessity-driven entrepreneurship has a negative impact on sustainable development what is in line with some earlier research (Kuckertz & Wagner, 2010).[19] Their conclusion was that entrepreneurs in the early stage of entrepreneurial activity are using less innovative solutions and less environmentally friendly technologies and methods of production, as previously mentioned by the literature, entrepreneurial activity cannot simultaneously achieve profits and sustainability goals without implementing appropriate ecosystem conditions. Also, it was clear that to attain the maximization of sustainable development of a country, governments should make efforts to prioritize the SDGs' implementation and incorporate them into their national agendas.

Youssef et al. (2018)[20] demonstrate that the relationship between entrepreneurship and sustainable development becomes substantially favorable when innovation and institutional quality are at their highest levels. In addition, they reveal that opportunity detection serves as the foundation for innovations, which play a crucial role in sustainable-oriented businesses. Nevertheless, above the institutional aspects, some important questions should be answer by the entrepreneur(s) before the business plan design (Figure 8.3).

Furthermore, in the context of sustainable development, entrepreneurial activity has been addressed through various streams in the literature, among which are ecopreneurship (a concept presented in Chapter 2), environmentally orientated entrepreneurship, social entrepreneurship, and sustainable entrepreneurship.[21] But all have the same purpose behind: ethical behavior for present and future generations.

Besides the ethical value associated of this type of entrepreneurial activity, one related impact is having also more international customers, bringing resources into the economy and generating further business. A high-export orientation business as one that anticipates 25 percent or more of its revenue coming from outside the country (GEM, 2022). Considering the international

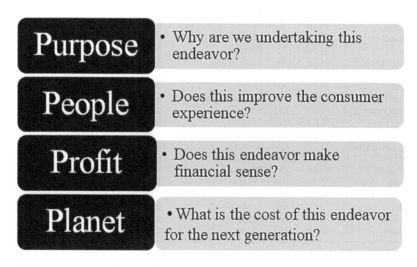

Figure 8.3 Entrepreneurial SDG-oriented questions

market, it is worth mentioning that actions to support the UN SDGs typically scored higher in high-income economies. Overall, three Level A economies (Norway, France, and Israel), one Level B (Taiwan), and one Level C (India) scored highest. In contrast, three Level C (Iran, Togo, and Tunisia), plus two Level B economies (Oman and Romania), scored lowest.

Based on the literature on organizational legitimacy and empirical findings from research on business ethics, results indicate that individual sustainability orientation can indeed explain entrepreneurial intention to some degree but the exploitation of opportunities for sustainable entrepreneurship can be encouraged seems to be – given the considerable complexity inherent to such opportunities – through entrepreneurial education (Kuckertz & Wagner, 2010).

Box 8.3   Quick review on SDG-oriented entrepreneurship

- Societal issues concern the potentially negative consequences of global warming, besides many industrialized countries are experiencing mass unemployment or wrestling with the challenges resulting from an increasingly globalized economy and society.
- Cultural values of post-materialism have a significant effect on the types of value creation corroborated by entrepreneurs.
- Entrepreneurship is an essential driver of societal health and wealth, being a powerful engine of economic growth and promoting innovation to exploit new opportunities, but to also address some of society's greatest challenges, such as the UN Sustainable Development Goals (SDGs).
- The SDGs were designed to reconcile environmental protection with socioeconomic development.
- The SDGs exist in a framework of 17 goals, 169 targets and 247 indicators, and were adopted by the UN General Assembly in 2015 to replace the expired Millennium Development Goals (MDGs).
- The emerging stream on sustainable entrepreneurship examples adds a new dimension to the general promise of entrepreneurship.
- Entrepreneurial endeavor is no longer supposed to merely result in economic success.
- Sustainable entrepreneurs manage by balancing economic health, social equity and environmental resilience through their business (triple bottom line).

Entrepreneurship and innovation in low-carbon economies

Mitigation of climate change is a transformative agenda requiring immediate governmental action. Using fundamental climate policies, such as carbon pricing and market-based instruments, regulatory action, and targeted support for innovation in low-carbon, sustainable technologies, it is remarkable that some nations are reducing emissions. Some essential issues about public policies are presented in the 2015 Report of Ministerial Council Meeting of the Organisation for Economic Co-operation and Development (OECD).[22]

As governments and businesses are becoming aware of the urgency of climate action and the need to manage a delicate balancing act: between greenhouse gas emissions and removals, between supply and demand of labor and capital, and between costs and benefits to achieve both sustainable development and economic performance, there are plenty discussions about the "transition to net-zero" within and out of academic environment.

In this context, specific businesses, such as innovative, clean technologies and automobiles with low emissions, will receive significant funding. And as capital changes, so will the labor, as some industries decrease, and others grow. In the energy sector alone, an estimated 14 million new employments will be created by 2030, while fossil fuel production as we know it could lose 5 million positions.

On the other hand, it is necessary to evaluate the immediate and long-term social and economic costs of a transition to net-zero emissions, in a process that must ensures that the transition to a low-carbon economy is inclusive, equitable, and that no one is left behind. Moreover, it is important to guarantee that organizations can reskill and upskill their workforces to make them more equipped and change-resistant and that they are monitoring and managing these risks and opportunities, as well as integrating these new strategies across their core businesses.

Low-carbon development strategy for the long term should consider not only the roles of the business sector but also the different spheres of government to get the maximum neutralization of global greenhouse gas (GHG) emissions by 2050. In 2023, Canada's largest bank (RBC) invests \$8 million in a global carbon markets company while the fastest growing social media platform joins the race to net zero.[23]

The transition to net-zero emissions intends to reduce impacts on the environment and, at the same time, promote the development of countries. One of the pillars of this change is the search for the reduction of greenhouse gas (GHG) emissions, with the expansion of the use of clean energy and attribution of costs to the impacts generated by the emission of polluting gases with the carbon credit.

More broadly, the low-carbon economy encourages the rational use of natural resources in renewing energy matrices and the circularity of production. Therefore, process innovation and technological development are essential allies to reduce harmful impacts on the planet, where companies and governments[24] are aligned with the 2030 Agenda – the Sustainable Development Goals.[25] The main challenges to the low-carbon economy transition can be observed in Figure 8.4:

In Brazil, like other emerging economies, considering public policies to overcome the challenges of low-carbon economy transition, they should address four main goals:

- *Pillar 1. Energy transition*
  Increase the percentage of renewable energies and biofuels in the energy matrix, by maintaining investments in renewable energies, strengthening the biofuels program, and policies and investments in new energies, such as hydrogen, carbon capture and storage (CCS), and offshore wind, to accelerate the energy transition in all countries.
- *Pillar 2. Carbon market*
  Create and implement a regulated carbon market in developed economies and developing countries, in the form of an emissions trading system, under the cap and trade rationale to contribute to the goals established by the Paris Agreement.
- *Pillar 3. Circular economy*
  Increase the productivity and competitiveness of each country's industry by promoting and valuing practices aligned with the circular economy concept, contributing to the reduction of GHG emissions.
- *Pillar 4. Forest conservation*
  Increase the effectiveness of government actions in the fight against illegal deforestation and fires. Providing Brazilian leadership with remote sensing technologies with command-and-control actions based on scientific data and intelligence. Additionally, coordination and integration of efforts by federal, state, and municipal governments will increase efficiency.

Definition

- broad and integrated country strategy to reduce emissions
- policies that create a favorable environment for investments

Establishment

- of institutional governance (government and the productive sector)
- greater transparency and compliance (commitment- Paris Agreement)

Elaboration

- decarbonization plan for the country (with the productive sector)
- based on sectorial plans that consider its specificities

Investments

- Research, development, and innovation - R&D&I
- targeting new low-carbon technologies such as hydrogen and carbon capture and storage

Development

- of an urban infrastructure based on low-carbon technologies (mobility, construction, lighting, basic sanitation, etc.)

Figure 8.4 Worldwide challenges to the low-carbon economy transition

OECD region: new environmental knowledge, green venture creation and financing

Potential entrepreneurs can be exposed to new and uncommercialized knowledge "by participation in formal R&D partnerships as well as through supplier – customer relationships, professional associations and mobile human capital" (Feldman & Kelley, 2006, p. 1510)[26] as well as in other channels. Frequently, green businesses result from knowledge and innovation collaborations with various parties, including companies from a wide range of industries, research institutions, governmental bodies, and nonprofit organizations.[27] (Doblinger et al., 2019).

In a paper titled "Entrepreneurs for a Low Carbon World: How Environmental Knowledge and Policy Shape the Creation and Financing of Green Start-ups," Cojoianu et al. (2020)[28] through the lens of the knowledge spillover theory of entrepreneurship (KSTE), technology, and innovation studies have argued that the primary source of entrepreneurial opportunity in the low-carbon energy transition is new environmental knowledge created but uncommercialized in established companies or research organizations. Investigating how different types of environmental policies and new regional environmental knowledge affect new venture creation in and financing of green (low carbon), brown (fossil fuel) and gray (unrelated to natural resources) technologies across 24 OECD countries and 293 regions over the period 2001–2013. Their results demonstrated that new regional environmental knowledge positively impacts new venture creation (green and gray industries). This highlight the importance of the existing infrastructure, as new entry across all sectors is facilitated by the presence of an increased number of regional research institutes. Also, it seems that a more stringent environmental policy regime negatively impacts the creation of new ventures across sectors, strongly discouraging new fossil fuel ventures. However, once entrepreneurs decide to start a new business, stringent environmental policies have on aggregate a positive effect on new venture financing across sectors, particularly through feed-in-tariffs and emission standards.

In the next section of this chapter, some examples are provided related to the perspective of entrepreneurship scholars and knowledge theorists,[29] who have attributed the creation of new firms to the entrepreneur's ability to coordinate a range of inputs, including heterogeneous knowledge about technology, people, and processes.

Entrepreneurs for a low-carbon world: innovation and ecopreneurs

Electricity is a form of energy that occurs naturally, so it is not considered an "invention." However, Benjamin Franklin is credited for establishing the link between lightning and electricity. Electricity has been around for over 2000 years. Ancient Greeks observed that stroking fur on fossilized tree resin (amber) generated an attraction that was subsequently termed *static electricity*. In the 1930s, scholars and archeologists unearthed pots that held copper that they believed to have been ancient batteries used to provide light.

Electricity security matters more than ever because it would be tough to imagine our modern societies without a secure electricity supply. While it only accounts for a fifth of primary energy use today, it is indispensable for the 24/7 and increasingly digital economy and daily life. The effects of a prolonged power outage extend much beyond the power system or the value of the lost energy purchase itself. How can we live in a digital age without electricity?

Rising energy prices provide a new impetus to more sustainable production and consumption, important parts of the SDGs[30]. In 2021 and 2022, GEM introduced questions related to the role that social and environmental considerations play in the long-term decision-making of entrepreneurs in relation to new businesses as well as questions about awareness of the SDGs and whether these play a part in business priorities and strategies.[31] With some exceptions, the results have shown that less than 1 in 10 new business starters were aware of the SDGs in 5 out of 9 Level C economies, 1 of 12 Level B economies, and none of 13 Level A economies. A similar pattern was found with established business owners, with more than a third of those running an established business aware of the SDGs in just four economies (Poland, Norway, Romania, and China), and less than 1 in 5 aware in eight Level C economies, six Level B, and four Level A economies (details at GEM Adult Population Survey, 2022).

Related to this research, representative samples of 399 enterprises in Colombia and 413 businesses in Egypt in 2021 were investigated in 2021.[32] According to the owner-managers, they frequently had strategies that included business operations' social and environmental implications (moreover, sometimes precedence over financial goals). In addition, socially beneficial and environmentally protective behaviors were less prevalent in Egypt, maybe due to more policies supporting the SDGs in Colombia.

Directly and indirectly, new enterprises can contribute to attaining the SDGs, as some business are created or strategic redesigned to provide employment opportunities to underrepresented minorities (see Chapter 7, DEI and HRM), or to directly tackle issues such as plastic pollution or climate change, examining the percentage of persons who start or run new firms who always consider environmental impacts when making decisions about the future of that business can provide some insight into the recent expansion of environmental consciousness the results showed higher commitment. GEM 2022 presented that of the 38 economies answering this question in both years, that proportion has increased in 23 of them.

New businesses are essential as a trend for cultural change, not just for what they offer now but especially for their high-growth potential and relevance in emerging economies. In addition to employment, the second positive consequence of a new firm's creation is innovation in products and/or processes, or innovation in products and/or processes.

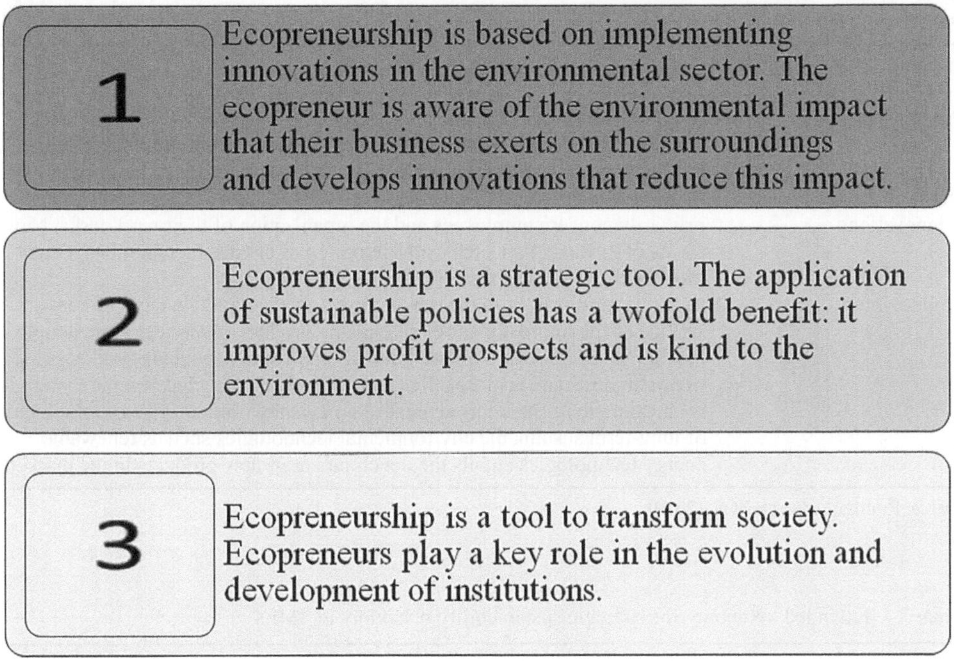

| 1 | Ecopreneurship is based on implementing innovations in the environmental sector. The ecopreneur is aware of the environmental impact that their business exerts on the surroundings and develops innovations that reduce this impact. |

| 2 | Ecopreneurship is a strategic tool. The application of sustainable policies has a twofold benefit: it improves profit prospects and is kind to the environment. |

| 3 | Ecopreneurship is a tool to transform society. Ecopreneurs play a key role in the evolution and development of institutions. |

Figure 8.5 Ecopreneurship approaches
Source: Rodríguez-García et al. (2019).

Large firms such as Walmart, GE, Kraft, or Toyota have taken on the challenge of building sustainability into their mainstream business, but for more than two decades (Gerlach, 2003[33]), the need to approach the analysis of the role of sustainable entrepreneurs in implementing sustainable development from the perspective of innovation was pointed out, concluding that successful sustainable innovation occurs when entrepreneurial actors acquire competitive advantages (i.e., they have economic success) by applying innovative environmental and/or social practices.

Eco-innovation can be the answer to this challenge.[34] This new stream of research has explored corporate strategies that focus on the environmental dimension, without overlooking other ones (social and economic). Still, priority is given to addressing the effect of the negative externalities of firms' economic activity on these firms' immediate surroundings (Table 8.3).

The industry is a significant driver of socioeconomic growth. Growing ecological and social consciousness among entrepreneurs has led to a paradigm shift from traditional to sustainable entrepreneurial practices. The nexus between innovation, entrepreneurship, and sustainable development[35] by several managerial and economic studies sponsors indicates that innovation and entrepreneurship are the most effective tools to diffuse sustainability values and economic security simultaneously.

Eco-innovation (e.g., eco-design, cleaner production) and sustainability-oriented innovations (SOIs), that means, the integration of ecological and social aspects into products, processes, and organizational structures had been analyzed in the context of large firms for a long time, but recently, the specificities of SOIs in small and medium sized enterprises (SMEs) as they are increasingly recognized as central contributors to sustainable development.[36] Klewitz and Hansen (2014) identified two major building blocks of SOI practices in SMEs: the SMEs

Table 8.3 Types of eco-innovation

Eco-innovation level	Description
Process innovations	These innovations relate to the production of goods and services. The goal is usually to enhance eco-efficiency. In most cases, these improvements are based on the use of more environmentally friendly production technologies.
Organizational innovations	These innovations relate to restructuring within the firm. These innovations primarily concern employees and the organization of their work tasks. New forms of management such as the adoption of environmental management models also fall into this category.
Product innovations	These innovations refer to the development of a completely new product or service or the improvement of an existing product or service. For example, ecological design could offer a good alternative to producing products that use natural resources more efficiently. The use of recycled organic materials is an example of the improvement of an existing product. The development of long-term sustainable environmental technologies such as renewable energy technologies entails the development of new products in the market.

Source: Rodríguez-García et al. (2019).

Table 8.4 Extended taxonomy for strategic sustainability behaviors in SMEs

Strategic behavior	Profit function	Goals	Innovation types	Interaction with external actors
Resistant	Ignorance of environmental or social factors	Compliance	–	–
Reactive	Environmental/social factors cause costs	Compliance and limited action beyond	Process improvements	Very low
Anticipatory	Consideration of environmental/social factors can reduce costs	Ahead of compliance and tangible cost reductions	Incremental process and organizational innovations	Low
Innovation-based	Consideration of environmental/social factors contribute to market success	Differentiation	Incremental process organizational, and incremental (limited radical) product innovations	Medium
Sustainability-rooted	Integration of economic, environmental, and social aspects define core business	Market transformation	Radical product, process, and organizational innovations (business model innovation)	High

Source: Klewitz and Hansen (2014).

strategic sustainability behavior and the pursued innovation types. Their results can be observed in Table 8.4.

As obtainable by these authors, SME strategic sustainability behavior ranges from resistant, reactive, anticipatory, and innovation based to sustainability rooted. Furthermore, on the process of strengthening the innovative capacity for SOIs of SMEs in a previous work they had shown how public private partnerships support SMEs in building up absorptive capacity, as the discussion on SOIs of SMEs often revolves around learning and knowledge as specific resources for innovation. Besides, the literature review shows that large companies can adopt the new and more radical sustainability strategies of the SMEs through acquisition to thereby engage more rapidly in disruptive change.

Box 8.4   Quick review on low-carbon economy transition and sustainable oriented business

- It is necessary to evaluate the immediate and long-term social and economic costs of a transition to net-zero emissions, in a process that must ensure that this is inclusive, equitable, and that no one is left behind.
- Considering public policies, to overcome the challenges of low-carbon economy transition, they should address four main goals: energy transition, carbon market, circular economy, and forest conservation.
- New environmental knowledge is positively related with the creation of new green ventures, emphasizing the role of universities and research centers to foster green technologies.
- New regional brown venture entry in the OECD region significantly and negatively correlates with stricter environmental policy.
- Feed-in-tariffs and emission standards are significantly and positively related to new regional green *venture capital financing*, across different investment stages and green sub-markets.
- Despite there being fewer factors considered when deciding whether to establish their own business in the green industry, environmental policy has become increasingly relevant for the financing of green startups.

Some further considerations about innovation, entrepreneurship, and sustainability are discussed in the following sections.

Challenge 1: energy

As mentioned earlier in this chapter, energy costs and usage are increasing in many countries, and it is relevant. Public policies must create favorable conditions for private investments by adopting carbon pricing mechanisms. In this way, internalizing and monetizing greenhouse gas emissions would be possible. As a highlight, there are more than 60 proposed pricing mechanisms. But, in 2021, the voluntary carbon market grew at a record pace, reaching $2 billion – four times its value in 2020 – and the pace of purchases is still accelerating in 2022. By 2030, the market is expected to reach between $10 billion and $40 billion.[37]

Brazil is on the list of countries that generate employment in the field of renewable energy alongside the United States, China, India, Japan, and Germany. Due to favorable climatic conditions, Brazil and other countries can be prominent in the world market in transitioning to a low-carbon economy. In addition to the abundance of water, which enables energy generation through hydroelectric plants, the country has a strategic position that facilitates the generation of solar energy almost throughout the year and in all states. In addition, the Brazilian coast and the Northeast region are privileged in the quality of the winds, facilitating wind energy generation.

For this transition to be satisfactory, expanding investment in the global economy towards low-carbon sectors is necessary, which should occur through the engagement of investors aligned with the decarbonization targets proposed by the Paris Agreement. In the United States, for example, the Recovery and Reinvestments Act in 2009 generated a series of social and economic benefits, including the generation of approximately 900,000 clean energy jobs in the country from 2009 to 2015.

The financial market is already aware of the risks of investing in activities that generate emissions. Therefore, they seek to invest in new businesses aligned with sustainability. As a result, sustainable companies are already outperforming their competitors. Organizations committed to renewable energy have better profit margins and can generate an 18 percent higher return on investment than companies that are not committed.

With the advance of global warming, world organizations and government representatives began to organize themselves to find viable alternatives for reducing these harmful gases. Until 2012, almost 70 percent of the energy produced worldwide was from fossil fuels and only 21 percent from renewable sources. The good news is that pursuing low-carbon growth is the best way to reap lasting economic and social benefits.

The trend is that the energy demand will continue to grow in the coming years. Therefore, searching for low-carbon options is a way to maintain production and simultaneously reduce negative impacts. There is a global initiative called We Mean Business in which more than 1400 companies have committed to reducing their GHG emissions through tangible actions.

In addition, the international Paris Agreement was also an essential step towards the transition to a low-carbon economy. Although this change is taking place gradually in the United States, it is already possible to see the results. The renewable sector already creates jobs 12 times faster than other sectors of the economy. In addition, with accelerated growth, the costs of generating both solar and wind energy have decreased.

A multilateral institution, the IEA[38] was established as the main international forum for energy cooperation on a variety of issues such as security of supply, long-term policy, information transparency, energy efficiency, sustainability, research and development, technology collaboration, and international energy relations. At its website, one can find information about GHGs from the energy sector for over 190 countries and regions.[39]

In the United States, most of the emissions of human-caused (anthropogenic) GHGs come primarily from burning fossil fuels – coal, natural gas, and petroleum – for energy use. Economic growth (with short-term fluctuations in growth rate) and weather patterns that affect heating and cooling needs are the main factors that drive the amount of energy consumed. Energy prices and government policies can also affect the sources or types of energy consumed.

Although people are still hesitant to acquire electric or hybrid vehicles due to the expensive purchase price, lengthy battery recharge times, low autonomy (driving range), and scarcity of charging stations. But, as technology evolves, energy efficiency improves simultaneously as repair and maintenance costs are reduced. Moreover, the designation of specific parking spots, and the provision of tax incentives the results indicate that automakers favor a gradual introduction of Evs.

This market has increased worldwide, as customers demonstrate more environmental consciousness today. Publicly accessible chargers worldwide approached 1.8 million charging points in 2021, of which a third were fast chargers, and nearly 500,000 chargers were installed in 2021. Environmental policies on climate change and directives for the potential use of renewable energy sources to power electric vehicles could tip the balance in favor of electric cars.

Industry participants are accelerating the pace of automotive technological innovation as they develop new concepts for electric, connected, autonomous, and shared mobility. Over the

Table 8.5 Electric vehicle (EV)-inspired entrepreneurship

EV Business Ideas

---

1. Start an electric car charging station
2. Become an electric car batteries refurbisher
3. Start an EV shop
4. Start an electric car diagnostic center
5. Become an electric car power bank manufacturer
6. Start an electric car repair and servicing garage
7. Start a blog for EV enthusiasts
8. Become an EV battery manufacturer
9. Start an electric car spraying and branding workshop
10. Become an EV charger distributor
11. Become an EV powertrain manufacturer
12. Start an electric car dealership
13. Start an EV mechanical engineering course
14. Start a self-driven EV taxi
15. Start an electric car tracker installation and repair
16. Start an electric car towing business
17. Start an EV car wash

Source: www.starterstory.com/electric-car-business-ideas

past decade, the industry has attracted more than $400 billion in investments, with roughly $100 billion arriving since the beginning of 2020. This funding is designated for companies and startups working on electrifying mobility, vehicle connectivity, and autonomous driving technology.

As an additional information, electromotive power started in 1827 when Hungarian priest Ányos Jedlik built the first crude but viable electric motor, which he used to power a small car.[40]

The global electric car market is growing exponentially, and industry estimates show that in the next decade, 45 percent of new car sales could be electric. Table 8.5 displays some business opportunities.

Challenge 2: waste

Leo Baekeland, a Belgian chemist (and marketer), invented the first completely synthetic plastic in 1907, and 20th-century citizens witnessed a revolution in products and goods by introducing synthetic plastics in almost all aspects of daily life.

In the early 1930s, polyethylene, the most abundant plastic in the world, was devised as a wonder material that was strong, flexible, and heat-resistant. During the post-war period, plastic began to supplant the more expensive paper, glass, and metal used in disposable items, such as consumer packaging.

Plastic is difficult to dispose of due to its chemical properties and durability, with some types requiring thousands or even tens of thousands of years to biodegrade in landfills. As the degradation of plastics into microscopic particulates pollutes our ocean, air, and ecosystems, the degradation itself is an even more significant environmental concern. The effects of microplastic deposits on our health are not entirely understood.

In the 21st century, when environmental awareness is on the rise, recycled plastic items have even become marketable and fashionable, with the original use of the material often listed on the product.

The three Rs – reduce, reuse, and recycle – are three approaches, and the most environmentally preferred. Reducing, reusing, and recycling plastic waste helps save landfill space by keeping useful materials out.

1 Recycle plastic entrepreneurship example

At the Massachusetts Institute of Technology, female entrepreneur and scientist Svetlana V. Boriskina oversaw the team that created polyethylene textiles. According to her, she was initially drawn to the polymer because it permits infrared radiation or body heat to escape, thereby cooling the wearer. After that, however, textile experts were skeptical that polyethylene, a known moisture-blocking material, could produce a comfortable fabric.

The team of Boriskina discovered that standard textile industry apparatus could be used to produce polyethylene fibers and yarns, which could then be knitted or woven into textiles.[41] The polyethylene on the surface of the filaments is oxidized during the extrusion process, which confers moisture-wicking properties. Because the interior of the fibers is hydrophobic, moisture does not penetrate but rather rapidly dissipates. Besides, polyethylene can be water-wicking, and this research is a significant step towards its use as a recyclable textile.

Boriskina states that the extruded polyethylene fibers are soft, silky, and cold to the touch. However, they can be manufactured to resemble cotton or fleece. In addition, the white fibers can be dyed using an eco-friendly procedure that involves the addition of a coloring agent during extrusion. While the recyclable material will not be featured in any upcoming ready-to-wear collections, and most important, MIT will spin off a startup company to create the fabric. The entrepreneur is working with the US Army, NASA, and athletic apparel manufacturer New Balance to develop applications for the material.[42]

2 Reuse plastic and organic fibers as an entrepreneurship example

As urban residents, we may have lovely gardens, windowsills, and balconies, but plastics are contaminating the land and seas. Plant pots are typically manufactured from high-density polyethylene (HDPE) or polypropylene, which are more difficult to recycle than polyethylene terephthalate (PET), the material used to create plastic beverage bottles.

Vasart is a 100 percent Brazilian company dedicated to the research, creation, and development of innovative products and services that promote a harmonious relationship between the individual and nature.[43] One of its main objectives is the production of pieces that transform environments into places of well-being and pleasure, such as collections of contemporary vases, accessories, and exclusive, signed, and patented furniture. Furthermore, with new sustainable ways in mind, Vasart has partnered with Therpol and Plataforma Circular to develop a circular collection of pots, Vasart Renova Therpol, which is produced using Therpol biotechnology and fabric fibers (of old pair of jeans) combined with polyethylene. These pots can be used outdoors and indoors, as they are resistant to sunlight and rain thanks to their high-quality material.

Founded in 2004, it is the first brand in Brazil, in the area of roto-molded vessels, to launch products with green polyethylene for the national public, with the *I'm green certificate*. In addition, it also uses 50 percent recycled material in the composition of all its parts, based on the principles of the circular economy, which removes tons of garbage from our planet.

As with gardeners, there will be no immediate answers, but top management teams of the food packaging industry, who are worried about the environment, can make small changes that will make a difference.

3 Reduce plastic as an entrepreneurship example

The capacity to increase cost savings, environmental friendliness, and consumer benefits has demonstrated skinny design packaging to be an effective method for maximizing product volume and performance. A roundtable with McKinsey consultants and product designers pointed out the advantages of making product packaging smaller: less material and shipping/ costs, and more product on the shelf, so fewer stockouts, along with a reduced ecological footprint.

The specialist in *McKinsey Talks Operations* on March (2023) presented another suggestion of reducing packages of ordinary products.[44] Water has just witnessed some evolution. Bottled water is a popular beverage, and it was originally packed in a matrix-style bottle that was larger and thicker. Depending on the brand, price point, and other factors, it has changed over time into a smaller, thinner, lighter-weight bottle wrapped in a honeycomb pattern which is asymmetrical. This can result in a 10–15 percent improvement in cube efficiency or shelf-holding capacity, which is significant. For a retailer, it has multiple meanings. First, there is more on the shelf and if happens a delayed delivery or a sudden increase in demand, 10–15 percent more inventory can be made available on the shelf. The second benefit is that the journey for the employee filling the shelf is now 10–15 percent shorter.

Another innovation could be the shape of the package, as water bottles usually have rounded shape. They have about 78 percent packing efficiency, whereas triangles and squares can be 100 percent. Substitute the plastic bottle to a more sustainable one is the last frontier. The challenge is to find a balance between customer satisfaction and material cost and ESG impact, but Brazilian "Agua na Caixa" ("water in box," in English) is reaching that point.

Box 8.5   Water in box: reducing plastic waste

"Água na Caixa" launched by cousins Fabiana Tchalian and Rodrigo Gedankien, in January 2021, aims to serve consumers looking for brands with greater environmental responsibility.

During a trip to the United States, in 2016, Brazilian entrepreneur Fabiana Tchalian ordered water and toast at a cafe. The water came in a box, which she had never seen before, and her immediate thought was that it could also be well accepted in Brazil. Thus came the idea of Água na Caixa, a Brazilian startup that sells mineral water in Tetra Pak boxes.

The product is reusable, fully recyclable, and made with 88 percent renewable material. The company, headquartered in Pinhalzinho, a city that is part of the so-called Water Circuit in the interior of São Paulo, has expanded its sales to the capital of the state (in January 2021).

After the ramp-up of operation, the company began its "second phase" of development, delivering the product directly to suppliers such as restaurants, cafes, bars, and hotel chains. The original business plan was to have a presence in at least a thousand points of sale across the country by 2021. But due to the COVID-19 pandemic, they decided to focus on e-commerce, like Amazon, Mercado Libre/MarketPlace, and some Brazilian counterparts, like drugstores, supermarkets, and retail companies. Today (2023), Água na Caixa is present at more than 3500 points of sale.

It is worth mentioning that the company calculates its carbon footprint in partnership with Way Carbon and finances the Reduction of Deforestation and Forest Degradation project in Pará to offset the footprint. As a result, it became Brazil's first and only carbon-neutral mineral water company.

Source: www.aguanacaixa.com.br/.

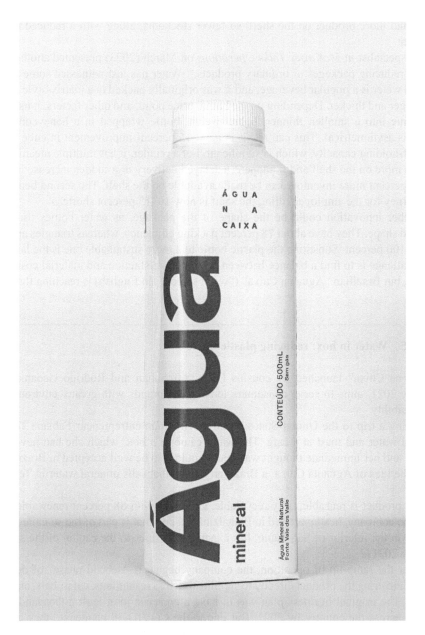

Figure 8.6 Água na Caixa

Source: Água na Caixa

Besides Brazil, this initiative exists in the United States (https://boxedwaterisbetter.com/) and South Africa (https://waterinboxes.com/). Water in Boxes company's cartoon packing is 76 percent recyclable and biodegradable, composed of renewable resource trees sourced from responsibly managed forests (Forest Stewardship Council [FSC] approved). A product certified by the FSC[45] meets the "gold standard" of ethical production. This FSC-certified wood is harvested from forests that are responsibly managed, socially beneficial, environmentally conscious, and economically viable.

Challenge 3: water

Governments, researchers, and citizens of urban regions or local agriculture communities are eager to monitor, protect, and restore their local freshwater resources, as freshwater is indispensable for life on Earth. FreshWater Watch,[46] is a global initiative managed by Earthwatch Europe, an environmental charity with a scientific focus. They enable organizations worldwide to assess the condition of their rivers, lakes, streams, ponds, wetlands, and reservoirs. The resulting data provide the solid evidence to support efforts to enhance water quality and management.

Since the launch of FreshWater Watch in 2012, Earthwatch has expanded this flagship initiative to include volunteers, research organizations, businesses, governments, and schools worldwide. According to FreshWater Watch, water saving is substantial because fresh, clean water is a limited and costly resource. As a homeowner, you're probably already well aware of the financial costs of inefficient water use. Moreover, water scarcity can halt business operations, disrupt supply chains, raise the costs of raw materials, and put employee health and safety at risk. So, the conservation of this natural resource is critical for the environment – and our civilization.

Using freshwater from agriculture, industry, and the domestic sector places the most significant pressure on natural systems, both in quantity (withdrawals) and quality (impact of wastewater discharges). After agriculture, the two major water users for development are industry and energy (20 percent of total water withdrawals), which are transforming the water use patterns in emerging market economies. Water and energy share the same demographic, economic, social and technological drivers.

By altering behavior, modifying and/or replacing equipment with water-saving equipment, industries can reduce their overall water consumption and increase their internal reuse. Moreover, to ensure the strategies, optimize water use, and reduce costs, it is necessary to assess current water consumption and establish objectives. As water conservation is the practice of using water efficiently to reduce unnecessary water usage, one way to reduce the amount of clean (treated) water is to redesign the productive process in the industry.

In *McKinsey Talks Operations* (March 2023[47]), one example brought by the specialists was healthcare items and water wastage. Shampoo is a suitable illustration of this concept, as 90 percent of the product is actually water. Producers fill large bottles with 90 percent water and a few chemicals. They place the bottles on pallets, ship them worldwide, primarily transporting water, and then place them on a shelf in a Walmart or equivalent where water takes up most of the space. They present an alternative solution: shipping a dehydrated powder in substantially smaller packaging. Consequently, reduced packing has a less environmental impact in many ways: it could be loaded onto smaller transport vehicles, reducing our environmental effect, and placing it in a store with minimal space requirements. Besides, it will also impact landfills after use.

It is important to mention that, when the consumer uses it in the shower, it will foam, and the sensation remains pleasant. Therefore, the consumer experience is unaffected, while the cost and environmental impact are improved.

In Brazil, a different alternative is already gaining market, where healthcare products come in bars not in plastic bottles. This business idea has many environmental gains: less water in production, skinny packing advantages, and reduced use of plastics.

Box 8.6   "Zero waste" cosmetics

In 2017, Andreia Quercia and Victor Falzoni, who were friends from university, decided to start a business that would help people reduce their environmental impact and the overall plastic pollution generated by the CPG industry (consumer packaged goods). After long research, they learned that more than 80 percent of what's in a traditional Brazilian shampoo bottle is water, and that's the only reason plastic packaging is required – to carry mainly water around. So, the duo decided to tackle the plastic problem in the cosmetic industry, by creating solid products – without all the water in them, a trend named waterless beauty.

After 2 years of research and development, they founded B.O.B. (Bars Over Bottles), which translated to Portuguese is "barras ao invés de garrafas." In 2019 they launched the brand with three types of shampoo and two types of conditioners, all wrapped in paper packaging, no plastic required. The brand's goal is to enable us to have a "plastic-free bathroom" and today, the company already sells different personal care bars, for skin, body, and hair care. Through social media networks, they encourage and educate their community to have a minimalist bathroom and generate less waste, reducing individual environmental impact.

Currently, the B.O.B. sells on average 75,000 beauty bars monthly and has a team of over 40 people working in the areas of cosmetic R&D, supply and logistics, marketing, technology, and back office. For the company's future, the founders intend to expand the personal care line portfolio, and increase their purpose to engage more and more people to reduce waste and have a "plastic-free bathroom," besides expanding sales to other countries.

Source: www.barsoverbottles.com/.

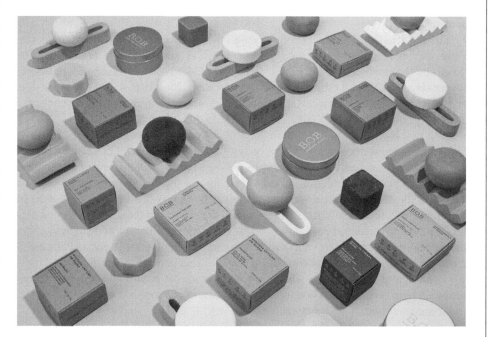

Figure 8.7 B.O.B. products
Source: sent by the owners (https://www.usebob.com.br/)

The capacity to increase cost savings, environmental friendliness, and consumer benefits has demonstrated skinny design packaging to be an effective method for maximizing product volume and performance. This roundtable with McKinsey consultants and product designers pointed out the advantages of making product packaging smaller: less material and shipping/ costs, more product on the shelf, so fewer stockouts, along with a reduced ecological footprint.

Waste and water reduction in the industry are gateways to a better future. Besides unnecessary water utilization in some products, the less packing is used; the less packaging material is needed to purchase. So in this sense, it saves money.

Besides, freight savings are essential to be competitive due to the cost of terrestrial transportation, which has substantially ascended in recent years. In addition, the greater the quantity of a product that can fit in a container or truck, the lower its unit cost.

Nevertheless, this needs to be noticed during the product's design process. Additionally, reduced transportation means less CO_2 emissions by diesel as it is possible to have more items on the truck. This scenario also implies an additional benefit for the climate change goals of nations.

Box 8.7   Quick review on energy, waste, and water sustainability-oriented business

- Before starting an entrepreneurial activity, with sustainability purpose it is important to answer the question: How do I make this better, not just for me, but for my customer and the next generation?
- It has never been so important to protect our freshwater environments. This is acknowledged by the UN Sustainable Development Goals, in particular in Goal 6: "Ensure availability and sustainable management of water and sanitation for all."
- The two most essential issues with freshwater are its quantity (or scarcity) and its quality. In this sense, using freshwater in industry and daily life should be continuously evaluated and reduced when possible.
- Through skinny design, different advantages are present: the consumer experience element, the store stocking element, the cost freight reduction element, and a significant sustainability benefit as well.
- Balancing business operation and product design with ESG and other demands beyond just profitability and usability is a reality for many firms.
- Consumer behavior and awareness are changing as more people accept alternative and sustainable mobility modes.
- Mainstream EVs will transform the automotive industry and help decarbonize the planet.
- In the sustainability-oriented business, there is a responsibility concerning employees, customers, suppliers, and a broader society.

Challenge 4: biodiversity

Biodiversity – the variety of life on earth – is essential to the daily well-being of billions of people. It provides many ecosystem services, including food, clean water and oxygen, the cycling of nutrients, and the sequestration of carbon. The enormous economic value of these services, which is frequently overlooked in decision-making, should also be highlighted.

A high level of biodiversity indicates a healthy ecosystem, which provides businesses with value and resilience. Everyone is intrinsically reliant on ecosystems. The outputs or processes nature provides benefit humans directly or indirectly and improves social welfare. Notable examples include refuse decomposition, crop pollination, flood control, water purification, and carbon sequestration, among others. The OECD (2020) estimates that ecosystem services are worth between $125 trillion and $140 trillion annually, equivalent to approximately 1.5 times the global GDP.[48]

In addition, businesses that desire to define a biodiversity policy as part of their nature ambition can outline their commitment and approach to biodiversity consideration and prioritization. However, this should be conducted through specific strategies, such as ending deforestation and promoting regeneration, which is linked to an overarching hierarchy of mitigation approach.

Companies should maintain a perspective of climate, social equity and justice, and human rights for their strategies to produce credible and ambitious outcomes. When addressing these issues, organizations must adopt a holistic approach that considers the interconnectedness of nature and biodiversity to catalyze action and progress that benefits people and the planet.

In 2021, the UN Convention on Biological Diversity proposed that "all businesses (public and private, large and small) assess and report on their dependencies and impacts on biodiversity, from local to global, and progressively reduce negative impacts, by at least half, and increase positive impacts, reducing biodiversity-related risks to businesses and moving towards a more sustainable business model." (CBD, 2021, p. 106).[49] The draft also states that "urgent global, regional, and national policy action is required to transform economic, social, and financial models so that the trends that have exacerbated biodiversity loss will stabilize in the next decade (by 2030)" (CBD, 2021, p. 40).

Consequently, higher education institutions (HEI) – such as universities and research centers – can be considered essential innovation drivers for ecopreneurship. Although the opening case in this chapter in Peru (Box 8.1) and another in New Zealand (Box 8.8) prove this, there are some difficulties to overcome in many countries. Considering the role of HEI and business engagement in emerging economies like Brazil, Aguiar and colleagues (2023)[50] highlighted the needs:

- To overcome current issues: offsets, licensing, and private reserves are fronts for engagement between academia and businesses in Brazil;
- To engage in new opportunities: sustainable bioeconomy, access and benefit sharing (ABS), and environmental, social, and corporate governance are topics whereby academia-businesses partnerships in Brazil can innovate.

Besides, a mindset shift in academia and corporations will be required to foster sustainable businesses from a biodiversity perspective, as presented in Figure 8.8.

Some scholars point out that in Brazil, the low absorption capacity of technology at the national level acts as a complement or substitute for businesses in technology development. Also, lengthy bureaucratic does not help progress.

In a study called "University-Industry Technology Transfer from a Brazilian Perspective," these authors discovered that it is embryonic. Besides, even after a considerable increase in intellectual property (IP) required in the last few years, the academic research outcomes are not being absorbed effectively by the industries because an insignificant percentage of the patents go to the market (Viana et al., 2018[51]).

Another critical issue regarding IP ownership in biodiverse countries is traditional knowledge. The Nagoya Protocol addresses genetic resources where indigenous and local communities have the established right to grant access to them.

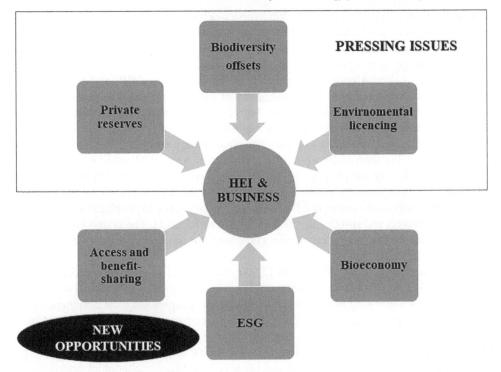

Figure 8.8 Biodiversity conservation and management

After the global commitments to Sustainable Development of the UN Conference on Environment and Development[52] (UNCED), held in June 1992 (Rio 92), Brazil ratified the decisions of the Convention on Biological Diversity (CBD), enacting Decree no. 2519, of March 16, 1998. Worldwide, the significant new milestone was the Nagoya Protocol in the CBD.[53] The Conference of the Parties created the agreement to the CBD at its tenth meeting (COP 10), which took place in Japan (2010), and entered into force on October of 2014. Brazil ratified the Protocol on March of 2021, joining 130 other countries.

The Nagoya Protocol aims to be an international agreement regulating the "Access to Genetic Resources and the Fair and Equitable Sharing of Benefits Arising from Their Use" (access and benefit sharing [ABS]). In other words, it establishes the guidelines for commercial relations between the country providing genetic resources and the one that will use them, covering points such as payment of royalties, the establishment of joint ventures, and the right to transfer technology and training.

Heinrich et al. (2020) show examples of a National Benefit Sharing Fund in other countries, mentioning that in April 2020,[54] 1233 internationally recognized certificates of conformity from 22 countries were published. The vast majority were issued by India (741) or France (233). Latin American countries include Panama (20), Peru (16), Mexico (8), Guyana (5), Uruguay (3), Guatemala and the Dominican Republic (2 each), and Argentina (1). The authors conclude that the implementation of the Nagoya Protocol (NP) and new forms of international collaboration in ABS often remain without a concrete proposal, especially in the context of public policies. In addition, the vision and implementation specific to this international treaty vary from country to country, leading to additional challenges (Heinrich et al., 2020).

Although China, India, and Brazil are biodiversity-rich and, since biotechnology promised to turn DNA into gold, their biotech sectors have shaped these countries with the principle of "common heritage of mankind" and the absence of ABS rules for genetic resource (GR) utilization. Furthermore, the governance of GRs is differently expressed in the three countries – but in common is the lack of alternatives to accrue rents from the possession of GRs and develop in time domestic biotech sectors capable of competing in world markets (Muzaka & Serrano, 2019).[55]

The preliminary literature review showed, for the most part, reflections on the legal and biodiversity aspects insufficient for the magnitude of the challenge.[56,57,58,59]

Some organizations are helping to gather data about natural resources. The Intergovernmental Science-Policy Platform on Biodiversity and Ecosystem Services (IPBES) is an independent intergovernmental body comprising over 130 member governments created in 2012 to provide policymakers with objective scientific assessments about the state of knowledge regarding the planet's biodiversity, ecosystems, and the contributions they make to people, as well as options and actions to protect and sustainably use these vital natural assets. The IPBES Global Assessment of Biodiversity and Ecosystem Services represents the landmark product of the first work program of IPBES (2014–2018)[60].

Based on the systematic review of about 15,000 scientific and government sources, the report published in 2019 also draws (for the first time ever at this scale) on indigenous and local knowledge, particularly addressing issues relevant to indigenous peoples and local communities.

To increase the policy relevance of the report, the assessment's authors have ranked, for the first time at this scale and based on a thorough analysis of the available evidence, the five direct drivers of change in nature with the largest relative global impacts so far. These culprits are, in descending order: (1) changes in land and sea use, (2) direct exploitation of organisms, (3) climate change, (4) pollution, and (5) invasive alien species.

Businesses such as food and agribusinesses, apparel, forestry industries, and packaging industries use species and ecosystem services as essential inputs in their production processes. Also, they rely on healthy ecosystems to treat and disperse waste, maintain soil and water purity, and help regulate air composition. Considering these societal and industrial benefits and the associated values of these ecosystems is crucial to protect biodiversity when evaluating land use opportunities and new endeavors.

Investors are also increasingly considering how to address biodiversity as part of their assessments and how they direct capital towards companies that can demonstrate and report on their biodiversity strategy. The Taskforce on Nature-Related Financial Disclosures (TNFD)[61] has recently launched the beta version of the TNFD framework, which is designed to help businesses understand their biodiversity risks and opportunities, and how to disclose their performance. This is expected to catalyze investor action in a similar way to the Task Force on Climate-Related Disclosures (TCFD)[62].

So, rather than allowing biodiversity risks to manifest in mainstream business, top management teams can take proactive measures to enable their company to remain at the forefront of the sector. Some tangible benefits of such action include funding, penalties avoidance, decreased costs of the reduced need for inputs to combat biodiversity degradation, and an intangible value: better reputation. In addition, there is increased brand recognition due to the implementation of conservation initiatives.

Cambridge Institute for Sustainability Leadership (CISL)[63] is a key partner in helping to demonstrate the power of business action to reverse nature loss. The most successful companies recognize that the environment is essential to business success. However, the global upward tendencies in consumption, population, and economic growth can pressure the environment's health. This modus operandi creates long-term hazards for businesses, consumers, and society, which rely on nature, so, universities can provide research information and strategy-building capacity to establish sustainability solutions and generate widespread momentum.

For example, CISL presents three successful cases:

* Olam International: Reconciling wild nature with large-scale plantations
* Mondi: Implementing mitigation measures in production landscapes
* Asda: Cooperating for biodiversity.

Table 8.6 shows that they are doing much more than this at these companies where biodiversity protection is part of the strategy and is observed in their purpose and everyday activities.

Conducting a nature assessment is the best method for businesses to gain knowledge about nature and biodiversity. The evaluation provides information on the most significant environmental issues and enables enterprises to prioritize action. The outcomes of this analysis will help

Table 8.6 Biodiversity-related business examples

Biodiversity protection as business strategy

Name	Olam International	Mondi	Asda
Purpose	We seek to re-imagine global agriculture and food systems. Our mission is to drive transformation in our sector, in an ethical, socially responsible and environmentally sustainable way.	We aim to operate as a responsible business, applying responsible governance at all our operations and relying on clear frameworks to communicate, measure, improve, and deliver against our ambitious sustainability commitments. We contribute to global SDGs.	Our promise is to build a better world and a more sustainable future through everything we do. *Strategy & Commitments* • Nature • Waste • Value • George For Good: Fibre Sourcing • George For Good: Waste • George For Good: Packaging • Health • Supporting Local Communities • Colleagues • Supply Chain Communities • Ethics and Compliance • Economic Contribution
Website	www.olamgroup.com/	www.mondigroup.com	www.asda.com/creating-change-for-better/better-planet
Country	Operating in 60+ countries	Globally (most in Europe)	England and Wales
Activities	Food and agribusiness, supplying food ingredients, feed, and fiber to 20,900 customers worldwide, ranging from multinational organizations with world famous brands to small family-run businesses.	Managing forests and produce pulp, paper and films to develop effective and innovative industrial and consumer packaging solutions. Leading brands around the world rely on our innovative technologies and products across a variety of applications, including personal care components, stand-up pouches, super-strong cement bags, clever retail boxes and office paper.	Groceries, clothing/apparel (brand: George) and mobile

risk management and safeguard access to ecosystem services through nature-based solutions that mitigate detrimental impacts, safeguard communities, and protect and regenerate biological diversity.

The term bioeconomy can be defined as comprising "those parts of the economy that use renewable biological resources from land and sea – such as crops, forests, fish, animals, and micro-organisms – to produce food, materials and energy" (EU Commission, n.d.)[64]. The bio-economy is promoted as a means to create wealth, address a variety of environmental pressures through the reduction and re-integration of waste streams (circular economy), generate new value from waste, and create a plethora of economic opportunities through the science, design, and development of production and processing facilities and industries that are more resilient (Bosman & Rotmans, 2016)[65].

After the 2009 OECD call for a global transition towards a bioeconomy, which resulted in several nations adopting national or regional strategies to develop their bioeconomy, New Zealand stands out due to its sizeable biological resource base and a well-established cultural heritage in farm production, including a comparative advantage in livestock production, should make it well-positioned for bioeconomy-based wealth creation.

Box 8.8   New Zealand's bioeconomy

It is common sense that new technologies cannot immediately compete on the market against established technologies. This problem is crucial for many new technologies with sustainability promises for energy, transportation, and agriculture. The current primary sector economic model for New Zealand, based predominantly on agricultural products from a livestock base and supplemented by forestry and horticulture, is under pressure from both environmental limits and increasing backlash from a concerned public. A bio-economy is based upon the principle of circularity and integration, and a continued sec-toral mentality will impede innovation in this area. Sector bodies exist to promote the development and continuation of their own sector, and in New Zealand research bod-ies. In addition to universities and independent research organizations, Crown [Govern-ment] Research Institutes (CRIs) were established in their current form in 1992. Each of the CRIs is aligned with a productive sector of the economy or a grouping of natural resourcesffortffort to diversify the sectors away from sheep and beef, poultry, apples and kiwifruit, and wine production into some new species, varietals, and consumer-driven markets provides a broader platform for a selection to expand and grow the bioeconomic resource base. In forestry, the historical dependence on single species (Radiata pine) and single market production (tangible forest products) are expanding into ecosystem ser-vice provision (recreational tourism and adventure parks, carbon trading, and riparian and catchment level water quality payment for services), bio-polymer development, as well as diversified production from under-cropping.

Despite significant inroads by the primary sector towards sustainable resource man-agement, alternative bioeconomic pathways will be required to supplement and trans-form conventional production to maintain the country's prized "clean and green" image. A range of promising niche developments has emerged to enable a gradual transition, pre-senting an exciting picture of innovation and creativity. But for the full benefits of a bio-economy to be realized, including a reduction in waste, GHG emissions, added value, and production efficiency, the scale and interconnection need to be increased considerably.

Supportive infrastructure in New Zealand in terms of dedicated R&D programs into emergent sector issues (e.g., the native freshwater crayfish, kiwifruit, aquaculture, and honey production) has proven essential to enable quality production. In addition, government support and incentives for firms to penetrate emerging sectors (e.g., biotech grants, R&D consortia, and even afforestation grants and support for new vineyard plantings) can allow the sectors to operate at scale and support establishment and credibility. Many potential contributions to a bioeconomy will begin as a niche production, with the niches ultimately driving the system forward in a new direction. Schot and Geels (2008) concluded that if such niches were constructed appropriately, they would be building blocks for broader societal changes towards sustainable development.[66] Support is required across sectors, especially from mainstream producers, for niche industries to perform.

Source: Our Land and Water. (2017). *New Zealand's Policies in Bioeconomy*. https://ourlandandwater. nz/wp-content/uploads/2017/06/BioeconomyResearchPolicy-1.pdf

Environmental sustainability can be defined "as a condition of balance, resilience, and interconnectedness that allows human society to satisfy its needs while neither exceeding the capacity of its supporting ecosystems to continue to regenerate the services necessary to meet those needs nor by our actions diminishing biological diversity" (Morelli, 2011)[67].

This definition puts limit to the growth of economic activities without causing damage to life supporting system in the environment. If entrepreneurs at any level continue to produce, the capacity of supporting ecosystems become endangered if restrictions are not laid on the rate of natural resources usage.

Figure 8.9 displays a theoretical model to analyze bioeconomy.

Box 8.9   Quick review on biodiversity protection as business strategy and bioeconomy

- Biodiversity fundamentally underpins the benefits that businesses derive from natural capital and supports the key ecosystem functions that ensure the delivery of business operations and productivity.
- Although our present economic model takes biodiversity as an infinite resource, new business strategies will determine the ability to achieve the goals of the 2030 Agenda.
- A comprehension of the relevance of biodiversity and how this is factored into the decision-making process is needed.
- Companies can take immediate action by assessing their nature impacts and dependencies and developing nature-based solutions that mitigate adverse effects, protect communities, and preserve and regenerate biological diversity.
- The impact of biodiversity loss can be extensive and often unrealized, causing disruption to supply chains, increasing regulatory compliance costs and potentially eroding social license to operate.
- Businesses should act now to understand their biodiversity risks and opportunities, build internal accountability, and disclose their actions to improve their reputation and brand value.

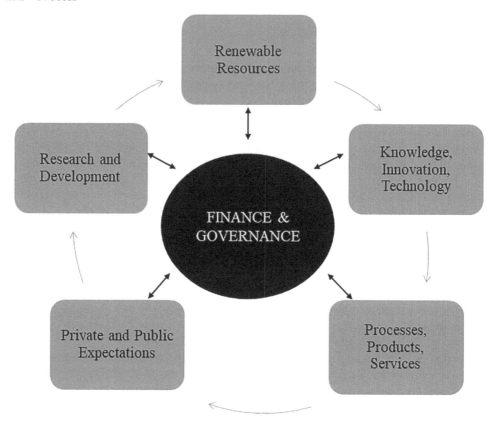

Figure 8.9 A conceptual framework for bioeconomy analysis
Source: Adapted from Maciejczak (2015).[68]

Conclusion

Although the evolving concept of CSR touches on organization's strategic impact on social and environmental performance, it is skewed in the direction of calibrating the firm's performance in line with business standards, norms, regulations, and stakeholder demands (Chapter 7), sustainability-driven entrepreneurs, and managers as the core movers of sustainable production and consumption.

Businesses managers and entrepreneurs are aware of their crucial position in resolving difficult and complex problems such as climate change, water and energy saving, and adequate waste disposal, making the three Rs priority. In recent years, there have been modifications to the employer-employee relationship. The emphasis has shifted from merely accomplishing goals to discovering nature-based solutions.

As we have seen previously in this book, besides the worldwide engagement and struggle against climate change, everyone is also interested in managing workplace diversity, equity, and inclusion (DEI).

We are more aware of the dependence of markets on thriving social and environmental systems. Additionally, businesses are cognizant of the environmental effects of their productions. What exactly are these challenges, and how can they be overcome?

The current opportunity to transform the way we move fundamentally results from changes in three main areas: regulation, consumer behavior, and technology. To tackle climate change, the carbon emissions from producing and operating an EV are typically less than those of producing and operating a conventional vehicle. EVs in urban areas almost always pollute less than internal combustion vehicles. Due to these characteristics they are increasingly appealing to consumers.

Skinny packing is an exciting idea, and it can work on some products to engage with customers. And in terms of sustainability, the business can claim that this is fair trade, ethically sourced, and most of all, their products use sustainable packaging. That could significantly impact consumers, and a growth rate in sales is also expected.

Biodiversity is increasingly recognized for its role in building resilience against climate change, supporting communities and livelihoods, and for its essential role in underpinning society and the economy. Some important organizations like OECD, TNFD, and TCFD are committed to pricing environmental services and set standards, which will enable businesses and financial institutions to put the value of biodiversity at the heart of decision-making. Consequently, there are some examples of organizations that have biodiversity conservation as part of their strategy.

In this context, economic activities run by profit-oriented managers and entrepreneurs are considered to be at the root of social and ecological crisis and hence, hamper sustainable development. Using command-and-control mechanisms to mitigate the negative environmental and social impacts of business, the government, policymaking institutions, and civil societies assume a central role in shaping a sustainability-focused industry from this perspective.

Nevertheless, the overlapping yet conceptually distinct terms "green" entrepreneurship, "social" entrepreneurship, and "institutional" entrepreneurship are incorporated to understand how entrepreneurs induce sustainable innovations to meet the objectives of social benefits and profit maximization in the context of changing market indicators.

Sustainable entrepreneurship is a broad concept in which corporate leaders are driven by environmental and social consciousness to establish and operate businesses to produce environmental, economic, and social value right from the start, as opposed to incorporating environmental and social practices in later phases of production (e.g., using a portion of excess revenues) to comply with standards and legal regulations/norms.

Discussion questions

1 What are the specific management skills to meet the challenges of developing enterprises that support vulnerable communities on the SDGs?
2 What are the individual and group characteristics of entrepreneurship aligned with SDGs, and how do these entrepreneurs create value?
3 What are the different SDG-driven business models, and how do they differ from traditional development projects or commercial enterprises?
4 What issues and opportunities should a company prioritize when using sustainability as a strategy for business operation?
5 Where should companies invest their time, resources, and money to drive the greatest sustainable impact through their business processes (e.g., food industry)?
6 When do corporate sustainability issues require companies to explore collaborations within and with other organizations to fulfill commitments and reach established goals?

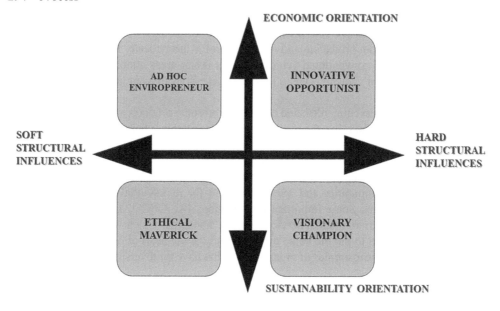

Figure 8.10 Ideal forms of green entrepreneurs

Source: Haldar (2019).

Table 8.7 Key terms

Access and benefit sharing (ABS)	Environmental sustainability
Bioeconomy	Low-carbon economy
Eco-innovation	Skinny design

Table 8.8 Glossary

Access and benefit sharing (ABS)	A fair and equitable sharing of benefits arising from their use, defining the guidelines for commercial relations between the country providing genetic resources and the one that will use them, covering points such as payment of royalties, the establishment of joint ventures, and the right to transfer technology and training
Bioeconomy	Those parts of the economy that use renewable biological resources from land and sea – such as crops, forests, fish, animals, and micro-organisms – to produce food, materials, and energy
Eco-innovation	Eco-innovation (e.g., eco-design, cleaner production) and sustainability-oriented innovations (SOIs), which means the integration of ecological and social aspects into products, processes, and organizational structures
Environmental sustainability	A condition of balance, resilience, and interconnectedness that allows human society to satisfy its needs while neither exceeding the capacity of its supporting ecosystems to continue to regenerate the services necessary to meet those needs nor by our actions diminishing biological diversity
Low-carbon economy	Also decarbonized economy; an economy based on energy sources that produce low levels of greenhouse gas emissions
Skinny design	In skinny design products packaging, the goal is to produce them smaller, with less material and shipping/costs. Because of this, more products could be on the shelf, so fewer stockouts, along with a reduced ecological footprint.

Notes

1 The SDG Partnership Guidebook. (2020). *A Practical Guide to Building High Impact Multi-Stake-holder Partnerships for the Sustainable Development Goals*. Darian Stibbe and Dave Prescott, The Partnering Initiative and UNDESA 2020. Retrieved from https://sdgs.un.org/sites/default/files/2022-02/SDG%20Partnership%20Guidebook%201.11.pdf
2 http://sdg.iisd.org/commentary/guest-articles/the-contested-legacy-of-rio20/
3 United Nations Development Programme. (2001). *Human Development Report 2001: Making New Technologies Work for Human Development*. Oxford, UK: Oxford University Press. https://doi.org/10.18356/2e565da3-en
4 Pearce, J., Grafman, L., Colledge, T., & Legg, R. (2019). Leveraging information technology, social entrepreneurship, and global collaboration for just sustainable development. *HAL-02120513*, 201–2010. Retrieved from https://hal.science/hal-02120513
5 Development Education Project. (2007). *Why Should We Teach about Sustainable Development?* Retrieved from www.dep.org.uk/scities/rationale/whyteach.php
6 Cohen, B., Smith, B., & Mitchell, R. (2008). Toward a sustainable conceptualization of dependent variables in entrepreneurship research. *Business Strategy and the Environment*, 17(2), 107–119. https://doi.org/10.1002/bse.505
7 Dean, T.J., & McMullen, J.S. (2007). Toward a theory of sustainable entrepreneurship: Reducing environmental degradation through entrepreneurial action. *Journal of Business Venturing*, 22(1), 50–76. https://doi.org/10.1016/j.jbusvent.2005.09.003
8 Shepherd, D.A., & Patzelt, H. (2011). The new field of sustainable entrepreneurship: Studying entrepreneurial action linking "what is to be sustained" with "what is to be developed." *Entrepreneurship Theory and Practice*, 35(1), 137–163. https://doi.org/10.1111/j.1540-6520.2010.00426.x
9 Belz, F.M., & Binder, J.K. (2017). Sustainable entrepreneurship: A convergent process model. *Business Strategy and the Environment*, 26(1), 1–17. https://doi.org10.1002/bse.1887
10 Munoz, P., & Cohen, B. (2018). Sustainable entrepreneurship research: Taking stock and looking ahead. *Business Strategy and the Environment*, 27(1), 300–322. https://doi.org/10.1002/bse.2000
11 Hall, J.K., Daneke, G.A., & Lenox, M.J. (2010). Sustainable development and entrepreneurship: Past contributions and future directions. *Journal of Business Venturing*, 439–448. https://doi.org/10.1016/j.jbusvent.2010.01.002
12 Sarango-Lalangui, P., Santos, J.L.S., & Hormiga, E. (2018). The development of sustainable entrepreneurship research field. *Sustainability*, 10(6). https://doi.org/10.3390/su10062005
13 Elkington, J. (1998). Partnerships from cannibals with forks: The triple bottom line of 21st-century business. *Environmental Quality Management*, 8(1), 37–51.
14 Sachs, J., Schmidt-Traub, G., Kroll, C., Lafortune, G., & Fuller, G. (2018). *SDG Index and Dashboards Report 2018, Bertelsmann Stiftung and Sustainable Development Solutions Network*. New York. Retrieved from www.sdgindex.org/reports/sdg-index-and-dashboards-2018/
15 Riti, J.S., Dankumo, A.M., & Gubak, H.D. (2015). Entrepreneurship and environmental sustainability: Evidence from Nigeria. *Journal of Economics and Sustainable Development*, 6(8), 130–140. Retrieved from https://core.ac.uk/download/pdf/234646994.pdf
16 Huđek, I., & Bradac Hojnik, B. (2020). Impact of entrepreneurship activity sustainable development. *Problemy Ekorozwoju*, 15, 175–183. https://doi.org/10.35784/pe.2020.2.17
17 https://unglobalcompact.org/
18 Huđek, I., & Bradac Hojnik, B. (2020). Impact of entrepreneurship activity sustainable development. *Problemy Ekorozwoju*, 15, 175–183. https://doi.org/10.35784/pe.2020.2.17
19 Kuckertz, A., & Wagner, M. (2010). The influence of sustainability orientation on entrepreneurial intentions – investigating the role of business experience. *Journal of Business Venturing*, 25(5), 524–539. https://doi.org/10.1016/j.jbusvent.2009.09.001
20 Youssef, A.B., Boubaker, S., & Omri, A. (2018). Entrepreneurship and sustainability: The need for innovative and institutional solutions. *Technological Forecasting and Social Change*, 129, 232–241. https://doi.org/10.1016/j.techfore.2017.11.003
21 OECD-Organisation for Economic Co-Operation and Development. (2010). *SMEs, Entrepreneurship and Innovation. OECD Studies on SMEs and Entrepreneurship*. Paris: OECD Publishing.
22 Organization for Economic Cooperation and Development – OECD. (2015). Aligning policies for the transition to a low-carbon economy. In *OECD Ministerial Council Meeting*. Retrieved from www.oecd.org/env/Aligning-policies-for-the-transition-to-a-low-carbon-economy-CMIN2015-11.pdf

23 Retrieved March 21, 2023, from https://carboncredits.com/canadas-largest-bank-rbc-invests-8m-in-clearblue-markets/

24 www.undp.org/destination-2030-accelerating-progress-sustainable-development-goals

25 www.un.org/sustainabledevelopment/wp-content/uploads/2023/02/SDG-Stimulus-to-Deliver-Agenda-2030.pdf

26 Feldman, M.P., & Kelley, M.R. (2006). The ex-ante assessment of knowledge spillovers: Government R&D policy, economic incentives and private firm behavior. *Research Policy*, 35, 1509–1521. https://doi.org/10.1016/j.respol.2006.09.019

27 Doblinger, C., Surana, K., & Anadon, L.D. (2019). Governments as partners: The role of alliances in US cleantech startup innovation. *Research Policy*, 48(6), 1458–1475. https://doi.org/10.1016/j.respol.2019.02.006

28 Cojoianu, T.F., Clark, G.L., Hoepner, A.G.F., Veneri, P., & Wójcik, D. (2020). Entrepreneurs for a low carbon world: How environmental knowledge and policy shape the creation and financing of green start-ups. *Research Policy*, 49(6), 103988. https://doi.org/10.1016/j.respol.2020.103988

29 Alvarez, S.A., & Busenitz, L.W. (2001). The entrepreneurship of resource-based theory. *Journal of Management*, 27(6), 755–775. https://doi.org/10.1007/978-3-540-48543-8_10

30 https://sdgs.un.org/goals

31 GEM-Global Entrepreneurship Monitor. (2023). *Global Entrepreneurship Monitor 2022/2023 Global Report: Adapting to a "New Normal."* London: GEM. https://gemconsortium.org/file/open?fileId=51147

32 Lui, Y., Samsami, M., Meshreki, H., Pereira, F., & Schøtt, T. (2021). Sustainable development goals in strategy and practice: Businesses in Colombia and Egypt. *Sustainability*, 13(22), 12453. https://doi.org/10.3390/su132212453

33 Gerlach, A. (2003). Sustainable entrepreneurship and innovation. In *Proceedings of Corporate Social Responsibility and Environmental Management Conference 2003 in Leeds.* Retrieved from https://andersabrahamsson.typepad.com/sustainable%20entrepreneurship%20and%20innovation.pdf

34 Rodríguez-García, M., Guijarro-García, M., & Carrilero-Castillo, A. (2019). An overview of eco-preneurship, eco-innovation, and the ecological sector. *Sustainability*, 11(10), 2909. https://doi.org/10.3390/su11102909

35 Haldar, S. (2019). Towards a conceptual understanding of sustainability-driven entrepreneurship. *Corporate Social Responsibility and Environmental Management*, 26(6), 1157–1170. https://doi.org/10.1002/csr.1763

36 Klewitz, J., & Hansen, E.G. (2014). Sustainability-oriented innovation of SMEs: A systematic review. *Journal of Cleaner Production*, 65, 57–75. https://doi.org/10.1016/j.jclepro.2013.07.017

37 www.bcg.com/publications/2023/why-the-voluntary-carbon-market-is-thriving

38 www.iea.org

39 www.iea.org/data-and-statistics/data-product/greenhouse-gas-emissions-from-energy-highlights

40 Guarnieri, M. (2012). Looking back to electric cars. In *2012 Third IEEE History of Electro-Technology Conference (HISTELCON)*, Pavia, Italy, pp. 1–6. doi: 10.1109/HISTELCON.2012.6487583.

41 Alberghini, M. et al. (2021). Sustainable polyethylene fabrics with engineered moisture transport for passive cooling. *Nature Sustainability*, 4, 715–724. https://doi.org/10.1038/s41893-021-00688-5

42 American Chemical Society. (2023). Could polyethylene be the sustainable fabric of the future? *Chemical & Engineering News*, 99(10). Retrieved from https://cen.acs.org/magazine/99/09910.html

43 https://thinkplasticbrazil.com/en/vasart-develops-a-circular-collection-of-100-recyclable-plant-pots/

44 McKinsey Talks Operations Podcast. Retrieved from www.mckinsey.com/capabilities/operations/our-insights/skinny-design-smaller-is-better-2023?cid=other-eml-dre-mip-mck&hlkid=e7f7db3bb7684578a1ccac4fd1b55be0&hctky=13503040&hdpid=68ccee88-d6e3–41ee-b22f-496ce9a21ecb#/

45 https://fsc.org/en/businesses/wood

46 www.freshwaterwatch.org/

47 McKinsey Talks Operations Podcast. Retrieved from www.mckinsey.com/capabilities/operations/our-insights/skinny-design-smaller-is-better-2023?cid=other-eml-dre-mip-mck&hlkid=e7f7db3bb7684578a1ccac4fd1b55be0&hctky=13503040&hdpid=68ccee88-d6e3–41ee-b22f-496ce9a21ecb#/

48 OECD. (2020). *Biodiversity: Finance and the Economic and Business Case for Action.* Retrieved from www.oecd-ilibrary.org/sites/a3147942-en/index.html?itemId=/content/publication/a3147942-en

49 CBD. (2021, September 3). First draft of the post-2020 global biodiversity framework. *Convention on Biological Diversity/WG2020/3/3*. Retrieved from www.cbd.int/doc/c/abb5/591f/2e46096d3f0330b08ce87a45/wg2020-03-03-en.pdf

50 Aguiar, A.C.F., Scarano, F.R., Bozelli, R.L., Branco, P.D., Ceotto, P., Farjalla, V.F., Loyola, R., & Silva, J.M.C. (2023). Business, biodiversity, and innovation in Brazil. *Perspectives in Ecology and Conservation*, 21(1), 6–16. https://doi.org/10.1016/j.pecon.2022.12.002

51 Viana, L.S., Jabur, D.M., Ramirez, P., & da Cruz, G.P. (2018). Patents go to the market? University-Industry technology transfer from a Brazilian perspective. *Journal of Technology Management & Innovation*, 13(3), 24–35. https://doi.org/10.4067/S0718-27242018000300024

52 https://sdgs.un.org/ (former: https://sustainabledevelopment.un.org/milestones/unced)

53 www.cbd.int/abs/

54 Heinrich, M. et al. (2020). Access and benefit sharing under the Nagoya Protocol – Quo vadis? Six Latin American case studies assessing opportunities and risk. *Frontiers in Pharmacology*, 11, 765–784. https://doi.org/10.3389/fphar.2020.00765

55 Muzaka, V., & Serrano, O.R. (2019). Teaming up? China, India and Brazil and the issue of benefit-sharing from genetic resource use. *New Political Economy*, 25, 734–754. https://doi.org/10.1080/13563467.2019.1584169

56 Aguilar, C.G., & Alfaro, M. (2015). Los recursos naturales de los pueblos indígenas y las empresas: estándares interamericanos y jurisprudencia chilena. *Anuario de Derechos Humanos*, 183–193. ISSN 0718-2058 No. 11 (Santiago: Universidad de Chile).

57 Celi, A. (2016). Análisis jurídico del ordenamiento jurídico internacional sobre protección de los recursos genéticos: desafíos y perspectivas en Uruguay a partir de la implementación del protocolo de Nagoya. *Revista de Direito Internacional*, 13(2), 117–131. https://doi.org/10.5102/rdi.v13i2.4055

58 Dutfield, G., & Suthersanen, U. (2019). Traditional knowledge and genetic resources: Observing legal protection through the lens of historical geography and human rights. *Washburn Law Jourbnal*, 58, 399–447. Retrieved from https://contentdm.washburnlaw.edu/digital/collection/wlj/id/7108/rec/64

59 Friso, F. et al. (2020). Implementation of Nagoya Protocol on access and benefit-sharing in Peru: Implications for researchers. *Journal of Ethnopharmacology*, 259, 112885. https://doi.org/10.1016/j.jep.2020.112885

60 IPBES. (2019). *Global Assessment Report on Biodiversity and Ecosystem Services of the Intergovernmental Science-Policy Platform on Biodiversity and Ecosystem Services* (p. 1148), edited by E.S. Brondizio, J. Settele, S. Díaz, & H.T. Ngo. Bonn, Germany: IPBES Secretariat. https://doi.org/10.5281/zenodo.3831673

61 https://tnfd.global/

62 www.unepfi.org/climate-change/tcfd/

63 www.cisl.cam.ac.uk/business-action/business-nature/natural-capital-impact-group/doing-business-with-nature/business-and-biodiversity

64 EU Commission. https://ec.europa.eu/research/bioeconomy/index.cfm

65 Bosman, R., & Rotmans, J. (2016). Transition governance towards a bioeconomy: A comparison of Finland and the Netherlands. *Sustainability*, 8(10), 1017. https://doi.org/10.3390/su8101017

66 Schot, J., & Geels, F.W. (2008). Strategic niche management and sustainable innovation journeys: Theory, findings, research agenda, and policy. *Technology Analysis & Strategic Management*, 20(5), 537–554. https://doi.org/10.1080/09537320802292651

67 Morelli, J. (2011). Environmental sustainability: A definition for environmental professionals. *Journal of Environmental Sustainability*, 1(1), Article 2. https://doi.org/10.14448/jes.01.0002

68 Maciejczak, M. (2015). How to analyse bioeconomy? Polish association of agricultural economics and agribusiness. *Stowarzyszenie Ekonomistow Rolnictwa e Agrobiznesu (SERiA)*, 6(6). https://doi.org/10.22004/ag.econ.233499

9 Marketing, technology, and entrepreneurship

Learning objectives

1 Learn the essentials of marketing
2 Comprehend aligning marketing strategies with business objectives
3 Effectively apply the steps from the marketing timeline
4 Examine financial effects and viability of social media and digital business initiatives
5 See how to fine-tune branding with management strategies.

Box 9.1   Tesla

Elon Musk, the CEO and founder of Tesla Motors, stated that the company's strategy was to "enter at the high end of the market, where customers are willing to pay a premium, and then drive down the market as quickly as possible to higher unit volume and lower price with each successive model" (2006)[1].

Anyone wishing to purchase a luxury car with a contemporary appearance that is also an electric vehicle frequently chooses a Tesla car. These cars have evolved into a status symbol in addition to being more environmentally friendly than the regular gas-powered sedan, especially given their price.

A competitive advantage provided by companies with a clearly defined strategy that aligns with their mission and vision has helped Tesla become a potential leader in the electric vehicle industry (Collis & Ruckstad, 2008).[2] The Model S, the automobile that earned the Motor Trend Car of the Year award, is a prime example of Tesla's dedication to design, engineering, software, and technological innovation. The company's dedication to providing exceptional customer care through its Super Charger networks and battery exchange facilities is just as strong. By making their patents available to the industry and partnering with companies like Panasonic, Daimler, Toyota, and Solar Edge, to mention a few, Tesla has advanced the idea of open innovation.

Using an incremental product innovation strategy, external and internal factors like market demand, creative culture, and leadership and teamwork support the innovation strategy of the company.

Tesla also integrated innovation into its business canvas model and created value for its customers. Because of this, its owners stand out: Tesla's car has many benefits, such as a smaller carbon footprint, increased performance, advanced technology, and social status.

DOI: 10.4324/9781003405740-14

Figure 9.1 Tesla

So, if you're looking for a high-tech performance car, a Tesla could be perfect for you. In addition, celebrity environmentalists like Leonardo DiCaprio, Arnold Schwarzenegger, and Al Gore have also made this vehicle a statement of eco-friendly transport, and although road transportation is not considered the leading source of greenhouse gas emissions, it contributes to the major part of the emissions.

In summary, Tesla's brand recognition and perceived elite status increase demand for these vehicles. The key factors that drive demand for all electric vehicles are the cost of gasoline, the available features (all-wheel drive, sedan versus larger vehicles), the availability of battery charging stations, and the appeal of the "green" movement make this car bestselling luxury brand in the United States last year, according to data reported by Automotive News.[3]

In the United States at the beginning of 2023, Tesla reduced the prices for all their models, making ownership possible for more people. The base Model 3 was slashed by $4000, and the most expensive Model X dropped in price from $120,990 to $99,990.[4] This is exactly what Musk predicted would happen.

Source: https://financebuzz.com/is-a-tesla-worth-it

Questions for discussion: Tesla's case

1　Electric vehicle (EV) reliability problems are frequently reported by drivers; however, for the first time, the rate of EV problems is lower than the rate of non-EV problems. Are urban areas prepared to adopt these cars in 20 percent of fleets today?

2 Since 2022, many original equipment manufacturers (OEMs) in the EV sector have struggled to keep up with market demand. Besides, there is no universal standard charging socket for direct current fast-charging. OEMs argue that setting no standard early on is good as it allows manufacturers to experiment and drives innovation. However, as a long-term solution, this is detrimental to the consumer. What is your opinion on innovation and industry standards?

3 Climate change reports drove an upheaval in the automobile sector, forcing established auto brands to reconsider their strategies and evolve. The main query, though, is whether the market and the brands have been able to resolve customer worries related to EV adoption. Discuss it with your colleagues.

4 The automotive industry has seen the resurgence of EVs in recent years due to new entrants like Tesla painting a different picture for the automobile sector with their high-performance EVs that utilize cutting-edge technology and also due to growing fuel prices and environmental concerns. So which aspect do you value most about EVs? List the pros and cons of EVs (like in a marketing campaign).

Introduction

Many businesses' strategies revolve around digital marketing, and the technology that underpins these initiatives is always developing. The expanding significance of long-run educational content, chatbots and live chat, and voice search are a few trends that are changing the game. While many marketing principles remain constant over time, organizations' methods for success in marketing have changed significantly. Advertising in newspapers and television used to be commonplace, but social media, artificial intelligence, and digital advertising are now essential components of commercial marketing strategies.

This chapter focuses on the know-how and tools for entrepreneurs, particularly those in developing countries, to successfully market their products or services. We will present marketing concepts and their application for entrepreneurs, in order, to advance their objectives. Furthermore, topics on the background information on the role of marketing for businesses success, characteristics of marketing, and marketing by entrepreneurs in developing countries will be discussed. We will also assess how enterprises could identify their business and clients in order to better construct their marketing positioning and branding placement.

Nowadays, entrepreneurs who stay ahead of the curve might even find new heights of marketing success. Digitalization has dramatically changed the company's focus.[5] Thus, entrepreneurs should now concentrate on engaging more consumers with their products. How does marketing play a role?[6]

Box 9.2   The role of marketing by the father of management thinking

There will always, one can assume, be need for some selling. But the aim of marketing is to make selling superfluous. The aim of marketing is to know and understand the customer so well that the product or service fits him and sells itself. Ideally, marketing should result in a customer who is ready to buy. All that should be needed then is to make the product or service available.

Peter Drucker

Main aim of marketing

Figure 9.2 Changing trends in marketing

Furthermore, we will analyze the marketing mix (price, place, and promotion) and go over a few customers loyalty plans appropriate for startup businesses. Small and medium-sized companies and entrepreneurs face many of the same marketing issues. Entrepreneurship is a process that aims to establish an enterprise as a small, medium, or large enterprise, as we covered in the previous chapters.

As stated earlier, both developed and developing nations' economies greatly benefit from the contributions of entrepreneurs. Entrepreneurs have contributed by creating a thriving manufacturing sector (China, for example), an emerging regional economy, capturing the global market through more significant exports, and creating job opportunities. A decade ago, the OECD 2013 Report indicated the important role of entrepreneurs for sustainable growth is due to their effectiveness in promoting innovation and providing employment opportunities. The challenge, however, until today is the availability of adequate financing to fund the inception and progressive growth of a business owing to the specific characteristics and challenges faced by new enterprises. In this sense, OECD has now an initiative – the Center for Entrepreneurship, SMEs, Regions and Cities[7] – to help local and national governments to foster entrepreneurs and small and medium-sized enterprises, promoting inclusive and sustainable regions and cities, boosting local job creation and implementing sound tourism policies. The OECD SMEs and Entrepreneurship Strategy (2022) highlights some recommendations.[8]

Considering small and medium enterprises entrepreneurial owner's reality (mainly in emerging economies), the official marketing models and processes, sophisticated marketing theories may not be suitable. However, it's critical to comprehend how business owners in developing nations could use marketing to connect with consumers and expand their market share.

Definition of marketing

According to the American Marketing Association, marketing is the:

> Activity set of institutions and processes for creating, communicating, delivering, and exchanging offerings that have value to customers, clients, partners, and society at large.

Marketing plays a central role in business success; most aspects of a business depend on a successful marketing campaign.[9] According to Peter Drucker, the aim of good marketing is to make selling unnecessary.[10] Marketing that is customer oriented has a higher success rate than marketing that is product oriented. The seller's aim should be to sell what they make, and the marketer's objective is to make what they can sell. Without marketing, an entrepreneur may not be able to be successful in expanding and prospering. By producing dimensions in one or more

Figure 9.3 Marketing

of the marketing mixes, companies can sell more to an existing customer or expand the number of customers, particularly for low budget entrepreneurs, whose marketing resources and planning process are limited. In addition, a marketing plan is essential in building an organization's reputation and product awareness.

Marketing efforts such as effective communication and offering quality products and services can build a business's reputation and expand market share and therefore increase sales and revenue. A successful marketing plan for an entrepreneur is essential. Generally, entrepreneurs have many more challenges in marketing their product or service because they do not have a record to stand on compared to developed companies.

Characteristics of marketing in developed and developing countries

The majority of entrepreneurs are independent because they have an idea, a product or service, and perhaps a few partners or workers. Also, (co-)owners may uniquely operate their business, particularly in a developing nation. However, they generally have a lack of expertise in the field and other resources. Resources include not just money, but facilities (like buildings), technology, equipment, specialists, professionals, and knowledge. One of the critical causes of high failure rates is the operational mediocrity that results from a lack of declared resources.

Nevertheless, public policies can make it easy. In Brazil, a specific nonprofit private entity associated with the federal government and created in 1972, has the mission of promoting the sustainable and competitive development of small businesses and to foster entrepreneurship, providing guidance to help small businesses to grow and generate more employment, helping to develop the Brazilian economy, Brazilian Service of Support for Micro and Small Enterprises the (SEBRAE)[11]

Without government support, it is understandable that these challenges could be much greater in developing countries because without specialists, many tools of marketing may not be available and therefore make it difficult to survive or expand.

Creating and applying a plan determines the potential success of any business, new or established.[12,13] A strategy typically consists of short- and long-term acknowledgment and response to any challenges or opportunities coming from the given business environment.[14] For example, the strategy could be the set of decisions for resource acquisition and allocation. Strategies relating to the marketing function are thus highly essential for any new enterprise, therefore developing a marketing strategy is crucial for each new business. Marketing success for the brand will help to create customer trust, position the brand in the appropriate market category, and ultimately result in increased revenues.

Networking and positive word of mouth is the first stage and most efficient for an entrepreneur or an SME. Numerous additional marketing channels and platforms are effective in grabbing a potential customer's attention. They are not, however, persuasion-based marketing

Major reasons for high failure rates among new enterprises

Figure 9.4 Failure reasons

strategies. Compared to other conventional marketing channels, word of mouth has a more significant impact on people as a whole.

In nations with accessible, low-cost, and user-friendly technology and communication, business owners could use social media to stay in touch with their clients. Being active on social media platforms like Instagram, Facebook, Twitter, YouTube, LinkedIn, and online blogs, for instance, is very effective because it allows the target market to express their opinions about the goods and services the company offers, completely changing the way information is shared between buyers and sellers and enabling immediate communication. The business may become more "customer-centric" as a result of this. But, of course, selling a product that fulfills customer demand is simpler than convincing customers to purchase whatever the corporation believes to be the most profitable.

The firm may have a lower profit per unit of the sold product by meeting client demands. However, sales of the product will increase consistently and quickly. By considering customer feedback and opinions when creating a product, business owners may innovate even more and create something that will be more popular and in more demand. A business owner wants to make money, so they carefully consider their positioning and branding while ensuring their consumers are happy.

The thoughtful product branding and positioning could be embodied in alignment between the company's mission statement, CSR, and actual activities, as reported by the media. So, it could affect customers' awareness and satisfaction, which are important for marketing campaigns to be successful (see Dove's strategy in Chapter 7 for an example).

It is worth mention that even when various marketing tactics and strategies are used, most small business owners and entrepreneurs need proper and formal marketing practices. Customer service, intuition, and environmental awareness must all be prioritized highly. Without a structured organizational role to handle marketing operations, entrepreneurs and SMEs are more likely to rely on a single person or a small group of people who are unwilling to consult outside specialists and make judgments based only on instinct and enthusiasm. There is little chance that you possess the necessary knowledge. As a result, the majority of marketing strategies used in that setting are applied inconsistently.

In addition to those generic features, enterprises face other threats:

1 They are affected by both the external and internal environment due to globalization and internationalization of the marketplace, so they may be forced to compete domestically and internationally.

2 Most entrepreneurs acknowledge that they need to gain more, faster, and better marketing knowledge and information, but they lack access to resources or are reluctant to pursue these needs.
3 Not all entrepreneurs are able to clearly articulate the fundamental issues below, which are essential for a successful marketing strategy (4Ps).

From this perspective, we will present some marketing fundamentals in the following sections.

Marketing mix – 4Ps

The *Economic Times* defines the marketing mix as a set of actions or tactics a company uses to establish its products, services, and brand on the market. Decisions about the product, place, price, and promotion of a brand are essential and must be taken prior to any marketing activity being set in motion. In a way, your marketing mix is the general plan or template for your marketing strategy, as it encompasses analysis of both internal and external strategic decisions.

Products and services

A definition of the primary products and services is also needed for the successful execution of any strategy. Offering multiple products or services increases the chance of attracting a larger customer target market. However, enterprises need to focus on marketing the most profitable or most frequently sold product or service, because it is part of the internal factors of an organization's operations, so the entrepreneur in charge has control over it. Now it is important to understand the competitive landscape. Knowledge about the difference between the enterprise and its competitors is essential for marketing the enterprise products more effectively and finding the one characteristic which differentiates your product from all other competitors on the market.

To ensure that their company keeps up with possible rivals, an entrepreneur must examine the relevant sector extensively and evaluate the price, quality, product offerings, and marketing approach. Attempting to identify the sources of differentiation may also help. It's important for businesses to keep tabs on the marketing budgets, couponing, promotions, social media activity, websites, and packaging of their concurrence.

Box 9.3 Quick review on marketing fundamentals

- Marketing plays a central role for business success: most aspects of a victorious entrepreneurial activity depend on an adequate marketing campaign.
- Two of the main reasons for high failure rates among SMEs and entrepreneurs are lack of government support and their operational mediocrity and/or resources.
- The potential success of a new enterprise (or any enterprise) depends upon the formulation and implementation of a strategy.
- To build customers' trust and to position the brand in the right segment of the marketing, targeting the right people from this segment and increasing the brand reputation are primary objectives of a marketing efficient strategy.
- The trend in marketing efforts is moving towards "customer-centric" positions from the previous products-centric and sales-centric positions.

- Networking along with positive word of mouth are the first stages and until now efficient enough for an entrepreneur or SME.
- Social media changes how customers and businesses share information because it lets companies respond quickly to new customer needs.

Big data technologies and analytics enable new digital services and are often associated with superior performance. But firms investing in big data often fail to attain those advantages. Considering how and when big data pay off, marketing scholars have been investigating this issue.[15] The authors conceptualize and operationalize three important big data marketing affordances: customer behavior pattern spotting, real-time market responsiveness, and data-driven market ambidexterity. They concluded that managers must identify those actors within their organization who are in the best position to actualize BTDA marketing affordances and empower them with the responsibility to take actions.

Almost every element of human life has been transformed by new technologies, including the strategies businesses use to promote goods and services to customers. More radical technologies are developing alongside well-known ones like the internet, more powerful computers, mobile devices and applications, and social media. These technical developments are having a significant impact on the practice of marketing.[16] These developments are related to artificial intelligence (AI) (Davenport, 2018),[17] the internet of things (IoT) (Hoffman & Novak, 2018)[18], and robotics (Mende et al., 2019)[19].

The review "The Future of Technology and Marketing: A Multidisciplinary Perspective" by Grewal et al. (2020) shows that the literature is arranged into six significant, major categories

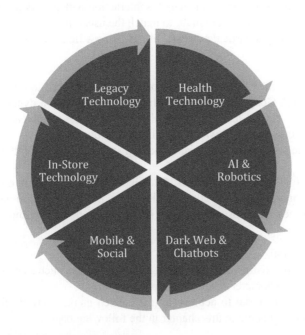

Figure 9.5 The future of technology in marketing

Source: Grewal, D. et al. (2020). The future of technology and marketing: A multidisciplinary perspective. *Journal of the Academy of Marketing Science*, 48, 1–8. https://doi.org/10.1007/s11747-019-00711-4

of research, including health technology, AI and robotics, the dark web and chatbots, mobile and social, in-store technology, and legacy technology.[20] However, they obviously cannot be comprehensive in terms of covering all cutting-edge technological innovation applications (see Figure 9.4).

In a similar way of the research agenda, the link between marketing and technology is present in business strategies, depending on the budget. While an entrepreneur may need more finance to hire specified professionals to do the tracking and compiling, the rapid technological development of the 21st century, like software and AI, allows the enterprise to do this, spending less money or time on it.

AI in marketing (also called "artificial intelligence marketing") is a strategy of leveraging data and machine learning to deliver campaigns that help achieve a brand's goals more effectively. Today, many marketers utilize AI in market research, data science, and real-time campaign analysis.[21]

AI in marketing includes the follow:

- Data analysis is the process of gathering and sorting through massive volumes of marketing data from numerous programs and initiatives that would otherwise need to be done by hand.
- Developing human-like language for customer service bots, experience personalization, and other uses is known as natural language processing (NLP).
- Media buying: predict the best ad and media placements for a company to reach its target audience and maximize the return on investment from its marketing plan.
- Automated decision-making: based on historical data or external data inputs, AI marketing solutions assist businesses in determining which marketing or business growth plan to employ.
- Writing both brief and lengthy content for a marketing strategy, such as video subtitles, email subject lines, online copy, blogs, and more is known as content generation.
- Real-time personalization: modifying a user's interaction with a marketing resource, such as a web page, social media post, or email, to match the user's previous preferences in order to nudge them into doing a particular action, like clicking a link, signing up for something, or making a purchase.

Additionally, you have probably seen an AI content generator used to create marketing copy, posed a query through Google Analytics Intelligence, or launched a dynamic search ad campaign in Google Ads. Now, ChatGPT is one of the possibilities to increase marketing performance for entrepreneurs and SME which have limited resources.

In early 2023, the most straightforward marketing strategies using ChatGPT are:[22]

1 Making a copy for marketing materials: ChatGPT can assist business owners with writing copy for any of marketing materials: Emails, blogs, product descriptions, copy for advertisements, headlines for websites, copy for social media posts, and more. Some examples include:

- Create the material
- Make changes to existing content to give it a specific tone, such as making it more exciting for a specific character or more ominous
- Enhance current material to achieve a goal (search engine optimization, for example). This definition will come in this chapter in the following pages.

2 Obtain suggestions for marketing tools: numerous "top ten" lists are available online for almost every tool.

3 Creation of content: find inspiration for blog posts, manuals, white papers, and e-books. One can use it to research a subject, compile a list of the best articles on a specific topic, ask it to simplify a complicated thought, or ask for post ideas based on subjects or existing material.
4 Learn formulas and efficiencies: ChatGPT can assist by teaching shortcuts to speed up data processing and analysis, like regular expressions, spreadsheet formulas, etc.
5 Make consumer surveys: create a survey or poll to continue learning more about the audience and clients and gathering client feedback.
6 Learn about chatbots: these are an excellent method to create leads, engage visitors, and get feedback by adding chat to the website.

McCormick (2023) emphasizes that it is essential to remember that the responses that ChatGPT creates is a starting point for brainstorming. Then, the business owners must customize the copy to their target audience and brand voice.

But how to achieve a perfect marketing mix? The traditional approach is presented next, showing the four key factors every marketer should use to guide their campaign strategy.

Place

Although specificities differ significantly from product to product, around one-fifth of a product's cost is spent on getting it to the client. The concept of place concerns different ways of moving and storing things before making them available to the client. A well-designed distribution system is required to get the appropriate product to the right place at the right time. Some manufacturers may find it more cost-effective to sell through wholesalers, who then sell to retailers, while others may prefer to sell to customers or retailers directly.

Distribution is important because it is the channel to get the product or service to the target audience.[23] The two common channel options are direct and indirect channels. Entrepreneurs could choose to sell directly to their customers without the involvement of any intermediary. The examples include direct sales force, mail, and online store. They may also select one or more intermediaries like an agent, broker, dealer, distributor, wholesaler, or retailer to reach their customers. Evolution of new technology, communication, and means of transportation impact where an entrepreneur will locate, online or in store.

An online store typically includes product descriptions, pricing, pictures, contact information, the company logo, and a brief business description. In addition, companies must open a merchant account, choose a valid payment method (e.g., Visa, Mastercard, or PayPal), choose shipping carriers, and establish shipping costs.

The e-commerce platform is now widely used worldwide since, during the pandemic, its sales experienced an unparalleled rise. However, the e-commerce industry has begun to return to pre-pandemic levels with the easing of restrictions and the reopening of physical businesses. Data on web traffic to e-commerce and direct-to-consumer (DTC) sites in the US likewise show a diminishing trend. In the US, in-store sales have been rising at the same time.

In 2023, inflation in many nations is at its greatest, wages are rising, and unemployment is at record lows. Shipping, fulfillment, labor, and customer acquisition expenses are all rising regarding e-commerce. Consequently, digital prices have been rising, albeit not as much as retail pricing. The Visa Spending Momentum Index has crossed the 100-point threshold, indicating that consumer confidence is waning and that consumers are spending less than they did a year ago. e-Commerce's share of overall retail sales is approaching pre-pandemic levels. How the economy is doing affects several things.[24]

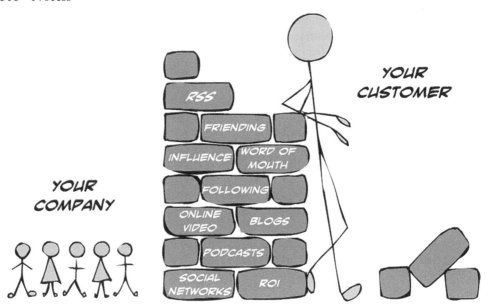

Figure 9.6 Customer

Box 9.4   Everything revolves around your customer

It has been proven in several consumer studies in developed countries that a vast majority of them will pay for a better service. Since a great experience is a known cause for increasing the brand loyalty and word-of-mouth referrals, you will also be happy to hear that Nielsen[25] reported personal recommendations as far more trustworthy (and effective) than ads from a consumer standpoint.

If you can't go toe-to-toe with the big guys on price, amazing services should be your winning proposition.

As a result, the e-store must be properly planned to embrace that service dimension and cater to the consumer's specific needs. Security is noteworthy for avoiding data leaks and compromising sales.

Also, navigability, or the ability for users to use the site quickly and easily, is the most crucial component of an e-store site's design.[26] The site layout should be simple and clear so that the customer can have a user-friendly experience. Also, an e-store site's important feature is interactivity between the user and the site itself. Businesses need to have a frequently asked question (FAQ) section to handle the questions that might be normally asked by the customer.

In addition, the web atmosphere is fundamental in changing shoppers' mood and creating a pleasant emotional experience. Music and visuals such as 3D displays and downloadable video clips are usually used to make an online storefront visually compelling.[27] A majority of the customers prefer a quick and accurate display of information about product and price. In many developing countries these methods of marketing and sales are used.

It is not necessary to hire specialists because, in the market, there are some e-commerce website builders with the following features:

- Drag-and-drop capabilities
- Mobile-optimization options
- Search engine optimization analytics
- Traffic analytics
- Payment processing capabilities
- Inventory tracking
- CRM integration
- SSL security
- Coupon creation tools
- Social media integration
- Live chat functionality.

These features will simplify processes, improve customer satisfaction, and help with the success of the experience in the online business store. Some of these builders are free or start with prices like $1/month.

In 2023, the best e-commerce website builders for creating a beautiful, customizable, and responsive online store from scratch (where no coding skill is required) considered to be intuitive online store builders to support inventory, payment, shipping, and more are the following:[28]

- Wix (www.wix.com/)
- Ionos (www.ionos.com/)
- Shopify (www.shopify.com/)
- Bluehost (www.bluehost.com/)
- Web.com (www.web.com/)
- Network Solutions (www.networksolutions.com/).

Consequently, it is possible to design a comprehensive online site using an e-commerce site builder which comprises all the features businesses owners and online consumers require, including specific product pages and a seamless shopping experience using easy online payment.

In addition, a website's search engine optimization can be boosted, as well as page loading speed, website traffic, and lead generation, with the help of a trustworthy builder. After all, if an appealing, useful e-commerce website that captures the audiences' attention is needed to surpass the competition, only an e-commerce website builder can help if the business still needs a web developer.

Apart from web store design, Martin notes that businesses need to ensure a reliable supply source of goods.[29] A common problem that many owners of e-commerce websites have is when their supplier closes shop or runs out of stock. Therefore, businesses must have a backup plan in place to be ready for any eventuality. The online store's success also depends on picking a reputable web host. Businesses can choose from a wide range of e-commerce websites offering hosted services and online apps based on subscriptions.

Small businesses regularly use e-commerce platforms like BigCommerce, Yahoo Small Business, eBay, Amazon, Alibaba, and others. Depending on the quality of service, each site has a distinct price range. Many of them have also made traffic-generating tools, mobile and social commerce alternatives, and integration with social media sites available. The consumer, the product, the environment, and the business goals are factors to consider while picking channels.

To establish the most effective strategy to target a potential customer, business owners need to understand their characteristics, including who they are, where they are from, and when and how they often shop.[30]

It is obvious that a product's physical appeal and presentation are key factors in attracting customers. Signaling and in-store marketing help to build your company's brand, but they are much less successful at attracting new clients. Therefore, a frequent tactic is first to run adequate (but not expensive) marketing and advertising to get customers to look at the goods inside the store, and then run heavy marketing and promotion there.

Pricing

Pricing is the primary predictor of profitability compared to the other three components of the marketing mix – product, promotion, and place – which impact marketing costs; developing a pricing strategy is an essential duty for a company. Setting the appropriate pricing is a difficult choice that must be carefully considered. Pricing that is too expensive will turn away clients, while pricing that is too cheap could give customers the impression that the product is of inferior quality.[31]

Price and input costs are related. Prices can be set to maximize profits and minimize unprofitable items or services by considering the cost of each good and service[32] So, to determine their product's overall costs for adequate pricing, businesses must evaluate every component's material, labor, and overhead costs.

A newly established business or product launch requires careful consideration when choosing an entrance pricing plan. Pricing is a key element of marketing, and how you enter the market will determine how your clients will respond at first. The ideal pricing approach typically depends on your short- and long-term objectives and your strengths and weaknesses in particular markets, as can be seen in Box 9.5.

Box 9.5   The right price

Selecting the right entry pricing strategy is critical for a new business or product launch. Pricing is a primary marketing component, and what you enter the market with dictates your customer's initial reaction.

Moreover, pricing is a crucial element of a successful marketing plan. Your product and service prices have an impact on sales, cash flow, earnings, and the market perception of your brand. Therefore, you should have a well-thought-out long-term pricing strategy in place before launching a new product or business to maximize client growth, revenue, or profitability, depending on your company's goals. Some examples include the following:

- *Penetrative*: Penetration pricing is aptly named, as it is a strategy specific to market entry. The premise is to offer very low up-front prices to attract customer from competitors or in the open market.
- *Skimming*: Price skimming is a common contrasting approach to penetration; you start with a premium price point to optimize short-term profit from the most aggressive customers.
- *Premium*: Premium pricing is a specific approach to launch high early prices you intend to maintain. This coincides with a high-end product and service offering that you believe has a large enough market to sustain your business over time.

- *Competitive*: When companies are more concerned about entering the market with competitive prices, they build meaningful relationships based on "non-price" factors such as product quality, service, patented features, environmental and civic involvement, and distinct benefits.
- *Pricing based on value*: A pricing technique known as "value-based pricing" bases prices on the target market's estimation of the value in comparison to competing brands. For instance, you might set the price of your product at or close to $30 if buyers thought $30 was a fair price. If more sophisticated items are introduced to the market later in the product life cycle, customer perceptions of value may decline.
- *Profitability*: Techniques like target return pricing and cost-plus pricing emphasize long-term profit maximization. Essentially, you establish prices based on the ideal level of earnings you anticipate achieving in the long run. For example, if your objective is to make a 20 percent profit throughout a product, you must predict how long early demand will persist at higher prices with a 30 to 40 percent profit margin. Additionally, it would be best to consider the possibility of discounting leftover inventory towards the end of the life cycle for little to no profit.

To have an effective initial price, market research is essential before the debut of a product. In addition, it would help if you continuously kept an eye on how demand is changing due to new product options becoming available and dwindling consumer interest in your offering.

Read more at https://smallbusiness.chron.com/entry-pricing-strategy-61428.html

Pricing is the primary predictor of profitability compared to the other three components of the marketing mix – product, promotion, and place – which impact marketing costs; developing a pricing strategy is an essential duty for a company. Setting the appropriate pricing is a difficult choice that has to be carefully considered. Pricing that is too expensive will turn away clients, while pricing that is too cheap could give customers the impression that the product is of inferior quality. Price and input costs are related. Prices can be set to maximize profits and minimize unprofitable items or services by considering the cost of each good and service. So, to determine their product's overall costs for adequate pricing, businesses must evaluate every component's material, labor, and overhead costs.

When an enterprise is mainly serving customers who are price sensitive, or when it enjoys a reduction in production and marketing costs with an increase in volume, it can charge a low initial price. If the target audience has a strong desire for the products and can afford to pay higher prices, the enterprise can afford a higher ceiling on price.[33] Of course, the enterprise should not be under competitive pressure.

Another strategy of pricing is discovering what your competitors are charging their customers. This provides enterprise a range within which they could set a price. When conducting the competitive analysis, the enterprise should assess not just the pricing, but also the whole package that includes the targeted customers, and other value-added services your competitor offers.

Small businesses are commonly believed to underprice. It is largely because they don't exert the operational efficiency larger players normally have, thus have an incorrect analysis of their costs. Therefore, rather than comparing the product/service price of large competitors, small businesses could add other differentiators that add value and justify higher prices.

Figure 9.7 Price

For example, they could increase the product's value proposition by enhancing its exclusivity, locating the product at the point of sale such as in a convenience store, additionally providing helpful, knowledgeable, friendly customer service.[34]

According to Crane, it is easier to set a higher initial price and lower the price over time than the reverse.[35] To raise the price, enterprises should communicate with customers the uniqueness and value of their products and services.[36,37] A useful alternative is to offer the customer a variety of choices such as off-peak pricing or tiered pricing, where the prices vary depending on attachments to the product.

The price should not be set in isolation; it should be integrated with product, promotion, and place to form a coherent mix that provides superior customer value. For example, for businesses that want to adopt low-end competitive pricing, the strategy needs to focus on reducing the costs. Entrepreneurs need to bargain to get the best possible price for the merchandise, locate the business in an inexpensive location, closely control inventory to minimize storage cost, limit product lines to best-selling items, and produce advertising to focus on "price specials."[38]

Price deals

Price deals are often used to get people to try out new products or lines that are being added, to attract new customers to an existing product, or to get current customers to buy more and use the product faster. Price reductions are most successful when the consumer's primary concern is price or when brand loyalty could be more present or higher. Keeping everything else the same, cheap goods typically have low quality.

Buyers may learn about price discounts either at the point of sale or through advertising. At the point of sale, price reductions may be posted on the package, on signs near the product, or in storefront windows. Many forms of advertisements can be used to inform consumers of upcoming discounts, including radios, newspaper, and social media. Existing customers treat discounts as rewards and often respond by buying in larger quantities. Price discounts alone, however, usually do not appeal to first-time buyers.

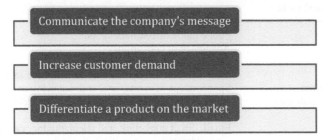

Communicate the company's message

Increase customer demand

Differentiate a product on the market

Figure 9.8 Marketing strategy

Discounts, bonus pack deals, refunds or rebates, and coupons are the primary categories of price deals. Price reductions provide immediate value to customers, creating a clear incentive for them to make a purchase. Price reductions, however, are simple for the competition to match and, if utilized repeatedly, can damage a brand's reputation.

Promotion

The traditional marketing mix is composed of four mixed facets, known as the four Ps: price, product, placement, and promotion. There are different theories about where social media fits into this model. It could lay in the promotional sector with public relations and advertising or in a fifth category all its own, consumers. Nowadays, as more and more businesses have become consumer centric, it is not surprising that buyers' power has increased dramatically. These days customers are more informed, connected, and thus are empowered more than ever before.

Understanding this trend and embracing it in their marketing strategy is essential. Thus, it is important for entrepreneurs to understand that a marketing strategy does not comprise promotion. Promotion is simply the means of raising customers' awareness of the product or service the company offers. Nevertheless, the company needs to formulate a viable marketing strategy which could be communicated to the customer through the means of promotion. The result of establishing a marketing strategy is a well-defined company mission statement which is communicated to consumers through promotion. The strategy typically has three main objectives: communicate the company's message, increase customer demand, and differentiate a product on the market.

Promotion is also part of the promotional mix or plan, which also constitutes advertising, direct marketing, sales promotion, and publicity. Others have identified a marketing communication mix:

> Marketing communications is the means by which firms attempt to inform, persuade, and remind consumers – directly, or indirectly – about the products and brands that they sell.[39]

The marketing communication mix consists of eight major types of communication, mainly divided between personal and nonperson channels. The personal channels could have three major sources: company (advocate), an independent third party (expert), or a simple social contact, for instance, your neighbor. On the other hand, the nonperson communication channels comprise media, atmospheres, and events.[40]

- Media channels include print, broadcast, display (billboards, posters, symbols), and electronic media.
- The atmosphere is in regard to the office environment a company portrays systematically in front of potential customers or stakeholders (website).
- Events have become the mainstay of small-business marketing attempts.

Table 9.1 Promotional tools

Advertising	Public mode of communication
	Advantage of concurrency
Sales promotion	Coupons, contests, premiums, etc.
	Gain attention through calling the consumer to act
Events and experiences	Sponsorships of sports, arts, entertainment, or cause events
Public relations and publicity	News stories are typically viewed as more reliable and authentic to consumers
Direct marketing	Email, direct marketing, and telemarketing; usually customizable as addressed to a specific individual
Interactive marketing	A company which supports the two-way communication between its customers and itself
Word-of-mouth-marketing	Still one of the most utilized and beneficial channels of a company seeding its message in customers' minds
Personal selling	Requires a live, immediate, and interactive relationship between individuals; personal selling leads to relationships

To make itself visible, gain attention, and mainly communicate its message to the market, a company might take advantage of the promotional tools listed in Table 9.1.

Box 9.6   Quick review on fundamentals of marketing mix

- Every business faces threats from both the external and internal environments.
- Most entrepreneurs acknowledge that they need to gain more, faster, and better marketing skills and information to stay ahead of the competition.
- Decisions about the product, place, price, and promotion of a brand are essential and must be taken prior any marketing activity is set in motion.
- An entrepreneur must compare and thoroughly analyze the given industry and compare price, quality, product offer, and marketing strategy to ensure their business is keeping up with potential competitors.
- Evolution of new technology, communication, and mean of transportation impacts where an entrepreneur can be located, either online or physical store.
- Enterprises may be serving customers who are price sensitive or are in need of a product. For businesses that want to adopt a low-end competitive pricing, the strategy needs to focus on reducing the costs.

Despite which channel a company wishes to utilize, it is essential for the company message to be consistent and well integrated with the company's strategy.[41] For this reason, it is important to play fair.

In recent years, the aggravation of environmental problems has led companies to seek the development and commercialization of green products. Nevertheless, some companies mislead their stakeholders through a phenomenon called *greenwashing*.

As used in the corporate world, greenwashing is an organization's attempt to present itself as being more environmentally friendly than it actually is. The Nielsen Media Research[42] a decade ago presented that 66 percent of global consumers were willing to pay more for environmentally friendly products. When these customers perceive companies as socially responsible, they may be more willing to buy the products from these firms at a higher price.

Greenwashing was first accused in 1986 by activist Jay Westerveld, when hotels began asking guests to reuse towels, claiming that it was a company water conservation strategy, although did not have any environmental actions with more significant environmental impact issues, it was just cost saving.

So, marketing should evaluate if a firm is environmentally concerned if it produces significant amounts of pollution or engages in actions that are unfavorable to the environment. To have sustainability a value, they might implement "green" initiatives like planting trees or upgrading the energy efficiency of their structures. However, these initiatives frequently have no meaningful environmental impact and are merely window dressing.

The practice of greenwashing, which can also be called "social washing," is pernicious for various reasons. First, businesses that exaggerate their environmental policies may mislead customers into choosing one product over another because they think it is better for the environment when in fact, the opposite may be true. This can lead people to make impulsive purchases without considering whether or not they are genuinely helping the environment.

Stakeholders and society as a whole are calling for governance, and demanding transparency in disclosure of information regarding the environmental impact of companies' activities. This communication must be dynamic, through different channels and with the purpose of educating awareness.[43]

TerraChoice[44] reported that 95 percent of products claiming to be green in Canada and the United States committed at least one of the "sins of greenwashing," from the sin of "the hidden trade-off" to the sin of "worshiping false labels." The complete TerraChoice list is presented in Table 9.2.

Table 9.2 Greenwashing's sin

Greenwashing's sin	Description
Sin of the hidden trade-off	A claim suggesting that a product is green based on a narrow set of attributes without attention to other important environmental issues. Paper, for example, is not necessarily environmentally preferable because it comes from a sustainably harvested forest. Other important environmental issues in the paper-making process, such as greenhouse gas emissions or chlorine use in bleaching, may be equally important.
Sin of no proof	An environmental claim not substantiated by easily accessible supporting information or by a reliable third-party certification. Common examples are facial tissues or toilet tissue products that claim various percentages of post-consumer recycled content without providing evidence.
Sin of vagueness	A claim that is so poorly defined or broad that its real meaning is likely to be misunderstood by the consumer. All-natural is an example. Arsenic, uranium, mercury, and formaldehyde are all naturally occurring, and poisonous. All natural isn't necessarily green.
Sin of worshiping false labels	A product that, through either words or images, gives the impression of third-party endorsement where no such endorsement exists – fake labels, in other words.
Sin of irrelevance	An environmental claim that may be truthful but is unimportant or unhelpful for consumers seeking environmentally preferable products. CFC-free is a common example, since it is a frequent claim despite the fact that CFCs (chlorofluorocarbons) are banned under the Montreal Protocol.
Sin of lesser of two evils	A claim that may be true within the product category but that risks distracting the consumer from the greater environmental impacts of the category as a whole. Organic cigarettes or fuel-efficient sport-utility vehicles could be examples of this sin.
Sin of fibbing	Environmental claims that are simply false. The most common examples are products falsely claiming to be Energy Star certified or registered.

Even reputable businesses can occasionally mislead customers by using ambiguous wording that leads to misunderstanding or confusion, and many organizations fall prey to the greenwashing temptation when it comes to promoting their sustainability efforts.

Moreover, a growing number of enterprises are susceptible to what is commonly called *greenblushing*. Greenblushing is the opposite of greenwashing; instead of providing buyers with misleading information about their sustainability efforts, businesses who engage in greenblushing don't share much information about their efforts to promote social and environmental sustainability or the environmentally friendly features of their products.

For effective sustainability claims, there are consultant in the market, like UL Solutions which helps companies to demonstrate safety, enhance sustainability, strengthen security, deliver quality, manage risk and achieve regulatory compliance. At their website there is a white paper to be used as a starting point.[45]

Advertising

Advertising is essential for any business, especially for entrepreneurs. Giorgi and Rahman state that firm's informality is pervasive in developing countries; low benefits and high indirect costs are the main barriers to formality.[46]

Advertising's high barrier to entry reinforces exclusivity and brand prestige, makes the competition a lot easier, and makes acquiring market share easier.[47]

To boost sales for beginners, there are some platforms on the internet that can help entrepreneurs and SMEs to make ads on social media.[48] An example would be showing how to

Figure 9.9 Advertising

create successful Instagram ads by addressing an audience that is ready to shop on the platform (https://blog.hootsuite.com/instagram-ads-guide/).

Psychological pricing

In marketing, brand equity refers to a brand's intrinsic value, or the perceived social value of a well-known brand name. Due to consumers' perceptions that products from well-known brands are superior to those from lesser known brands, the owner of a well-known brand name can make more money just by virtue of brand recognition.

How do you measure an intangible object such as brand equity?

When the customer experience provided by the brand is measured over numerous iterations and it endures over time, it results in the creation of brand loyalty. Today, customers can (and do) easily communicate the strength of their brand attitude to others via customer reviews and social sharing.

Brand recognition is hugely responsible for a customer to recognize a psychological feeling of what it stands for. For example, when we hear Apple, we instantly recognize its superiority in design and technology. Similar brands such as Tesla and Bentley bring a feeling of prestige and luxury while not all companies compete for the same recognition. Toyota stands for durability, BMW for performance, Honda for safety,[49] Samsung for technology, and Spirit Airlines for its affordability.

While measuring a company's brand equity the main question is: "How much will a consumer pay for a product or service that is branded over other that is not?" So, market research that focuses comparative tracking among competitive brands or products against a benchmark should be conducted.

Besides, quantitative and qualitative surveys should be employed to ensure that customer recognize the brand for its stated vision and promises. In this sense, product/service differentiation is a linchpin for brand loyalty, while confidence in a brand's stated "promises" keeps customers to choose other products from the same brand.

Box 9.7   Psychological pricing

In the article, Lisa Hephner shares key statistics on purchase habits of Americans during the holiday months of November and December. It is well known to every retailer (online and offline) the importance of these 2 months. Lisa writes about promotional ideas for SMEs.

While large retailers have the money to advertise, hold billboards and flyers, small retailers can also compete using creative ideas.

- Number 9: Ever wonder why you see so many prices, and particularly sale prices, that end in 9? The simplistic theory is that most people suffer from a "left digit effect," in which they give more weight to the left most number in a price such that "$59.99" is thought of as $50 and is processed by the brain as significantly lower cost than an item priced at $60 would be.
- Anchoring, framing, and relative pricing: Anchoring refers to the brain's tendency to rely most heavily on the first piece of information it encounters when making a decision and to give less weight to all the details it gathers later, no matter how objectively persuasive.

- Innumeracy (your customers won't do math): Studies have shown that in general people just won't do unprompted math, and as a result clever (and even not so clever) pricing schemes can end up giving customers a perception of value when it is not really there. That's why customers immediately perceive the value of "buy one get one free" offers, but struggle with the value of "half off" or "50 percent off" promotions. (Yes, the latter two are the same.)
- Strategic coupon use: Even more than sale prices, people love coupons! According to a Forrester research study on coupons, 60 percent of respondents agreed that they "love to receive digital coupons" and 50 percent report being more likely to visit a store if they receive a coupon.

See more information at https://paysimple.com/blog/the-small-business-guide-to-holiday-sales-and-promotions/

In terms of marketing, anchoring is commonly leveraged by displaying very high "regular" prices that are crossed out or otherwise replaced by significantly lower sale prices.

Entrepreneurial marketing

Marketers must distinguish between entrepreneurial activities used by previously established organizations and those utilized in marketing strategies when establishing a business, for example. Therefore, the emphasis of both this chapter and the entire book is on entrepreneurship as it relates to starting new enterprises. Nevertheless, it is important to understand the concept of *entrepreneurial marketing* (EM) as well:

> EM draws on the work of both marketing and entrepreneurship scholars by focusing on how individuals and management teams accept the risk to innovatively and proactively leverage resources to create value in the marketplace.[50]

Also, when traditional marketing methods don't work for small and medium-sized businesses, entrepreneurs have to unlearn them and replace them with new, creative ideas and activities, such as EM. In a study of Kosovo's small and medium-sized businesses (SMEs) and how they are affected by EM dimensions, respondents frequently have a strong opportunity focus and know the value of resource leveraging.[51] But even though respondents think that creating value is an essential part of entrepreneurial marketing, they are cautious when taking risks and don't usually show initiative, innovation, or a focus on the customer.

In Table 9.3 you can find a framework which categorizes EM according to its main locus – *vertical* (as a strategy, coming from top management); *horizontal* (culture and process, when it is across the organization, and *temporal* (as a response to an environmental macro factor).

Box 9.8   The value of sustainable business

This talk presents some advanced commercial prospects while positively impacting the world. Marga Hoek, a three-time CEO and a winner of multiple golden awards as an author, discusses the importance of sustainable business and uses numerous examples from other countries to support her viewpoint. Through this session, you will learn about the chances for sustainability currently available in the corporate world and how it may benefit firms creating brand value as well.

You can check in more details the full DLC Talk in this link: https://www.youtube.com/watch?v=p8loWMkOu28 (The value of sustainable business | Marga Hoek | DLC Talks

About DLC: Founded by Jimmy Mistry, Della Leaders Club aims to create a global community of transformative leaders who want to evolve from a life of success to a life of significance. Della Leaders Club – Worlds 1st Business Platform is a global community of entrepreneurs, professionals, and young leaders that brings people together to positively impact the world.[52]

Marketing timeline

A corporation must define its own business and analyze the business environment it desires to operate in, including the industry, key stakeholders, and competitors, before presenting its mission statement and company message to the market. Consequently, an analysis of the customers the company aspires to offer its products or services is needed; in other words, an identification

Figure 9.10 Low price

Table 9.3 Entrepreneurial marketing

Locus	Role of EM	Area of focus	Illustrative example
Vertical	As strategy	EM as a disposition of the top management team. EM fundamentally must reflect both the needs of the customer and the entrepreneur. EM as strategy making heuristic.	P&G's incoming CEO in the late 1990s forced the product managers to "burn the boats," give away IP, and stop supporting the big brands to become more innovative.
Horizontal	As culture and process	EM residing across functional areas and business units. EM being across the organization as culture	42 Below vodka's social media and CRM strategy for marketing
Temporal	As response	As a strategic response to environmental turbulence	Walmart's entry into health, organic, and now locally produced food

Source: Adapted from Wales, Monsen, and McKelvie (2011).

of the *target market*. To best analyze the business environment, an enterprise might use a variety of tools (e.g., PESTEL, RBV, 4Ps, 5Ps).

Due to globalization, geographical boundaries have been blurred and in combination with the rapid technological development of the century, these tools have become easily available online, thus decreasing the barriers to entry in some industries where marketing and differentiation could bring a lot of profit.[53] This is particularly beneficial to entrepreneurs as it gives them almost equal access to information, the utilization of which is which is essential for the success of the business as marketing knowledge could be a source of competitive advantage.[54, 55]

After the analysis has been conducted, the new company will possess valuable information on how to proceed further with positioning its brand on the market. However, this is not the last step. If the company has done all the steps above, it will be able to position itself on the market in the most profitable way through organizing a marketing campaign. However, the marketing campaign needs to correspond to the position that the company wants to take in customers minds. Hence, it is highly important for the company to conduct this prior research to better comprehend where the highest need for the certain product or service is and how to best position itself in people's minds to gain the most profit.

Once the marketing campaign is in motion, marketers must closely follow customers' response to the product or service or both and provide the company with feedback on customers' feedback and further positioning strategies. Even after the campaign is over, the company must take the necessary measures to establish the return on investment on marketing (ROMI), as "you cannot manage what you cannot measure" (Peter Drucker) and gain valuable insights on how it should continue its marketing efforts in the future, which channels were most successful, etc.

Step 1: defining your mission – "what business are we in"?

Defining your business niche is the most critical but overlooked aspect of building a successful marketing campaign. This is important because developing through their products and or services, an enterprise creates effective and realistic marketing. However, they must be clear and

Figure 9.11 iPhone

fully understand the need that the product or service satisfies. This is particularly important for entrepreneurs since most of them have limited marketing budgets and resources.

Box 9.9   An entire generation's very first iPhone

The best product strategy that Apple employs is coming up with very good products. They call it the "great product" strategy. By continuing to hold on to high standards of quality, Apple refuses to get on the bandwagon that most other device makers are using, and for years it opted to stick to offering the most expensive products that have a lot more, and better, things to offer. One of the main advantages of iOS is its usability. The other is design. The use of Apple's smartphones in the US and worldwide is so widespread that iPhone has become a household name like Kleenex, being a product that separated the smartphone market in two: iPhone and everything else.

Following the initial release of the iPhone (first generation), Apple Inc. introduced the iPhone 3G and iPhone 4 in the years that followed. The iPhone 5 was designed with a touchscreen and marketed as the 6th generation iPhone, released on September 21, 2012. The iPhone 14 has Dynamic Island and Always-On Display, and the 48 MP camera are the innovations of iPhone 14 Pro and Pro Max; the phones were launched in 2023. It is important to notice that Apple's ads always show cool, trendy, laid-back people and emphasize how easy everything is with their products, above its quality. A big reason why consumers choose Apple in the first place is because of the company's marketing.

Identifying the target market and product type are essential because they will influence other aspects of the marketing strategy and the business overall. If an enterprise's target market consists of people with a high level of income, then it does not need to put a lower price tag on its products. If the enterprise wants to have a high volume–low price business, the price might be the key criterion for advertising. These enterprises should target a wider customer pool, nevertheless, no matter the business focus; the enterprise needs to conceive a proper balance between price and quality.

Both types of strategies have their advantages and disadvantages. Entrepreneurs must identify the best fit, the design needs, and their respective marketing campaigns to attract the right kind of customers.

Step 2: identifying the client (target market)

After having an overview of your business, it is important to delve deeper into identifying the ideal target market. By identifying and understating an ideal client, an enterprise can design a marketing strategy and customize it to fit consumer needs. Demographic and psychographic information is often used to identify the target market. Generally, people with similar demographic backgrounds tend to behave similarly and companies can benefit from this similarity. For example, teenagers may have different information search channel compared to middle-aged people; demographics information could direct an enterprise when choosing marketing mediums.

Customer profile and characteristics assist in understanding the potential market. The important attributes to analyze are listed in Table 9.4.

Different methods will be used to acquire this information.[56] [57]

After knowing the rational dimension of customers, it is also critical to know the emotional side, which indicates the psychographics about customers. Psychographics segmentation illustrates a group's attitudes and behaviors and gives ideas on how customers are likely to make decisions based on who they might like and trust.[58] By adding the psychographics of customers, an enterprise can target customer more accurately and gain a deeper understanding of their needs. An enterprise can get to know how customers feel and act by knowing their hobbies and interests. This kind of information is often obtained through open-ended questions in surveys and observations of sales.

Figure 9.12 Target market

Table 9.4 Customer profile

Demographic segmentation	Psychographics segmentation
Age and gender	Personality and values
Email address, phone number, zip code	Interests
Education and income levels	Lifestyle
Occupation and ethnic background	Behavior

Also, social media sites like Facebook are helpful in gaining both demographics and psychographic information. An enterprise can learn about web analytics related to the types of customer and their opinions/comments.

An important point to pay attention is that an enterprise should not waste efforts in attracting all types of customers. This is not a successful client acquisition strategy. An enterprise target market should be specific enough so that the enterprise can produce products and services tailored to the targeted customers' unique needs. Also, specific markets are easier for an enterprise to reach. Since there are many trade associations, publications, and mailing lists available for a certain market, it is easy for a business to customize their marketing efforts according to the client's needs and wants.[59]

It is essential to understand and differentiate a prime customer's base. *Typical* customers are those who frequently purchase from a given business. *Prime* customers tend to have fewer transactions but make up a larger portion of your profit. One easy way to differentiate customer is to track the purchase history and generated revenues of your existing customers' bases.[60]

Step 3: analyze the environment

The marketing mix 4 Ps are product, place, promotion, and price.

Product

For a business to increase its market share, product expansion is essential. Product expansion takes different forms including upgrading existing products, adding new products to the product line, expanding new product lines, and selling products in new markets.[61] Having multiple product lines is beneficial because it contributes to diversifying the risks. The more products in a product line, the more the company is likely to attract customers with different preferences, which would result in higher profits.

An increase in product lines will lead to diversification and minimization of the risk. Still, this may take away the company's focus from utilizing its strengths effectively, which may lead to dilution of its quality and services. Therefore, clearly defining the boundaries between core business and diversification is essential. Expanding product lines improve customer base and loyalty as they may purchase more products and engage more with the companies.[62] This is true, especially if products and services are complementary.

Nonetheless, product expansion may have its downside in cannibalizing sales revenue of the existing products assuming they are not complementary. It is also generally believed to be

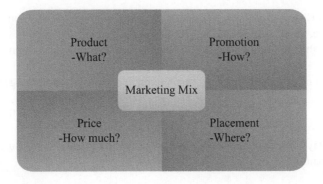

Figure 9.13 Marketing mix

time-consuming and expensive to diversify. Therefore, expansion of products or services would make more sense when an enterprise has a certain degree of maturity. A strategic expansion is the acquisition of growth opportunities relative to competitors and that depends upon the favorability of market conditions.[63,64]

There are several steps enterprises need to follow to safely expand their product lines. First, businesses should discover the specific needs of their customers, and the best method is to conduct a competitive analysis.[65] They can track their competitors' brochures and other marketing materials to find out what they are currently offering.[66]

A useful guide is to rethink the psychographics such as attitudes and fears and also the demographics such as age, gender, household income, education, and buying habits of your target market, then analyze companies which have reached the same group.

The blue ocean strategy is another strategy that the firm can use to raise the chances and level of success. Blue ocean would utilize strategies such as offering insights on innovative positioning of new ventures, such as extension of the product line and the tools to make it possible.

Another approach in identifying demand for a product is similar to what Apple did. They foresaw the future application of technology in communication and entertainment and created the iPhone with its unique characteristics, thus creating and satisfying customers' needs. Many of the new apps, social media, etc. that entrepreneurs have been creating are done without in-depth old-fashioned marketing research.

Linton believes that observing customers' feedback on social media sites generates helpful insight into customers' needs and preferences. Significant comments favoring certain product features provide a useful guide for any businesses in product expansion.[67] Also, businesses could invite customers to collaborate or contribute to product development. Covel suggests that businesses talking directly to customers in a casual, authentic atmosphere can help them discover features of the product they like and the items that might be convenient to have in addition to what they are buying.[68]

Moreover, companies could offer incentives like discounts for purchase to encourage more consumers to participate. Generally, it is better if a third party is in charge of conducting information interviews to ensure more objective and accurate information. Last, it is essential that businesses also use market research data and continuously improve upon their relationship with suppliers, distributors, and pretty much every stakeholder in the value chain.

For instance, Nornberg believes that distributors are valuable in offering information on what competitors are doing.[69] Also, they could enable an enterprise to assess the best distribution channels for selling its products to new markets.

Branding or "brand myopia"

The technological revolution has provided a two-way connection between brands and consumers. Therefore, an effective branding strategy could provide a company with a competitive advantage in a highly competitive market. Typically, branding has been defined as follows:

> The promotion of a particular product or company by means of advertising and distinctive design.
>
> (Oxford Dictionary)

However, nowadays, a more precise definition is presented by the online Business Dictionary, which defines branding as:

The process involved in creating a unique name and image for a product in the consumers' mind, mainly through advertising campaigns with a consistent theme. Branding aims to establish a significant and differentiated presence in the market that attracts and retains loyal customers.

The underlying difference in the two definitions is the fact that while the first centers' *promotion* as a branding strategy, the latter focuses on consumers. In other words, it outlines promotion as simply the way a company communicates its previously established image ("brand") in consumers' minds. This should be the definition of branding all entrepreneurs understand to further build and develop it according to other internal and external factors.

Box 9.10   Quick review on customer-oriented marketing

- Price deals are usually intended attract new buyers or to persuade existing customers to increase their purchasing.
- Marketing communication is the means by which firms attempt to inform, persuade, and remind customers about the products and brands that they sell.
- The main types of price deals include discounts, bonus pack deals, refunds or rebates, and coupons.
- These days customers are more informed, connected, and thus are empowered than ever before.
- Society as a whole calls for openness in the disclosure of information regarding how businesses' operations affect the environment. In this context, greenwashing is a risk for a business.
- Real green claims would suffer from greater skepticism since it is hard for customers to differentiate the reliability of green marketing initiatives.
- Today's technological tools have decreased the barriers to entry in some industries, where marketing and differentiation could bring a lot of profit.
- Once the marketing campaign is in motion, marketers must closely follow customers.
- SME resources should be focused on identifying target markets and product types that will influence other aspects of the marketing strategy and the business overall.
- Demographic and psychographic information is often used to identify the target market. Customer profile and characteristics also assist in understanding the potential market.
- Expanding product lines improves the customer base and loyalty as they may purchase more products and engage more with the company.
- It is essential that business also use market research data and continuously improve upon their relationship with suppliers, distributors, and pretty much every stakeholder in the value chain.

Nevertheless, branding should not be perceived as an end in itself or merely a management tool, which if managed successfully could assist in the achievement of organizational objectives. This managerial fault has lately been coined as "branding myopia," where brands are viewed as an end in themselves.

In their core, brands are symbols around which company's stakeholders (e.g., consumers, competitors, and suppliers) construct identities for certain products.[70] Entrepreneurs should also consider the external (macro) environment. Currently, major anti-branding movements and anti-globalization activities have illustrated people's antipathy of large corporations. This could be highly beneficial for entrepreneurs who understand and utilize it to their advantage through an effective branding strategy.

Imagine if market characteristics were divided between order winners and order qualifiers, where the winners would get the most beneficial market characteristics and qualifiers would be the requirements. In such a scenario, having a brand is no longer seen as an order winner. Technology and globalization have transformed it to an order qualifier, as having a brand is no longer enough. Therefore, it is important for any company to know how to gain more brand equity.

Now, brands are embodied by products but enacted by customers. Moreover, as brands nowadays have multiple dimensions, their meaning varies with the passage of time and in accordance with the many stakeholders. In the branding process, the initial steps are of crucial importance as they are key to successful management of a brand evolution, which requires that "the brand does not lose its roots in the past."[71]

Technology and marketing

Previously in this chapter, the relation between marketing and new technologies had been discussed, highlighting the potential of AI. Despite its practical use as a tool for marketing, researchers are dealing with theoretical frameworks.[72] Huang and Rust (2021) develop a three-stage framework for strategic marketing planning, incorporating multiple artificial intelligence (AI) benefits:

- Mechanical AI for automating repetitive marketing functions and activities;
- Thinking AI for processing data to arrive at decisions;
- Feeling AI for analyzing interactions and human emotions.

This framework lays out the ways that AI can be used for marketing research, strategy (segmentation, targeting, and positioning [STP]), and actions. At the marketing research stage, mechanical AI can be used for data collection, thinking AI for market analysis, and feeling AI for customer understanding. At the marketing strategy (STP) stage, mechanical AI can be used for segmentation (segment recognition), thinking AI for targeting (segment recommendation), and feeling AI for positioning (segment resonance). At the marketing action stage, mechanical AI can be used for standardization, thinking AI for personalization, and feeling AI for relationalization. Figure 9.14 shows an overview of the potential of AI in marketing.

According to Pew Research Center survey statistics, 81 percent of Americans use the internet every day, with 28 percent indicating they are online "almost constantly." This reliance on digital tools pervades the commercial world as well. The epidemic has hastened online purchasing patterns, and many businesses rely on software-as-a-service (SaaS) and platform-as-a-service (PaaS) platforms to keep their operations running smoothly. Such dependence on technology presents new opportunities for entrepreneurs, but it also necessitates that companies use the correct digital tools and technologies themselves.

Many social networking platforms are available, and many more are evolving. An entrepreneur should be forward-looking and identify where social networking will be in the future and how it can be used efficiently.[75] The question is where to commit and allocate time and resources.

Social networking has always been a vital part of promoting businesses for SMEs since it is an effective way of making one's mark.

Marketing Action

- Standardization (mechanical AI)
- Personalization (thinking AI)
- Relationalization (feeling AI)

Marketing Research

- Data collection (mechanical AI)
- Market analysis (thinking AI)
- Customer understanding (feeling AI)

Marketing Strategy

- Segmentation (mechanical AI)
- Targeting (thinking AI)
- Positioning (feeling AI)

Figure 9.14 AI and strategic marketing decisions

Source: Huang and Rust (2021).

People quite simply prefer doing business with people they know and like, so cementing a relationship in person can translate an unenthusiastic relationship into a long-term and mutually beneficial one.

Social networks will drive value. The principal benefit of new social platforms is that today's knowledge workers have connected to each other and consumers. Social media platforms such as Facebook and Twitter accounts provide abandoned opportunities for marketing online. The beauty of online marketing is that it will level the playing field between a Fortune 500 company and a small business, holding everything else constant.

As social media has increased in importance, many businesses have been forced to assign social networking tasks to current staff. This leads to inconsistencies between organizations as one company may have an administrator, another business owner, and another member of the marketing staff handling updates.[76] With the rise of social media, it has been much easier and helps to enhance communication. Entrepreneurs could use free tools to keep customers updated about their business, communicate and build a relationship with customers and making customers "know, like, and trust" their business.[77] Social media marketing is also the resource of word-of-mouth promotions. When prospects obtain the positive responses from satisfied customers through social media, word-of-mouth has already been proliferated.[78]

Whether a video, a blog post or a status update, content is the engine of the social web; if enterprise produces and shares useful content, your community will be more likely to become customers, and this would result in repeat customers for the enterprise. To be able to create appropriate and effective content, an enterprise needs to understand the needs and mindsets of its customers. One useful way to do this is using social media sites to monitor what people are discussing about your enterprise, in terms of product and quality when compared to competitors. Table 9.5 presents the main tools for entrepreneurs. In addition, businesses need to frequently

Table 9.5 Technologies for entrepreneurs

Cloud native technology	"Cloud native tech offers speed, scalability and elasticity that businesses of all sizes can leverage to their advantage. The ability to build and run cutting-edge solutions that are hosted on public, private or hybrid cloud environments and leverage containers, microservices, immutable infrastructure, APIs and serverless computing is now mainstream" (Karan Nangru, founder of StatusNeo).
	Enterprise businesses, as well as entrepreneurs, have one focus in common – business transformation. In most cases, technology enables this transformation, while cloud native platform services accelerate it.
Marketing tools[73]	Successful entrepreneurs must use each of these tools if they want to reach their customers. Social media, email campaigns, search engine optimization, and pay-per-click are all significant sources of traffic and customers for brands. Of course, many startups do not have the financial resources to hire an advertising agency. The good news is that marketing tools make each task easier and more affordable to manage.
Machine-powered data monitoring	One of the greatest points of interest of advanced tech instruments is their capacity to gather information. By learning more about your clients or the efficiency of your forms, you'll be able make key changes to your commerce to move your productivity forward.
	"Machine-learning computer program empowers the investigation of typical behavior for measurements inside your framework. Utilizing this pattern, machine-learning modeling can moreover decide whether any changes that take put are anomalous. These variations from the norm trigger proactive alarms so you gotten to be mindful of vital patterns affecting your business' biological system. By turning numbers and information into significant data, business visionaries can take quick activity to move forward their commerce" (Victor Zhang, co-founder of Orbiter).
Customer relationship management software	Since clients are so critical, it ought to barely be astounding that there's a complete fragment of tech devices devoted to them. Customer relationship administration (CRM) computer programs give companies more prominent control in how they handle these imperative connections.
	CRMs collect a wide extend of data that can support your deals, group change over leads into deals, or progress client retention metrics. For illustration, following client touch focuses along with your brand will help deals staff know which prospects are most likely to change over, so they can prioritize client outreach suitably.
	When utilized viably, CRM devices can make an enormous distinction for your foot line. A study from Capterra found that 47 percent of CRM clients said the program "essentially progressed" maintenance and client fulfillment.
Basic automation	There are only 24 hours in a day; nevertheless, entrepreneurs often feel like they need an extra hour or three to get everything done. This is especially true for solopreneurs, who must manage a whole business on their own; automation solutions or the utilization of a virtual assistant are crucial.
	With strategic automation, you can open up a lot of time for tasks that have a greater contribution to your bottom line.

Source: Social Networking.[74]

produce content using social platforms to educate customers, satisfy customers' informational needs, solve their issues and problems, engage them, and entertain them.[79,80]

By participating in community activities, the enterprise will increase visibility and reputation. This shows to the customers that the enterprise cares about them and thus helps the enterprise to become the opinion leader in that respective area. To increase the visibility of the enterprise, it should also build relationships with the person or businesses which write about the industry, company, and products.[81] This is applicable because many of them are willing to connect with the organization. However, the enterprise should not expect them to directly advertise like posting corporate materials. Instated, the enterprise could offer them the critical information that complements their current work. Due to the fast dissemination of information, entrepreneurs should pay special attention to the negative comments on social platforms. The enterprise should investigate what really happened, explain to the customers, apologize, and make efforts to improve their reputation.

With social media, entrepreneurs and SMEs are able to use free and low-cost social tools to help increase word-of-mouth advertising while decreasing the need for more expensive outbound advertising platforms like the Yellow Pages, cable television ads, etc.[82] The popular social media sites used by entrepreneurs include YouTube, Telegram, TikTok, Facebook, Twitter, Pinterest, Instagram, LinkedIn, and Google+. However, they still require a major time commitment from the enterprise to work properly.[83]

Companies should therefore not try to be active in every platform (see Table 9.6 for an e-commerce examples), instead focusing time and resources on the social media channels that generate the highest return on investment for the business. To identify the sites that are most effective for an enterprise, it needs to experiment with different sites and track which sites offer the highest return in traffic.[84]

Also, different social networking sites require users to operate in different ways. For example, an enterprise may use Pinterest to share their products' image but use Twitter to share industry news as well as employment opportunities.[85] When an enterprise has a presence on multiple social networking sites, it is useful to use third-party tools like HootSuite.com and TweetDeck that can operate multiple social media platforms at once.[86]

Social media marketing takes new skills and most of us can acquire skills to manage it. By definition, it is accessible.[87] Investment in social media will become a necessity, not a luxury. Businesses are already coming to terms with the need to integrate their social media efforts with their content strategy and are seeing the impact of social media in terms of lead generation, referral traffic, and revenue.[88]

Businesses need to be aware that it can take a long time to build up a social network, expand customer base, and generate enough leads to keep in business. Business should therefore not rely on them as a sole source of doing business. In addition, entrepreneurs need to extract information and data from social media to drive business strategy.[89]

It is feasible to analyze and measure the business environment as technology has been advancing almost exponentially every 2 years, in accordance with Moore's law.[90] Terms such as *big data* and *business analytics* have attracted worldwide attention due to the benefits their utilization brings to the company.[91] Some have even called it the "big data revolution," which has irrevocably transformed how marketing is done and seen.[92] For about two decades now, search engines have proliferated (Google being in the center) and revolutionized online research. In an era in which libraries are primarily used for the Wi-Fi signal rather than the books they offer, technology has certainly taken its turn. Thus, conducting a business environment analysis has become easier than ever which contributes to the simplification of creating a marketing strategy (a comprehensive marketing plan) which is created based on the prior analysis of the business environment and with a focus on the marketing mix.

As far as branding is concerned, technology has now made it possible for companies to precisely analyze the impact of its potential branding strategy on the sales volume. Through a recently presented approach, called the centrality-distinctiveness (C-D) map, for the first time offers companies with a direct physical measurement of how their brand is perceived on the market. The successful utilization of this tool might bring better insights into the desired market position, resource allocation, and overall brand strategy.

Box 9.11   Quick review on branding

- Branding should not be perceived as an end in itself or merely a management tool, which if managed successfully could assist in the achievement of organizations' objectives.
- It is important for any company to know how to gain more brand equity.
- Social networking has always been a vital part of promoting business for SMEs since it is an effective way of making your mark.
- To be able to create appropriate and effective content, an enterprise must understand the needs and mindsets of its consumers.
- Enterprises could offer its customers critical information that complements their current products and the company's vision.
- Green products can be sold at a premium, making them more expensive, which can lead consumers to overpay, but greenwashing can lead to a loss in consumer trust, as the company is viewed as disingenuous and unreliable.
- Greenwashing is deceitful and unethical because it misleads investors and consumers that are genuinely seeking environmentally friendly companies or products, so branding (marketing campaigns) and documents disclosure should be aware of it.
- With social media and self-made institutional websites, entrepreneurs and SMEs are able to use free and low-cost social tools over the more expensive outbound advertising platforms.

Source: DeVault (2018).[93]

After choosing a geographic market and a customer segment, a company must conduct a "survey on consumers' perception of the brand's centrality and distinctiveness."[94]

- Unconventional brands – possess unique characteristics (e.g., Tesla). Mainly a niche strategy;
- Peripheral brands – "Me too" strategy; inadequate distinction, thus not a top choice (e.g., Kia, Mitsubishi), but still quite profitable;
- Aspirational brands – wide appeal and high differentiation (e.g., for beer – 62 percent of unit sales);
- Mainstream brands – first to mind in a category but still indistinctive, thus lacking pricing power. Nevertheless, still popular and bought by consumers (e.g., Ford, Chevrolet).

Increased centrality is usually considered as a sales booster, while the distinctiveness of a brand is associated with the higher end niche brands, thus sales volume is lower. Nevertheless, distinctiveness is important as it has the price advantage in the long term. For further examples of how different companies perform on the C-D map, please visit https://hbr.org/2015/06/a-better-way-to-map-brand-strategy

Search engine optimization

Building a website is like building a house. When built properly, they combine interdependent components into a functional and attractive whole. In a house, the components are things like plumbing and ventilation; in a website, they are things like search engine optimization (SEO)

Figure 9.15 The process of SEO

and navigational structure.[95] SEO has evolved over the past few years with a greater emphasis on the quality of the actual content.[96]

Good SEO is essential for building credibility and positioning your company as an industry leader.[97] SEO is the process of affecting the visibility of a website or a web page in a search engine's "natural" or un-paid ("organic") search results. Businesses need to have an SEO plan to increase organic search via blogs, web content, etc. Basically, this can be applied to any business model. In general, the earlier (or higher ranked on the search results page) and more frequently a site appears in the search results list, the more visitors it will receive from the search engine's users.

Therefore, businesses need to consider how search engines work, what people search for, the actual search terms or keywords typed into search engines, and which search engines are preferred by their targeted audience through social media. Optimizing a website may involve editing its content to contain various social networks, HTML, and associated coding to both increases its relevance to specific keywords and to remove barriers to the indexing activities of search engines. Promoting a site to increase the number of backlinks, or inbound links is another SEO tactic.[98]

Before summarizing, we would like to discuss how entrepreneurs could use the marketing advice and suggestions provided above to increase their market share. While some people use the terms "entrepreneur" and "small business owner" synonymously, there are still differences between the entrepreneurial venture and the small business. First, an entrepreneur(s) is a person(s). A small business is an organization/entity which is created by an entrepreneur(s). Therefore, small businesses generally are larger in size and have higher access to resources than entrepreneurs. In addition, small businesses may have different objectives and views than entrepreneurs. Therefore, entrepreneurs need to choose the right combination of strategies based on their own capabilities and goals.

Box 9.12   Quick review on SEOs

- Enterprises need to identify the sites that are suited for most return of investment (ROI); initially they need to experiment with different sites and tracks which sites offer highest return in traffic.
- Investments in social media will become a necessity, even more after the habit of online purchase acquired during pandemic COVID-19.
- For about two decades now, search engines have proliferated and revolutionized online research.
- The centrality-distinctiveness (C-D) map can offer companies with a direct physical measurement of how their brand is perceived on the market. The successful utilization of this tool can bring better insights on the desired market position, resource allocation, and overall brand strategy.
- Good SEO is essential for building credibility and positioning your company as a leader in the segment.
- Businesses need to have an SEO plan to increase organic search via web contents.
- HTML and associated coding are required to both increase SEO's relevance to specific keywords and to remove barriers to the indexing activities of search engines.

Conclusion

Given the crucial role that marketing plays in business success and the unique traits of entrepreneurs, it is essential to create a thorough marketing plan that emphasizes technology and marketing strategy. Entrepreneurs must decide on their product focus (quality vs. quantity), their primary goods and services, and the competitive environment in order to comprehend their firm. To determine who their customers are, entrepreneurs need to gather demographic information, analyze psychographic traits, and tell the difference between their typical and ideal customers. Entrepreneurs might think about options like improving current products, introducing new products to their product line, expanding into new product categories, offering novel products, and selling products in new markets for product expansion. Entrepreneurs have many choices for how to sell their products. They can open an online store, a physical store, or both.

In either case, business owners must create the content of their stores to draw customers and improve their shopping experiences. For example, entrepreneurs could use radio, newspaper, and online advertising for promotion.

They can also get in touch with their customers directly through direct mail, social media, and advertising at events. Additionally, business owners can encourage client purchases by using sales promotions, including price cuts, bonus pack coupon publications, continuity programs, and sampling. Entrepreneurs must evaluate the cost structure, comprehend their positioning strategy, and analyze the pricing from competitors in order to build a successful price strategy. Additionally, business owners might create tiered customer loyalty programs by providing a variety of benefits to draw in and keep customers. Finally, entrepreneurs must combine all the components to build a unified message to develop an effective marketing plan.

Discussion questions

1   What is the definition of marketing, and how has it changed over time?
2   Did you find marketing theories relevant in this chapter?

Marketing, technology, and entrepreneurship 333

Table 9.6 Online-store

- Online transactions for many products, growing exponentially.
- Customers are attracted to online shopping because they can easily conduct an information search and price comparison.[99]
- Having an online store is attractive to businesses because it allows the enterprise to reach a wider range of customers both in the country and internationally.
- Provides convenience for your customers since they can access the enterprise's website 24/7 at any place as long as an online connection is given. It is also believed to be cost-effective because the reduction in costs of face-to-face sales force and premise.
- Intuit indicates that physical stores usually have limited space for storing products, thus, by having online stores, businesses could choose to store the products in warehouses, thereby offering a wider range of products and keeping costs down. A complement to the warehouse model could be showrooms in selected high traffic locations.[100]

Table 9.7 Key terms

Marketing	Target market
Strategy	Return on investment on marketing (ROMI)
Marketing mix	Psychographics segmentation
Price deals	Brand myopia
Marketing communications	Big-data and business analytics
Entrepreneurial marketing	Search engine optimization (SEO)

Table 9.8 Glossary

Marketing	Activity set of institutions and processes for creating, communicating, delivering, and exchanging offerings that have value to customers, clients, partners, and society at large.
Strategy	Typically consists of short- and long-term acknowledgment and response to any challenges or opportunities coming from the given business environment.
Marketing mix	A set of actions or tactics a company uses to establish its products, services, and brand on the market.
Price deals	Are usually intended attract new buyers or to persuade existing custom to increase their purchases.
Marketing communications	The means by which firms attempt to inform, persuade, and remind consumers – directly or indirectly – about the products and brands that they sell.
Entrepreneurial marketing	Draws on the work of both marketing and entrepreneurship scholars by focusing on how individuals and management teams accept the risk to innovatively and proactively leverage resources to create value in the marketplace.
Target market	The specific group of consumers or businesses that a product or service is intended to serve.
Return on investment on marketing (ROMI)	A financial performance measure used to evaluate the effectiveness of a company's marketing activities.
Psychographics segmentation	Illustrates a group's attitudes and behaviors and gives ideas on how customers are likely to make decisions based on who they might like and trust.
Brand myopia	A narrow or short-sighted focus on a company's current products or brand, without considering broader market trends or changes in consumer preferences.
Big-data and business analytics	"Big data" is a large volume of structured and unstructured data that are generated from various sources, such as social media, sensors, transactions, and machines. "Business analytics" is the process of analyzing these large data sets using statistical and quantitative methods to extract insights and improve business decision-making.
Search engine optimization (SEO)	The process of optimizing a website or a web page to improve its visibility and ranking on search engines.

3   What is the relationship between marketing, technology, and entrepreneurship?
4   Describe the first two steps a company must undertake prior to formulating a marketing strategy.
5   Provide a few examples of how technology has transformed marketing.
6   Write a short case that illustrates at least two important topics from this case.

Notes

1   Musk, E. (2006, August 2). *The Secret Tesla Motors Master Plan (Just between You and Me)*. Blog. Co-Founder & CEO of Tesla Motors. Retrieved from www.tesla.com/blog/secret-tesla-motors-master-plan-just-between-you-and-me
2   Collis, D.J., & Rukstad, M.G. (2008). Can you say what your strategy is? *Harvard Business Review*, 86(4), 82–90.
3   www.caranddriver.com/news/a42938734/tesla-best-selling-luxury-brand-2022/
4   https://moneywise.com/insurance/auto/afford-tesla-even-if-not-rich
5   Kumar, V., & Gupta, S. (2016). Conceptualizing the evolution and future of advertising. *Journal of Advertising*, 45(3), 302–317. https://doi.org/10.1080/00913367.2016.1199335
6   Kozielski, R. (2016). Determinants of business success – theoretical model and empirical verification. *Folia Oeconomica Stetinensia*, 16(1), 274–285. https://doi.org/10.1515/foli-2016-0018
7   www.oecd.org/cfe/
8   https://legalinstruments.oecd.org/en/instruments/OECD-LEGAL-0473
9   Lorette, K. (2013). *The Importance of Marketing for the Success of a Business* [Online]. Retrieved from http://smallbusiness.chron.com/importance-marketing-success-business-589.html
10 Swaim, R. (2013). Peter Drucker on Sales and Marketing. *PEX Process Excellence Network*. Retrieved from www.processexcellencenetwork.com/organizational-strategies-for-innovation-continuou/columns/peter-drucker-on-sales-and-marketing/
11 www.sebrae.com.br/sites/PortalSebrae/canais_adicionais/sebrae_english
12 Miles, R., & Snow, C. (1978). *Organizational Strategy, Structure, and Process*. New York: McGraw-Hill.
13 Porter, M.E. (1980). *Competitive Strategy*. New York: The Free Press.
14 Knight, G. (2000). Entrepreneurship and marketing strategy: The SME under globalization. *Journal of International Marketing*, 8(2), 12–32. www.jstor.org/stable/25048805
15 De Luca, L.M., Herhausen, D., Troilo, G., & Rossi, A. (2021). How and when do big data investments pay off? The role of marketing affordances and service innovation. *Journal of the Academy of Marketing Science*, 49(4), 790–810. Retrieved from https://link.springer.com/content/pdf/10.1007/s11747-020-00739-x.pdf
16 Grewal, D., Hulland, J., Kopalle, P.K., & Karahanna, E. (2020). The future of technology and marketing: A multidisciplinary perspective. *Journal of the Academy of Marketing Science*, 48(1), 1–8. Retrieved from https://link.springer.com/article/10.1007/s11747-019-00711-4#Bibl
17 Davenport, T.H., & Ronanki, R. (2018). Artificial intelligence for the real world. *Harvard Business Review*, 96(1), 108–116. http://blockqai.com/wp-content/uploads/2021/01/analytics-hbr-ai-for-the-real-world.pdf
18 Hoffman, D.L., & Novak, T.P. (2018). Consumer and object experience in the internet of things: An assemblage theory approach. *Journal of Consumer Research*, 44(6), 1178–1204. https://doi.org/10.1093/jcr/ucx105
19 Mende, M., Scott, M.L., van Doorn, J., Grewal, D., & Shanks, I. (2019). Service robots rising: How humanoid robots influence service experiences and food consumption. *Journal of Marketing Research*, 56(4), 535–556. https://doi.org/10.1177/0022243718822827
20 Grewal, D. et al. (2020). The future of technology and marketing: A multidisciplinary perspective. *Journal of the Academy of Marketing Science*, 48, 1–8. https://doi.org/10.1007/s11747-019-00711-4
21 www.marketingevolution.com/marketing-essentials/ai-markeitng#:~:text=AI%20marketing%20uses%20artificial%20intelligence,efforts%20where%20speed%20is%20essential
22 McCormick, K. (2023, April 5). 6 ways to use ChatGPT for small business marketing (+6 ways not to use it). *Industry News & Insights Blog*. Retrieved from www.wordstream.com/blog/ws/2023/03/06/how-to-use-chatgpt-for-small-business-marketing#:~:text=You%20can%20use%20ChatGPT%20to,social%20media%20captions%2C%20and%20more

23 Jobber, D. (2010). *Principles and Practice of Marketing* (6th ed.). New York: McGraw-Hill.

24 https://influencermarketinghub.com/state-of-ecommerce-pandemic/

25 https://annualmarketingreport.nielsen.com/download-report/

26 Dennis, C., Fenech, T., & Merrilees, B. (2004). *E-Retailing*. New York: Routledge.

27 McCue, T.J. (2010). *BigCommerce Review: Building a Small Business Online Storefront [Online]*. Retrieved from http://smallbiztrends.com/2010/08/bigcommerce-review-building-a-small-business-online-storefront.html

28 https://software.fish/hosting-services/best-ecommerce-site-builders

29 Martin, S. (2012). *For Your Small Business: Opening an Online Store [Online]*. Retrieved from www.expand2web.com/blog/for-your-small-business-opening-an-online-store/

30 Crane, F.G. (2010). M*arketing for Entrepreneurs: Concepts and Applications for New Ventures*. California: SAGE Publications, Inc.

31 Crane, F.G. (2010). *Marketing for Entrepreneurs: Concepts and Applications for New Ventures*. California: SAGE Publications, Inc.

32 Beesley, C. (2012). *How to Price Your Small Business' Products and Services [Online]*. Retrieved from February 10, 2013, from www.sba.gov/community/blogs/how-price-your-small-business%E2%80%99-products-and-services

33 Zahorsky, D. (2013). *Pricing Strategies for Small Business [Online]*. Retrieved March 20, 2013, from http://sbinformation.about.com/cs/bestpractices/a/aa112402a.htm

34 Zahorsky, D. (2013). *Pricing Strategies for Small Business [Online]*. Retrieved March 20, 2013, from http://sbinformation.about.com/cs/bestpractices/a/aa112402a.htm

35 Crane, F.G. (2010). *Marketing for Entrepreneurs: Concepts and Applications for New Ventures*. California: SAGE Publications, Inc.

36 Berthon, P., Holbrook, M.B., Hulbert, J.M., & Pitt, L. (2007, January 1). *Viewing Brands in Multiple Dimensions*. Retrieved from https://sloanreview.mit.edu/article/viewing-brands-in-multiple-dimensions/

37 Kozielski, R. (2016). Determinants of business success – theoretical model and empirical verification. *Folia Oeconomica Stetinensia*, 16(1), 274–285. https://doi.org/10.1515/foli-2016-0018

38 Beesley, C. (2012). *How to Price Your Small Business' Products and Services [Online]*. Retrieved February 10, 2013, from www.sba.gov/community/blogs/how-price-your-small-business%E2%80%99-products-and-service

39 Rao, N. (2014, June 9). *Marketing Communication: Channels and Promotion Tools*. Retrieved from http://nraomtr.blogspot.com/2011/12/marketing-communication-channels-and.html

40 Kotler, P. (2014). *Kotler On Marketing*. [Place of publication not identified]: Free Press. Print.

41 Batra, R., & Keller, K.L. (2016). Integrating marketing communications: New findings, new lessons, and new ideas. *Journal of Marketing*, 80(6), 122–145. EBSCOhost, https://doi.org/10.1509/jm.15.0419

42 *Nielsen Media Research*. (2015). Retrieved from www.nielsen.com/us/en/insights/reports/2015/the-sustainability-imperative.html

43 de Freitas Netto, S.V. et al. (2020). Concepts and forms of greenwashing: A systematic review. *Environmental Sciences Europe*, 32, 19. https://doi.org/10.1186/s12302-020-0300-3

44 TerraChoice. (2010). *The Sins of Greenwashing: Home and Family Edition*. Retrieved from http://sinsofgreenwashing.org/fndings/the-seven-sins/

45 www.ul.com/insights/making-effective-sustainability-claims

46 Giorgi, G., & Rahman, A. (2013, September). *SME's Registration: Evidence from an RCT in Bangladesh*. Elsevier Science Ltd. Retrieved from http://search.proquest.com/abicomplete/docview/1417004268/141BD3756D63D43EA7D/35?accountid=8576

47 Stone, K.E. (2012, September 18). Why traditional marketing trumps social media, and what to do about it. *Forbes*. Retrieved from www.forbes.com/sites/yec/2012/09/18/why-traditional-marketing-trumps-social-media-and-what-to-do-about-it/

48 Macready, H. (2023, February 13). *8-Step Guide to Using Instagram Ads. 2023 Edition*. Blog. Retrieved from https://blog.hootsuite.com/instagram-ads-guide/

49 https://youtu.be/_SjJ-udx9xw

50 Miles, M., Gilmore, A., Harrigan, P., Lewis, G., & Sethna, Z. (2014). Exploring entrepreneurial marketing. *Journal of Strategic Marketing*, 23(2), 94–111. https://doi.org/10.1080/0965254x.2014.914069

51 Sadiku-Dushi, N., Dana, L.P., & Ramadani, V. (2019). Entrepreneurial marketing dimensions and SMEs performance. *Journal of Business Research*, 100, 86–99. https://doi.org/10.1016/j.jbusres.2019.03.025

52 https://dellaleaders.com/

53 Kumar, V., & Gupta, S. (2016). Conceptualizing the evolution and future of advertising. *Journal of Advertising*, 45(3), 302–317. https://doi.org/10.1080/00913367.2016.1199335

54 Polanyi, M. (1966). The logic of tacit inference. *Philosophy*, 41(155), 1–18. https://doi.org/10.1017/S0031819100066110

55 Kozielski, R. (2016). Determinants of business success – theoretical model and empirical verification. *Folia Oeconomica Stetinensia*, 16(1), 274–285. https://doi.org/10.1515/foli-2016-0018

56 Hoxie, M. (2011). *90 Days to Success Marketing and Advertising Your Small Business*. Boston: Course Technology, Cengage Learning.

57 Joseph, J. (2012). The experience effect for small business: Big brand results with small business resources. *Books24x7 Version*. Retrieved February 1, 2013, from http://common.books24x7.com.ezp.bentley.edu/toc.aspx?bookid=45346

58 Joseph, J. (2012). The experience effect for small business: Big brand results with small business resources. *Books24x7 Version*. Retrieved February 1, 2013, from http://common.books24x7.com.ezp.bentley.edu/toc.aspx?bookid=45346

59 Jantsch, J. (2006). Duct tape marketing: The world's most practical small business marketing guide. *Books24x7 Version*. Retrieved January 22, 2013, from http://common.books24x7.com.ezp.bentley.edu/toc.aspx?bookid=37673

60 Jantsch, J. (2006). Duct tape marketing: The world's most practical small business marketing guide. *Books24x7 Version*. Retrieved January 22, 2013, from http://common.books24x7.com.ezp.bentley.edu/toc.aspx?bookid=37673

61 Jobber, D. (2010). *Principles and Practice of Marketing* (6th ed.). New York: McGraw-Hill.

62 Linton, I. (2013). *Four Reasons to Expand a Product Line [Online]*. Retrieved March 15, 2013, from http://smallbusiness.chron.com/four-reasons-expand-product-line-55242.html

63 Kulatilaka, N., & Perotti, E.C. (1998). Strategic growth option. *Management Science*, 44, 1021–1031. https://doi.org/10.1287/mnsc.44.8.1021

64 Sharifi, H., Ismail, H.S., Qiu, J., & Tavani, S.N. (2013). Supply chain strategy and its impacts on product and market growth strategies: A case study of SMEs. *International Journal of Production Economics*, 145(1), 397–408. https://doi.org/10.1016/j.ijpe.2013.05.005

65 Gordon, K.T. (2004). *Pros and Cons of Expanding Your Product Line [Online]*. Retrieved February 20, 2013, from www.entrepreneur.com/article/71094

66 DeLeon & Stang. (2009). *Four Tips for Expanding the Product Line Develop a Logical Plan for New Launches [Online]*. Retrieved March 1, 2013, from www.deleonandstang.com/news-articles/managers-edge-article/four-tips-for-expanding-the-product-line/

67 Linton, I. (2013). *Four Reasons to Expand a Product Line [Online]*. Retrieved March 15, 2013, from http://smallbusiness.chron.com/four-reasons-expand-product-line-55242.html

68 Covel, S. (2008). *Tips: How to Expand Your Product Line [Online]*. Retrieved February 21, 2013, from http://online.wsj.com/article/SB121927283771758259.html

69 Nornberg, V.M. (2013). *3 Sure-Fire Ways to Expand Your Product Line [Online]*. Retrieved March 15, 2013, from www.inc.com/vanessa-merit-nornberg/growth-strategies-sure-fire-ways-to-expand-your-product-line.html

70 Berthon, P., Holbrook, M.B., Hulbert, J.M., & Pitt, L. (2007, January 1). *Viewing Brands in Multiple Dimensions*. Retrieved from https://sloanreview.mit.edu/article/viewing-brands-in-multiple-dimensions/

71 Berthon, P., Holbrook, M.B., Hulbert, J.M., & Pitt, L. (2007, January 1). *Viewing Brands in Multiple Dimensions*. Retrieved from https://sloanreview.mit.edu/article/viewing-brands-in-multiple-dimensions/

72 Huang, M.H., & Rust, R.T. (2021). A strategic framework for artificial intelligence in marketing. *Journal of the Academy of Marketing Science*, 49(1), 30–50. https://doi.org/10.1007/s11747-020-00749-9

73 Patoli, Z. (2022, November 9). Council post: Why digital marketing is important for business owners. *Forbes*. Retrieved March 29, 2023, from www.forbes.com/sites/forbesagencycouncil/2021/08/02/why-digital-marketing-is-important-for-business-owners/?sh=2fcab12c6f86

74 www.entrepreneur.com/science-technology/5-types-of-technology-all-entrepreneurs-need-access-to-in/358821

75 DeMers, J. (2013, September 24). *The Top 7 Social Media Marketing Tips that will Dominate 2014*. Retrieved from www.forbes.com/sites/jaysondemers/2013/09/24/the-top-7-social-media-marketing-trends-that-will-dominate-2014/

76 Hendricks, D. (2013, October 16). How social media campaigns will change in 2014. *Forbes*. www.forbes.com/sites/drewhendricks/2013/10/16/how-social-media-campaigns-will-change-in-2014/

77 Roeder, L. (2013). *Social Media Marketing: A Small Business Primer [Online]*. Retrieved February 20, 2013, from http://lkrsocialmedia.com/social-media-marketing/

78 YEC. (2023, March 8). Council post: What relationship marketing can mean for your business. *Forbes Magazine*. Retrieved from www.forbes.com/sites/theyec/2023/03/07/what-relationship-marketing-can-mean-for-your-business/?sh=4efbbdc14831

79 Bodnar, K. (2013). *Generating Small Business Customers with Social Media Marketing: Small Business Case Studies [Online]*. Retrieved February 20, 2013, from www.hubspot.com/Portals/53/docs/small-business-social-media-ebook-hubspot.pdf

80 Hartman, D. (2013). *Operations Strategy for Product Expansion [Online]*. Retrieved February 16, 2013, from http://smallbusiness.chron.com/operations-strategy-product-expansion-25609.html

81 Scott, D.M. (2011). *The New Rules of Marketing and PR*. New Jersey: John Wiley & Sons, Inc.

82 Juon, C., Greiling, D., & Buerkle, C. (2011). *Internet Marketing from Start to Finish: Drive Measurable, Repeatable Online Sales with Search Marketing, Usability, CRM, and Analytics*. Indianapolis, IN: Que Publishing.

83 Sinelnikov, D. (2023, February 16). Council post: Using social media and digital marketing metrics to develop or change your brand image. *Forbes*. Retrieved March 28, 2023, from www.forbes.com/sites/forbesagencycouncil/2023/02/15/using-social-media-and-digital-marketing-metrics-to-develop-or-change-your-brand-image/?sh=7c0e80c419bf

84 Roeder, L. (2013). *Social Media Marketing: A Small Business Primer [Online]*. Retrieved February 20, 2013, from http://lkrsocialmedia.com/social-media-marketing/

85 Hartman, D. (2013). *Operations Strategy for Product Expansion [Online]*. Available at: Retrieved February 16, 2013, from http://smallbusiness.chron.com/operations-strategy-product-expansion-25609.html

86 Roeder, L. (2013). *Social Media Marketing: A Small Business Primer [Online]*. Retrieved February 20, 2013, from http://lkrsocialmedia.com/social-media-marketing/

87 Shaughnessy, H. (2012, April 12). Marketing 2015: Be prepared to be surprised. Very surprised. *Forbes*. Retrieved from www.forbes.com/sites/haydnshaughnessy/2012/04/12/marketing-2015-be-surprised-be-very-surprised/

88 DeMers, J. (2013, September 24). The top 7 social media marketing tips that will dominate 2014. *Forbes*. Retrieved from www.forbes.com/sites/jaysondemers/2013/09/24/the-top-7-social-media-marketing-trends-that-will-dominate-2014/

89 Hoxie, M. (2011). *90 Days to Success Marketing and Advertising Your Small Business*. Course Technology, Cengage Learning. [Online]. Retrieved February 20, 2013, from http://lkrsocialmedia.com/social-media-marketing/

90 Friedman, T. (2016). *Thank You for Being Late*. New York: Farrar, Straus and Giroux.

91 Wedel, M., & Kannan, P. (2016). Marketing analytics for data-rich environments. *Journal of Marketing*, 80(6), 97–121. https://doi.org/10.1509/jm.15.0413

92 Kumar, V., & Gupta, S. (2016). Conceptualizing the evolution and future of advertising. *Journal of Advertising*, 45(3), 302–317. https://doi.org/10.1080/00913367.2016.1199335

93 DeVault, G. (2018, September 4). *Measuring Brand Equity*. Retrieved from www.thebalancesmb.com/how-to-measure-brand-equity-2296827

94 Bagga, C.K., & Dawar, N. (2015). A better way to map brand strategy. *Harvard Business Review*, 90–97. Print.

95 Shorr, B. (2013, June 26). 10 ways companies screw up their websites. *Forbes*. Retrieved from www.forbes.com/sites/allbusiness/2013/06/26/10-ways-companies-screw-up-their-websites/

96 Simon, D. (2013, May 9). 10 SEO tips for 2013. *Forbes*. Retrieved from www.forbes.com/sites/dansimon/2013/05/09/10-seo-tips-for-2013/

97 Hall, J. (2013, September 4). What every leader needs to know about SEO. *Forbes*. Retrieved from www.forbes.com/sites/johnhall/2013/04/09/what-every-leader-needs-to-know-about-seo/

98 In basic link terminology, a backlink is any link received by a web node (web page, directory, website, or top level domain) from another web node. Backlinks, incoming links, inbound links, inlinks, and inward links present incoming links to a website or web page.

99 Juon, C., Greiling, D., & Buerkle, C. (2011). *Internet Marketing from Start to Finish: Drive Measurable, Repeatable Online Sales with Search Marketing, Usability, CRM, and Analytics*. Indianapolis, IN: Que Publishing.

100 Intuit. (2013). *Why Ecommerce Solutions? [Online]*. Retrieved March 1, 2013, from www.intuit.com/ecommerce/create-your-online-store/

10 Financing opportunities and challenges

Learning objectives

1 Recognize the value of finance for entrepreneurs
2 Understand prospective funding sources
3 Consider the financial life cycle
4 Analyze financial constraints and entrepreneurship development
5 Discuss the role of public policy in the source of funding for entrepreneurship.

Box 10.1   Banking reimagined through microfinancing

Dr. Muhammad Yunus is a Bangladeshi social entrepreneur, banker, economist, and civil society leader who was awarded the Nobel Peace Prize for founding the Grameen Bank, which pioneers the concepts of microcredit and microfinance. Grameen Bank was founded in 1976 in Dhaka, Bangladesh, with the main aim to provide credit to the poorest of the poor in rural Bangladesh without any collateral. From its origins as an action-research project in 1976, Grameen Bank has grown to provide collateral-free loans to 7.5 million clients in more than 82,072 villages in Bangladesh, 97 percent of whom are women.

Introduction

The growth of a nation's infrastructure, agribusiness, legal systems, financial systems, regulatory bodies, and economic and social policies are integral components. While the general business environment has a significant indirect impact on all businesses and entrepreneurs operating in that environment, this chapter concentrates on the factor that has a direct, measurable effect on entrepreneurial growth: access to capital.

This chapter examines entrepreneurs' opportunities, obstacles, and limitations in pursuing financing. It emphasizes the significance of securing funding for entrepreneurial expansion. From an economic standpoint, micro constraints and macro constraints are distinguished (i.e., direct vs. indirect constraints). In their pursuit of financing, there is a distinction between startup entrepreneurs and large enterprises based on volume. From a global standpoint, the discussion should be framed in terms of a developing nation. While developed countries are discussed as a point of reference, it is assumed that the reader is familiar with the general business environment in a developed nation and is able to comprehend the unique systemic problems in developing countries.

DOI: 10.4324/9781003405740-15

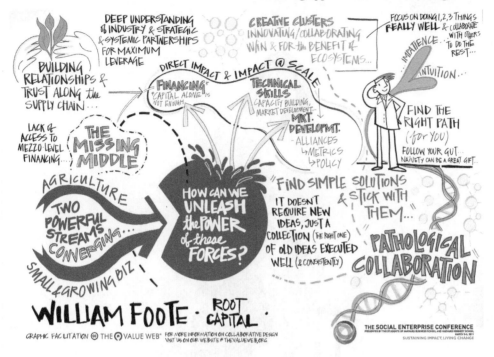

Figure 10.1 Challenge of new business finance

Source: dpict.info, licensed under CC BY-NC 2.0.

Finally, the interaction between macro (i.e., indirect) and micro (i.e., direct) constraints and the business-friendly environment will be analyzed to demonstrate that access to credit for entrepreneurs is a systemic and circular issue.

Can undertaking entertainment aimed at knowledge about personal finance and small business be a good deal?

Box 10.2   Me Poupe!

Nathalia Arcuri is a Brazilian woman entrepreneur, journalist, financial expert, influencer, philanthropist, and the inventor of Me Poupe!, the world's largest financial entertainment platform. From content in a YouTube channel[1] to technology, Me Poupe! ("Spare me!" in English) has made it easy for consumers to comprehend complex financial and investing ideas; her organization assists over 21 million people monthly in improving their financial lives. Nathalia believes that education is the first step towards genuine financial independence, and she aims to liberate individuals through democratic access to high-quality information.

The Brazilian financial market was disrupted by Nathalia's application of the concept of entertainment to financial education. In the past 4 years, her work at the forefront of financial literacy has earned her a number of honors. Me Poupe! democratized access

Figure 10.2 Nathalia Arcuri, founder of Me Poupe!

to personal finance content simplified complex concepts, and has more than 5.5 million active YouTube viewers on its platform. She is an author, behavioral economics student, and choice architecture specialist. "Spare me" the bibliography! 10 measures to ensure you never run out of cash.[2]

As a further step, Me Poupe!, the financial education company, announced on February 2023 the reorganization of its business model with the addition of entrepreneur Andreas Blazouzakis, expert in cryptocurrencies, blockchain, and NFT (non-fungible tokens), who will act as Nathalia's co-CEO.

The corporation justifies the redesign as a natural progression to pave the way for developing new solutions that can be scaled out on a large scale and with low-cost population access.

Regarding the Me Poupe! courses, the company stated that they will continue to be sold, but the goal is for private businesses to fund the courses for their employees and customers. A corporation adds that the Me Poupe! content on social networks will continue to be made freely available. Nevertheless, the main product of Me Poupe! becomes their application, named as the original brand.

The application will be a financial market aggregator employing open finance technology, artificial intelligence, and Web 3.0 in conjunction with the firm's principles and values. The new Me Poupe! App will be released in April, and its features will be introduced in phases.

The company intends to demonstrate that raising investments and financial health is possible without abandoning a sustainable approach in business.

There will be discussions later in the chapter on each of the previously mentioned principles, and it may be helpful to provide an example to illustrate each of them. Imagine an entrepreneur who is attempting to secure funding for their enterprise. They visit the bank and submit a loan application. Entrepreneurs face only direct credit constraints, such as a credit score, in developed countries (e.g., the United States). ssume the entrepreneur's credit is excellent. The bank checks their credit to determine whether or not they are creditworthy. After reviewing the business proposal, credit information is used to approve a loan.

Consider the same situation for a bad-credit entrepreneur in a developing nation (e.g., Ethiopia). The entrepreneur visits the bank, but the institution is unable to assess their creditworthiness (because there is no central credit bureau and information-sharing between banks is limited). Therefore, the bank requests that they use their home as collateral for the loan. Now, if the entrepreneur agrees to the loan and then goes bankrupt a few months later, the bank attempts to sell the entrepreneur's house to repay the loan, but it turns out that the entrepreneur fraudulently pledged the house to obtain the loan. Due to the absence of collateral, the bank must record the loan transaction as a loss. Again, there are a variety of possible positive and negative outcomes. Do you believe the banks in the second scenario will lend to small businesses again without collateral? Most likely not. In this particular fact pattern, however, the problem has become systemic. Due to the weak legal system, property rights, and lack of credit information sharing in developing nations, the bank cannot accurately assess risk. Therefore, indirect constraints significantly impact entrepreneurs' overall access to capital in these nations.

Although these examples are extreme, they illustrate the diversity of potential causes of credit restrictions. In developed nations, well-established legal systems, clearly delineated property rights, and central credit bureaus impose limitations (e.g., credit score). These are the most influential factors in lending decisions (see Table 10.1). In developing nations, however, indirect constraints (e.g., an underdeveloped legal system, inadequate property rights, and a lack of information sharing) have a much more significant impact on lending decisions.[3]

Table 10.1 Well-established, versatile business environment

A well-established, versatile business environment is defined as an environment that has:
Well-established legal and regulatory bodies
Well-defined property rights
Effective contract enforcement
Competitive markets (product, labor, and capital)
Legal framework that allows for relatively easy entry and exit of enterprises.[4]

Figure 10.3 Entrepreneurship in China

Source: Ken Lund, licensed under CC BY-SA 2.0.

While many constraints are considered circular (e.g., a developed legal system is required for financiers to have confidence in lending money), the scope of this chapter will be limited to the direct constraints of obtaining financing while touching on the indirect effects of other restrictions (e.g., an underdeveloped legal system, ineffective government policy).[5] Beck (2014) argues that financial systems play a crucial role in an economy's development, so allocating savings to this use would be a good use of funds.[6]

Financing life cycle

In the United States and most developed countries, there are multiple sources of funding available for entrepreneurs. Figure 10.3 represents the life cycle of financing which links revenue and stages of the products or services. The initial funding has to come from the wealth and income of funders and immediate family and friends. Of course, angel investors or community funding are other options.

Crowdfunding has become an increasingly popular way for entrepreneurs to obtain funding for their ventures. Brown et al. (2018) highlighted the importance of improvisational entrepreneurship in equity crowdfunding campaigns, as entrepreneurs must constantly adapt to the needs and expectations of their investors.[7]

As the product or services move further towards the output stage, other sources of funding from angel investors and venture capital will become available. When the product or services

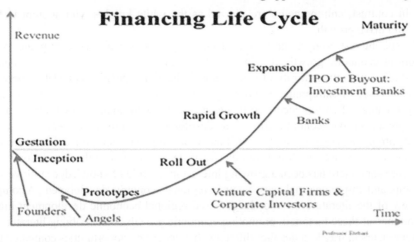

Figure 10.4 Financing life cycle

are reaching what is called "roll out" stage, then additional sources of funding such as banks and IPO will become available. In most developing countries, the primary sources of funding are family, friends, and banking institutions. In some countries, governments may provide some initial seed funding. In the following sections we will discuss intuitional, regulatory, and cultural constraints that exist in the developing countries and suggest solutions.

Companies typically go through four stages in their finance life cycle, from startup to maturity and decline. In the startup stage, companies often rely on personal savings, loans from friends and family, and government grants to fund their operations, while in the growth stage, they may seek funding from angel investors, venture capitalists, or crowdfunding platforms. As the company reaches maturity, it may turn to debt financing or equity financing through initial public offerings (IPOs) to fund expansion and acquisitions. Finally, in the decline stage, companies may divest assets or engage in restructuring to manage debt and cash flow. Entrepreneurs and investors must understand the finance life cycle to make informed decisions about financing strategies and the timing of financing activities. One key extant literature finding is that firms tend to shift from investment and growth to more conservative strategies as they mature.

Moreover, the corporate life cycle has considerable effects on various aspects of the company's operations, including financial reporting, corporate disclosures, corporate investment, financing, dividends decisions, and corporate governance. The way a company communicates with its stakeholders, such as shareholders, regulators, and customers, may vary depending on its life cycle stage. In addition, a company's financing decisions, such as debt or equity financing, are often influenced by its life cycle stage. Finally, a company's corporate governance and socially responsible behavior may also be impacted by its life cycle stage. Thus, understanding the finance life cycle and its impact on a company's operations is essential for entrepreneurs, investors, and policymakers.

Entrepreneurial growth and a country's economic development

The common perception is that entrepreneurs power economic growth and innovation and help developing nations achieve economic parity. Large corporations are frequently portrayed as corrupt and a representation of those in power, thereby losing the trust of the average person. In contrast, entrepreneurs are viewed as the white knights who attempt to balance equality and drive growth.

Lobbyists, interest groups, and policymakers frequently declare that entrepreneurs are the generators of economic growth. In addition, there have been some micro-studies and cross-country studies, with the majority of conclusions indicating a positive correlation between the growth percentage of entrepreneurs and the growth rate of a country; this means that a higher growth percentage of entrepreneurs correlates positively with higher growth rates, suggesting that entrepreneurs drive economic growth and development.[8] A limited amount of research suggests that entrepreneurs significantly contribute to development. Still, the evidence needs to be more conclusive because a multitude of other variables could explain the correlation.[9]

In recent years, there has been a growing interest in the role of knowledge spillovers, entrepreneurship, and entrepreneurial ecosystems in regional economic development. A comprehensive review of the literature on knowledge-based regional economic development highlights the importance of these factors in promoting economic growth.[10] An evolving literature argues that entrepreneurs in fragile states face different challenges and opportunities compared to those in more stable and developed countries. These literatures emphasize the crucial role of entrepreneurship and knowledge-based factors in promoting regional economic development, highlighting the need for policymakers to create supportive ecosystems that foster entrepreneurial activities and knowledge spillovers.[11]

However, research has found that a better indicator of development and growth is an overall positive environment conducive to doing business. In other words, the number of entrepreneurs is not as strong an indicator of development and growth as is a well-established and versatile business environment.

When an environment conducive to doing business is in place, both entrepreneurs and large enterprises flourish. Therefore, perhaps more important than ensuring a level playing field for entrepreneurs (e.g., through the use of entrepreneurial special subsidies) is ensuring the proper framework is established to conduct business (e.g., an established legal system, competitive regulations). Policies focused on overall business improvement are aimed to better serve entrepreneurs than are policies directly focused on subsidizing certain market demographics. Additionally, overall business improvement is more sustainable and requires less administration by policymakers.

To emphasize the importance of conducive business and financial environments, it may be helpful to review a few examples which illustrate why it is quintessential.

Although the breadth of a good business environment is sprawling, of particular note to an overall conducive business environment is the ease of entrance and exit of enterprises. This may be of particular interest to active entrepreneurs and inexperienced entrepreneurs looking to break into a market. If the business environment has higher barriers to entry, it will be less conducive for new entrepreneurs to enter the market. From this perspective, it is important for policy to keep barriers to entry low (e.g., through regulation of low registration costs) rather than subsidizing those barriers for certain groups (e.g., subsidizing registration costs for entrepreneurs). A subsidy is not sustainable and will only temporarily fix the problem. However, regulating registration costs so they remain low across the board is sustainable. The market has a way of self-correcting when proper regulations are in place.

Using the regulation of registration costs as an illustration, Italy and the United Kingdom provide us with real-world examples of how two distinct regulatory strategies can produce vastly different outcomes for entrepreneurial development and overall economic growth. Excessive registration fees hinder competition and impede the development of entrepreneurs. In other words, a high cost of doing business discourages market entry. On the other hand, low registration fees create a more conducive business environment and make a market more alluring to potential entrants. The countries illustrate the importance of regulatory influence and a business-friendly environment in influencing economic growth and development.[12]

Italy has taken the approach to make registration costs high. Conversely, the UK has taken the approach to keep registration costs low.[13] The two approaches produce inefficient and slow-growing entrepreneurs in Italy and rapid entrepreneurial growth in the United Kingdom. Moreover, this indicates that market-enabling policies, such as low registration fees, encourage entrepreneurial development, contributing to the UK's overall economic growth. In many developing nations, administrative procedures are lengthy, cumbersome, and time-consuming.

Box 10.3   Quick review on business environment and finance

- Access to finance has a direct measurable impact on entrepreneurial growth.
- Entrepreneurs face opportunities, obstacles, and constraints in their pursuit to obtain finance.
- Entrepreneurial credit access is a systemic and circular problem, giving indirect constraints with significant impact on the overall access to finance for entrepreneurs, primarily in developing countries.
- In most developing countries, the primary sources of funding are family, friends, and banking institutions.
- Policies focused on overall business improvement are aimed to better serve entrepreneurs than are policies directly focused on subsidizing certain market demographics. Additionally, overall business improvement is more sustainable and requires less administration by policymakers.
- A well-established and versatile business environment is a stronger indicator of development and growth than the number of entrepreneurs.

While unintended, these barriers (e.g., registration costs) have a disproportionately negative effect on entrepreneurs when compared to larger enterprises which have the infrastructure in place to absorb such high costs. Therefore, even if the UK were to subsidize registration costs for entrepreneurs (e.g., through tax incentives), a better approach to the problem is to implement regulations that foster the overall business environment without giving certain groups any special incentives.

Legal framework and property rights

Legal framework and property rights are related to the financial constraints of entrepreneurs; they are critical in shaping entrepreneurs' financing options, with a supportive framework and property rights regime increasing the availability of external financing.[14] Inclusive institutions that promote equality and fair competition foster an environment where investors are willing to fund innovative ventures.[15] Financial institutions and policies also provide access to capital,[16] including crowdfunding, venture capital, angel investors, and government programs.[17]

Knowing that, imagine a small business needing a loan to buy a business facility. The entrepreneur has a 25 percent cash down payment but needs a loan to finance the rest of the purchase of the facility. The small business goes to a bank to acquire a loan. The bank will require a laundry list of items, such as audited financial statements of the business, to ensure the business can service the debt (i.e., pay the note to the mortgage). Additionally, the small business owner is expected to put a hefty down payment on the property and will be asked to provide references of good character and credit since many developing countries lack centralized credit bureaus that share credit information. After all the due diligence is completed and the legal documents are signed, the mortgage note serves as legal proof of the bank's ownership in the property. The business owner will pay back the note and, upon final payment, receive the title to the property.

Bridging the gap of inequality supporting women entrepreneurs is a global challenge.

Box 10.4   Women entrepreneurs' finance initiative

The UN Development Programme (UNDP) is the UN's global development agency. It works in nearly 170 countries to provide knowledge, experience, and resources to help create country-owned solutions to global and national challenges. UNDP manages the UN development system, ensuring greater UN coherence at the country level. Funded entirely through voluntary contributions, UNDP manages an annual budget of some $5 billion, including roughly $1 billion of core resources that support basic program activities, technical expertise, and the global country networks needed to deliver worldwide programming.

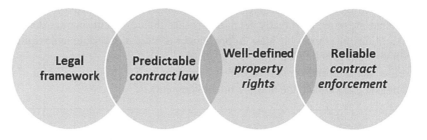

Figure 10.5 Elements of law and economics

However, the entire process described means nothing without the following (see Figure 10.5).

If the borrower defaults on their loan, the financial institution will seek redress through the court and the legal system. If the borrower defaults on the loan, the bank has no recourse absent the requisite framework. This creates a substantial risk for the lender.[18] Consequently, from the lender's perspective, it is highly risky to lend to the entrepreneurs in an environment that lacks the necessary legal framework. So, why would a lender provide financing to entrepreneurs? Often times, they will not.

Proper legal infrastructure is more than important to lenders in the context of loaning capital to entrepreneurs; it is essential. Although this is not a problem unique to them, entrepreneurs receive a disproportionate benefit (with regards to financing) by having a strong legal framework in place. This is because lenders are more likely to make concessions for larger enterprises – even if the legal framework is not in place – whereas they would not do so for entrepreneurs.

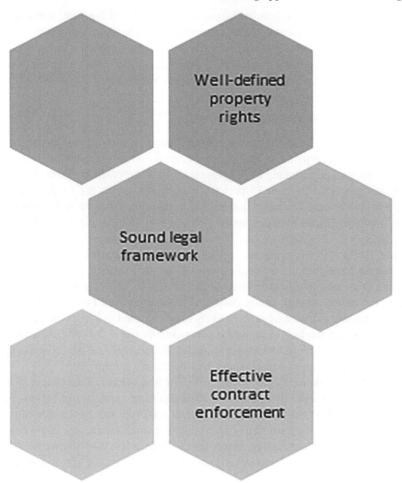

Figure 10.6 Necessary variables

This is a function of the size of the transactions (i.e., the amount of profit the bank stands to make) as well as enterprise transparency and reputation (large corporations are more likely to be established and comply with lending requirements).

A similar concept can be applied to the registration costs previously discussed. Although high registration costs affect entrepreneurs and large enterprises alike, the effects are far more profound for entrepreneurs than they are for large enterprises. This is because large enterprises are in a better position to absorb the impact of the high cost.

Conversely, high registration costs could make or break entrepreneurs when deciding whether or not to enter a market or entering a shadow economy in developing countries.

Research has shown that the institutional environment plays a crucial role in shaping entrepreneurial activity and its impact on economic growth, particularly in developing countries. An enabling business environment that enables easy procedures to start a new business, private credit coverage, and access to communication can foster entrepreneurial activity driven by opportunity. A favorable institutional environment can create opportunities for entrepreneurs to flourish and contribute to economic growth. For instance, simplified procedures for business registration and licensing can minimize the cost of starting a new business, while access to private credit coverage can help entrepreneurs secure funding for their ventures.[19]

The previously discussed points illustrate that an overall conducive business environment benefits growth and development significantly, and entrepreneurs stand to gain a disproportionately larger benefit from an overall conducive business environment.

Financial barriers and entrepreneurial growth

This section serves to expand on the entrepreneurial trends and constraints that were alluded to in previous sections and provide additional insight into the issues. Enterprises and entrepreneurs have consistently ranked financing as the biggest obstacle preventing growth. Specifically, the cost of financing is rated by over 35 percent of entrepreneurs as the single biggest obstacle hindering growth. (It should be noted that most entrepreneurs surveyed in this study were from developing countries, rather than developed.) This is of particular importance for two reasons (see Table 10.2).

Therefore, the lack of financing availability has a higher negative impact on startup entrepreneurs than on large companies. Studies have shown that financing obstacles tend to affect entrepreneurs more profoundly than large firms. This is consistent with other findings noted earlier (e.g., the impact of registration costs and legal framework on entrepreneurs). In other words, the availability of financing is more likely to be extended to larger enterprises rather than smaller ones; however, the lack of finance is exponentially worse for entrepreneurs as opposed to large enterprises. The lack of financing availability has nearly twice the constraining effect on the growth of entrepreneurs as it does on the growth of large enterprises.

As a result of the unavailability of finance, smaller firms tend to finance less through traditional financing sources and rely more on internal equity or capital contributions from entrepreneurs' friends and families. The lack of financial resources can be a major impediment to the growth of entrepreneurs, particularly for young and small businesses in developing countries.[20] In developing countries, entrepreneurs tend to finance less than 10 percent of their needs through bank finance, as opposed to larger institutions which finance upwards of 20 percent.[21]

Table 10.2 Financing preventing growth

First	Second
Financing costs rank highest and therefore are considered to be of prime importance to entrepreneurs.	There is a direct relationship between the availability of finance and entrepreneurial growth. The two have a positive correlation which is directly measurable.
Corruption, legal issues, regulation, high taxes, technological barriers, and any other noteworthy constraints simply pale in comparison to financing in terms of growth constraints.	Therefore, not being able to obtain financing will have a direct negative impact on entrepreneurial growth. Since finance is directly correlated to entrepreneurial growth, it provides empirical evidence for policymakers and financial institutions. This is much different than trying to measure the indirect effects of something.
This is not to say that any of these issues are not in and of themselves constraining. However, when 35 percent of surveyed respondents rank cost financing as the single most constraining element they face, it shows the magnitude of importance of the issue.	For example, if one was trying to measure the result on entrepreneurial growth due to the reduction in corruption, it would be very hard to make direct attributes. This is because there are many confounding variables in the equation, all of which may be the dependent variable.

This is partially due to the cost of financing (i.e., fixed transaction costs are too expensive for smaller firms) and partially due to credit availability (i.e., institutions are reluctant to lend to entrepreneurs). They also find that government has an important role to play in "funding and management, but less so in risk assessment and recovery."

With respect to credit availability, entrepreneurs tend to struggle with financing obstacles such as collateral requirements, bank paperwork, interest rate payments, and the need for audited financial statements. We can call these types of obstacles "red tape." As a result of this red tape, banks are not able to service entrepreneurs. The bank views entrepreneurs as highly risky, and the return on investment simply is not there from the lender's perspective.

Businesses incubators

As discussed, earlier entrepreneurship development is affected by multiple factors, and one of the most critical is the perspective of lenders. Research shows that access to capital is a significant barrier for many entrepreneurs, particularly for those from disadvantaged backgrounds.[22, 23] This creates a gap that can be filled by business incubators, which provide resources and guidance to startups and entrepreneurs.[24] One of the ways incubators can help entrepreneurs finance their ventures is by connecting them with investors or providing access to funding sources, offering training programs to develop effective business plans and pitches to potential investors. In addition, incubators may provide access to shared resources and facilities, such as office space, equipment, and administrative services, which can cut costs. Overall, incubators can play a vital role in helping entrepreneurs overcome financial barriers and access the resources they need to turn their ideas into successful businesses.

Furthermore, government policies play an essential role in shaping the environment for entrepreneurship, either by providing funding or by creating a favorable regulatory climate.[25] This can include measures such as tax incentives, subsidies, or streamlined processes for starting a business. However, incubators also face several challenges, including a lack of funding, inadequate access to financing, and regulatory hurdles, which can hinder their ability to support entrepreneurship.[26, 27] Despite these challenges, the literature emphasizes the crucial role of incubators in fostering entrepreneurship and innovation, and as a key element to establish a bridge to capital access.

The circular problem

The ironic part of this red-tape problem is that it is somewhat circular. Entrepreneurs require loans to acquire assets, but they need assets as collateral to obtain a loan. The issue may be considered institutional or systemic. Many entrepreneurs need more capital to be credit constrained.

When credit constrained, entrepreneurs' growth is not constrained by lack of sales, market conditions, or competition. In this sense, growth is restricted by their inability to obtain financing.

In a study conducted in the developing nation of India, comprehensive loan information for over 250 entrepreneurs was analyzed. The loans were issued as part of a subsidized lending program designed to extend credit to Indian business owners. However, the detailed loan data analysis revealed that the expansion of these businesses was exclusively constrained by credit.[28] In other words, if financing was available, their firm would be able to grow. However, since financing was not available, the entrepreneurs were not able to grow. In this sense, the only thing impeding growth was the availability of capital.

The effect the infused capital (i.e., the loan) had on each business was tracked and the results were surprising. The analysis showed that sales increased proportionately to the amount of credit received, thus proving the credit constraints facing these companies was truly preventing growth.[29] While the results of this study showed that these Indian firms were indeed credit constrained, it should be noted that subsidized credit is not necessarily the solution to alleviate this problem. A more detailed discussion surrounding this policy will be presented in future sections.

Lender perspective, environment, and the role of government

So far we have discussed how capital markets affect entrepreneurs. However, to better understand the credit market, it is important to look at how lenders are affected by entrepreneurs. By analyzing the reverse relationship (i.e., entrepreneurs' effect on the lenders), the stage will be set for a discussion on policy. From a lender perspective, banks are typically risk-averse. High risk requires a higher rate of return on their investment. Therefore, a loan for an entrepreneur will innately have a higher interest rate than that of a large developed enterprise. This is due both to the size of the loan (the absolute return on investment amount) as well as the interest rate on the loan (the rate of return for the bank).

Box 10.5   Thailand; the best country to start a business

Deidre McPhillips (March 7, 2017), a writer for *USA Today*, discusses the top places in the world to start a business in 2017. Many might instantly think it could be America because it has the highest GDP or the "world's best economy," but that would be wrong. McPhillips gives us a ranking and explains the top countries and why.

Figure 10.7 Thailand

Source: Keith "Captain Photo" Cuddeback, licensed under CC BY-NC-ND 2.0.

In 2017, Thailand was ranked the best place to start a company for the second year in a row. For instance, in Thailand it only takes about 26 days to start and run a company. Also, starting a company only costs 6.6 percent of the average income per capita in Thailand. This means that if you assume you are making about average income in Thailand, it will only cost about 6 percent of your yearly income to create and run a business.

Following Thailand, the best countries to start a company in descending order to five are China, Malaysia, India, and Indonesia. It's interesting when reviewing the next four because in somewhere like Malaysia (third best), it only takes 18 days to start a company. Although this is much faster than Thailand, there are many other factors about Thailand that makes it better than all of the rest.

Source: Radu (2018).[30]

The relationship between interest rates and risk is not always linear. A linear relationship would cause interest rates for riskier entrepreneurs to surge. Almost every entrepreneur would have access to financing, and the interest rates for the most risky entrepreneurs would be absurdly exorbitant. The lender would prefer not to lend at this time. This is because there is a pinnacle where two types of risk – selection risk (i.e., the risk that the lender will select an unworthy borrower) and default risk – become so high that the lender would prefer not to lend. Unfortunately, when this approach is applied by lenders, it means that some qualified borrowers will be left out.

This is an opportunity cost that lenders are willing to accept. Simply stated, a financial institution will be able to serve a maximum number of entrepreneurs based on the amount of funds

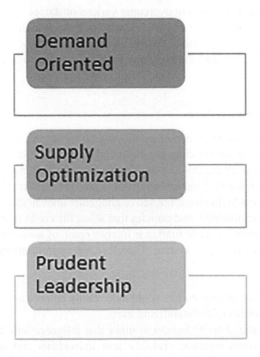

Figure 10.8 Three categories of policies

Figure 10.9 Needs cycle

available. We can extend the concept of production possibility frontier (PPF) from economics to finance and define an access possibility frontier.[31] The objective of lenders is to maximize their lending opportunities. The access possibility frontier for entrepreneurs is the proportion of plausible loan applicants that any financial institution could prudently serve, given all other variables.

By defining the maximum number of loan applicants that financial institutions can serve, the environment can be better analyzed to identify systemic issues in the credit market.[32] No two economies are precisely alike. Therefore, proposing a general solution for all credit markets is inappropriate. The three fundamental categories of policies that affect capital markets are described below. Each policy has been generalized, and each market will require a tailored approach and multifaceted solutions to overcome various obstacles.

However, generalizations can be made to classify policies into three categories: (1) market developing, (2) market enabling, and (3) market harnessing.[33] A discussion about each type of policy, examples of solutions, and the problems each policy aims to address are detailed in the following.

Capital market developing policies

Every developing country needs a market developing policy. In this sense, the breadth of these types of policies is seen as the baseline for the sound financial capital market framework (see Figure 10.8). Market developing policies are the baseline for lending. These types of policies are the framework for all lending and are designed to provide significant depth and breadth. An environment where access to finance is limited or altogether unavailable would require a significant overhaul of rules, regulations, and policies that affect the credit market.[34]

For example, a non-existent credit market is likely a result of weak contract law, information asymmetry, and an ineffective legal system. Therefore, the appropriate market developing policies would focus on:

1 Improving contract law so that lenders could more easily enforce collateral rights and reduce the administrative burden of collateralizing loans.
2 Establishing a centralized credit bureau to make due diligence and lending decisions more streamlined. This would enhance visibility into individuals and organizations and also increase competition among lenders.

3 Strengthening the legal system and contractual enforcement. As previously discussed, an efficient legal system and contractual enforcement methods give lenders confidence and is an essential part of the development of capital markets.
4 In this process, the rights and recourse for borrowers are defined and described.

Capital market enabling policies

Capital market enabling policies foster the breadth of access to finance. Therefore, the application of such policies would be applicable to environments where there is (1) capital demand originated problems, (2) supply suboptimization, or (3) prudent lending by credit suppliers. In the following is a discussion of each environment and the appropriate policies to address such environments.

Contextual capital demand originated problems

An environment has a demand originated problem when there is not enough demand for capital lending. This is often the result of self-exclusion by entrepreneurs. Self-exclusion happens when entrepreneurs do not apply for lending due to a self-perception that obtaining financing is impossible.

This is a complex issue in which cultural and social perceptions (among other perceptions) influence the entrepreneur's sense of self. For various reasons, early-stage entrepreneurs need

Figure 10.10 UNDP

Source: UNDP. (n.d.) About us. Retrieved from www.undp.org/content/undp/en/home/about-us.html

help procuring funding from financial institutions and private venture capital. In developing countries, it is much more difficult for enterprises to obtain funding due to institutional barriers and financial constraints. In general, entrepreneurs' initial sources of capital are immediate family members and close acquaintances.[35] Due to the underdeveloped financial markets and related private and public institutions in developing nations, immediate family members and acquaintances play a more significant role in funding entrepreneurship. Overall, entrepreneurs in developing countries are at a disadvantage compared to those in developed nations due to weak or nonexistent contract laws that define the roles of fund demanders and fund providers.

Therefore, holding everything else constant, potential success rates in acquiring sustainable funding is lower for entrepreneurs in developing countries compared to developed countries.

Nowadays, it is clear that to make better financial choices, one should be trained besides using judgment. Financial literacy is the possession of the set of skills and knowledge that allows an individual to make informed and effective decisions with all of their financial resources to form a good business, as we saw earlier in the opening case of this chapter.

Box 10.6   Entrepreneurship and financial literacy: how money works?

In the TED Talk "Financial Literacy & The Social Media Generation," some cultural aspects about dealing with money are presented. Nelson Soh posits that the generation born in and after 1985 is unique because of its sense of entitlement, need for instant gratification, and access to easy credit, leading to predicted harmful behaviors like being easily persuaded by social media, addicted to material things, and financially illiterate. He tells his turnaround story of entrepreneurship and becoming a financial literacy expert at www. youtube.com/watch?v=MoFj7meoHkY

Financial illiteracy is also another major problem of self-exclusion. For example, some entrepreneurs mix personal accounts with the company's accounts or do not keep books and records. Therefore, financial transparency does not exist and there is an information asymmetry between the entrepreneur and the lender. In such a situation, the financial illiteracy of the entrepreneur causes opaqueness of the business entity and therefore the lender is unable to properly assess the entity's creditworthiness.[36] This type of problem creates low demand for capital lending because financially illiterate candidates often self-exclude themselves from the market.

Supply suboptimization

A market suffers from suboptimal supply when creditors cannot service a sufficient proportion of the market. Thus, creditors operate below the access possibility frontier and do not explore all market opportunities entirely. In addition, numerous causes of suboptimal supply, such as stringent regulatory policies, make it difficult for lenders to pursue and exploit entrepreneurial lending opportunities to their maximum potential. This type of environment requires market-enabling policies to be implemented in order to develop the credit markets.[37]

To combat supply suboptimization, regulatory bodies could reduce interest rates. The availability of cheap capital would enable lenders to investigate non-traditional lending options, such as lending to entrepreneurs. In addition, the minimal cost of capital would make it financially beneficial for banks. Reducing the capital reserve requirements of banks is another example of a regulatory policy that, if implemented, would combat supply suboptimization. The minimum quantity of cash a bank must maintain on hand is regulated.

High capital reserve requirements will exacerbate the issue if a market suffers from subsupply optimization. In contrast, reducing capital reserve requirements injects currency into the economy and the hands of entrepreneurs. However, if capital requirements are reduced, regulatory bodies must ensure that the surplus capital is distributed equitably between entrepreneurs and large businesses. In other words, controls must be in place to ensure that the regulator's objectives are met. A straightforward control would be to finance entrepreneurs with a certain percent of capital.

Lending policies

Similar to the supply suboptimization discussed earlier, prudent lending by creditors will lead to an underserviced capital market. The cause, however, is often a result of a weak economy, high cost of lending, instability in the currency and the government, and/or rapid inflation.[38] This type of environment calls for stability in the economy, government, and market-enabling policy implementation.

Capital market environment

The three capital market environments discussed earlier all call for market-enabling policies in order for capital markets and the entrepreneurs they serve to develop, grow, and prosper. Although each policy will be tailored to suit each specific environment, all policies will have the same underlying objective: to develop the credit markets and enable access to finance. Policies aimed to combat demand-originated problems would focus on public awareness, changing cultural trends, and encouraging financial literacy.

Policies of this nature could include free financial literacy courses and continuing education classes aimed to educate entrepreneurs. Through these policies and programs, the environment will begin to change and develop, thus reducing self-exclusion levels among entrepreneurs.

Policies addressing supply suboptimization and prudent lending are generally more robust. More robust policies are partially a result of these problems (e.g., prudent lending and supply suboptimization) being a larger hindrance to market growth and partially a result of policy effectiveness in these areas. From a policy perspective, effective policy is more easily implemented in combating prudent lending than it is in combating demand-oriented problems, as demand-oriented problems have significant cultural and social obstacles that mitigate the effectiveness of the policy (see Figure 10.7).

One example is the European Union's capital markets union (CMU), which aims to create a single market for capital in the EU. The goal is to integrate and deepen the capital markets of member states, which would make it easier for companies and investors to raise capital and invest across borders. This intend to provide more funding options for SMEs and startups, diversify funding sources, and reduce dependence on bank financing. The initiative involves measures such as harmonizing regulation and supervision, promoting cross-border investment and trading, and improving access to information and advice. The CMU is viewed as a vital component of the EU's strategy to strengthen the Economic and Monetary Union and promote growth, innovation, and competitiveness.[39]

Effective market-enabling policies for addressing supply suboptimization and prudent lending can be found primarily in the realm of informational frameworks. Creating a centralized credit registry, for instance, would improve the flow of information between lenders and

Figure 10.11 Entrepreneurship train

Source: GES 2016 Silicon Valley, marked with Public Domain Mark 1.0.

increase competition among lenders. Increased competition would allow more lenders to service entrepreneurs. Leasing and factoring could be added to another regulatory framework. These policies are excellent examples of how entrepreneurs receive disproportionate advantages relative to large businesses. In other words, entrepreneurs would be the primary beneficiaries of such policies even though they do not provide specific benefits or incentives to entrepreneurs. Leasing and factoring are advantageous to less established businesses.

Factoring is a financial transaction where a company sells its receivables, at a discount, to a third party.[40] The third-party gains by capitalizing on the difference between the discount (amount paid) and the receivables' value. (the amount they collect). The benefits to the SME include reduced collection costs and immediate payment, as opposed to waiting 3 to 6 months to receive payment.

Box 10.7   Lending and policies

- The problem of acquiring loans can be viewed as institutional or systemic: entrepreneurs need loans to buy assets, yet they need assets for collateral in order to get a loan.
- Sales increase proportionately to the amount of credit received.
- Banks are typically risk-averse; a loan for an entrepreneur will innately have a higher interest rate than that of a large developed enterprise.

- The access possibility frontier for entrepreneurs is defined as the maximum share of viable loan applicants that could be served by any financial institution prudently given all other existing variables.
- There are three basic types of policies that affect capital markets: market developing policies that serve as a baseline for lending; capital market enabling policies that foster the breadth of access to finance; and capital market harnessing policies, where lending standards are not prudent enough.
- An environment has a demand-originated problem when there is not enough demand for capital lending.
- Potential success rates in acquiring sustainable funding is lower for entrepreneurs in developing countries compared to developed countries.

Policies that enable factoring and allow for transparent information flow directly benefit entrepreneurs. Larger enterprises often have less of a need to factor receivables because the organization is large enough to absorb the waiting time during collection.

Entrepreneurs, on the other hand, are often credit constrained and need to collect receivables quickly in order to meet their cash flow obligations (e.g., working capital requirements, accounts payable, debt service).[41]

Similarly, policies enabling leasing greatly benefit entrepreneurs. Leasing is a way to obtain necessary business assets while minimizing upfront costs. For example, if an SME needs a piece of machinery, it has two basic options: buy or lease. Buying the asset would require a large initial investment and potentially financing. Additionally, it commits the business to ownership where ownership may not be required or desired (e.g., long-term technology assets that may be rendered obsolete).[42] Alternatively, leasing provides lower initial costs, flexible repayment structure (often times tailored to the cash flow of the asset), fixed or variable interest rates, and some accounting/tax benefits depending on the SMEs situation. Leasing typically makes more sense for credit-constrained entrepreneurs. However, if the necessary policies are not in a place that allows for leasing, entrepreneurs will not be able to reap the benefits.

Capital market harnessing policies

The environment

Environments in need of market harnessing policies are those where lending standards are not prudent enough. In this environment of excess access, lenders grant loans to a larger share of applicants above the warranted interest rates, risk premiums, and other economic variables.

These types of environments can be risky because it can overextend financial institutions and their insurers and have a devastating effect on the overall health of credit markets. "Costly regulations hamper the creation of new firms, especially in industries that should naturally have high entry."[43] The credit market associated with the subprime mortgage crisis in the United States is the most recent example of such excess access. As a result, lenders should have exercised prudent lending practices and granted loans to applicants who lacked creditworthiness. The problem was exacerbated by mortgage securitization, independence issues at the corporate entity level, and valuation issues. However, the root of the matter was the excessive availability of credit.

Figure 10.12 Entrepreneurship and environment
Source: Tom à la rue, licensed under CC BY-SA 2.0.

Public policies

Government policy is especially important when it comes to market harnessing strategies. These policies have to balance market enablement, which allows for growth and prosperity, with harnessing corporate greed and risk. If left unregulated, lenders would be pushed towards an unsustainable equilibrium and eventually to collapse. A typical policy that would harness risk in the credit market would focus on raising the necessary cash required to be held on deposit. Higher deposit amounts mean a bank cannot lend as much and is more likely to exhibit diligence in lending, thus lending to only the best candidates. Other policies include adjusting interest rates, regulating new entrants, and revising the foreign policy.

The role of government in policymaking

All previously discussed policies necessitate government intervention. The government formulates and implements policies. A government needs to have the necessary infrastructure to formulate and implement policy. However, how much intervention is required? There are a variety of political, ideological, and theoretical viewpoints and opinions regarding the government's function in the business world. In the context of entrepreneurship finance, the government's role must achieve a balance between facilitating credit and funding markets without unduly transferring risks to the government.

Nevertheless, in the developing countries, the role of government in terms of providing financial incentives and appropriate regulations that result in expansion of entrepreneurial activities is essential.

Pandemic effects on entrepreneurial finance

Entrepreneurial finance has been significantly affected by the COVID-19 pandemic. The pandemic has caused a great deal of uncertainty and disruption, resulting in a decline in the availability of funding for entrepreneurs. The COVID-19 crisis has impacted the market for entrepreneurial finance in major markets, leading to a significant decrease in funding for start-ups and early-stage ventures.[44] This is consistent with findings from literature, which describe that the pandemic has led to a tightening of credit conditions, making it more difficult for entrepreneurs to secure funding.[45] It was noted that the pandemic has resulted in a shift in investor preferences towards more established firms with a proven track record, leaving early-stage ventures struggling to secure funding.[46] In response to these challenges, policymakers and financial institutions have implemented various measures to support entrepreneurs during these difficult times. For instance, some authors and analysts suggest that in times of crisis, governments can provide financial assistance to entrepreneurs in the form of grants and loans, while financial institutions can offer moratoriums on loan repayments and extend credit lines. However, there is a need for further research to evaluate the effectiveness of these measures and identify the most appropriate strategies to support entrepreneurial finance during times of crisis.[47]

In this regard it is relevant to shed light in some policy measures taken in response to the COVID-19 pandemic and its impact on entrepreneurs specifically to support bank lending conditions. Evidence shows that without funding cost relief and capital relief associated with the pandemic response measures, banks' ability to supply credit would have been severely affected, making it harder for entrepreneurs to obtain the necessary funding to sustain their businesses. However, the coordinated intervention by monetary and prudential authorities amplified the effects of the individual measures in supporting liquidity conditions and helped to sustain the flow of credit to the private sector. These findings emphasize the importance of government policies that support entrepreneurs during crises and help maintain a healthy lending environment.

Conclusion

This chapter has presented fundamental ideas in the area of entrepreneurial finance in developing countries, discussed credit constraints and obstacles that entrepreneurs face, analyzed various market environments and policies that create such environments, and opined upon regulatory solutions to each market. The common themes throughout this chapter include entrepreneurs being disproportionately hurt by the lack of financing availability, leading to the conclusion that entrepreneurial growth is largely dependent on access to finance (i.e., entrepreneurs in developing countries are credit constrained), and the necessary regulatory intervention needed for the overall credit market rather than subsidized point solutions. Entrepreneurs, therefore, must have a clear understanding of the environment and its surrounding bank and governmental policies in order to be able to fully benefit from it. An assessment of the potential for credit availability is needed, and financial books of new firms must be regularly updated in order to decrease the so-called self-exclusion process. This should be a priority to any business as an increased self-exclusion typically leads to missed opportunities and lost profit.

Discussion questions

1 Discuss funding challenges that entrepreneurs are facing.
2 State potential sources of funding and their mission.
3 Examine the financial life cycle.
4 Provide some examples of successes and failures of entrepreneurs due to funding.
5 Discuss the role of governments as a potential source of funding for entrepreneurship in most countries, especially developing countries.

Table 10.3 Key terms

Financing life cycle	Property rights
Barriers to entry	Access possibility frontier
Legal framework	Demand-originated problem
Leasing	Capital markets union
Registration costs	

Table 10.4 Glossary

Financing life cycle	Comprises the stages between gestation and maturity of a business.
Barriers to entry	An economic barrier to entry is a fixed cost that must be incurred by a new entrant into a market, regardless of production or sales activities, that incumbents do not have or have not had to incur. Due to the fact that entry barriers safeguard incumbent firms and restrict competition in a market, they can contribute to price distortions and are therefore crucial when discussing antitrust policy.
Legal framework	Legal framework and property rights are related to the financial constraints of entrepreneurs; they are critical in shaping entrepreneurs' financing options, with a supportive framework and property rights regime increasing the availability of external financing.
Leasing	A lease is a contractual agreement in which the user (known as the lessee) pays the proprietor (known as the lessor) for the use of an asset. Real estate, structures, and vehicles are common leased assets. Additionally, industrial or commercial apparatus is leased. The lessor is the asset's legal proprietor, while the lessee obtains the right to use the asset in exchange for regular rental payments.
Registration costs	To register a new company or organization, the owner must pay fees. In most cases, the total cost to register a new business varies depending on country, state, and business structure. The information needed to register typically includes the business name and location.
Property rights	Property rights define the theoretical and legal ownership of resources and the permissible uses of those resources. Individuals, corporations, and governments are able to own property. These rights define the benefits that come with property ownership.
Access possibility frontier	The proportion of plausible loan applicants that any financial institution could prudently serve, given all other variables.
Demand-originated problem	An environment has a demand-originated problem when there is not enough demand for capital lending.
Capital markets union	A plan to create a single market for capital. The aim is to get money – investments and savings – flowing across the EU so that it can benefit consumers, investors, and companies, regardless of where they are located (https://finance.ec.europa.eu/capital-markets-union-and-financial-markets/capital-markets-union_en).

Notes

1 Retrieved from www.youtube.com/channel/UC8mDF5mWNGE-Kpfcvnn0bUg
2 Retrieved from www.weforum.org/people/nathalia-arcuri
3 Aghion, P., Fally, T., & Scarpetta, S. (2007). Credit constraints as a barrier to the entry and post-entry growth of firms. *Economic policy*, 22(52), 732–779. Wiley Centre for Economic Policy Research Center for Economic Studies, CESifo Group Maison des Sciences de l'Homme. https://doi.org/10.2307/4502214
4 Beck, T., & Levine, R. (2005). Legal institutions and financial development. In *Handbook of New Institutional Economics* (pp. 251–278). Boston, MA: Springer.
5 Banerjee, A.V., & Duflo, E. (2014). Do firms want to borrow more? Testing credit constraints using a directed lending program. *The Review of Economic Studies*, 81(2), 572–607. https://doi.org/10.1093/restud/rdt046
6 Beck, T. (2014). Finance, growth, and stability: Lessons from the crisis. *Journal of Financial Stability*, 10, 1–6. https://doi.org/10.1016/j.jfs.2013.12.006
7 Brown, R., Mawson, S., Rowe, A., & Mason, C. (2018). Working the crowd: Improvisational entrepreneurship and equity crowdfunding in nascent entrepreneurial ventures. *International Small Business Journal*, 36(2), 169–193.
8 Beck, T., & Demirguc-Kunt, A. (2006). Small and medium-size enterprises: Access to finance as a growth constraint. *Journal of Banking & Finance*, 30(11), 2931–2943. https://doi.org/10.1016/j.jbankfin.2006.05.009
9 Beck, T., & Torre, A.D. (2006). The basic analytics of access to financial services. *Policy Research Working Papers*. https://doi.org/10.1596/1813-9450-4026
10 Qian, H. (2018). Knowledge-based regional economic development: A synthetic review of knowledge spillovers, entrepreneurship, and entrepreneurial ecosystems. *Economic Development Quarterly*, 32(2), 163–176.
11 Amorós, J.E., Ciravegna, L., Mandakovic, V., & Stenholm, P. (2019). Necessity or opportunity? The effects of state fragility and economic development on entrepreneurial efforts. *Entrepreneurship Theory and Practice*, 43(4), 725–750.
12 Beck, T., Demirgüç-Kunt, A., & Martinez Peria, M. (2008). Bank Financing for SMEs around the World: Drivers, Obstacles, Business Models, and Lending Practices. *Development Economics*.
13 Beck, T., Demirguckunt, A., & Maksimovic, V. (2008). Financing patterns around the world: Are small firms different? *Journal of Financial Economics*, 89(3), 467–487. https://doi.org/10.1016/j.jfineco.2007.10.005
14 Fuentelsaz, L., Maicas, J.P., & Montero, J. (2018). Entrepreneurs and innovation: The contingent role of institutional factors. *Journal of Business Research*, 86, 115–122. https://doi.org/10.1016/j.jbusres.2017.12.030
15 Acemoglu, D., & Robinson, J.A. (2012). *Why Nations Fail: The Origins of Power, Prosperity, and Poverty*. Crown Books.
16 Cosh, A., & Zhang, J. (2017). Innovation and the financing of young firms: Evidence from the UK. *Journal of Financial Management, Markets and Institutions*, New York: Crown Business, 5(1), 107–129.
17 Shepard, A. (2019). The importance of intellectual property rights in the knowledge-based economy. In *Innovation in the High-Tech Economy* (pp. 63–79). Cham: Springer. https://doi.org/10.1007/978-3-030-04091-8_4
18 Beck, T., & Demirguc-Kunt, A. (2006). Small and medium-size enterprises: Access to finance as a growth constraint. *Journal of Banking & Finance*, 30(11), 2931–2943. https://doi.org/10.1016/j.jbankfin.2006.05.009
19 Urbano, D., Audretsch, D., Aparicio, S., & Noguera, M. (2020). Does entrepreneurial activity matter for economic growth in developing countries? The role of the institutional environment. *International Entrepreneurship and Management Journal*, 16(3), 1065–1099.
20 Guo, K., & Rasheed, A.A. (2021). Entrepreneurial finance, network resources, and firm growth: Evidence from China. *Asia Pacific Journal of Management*, 38(1), 123–150.
21 Beck, T., Klapper, L.F., & Mendoza, J.C. (2010). The typology of partial credit guarantee funds around the world. *Journal of Financial Stability*, 6(1), 10–25. https://doi.org/10.1016/j.jfs.2008.12.003
22 Davidsson, P. (2015). Entrepreneurial opportunities and the entrepreneurship nexus: A re-conceptualization. *Journal of Business Venturing*, 30(5), 674–695.

23　Shane, S. (2018). *The Illusion of Entrepreneurship: The Costly Myths that Entrepreneurs, Investors, and Policy Makers Live by.* New Haven: Yale University Press.

24　Li, C., Ahmed, N., Qalati, S.A., Khan, A., & Naz, S. (2020). Role of business incubators as a tool for entrepreneurship development: The mediating and moderating role of business start-up and government regulations. *Sustainability*, 12(5), 1822.

25　Bozhikin, I., Macke, J., & da Costa, L.F. (2019). The role of government and key non-state actors in social entrepreneurship: A systematic literature review. *Journal of Cleaner Production*, 226, 730–747.

26　Ganco, M., Ziedonis, R.H., & Agarwal, R. (2017). More stars stay, but the brightest ones still leave: Job hopping in the shadow of patent enforcement. *Strategic Management Journal*, 38(10), 2050–2071. https://doi.org/10.1002/smj.2639

27　Zheng, H., Wei, J., Zhao, Y., & Wang, H. (2021). How do incubators promote start-ups' innovation performance in the context of innovation ecosystem? An empirical study from China. *Journal of Business Research*, 128, 261–272. https://doi.org/10.1016/j.jbusres.2021.01.041

28　Benavente, J.M., Galetovic, A., & Sanhueza, R. (2006). Fogape: An economic analysis. *Working Papers*. Retrieved from https://ideas.repec.org/p/udc/wpaper/wp222.html

29　Berger, A.N., & Udell, G.F. (1998). The economics of small business finance: The roles of private equity and debt markets in the financial growth cycle. *Journal of Banking & Finance*, 22(6–8), 613–673. https://doi.org/10.1016/s0378-4266(98)00038-7

30　Radu, S. (2018, January 23). *These Are the Top 5 Countries to Start a Business*. Retrieved from www.usnews.com/news/best-countries/best-start-a-business

31　Cetorelli, N., & Strahan, P.E. (2006). Finance as a barrier to entry: Bank competition and industry structure in local U.S. markets. *The Journal of Finance*, 61(1), 437–461. https://doi.org/10.1111/j.1540-6261.2006.00841.x

32　Cole, S. (2004). Fixing Market Failures or Fixing Elections? Agricultural Credit in India. *American Economic Journal: Applied Economics*, 1(1), 219–250.

33　Allen, F., & Gale, D. (2004). Competition and access to finance: International evidence. *Journal of Money, Credit and Banking*, 36(3), 453–480.

34　De la Torre, A., Soledad Martinez Peria, M., & Schmukler, S.L. (2008). *Bank Involvement with SMES: Beyond Relationship Lending*. The World Bank. https://doi.org/10.1596/1813-9450-4649

35　El Jadidi, J., Asgary, N., & Weiss, J. (2017). Cultural and institutional barriers for western educated entrepreneurs in Morocco. *CYRUS Chronicle Journal: Contemporary Economic and Management Studies in Asia and Africa*, 61–75.

36　Dinc, I. (2005). Politicians and banks: Political influences on government-owned banks in emerging markets. *Journal of Financial Economics*, 77(2), 453–479. Web.

37　Frame, W.S., & Woosley, L. (2004). Credit scoring and the availability of small business credit in low- and moderate-income areas. *The Financial Review*, 39(1), 35–54. Web.

38　Frame, W.S., Srinivasan, A., & Woosley, L. (2001). The effect of credit scoring on small-business lending. *Journal of Money, Credit and Banking*, 33(3), 813. Web.

39　Braun, B., Gabor, D., & Hübner, M. (2018). Governing through financial markets: Towards a critical political economy of capital markets union. *Competition & Change*, 22(2), 101–116.

40　Gormley, T.A. (2005). *Banking Competition in Developing Countries: Does Foreign Bank Entry Improve Credit Access?* Boston: Department of Economics, MIT.

41　Hallberg, K. (2000). *A market-oriented strategy for small and medium scale enterprises* (Vol. 63). World Bank Publications.

42　Khwaja, A.I., & Mian, A. (2005). Do lenders favor politically connected firms? Rent provision in an emerging financial market. *The Quarterly Journal of Economics*, 120(4), 1371–1411. Web.

43　Klapper, L., Laeven, L., & Rajan, R. (2006). Entry regulation as a barrier to entrepreneurship. *Journal of Financial Economics*, 82(3), 591–629. https://doi.org/10.1016/j.jfineco.2005.09.006

44　Brown, R., Rocha, A., & Cowling, M. (2020). Financing entrepreneurship in times of crisis: Exploring the impact of COVID-19 on the market for entrepreneurial finance in the United Kingdom. *International Small Business Journal*, 38(5), 380–390.

45　Groen, B., Popov, A., & Vladimirov, V. (2020). Financing constraints and unemployment: Evidence from the COVID-19 pandemic. *Journal of Financial Stability*, 53, 100971.

46　Chua, R.Y., Cohen, M., & Wood, M.C. (2021). Covid-19, recession and venture capital decision-making. *Journal of Business Research*, 124, 266–270.

47　Ratten, V., Jones, P., & Braga, V. (2020). Government policy measures to support small businesses during crises: A synthesis of international research. *International Journal of Disaster Risk Reduction*, 50, 101786.

11 Essentials of bookkeeping

Learning objectives

1 Learn the essentials of bookkeeping
2 Understand why entrepreneurs must keep financial records
3 Comprehend how to calculate fixed, variable, and total costs
4 Understand how to calculate profit
5 Examine budgeting and financial spreadsheets
6 Identify the main differences between for-profit and nonprofit organizations.

Figure 11.1 Lojas Americanas, Paratinga/Bahia-Brazil

Source: CC by Fronteira. https://commons.wikimedia.org/wiki/Category:Lojas_Americanas#/media/File:Lojas_Americanas,_Paratinga,_janeiro_de_2023_(2).jpg

DOI: 10.4324/9781003405740-16

Box 11.1   Alleged fraud at a Brazilian retailer Americanas SA puts three billionaires in the spotlight

Lojas Americanas in its traditional format was the company's first store model, presenting an average sales area of 1000 m² and an assortment of up to 60,000 items. Americanas.com is the largest online marketplace in Brazil, offering millions of products in over 40 categories. Customers have ranked this online store as having the finest customer service; it is the most beloved online store because it provides the best shopping experience and multiple delivery options. Consumers can purchase via the website, smartphone, or in-store kiosks and have their products delivered to their homes or to one of more than 1700 Lojas Americanas shops across the country. The brand is present in Brazilians' daily lives since this company is 94 years old with stores all over Brazil and conducts major e-commerce activity. The company's reference shareholders include the three billionaires (Jorge Paulo Lemann, Carlos Alberto Sicupira, and Marcel Telles) who created 3G Capital, which filed for bankruptcy in January 2023 after discovering about $4 billion in "accounting inconsistencies" and is now being investigated due to the possibility of fraud. The scandal erupted on January 11th, when the new chief executive of Americanas, Sergio Rial, reported that the retail giant had hidden R$20 billion ($4 billion) of debt over a decade and swiftly resigned.[1] Correcting the error swelled the firm's debt to $8 billion so, its shares lost 94 percent of their value. On January 19th it filed for bankruptcy after its cash reserves disappeared. In early February, the company's board of directors requested the dismissal of three directors and three executives following a court order for the seizure of corporate emails sent and received by managers and board members over the past decade.

Daniel Gerber, an attorney representing 20 minority shareholders in Americanas, said: "The fraud was malicious. It was a procedure orchestrated and accepted by all involved and which generated fantastic profits for the distribution of bonuses for years."

Brazilian banks such as BTG or Bradesco would pay Americanas suppliers in advance, and the company was responsible for the repayment of these loans, including interest payments. These interest transactions, however, were effectively hidden by the company accounting, not classified as financial debts. Analysts and minority shareholders are sure now that this practice, which resulted in higher reported profits, had persisted for decades, considering the actual indebtedness.

The company's board, auditing committee, and auditor PricewaterhouseCoopers (PwC) are already being criticized for their role in the disaster, with many stockholders facing massive losses and tens of thousands of employees facing an undetermined future. Fábio Coelho, the president of the Association of Capital Market Investors in Brazil, declares, "We should seek answers from those directly involved in approving the accounting records."

On the other hand, PwC denied commenting on any part of the case, including charges of fraud. Currently, the Americanas stores remain open, but the outlook for the corporation is grim. As a result of the controversy, only some experts are confident about the company's ability to restructure properly, and many believe it will struggle to get financing.

At the site of Americanas, is it possible to identify the ownership structure and everything expected from stakeholders' point of view: corporate governance practices and

Shareholders	Number of Shares	(%) Total
Reference shareholders	271,834,960	30.12%
Others	630,694,543	69.88%
Total Shares	902,529,503	100.00%

Figure 11.2. Ownership structure of Lojas Americanas

Source: https://ri.americanas.io/en/corporate-governance/ownership-structure/ Reference date: February 13, 2023.

Novo Mercado; rights of Americanas SA's common shares; regulation of the Brazilian securities market; and disclosure and use of information. The reference shareholders of the G3 group have one-third of the company's shares (Figure 11.2).

Besides improving corporate governance, the scandal demonstrated the need to strengthen the capabilities of the Brazilian Securities Commission (CVM). Despite the fact that the CVM has launched various investigations, it appears from what have been disclaimed by media that the accounting "irregularity" resulted from a standard practice among Brazilian shops.

Nonetheless, CVM stated that if any illegality was discovered, "each responsible party may be held accountable in accordance with the law and to the degree appropriate." It is estimated that more than 9000 creditors are waiting for the process when this debtor's assets will be measured and evaluated. Eventually, these assets may be used to repay some of the outstanding debt.

The internet has exponentially expanded the forms of economic interaction between companies, families, and individuals. Each of these economic actors can transact in different ways in various other locations worldwide. Precisely for this reason, the importance of accounting records' quality, relevance, accuracy, and objectivity has also increased exponentially.

In the example of Lojas Americanas there are 53 million customers, 1.7 billion items sold, half a billion transactions, and 150,000 sellers (data from the third quarter of 2022).[2]

Through Lojas Americanas, the financial resources of millions of buyers are transferred to tens of thousands of suppliers. As there is a mismatch of terms between these financial flows, banks act by lending and receiving part of the commercial flow; therefore, there are structurally bank debts that were not properly explained in the financial statements.

The volume achieved (via the internet) was such that this accounting weakness reached the level of billions.

The breadth, speed, and intensity that the internet offers to business require a systemic look from accounting. These large transactional hubs (e.g., Lojas Americanas) can generate large-scale crises, previously the monopoly of banks. Although every crisis opens up learning opportunities, accounting will need to address indicators that show the strength of these large transactional hubs.[3]

The literature shows that some corporate fraud motivations and drivers include agency theory, executive compensation, and organizational culture. Nevertheless, fraud's repercussions differ for various corporate stakeholders and could have spillover effects on other corporations, the political environment, and financial market participants.[4]

Questions for discussion: corporate fraud

1 Even though there is no commonly accepted definition, development banks generally define a fraudulent activity as any act or omission, including a misrepresentation, that intentionally or recklessly deceives or attempts to deceive a party to obtain a financial or other benefit or to avoid an obligation. Consequently, corporate fraud is an intentional act by one or more individuals to get an unjust advantage by using deception. In your opinion, who benefited most from this Americanas' accounting inconsistency?

2 According to Baker et al. (2020) fraud has five major elements: (1) it involves two parties – a fraudster and a victim, (2) a fraudster knowingly or unknowingly facilitates a false statement, (3) a fraudster accepts the statement being false, (4) a victim relies on the false statement or presentation, and (5) reliance on the presentation results in a damage or risk of damage to a victim. Describe the situation at Americanas, assigning a number (1 to 5) to the reference shareholders, the CFO, the auditor PwC, and the employees according to your perspective.

3 Compare the statements of four auditing companies in relation to fraud prevention in the document "Fraud and Going Concern Discussion Paper" (www.ifac.org/system/files/meetings/files/20210421-IAASB-Agenda-Item-3-A.2-Fraud-Question-1b.pdf).

Introduction

An entrepreneur who has an idea and passion to bring their product or service to the market needs to have some basic knowledge of accounting to be able to identify the bottom line, which is critical information for moving forward. An entrepreneur must make many decisions including identifying target customers, finding the best suppliers for raw materials, deciding how to get the product or service to market, and how products should be priced. Some of these decisions seem very intuitive, but it is very difficult to evaluate them without being able to measure how they affect the amount of money the business is generating. To do this, they must keep records of revenue and carefully identify and track expenses.

A budget is one of the most Important documents an entrepreneur must create, and it depends heavily on detailed records of expenditures and revenues (see Figure 10.2). It seems that bookkeeping is more intimidating to many entrepreneurs or small businesses than other aspects of running a business. In developing economies, entrepreneurs and small businesses often operate in the informal sector, avoiding the need to keep financial records for tax purposes. According to World Bank estimates, the informal sector represents 10 to 20 percent of the GNP in developed countries and more than 30 percent in developing ones.[5] This can discourage bookkeeping for those who do not understand the necessity of financial records for the success of any business.

This chapter will address two important questions related to bookkeeping for an entrepreneur. First, why must an entrepreneur keep financial records? Without the knowledge of financial feasibility of the business, it is hard to acquire support for growth. When we look at developed economies, the most important motivating factors for entrepreneurs is the need to obtain outside financing and reporting requirements from tax authorities.

In an environment lacking these objectives, entrepreneurs may think that bookkeeping will add unnecessary complexity to running their business. We will explain many benefits of keeping

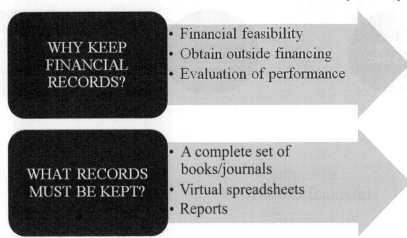

Figure 11.3 Relevance of accounting

complete and accurate account books and also the risks a business faces having no clear financial picture gleaned from accurate records.

The second question to be addressed is: What records must be kept? In other words, what is the minimum for a complete set of books? We will provide information for bookkeeping by clearly explaining the simple records that will provide the information needed to reap the benefits outlined (Figure 11.3).

Why is bookkeeping important?

Why does every entrepreneur need to have financial information about revenue and costs of the business and keep a complete and accurate set of books? Financial records tell the story of what is really happening in business as a whole. As a business owner, "Without a complete set of books, you find yourself trying to evaluate your business by looking at isolated areas, such as cash and inventory – these being the most observable, and also the most misleading."[6]

An example of how this can be a problem is the common practice entrepreneurs and SMEs take to base their prices on the cost of materials plus an arbitrary markup, without factoring in many costs that are harder to identify. Without tracking explicit costs (e.g., rent, utilities, insurance) and implicit costs (opportunity cost of an entrepreneur), the prices can be settled below an appropriate profit margin – sometimes even at a loss – without knowing it.

In other words, an entrepreneur can overestimate a business's profit. Therefore, knowing the cost of producing a unit of a product or service is essential. The *explicit cost* is a cost that is the source of the cash outflow for business activities to which the expense is recognized. These explicit costs are wage expenses, rent or lease costs, and the materials cost that are directly paid. An *implicit cost* is the opportunity cost to what an entrepreneur must give up to do this job. Total cost is explicit plus implicit costs, which are defined as *opportunity cost* in economics (see Figure 11.4).[7]

There are many reasons that bookkeeping is crucial beyond proper pricing. In Brazil, literature findings indicate that pricing policies influence the profitability of organizations and therefore,

Figure 11.4 Total costs

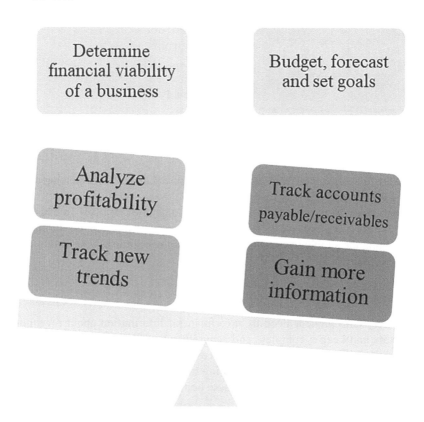

Figure 11.5 Record benefits

a more strategic look at the pricing process may constitute one aspect that cannot be overlooked by managers. The profitability and cost-effectiveness of business are highly attached to a pricing strategy that encompasses their internal capacities, skills, and corporate advantages against their competitors while also considering their customer's needs or how much they are willing to pay.[8]

Keeping complete and accurate financial records allows a business owner to complete the tasks outlined in Figure 11.5.

Generally, a business plan serves as a kind of "road map" for an entrepreneur. Financial records serve as a dashboard that shows financial viability and the adjustment of their practices and strategies as necessary. If outside financing is an option, financial records will almost certainly be required. Many entrepreneurs have to exploit outside initial funding. In this case, more detailed records increase the chances of securing a loan or persuading an investor. Also, for formal or registered businesses, financial records will be necessary for tax reporting.

Another good reason to keep financial records is the possibility to apply for governmental incentives for innovation, including R&D, capital expansion, energy sustainability, employment, and training.[9] The nature of these records will depend on the tax jurisdiction and form of business. This chapter does not intend to address the financial records necessary for tax purposes.

Bookkeeper and methods of bookkeeping

As stated before, bookkeeping entails the systematic recording of a company's financial transactions. With efficient bookkeeping, businesses can maintain track of all information on their books and make critical operational, investment, and financing choices. Bookkeepers are individuals who manage all transactions of an organization's financial data. With bookkeepers, businesses would be aware of their present financial standing and the transactions that take place within the company. The advantage of correct bookkeeping is to provide evidence to external users, such as investors, financial institutions, and the government, who want access to reliable information to make more informed investment or lending decisions.

Asymmetric information, also known as "information failure," occurs when one party to an economic transaction possesses greater material knowledge than the other party, and that is the reason why accounting disclosure and auditing are so important. An empirical study of 225 manufacturing companies listed on the Indonesia Stock Exchange from 2016 to 2018[10] found out that the more that companies make voluntary disclosures, there will be more interest by investors and stakeholders. The lower the information asymmetry, the better the quality of financial reporting will be. Vice versa, the higher the information asymmetry, the lower the quality of financial reporting.[11]

In this sense, the accuracy of a company's performance evaluation is enhanced by accurate bookkeeping. It also gives information for making general strategic decisions and serves as a benchmark for the company's revenue and income objectives. In conclusion, once a business is up and operating, it is essential to invest more time and resources in maintaining accurate records. To summarize, internal and external users of a corporate entity rely on accurate and trustworthy bookkeeping.

Usually due to the expense, many small businesses do not actually employ full-time accountants. Small businesses typically employ a bookkeeper or outsource the task to a professional organization. It is vital to highlight that many people who wish to start a new business need to pay more attention to the need of maintaining detailed records of every dollar spent.

The cash versus accrual accounting method

To correctly execute bookkeeping, businesses must first determine which accounting system they will use. Two fundamental accounting systems are available to companies: the cash basis of accounting and the accrual basis of accounting. The distinction between these accounting methods depends on when a corporation records a sale (money inflow) or purchase (money outflow) in its books.

	Cash Basis	*Accrual Basis*
Definition	Record transaction only when cash is actually received or paid	Record transaction when it occurs, even if cash is not received or paid
Example: You purchased 100 units of a product and will pay for it next month	No transaction recorded	Transaction recorded through an accounts payable (liability) account

Source: https://corporatefinanceinstitute.com/resources/accounting/bookkeeping-definition/

Setting prices

One of the most important reasons for an entrepreneur to keep careful financial records is to be able to set prices for goods or services at a level to make an appropriate profit. When determining what price will be charged, many variables need to be considered (e.g., competitors' prices, the willingness of customers to pay, what differentiating factors may justify a higher price, and what signals the prices are sending).

The details of this process were presented in Chapter 9 on marketing. For now, it is important for an entrepreneur to know how much it costs to produce each item and identify how much profit is made per unit, known as the *contribution margin*, when making these decisions. Contribution margin is defined as the selling price per unit minus the variable cost per unit (see Figure 11.6).

The contribution margin represents the portion of sales revenue that is not paid for variable costs and therefore contributes to the payment for fixed costs. Correctly calculating the cost of the product is important for setting an appropriate price that will cover all of the costs and provide enough revenue for reinvestment and growth. The amount of variable costs is also known as "cost of goods sold" (COGS).

In addition to direct material and direct labor represented in the COGS, entrepreneurs also have to understand the *indirect costs*, which are other expenses that must be paid to produce the product or services. This includes costs such as maintenance for the equipment, business trips, communication expenses, marketing campaigns, administrative work, the time spent researching new designs, among others.

While these costs cannot be attributed to an individual product, they contribute to a line of production; therefore, the costs should be an estimate per period and divided among the units of the products that are produced in a given timeframe.[12] Therefore, an entrepreneur has to know all costs, explicit and implicit, and incorporate them into setting their pricing mechanism.

Box 11.2   Environmental accounting for sustainable development

Scholars at the World Bank examined environmental and resource management concerns in the economic decision-making process.[13] They explored the linkages between development and environment with the understanding that when environment is concerned, someone will eventually have to bear the "external costs" of the current production and consumption activities. They feel that their approach will more accurately represent the true income of a country while the GDP fails to account for the negative effects on the environment.

Reading through the book, one can understand the overview of a variety of approaches, from constructing of environmental and resource accounts for developing countries, measurement of development using the sustainable social net national product approach, practical solutions towards correcting national income measures by taking into account the environmental losses, and much more.

Figure 11.6 Contribution margin

Increasing numbers of businesses and other organizations are incorporating environmental management into their plans to establish measures for addressing environmental challenges and to conduct environmental conservation efforts internally aligned with societal expectations. Environmental accounting is a supplementary tool for environmental management, and its information is not only utilized internally by businesses and other organizations. It is also disclosed to the public through environmental or sustainability reports.

Being one of the essential components of an environmental report, the disclosure of environmental accounting data enables parties employing this information to understand the company's stance on environmental conservation and how it precisely addresses environmental challenges. Concurrently, a more comprehensive understanding of the environmental information of enterprises and other organizations can be achieved.

The importance of environmental accountancy is essential for the quantitative management of environmental conservation operations, being an efficient method for developing and sustaining better company management. In other words, a corporation or other entity can accurately identify and quantify the investments and expenses associated with environmental conservation actions and prepare and analyze this information. Furthermore, environmental accounting plays a crucial role in supporting rational decision-making by enhancing the company's understanding of the potential return on these investments and costs. As a result, the company is not only able to increase the efficacy of its operations, but environmental accounting also facilitates rational decision-making.

In addition, companies and other organizations must be accountable to stakeholders, such as consumers, business partners, investors, and employees, while using environmental resources (e.g., public goods) for business purposes. The publication of environmental accounting data (public disclosure) is a fundamental aspect of accountability. Thus, environmental accounting assists businesses and other organizations gain the public's trust and confidence and earn a fair evaluation.

The three key facets are environmental conservation cost (monetary value), environmental conservation benefits (physical units), and the economic benefit associated with environmental conservation activities (monetary value).[14] So, environmental accounting is structured to identify, measure, and communicate a company's activities based on its environmental conservation cost or economic benefit associated with environmental conservation activities, considering the company's financial performance, which is evaluated in monetary value, and its environmental conservation benefits, the organization's environmental performance, which is measured in physical units as can be seen in Figure 11.7.[15]

It is worth to mention that internal and external roles and functions of environmental accounting are distinguished, but both relevant.

1 Internal functions

As a component of an organization's environmental information system, the internal function enables the management of environmental conservation costs, the analysis of the cost of environmental conservation activities versus the benefit obtained, and the promotion of effective and efficient environmental conservation activities employing appropriate decision-making.

2 External functions

The external function allows a corporation to influence the decisions of stakeholders, including consumers, investors, and local residents, by exposing the objectively measurable results of its environmental conservation actions.

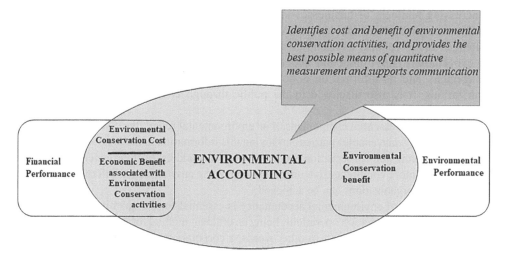

Figure 11.7 Environmental accounting

Source: Japan. Ministry of the Environment – MOE. (2002). Retrieved from www.env.go.jp/content/900453353.pdf

Budgeting

Once an entrepreneur has done a careful analysis of the expenses, then it will be possible to create an annual budget. A budget is one of the most important documents an entrepreneur can create, and it depends heavily on detailed records of expenditures and revenues.

The budget needs to underline the financial viability. In its most basic form, a budget is a documentation of how much money a business owner plans to spend (expenses) and make (revenues) over a given period of time. In the case of the annual budget, the timeframe would be a year. But such a simple description conceals its true power. For a carefully prepared budget, the process of determining the proper numbers needed to calculate the final expense figures can be quite illuminating. Additionally, an entrepreneur must carefully analyze the business and its market to work out a useful sales forecast.

At the end of a year, the budget serves as a concrete way to measure performance against goals and can be even more useful when it is used to compare progress to incremental targets throughout the year. By comparing monthly or quarterly figures to budgeted amounts, a business owner can see when things are not going as planned and take action to correct the course of action.[16]

Tracking expenses and revenue

To create a budget, an entrepreneur must project how much they will spend in the coming year and what volume would be expected to sell and at what price. This entails taking a closer look at previous years' budgets to determine how much it costs to run the business and carefully analyze past sales.

Everything in the expenses should be included, from the cost of materials to wages that have been paid in the previous year(s). In order to do this, an entrepreneur needs a detailed record of previous years' expenses. The break-even point is achievable when the total costs of production or services equals the total revenue received from sales.[17] Being able to calculate break-even for the year is essential. In a more straightforward way to explain, Break-even is the output level in which total revenue minus total cost (explicit plus implicit) is equal to zero (Figure 11.8).

Figure 11.8 Break-even point of a business

> The break-even theory[18] is based on the fact that there is a minimum product level at which a venture neither makes a profit nor a loss. This is a starting point for a successful entrepreneurial activity.

It is essential to mention that Rambo (2013) pointed out that despite the exponential growth in the number of small and medium-sized enterprises in sub-Saharan Africa since the 1990s, over two-thirds of these businesses failed to launch, resulting in negative micro- and macroeconomic effects. In an empirical study including 146 companies in Kenya that had been operating for between 1 and 5 years,[19] the author found that their break-even period varied between 3 and 40 months. The amount of financial management training was the most influential covariate, accounting for up to 12.1 percent of the variance in the break-even period. Financial management training accounted for 10.2 percent, marketing for 9.7 percent, educational attainment for 8.6 percent, capitation financing level for 7.5 percent, and company size for 6.0 percent. As one can see, accounting aspects are the most important among them.

Common sense states that an entrepreneur cannot operate in the long run if only the accounting cost is being covered (or it is at break-even point); they may do it only in the short run. While preparing the budget, it is important that the entrepreneur recognizes that not all costs are the same. Some have to be paid no matter how many products or services are produced, such as purchasing a new machine or renting a place – these expenses are known as *fixed costs*. Others, known as *variable costs*, depend completely on how many products are made. Variable costs include things such as the cost of raw materials or hourly wages for employees. Not every cost fits clearly into one category or another, which we will discuss in more detail later.

Entrepreneurs should first determine the total amount of fixed costs and based on the sales forecasts determine the total variable cost and therefore total cost. By going through this analysis, entrepreneurs can determine if the price that is set for the product is providing enough profit margin. Identifying areas for saving money and cutting costs represents the organization's long-term budget goals. For example, if by learning a new technique of production, time decreases from an hour to 45 minutes, money will be saved. This continuous improvement process is known as *kaizen budgeting* and was developed by Japanese companies to reflect the practice of improvement.[20]

Monitoring performance

In creating a budget, entrepreneurs have to set financial goals of the business. As the year progresses, they can compare the actual performance to the set targets. Many business owners will choose a regular schedule on which to go back to their budget, compare results, and adjust it if necessary. Most will go through this process at the end of each month, although the timing will depend on the cost of such analysis and the responsiveness of the business. Prior to the creation of a budget, the questions outlined in Figure 11.9 need to be answered by the entrepreneur.

Having accurate records helps to answer these questions to the best estimate. Ideally, an entrepreneur shall be able to go beyond the regular "yes" or "no" answers and will be further able to analyze the reasons for any unexpected results. It may also be helpful to compare the results, month to month. Developing a pro forma is essential for an entrepreneur.

For example, an entrepreneur can analyze and decide under different pricing scenarios what would be break-even, positive profit, or negative profit. Entrepreneurs should take note of which costs are having the most impact on profitability and identify any possible ways to keep these down and watch for any particular expenses that are rising. It may be useful also to compare the costs of the current period to the same period in previous years.

When analyzing sales, it can be useful to take note of trends which can be potential opportunities for growth or even threats to profitability. By tracking the sales of each type of product over the course of the year, entrepreneurs may notice that some are becoming more popular while others are selling less. These types of observations become most useful if entrepreneurs can identify possible reasons behind the patterns. For example, consider a business selling small clutches; if the sales of these small clutches started increasing in April, right around the time that a popular actress was seen with a similar style, the entrepreneur should consider producing

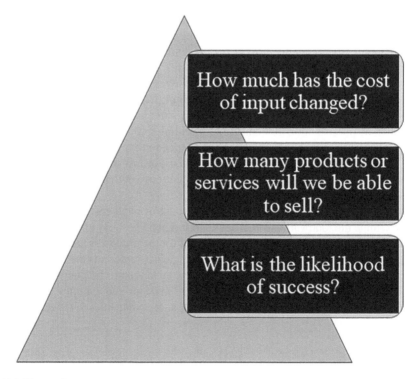

Figure 11.9 Key performance assessments

more in order to capitalize on its current trendiness. Conversely, if sales of a previously popular style have been dropping off, it may be time for the entrepreneur to try a new design more in line with what is becoming fashionable.

Outside financing

As stated before in this book (Chapter 10), it is important to have an accurate bookkeeping when looking for partners in the financial system. Banks and other sources of financing will usually require detailed financial records in order to determine whether or not to extend a loan to business and terms of the loan depend on the financial performance of the business.

Lack of these records is a major barrier to growth for many small businesses in developing economies.[21] Entrepreneurs may decide that to grow more quickly, a new machine is needed as soon as possible. To do this, the entrepreneur would have to ask for a loan from a bank. The bank will want to see documentation of the company's previous period's financial performance to decide how big of a risk they are taking by lending the money. The more evidence the organization shows that it's being profitable, the more likely it is for the bank to provide funds. The basic concept is displayed in Figure 11.10.

Figure 11.10 Base of accounting

Source: "Cash flow stock photo" by lendingmemo_com is licensed under CC BY 2.0. www.flickr.com/photos/146007056@N02/46462500542

Box 11.3   Accountant with an entrepreneurial bug

Accountants have the skills, experience, and knowledge necessary to provide services to a variety of individuals and organizations. Even though accountants are seen as well-paid professionals, many of them are venturing into side businesses in order to make additional income. According to Statista, "In 2011, the revenue of accounting, tax preparation, book-keeping, and payroll services in the U.S. ranged at approximately 120.44 billion U.S. dollars."[22] It was expected that revenue would increase to $160 billion by 2018.

While a large portion of revenue is generated by top accounting firms, such as Deloitte and PricewaterhouseCoopers, smaller operations are in a position to achieve great success as well.

According to MyTopBusinessideas.com, here are the top ten small business ideas for accountants and auditors to peruse:

Bookkeeping
Payroll service
Tax preparation service
Blogging
Freelance writing
Tutoring
Consulting/financial advisor service
Selling accounting software
Microfinance
E-commerce.[23]

Simply by having these records, entrepreneurs also demonstrate that their organization is mature enough and the people in charge are competent leaders of business with adequate financial controls in place. Lack of these factors could be a major concern for many banks and support agencies when dealing with entrepreneurs and small businesses in developing economies.[24]

Box 11.4   Quick review on accounting basics

- An entrepreneur needs to have some basic knowledge of accounting to be able to identify the bottom line, which is critical information for moving forward.
- Financial records tell the story of what is really happening in a business as a whole.
- Total cost is explicit plus implicit costs, which is defined as opportunity cost in economics.
- Financial records serve as a dashboard that show financial viability and to adjust their practices and strategies as necessary. They enable the entrepreneur to set prices for goods or services at a level to make an appropriate profit.
- The budget needs to underline the financial viability, which is a documentation of how much money a business owner plans to spend (expenses) and make (revenue) over a given period of time.

Decision-making

By keeping accurate financial records, entrepreneurs are able to make informed decisions. When deciding which items to produce more or less of, entrepreneurs are better off to have hard numbers instead of a general idea. Entrepreneurs can better anticipate when the company should have more inventory available for sale, or when it will be better to produce at lower volumes.

Entrepreneurs can set realistic goals and create feasible plans for expanding or investing in new equipment. When entrepreneurs need a loan or want to approach an investor, the documentation needed will be readily available.

What records should be kept?

Now that entrepreneurs are convinced that a complete and accurate set of books must be kept, the following sections explain the advantages of being precise. What records constitute the minimum needed to provide an accurate picture of the business's financial position? Answering this question as simply as possible should make an entrepreneur feel that bookkeeping is a manageable task. This section will attempt to outline the basic records needed for an enterprise as it starts growing.

Like businesses everywhere, the exact records needed, and the structure of the business in a developing economy, will depend on the type of business, as well as its size and complexity.[25] There are standards for accounting, usually defined per country, that are defined by organizations such as US GAAP (US generally accepted accounting principles), AASB (Australian Accounting Standards Board), ICAI (Institute of Chartered Accountants of India), and also the IFRS (International Financial Reporting Standards), whose standards provide a common ground for accounting comparison among different countries.[26]

Many startups in developed economies can invest in simple software such as QuickBooks that will walk them through setting up a basic chart of accounts and automate the double-entry process, but this may not be an option for entrepreneurs in developing economies. Without the aid of software, double-entry accounting may be unnecessarily complex to fill the needs of a small business. Most businesses will find that they need to track a few key categories of information (see Figure 11.11).

Budgeting, tracking expenses and revenue, and monitoring performance

In recent years, the importance of accounting and control to entrepreneurship and innovation has increased. The conventional worldview that defined accounting and control as nothing but detrimental to these two facets of management has been challenged by conceptualizations and recent empirical findings.[27] For example, a study of 131 startups in the US retail sector[28] demonstrates the role of strategy into the process of control systems adoption – consistent with contingency theory, the author of that study finds that fit between strategy and "additional controls" adopted is associated with improved performance. Moreover, Wijbenga et al. (2007),[29] analyzing 93 Dutch venture-backed startups, call attention to the impact of venture capitalists whose role goes beyond monitoring on the relationship between the use of cost control and financial performance. These evidence indicate a beneficial effect of formal systems on the growth of startup firms.

Management control systems are usually conceptualized as "formal, information-based routines and procedures managers use to maintain or alter patterns in organizational activities." For the company to have any chance to grow and succeed, accounting and control within startup companies has to be limited to bookkeeping under this view.

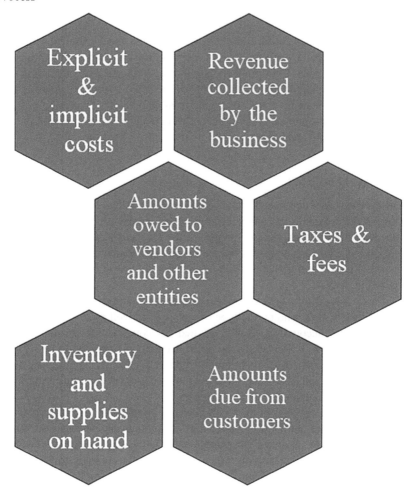

Figure 11.11 Meaningful information

While this information is easier to collect for established businesses, for a startup business, this data may not be as accurate. Accounts payable and receivables and cash on hand can be kept as simple journals. For simple businesses, expenses and revenues can be tracked in a single multi-column journal. Larger businesses with higher expenses and revenue categories may want to keep the two separate. Before creating the journal(s) to record this information, a business owner must take a careful look at the business and determine what expenses are incurred regularly. These must be broken into fixed costs (overhead) and variable costs that change with production levels. Inventory may be the most complex topic to tackle budgeting.

Many business owners may find that determining the expense categories is more difficult than maintaining their books over time and that learning the concepts behind inventory valuation is a challenge. However, taking the time to set up the records properly, in the beginning, will make the information they contain more useful.

Once an entrepreneur has learned some of these basic concepts related to bookkeeping and has set up the books, the entrepreneur will benefit from learning to compile the information into a basic income statement, also known as a profit and loss statement. This will allow entrepreneurs to use financial information in the books to evaluate the profitability of the business.

Box 11.5   The beauty of data visualization

Information can tell us stories, but they are useless without context. David McCandless turns complex data sets (like worldwide military spending, media buzz, Facebook status updates) into beautiful, simple diagrams that tease out unseen patterns and connections. Good design, he suggests, is the best way to navigate information glut and it may just change the way we see the world. Data analysis can even change our perception of reality. More details are available in the TED Talk at www.ted.com/talks/david_mccandless_the_beauty_of_data_visualization#t-1077985

Basics of bookkeeping: journal of revenues and expenses

Large businesses, particularly those that are traded on an exchange, may have strict requirements as to the form and content of the financial records they must keep, but smaller businesses have much greater leeway in making these decisions. However, no matter the size of the business, the primary question that a business owner must answer is "Which alternative provides the most useful information for decision-making purposes?" To help determine this, it is useful to consider two constraints: *cost-benefit* and *materiality*.[30]

There is always a price associated with collecting and storing information which must be weighed against the benefit of the information itself. For a large corporation, this will come in the form of elaborate enterprise resource planning systems, entire departments of additional employees, storage space, and independent auditors. An entrepreneur or a small business owner may invest in a software package to help keep track of finances or may choose to use paper journals, but the most important cost will frequently turn out to be time and effort. An entrepreneur needs to realize the importance of opportunity cost of the extra effort put into using paper journals.

When deciding how to structure the bookkeeping system, entrepreneurs should realize the benefit of adding an extra detail against the amount of time it will take to track it. If the additional information will not add enough value to justify the extra time, then it may be better off with a simpler system. Entrepreneurs can also weigh the value of the time against the cost of paying a bookkeeper to help track the finances. Advantages of hiring a bookkeeper would be avoiding unnecessary wasted time in analyzing laws and procedures that do not belong to the daily activities of the entrepreneur. Some small business owners may even be able to find a bookkeeper that is willing to take payment-in-kind. For example, an entrepreneur could trade a purse or sewing lessons for the services of a bookkeeper. Nevertheless, even if hiring a bookkeeper, the entrepreneur should have a basic knowledge of accounting to be able to understand the reports and make the best use of them.

Box 11.6   Quick review on financial records

- Break-even is the output level in which total revenue minus total cost (explicit plus implicit) is equal to zero.
- It is important that the entrepreneur recognizes that not all costs are the same: there are fixed and variable costs.
- Ideally, with proper records, an entrepreneur shall be able to go beyond the regular "yes" or "no" answers and will be further able to analyze the reasons for any unexpected results.
- Banks and other sources of financing will usually require detailed financial records and depend on the financial performance of the business.
- By keeping accurate financial records, entrepreneurs are enabled to make informed decisions; with this information, entrepreneurs can set realistic goals and create feasible plans for expanding or investing in new equipment.

An entrepreneur must also consider the impact that a transaction will have on the overall financial state of the business. This is known as *materiality*. For an entrepreneur or a small business, most transactions may be material, as each purchase or sale represents a larger percentage of activity than it does for a larger business.

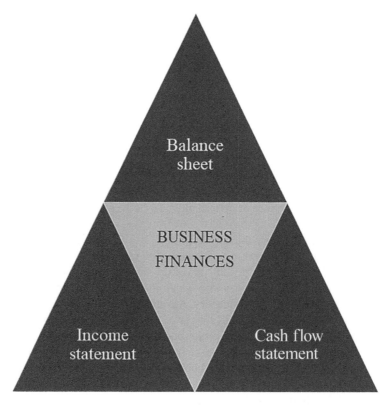

Figure 11.12 Financial Statement

This is especially true for small expenses that are incurred with some frequency. For example, this is easy to see with the materials used to make the products: each clasp may cost only a few cents, but it needs to be included in the cost of each purse. However, the same is true for the bus fare an entrepreneur pays when shopping for the clasps; while each trip may only be a small amount, this will add up over the course of a month or a year. In particular, for an entrepreneur or a small business that plans to grow, it is important to record even the small transactions as they add up eventually. This will allow the entrepreneur to see which expenses are growing fastest as the business becomes larger, as well as which sources of revenue are doing most to fuel the growth.

While larger businesses may benefit from a method known as *double-entry bookkeeping*, this practice would create more complications than it would be worth for most small businesses. For a startup, *single-entry bookkeeping* will allow an entrepreneur to capture all of the information needed to reap the benefits described in the previous section.[31]

At the heart of the single-entry bookkeeping system is the revenue and expense journal, in which entrepreneurs will record the details of all of the business transactions. Every time the business receives money from a customer or pays money to a vendor, it must be recorded in this journal. The revenue and expense journal should be structured in a way that is most useful, capturing all the material information at a level of detail that best informs the decision-making. Sometimes an expert – an accountant – is required (Figure 11.13).

The entrepreneur needs to decide whether to use a single journal for both revenues and expenses, or if it is better to keep two separate journals. This will be discussed in more detail in the following topics.

Figure 11.13 Accountant

Box 11.7   Hiring an accountant

The financial implications of business ownership are extensive yet critical to a company's success. Having a dependable, efficient accounting system can free up your time to focus on the things you love about your business.

Though one can outsource accounting, one has to explore accounting solutions that fit their needs and budget. Consider the following questions that will give you an understanding of your company's needs and help choose the best option:

- What is the size of my company? Small businesses generally have fewer than 20 employees.
- What technology is available to me and my employees?
- Is my understanding of basic accounting up to the task?
- Does my cash flow allow for accounting expenditures on a monthly or annual basis?
- How comfortable am I handing over sensitive business data to an individual or accounting service?
- Is daily data entry something that I or one of my staff can reasonably accomplish?
- Does my company operate in a complex tax environment that may be subject to audit?
- Do my competitors in the industry find a particular method to be most useful?
- Are there compatibility factors to consider with other technological processes that regularly occur, like payroll?

Note that the transactions entered in this journal do not include any instance when an entrepreneur withdraws money for personal use, as this is not an expense of running the business. Identifying revenue and expenses can present several difficulties for entrepreneurs in developing economies, many of whom operate in the informal sector. One of the biggest problems is identifying the expenses associated with the business and separating these from the business owner's cost of living, as the line is not always clear. This makes it even more important that an entrepreneur keeps careful records, beginning with the revenue and expense journal.

The journal can be either a book or an electronic spreadsheet. Traditionally, many small business owners have used a 12-column journal. See Figure 11.14 for what the first five columns should be.

The remaining columns should consist of categories of the expenses and revenues. Table 11.1 is a sample of the spreadsheet.

| Transaction identification | Date | Description | Revenue | Expense |

Figure 11.14 Journal

Table 11.1 Spreadsheet of book of account

Number	Date	Description	Revenue	Expense	Sales revenue	Class revenue
516	1/3/2015	Jana Silva	$275	–	$150	$125

At the end of each month, the entrepreneur will add up each revenue and expense category and record the results. Entering each revenue and expense twice provides a way to double check the accuracy of the entered amount. The sum of the revenue subcategories should equal the total revenue for the month and likewise for the expenses. It is important that entrepreneurs also keep all of the receipts to be able to review, if needed, and also for tax purposes.

An example of a basic revenue and expense journal is provided in Table 11.2.

If entrepreneurs find the need to track revenues and expenses in more detail, then the business needs to use more subcategories than a single revenue and expense journal can provide. In this case, the entrepreneur will set up a separate revenue and expense journal, each with as many subcategories as required. It is important to remember that the purpose of keeping financial records is to provide a business owner with the information required to analyze and evaluate the business performance and to make informed decisions. Entrepreneurs must determine the precise form that will best serve the specific needs of the business and can adjust the system as required.

Based on a sample of 144 responses from a survey of members of the Australian Association of Practice Managers (AAPM), King et al. (2010)[32] identified evidence linking primary healthcare business characteristics, budgeting practices, and business performance, finding that business performance was positively associated with written budgets. Budgeting ensures that a firm is spending the same as it is making, allowing it to plan for short- and long-term expenses. Moreover, factors identified by contingency-based research are useful for predicting a business's budgeting practices. Contingency-based research proposes that there is no single management control system (MCS) suitable for all businesses.[33]

As changes occur, entrepreneurs must take care of the financial records by incorporating the added complexity.[34]

Expenses

In the previous sections, we described many reasons why an entrepreneur needs to have detailed records of the expenses that have been incurred while running the business. We also described the categories into which costs can be divided. Entrepreneurs can use this information to set prices, create budgets, and analyze the financial status of the business.

While the implicit costs do not affect cash flow, they still must be included in any financial analysis to represent the true cost of running the business (see Figure 11.15). Another distinction that warrants a slightly more detailed explanation is that of *fixed* versus *variable* costs.

Furthermore, in addition to helping to establish prices, knowing the difference between direct and indirect costs can be instrumental in preparing your tax returns. This is because certain direct and indirect costs are tax-deductible.

Finally, it is worth mentioning that in the event your firm receives a grant, most will include their own rules pertaining to the type and amount of indirect costs that can be claimed, if any. This is true for government grants and other types of external funding.

Fixed and variable costs

Fixed costs are those which entrepreneurs will have to pay no matter how many units of product or services they are making. This includes the cost of production space (land) and its utilities or any insurance costs, among others. The fixed costs are the costs that do not change with the output, and entrepreneurs should cover them before producing anything. *Variable costs* are those that will increase with the level of production, usually on a per-unit basis.

Table 11.2 Spreadsheet of cash flow

| Company X | | | Type | | Revenue | | | Expenses | | | | |
No.	Date	Description	Revenue	Expense	Retail sales	Classes	Custom orders	Materials	Wages	Supplies and equipment	Travel	Misc.
	2/12/2015	Balance Fwd	2150.00	1810.00	1200.00	250.00	700.00	870.00	400.00	480.00	60.00	55.00
	2/12/2015	Sara	180.00		180.00							
417	2/14/2015	NI Fabric Co.		200.00				200.00				
Cash	2/15/2015	Bus Fare		5.60							5.60	
	2/18/2015	José Renato	60.00		60.00							
418	2/20/2015	J&J Supplies		90.00				70.00		20.00		
	2/21/2015	Marah Ferreira	250.00		125.00	125.00						
	2/21/2015	Isadora Silva	180.00		80.00	100.00						
	2/21/2015	Jana Santos	120.00		120.00							
419	2/22/2015	Martha Harte		100.00					100.00			
TOTAL			2940.00	2205.60	1765.00	475.00	700.00	1140.00	500.00	500.00	65.60	55.00

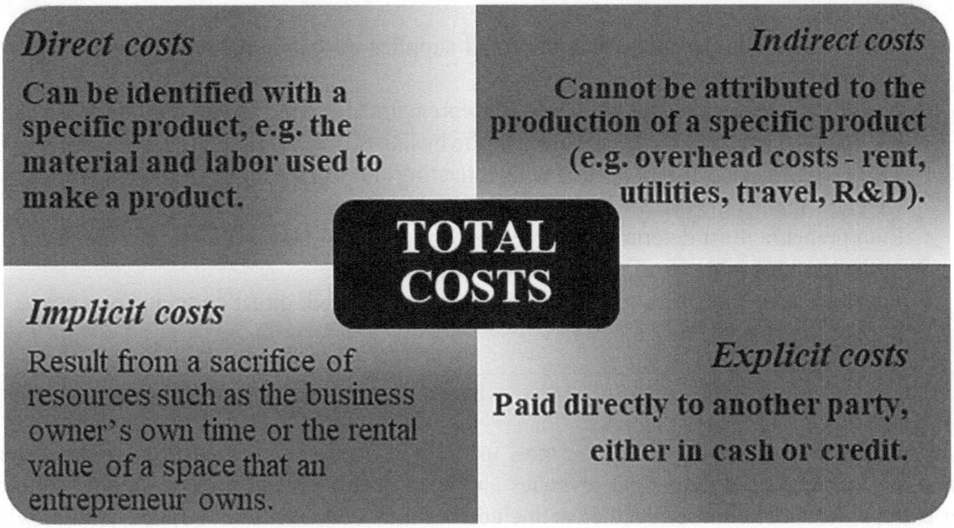

Direct costs	Indirect costs
Can be identified with a specific product, e.g. the material and labor used to make a product.	Cannot be attributed to the production of a specific product (e.g. overhead costs - rent, utilities, travel, R&D).

TOTAL COSTS

Implicit costs	Explicit costs
Result from a sacrifice of resources such as the business owner's own time or the rental value of a space that an entrepreneur owns.	Paid directly to another party, either in cash or credit.

Figure 11.15 Total costs

Note that if an entrepreneur increases production enough, they must move to a larger space and, thus, increase their rental expenses; however, rent is not considered a variable cost because it does not increase with each unit increase in production. With large enough increases in production and a long enough timeline, almost any cost will go up, so we may only consider whether a cost is fixed in the short term. Any direct materials and direct wage labor will be variable costs for the same reason. In the long run, theoretically, there is no fixed cost for businesses.

Some costs may not be either fixed or variable but have properties of both. Consider electricity. Whether a business produces any product or services, the entrepreneur will have to pay a base amount to the utility company. The more product or services produced, the longer the lights need to be kept on, and the more equipment is kept running, the bills will go up proportionally, holding everything else constant.

Sales and revenue

While it is crucial that entrepreneurs track expenses carefully, it is just as important to keep detailed records of revenue. Many of the points of analysis discussed in previous sections require information relating to sales and revenue: tracking overall trends such as seasonality, comparing different methods or locations of sales, or analyzing the popularity and profitability of various products and services.

Box 11.8   Quick review on cost accounting

- There are standards for accounting, usually defined country by country.
- Most businesses will find that they need to track a few key categories of information: explicit and implicit costs, revenue collected by the business, amounts owed to

vendors and other entities, inventory and supplies on hand, and amounts due from customers.
- A profit and loss statement will allow entrepreneurs to use the financial information in the books to evaluate the profitability of the business.
- There is always a price associated with collecting and storing information that must be weighed against the benefit of the information itself.
- Entrepreneurs must determine the precise form that will best serve the specific needs of the business and can adjust the system as required.
- There are four categories into which costs can be divided: direct costs, indirect costs, implicit costs, and explicit costs.

Exactly which comparisons will be most useful will depend on the specific business, thus each entrepreneur must determine revenues and keep detailed records. As mentioned before, an entrepreneur can choose whether to include revenue collections in a single journal with expenses or to capture enough detail about the sources of income in a separate journal. While there are specific rules governing what needs to be reported as income for tax purposes, entrepreneurs should realize that there is an infinite amount of flexibility in the records they keep for themselves.

If an entrepreneur feels the need to know both types of revenue the business is collecting (e.g., sales, service) and its sources (e.g., markets, fairs, online), they can create a journal that allows the tracking of both, simply by including both sets of subcategories and entering each transaction three times instead of two.

Along with information on how much is collected from the customers, entrepreneurs may want to take time to record information about *who* their customers are. While this is not a purely financial record, it can also help to analyze sales and identify purchasing trends according to customer categories. By tracking demographic information, the entrepreneur can learn more about the characteristics of people buying their products: their age, where they live, where they heard about the products, etc. Entrepreneurs can use this information to try to target future sales to similar kinds of people. These records can also help to identify who their regular customers are or if certain customers are helping to spread the word about the company, enabling entrepreneurs to send targeted messages to these key supporters.

Entrepreneurs may want to contact and let regular customers know when a business has a new product they might like or send them a birthday card with a discount coupon to show gratitude. Customer loyalty impacts almost every metric important to running a business. As a rule, new customers tend to cost more to acquire and don't spend as much money as loyal customers.

Accounts payable

In addition to cash transactions, many entrepreneurs and small businesses take advantage of credit extended by vendors or will invoice customers and allow payment within a set timeframe. Businesses that use these extended payment terms must keep records of these transactions separately from the journal of revenue and expense (Figure 11.16).

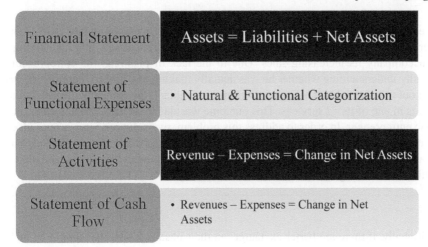

Financial Statement	Assets = Liabilities + Net Assets
Statement of Functional Expenses	• Natural & Functional Categorization
Statement of Activities	Revenue – Expenses = Change in Net Assets
Statement of Cash Flow	• Revenues – Expenses = Change in Net Assets

Figure 11.16 Financial reports

Box 11.9 Accountant consultants can improve revenue performance

Figure 11.17 Accounting consultant

Source: "wocintech (microsoft) – 43" by WOCInTech is marked with CC0 1.0.

https://openverse.org/en-gb/image/f5c30780-aec7-4ac0-bcbc-00783e4a59f4?q=women%20typing%20in%20computer

A cleaning products trading company started its service operation in late 2015 in Brazil. After about 6 months of being in operation, the entrepreneur saw that his earnings did not accompany its increasing sales. Due to the lack of planning, the entrepreneur had difficulty understanding whether he was actually making any profit. Therefore, he had to reach out to a specialist. Through help from a consultant, the company identified that the profit is in one of its 12 services. This outcome was due to its high variable costs, mainly by the entrepreneur. In order to address this problem, two solutions were proposed: either just market one service and increase its prices and sales (which is very unlikely) or cut its variable cost. This short summary highlights the high importance of understanding the details of accounting.

Additionally, if there are barter exchanges in their business, then that should be included in the spreadsheet. An enterprise may have multiple vendors; therefore they should create a record for each vendor that allows paying on the account. This should include all relevant information about the vendor, such as the name of the company, address, and phone number. Along with information about the vendor, an entrepreneur should create a chart to record the details of each credit transaction and include the following information:

- Transaction or invoice date
- Invoice number (if applicable)
- Amount of the transaction
- Due date or transaction terms
- Date paid.

For an account that pays down incrementally, entrepreneurs will also want to include columns for amount paid and account balance. An example of an account record for accounts payable follows the structure shown in Table 11.3. It is important that the entrepreneur tracks the accounts payable carefully and remembers to incorporate them in the planning process. If the accounts payable are growing faster than the revenue stream, it may mean that business is trying to grow faster than the customer base can support it.

Managing accounts payable well is crucial for maintaining good relationships with suppliers.

Table 11.3 Accounts payable

Accounts Payable: Account Record						
Vendor: Que Beleza Fabric				**Contact:** Sandra		
Address:				**Phone:** (21) 9999		
Trans. Date	*Invoice No.*	*Amount*	*Date Due*	*Date Paid*	*Amount Paid*	*Account Balance*
2/19/2021	56	$ 600.00	3/19/2015	3/15/2015	$ 600.00	$ –
3/20/2021	68	$ 625.00	4/20/2015	4/10/2015	$ 625.00	$ –
4/15/2021	82	$ 900.00	5/15/2015	5/15/2015	$ 600.00	$ 300.00

Accounts receivable

It is defined as the amounts a business needs to receive because it has sold its goods or services on credit to a customer (down payment). In this case, businesses will create a record for each customer who pays on an account and will track the amount that is due and how long it takes to collect it. The record will look very similar to that created for accounts payable and an example is shown in Table 11.4.

When extending credit to a customer, it is important that the business makes clear the expected timeframe for repayment and monitors when payments are not coming in as expected.

Inventory

In the process of making a product or a service, an entrepreneur purchases and stores the materials that will be used to create them. To track the costs of a product, businesses must first track the costs of these materials. Additionally, a business must keep a record of the finished products that are available for sale. Inventories can be divided into three types: raw material, work in progress material, and finished goods which are not sold yet.[35] For a business that purchases finished products and resells them, their inventory will consist of *merchandise* available for sale. Some businesses may be required to track the value of their inventory for tax purposes, but it is important for an entrepreneur to track this information for its own use as well.

While the systems used to value inventory in large companies can be very complex, a small business will generally use one of two methods: *specific identification* and *first-in-first-out* (FIFO). Specific identification can be used for items such as the product or services that an entrepreneur makes, or any one of a kind, easily tracked product. FIFO is used for items that are bought in larger quantities and may not be traced easily. FIFO costing assumes that the first item to be placed into inventory is the first item to be used or sold. Accounting textbooks used in college can be a good source of information (Figure 11.18).

Accounting auditing

Auditing often refers to financial statement audits or an objective study and evaluation of a company's financial accounts – frequently conducted by a third party (external auditor).

An audit is a crucial accounting term that refers to reviewing and confirming a company's financial records. It ensures that financial information is accurately and fairly disclosed and are conform to the applicable accounting rules.[36]

Table 11.4 Accounts receivable

Accounts Receivable: Account Record							
Customer:	Marisa Monte			**Phone:**	(21) 9999999		
Address:							
Trans. Date	*Invoice No.*	*Amount*	*Date Due*	*Date Paid*	*Amount Paid*	*Account Balance*	
5/3/2021	150	$ 125.00	6/3/2015	5/28/2015	$ 125.00	$ –	
11/15/2021	215	$ 150.00	12/15/2015	12/17/2015	$ 150.00	$ –	
3/12/2021	232	$ 100.00	4/12/2016			$ 100.00	

Figure 11.18 Accounting college textbooks

Source: "Boring accounting college textbooks" by m01229 is licensed CC. www.flickr.com/photos/39908901@N06/8279563428

The three most essential financial statements are:

- Income statement
- Balance sheets
- Cash flow statement.

Financial statements are designed to offer valuable information to the following audiences:

- Creditors
- Clients
- Suppliers
- Associates
- Shareholders
- Government entities.

A company's operating, investing, and financing activities are reflected in its financial statements through various recorded transactions. Because the financial statements are generated internally, there is a considerable danger of fraud on the part of the statement preparers. Besides, without appropriate restrictions and standards, preparers can readily mislead a company's financial status to make it appear more profitable or successful than it is (see Box 11.1 for an example).

There are three primary audit types:

1 Internal auditing: conducted by company or organization workers. These audits are not shared outside the organization. They are instead designed for usage by management and other internal stakeholders and are needed for improving the company's decision-making process.
2 Conducted by external organizations (independent) and other parties to provide an impartial assessment that internal auditors may be unable to do. For example, external financial audits are used to determine whether a company's financial statements contain any material misstatements or inaccuracies. There are numerous well-established accounting companies that do external audits for a variety of businesses. The Big Four – Deloitte, PricewaterhouseCoopers (PwC); Ernst & Young (EY), and KPMG – are the most well-known working worldwide.[37]
3 Governmental audits: are conducted to ensure that financial statements have been appropriately generated and do not misrepresent a company's taxable income.

Box 11.10   Developing an accounting and auditing architecture in the MNA region

Countries in Middle and North Africa are working with the World Bank to strengthen their international and national financial architecture. The World Bank Group wants to help create an environment in which commercial business can thrive in these nations.

Figure 11.19 Developing an accounting and auditing architecture in the Middle and North Africa – MNA region

Source: "IFLA HQ" is licensed under CC BY-SA 2.0. www.flickr.com/photos/ifla/34825187222/in/photostream/

Thus, Financial Management (FM) has been founded with its key components being to ensure development process, accountability, and efficiency in the management of public resources and promoting private investment and growth. Middle and North Africa (MNA) FM's focus on engaging with MNA countries' systems and working closely with counterparts and other partners to build in-country capacity as they work to ensure the financial integrity of their operations. Since conditions in one country can affect the financial environment of a region or even the world, the World Bank works to strengthen the international and national financial architecture.

These key partnerships have been working towards creating a strong financial architecture by bringing in corporate financial reporting to defined standards. Tapping into its broad and detailed knowledge in accounting, financial management, and auditing, the World Bank hopes to improve financial reporting and bring international standards into practice. It also has both accounting and auditing resources to analyze the country's strengths and weaknesses in financial reporting, compare national accounting and auditing standards with international standards, examine compliance with national standards, and evaluate the strength of enforcement mechanisms. This analysis will help to address gaps and also includes policy recommendations.

Since investors and lenders need reliable financial information to make sound decisions about financing, the World Bank hopes good corporate financial reporting will help promote investment, develop markets, and improve access to credit.

Questions for discussion: accounting and auditing case

1 What initiatives could small business owners make to ensure good corporate financial reporting procedures are followed in their company?
2 List reports that an investor might review before taking the decision to invest in any venture.

Source: Msadek (2009).[38]

US accounting and international accounting

Despite major efforts by the Financial Accounting Standards Board (FASB) and the International Accounting Standards Board (IASB), significant variances remain between United States and international accounting methods. The IASB has consolidated international practices in the International Financial Reporting Standards (IFRS) used worldwide. The IFRS was created to have a common accounting language so that businesses and accounts can be understood from company to company and country to country.

In the United States, FASB establishes and organizes financial reporting methods within the context of generally accepted accounting principles (GAAP).[39] The major accounting differences between GAAP and IFRS are:

* Inventory:

  * Under GAAP, inventory is carried at the lower of cost or market, with the market being defined as the current replacement cost, with some exceptions. Inventory under IFRS is

carried at the lower of cost or net realizable value, which is the estimated selling price minus costs of completion and other costs necessary to make a sale.[40]

- US companies are allowed to use "last in, first out" (LIFO) as an inventory-costing method. A competing set of accounting rules used in the majority of the world prohibits LIFO.[41]

Both systems allow for the first-in, first-out method (FIFO) and the weighted average-cost method.[42]

- Financial statements: Companies that report under IFRS are required to compile and publish a balance sheet, income statement, changes in equity document, cash flow statement, and all associated footnotes. The FASB requires all of these as well and adds in statements about comprehensive income.[43]
- Investments: Recognizing income or profits from an investment. Under GAAP it is mostly dependent on the legal form of the asset or contract; under IFRS the legal form is irrelevant and only depends on when cash flows are received.[44]
- Methodology: GAAP is considered to be rules based, meaning rules are made for specific cases and do not necessarily represent a larger principle. IFRS is principles based and, in that way, more consistent.[45]
- Depreciation of long-lived assets: GAAP does not allow for assets to be revalued; IFRS allows for some revaluation based on fair value, as long as it is completed regularly.[46]

Figure 11.20 shows the eight steps of the accounting cycle: identifying transactions, recording transactions in a journal, posting, the unadjusted trial balance, the worksheet, adjusting journal entries, financial statements, and closing the books.

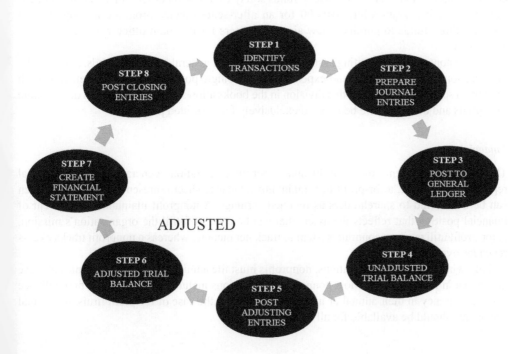

Figure 11.20 Accounting cycle

Accounting for nonprofit organizations

Ownership is one of the fundamental accounting differences between for-profit and nonprofit corporations. Equity is individuals' and entities' ownership (percentages or shares) of a for-profit corporation. In the company's accounting system, the owner's stock or percentage of ownership is documented and may rise or decrease over time. As a result, the owners listed on the books have the right to benefit from the company's activities by receiving dividends or profit distributions or by increasing the number of their ownership shares or percentages due to the company's market success.

It is important to remind that *no one owns* a nonprofit organization. Even if it is formed by one group or is served by its board of directors, these do not own any portion of the business. Following the state's laws in which the nonprofit is established, the board, officers, and employees manage the organization as a public trust. This indicates that in their journal, there are no accounts for owner's equity or retained earnings in the organization's accounting system.

Income and expenses accounting

As stated before in this book, in a general ledger (a single, self-balancing account that represents the business activity of a single organization), for-profit corporations record revenue and expenses typically associated with the sale of products and services. A nonprofit organization does not offer for-profit goods and services that can be accounted for using a standard chart of accounts and general ledger.

Usually, a nonprofit organization's money comes from donations and grants. However, numerous sorts of donations are restricted in their usage, and grants frequently have a self-contained budget that enables the use of funds solely for the agreed-upon in the grant contract. For instance, if a grant allots $10,000 for an after-school dance program, a nonprofit can only use those funds to purchase new air conditioners for the main office with the grantor's agreement.

Thus, a nonprofit's accounting system often consists of general ledgers or funds, allowing the organization to trace revenues and expenditures to a single point of origin. Theoretically, each fund has a separate budget, and this division in the books allows the organization to demonstrate that grants and donations are being used exclusively for permitted purposes.

Financial reports

The accounting systems of for-profit and nonprofit corporations generate different financial reports. For example, a for-profit firm maintains a balance sheet representing its assets, which can be transferred to shareholders as retained earnings. A nonprofit maintains a statement of financial position that reflects the assets that can be used to fulfill the organization's mission. A for-profit utilizes its accounting system to track net income, whereas a nonprofit tracks excess revenues over expenses.

Following each state's regulations, nonprofits must file annual statements (examples of these are shown in Figure 11.15). Most nonprofit organizations include these remarks of compliance and transparency in their annual or impact reports. As in the case of for-profit firms, the annual statements should be available for all stakeholders.

Besides, nonprofits also have a primary responsibility to their donors when filing and sharing these financial statements. Therefore, organizations must follow basic accounting practices when filing these statements and find ways to share these details in ways donors can understand.

Moreover, information like *Financial Statements* also assists nonprofit organizations in determining their path. As a result, board members can better comprehend the growth potential of the organization and uncover prospective financial possibilities and strategies to manage financial challenges.

Remember, "assets" are what the organization owns, which include office supplies and equipment, event supplies, cash, donations, grants, and property. On the other hand, "liabilities" are what the nonprofit organization owes, including long-term liabilities (e.g., car loans and mortgages) or current liabilities, which cover accounts payable debt like salaries and immediate payments.

It is important to highlight that legislation does not allow nonprofits to make a profit, so, liabilities and assets must balance. Net assets are any assets left over after subtracting the liabilities and can come from current and prior fiscal years and comprise anything of value. In the United States nonprofits are not required to itemize their net assets.

The *Statement of Functional Expenses* provides benefactors with further information about how the organization spends its money. To make this task effortless, any expenses incurred by a nonprofit organization must include natural and functional categorization. Therefore, these expenses must be categorized as programs, fundraising, and management (e.g., wages, events, administrative expenditures).

The *Statement of Activities* is used by nonprofit organizations to analyze changes in their net assets and to report income and spending for the accounting period. Directions can be obtained from GAAP and IFRS practices to ensure that the classification of net assets is accurate. A more straightforward way is to classify them as having or lacking donor restrictions.

The significant distinction between nonprofit and for-profit corporations filing a statement of activities is their gross receipts. As revenue, nonprofits use gross receipts rather than gross sales. The organization's net assets are its revenues minus its expenses and cash or accrual accounting can be used to record revenue and expenses by nonprofit organizations. Yet, they frequently adopt the accrual technique because this method allows nonprofits to report revenue as it is earned.

The *Statement of Cash Flow* illustrates how cash enters and exits an organization, providing board members and leaders (or managers) with a better understanding of the available funds for spending. The cash flow in nonprofit organizations can be split in three:

- Operational money: Revenue (like donations, services, and product sales) or expenses (employees' salaries and expenditures on equipment and supplies);
- Investment: Income (amount of interest earned) or expenses (like the acquisition of long-term investments and any payments made in the long term, as in real estate or machinery);
- Financing: Income (earnings and interests) or expenses (the interest paid on loans).

Knowing these fundamental accounting distinctions between for-profit and nonprofit organizations can prevent unpleasant surprises and guarantee that the company complies with state and federal laws for financial accountability and transparency.

Figure 11.21 Wells Fargo Bank

Source: "Wells Fargo Bank" by JeepersMedia is licensed under CC BY 2.0.
www.flickr.com/photos/39160147@N03/14451483160

Box 11.11   Wells Fargo: a case on responsible leadership

Wells Fargo, led by CEO and Chairman John Stumpf, pressured its employees into unethical business practices by conditioning them to go after cross-selling opportunities no matter how detrimental to the customer. By putting such an emphasis on cross-selling and by tying financial performances to unrealistic sales targets, Wells Fargo forced lower-level team members to falsify cross-selling occurrences of their customers so that they could earn bonuses and keep their jobs. This created many negative effects to the customers, including incurring fees for unconsented services, as well as reducing credit scores. To combat negative publicity from these behaviors and the recently fired employees' concerns expressed in the media, Wells Fargo publicly denounced these practices by pointing towards their "Vision, Values, and Code of Ethics" which they hid behind while committing unethical conduct. In addition, they worked quickly to get rid of employees who opposed these practices through a "can the whistleblowers" process by encouraging them to use their ethics hotline and then finding trumped-up charges to fire any employees who utilized it.

   When all of these problems came to light, Wells Fargo failed at scapegoating individual employees for the falsified cross-selling occurrences; leadership was rightfully forced to shamefully resign, and the executive who reported financial misconduct and electronic fraud to the company's whistleblowing channel was fired in 2019. In September 2022, the financial company Wells Fargo was ordered to pay $22 million by the US Department of Labor for violating whistleblower protection laws by improperly firing a senior manager of its commercial banking segment who worked in the Chicago area.

The key problem in this case is the lack of accountability and responsibility of management and executives for the actions that took place under their control. In 2011, Stumpf knew there was a problem but ignored it until the problem became too large to ignore. Several problems are observable. First, it was the top-down pressure from executives. Second, HR executives were being given tips on how to handle the whistleblowers of the company by completely disregarding the dispute resolution policy of Wells Fargo and finding ways to work around the truth in order to get rid of employees who refused to comply with unethical behaviors. Finally, top management strayed from the code of ethics and vision of the company.

Questions for discussion: responsible leadership case

1 If new management were to replace the current one, what checks and balances should be adopted to combat any future mishandling of power?
2 How much control should the HR department possess in a business/company?
3 What decision capabilities should the future HR department of Wells Fargo possess?
4 Relate the agency theory with this case.

For additional information, please view some explanations of the bookkeeping process at the following links:

www.youtube.com/watch?v=5rm1ztHuic8
www.youtube.com/watch?v=yYX4bvQSqbo

Box 11.12   Quick review on bookkeeping for for-profit and nonprofit organizations

• Keeping detailed records of revenue is important to track overall trends such as seasonality, comparing different methods or locations of sales, or analyzing the popularity and profitability of various products and services.
• There is an infinite amount of flexibility in the records kept for themselves, besides those reported as income for tax purposes.
• Accounts payable are transactions that take advantage of credit extended by vendors or will invoice customers and allow payment within a set timeframe. Managing them well is crucial for maintaining good relationships with suppliers.
• Accounts receivable are the amounts a business needs to receive because it has sold its goods or services on credit to a customer (down payment).
• Inventories can be divided into three types: raw material, work in progress material, and finished goods which are not sold yet.

- Nonprofit organizations and for-profit businesses have different financial objectives, and their accounting processes differ.
- For-profit firms generate revenue primarily through sales, they generate revenue primarily through donations and grants. Nevertheless, financial reports should be reported rather concisely and transparently in both cases.

Concluding remarks

The importance of keeping complete and accurate financial records for any business, large or small, cannot be overstated. These records provide a way to analyze past performance and serve as a basis for future planning and forecasting. Without carefully tracking expenses, a business cannot set prices to identify its profitability. Sales records allow a business to be most responsive to the customers' needs and to tailor offerings to the market's needs. Additionally, good bookkeeping may allow an entrepreneur to access additional sources of capital, through outside investors or bank loans.

Understanding terms like assets, liabilities (third parties), and equity (revenue, expenses, dividends) is fundamental to start a general ledger database (records of journal). Also, firms should execute some calculations as the unadjusted trial balance (close one account year), closing balance (the cumulative total of all transactions), and adjusting entries (journal entries that bring the books in line with the accrual method of accounting). For the adjusted trial balance, both accrual methods, IFRS and GAAP, are accepted in the United States. Worldwide, the three main financial statements are the balance sheet, income statement, and cash flow statement.

Nonprofit organizations, like for-profit enterprises, must detail their income and expenses for complete financial transparency. Accounting may facilitate the efficient operation of charitable organizations, indirectly providing many opportunities to bring about change for those in need. On the other hand, nonprofit organizations and for-profit corporations operate under distinct sets of financial accounting regulations. Nonprofit organizations are primarily concerned with accounting for the funds they receive, whereas for-profit enterprises are focused on sustaining profitability.

Although bookkeeping may be one of the most intimidating aspects of running a business for many entrepreneurs and SMEs, it does not need to be daunting. The basic records necessary to capture the activity of business are simple to keep, so long as they are set up properly in the beginning. Setup should not be difficult once the business owner understands how the records will be used; the careful examination of the business during this process can be useful in and of itself.

Accounting for for-profit or nonprofit organizations may require the help of professionals who understand accountancy definitions and have solid educational backgrounds: the accountants. Accountants can maintain the organizations' records in line with state and federal regulations and assist a business in developing strategies and making choices.

Discussion questions

1 Why is learning bookkeeping required?
2 Select a small or medium size firm and analyze its budget.
3 What is the explicit and implicit cost?
4 Describe economic and accounting costs and analyze their implications for entrepreneurship.
5 Are there differences in terms of the application of these issues for developed and developing countries?

Table 11.5 Key terms

Explicit cost	Cost-benefit and materiality
Implicit cost	Materiality
Contribution margin	Double-entry bookkeeping
Cost of goods sold (COGS)	Direct costs
Break-even	Indirect costs
Fixed costs	Accounts receivable
Variable costs	Inventories
Kaizen budgeting	FIFO (first in, first out)
Nonprofit organization	LIFO (last in, first out)

Table 11.6 Glossary

Explicit cost	A cost that is the source of the cash outflow for business activities to which the expense is recognized.
Implicit cost	The opportunity cost to what an entrepreneur must give up to do this job.
Contribution margin	The selling price per unit minus the variable cost per unit.
Cost of goods sold (COGS)	The amount of variable costs.
Break-even	The output level in which total revenue minus total cost (explicit plus implicit) is equal to zero.
Fixed costs	The costs that do not change with the output and entrepreneurs should cover them before producing anything.
Variable costs	The costs that will increase with the level of production, usually on a per-unit basis.
Kaizen budgeting	Continuous improvement process developed by Japanese companies to reflect the practice of improvement.
Nonprofit organization	An organization whose mission and purpose are to further a social cause and provide a public benefit. They include NGOs, hospitals, universities, national charities, and foundations.
Cost-benefit and materiality	Two constraints for decision-making.
Materiality	The significance or importance of information or events in relation to a particular context or situation.
Double-entry bookkeeping	An accounting method used to record financial transactions in which every transaction is entered into at least two accounts, resulting in a balanced equation, benefiting larger companies.
Direct costs	Expenses that can be directly attributed to a particular product, service, or project.
Indirect costs	Other expenses that must be paid to produce the product or services.
Accounts receivable	The amounts a business needs to receive because it has sold its goods or services on credit to a customer (down payment).
Inventories	Divided into three types: raw material, work in progress material, and finished goods which were not sold yet.
FIFO (first in, first out)	This method is used for items that are bought in larger quantities and may not be traced easily. The costing assumes that the first item to be placed into inventory is the first item to be used or sold.
LIFO (last in, first out)	This method assumes that the most recent products in a company's inventory have been sold first and uses those costs instead.

Notes

1 Harris, B. (2023, February 6). How the $3.9bn Americanas scandal has shaken corporate Brazil Mysterious financial hole at heart of retailer has pitted banks against billionaires. *Financial Times*. Retrieved from www.ft.com/content/e7178ec4-1530-4c51-a5b1-cfacabe6c832

2   Retrieved January 28, 2023, from https://ri.americanas.io/informacoes-aos-investidores/central-de-resultados/

3   Araújo, L.J.S. (personal communications in January, 2023). Professor of Department of Accounting and Actuarial Sciences at FEA-USP Universidade de São Paulo. Contact: ljsimoes@usp.br

4   Baker, H.K., Purda-Heeler, L., & Saadi, S. (Ed.) (2020). *Corporate Fraud Exposed*. Bingley: Emerald Publishing Limited. https://doi.org/10.1108/978-1-78973-417-120201036

5   Benjamin, N. (2014, May). *Informal Economy and the World Bank*. World Bank. Retrieved May 25, 2017, from Web. http://documents.worldbank.org/curated/en/416741468332060156/pdf/WPS6888.pdf

6   Kamoroff, B. (2008). *Small Business Operator: How to Start Your Own Business, Keep Your Books, Pay Your Taxes and Stay out of Trouble*. Laytonville, CA: Bell Springs Publishing. Print.

7   Gwartney, J.D., Stroup, R.L., Sobel, R.S., & Macpherson, D. (2008). *Economics: Private and Public Choice*. Cincinnati: South-Western College Publishing. Print.

8   De Toni, D., Milan, G.S., Saciloto, E.B., & Larentis, F. (2017). Pricing strategies and levels and their impact on corporate profitability. *Revista de Administração*, 52(2), 120–133. https://doi.org/10.1016/j.rausp.2016.12.004. Retrieved from www.sciencedirect.com/science/article/pii/S0080210716308299

9   Survey of Global Investment and Innovation Incentives. (2017, March). Retrieved May 25, 2007, from www2.deloitte.com/global/en/pages/tax/articles/global-investment-and-innovation-incentives-survey.html

10 Suharsono, R.S., Nirwanto, N., & Zuhroh, D. (2020). Voluntary disclosure, financial reporting quality and asymmetry information. *Journal of Asian Finance, Economics and Business*, 7(12), 1185–1194, 1185. Online ISSN 2288-4645; https://doi.org/10.13106/jafeb.2020.vol7.no12.1185

11 Moerman, D.E. (2006). The role of information asymmetry and financial reporting quality in debt trading: Evidence from the secondary loan market. *Journal of Accounting and Economics*, 46(2–3), 240–260. https://doi.org/10.1016/j. jacceco.2008.08.001. Retrieved from www.sciencedirect.com/science/article/abs/pii/S0165410108000505

12 Newman, P. (2006, September 15). *Setting Competitive and Profitable Prices*. Retrieved April 9, 2009, from www.entrepreneur.com/article/167198

13 Ahnad, Y.J., & Lutz, E. (1989). Environmental accounting for sustainable development. In *The World Bank Symposium* (p. 118). Washington: The World Bank.

14 Kokubu, K., & Nashioka, E. (2005). Environmental management accounting practices in Japan. In P.M. Rikhardsson, M. Bennett, J.J. Bouma, & S. Schaltegger (Eds.), *Implementing Environmental Management Accounting: Status and Challenges. Eco-Efficiency in Industry and Science* (Vol. 18). Dordrecht: Springer. https://doi.org/10.1007/1-4020-3373-7_16

15 Japan. Ministry of Environment – Moe. (2002). *Environmental Accounting Guidelines 2002 Version*. Tokyo. Retrieved from www.env.go.jp/content/900453353.pdf

16 Horngren, C.T., Datar, S.M., Rajan, M.V., & Foster, G. (2008). *Cost Accounting: A Managerial Emphasis* (p. 221). Hoboken: Prentice Hall. Print.

17 Rambo, C.M. (2013). Time required to break-even for small and medium enterprises: Evidence from Kenya. *International Journal of Management and Marketing Research, The Institute for Business and Finance Research*, 6(1), 81–94. Retrieved from www.theibfr2.com/RePEc/ibf/ijmmre/ijmmr-v6n1-2013/IJMMR-V6N1-2013-5.pdf

18 Ndaliman, M.B., & Suleiman, U.Y. (2011, June). An economic model for break-even analysis conference. In *2nd International Conference on Mechanical and Manufacturing Engineering (ICME 2011)*. Putrajaya, Malaysia: PICC.

19 Rambo, C.M. (2013). Time required to break-even for small and medium enterprises: Evidence from Kenya. *International Journal of Management and Marketing Research*, 6(1), 81–94. Retrieved from www.theibfr2.com/RePEc/ibf/ijmmre/ijmmr-v6n1-2013/IJMMR-V6N1-2013-5.pdf

20 Horngren, C.T., Datar, S.M., Rajan, M.V., & Foster, G. (2008). *Cost Accounting: A Managerial Emphasis* (p. 221). Hoboken: Prentice Hall. Print.

21 Bartlett, W., Bateman, M., & Vehovec, M. (2002). *Small Enterprise Development in South-East Europe: Policies for Sustainable Growth*. Boston: Kluwer Academic. Print.

22 Statista. (2014). *Revenue of Accounting, Tax Preparation, Bookkeeping, and Payroll Services (NAICS 5412) in the United States from 2008 to 2018 (in Million U.S. Dollars)*. Statista Research Department. Retrieved from www.statista.com/forecasts/311178/us-accounting-tax-preparation-bookkeeping-and-payroll-services-revenue-forecast-naics-5412

23 Top 10 Small Business ideas for Accountants & Auditors 2018. (n.d.). Retrieved from www.profitableventure.com/accountants-and-auditors/

24 Diaz-Briquets, S., & Weintraub, S. (1991). *Migration, Remittances, and Small Business Development: Mexico and Caribbean Basin Countries*. Boulder: Westview. Print.

25 Lawrence, S. (1996). Accounting problems of developing countries. In *International Accounting* (p. 421). Boston: Cengage Learning Business Press.

26 International Financial Reporting Standards. (2017, May 18). *In Wikipedia, The Free Encyclopedia*. Retrieved from https://en.wikipedia.org/w/index.php?title=International_Financial_Reporting_Standards&oldid=78101246

27 Davila, A., Foster, G., & Oyon, D. (2009). Accounting and control, entrepreneurship and innovation: Venturing into new research opportunities. *European Accounting Review*, 18(2), 281–311. https://doi.org/10.1080/09638180902731455. Retrieved from www.tandfonline.com/doi/abs/10.1080/09638180902731455?journalCode=rear20

28 Sandino, T. (2007). Introducing the first management control systems: Evidence from the retail sector. *The Accounting Review*, 82(1), 265–293. Retrieved from www.jstor.org/stable/30243464

29 Wijbenga, F.H., Postma, T.J.B.M., & Stratling, R. (2007). The influence of the venture capitalist's governance activities on the entrepreneurial firm's control systems and performance. *Entrepreneurship: Theory and Practice*, 31(2), 257–277. https://doi.org/10.1111/j.1540-6520.2007.00172.x. Retrieved from https://journals.sagepub.com/doi/10.1111/j.1540-6520.2007.00172.x

30 Kieso, D.E., Weygandt, J.J., & Warfield, T.D. (2010). *Intermediate Accounting*. Hoboken, NJ: John Wiley & Sons. Print.

31 Fox, J. (1994). *Accounting and Recordkeeping Made Easy for the Self-Employed*. New York: John Wiley. Print.

32 King, R., Clarkson, P.M., & Wallace, S. (2010). Budgeting practices and performance in small healthcare businesses. *Management Accounting Research*, 21(1), 40–55. https://doi.org/10.1016/j.mar.2009.11.002. Retrieved from www.sciencedirect.com/science/article/abs/pii/S1044500509000602

33 Covaleski, M., Evans III, J., Luft, J., & Shields, M. (2006). Budgeting research: Three theoretical perspectives and criteria for selective integration. *Handbooks of Management Accounting Research*, 2, 587–624. https://doi.org/10.1016/S1751-3243(06)02006-2. Retrieved from www.sciencedirect.com/science/article/pii/S1751324306020062

34 Pinson, L. (2007). *Keeping the Books*. Chicago: Dearborn. Print.

35 Brigham, E.F., & Houston, J.F. (2012). *Fundamentals of Financial Management*. Boston: Cengage Learning.

36 https://corporatefinanceinstitute.com/resources/accounting/what-is-an-audit/

37 https://big4accountingfirms.org/the-top-accounting-firms-in-the-world/

38 Msadek, S. (2009, March). *Accounting and Auditing Practices & Development Effectiveness. MENA Knowledge and Learning Quick Notes Series No. 4*. Washington, DC: World Bank. Retrieved from https://openknowledge.worldbank.org/bitstream/handle/10986/10993/517920BRI0MENA10Box342050B01PUBLIC1.pdf?sequence=1&isAllowed=y

39 American Institute of Certified Public Accountants. *Is IFRS That Different from U.S. GAAP?* Durham: American Institute of Certified Public Accountants. Retrieved from: http://www.ifrs.com/overview/General/differences.html

40 Grant Thornton. *Comparison between U.S. GAAP and IFRS Standards* (pp. 57–59). Chicago: Grant Thornton LLP.

41 American Institute of Certified Public Accountants. *International Financial Reporting Standards*. Durham: American Institute of Certified Public Accountants. Retrieved from: https://www.ifrs.com/pdf/IFRSUpdate_V8.pdf

42 U.S. Securities and Exchange Commission. *A Comparison of U.S. GAAP and IFRS* (pp. 20–21). Washington: U.S. Securities and Exchange Commission. Retrieved from: https://www.sec.gov/spotlight/globalaccountingstandards/ifrs-work-plan-paper-111611-gaap.pdf

43 Grant Thornton. *Comparison between U.S. GAAP and IFRS Standards* (pp. 16–20). Chicago: Grant Thornton LLP.

44 Ernst & Young. *US GAAP Versus IFRS: The Basics* (pp. 22–23). London: Ernst & Young. Retrieved from: file:///C:/Users/UAB%20UNIFESP/Downloads/ey-ifrs18670-231us-08-23-2023.pdf

45 U.S. Securities and Exchange Commission. *A Comparison of U.S. GAAP and IFRS* (pp. 8–11). Washington: U.S. Securities and Exchange Commission. Retrieved from: https://www.sec.gov/spotlight/globalaccountingstandards/ifrs-work-plan-paper-111611-gaap.pdf

46 Ernst & Young. *US GAAP versus IFRS* (p. 15). London: Ernst & Young. Retrieved from: file:///C:/Users/UAB%20UNIFESP/Downloads/ey-ifrs18670-231us-08-23-2023.pdf

12 Cases

Case I

Philips Company, the Dutch multinational conglomerate (1891–present)

Introductions and background

In the following longitudinal case, we are evaluating Philips Company since its inception in 1891. We examine the company from the perspectives of the main topics of each chapter of the book. In otherwards, the company is evaluated through the lenses of the important subject's overtime. This case may serve as a review of the book through Philips, a creative and sustainable company for more than a century. In general, the case is organized as a review of the chapter. At the end of the case, we have added a few questions for discussions and evaluation.

The company Philips was founded in 1891 by Gerard Philips and his father Frederik Philips. Gerard had an early interest in electronics and engineering. He frequently got business help from his brother, and this became a family business. Gerard supported education and social initiatives in Eindhoven[1] in the Netherlands. He enrolled in the mechanical engineering department at the Polytechnic School. Before going into business with his father, Gerard joined the Anglo-American Brush Electric Light Corporation which was one of the largest electric lighting companies at the time. He combined the activities of an entrepreneur-manufacturer with the work of a manager and constructor. He didn't only excel in the engineering labor department; he also did a lot of research because he realized that an innovation can only be successful if a person has knowledge and not only experience. He also held several other supervisory positions. On January 8, 1917, the senate of the Technische Hoogeschool in Delft, through the promoter W. Reinders, awarded him the doctorate honoris causa in technical sciences. Overall, Gerard can be described as a driven entrepreneur who excelled in various departments. He also took advantage of the education he received and applied his success throughout his entrepreneurship. Some people have different opinions on whether you need an educational experience to be a successful entrepreneur; Gerard would argue that with education comes knowledge, and that's what puts you ahead of others.

Anton Philips was born on March 14, 1874. He was the co-founder of Philips along with his brother Gerard and their father Frederik. During World War I Anton Philips took advantage of the boycott on German goods, which occurred in multiple countries. This was a big boost in sales for Philips. They were supporters of multiple educational and social programs/facilities. Anton brought his son Frits and son-in-law Frans Otten into the company. During the Nazi Occupation in World War II, Anton, Otten, and multiple other family members escaped to the United States. Anton's son Frits decided to stay and manage the company during occupation. He

DOI: 10.4324/9781003405740-17

Figure 12.1 Philips at Eindhoven
Source: www.flickr.com/photos/56537760@N03/30961706956

was imprisoned at the Vught concentration camp. Frits was able to save 382 Jews by claiming them indispensable to his factory, which allowed all of them to leave the camp. He was awarded the Order of Saint Sava by the State of Israel in 1996.[2] Anton Philips died in Eindhoven, the Netherlands, on October 7, 1951.

Philips Company mission and values

Philips is very focused on not only improving the lives of employees, but also the lives of others. When looking for an employee to join the team at Philips, not only should the employee have adequate experience in the health technology field, but they should also have the personality to join a socially responsible environment that focuses on improving the lives of others. The Philips mission is to make people's lives better through meaningful innovation. Keeping this promise depends on their passionate, inspirational, collaborative, and diverse team. Being like-minded, motivated, and focused allows them to create a healthier, more connected society while transforming themselves personally and professionally.

Philips operates in several different markets, including healthcare, lighting, and consumer electronics. As a company that values innovation and technology, Philips places a significant emphasis on training its employees to stay up to date with the latest industry trends and best practices. The company offers a variety of training programs and resources for its employees. One of the primary ways that Philips trains its employees is through its Learning Management System (LMS). This system allows employees to access a wide range of online training courses, which cover topics such as leadership development, technical skills, and compliance training. The LMS also provides employees with personalized learning plans and tracks their progress, allowing them to focus on areas where they need the most improvement. Philips helps their employees track themselves to help improve their work, making it easier to find placements for employees. In addition to online training, Philips also offers in-person training programs, including workshops, seminars, and conferences. These events provide employees with opportunities to learn from industry experts, network with colleagues, and share best practices. Philips also encourages its employees to take advantage of external training opportunities, such as industry certifications and courses offered by universities and other educational institutions. Through these training Philips ensures that its workforce is equipped with the skills and knowledge necessary to drive innovation and maintain its position as a leading technology company.

Globalization

Philips has embraced globalization and leveraged its benefits to become a leader in the technology and healthcare sectors.[3] Philips has adopted several entrepreneurial strategies in the age of globalization, such as innovation, collaboration, and market expansion. Innovation has been the driving force behind Philips' success, as the company constantly invests in research and development (R&D) to create cutting-edge products and services. Globalization has also allowed Philips to expand its market presence across the globe. The company's operations span over 100 countries, with manufacturing and R&D centers in Europe, North America, and Asia. Philips has strategically acquired and merged with local companies in emerging markets to strengthen its foothold and better cater to the needs of its diverse customer base.

As a global company, Philips has recognized the importance of adapting to cultural differences and has incorporated this into its corporate culture. The company promotes inclusivity and diversity, ensuring that its employees feel valued and respected, regardless of their cultural background. This has not only allowed Philips to attract a diverse workforce but has also facilitated its understanding of local markets and the development of tailored products and services.

Philips has established manufacturing facilities and sourcing networks in various countries to ensure that its products are available and affordable in different markets. By sourcing locally, Philips has been able to adapt to local market conditions, leverage local resources and talent, and reduce production costs. Additionally, Philips has established partnerships with local distributors and retailers in different countries to ensure that its products are widely available and accessible to consumers. The company has also invested in online channels, such as its e-commerce platform, to reach customers in remote or underserved regions. Their website reaches more than 57 countries in more than 35 languages, all while making adaptations to local market preferences.

R&D is a main focus for the company. The companies must continually invest in R&D to remain competitive and that the global market provides opportunities for collaboration and knowledge sharing. The company's areas of expertise, such as electronics, healthcare, and lighting, have led to products such as its Sonicare toothbrush, Hue smart lighting system, and magnetic resonance imaging machines. Philips Company's innovation has helped it maintain a competitive edge in the global market.

Philips has acquired and partnered with local companies, such as Respironics in the United States and WOOX Innovations in China, to gain a better understanding of the local market and to leverage their local expertise and networks. These acquisitions and partnerships have allowed the company to expand its product offerings and increase its market share in different regions.

Philips has successfully expanded its brand globally through its various globalization strategies. By developing a strong global supply chain, vast and secure global distribution networks, a focus on innovation, and acquiring/partnering with local companies, Philips has been able to adapt to local market conditions and reach customers in different regions. As a result, Philips has established itself as a leading multinational technology company with a presence in over 100 countries.

Expansion into Africa and Middle East market

Philips wanted to turn struggles for the African community into opportunities, and by that, the company decided to turn health services in Africa to an easy process by partnering with the government of Kenya and the UN in order to make the process smoother.[4] This initiative aimed at strengthening primary and community-based healthcare in Africa, and as the leading health technology company, Philips is coming on board as the first private sector partner to establish a Sustainable Development Goals Partnership Platform in Kenya for accelerating primary healthcare transformation in support of universal health coverage. This unique partnership will bring opportunities from both sides as the government will provide executive leadership, development partners, private sector organizations and civil society to investigate chances for accelerating universal access to primary healthcare services in Kenya.[5] This collaboration mainly focuses on improving the gaps in human resources, healthcare financing, essential medicines, medical supplies, health information, and the use of technology. Philips is providing full support to this by working on establishing a common fact-based approach to primary healthcare, by improving current and future healthcare needs, designing, and implementing transformative initiatives in pursuit of the platform's ambitions. What is good about Philips's expansion in Africa is that they believe that strengthening local healthcare systems is central, and they have been dedicated to advancing primary healthcare in Africa for a long time, with a strong focus on mother and child care.[6]

Also, Philips is collaborating with the UN Population Fund (UNFPA) and the government of the Republic of Congo to improve access to maternal and child healthcare for a target population of 500,000 inhabitants. A company like Philips and how focused they are on the African market should be taken as an example of how a fast-driven industry should be. All companies should look forward to improving a lot of markets throughout the world, especially third world countries, and to give them as many opportunities as other advanced markets have. Philips is also taking huge steps in the Middle East and Turkey by introducing new advanced technologies to the markets. They have faced many political instability and major competitors throughout the process, but that has not stopped them from expanding in the region. Philips is committed to making the world healthier.

Innovation and creativity

Throughout the 1900s, Philips expanded greatly and became the largest private employer in the Netherlands. The company held its values of research, curiosity, and social responsibility high in its business model, and eventually began producing technologies for the post-war world. Their product line soon expanded to include small projectors, cassette players, and eventually, the groundbreaking compact disc (CD). In the late 1900s, Philips technology began entering the medical field and soon became the leader in health technology through to the 2010s. Their business strategy today is centered around continued, people-focused innovation in the healthcare industry.

In reflecting on the history of Philips Company, it is evident that creativity and innovation have played a crucial role in the success of the business. The brand's innovation began with the creation of the company itself and the decision to explore new technologies in the electricity industry. Their initial plan of creating cost-efficient, reliable light bulbs was at first considered bold; however, Philips was able to prove to consumers over time that their brand was dedicated to continued innovation and delivering value through their wide range of products. Transitioning from light bulbs to entertainment products and now to health technology, Philips has demonstrated a clear ability to think outside of the box and find new ways to meet changing consumer needs.

Successful entrepreneurs must have an innovative mindset in order to identify unmet market needs and develop a creative solution to meet them. As seen by the history of Philips, the company has been innovative since the beginning. From selling light bulbs to creating new medical technologies, Philips Company reflects a long line of innovative, curious individuals who are constantly looking to solve consumer problems.[7]

Governance and strategy

Philips has built foundations for a sustainable organization that has last since 1891. Effective corporate governance is an issue that has really only been heavily looked at in recent years. Prior to this, investors and stakeholders only cared about profits. However, now companies are required to fully embrace effective corporate governance, and Philips definitely does. First, Philips holds annual shareholder meetings to understand shareholder opinions on various issues and how they hope the company should go forward. The firm has employed strict risk management principles and procedures that stem across the entire firm to ensure safe products and the mitigation of various financial risks. The firm also hires external auditors to validate the firm's financial statements and notes to the financial statements to ensure that the firm is not committing fraud and that the data they are presenting is accurate. Philips focuses on fair and equitable hiring practices that have an emphasis on diversity and creating an inclusive environment for LGBTQ+ members. However, we did notice that Philips has a noticeable lack of diversity on their executive committee, as there are only two women, and it consists of mostly white men. In terms of the past, there is a lack of available data on prior governance issues, but it is clear that the firm now has a focus on creating a diverse and inclusive environment.

Philips has made a point to have a consistent policy that optimizes their governance in line with Dutch, US, and international best practices. They want to give long-term value to the shareholders and customers, and they live up to the standards of ethics and governance that are kept highly in their culture. Philips has a board of management and a supervisory board that both have accountable and able-bodied workers that aim to meet their high standards and continue the connection between their staff, shareholders, and employees. The board of management is supported by key officers that consult their executive committee by being transparent, honest, and understanding to their shareholders and the people above them.[8] The Philips business system defines how they work together to reach the needs of their customers and it helps them strive towards company goals. The model consists of key components that are performance, strategy, governance, culture, processes, and people.[9]

Philips underwent a transformation to refocus itself on healthcare and technology for the reasons of growing population and high demand for access to healthcare. They are focusing on growth but have a heavy emphasis on providing value and creating sustainable growth. They achieve this growth by investing and utilizing state-of-the-art technology, which not only creates value but allows for patients to have one less thing to worry about. This goes both for hospital care and for care at home because they have a diversified number of products depending on the needs of the customer. That's why they focus on smaller products, but anything they create has huge potential to help a large number of customers. Then with improved execution, the patient's safety and quality is the main goal of their innovation and embedded into their culture. Supply chain reliability is major because they shifted from one size fits all to more of a one-on-one business and products. A simplified operating model allows for more flexibility and is able to focus more on the patients.

On Philips' "Strategy" web page, they state theirs is a "strategy of focused organic growth, founded on clear choices in business and innovation, and improved execution." Because strategy and leadership are closely linked, it can be inferred that the leadership behind Philips made the conscious decision to develop along with the times as one of the most influential technology companies in the world. They say, for example, that "over the past 10 years, Philips has undergone a transformation to reshape its portfolio and become a focused health technology company." Such a focused strategy is needed in an ever-shifting and increasingly globalized world.[10]

Corporate social responsibilities

According to Philips, they are committed to supporting sustainability and strive for social accountability to employees, stakeholders and consumers. The company is focused on doing business responsibly and sustainably as part of their CSR and HRM strategy with commitments to environmental, social and corporate governance (ESG).

From an environmental standpoint, Philips is making strides to take climate action. By doing so, they are working with suppliers to take appropriate steps in regard to minimizing their environmental footprint (e.g., reducing carbon emissions) as well as creating EcoDesigns for their products. Philips uses the UN Sustainable Development Goals (SDGs) to ensure they are embedding sustainability into their deeper work culture. They achieved all their environmental targets back in 2020 and hope to keep proceeding in the future.

From a social standpoint, Philips will work alongside Movember for the first time this year to help better men's life. In fact, they state that they want to improve "2.5 billion lives per year, with 400 million in underserved communities by 2030." Since "Movember has funded more than 1250 men's health projects around the world focused on mental health and suicide prevention, prostate cancer and testicular cancer," Philips decided to donate $400,000 to the organization this year. This is a great social policy to have as men's health, especially mental health, has been demanding more recognition from society as what men feel is usually discredited or completely ignored. The company's commitment to sustainability and social accountability demonstrates how a responsible and forward-thinking organization can make a positive impact on society and the environment.

By aligning with the UN Sustainable Development Goals and focusing on both environmental and social aspects, Philips has showcased its dedication to addressing pressing global challenges.[11] The company's collaboration with Movember, for instance, illustrates its strong commitment to improving men's health and well-being.

Philips' success in achieving its environmental targets and its ongoing efforts in the areas of CSR and HRM serve as an inspiring example for other businesses to follow. As demonstrated by Philips, incorporating sustainable and socially responsible practices into a company's core strategy is not only beneficial for the environment and society but can also contribute to the overall success and reputation of the organization. By prioritizing ethics, CSR, and HRM, companies can create lasting value for their stakeholders and play a crucial role in shaping a better future for all.

Marketing

The company has a great marketing strategy to supply and have high sales, considering its primary target market is the high middle class. Today, Philips has several different products but focuses on the technology sector, specifically in lighting and healthcare.[12]

Philips has incredible marketing strategies, focusing on simple but good-quality materials and products. For starters, the firm's mission is to "improve people's lives through meaningful innovation."[13] With that, across all countries where they sell its products, it focuses on promoting a better quality of life for its consumers. Philips has their own e-commerce and sells to third parties, such as Amazon. Their marketing strategy focuses primarily on promoting innovation and what is necessary for consumers' lives. They are aware of all the changes that should be made to consumers' daily life, and then they work to benefit and promote a better quality of life with their products. Furthermore, Philips offers competitive pricing, prices that are similar to its competition, despite having better quality products than their rivals.[14]

Philips focuses mainly on social media and internet advertisement for their marketing strategy. This is because they have already made a name for themselves and need to maintain their quality. However, they use the internet to engage with more customers or make already existing customers aware of all their products. The internet today is one of the most used media sources for advertisement, which plays a significant role in promoting any brand. Further to internet marketing, the company has started to focus on sustainability to connect with consumer's values on a more personal level as well. Philips is able to keep up with the latest trends which has allowed them to take a favorable position and a key portion of the market share.

Financing

Philips was financed by a banker based in Zaltbomel, Netherlands, who provided Gerard Philips and his father with an empty factory building. Gerard Philips and his father began producing lamps in this factory. After a few years of business, the company faced many issues with the threat of bankruptcy. To help this issue, Gerard brought his brother, who had an innovative spirit, into the business, and he came up with revolutionary ideas that would cause their business to grow and gain a larger customer base. As the company started reaching its roll out stage, it began to partner with other companies such as Osram Licht AG to create new products and reach new markets. These partnerships allowed for Philips to repay their debt and come out of the threat of bankruptcy. The company also had to be spontaneous during World War II. The Philips family took a large amount of money with them to the US and operated their business successfully throughout WW2 from overseas as North American Philips Company. During times of political upheaval, it is important for a business to change its operations to become more efficient. In the 1980s Philips saw their profit margin decrease rapidly, which caused them to create a plan to help their business. They created various joint ventures with other companies to help support their company. More recently, Philips decided to change their focus from electronics to healthcare to better support the world they are in and help their company thrive.

This took financial restructuring to ensure that it would be feasible and generate higher returns in the future. Philips used a combination of bonds, forward contracts, leases, and loans from banks to fund their business activities, and through their innovative products and talented team, they were able to avoid bankruptcy and continue to strengthen.[15]

In its early years, the firm mostly depended on equity funding from family and friends, a common financing strategy for startups. This first cash investment enabled the firm to engage in R&D, resulting in the development of novel goods and the subsequent growth into new markets.

The Philips Company had developed greatly by the early 20th century and needed extra money to continue its expansion. The book points out that established enterprises frequently seek equity funding through public offerings in order to have access to bigger capital pools. The Philips Company went public in 1912, placing its shares on the Amsterdam Stock Exchange.[16] This action supplied the company with the capital it needed to create subsidiaries in Europe and North America, allowing it to become a worldwide player.

The history of the Philips Company also demonstrates how firms may use equity finance to buy and invest in other enterprises, a technique highlighted in the book as well (Asgary et al., 2019). Throughout the 1920s and 1930s, for example, the company purchased many radio makers, acquiring a dominant position in the radio market. Later, in the 1960s and 1970s, it used its strong financial position to invest in the emerging semiconductor industry. These acquisitions not only diversified the company's product line but also offered access to new technology and markets.

Even though Philips has been around since 1891, most of the available data on the company's financials only dates to around 2009. The company initially started out as a lighting company and then concentrated on electronics, but today it is a company focused on healthcare and medical technology. With that in mind, it has had some variance in revenue and sales from 2009 to 2022. From the data available in Figure 12.2, Philips had revenue of roughly €18.15 billion in 2009, and with the success and expansion of its business units, the company reached a peak

Philips' revenue worldwide from 2009 to 2022

(in billion euros)

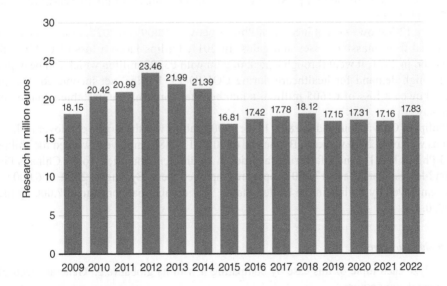

Figure 12.2 Philips revenue graph

Source: www.statista.com/statistics/272107/philips-revenue-worldwide-since-2006/

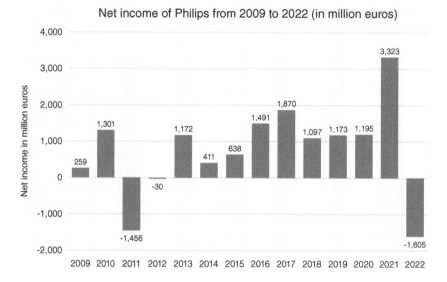

Figure 12.3 Net income of Philips 2009–2022, in million euros

Source: www.statista.com/statistics/272109/philips-electronics-net-income-worldwide-since-2006/

revenue of €23.46 billion in 2012. In April 2017, Philips Lighting became a discontinued operation due to sell-downs by Philips and would become a stand-alone company. The figures since 2015 have been restated accordingly, which also represents the drop in revenue to €16.81 billion that year. Since then, the company has had slow but steady growth even as it dealt with supply chain shortages and other issues due to the COVID-19 pandemic from 2020 to present and as it continues to deal with the Philips Respironics recall and impacts of the Russia-Ukraine war in 2022 and beyond.

Figure 12.3 shows the net income of Philips between 2009 and 2022. In fact, the company fluctuated from massive losses and gains. In 2011, Philips faced a loss of €1456 million. However, in 2021, it went through a peak of gain with €3323 million which can be explained by the high demand for healthcare during COVID-19. Philips' net income for the end of 2022 showed a loss of €1605 million, a number that confirms the unstable situation of the company.

Philips & Co was founded in 1891. In the 1900s Philips was the largest employer in the Netherlands with over 2000 workers. By the end of 2011, 121,888 employees worked for Philips. By 2013 Philips had 111 manufacturing facilities in 26 different countries. Today China is Philips' second-largest market and 17,500 people are employed there. By August 2020, 156,000 people were employed by Philips in the United States. That number ballooned to 187,000 by the end of 2020.

Discussion questions

1 Analyze each topic of this case by comparing it with its global (e.g., General Electric) and regional competitors.
2 Examine how the company has overcome its challenges through time.
3 Draft a case similar to this one.

Case II

Entrepreneurship in education: the case of ESCA Ecole de Management[17]

In recent years, there has been a growing interest in promoting entrepreneurship in Africa as a driver of job creation, poverty reduction, innovation, and global competitiveness. Several studies have identified the challenges faced by entrepreneurs in Africa, including limited access to capital, poor infrastructure, inadequate legal and regulatory frameworks, and a lack of entrepreneurial skills and education.[18] Despite these challenges, there are numerous examples of successful African entrepreneurs who have created innovative businesses that have had a positive impact on their communities.[19] ESCA Ecole de Management is one of these examples that has marked the higher education area in Africa, and Morocco in particular. The school is the first independent business school recognized by the State in Morocco and the first AACSB accredited in French-speaking Africa. First ranked in Morocco by Eduniversal 2022, it is located at the heart of Casablanca Finance City, the most important financial hub in Africa that comprises the headquarters of national and international financial institutions and companies, with a campus that has a capacity of more than 2000 students. ESCA Ecole de Management has demonstrated its leadership in Moroccan higher education thanks to its deep entrepreneurial spirit and innovative culture.

The edupreneurship spirit

ESCA Ecole de Management was founded by Thami Ghorfi, one of the most prominent edupreneurs in Morocco. After his graduation from ISG-Paris and ESSEC Business School, Thami started his entrepreneurship journey by launching several businesses delivering marketing and management consulting services and achieving editing projects. In 1992, he decided to return to Morocco and create ESCA Ecole de Management, a school that started with around 70 students in a small office in downtown Casablanca to become, 30 years later, the leading business school in French-speaking Africa. Recently, Thami has also succeeded in establishing an international primary and secondary institution that is already bringing real value to hundreds of students and preparing an expansion project to extend its capacity. In parallel to his contribution to the education sector, Thami has also been active in the media (radio and TV) by developing and hosting programs such as "Entreprendre," "Challenger," and "Libre Echange" to promote entrepreneurship and the best management practices in Morocco. In 2007, in the context of the liberalization of the audio-visual sector, he created one of the largest radio stations in Morocco, named "ASWAT" ("voices" in Arabic), as a way to contribute to strengthening the Moroccan identity in an increasingly globalized world and promoting modern values (e.g., personal advancement, gender equity, social justice).

Thami was distinguished in 2017 as Chevalier of Academic Palms by the French government for his contribution to the education sector. He also received the Education and Training Award of the Africa Economy Builders (Cote d'Ivoire), and a doctorate honoris causa from Grenoble Ecole de Management. He has been appointed as a member of the Moroccan Higher Council for Education, Training and Scientific Research, and an expert member of the Economic, Social and Environmental Council of the Kingdom of Morocco. He also acts as a member of the AACSB Initial Accreditation Committee. He has accumulated an extensive international experience in education management as chair of the AACSB[20] Middle East and North Africa Advisory, a member of the EDAF (EFMD Deans Across Frontiers) Committee,[21] and a member of the Advisory Board of the GBSN.[22] Through his position as vice president of the ALAMANA

Foundation, a leading microfinance organization in the Middle East and North Africa (MENA) region, he is strongly involved in promoting social and economic inclusion.

All these efforts reflect the importance of edupreneurship in developing countries. Thami firmly believes that education is a key change agent that could strengthen the African economy and modernize its societies. He often reminds his audience that business schools are "Schools for Businesses for Societies." On the one hand, they can play a fundamental role in encouraging innovation and entrepreneurship and consequently, fostering value creation through the launch of more businesses and the reinforcement of existing ones. By doing so, business schools contribute to the economic growth and the competitiveness of organizations. On the other hand, business schools can contribute to their societies by promoting dimensions such as gender equity, youth advancement, social inclusion, and sustainable development. They are responsible for preparing people who should behave ethically and support responsible values within companies. In addition, developing the entrepreneurship spirit among students gives them the self-confidence to take initiative and gain control over their professional futures. It helps young people to adopt the culture of performance and positive attitudes such as ambition, determination, autonomy, creativity, and risk-taking. Thus, the role of entrepreneurship education is crucial in achieving numerous SDGs in Africa.

Teaching entrepreneurship at ESCA

Entrepreneurship has been identified as a key driver of economic growth and social advancement in many developing countries. Around 98 percent of Moroccan companies are SMEs employing more than 70 percent of the Moroccan workforce but with only 40 percent of revenues generated in 2022.[23] To promote entrepreneurship, ESCA Ecole de Management has introduced many innovative programs and practices. First, the school has adopted in all its programs a learning goal that aims at developing the student entrepreneurship spirit. Thus, at the end of their programs, students are able to detect entrepreneurship opportunities and exploit them to lead their initiatives to a successful output, despite the associated risks and constraints. The school seeks to prepare students to successfully start a business and/or to effectively manage intrapreneurship projects as a member of an established organization. In this perspective, students follow many entrepreneurship-related modules taught within the programs (e.g., entrepreneurship, innovation and business models, design thinking).

Also, students are engaged in numerous student society activities where they develop and demonstrate their ability to carry out entrepreneurial projects. During their studies at ESCA Ecole de Management, they initiate and achieve in teams, business, cultural, sports, or other social projects in their environment. ESCA students also participate in entrepreneurship competitions (e.g., MTN Entrepreneurship Challenge, ENACTUS, University of San Diego Social Innovation Challenge). By doing so, the school has opted for a teaching through entrepreneurship approach that leverages an experiential learning process to allow students to practice entrepreneurial activities during their studies.

ESCA Ecole de Management has also distinguished itself through its intellectual contributions. It has established a research group focused on entrepreneurship, and succeeded, in collaboration with companies (e.g., Orange) and international partners (e.g., American University in Cairo, American University of Beirut), in launching two research chairs, one on digital innovation and the other on family businesses. The school has also founded an African Academic Association on Entrepreneurship with five other first-class African business schools,[24] and a regional consortium[25] on family business within the MENA region. Besides this, the school has been part of international consortia (funding projects) dedicated to entrepreneurship (e.g.,

FEFEDI, Porefire, Maghrenov), as an education and research provider. Finally, ESCA Ecole de Management has established an incubator within an entrepreneurship and innovation center located on its campus.

As a result of these efforts, ESCA Ecole de Management has succeeded in educating and supporting many entrepreneurs through its programs. Around 10 percent of its graduates start a business after their graduation, which is significant in Morocco given the contextual constraints. The school has also contributed through its research and intellectual activities by focusing on topics like social innovation, women's entrepreneurship, and family businesses. Several books have been published on entrepreneurship and family business topics. ESCA faculty have also written business cases highlighting successful Moroccan entrepreneurs (three of them have received the EFMD Case Writing Award). For instance, we can note a book gathering 18 case studies on innovation and entrepreneurship in the Maghreb. The school has also organized and promoted international events on entrepreneurship such as the GBSN Teaching Entrepreneurship Summit, the Digital Society Forum with Orange, the Durar MENA Program supporting Design and Creativity, and the ESCA EM Colloquium on Entrepreneurship and Innovation. In addition, ESCA Ecole de Management has designed and delivered customized programs, in partnership with the Moroccan pharmacists and dentists association, to develop their members' entrepreneurship skills and support their projects.

Through all these initiatives promoting entrepreneurship skills and mindsets, ESCA Ecole de Management seeks to contribute to the economic and social development of its region by tackling three issues, namely youth employment, gender inequity, and the lack of competitiveness of local family businesses. Youth unemployment in the Arab world is about 23 percent, compared to the global average which is 13.7 percent.[26] In Morocco, 76.1 percent[27] of those aged 15–24 years old are unemployed. Entrepreneurship education can help young people improve their financial situations and meet their social aspirations. In terms of gender inequity, the Arab world has the largest gap, with 12 out of the 30 countries ranked at the bottom of the Global Gender Index ranking.[28] Also, women's entrepreneurship is almost half that of men in Arab countries.[29] In Morocco, only 16 percent[30] of SMEs are led by women, who are mainly driven by necessity and/or social motivations. Terjesen and Lloyd (2015)[31] have shown that a large number of women hesitate to launch startups because of their lack of entrepreneurial skills. Entrepreneurship education, in this case, supports women entrepreneurs in the region by equipping them with the right tools and mindsets. So, they can not only be able to launch their businesses but also target international markets with more sophisticated offerings (e.g., technology) and distinctive value propositions. Finally, ESCA Ecole de Management aims at supporting family businesses as one of the main contributors to the GDP of Arab countries (90 percent of companies, 60 percent of the GDP, and 80 percent of the workforce in the Middle East[32]). Entrepreneurship education can help family businesses reinforce their global competitiveness through effective governance and HR practices, internationalization strategies, innovation, etc.[33]

ESCA Ecole de Management: the international ambition

Internationalization is one of the most important strategic axes for the development of ESCA Ecole de Management. The school started its internationalization as early as 2003, which was, at that time, a non-conventional approach in Morocco and in Africa in general. More precisely, the school has been internationalizing its learning activities through programs focused on international business and embedded with diverse mobility opportunities for students and faculty (e.g., exchange semesters, study trips, dual degrees, internships abroad, summer programs). For instance, undergraduate students of the Grande École Master Program have 300 seats available on annual basis for exchange programs thanks to the school's international partnerships (more than 130 partners in 2022). They are also able to obtain a double degree, in particular with institutions such as Tongji University, Neoma Business School, and Kedge Business School. Alongside this, they have the opportunity to carry out their internships in companies based abroad. For specialized master's students, study trips have been integrated into the academic paths in collaboration with the school's partners, for destinations such as Paris and Grenoble (France), Brussels (Belgium), Johannesburg and Cape Town (South Africa), Mumbai (India), Buenos Aires (Argentina), and Istanbul (Turkey).

In addition, ESCA Ecole de Management has set up an innovative collaboration system called COIL (Collaborative Online International Learning) to deliver joint courses with its academic partners (e.g., Robinson College of Business at Georgia State University, ESDES Lyon Business School) and allow group projects between its students and their international peers. This initiative was initially developed with Georgia State University as an alternative to Virtual Global Study Tours and has been awarded in the United States. The school has also distinguished itself by developing programs like "Doing Business in Morocco and MENA Region" and "Doing Business in Africa." These are Global Study Tours offered to its international partners such as Stern School of Business (New York University) and Stellenbosch University. Such seminars share with students and leaders from different countries (e.g., France, United States, Canada, South Africa) key knowledge and practices about the business world in emerging contexts and more particularly in Morocco.

Thanks to its long-standing international commitment, ESCA Ecole de Management has gained global recognition for its academic excellence and intellectual contribution focused on business in Africa. The school is now looking for another level of achievement in terms of internationalization. ESCA Ecole de Management aims at developing further its activities in Africa and attracting more international students to its campus. Currently, most of the foreign regular students come from French-speaking sub-Saharan African countries, and students from Europe, North America, and Asia mainly come for exchange semesters. The school also seeks to foster its research activities by increasing external funds and joint projects at the international level. This is very important when we consider that research activities are mainly financed by the school.

Discussion questions

1 Why is entrepreneurship important for developing countries?
2 What are the challenges that entrepreneurs face in developing countries?
3 What are the types of entrepreneurship that could bring value to developing countries?
4 How can ESCA promote entrepreneurship and increase its impact in its region?
5 Could you suggest other practices to teach entrepreneurship?
6 How can ESCA further achieve its international ambition?

Case III

Making a difference: the case of CYRUS Institute of Knowledge

The CYRUS Institute of Knowledge (CIK) started as an entrepreneurial initiative with the aim of making a difference in the life of junior scholars, especially from developing countries. CIK's aim has been to build bridges between scholars and practitioners in developed and developing countries to advance scientific-based knowledge. CIK was founded by Nader and Jila Asgary

Figure 12.4 CIK logo

in March of 2012 as an educational, scientific, and nonprofit tax-deductible organization in the United States. It is a secular and nonpartisan organization.

CIK has created an intellectual atmosphere for scholars and practitioners to engage in educational activity and generate theoretical and applied knowledge in management sciences, economic development, sustainable growth, and related disciplines globally. CIK also provides educational services and training to individuals and organizations to advance their goals and objectives. CIK's competitive edge is the areas of specialization, knowledge, and interest of its members and their cultural awareness about the regions.

CIK vision and values

CIK's vision is "to cultivate the discourse on human capital potentials for better living." CIK's values support its vision and mission. These values are as follows:

Passion: We are enthusiastic and passionate in advancing knowledge. Our goal is to enrich human resource strengths and potential growth.
Commitment: We live embrace by strong commitment to create an institute that strives in supporting scholars, businesses, and organizations to succeed.
Excellence: Our ambition is to deliver the highest levels of quality work! We lead by example to achieve our vision and goals and we work hard to exceed expectations.

Namesake

Cyrus the Great, the founder of the Persian Empire, was born in 600 BC and died in 530 BC. Due to his efforts and under his leadership, the Middle East and Central Asia enjoyed tolerance, prosperity, and peace. Cyrus allowed foreigners who had been forcibly relocated, including the Jews of the Babylonian captivity, to return home. Cyrus respected the traditions and religions of those who lived in his country; as a result, he is celebrated as an enlightened and tolerant leader.

A hallmark of Cyrus' administration was religious freedom and the respect for the customs of ethnic minorities, a fact acknowledged by ancient Jewish historians. Combining these missions with Cyrus' wise and fruitful economic policies, the Middle East and Central Asia emerged as the pinnacle of early civilization. Cyrus was a great man who also harbored a spirit of humility, Cyrus asked to be buried in earth, rather than encased in silver or gold, as was the tradition.

It is quite suitable to highlight a quotation from Cyrus the great here: "I was never the plaything of fear or greed. Though I had the advantage of royal birth, it was through my own efforts that I reordered the world as I wished it to be, and conquered far more by the force of my mental powers than by the strength of my sinews" (Larry Hedrick, 2006). Knowledge is power!

Figure 12.5 CIK mission

Figure 12.6 CIK values

Figure 12.7 Cyrus Cylinder

A man of many achievements in life, in death he acknowledged he was a man, like any other, and insisted on being treated accordingly. This empathy for all humanity marks Cyrus' greatness and inspires us to recall his achievements when we attempt, in some small way, to contribute to the knowledge generation, peace, and prosperity of the Middle East, North Africa, and Central Asia. For further information, see several comprehensive articles at www.iranicaonline.org/articles/cyrus-index.[34]

CIK performance since inception

Conferences

So far, CIK has been focusing on international conferences and publishing scholarly studies. Since December of 2012, CIK has organized ten domestic and international conferences. The strategy has been to have one domestic conference at a higher education institution in Boston/ Cambridge, Massachusetts, and one at a university outside the United States. CIK has organized conferences in the United States at Harvard University, Massachusetts Institute of Technology (MIT), and Hult International Business School in Cambridge, Massachusetts. Internationally, conferences have been hosted by Hult International Business School in Dubai, the American University in Cairo Egypt, ESCA Ecole de Management in Casablanca, Morocco, and at UNINOVE University in Sao Paulo, Brazil.[35] During most of the COVID-19 lockdowns, CIK and the International Symposium on Management, Projects, Innovation and Sustainability (SINGEP) organized joint online conferences with accepted submission of more than 500, jointly. The conference's executive committees have been diverse and international.

For most of these conferences, CIK had multiple domestic and international universities as cosponsors for each conference.[36] Their faculty and graduate students presented and participated in the conference. These institutions also provided financial assistance and other services to the conference. Generally, the themes of the conferences have focused on entrepreneurship, innovation, responsible leadership, and economic development. For each conference, CIK and its partners planned plenary panels for each conference to debate important long-term issues such as the new era of globalizations and entrepreneurship, higher education's challenges during COVID-19, and environmental changes. The topics for which CIK has received scholarly work are the following: entrepreneurship; innovation and development; environmental changes, business development, and governance; natural resources and sustainable development; leadership and cultural characteristics; women and business development; higher education institutions; ethics and social responsibility; institution and development; and organization and cultural issues.

Journal: CYRUS Global Business Perspectives

CYRUS Global Business Perspectives (CGBP), formerly the *CYRUS Chronicle Journal* (CCJ), started in 2014.[37] Since then, CIK has published seven volumes of scholarly studies. The editorial board of the CGBP sets the editorial policy and topics of interest, which is similar to other journals. The CGBP editorial board is supported and advised by an advisory board, which aims to enhance the journal's quality and reputation. The academic credentials of the editorial board and the advisory board consist of professors from well-known institutions of higher education, who have had many years of academic and professional experience. The editorial and advisory board members are from many different nationalities, which make CIK a truly international organization.[38] Also, the CGBP's advisory board comprises accomplished experts offering innovative advice and dynamic perspectives. The diverse range of knowledge(s), skills, and abilities of the members of the board are receptive and open to new ideas. In general, both boards include members that can work within flexible structures, have different scholarly interests, and all aspire to accomplish the goals of the organization. The board aligns with common interests in active participation, shared mission, and direct influence on students, faculty, and other board members.

CIK post-doctoral opportunities

CIK provides post-doctoral fellowships to qualified candidates. The positions are open to PhD graduates who are interested in advancing their research capabilities during their post-doctoral studies. CIK associates who are highly accomplished and well-known scholars have expressed interest to contribute to the advancement of future generations. The names and areas of specialization of CIK associates are provided on the website. The post-doctoral positions are open to all domestic and international applicants. So far, CIK does not have the means to offer financial support; however, if needed, support for the applicant's visa is provided.

Aims and objectives – post-doctoral

1 Advance the scholarly capabilities of doctoral students, particularly from developing countries, through their collaboration with the experienced CIK associates
2 Enrich the international network and publication opportunities of post-doctoral fellows
3 Enhance post-doctoral fellows' job opportunities in their homeland and beyond
4 Deepen scientific knowledge-based studies.

Expected outcomes – post-doctoral

1 Accepted post-doctoral applicants will work closely with experienced scholars, which will lead to improvement of their research competencies and increase their publications' quality and quantity
2 Present their research output at the CIK seminars, at the CIK annual international conference, and at other organizations and associations
3 Publish scholarly output in peer-reviewed journals, including the CIK journal *CYRUS Global Business Perspectives*
4 Explore raising funds from the public and private sectors to support their research projects and scholars at the CIK.

CIK challenges

Similar to some other nonprofit organizations, CIK has had challenges in acquiring financial support to advance and grow faster. Currently, it is operating positively through some funding generated from conferences and individual contributions. The hope is to advance in this area as the reputation of the organization increases.

Conclusions

The CIK has been successful in operating for the past 12 years in terms of conferences and journal publications. It has enriched scholars and practitioners in this process. In addition, it has created a valuable brand and a network of scholars and institutions. So far, CIK has been financially viable. However, CIK has also faced challenges that have slowed the operational and financial growth. *Thanks to many from around the world who have contributed and are advancing the aim and objectives of the CIK.* The founder and the boards hope that in the near future CIK will be able to advance its vision which states "to cultivate the discourse on human capital potentials for better living."

Discussion questions

1 Examine CIK values and its implementation successes.
2 Has its theme of entrepreneurship been delivered effectively?
3 What are the challenges for a nonprofit such as CIK to operate in developed and developing countries?
4 What types of entrepreneurial activities could add more values to CIK?

5 How can CIK promote entrepreneurship globally?
6 How can CIK further achieve its aim and ambition?
7 Identify how CIK and other nonprofit organizations can acquire funds to advance its causes.
8 Read the book *Xenophon's Cyrus the Great: The Arts of Leadership and War* by Larry Hedrick (2006) and examine its applicability to leadership.

Notes

1 Huygens Institute. (2015, January 12). *Philips, Gerard Leonard Frederik (1858–1942). Resources.* Retrieved April 9, 2023, from https://resources.huygens.knaw.nl/bwn1880-2000/lemmata/bwn3/philips

2 Yad Vashem. *World Holocaust Remembrance Center*. Retrieved June 26, 2019, from http://db.yadvashem.org/righteous/family.html?language=en&itemId=4043449

3 Philips Again Recognized as a Clarivate Top 100 Global Innovator. (2021, November 19). *Philips*. Retrieved from www.philips.com/a-w/about/news/archive/standard/news/press/2021/20210226-philips-again-recognized-as-a-clarivate-top-100-global-innovator.html

4 Philips is Committed to Making the World Healthier. (2022, January 26). *Gulf News*. Retrieved February 22, 2022, from gulfnews.com/uae/health/philips-is-committed-to-making-the-world-healthier-1.1643188403767

5 Philips Partners with the Government of Kenya and the United Nations to Improve Access to Primary Healthcare in Africa. *Philips*. Retrieved from www.philips.com/a-w/about/news/archive/standard/news/press/2017/20170502-philips-partners-with-the-government-of-kenya-and-the-united-nations-to-improve-access-to-primary-healthcare-in-africa.html

6 Philips and the Dutch Development Bank FMO Combine Forces to Accelerate Universal Health Coverage in Africa. *Philips*. Retrieved April 10, 2023, from www.philips.com/a-w/about/news/archive/standard/news/articles/2021/20210308-philips-and-the-dutch-development-bank-fmo-combine-forces-to-accelerate-universal-health-coverage-in-africa.html

7 *About Us*. (2023, January 30). *Philips*. Retrieved April 6, 2023, from www.philips.com/a-w/about.html

8 Executive Committee. (2020, December 15). *Philips*. Retrieved from www.philips.com/a-w/about/executive-committee.html

9 Stewart, C. (2023, March 16). Philips number of employees worldwide by region 2020–2022. *Statista*. Retrieved from www.statista.com/statistics/496009/philips-number-of-employees-by-region/

10 ESG Governance | Philips. (2018, March 14). Our strategic focus. *Philips*. Retrieved from www.philips.com/a-w/about/our-strategy.html

11 ESG Environmental Sustainability | Philips. Retrieved from www.usa.philips.com/c-e/movember

12 Bhasin, H. (2019, May 29). Marketing strategy of Philips – Philips marketing strategy. *Marketing91*. Retrieved from www.marketing91.com/marketing-strategy-of-philips/

13 Bhasin, H. (2019, May 29). Marketing strategy of Philips – Philips marketing strategy. *Marketing91*. Retrieved from www.marketing91.com/marketing-strategy-of-philips/

14 Karthikeyan, A. (2023, March 21). Philips marketing strategy: Driving sustainability and sales. *StartupTalky*. https://startuptalky.com/philips-marketing-strategy/

15 Philips. (2023, March 29). *Wikipedia*. Wikimedia Foundation. Retrieved from en.wikipedia.org/wiki/Philips

16 Philips. (2023, March 29). *Wikipedia*. Wikimedia Foundation. Retrieved from en.wikipedia.org/wiki/Philips I.J. Blanken. (1999). *The development of N.V. Philips' Gloeilampenfabrieken into a major electrical group*. Zaltbommel, European Library, 1999. (Vol. 3 of The history of Philips Electronics N.V.). ISBN 90-288-1439-6; Asgary, N.H., & Maccari, E.A. (2019). *Entrepreneurship, Innovation and Sustainable Growth: Opportunities and Challenges* (1st ed.). Routledge. https://doi.org/10.4324/9780429261640

17 Authors: Thami Ghorfi, President & Imad-eddine Hatimi, Researcher at ESCA Ecole de Management.

18 Masurel, E., Montalvo Correa, M.E., & Fassin, Y. (2019). Entrepreneurship in Africa: A review of the literature. *International Journal of Entrepreneurial Behavior & Research*, 25(2), 212–238.

19 Adeleye, I., & Fakile, A.S. (2017). Entrepreneurship in Africa: Trends, opportunities, and challenges. In *Handbook of Research on Intrapreneurship and Organizational Sustainability in SMEs* (pp. 47–67). Hershey: IGI Global.

20 Association to Advance Collegiate Schools of Business.

21 European Foundation For Management Development.

22 Global Business School Network.
23 https://medias24.com/2021/10/04/tpme-38-de-la-valeur-ajoutee-et-74-des-emplois-declares-au-maroc-observatoire/#:~:text=En%202020%2C%20les%20micro%2Dentreprises,grandes%20entreprises%2026%2C3%25
24 American University in Cairo (Egypt), Lagos Business School (Nigeria), Strathmore Business School (Kenya), Stellenbosch University, and the University of Cape Town (South Africa).
25 American University of Beirut (Lebanon), American University in Cairo (Egypt), USEK (Lebanon), Ajman University (UAE), and ESCA EM.
26 www.ilo.org/wcmsp5/groups/public/-dgreports/-dcomm/documents/briefingnote/wcms_737672.pdf
27 www.hcp.ma/Note-d-information-a-l-occasion-de-la-journee-internationale-de-la-jeunesse-du-12-aout-2022_a3563.html
28 https://www3.weforum.org/docs/WEF_GGGR_2022.pdf
29 www.gemconsortium.org/report/gem-2019-2020-global-report
30 https://womeninbusiness.ma/2022/10/15/omtpme-voici-les-resultats-de-la-1ere-etude-sur-lentrepreneuriat-feminin-au-maroc/
31 Terjesen, S., & Lloyd, A. (2015). *The 2015 female entrepreneurship index*. Kelley School of Business Research Paper, n. 15–51, 2015.
32 www.pwc.com/m1/en/publications/family-business-survey.html
33 Ghorfi, T. (2017). *Entreprises Familiales: Des paradoxes aux opportunités* (p. 328). Casablanca: Editions La Croisée des chemins.
34 Cyrus the Great, The Art of Leadership and War, by Larry Hedrick. (2006). Retrieved from www.iranicaonline.org/articles/cyrus-index
35 https://cyrusik.org/conference/2023
36 https://cyrusik.org/conference/
37 https://cyrusik.org/cyrus-global-business-perspectives/about
38 https://cyrusik.org/cyrus-global-business-perspectives/editorial-board

Index

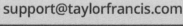

For Product Safety Concerns and Information please contact our
EU representative GPSR@taylorandfrancis.com Taylor & Francis
Verlag GmbH, Kaufingerstraße 24, 80331 München, Germany